Mixed Methods Applications in Action Research

This book is dedicated to my students. Over the years, students from diverse backgrounds, geographical locations, and academic disciplines inspired me to critically think about research, try new methods of inquiry, and apply innovative ideas to practice. This book is for them to test, apply, reflect, and generate ideas about how to integrate research and practice.

Mixed Methods Applications in Action Research

From Methods to Community Action

Nataliya V. Ivankova

University of Alabama at Birmingham

Los Angeles | London | New Delhi
Singapore | Washington DC

Los Angeles | London | New Delhi
Singapore | Washington DC

FOR INFORMATION:

SAGE Publications, Inc.
2455 Teller Road
Thousand Oaks, California 91320
E-mail: order@sagepub.com

SAGE Publications Ltd.
1 Oliver's Yard
55 City Road
London EC1Y 1SP
United Kingdom

SAGE Publications India Pvt. Ltd.
B 1/I 1 Mohan Cooperative Industrial Area
Mathura Road, New Delhi 110 044
India

SAGE Publications Asia-Pacific Pte. Ltd.
3 Church Street
#10-04 Samsung Hub
Singapore 049483

Acquisitions Editor: Vicki Knight
Assistant Editor: Katie Guarino
Editorial Assistant: Yvonne Mcduffee
Project Editor: Veronica Stapleton Hooper
Copy Editor: Alison Hope
Typesetter: C&M Digitals (P) Ltd.
Proofreader: Wendy Jo Dymond
Indexer: Jean Casalegno
Marketing Manager: Nicole Elliott

Printed in the United States of America.

Library of Congress Cataloging-in-Publication Data

Ivankova, Nataliya V.

Mixed methods applications in action research : from methods to community action / Nataliya V. Ivankova.

pages cm
Includes bibliographical references and index.

ISBN 978-1-4522-2003-1 (alk. paper)

1. Action research. 2. Education—Research—Methodology. I. Title.

LB1028.24.I83 2015
370.7—dc23   2014013501

This book is printed on acid-free paper.

SFI label applies to text stock

15 16 17 18 19 10 9 8 7 6 5 4 3 2 1

BRIEF CONTENTS

List of Figures and Tables   xiv

Preface   xvi

About the Author   xx

PART I. APPLYING MIXED METHODS IN ACTION RESEARCH   1

Chapter 1. Introducing Mixed Methods Research   3

Chapter 2. Introducing Action Research   26

Chapter 3. Applying Mixed Methods in Action Research   50

PART II. DESIGNING AND CONDUCTING A
MIXED METHODS ACTION RESEARCH STUDY   85

Chapter 4. Conceptualizing a Mixed Methods Action Research Study   87

Chapter 5. Designing a Mixed Methods Action Research Study   117

Chapter 6. Planning Integration of Quantitative and Qualitative
      Methods in a Mixed Methods Action Research Study   151

Chapter 7. Sampling and Collecting Data in a
      Mixed Methods Action Research Study   181

Chapter 8. Analyzing Data in a Mixed Methods Action Research Study   218

Chapter 9. Assessing Quality of a Mixed Methods Action Research Study   258

PART III. USING MIXED METHODS INFERENCES
TO INFORM COMMUNITY ACTION   295

Chapter 10. Planning and Implementing Action Using
      Mixed Methods Action Research Study Inferences   297

Appendix   328

Glossary   407

References   413

Author Index   425

Subject Index   435

DETAILED CONTENTS

List of Figures and Tables   xiv

Preface   xvi

About the Author   xx

PART I. APPLYING MIXED METHODS IN ACTION RESEARCH   1

Chapter 1. Introducing Mixed Methods Research   3
   Introduction   3
   Definitions of Mixed Methods Research   4
   Example of a Mixed Methods Research Study   6
   Rationales for Using Mixed Methods Research   10
   Evolution of Mixed Methods Research   13
   Current Status of Mixed Methods Research   14
   Philosophical Foundation of Mixed Methods Research 16
   Methodological Characteristics of Mixed Methods Research   18
      Number of Study Strands   18
      Timing or Type of Implementation Process   20
      Priority or Weighting of the Methods   20
      Integration or Mixing of Methods   21
   Summary   23
   Reflective Questions and Exercises   23
   Further Readings   24

Chapter 2. Introducing Action Research   26
   Introduction   26
   Definitions of Action Research   27
   Essential Features of Action Research   29
      Community Orientation   30
      Practical Focus   32
      Participation and Collaboration 33
      Reflection   33
      Empowerment   34
   Example of an Action Research Study   35

Conceptual Models of Action Research   37
   Select Models of Action Research   38
   Steps in the Action Research Process   42
Methodological Characteristics of Action Research   44
   Systematic   44
   Cyclical   44
   Flexible   46
   Multiple Data Sources   46
   Plan of Action or Intervention   47
Summary   47
Reflective Questions and Exercises   48
Further Readings   49

Chapter 3. Applying Mixed Methods in Action Research   **50**
Introduction   50
Connecting Mixed Methods and Action Research   52
   Following Principles of Systematic Inquiry   53
   Providing Comprehensive Information   53
   Being Pragmatic   53
   Being Dialectical   54
   Using Reflective Practice   55
   Applying Transformative/Advocacy Lens   55
   Using Quantitative and Qualitative Information Sources   56
   Being Cyclical   56
   Adopting a Collaborative Approach to Research   57
   Combining Insider–Outsider Perspectives   57
Advantages of Applying Mixed Methods in Action Research   58
Application of Mixed Methods in Action Research   59
   Mixed Methods Methodological Framework for Action Research 59
   Application of Mixed Methods in Published Action
      Research Studies   62
Examples of Five MMAR Studies   70
   Example A: MMAR Study in the Field of
      K–12 Education (Kostos & Shin, 2010)   70
   Example B: MMAR Study in the Field of Nursing
      (Glasson et al., 2006)   71
   Example C: MMAR Study in the Field of Social Work (Craig. 2011) 73
   Example D: MMAR Study in the Field of
      Higher Education (Sampson, 2010)   75
   Example E: MMAR Study in the Field of
      Health Care (Montgomery et al., 2008)   77

Summary   80

Reflective Questions and Exercises   81

Further Readings   82

**PART II. DESIGNING AND CONDUCTING
A MIXED METHODS ACTION RESEARCH STUDY**   **85**

Chapter 4. Conceptualizing a Mixed Methods Action Research Study   **87**

Introduction   87

Steps in an MMAR Study Process   88

Diagnosing Phase   89

Reconnaissance Phase   91

Planning and Acting Phases   92

Evaluating Action Phase   92

Monitoring and Revising Action Phase   93

Conceptualizing an MMAR Study   94

Identifying the Problem/Issue   95

Reviewing the Literature   96

Writing a Research Problem Statement   99

Developing a Study General Research Plan   101

Specifying Overall Study Purpose, Expected Outcomes,

   Objectives, and Research Questions   104

Considering Ethical Issues   110

Summary   114

Reflective Questions and Exercises   115

Further Readings   116

Chapter 5. Designing a Mixed Methods Action Research Study   **117**

Introduction   117

Current Mixed Methods Design Typologies   118

Typology of MMAR Study Designs   124

Key Methodological Dimensions of MMAR Study Designs   125

Basic MMAR Study Designs   128

Concurrent Quan + Qual MMAR Study Design   128

Sequential Quan → Qual MMAR Study Design   133

Sequential Qual → Quan MMAR Study Design   138

Multistrand MMAR Study Design   143

Summary   148

Reflective Questions and Exercises   149

Further Readings   150

Chapter 6. Planning Integration of Quantitative and Qualitative
    Methods in a Mixed Methods Action Research Study   **151**

Introduction   152

Integration or Mixing of Quantitative and Qualitative Methods   152

    Integration or Mixing in Mixed Methods Research   152

    Creating Meta-Inferences   154

    Points and Strategies of Methods' Integration   155

Integrating Quantitative and Qualitative Methods in
    MMAR Study Designs   156

    Integrating Methods in a Concurrent Quan + Qual
        MMAR Study Design   156

    Integrating Methods in a Sequential Quan →Qual
        MMAR Study Design   158

    Integrating Methods in a Sequential Qual →Quan
        MMAR Study Design   159

    Integrating Methods in a Multistrand MMAR Study Design   160

Developing Study Purpose and Research Questions for
    Reconnaissance and Evaluation Phases of an MMAR Study   161

    Study Purpose and Research Questions for
        Reconnaissance and Evaluation Phases   162

    Examples of Study Purpose and Research Questions
        for MMAR Study Designs in Reconnaissance
        and Evaluation Phases   164

Visual Presentation of MMAR Study Procedures   171

    Notation System for Visual Presentation of
        MMAR Study Procedures   171

Examples of Visual Diagrams in MMAR Study Designs   173

    Visual Diagram of a Concurrent Quan + Qual MMAR Study
        Design (Example A: Kostos & Shin, 2010)   173

    Visual Diagram of a Sequential Quan → Qual MMAR Study
        Design (Example E: Montgomery et al., 2008)   173

    Visual Diagram of a Sequential Qual → Quan MMAR Study
        Design (Example C: Craig, 2011)   174

    Visual Diagram of a Multistrand MMAR Study Design
        (Example D: Sampson, 2010)   178

Summary   178

Reflective Questions and Exercises   179

Further Readings   180

Chapter 7. Sampling and Collecting Data in a Mixed
    Methods Action Research Study   **181**

Introduction   182

Sampling in an MMAR Study   182
   Overview of Major Sampling Strategies and Sample
     Types in Research   182
   Sampling Considerations in an MMAR Study   185
   Approaches to Sampling in Mixed Methods Research   191
Sampling Schemes for MMAR Study Designs   191
   Sampling Scheme for a Concurrent Quan + Qual
     MMAR Study Design   191
   Sampling Scheme for a Sequential Quan → Qual
     MMAR Study Design   193
   Sampling Scheme for a Sequential Qual → Quan
     MMAR Study Design   194
   Sampling Scheme for a Multistrand MMAR Study Design   195
Data Collection in an MMAR Study   196
   Quantitative Data Sources   196
   Qualitative Data Sources   200
   Data Collection Considerations in an MMAR Study   206
   Integrating Quantitative and Qualitative Data in an MMAR Study   211
Summary   214
Reflective Questions and Exercises   215
Further Readings   216

Chapter 8. Analyzing Data in a Mixed Methods Action Research Study   218
Introduction   218
Analyzing Quantitative Data in an MMAR Study   219
   Descriptive Statistics Analytical Methods   220
   Inferential Statistics Analytical Methods   221
Analyzing Qualitative Data in an MMAR Study   232
   Process of Qualitative Data Analysis   233
   Coding and Theme Development   239
Mixed Methods Data Analysis in an MMAR Study   245
   Mixed Methods Data Analysis in a Concurrent
     Quan + Qual MMAR Study Design   246
   Mixed Methods Data Analysis in a Sequential
     Quan → Qual MMAR Study Design   247
   Mixed Methods Data Analysis in a Sequential
     Qual → Quan MMAR Study Design   250
   Mixed Methods Data Analysis in a Multistrand
     MMAR Study Design   252
Summary   254
Reflective Questions and Exercises   255
Further Readings   256

Chapter 9. Assessing Quality of a Mixed Methods Action Research Study   **258**

Introduction   258

Assessing Validity and Reliability of Quantitative Data and

    Their Interpretation in an MMAR Study   259

      Means of Assessing Quantitative Validity and Reliability   260

Assessing Trustworthiness of Qualitative Data and

    Their Interpretation in an MMAR Study   261

      Criteria for Assessing Trustworthiness in Qualitative Research   265

      Strategies for Assessing Trustworthiness of Qualitative Data and

        Their Interpretation in an MMAR Study   267

Addressing Quality Considerations Related to Action Research   270

      Insider versus Outsider Status of Practitioner-Researchers   272

      Objectivity versus Subjectivity When Studying One's Own Practice   273

      Generalizability versus Transferability of Study Results   274

Assessing Quality in an MMAR Study   275

      Quality Considerations in Mixed Methods Research   275

      Approaches to Assessing Quality in Mixed Methods Research   276

      Assessing Quality in an MMAR Study   284

Summary   290

Reflective Questions and Exercises   291

Further Readings   292

PART III. USING MIXED METHODS INFERENCES TO INFORM COMMUNITY ACTION   **295**

Chapter 10. Planning and Implementing Action Using

    Mixed Methods Action Research Study Inferences   **297**

Introduction   298

Using Meta-Inferences to Inform Action/Intervention in

    an MMAR Study   298

      Interpreting Meta-Inferences from an MMAR Study   299

      Examples of Interpreting Meta-Inferences in Different

        MMAR Design Studies   305

Developing and Implementing Action/Intervention in an MMAR Study   307

      Action Plan   308

      Levels of Action Planning   309

      Success and Challenges of Implementing

        Action/Intervention in an MMAR Study   314

Evaluating and Monitoring Action/Intervention in an MMAR Study   316

Disseminating MMAR Study Results   318

Developing a Proposal for an MMAR Study   321

Summary   324

Reflective Questions and Exercises   325
Further Readings   326

Appendix   **328**

Example A: MMAR Study in the Field of K–12 Education
(Kostos & Shin, 2010)   328
Example B: MMAR Study in the Field of Nursing
(Glasson et al., 2006)   342
Example C: MMAR Study in the Field of Social Work (Craig, 2011)   360
Example D: MMAR Study in the Field of Higher
Education (Sampson, 2010)   376
Example E: MMAR Study in the Field of Health Care
(Montgomery et al., 2008)   393

Glossary   **407**

References   **413**

Author Index   **425**

Subject Index   **435**

LIST OF FIGURES AND TABLES

FIGURES

1.1	A Conceptual Model of Mixed Methods Research	7
1.2	Visual Diagram of Ivankova and Stick's Mixed Methods Study Research Activities	22
2.1	Lewin's Basic Four-Stage Action Research Model	38
2.2	Lewin's Methodological Steps Action Research Model	39
2.3	Kemmis and McTaggart's Action Research Spiral	40
2.4	Elliot's Action Research Model	41
2.5	Stringer's Action Research Interacting Spiral	42
2.6	Mills's Dialectic Action Research Spiral	43
2.7	Steps in Action Research Process	45
3.1	Mixed Methods Methodological Framework for Action Research	61
3.2	MMAR Studies by Year of Publication	64
3.3	MMAR Studies by Subject Area or Discipline and Year of Publication	65
3.4	Research Activities in Kostos and Shin (2010) MMAR Study	72
3.5	Research Activities in Glasson et al. (2006) MMAR Study	74
3.6	Research Activities in Craig (2011) MMAR Study	76
3.7	Research Activities in Sampson (2010) MMAR Study	78
3.8	Research Activities in Montgomery et al. (2008) MMAR Study	80
4.1	MMAR Study Process Model	90
4.2	Logical Flow of Ideas in MMAR Study Research Problem Statement	100
5.1	Conceptual Model of a Concurrent Quan + Qual MMAR Study Design	130
5.2	Concurrent Quan + Qual MMAR Study Design Decision Flowchart	134
5.3	Conceptual Model of a Sequential Quan → Qual MMAR Study Design	135
5.4	Sequential Quan → Qual MMAR Design Decision Flowchart	139
5.5	Conceptual Model of a Sequential Qual → Quan MMAR Study Design	140
5.6	Sequential Qual → Quan MMAR Design Decision Flowchart	145
5.7	Conceptual Model of a Multistrand MMAR Study Design	146
6.1	Conceptual Model of Combining Integration Strategy in a Concurrent Quan + Qual MMAR Study Design	157

6.2 presents a conceptual model of a merging integration strategy in a concurrent Quan + Qual MMAR study design 158
6.3 Conceptual Model of Connecting Integration Strategy in a Sequential Quan → Qual MMAR Study Design 159
6.4 Conceptual Model of a Connecting Integration Strategy in a Sequential Qual → Quan MMAR Study Design 160
6.5 Visual Diagram of a Concurrent Quan + Qual MMAR Study Design 174
6.6 Visual Diagram of a Sequential Quan → Qual MMAR Study Design 175
6.7 Visual Diagram of a Sequential Qual → Quan MMAR Study Design 176
6.8 Visual Diagram of a Multistrand MMAR Study Design 177
7.1 Conceptual Diagram of a Concurrent Sampling Scheme for Quan + Qual MMAR Study Design 192
7.2 Conceptual Diagram of a Sequential Sampling Scheme for Quan → Qual MMAR Study Design 193
7.3 Conceptual Diagram of a Sequential Sampling Scheme for Qual → Quan MMAR Study Design 194
8.1 Visual Model of Qualitative Data Analysis Process in an MMAR Study 240
8.2 Conceptual Diagram of a Concurrent Quan + Qual Mixed Methods Data Analysis in an MMAR Study 248
8.3 Conceptual Diagram of a Sequential Quan → Qual Mixed Methods Data Analysis in an MMAR Study 250
8.4 Conceptual Diagram of a Sequential Qual → Quan Mixed Methods Data Analysis in an MMAR Study 252
9.1 Quality Assessment Domains within an MMAR Study Process Model 285
10.1 Multiple Entities that Shape Meta-inferences in a MMAR Study 300

TABLES

1.1 Reasons and Purposes of Mixed Methods Research 11
3.1 Reasons for Applying Mixed Methods in Select Action Research Studies 67
5.1 Recent Typologies of Mixed Methods Designs 120
6.1 Points and Strategies of Quantitative and Qualitative Methods' Integration in MMAR Study Designs 156
7.1 Examples of Descriptions of Select Sampling Strategies from Published MMAR Studies 186
7.2 Mixed Methods Data Collection in MMAR Study Designs 213
8.1 Statistical Tests and Statistics Frequently Used in Educational Research and Criteria for Choosing the Statistics for Hypothesis Testing 226
8.2 Example of Themes and Supporting Quotes in Zoellner et al. MMAR Study 234
8.3 Examples of Descriptions of Qualitative Data Analysis from Published MMAR Studies 236
8.4 Computer-Based Programs for Qualitative and Mixed Methods Data Analysis 243
9.1 Conceptual Models and Frameworks of Assessing Quality in Mixed Methods Research 280
9.2 Quality Assessment Criteria for Six Phases in an MMAR Study Process Model 286

PREFACE

PURPOSE OF THE BOOK

As with many texts, this book has emerged as a result of teaching a graduate-level course titled "Mixed Methods Approaches to Action Research" for students seeking practice-oriented research-based degrees. The goal of the course was to equip the students with the knowledge of designing and conducting an action research study that employed mixed methods. The term *mixed methods action research (MMAR) study* was coined during the class discussions and a methodological framework for conducting and designing an MMAR study was developed as the course evolved.

There are a number of common features between mixed methods and action research that make the integration of these two approaches possible within a given study. However, in spite of the growing number of published studies that have applied mixed methods in action research, there is a dearth of methodological advice in action research texts about how to systematically incorporate mixed methods. This book addresses this gap and provides a detailed guide on how to apply mixed methods in action research. It provides applied knowledge for designing and conducting an MMAR study that integrates the two methodological approaches (mixed methods and action research) in a practical and pragmatic manner. To meet the varied epistemological and professional needs of scholar-practitioners, this book has a multidisciplinary focus, provides both scholarly and practical orientation, and is applicable to broad audiences with different levels of research skills.

Application of mixed methods in action research helps secure a more systematic approach to the assessment of a problem and to the development, evaluation, and monitoring of an action/intervention in the process of fostering meaningful change. In times of evidence-based and data-driven calls for improvement, there is a need for action research that meets rigorous standards to generate scientifically sound and effective plans for action or intervention. When combined with mixed methods, action research helps practitioner-researchers develop "a new appreciation for a data-driven decision-making process" (Lyons & DeFranco, 2010, p. 149) by capitalizing on the strengths of both quantitative and qualitative methods. McNiff and Whitehead (2011) argued that without a solid research and knowledge base, action research often turns into "a form of personal-professional development" (p. 11). Mixed methods as a research approach can provide a rigorous methodological foundation for action research.

In this book, action research is viewed broadly as a cover term that embraces several approaches and that underscores its practical focus, community orientation, participatory and collaborative nature, emphasis on empowerment, and value of reflection (Herr & Anderson, 2005). Consistent with this view, *community* is defined broadly as inclusive of all types of communities from educational to professional to public. Thus, the major purpose of action research is seen to produce practical knowledge that will contribute to the increased economic, political, psychological, health, and spiritual well-being of persons and their communities, resulting in more equitable and sustainable relationships with the wider ecologic context of the society.

AUDIENCE FOR THE BOOK

With the growing interest in community-based participatory action research and scientific application of mixed methods in action research projects, this book is intended for a broad audience: from students who are learning how to conduct research in practical settings, to practitioners who are faced with the need to address pertinent issues in their professional practices, to community leaders who strive to inform policy changes, to college faculty who teach research methods and conduct funded research in collaboration with practitioner-researchers and community stakeholders. The purpose of the book is to provide applied knowledge of designing and conducting an MMAR study that integrates the two methodological approaches in a practical and pragmatic manner.

As such, the book can be used as a primary or supplemental text in graduate and upper-level undergraduate research methods courses that prepare scholar-practitioners to conduct action research and inform policy changes in various fields. This potential audience also includes a growing body of national and global distance learners who pursue graduate practice-oriented research-based degrees while continuing with their jobs. Indeed, the ability to conduct community needs assessment, developing and implementing a plan of action/ intervention utilizing both quantitative and qualitative methods in an informed and integrated way, is a skill that every scholar-practitioner must possess. A number of varied pedagogical features that the book contains make it appropriate for use as an instructional text aimed at developing those skills.

BOOK OUTLINE

The book's content is presented in three parts and follows the process of conceptualizing, designing, conducting, and using an MMAR study to inform community action/intervention. Within each part there are numerous illustrations to support the discussed information and provide opportunities for potential modelling.

Part I introduces mixed methods and action research and addresses the opportunities and advantages for integrating these two research approaches. It introduces the reader to the mixed methods methodological framework for action research and illustrates its application on published MMAR studies in different disciplines.

Part II presents an MMAR Study Process Model and addresses the steps to consider when designing and conducting an MMAR study, from its conceptualization stage to assessing the quality of the integrated study conclusions. It walks the reader through the process of developing a research problem statement, choosing a design, selecting sampling strategies and tools of data collection and analysis, and deciding on the quality assessment criteria appropriate for an MMAR study.

Part III discusses how to use the results from an MMAR study to inform community action/intervention. It exposes the reader to the logistics of interpreting meta-inferences as an MMAR study outcome, describes the process of action planning, and addresses the role of evaluation and monitoring in action/intervention implementation. It also offers the guidelines for developing a proposal for an MMAR study.

BOOK FEATURES

The book offers a number of features to enhance the reader's understanding and application of its content. Each chapter begins with learning objectives that guide the presentation of the information. The explanation of the concepts are illustrated by employing extensive examples of the application of mixed methods in action research, consisting of published studies, research protocols, and unpublished research proposals. Full texts of five featured published studies from different disciplines are included in the appendices. The terms are bolded in the text and their definitions are provided in the glossary. Cross-references are highlighted in the margins for the convenience of the reader. The book also has many applied practical tools:

- Scripts
- Templates
- Outlines
- Tips for practice
- Tables and boxes that summarize and organize important information
- Figures that depict conceptual models, design diagrams, and decision-making flowcharts of methodological procedures
- End-of-chapter summaries
- Reflective questions and exercises at the end of each chapter
- Further readings organized by main topics at the end of each chapter

ACKNOWLEDGMENTS

This book would not have been possible without the support, assistance, encouragement, and inspiration from many people. First and foremost I want to thank the graduate students in 'EPR 790 Mixed Methods Approaches to Action Research' course that I taught at the University of Alabama at Birmingham in Fall 2011: Debbie Blackstone, Wendolyn Conner-Knight, Jennifer Cunningham, Wanda Davis, Beth Hales, Dominique Prince, and Dale and Rebecca Stripling. Their constructive feedback was enormously helpful for conceptualizing, focusing, and structuring this book. The students' comments on the application materials and topical assignments helped me choose the right presentation format and keep an appropriate balance between a scholarly discussion of the book concepts and their practical application to real-life situations. Most important, the students allowed me to use their coursework related to designing an MMAR study. Excerpts from their research proposals are used to illustrate and explain some of the book's concepts.

I also want to thank Dr. Vicki Plano Clark for her encouragement with developing this book idea, her initial feedback to the book proposal, and her continuous emotional support during the book writing process.

I am very grateful to Dr. Sheldon Stick for his willingness to serve as a critical reader of the book manuscript and to provide constructive feedback on the clarity of the presented information.

I want to especially thank the SAGE team who assisted and supported me during the book writing and publishing process. My sincere gratitude goes to the publisher, Vicki Knight, who guided me in the entire process, for her continuous encouragement, lasting patience, instrumental support, prompt assistance, and always positive feedback. I also want to acknowledge Nicole Elliott, Anna Guico, Lauren Habib, Candice Harmon, Alison Hope, Veronica Stapleton Hooper, Yvonne McDuffee, and Jessica Miller for their assistance with this book project.

Special gratitude goes to the reviewers who provided valuable constructive feedback when reviewing the chapters as a work in progress. Their thoughtful comments helped improve the presentation of the book content, secure a logical flow of the ideas, and add to the depth and breadth of the discussed information.

REVIEWERS

Victoria D. Coleman, Walden University

Joan Engebretson, University of Texas Health Science Center-Houston

Anne J. Hacker, Walden University

Brigitte Harris, Royal Roads University

John H. Hitchcock, Ohio University

Juanita A. Johnson, Union Institute & University

Daniel Kmitta, Argosy University

D. Patrick Lenihan, University of Illinois at Chicago

Laura J. Meyer, University of Denver

Alberto M. Ochoa, San Diego State University

Barbara Kline Taylor, Western New Mexico University

Wendy G. Troxel, Illinois State University

Pamela M. Wesely, University of Iowa

Debby Zambo, Arizona State University

ABOUT THE AUTHOR

Nataliya V. Ivankova, Ph.D., is associate professor in the Department of Health Services Administration (School of Health Professions) and the Department of Acute, Chronic, and Continuing Care (School of Nursing) at the University of Alabama at Birmingham. She teaches graduate-level research methods courses, including courses on research design, survey, and qualitative and mixed methods research in conventional and online environments. She developed a course titled "Mixed Methods Applications in Action Research" that has served as a foundation for this book. She also mentors doctoral students, post-doctoral fellows, and junior faculty in their qualitative and mixed methods research, and serves as consultant, co-investigator, and methodologist on externally and internally funded mixed methods research projects. She has assisted with design and conduct of mixed methods studies in different areas including education, health services, nursing, and public health. Her primary research focus is on the applications of mixed methods research in social and behavioral sciences, including community-based participatory action research and implementation science. She has published more than 40 articles, has coauthored a number of book chapters, and is a contributing author to the second edition of *SAGE Handbook of Mixed Methods in Social & Behavioral Research.* Professionally, she serves as a member of several editorial boards, including the *Journal of Mixed Methods Research,* and is a founding co-editor of the *Mixed Methods Research* series with Sage Publications. Prior to coming to the University of Alabama at Birmingham, she was research projects coordinator in the Office of Qualitative and Mixed Methods Research at the University of Nebraska–Lincoln. During the first 18 years of her professional career, she served as a member of the faculty and as dean of admissions at the Izmail State University in Ukraine.

PART I

Applying Mixed Methods in Action Research

1

Introducing Mixed Methods Research

OBJECTIVES

By the end of this chapter, the reader should be able to

- Understand the essence of the mixed methods approach to research,
- Define mixed methods research,
- Identify the reasons for using mixed methods research,
- Describe the history of mixed methods research,
- Understand the current status of mixed methods research,
- Explain the philosophical foundations of mixed methods research, and
- Describe the methodological characteristics of mixed methods research.

INTRODUCTION

Mixed methods research is growing in its applications across social, behavioral, and health sciences (Ivankova & Kawamura, 2010). Originated to overcome the dichotomy of conventional **quantitative** and **qualitative methods**, mixed methods has become a popular research approach due to its ability to address the research problem more comprehensively (Creswell & Plano Clark, 2011; Teddlie & Tashakkori, 2009). In their editorial for an issue of the *Journal of Mixed Methods Research,* Tashakkori and Creswell (2008) attributed the popularity of mixed methods research to the influence of two parallel factors: the need to use all possible methods to answer complex study research questions and the complexity of the social phenomena that dictates the need to explore social phenomena from various facets and multiple perspectives. Indeed, by integrating quantitative and qualitative methods within a mixed methods approach, researchers can gain a more thorough understanding of the research problem under investigation and get more complete answers to the posed research questions. By conducting a mixed methods study, researchers can obtain statistical trends and patterns in the data and get individual perspectives that help explain these trends. In other words, by conducting a mixed methods study, researchers can address both confirmatory (verifying knowledge) and exploratory (generating knowledge) questions and get answers to "What?" "How?" and "Why?" questions at the same time (Teddlie & Tashakkori, 2009). This ability of mixed methods research to address a range of knowledge generation and knowledge verification questions within a single study may be appealing to practitioner-researchers, who encounter the need to seek more comprehensive solutions to complex practical problems and issues in their professional settings.

The strength and utility of mixed methods research is emphasized by its recognition as the "third methodological movement" (Teddlie & Tashakkori, 2003, p. 5), the "third research approach" (Creswell, 2003, p. 6), the "third research paradigm" (Johnson & Onwuegbuzie, 2004, p. 14), and the "third research community" (Teddlie & Tashakkori, 2009, p. 4). Reaching beyond the traditional quantitative-qualitative divide, mixed methods research capitalizes on the fact that qualitative and quantitative research approaches are complementary in nature. As an approach, mixed methods research has unique procedural characteristics, designs, strategies for integrative data collection and analysis, and validation techniques all aimed at generating quality "**meta-inferences**" (Teddlie & Tashakkori, 2009, p. 152), or study conclusions grounded in the integrated quantitative and qualitative results from the entire study. As Padgettt (2009) observed, mixed methods studies offer possibilities for "synergy and knowledge growth that mono-method studies cannot match" (p. 104).

> The process of developing meta-inferences is discussed in more detail in Chapter 6.

So, what is mixed methods research?

DEFINITIONS OF MIXED METHODS RESEARCH

In spite of the fact that mixed methods is a relatively new approach to research, there are many definitions of mixed methods research based on different criteria used to explain the nature of this approach. For example, Johnson, Onwuegbuzie, and Turner (2007) identified and analyzed 19 different published definitions of mixed methods research. In the first edition of the *Handbook of Mixed Methods in Social & Behavioral Research,* Tashakkori and Teddlie (2003) advanced the name of the approach as "mixed methods" and defined it as "a type of research design in which QUAL and QUAN approaches are used in types of questions, research methods, data collection and analysis procedures, and/or inferences" (p. 711). In the second edition of the *Handbook* (Tashakkori & Teddlie, 2010) that covered a range of topics related to the development, conceptualization, and application of mixed methods research over the recent decade,

Tashakkori and Teddlie emphasized the methodological aspects of mixed methods research. They defined mixed methods research as "the broad inquiry logic that guides the selection of specific methods and that is informed by conceptual positions common to mixed methods practitioners (e.g., the rejection of 'either-or' choices at all levels of the research process)" (p. 5). This definition emphasizes the distinctness and uniqueness of mixed methods approach to research at the methodological and conceptual levels in contrast to **mono-method approaches**, such as quantitative or qualitative.

In 2007 in their editorial to the first issue of the *Journal of Mixed Methods Research* the founding editors, J. Creswell and A. Tashakkori, provided a general definition of mixed methods research to embrace mixed methods researchers from different disciplines and research orientations:

> As an effort to be as inclusive as possible, we have broadly defined mixed methods here as research in which the investigator collects and analyzes data, integrates the findings, and draws inferences using both qualitative and quantitative approaches or methods in a single study or program of inquiry. (Tashakkori & Creswell, 2007, p. 4)

This editorial definition encompasses existing definitions of a mixed methods research approach and highlights the use of both quantitative and qualitative data, as well as meaningful **integration** of quantitative and qualitative methods within a study to generate conclusions about the research problem that are more credible and more persuasive. This definition of mixed methods research is adopted in this book and guides the discussion of how mixed methods can be applied in action research.

Most recently, Creswell and Plano Clark (2011) suggested describing mixed methods based on the principal characteristics that they identified through a consistent analysis of how researchers applied mixed methods in published mixed methods empirical articles. This definition of mixed methods research included six "core characteristics" (p. 5), presented in Box 1.1. According to the authors, this definition of mixed methods research "combines methods, a philosophy, and a research design orientation" (p. 5). Each of these characteristics is essential for designing and conducting a mixed methods study.

> Types and levels of integration of quantitative and qualitative methods are further discussed in Chapter 6 in relation to study designs.

While Creswell and Plano Clark's (2011) definition of mixed methods aims at incorporating multiple viewpoints, Greene (2007) offered a more practically oriented explanation of mixed methods as a way of viewing and understanding the social world. In her words, mixed methods is a form of inquiry that "actively invites us to participate in dialogue about multiple ways of seeing and hearing, multiple ways of making sense of the social world, and multiple standpoints on what is important and to be valued and cherished" (p. 20). This definition of mixed methods emphasizes broad applicability of mixed methods research to generating knowledge that is socially and mutually constructed within diverse contexts and that has practical value to everyone who is directly and indirectly involved in the process of inquiry.

In 2011 a team of mixed methods researchers from social and health sciences answered the call from the Office of Behavioral and Social Sciences Research of the National Institutes of Health (NIH) and produced a document that became officially known as *Best Practices for Mixed Methods Research in the Health Sciences*

BOX 1.1

Core Characteristics of Mixed Methods Research

- In mixed methods, the researcher collects and analyzes persuasively and rigorously both quantitative and qualitative data (based on research questions).
- In mixed methods, the researcher mixes (or integrates or links) the two forms of data concurrently by combining them (or merging them), sequentially by having one build on the other, or embedding one within the other.
- In mixed methods, the researcher gives priority to one or both forms of data (in terms of what the research emphasizes).
- In mixed methods, the researcher uses these procedures in a single study or in multiple phases of a program of study.
- In mixed methods, the researcher frames these procedures within philosophical worldviews and theoretical lenses.
- In mixed methods, the researcher combines the procedures into specific research designs that direct the plan for conducting the study.

Reprinted from Creswell and Plano Clark (2011, p. 5), with permission of SAGE Publications, Inc.

(Creswell, Klassen, Plano Clark, & Clegg Smith, 2011). In this report, the researchers provided a broad understanding of mixed methods as a research approach or methodology, building on previously reported multiple definitions of mixed methods research (see Box 1.2). Although developed primarily for those seeking funding for mixed methods projects in health sciences, a definition of mixed methods research that emphasizes its methodological and procedural aspects may be helpful for practitioner-reseachers in conceptualizing, designing, and conducting MMAR studies in different professional and community-based settings.

So, conceptually mixed methods can be presented as several overlapping spheres where quantitative and qualitative spheres connect with each other representing integration of the approaches and methods (Figure 1.1). The degree of integration may differ from study to study, depending on the research purpose, which is reflected in the figure by different dashed spheres representing mixed methods. The direction of the arrows indicates whether the study is a mono-method study—that is, quantitative or qualitative (solid horizontal arrows in quantitative and qualitative spheres pointing in opposite directions) or whether the study is a mixed methods study (dashed horizontal arrows pointing to each other).

So, how do the definitions of mixed methods research help understand what mixed methods research is?

EXAMPLE OF A MIXED METHODS RESEARCH STUDY

To better understand the nature of mixed methods research and its methodological characteristics, consider a synopsis of Ivankova and Stick's (2007) mixed methods study in the field of higher education presented in Box 1.3.

BOX 1.2

Best Practices Definition of Mixed Methods Research

For purposes of this discussion, mixed methods research will be defined as a research approach or methodology:

- focusing on research questions that call for real-life contextual understandings, multi-level perspectives, and cultural influences;
- employing rigorous quantitative research assessing magnitude and frequency of constructs and rigorous qualitative research exploring the meaning and understanding of constructs;
- utilizing multiple methods (e.g., intervention trials and in-depth interviews);
- intentionally integrating or combining these methods to draw on the strengths of each; and
- framing the investigation within philosophical and theoretical positions.

Reprinted from Creswell et al. (2011, p. 4), with permission of NIH Office of Behavioral and Social Sciences Research.

FIGURE 1.1   A Conceptual Model of Mixed Methods Research

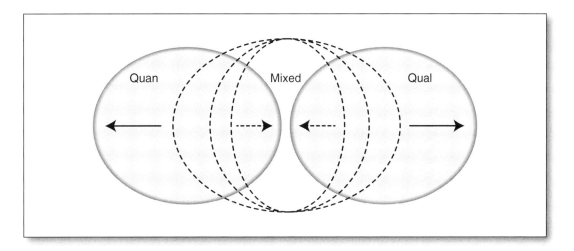

So, what makes Ivankova and Stick's (2007) research a mixed methods study? Following Tashakkori and Creswell's (2007) definition of mixed methods, the researchers collected and analyzed both quantitative data (Web-based survey) and qualitative data (individual telephone interviews, reflective notes, artifacts)

BOX 1.3

Example of a Mixed Methods Research Study

Ivankova and Stick (2007) conducted a mixed methods study to understand what impacts students' persistence in the Distributed (Online) Doctoral Program in Educational Leadership in Higher Education (ELHE-DE) offered by the University Nebraska–Lincoln. Three major theories of students' persistence, Tinto's (1975) Student Integration Theory, Bean's (1980) Student Attrition Model, and Kember's (1995) model of dropout from distance education courses, served as a theoretical foundation for this study.

The rationale for using a mixed methods research approach was that neither quantitative nor qualitative methods were sufficient by themselves to capture the trends and details of situations, such as the complex issue of doctoral students' persistence in the online environment. The priority in the study was given to the qualitative phase because it focused on in-depth explanations of the results obtained in the first, quantitative phase, and involved extensive data collection and analysis from multiple sources. The study consisted of two sequential phases, a quantitative phase followed by a qualitative phase. The study phases were connected while selecting four participants for qualitative case studies and developing the interview protocol based on the results from the statistical tests from the first phase.

In the first, quantitative phase, the researchers conducted a Web-based survey of all current and past students in the ELHE-DE program (N=278) to identify the predictive power of nine composite variables, representing selected internal and external factors to students' persistence in pursuing a doctoral degree online. The response rate to the survey was 74.5%. First, the participants' answers to separate items on the survey scales were analyzed using descriptive statistics. Next, a discriminant function analysis based on the participants' status in the program (Beginning, Matriculated, Graduated, and Withdrawn/Inactive) identified five factors best predicting the students' completion of the program: program quality, online learning environment, student support services, faculty, and self-motivation.

In the second, qualitative study phase, four case studies were used to explore the results from the statistical tests in more depth. One case representing each of the four participant groups (Beginning, Matriculated, Graduated, and Withdrawn/Inactive) was selected using a typical response and maximal variation sampling strategies. The data collection included multiple sources, such as semistructured telephone interviews, the researcher's reflective notes, academic transcripts and students' files, artifacts, and selected archival online classes. Four themes that emerged from the thematic analysis of each case and across cases using QSR N 6 software helped understand the role of the identified factors in the students' persistence in the program in more depth. The quality of the program and students' academic experiences with online learning emerged as the most important factors that helped the participants successfully matriculate in the program. Quality and online learning environment were also the reasons for withdrawal from the program. Two other themes—support and assistance, and self-motivation—contributed to understanding the reasons for students' persistence.

The quantitative and qualitative results from both study phases were integrated while interpreting the outcomes of the entire study. Based on these inferences, a preliminary model of students' persistence in an online doctoral program that included both internal and external factors was developed to contribute to other theories explaining students' persistence in online learning environments.

With kind permission from Springer Science+Business Media: Research in Higher Education, STUDENTS' PERSISTENCE IN A DISTRIBUTED DOCTORAL PROGRAM IN EDUCATIONAL LEADERSHIP IN HIGHER EDUCATION: A Mixed Methods Study, Vol. 48, 2007, pp. 93–135, Nataliya V. Ivankova and Sheldon L. Stick.

in this two-phase study. They integrated the quantitative results (statistically significant and nonsignificant factors) with qualitative findings (themes and categories) to better understand students' persistence in the ELHE-DE program. Based on the integrated results from the entire study, the researchers generated the conclusions or meta-inferences that allowed them to develop a preliminary model of students' persistence in an online doctoral program.

Consistent with Tashakkori and Teddlie's (2010) definition of mixed methods as a "broad inquiry logic that guides the selection of specific methods and that is informed by conceptual positions common to mixed methods practitioners" (p. 5), Ivankova and Stick's (2007) study used multiple quantitative and qualitative methods to address the study's research questions. The selection of methods was guided by the researchers' pragmatic philosophical views that rejected dichotomous either/or thinking (Johnson & Gray, 2010), with an emphasis on the constructivist qualitative methods that helped generate explanations to the initial statistical results.

Creswell and Plano Clark's (2011) core characteristics of mixed methods research also find reflection in Ivankova and Stick's (2007) study. Thus, the researchers systematically collected and analyzed both qualitative and quantitative data using rigorous procedures (discriminant function analysis and thematic cross-case analysis) to answer the study's quantitative and qualitative research questions. The researchers integrated the two forms of data sequentially by having the qualitative data collection build on the quantitative results—that is, the results from the initial statistical tests guided the development of the qualitative interview questions and the selection of typical cases for further multiple case study exploration. The researchers gave priority to the second, qualitative phase of the study because it focused on in-depth explanations of the results obtained in the first, quantitative phase and implied substantial data collection from different sources. The researchers used quantitative and qualitative methods in two sequential phases within a single study. The researchers framed the study procedures within their philosophical pragmatic and constructivist worldviews and theoretical lenses. Finally, the researchers combined the study procedures within a mixed methods sequential explanatory research design (Creswell & Plano Clark, 2011) that guided the implementation of the study—that is, quantitative and qualitative sampling, data collection, analysis, and validation.

To reflect Greene's (2007) socially oriented definition of mixed methods, Ivankova and Stick's (2007) study employed "multiple ways of seeing and hearing" by using quantitative and qualitative data collection and analysis, and "multiple ways of making sense of the social world" (p. 20) by interpreting and integrating the results from the entire study to make conclusions about students' persistence in an online doctoral program and to provide recommendations for developing potential intervention or planning action.

This discussion of what constitutes mixed methods research along with the analysis of Ivankova and Stick's (2007) mixed methods study lead to another question related to when using mixed methods is appropriate and what research situations can be best addressed by employing a mixed methods research approach.

RATIONALES FOR USING MIXED METHODS RESEARCH

The rationales or purposes for conducting mixed methods studies have been extensively discussed in mixed methods literature. Table 1.1 summarizes different views on the reasons and purposes of conducting mixed methods research. To begin, in their seminal paper on mixed methods evaluation designs, Greene, Caracelli, and Graham (1989) identified five broad reasons for applying mixed methods: triangulation, complementarity, development, initiation, and expansion (see Table 1.1 for the description of each reason). Greene and colleagues' paper boosted further discussion of the rationales for using mixed methods and the research goals that can be addressed by applying a mixed methods approach. The typology of five reasons advanced by Greene and colleagues is still frequently used by researchers to provide direction for a study and to help select an appropriate mixed methods design. Most recently, Creswell and Plano Clark (2011) discussed six research problems best suited for employing mixed methods. In each situation, an alternative data set is required to enhance understating of the research problem. In these authors' view, it is necessary to combine quantitative and qualitative methods when using one data set may be insufficient to answer the research questions, initial results require further explanation, exploratory findings from a small group of people need to be generalized to a larger population, the study design needs to be enhanced with a second method, a theoretical perspective needs to be employed to guide the study, or there is a need to address a complex research objective through multiple research phases. These six research situations justify the use of mixed methods and serve as the foundation for specific mixed methods designs that are discussed in Chapter 5. Similarly, Morse and Niehaus (2009) described the goals of adding a supplemental quantitative or qualitative component in mixed methods studies, such as to elicit another perspective or dimension, to obtain data or description that the first method cannot access, to enhance or add a second layer of description, to enable the testing of an emerging conjecture, and to provide explanation or supplemental evidence. In each of these research situations, an alternative component adds to the "scientific contribution" (p. 30) and the rigor of the research study.

Teddlie and Tashakkori (2009) emphasized three areas where using a mixed methods research approach can be more advantageous than using quantitative or qualitative methods alone. First, researchers can answer both confirmatory and exploratory research questions within the same study by integrating quantitative and qualitative methods. Second, researchers can generate stronger and more credible inferences or study conclusions by using integrated quantitative and qualitative study results. Third, researchers can explore more divergent viewpoints on the same issue by using quantitative and qualitative methods within a mixed methods approach.

To illustrate Teddlie and Tashakkori's (2009) point, the purpose of Ivankova and Stick's (2007) mixed methods study discussed in the previous section was to understand the factors that impact students' persistence in an online doctoral program. The researchers could not have achieved this purpose if they chose to conduct either a quantitative or a qualitative study. Therefore, the scope of the study required addressing both confirmatory and exploratory research questions. For example, if the researchers collected and analyzed only the quantitative

TABLE 1.1	**Reasons and Purposes of Mixed Methods Research**
Greene, Caracelli, & Graham (1989)[1]	• TRIANGULATION seeks convergence, corroboration, and correspondence of results from the different methods. • COMPLEMENTARITY seeks elaboration, enhancement, illustration, and clarification of the results from one method with the results from the other method. • DEVELOPMENT seeks to use the results from one method to help develop or inform the other method, where development is broadly construed to include sampling and implementation, as well as measurement decisions. • INITIATION seeks the discovery of paradox and contradiction, new perspectives of frameworks, the recasting of questions or results from one method with questions or results from the other method. • EXPANSION seeks to extend the breadth and range of inquiry by using different methods for different inquiry components.
Creswell & Plano Clark (2011)[2]	• A need exists because one data source may be insufficient. • A need exists to explain initial results. • A need exists to generalize exploratory findings. • A need exists to enhance a study with a second method. • A need exists to best employ a theoretical stance. • A need exists to understand a research objective through multiple research phases.
Morse & Niehaus (2009)[3]	• Elicit another perspective or dimension. • Obtain data that the first method cannot access. • Enhance description (how much many [sic], high, fast, loud, etc.). • Enable the testing of an emerging conjecture. • Provide explanation. • Obtain description that the first method cannot access. • Add a second layer of description. • Provide supplemental evidence.
Teddlie & Tashakkori (2009)[4]	• Mixed methods research can simultaneously address a range of confirmatory and exploratory questions with both the qualitative and the quantitative approaches. • Mixed methods research provides better (stronger) inferences. • Mixed methods research provides the opportunity for a greater assortment of divergent views.

[1]Reprinted from Greene et al. (1989), p. 259.

[2]Reprinted from Creswell & Plano Clark (2011), pp. 8–11.

[3]Reprinted from Morse & Niehaus (2009), p. 31.

[4]Reprinted from Teddlie & Tashakkori (2009), p. 33.

survey data they would have learned what factors that were external or internal to the program had significant or insignificant effects on doctoral students' successful matriculation in an online program. However, they would not know why certain factors that were identified as significant predictors of the doctoral degree completion in traditional campus-based programs (e.g., academic advising) had an insignificant effect on online students' persistence. Alternatively, the researchers could have chosen to conduct a qualitative multiple-case study and to explore in depth several students' experiences in an online doctoral program. They may have uncovered a lot of influencing factors and underlying reasons why students do or do not succeed in a specific online doctoral program. However, the qualitative study results may be relevant only to students who participated in the study and may not explain other doctoral students' experiences in similar programs. By using a mixed methods research approach and combining quantitative and qualitative methods within one study, Ivankova and Stick managed to generate stronger conclusions about what affected online doctoral students' persistence and why certain factors had a different effect in an online learning environment than they did in a traditional setting.

For example, in a follow-up qualitative study phase, Ivankova and Stick (2007) found that faculty teaching in the ELHE-DE program provided a lot of support and advice to online students enrolled in their courses; students often used such support in lieu of contacting their academic advisors. Besides, most of the students in the program were educational administrators who had to work long hours during the day. For these students, pursuing a doctoral degree online that offered flexibility and convenience was often the only choice to earn the necessary academic credentials. This positively affected students' motivation to persist in their studies. The students also valued support that their families and employers provided them by giving them time to study or allowing them to work from home. Finally, a systematic selection of the follow-up qualitative cases based on typical responses to the survey questions in four participant groups allowed the researchers to capture different views on the same issues and extend their findings to students with similar demographic characteristics in similar online programs.

Morse and Niehaus (2009) summarized the advantages that a study employing a mixed methods design offers: "It enables the completion of a single research project more expeditiously and efficiently than conducting a multiple methods design that entails a series of related research projects conducted over time" (pp. 14–15). Additionally, they viewed mixed methods studies as being stronger than mono-method studies because the use of an alternative quantitative or qualitative data set enhanced the study validity by "enriching or expanding" researchers' understanding of the research problem and by converging different perspectives (p. 14). In fact, Patton (2002) argued that studies that use only one method are more vulnerable to errors linked to that particular method compared to studies that use multiple methods in which different types of data help validate each other. Johnson and Turner (2003) referred to this advantage of mixed methods as a **fundamental principle of mixed methods research**. In their words, "methods should be mixed in a way that has complementary strengths and nonoverlapping weaknesses" (p. 299). By capitalizing on the complementary strengths of each method, mixed methods researchers can produce much stronger and more credible studies that (1) will yield more convergent or corroborating results about the studied phenomenon, (2) will eliminate or minimize potential alternative explanations of the findings, and (3) will explain the divergent aspects of the phenomenon of interest.

The seeming advantages of mixed methods research over mono-method quantitative and qualitative research approaches and its extensive applicability across disciplines lead to other questions: How old is mixed methods, and how has it developed as a research approach?

EVOLUTION OF MIXED METHODS RESEARCH

There is much discussion about how old or how young is mixed methods research. Creswell and Plano Clark (2011) considered mixed methods research to be relatively young. They dated its start as a research approach to the late 1980s and early 1990s, aligning it with the emergence of books and articles defining and describing mixed methods (Bryman, 1988; Creswell, 1994; Greene et al., 1989; Morse, 1991). It was at that time that social, behavioral, and health researchers began to conceptualize a mixed methods approach, the specific mixed methods designs, and the features that make it distinct from quantitative and qualitative mono-method approaches. Greene (2008) also referred to 20 years of the growing interest in mixed methods as a form of social inquiry. However, she insisted that social science researchers have long been using a variety of methods in their studies because "the practical demands of the contexts in which they worked called for both generality and particularity" (p. 7).

Some authors believe mixed methods research is much older. For example, Johnson and Gray (2010) pointed out that mixed methods was used by social science researchers as far back as the beginning of the 20th century when the quantitative approach was not yet considered a dominant research paradigm. To support their claim, they provided an example of Fry's book *The Technique of Social Investigation* published in 1934 in New York. The book contains separate chapters on quantitative and qualitative analysis, as well as on combining the methods. Johnson and Gray quoted Fry (1934), who said, "Time and again the really creative part of a social inquiry is deciding how different approaches should be combined to yield the most fruitful results (p. 136)" (Fry, as cited in Johnson & Gray, 2010, p. 87).

Teddlie and Tashakkori (2009) tracked the history of mixed methods research back to Aristotle and his peers who used qualitative descriptions along with quantitative assertions to study natural phenomena. Teddlie and Tashakkori wrote,

> In some ways, Aristotle might be viewed as a proto-mixed methodologist. First, he articulated the importance of a combination of inductive and deductive approaches to knowledge. Second, he noted that probabilistic (i.e., inductive) reasoning is perhaps the best we can do when studying human thinking and action (i.e., psychology). Third, he emphasized the importance of balancing extreme ideas in his principle of the golden mean. (2009, pp. 47–48)

In spite of these divergent views, many mixed methods authors agree that Campbell and Fiske's article published in 1959 prompted an interest in mixed methods and stimulated the development of its philosophical premises and methodological procedures. In that article, Campbell and Fiske introduced the multimethod approach and suggested that researchers should collect multiple quantitative measures and assess them with separate methods to study one psychological construct. The authors' discussion of the combination of different quantitative methods encouraged researchers from different disciplines to use multiple approaches to collect data within a single study, recognizing the limitations of using a single method. For example, Sieber (1973) combined surveys and fieldwork in sociology; Jick (1979) triangulated surveys, observations, semistructured interviews, and documents in psychology; Patton (1980) discussed mixing methods in experimental and naturalistic designs in evaluation, while Denzin (1978) supported the overall idea of using multiple methods to better understand the research problem. Creswell and Plano Clark (2011) called this time a formative period in the history of mixed methods research.

Further development of mixed methods was interrupted by the debate between quantitative and qualitative researchers, referred to as the "paradigm debate" (Teddlie & Tashakkori, 2009, p. 15). This debate stemmed from the idea of incompatibility between different philosophical worldviews and the quantitative or qualitative approaches (Reichardt & Rallis, 1994). According to this **incompatibility thesis**, combining quantitative and qualitative methods was not right because these methods had different underlying philosophical paradigms (Smith, 1983). However, an increased interest in the procedures for mixing different methods in the late 1980s and the acceptance of pragmatism as a philosophical foundation for mixed methods research caused the debate to stop gradually (Howe, 1988; Rossman & Wilson, 1985). Through their work in the 1990s, mixed methodologists were actively advocating for establishing a distinct mixed methods approach to research with its own designs and a set of procedures (Brewer & Hunter, 1989; Creswell, 1994; Greene et al., 1989; Morgan, 1998; Morse, 1991; Tashakkori & Teddlie, 1998). By 2003, when Sage published the first edition of the *Handbook of Mixed Methods in Social & Behavioral Research* mixed methods had been recognized as a third approach to research along with quantitative and qualitative approaches (Tashakkori & Teddlie, 2003). The publication of the *Handbook*, as pointed out above, has also registered an official term for this approach: *mixed methods*.

So, how does this recognition of mixed methods influence its adoption across disciplines?

CURRENT STATUS OF MIXED METHODS RESEARCH

No matter how old or how young mixed methods research is, it is important that it is rightfully recognized as an effective and advantageous approach to research. Mixed methods is now extensively applied in many social, behavioral, and health sciences disciplines. Ivankova and Kawamura (2010) searched five major library databases and identified 70 fields in which mixed methods research have been utilized between 2000 and 2008. The greatest frequency of studies that self-identified as mixed methods was in health and medicine, and in education. Similarly, Alise and Teddlie (2010) analyzed articles published in 2005 in highly respected professional journals in four disciplines. They reported a 16% prevalence rate for mixed methods studies in the applied disciplines of education and nursing, and a 6% prevalence rate in nonapplied, pure fields, such as psychology and sociology. There is also evidence that mixed methods research is crossing the boundaries of many traditionally quantitative fields, such as computer sciences, agriculture, library studies, ecological studies, psychology, business, and economics. It seems the growing need to address complex research problems, often from a multidisciplinary perspective, necessitated the need for a pragmatic approach that prompted the use of multiple research methods (Ivankova & Kawamura, 2010).

The growth of empirical mixed methods studies is supported by the emergence of numerous books and methodological articles devoted to conceptual and procedural issues of mixed methods research. Besides general and cross-disciplinary methodological discussions, there are also numerous articles devoted to mixed methods practices in specific disciplines (Ivankova & Kawamura, 2010). The second edition of the *SAGE Handbook of Mixed Methods in Social & Behavioral Research* (Tashakkori & Teddlie, 2010) is a reflection of the most current thinking about mixed methods research. Two cross-disciplinary international journals, the

Journal of Mixed Methods Research and the *International Journal of Multiple Research Approaches,* have been established in recognition of a mixed methods approach. Additionally, many discipline-based journals—for example, *Research in the Schools, Qualitative Inquiry, Qualitative Research in Accounting & Management, Health Services Research,* and the *British Journal of Health Psychology*—publish special issues devoted to mixed methods research.

The popularity of mixed methods research is also growing among the major funding agencies in the United States. Creswell (2010) considered this increased interest as "a helpful stimulus" for further development of mixed methods (p. 63). This interest goes back to 1999 when the NIH Office of Behavioral and Social Sciences Research issued the guidelines for the use of qualitative methods in health research in which several approaches for combining quantitative and qualitative research were discussed (NIH, 1999). In 2003 a U.S. National Science Foundation workshop emphasized the development of hybrid methodologies that combine the strengths of both qualitative and quantitative methods (Ragin, Nagel, & White, 2004), and the National Research Council of the U.S. National Academy of Sciences stipulated a sequence of three guiding research questions (qualitative-quantitative-qualitative) for scientific educational research (Shavelson & Towne, 2002). Workshops on mixed methods research have also been conducted by private U.S. entities, such as the Robert Wood Johnson Foundation (http://www.rwjf.org/) and William T. Grant Foundation (http://www.wtgrantfoundation.org/).

As discussed above, in 2011 the NIH *Best Practices for Mixed Methods Research in the Health Sciences* (Creswell et al., 2011) was published to guide NIH researchers on how to develop and evaluate scientifically sound proposals for mixed methods funded studies. NIH (http://nih.gov/) along with other funding agencies, such as the Agency for Healthcare Research and Quality (http://www.ahrq.gov/) and Patient-Centered Outcome Research Institute (http://www.pcori.org/) have also been extensively funding projects that utilized mixed methods. Plano Clark (2010) examined the abstracts of the proposals funded by NIH between 1997 and 2008 and discovered a steady increase in the use of mixed methods in funded projects. Twenty-seven percent of the funded NIH studies presented randomized controlled trials or experimental studies with qualitative components, which illustrated the applicability of mixed methods research in traditionally quantitative fields.

International recognition of mixed methods research is also growing. The number of mixed methods methodological discussions and empirical studies conducted in countries other than the United States is about 50%, with the United Kingdom, Canada, and Australia taking the lead (Ivankova & Kawamura, 2010). The Economic and Social Research Council in the United Kingdom plays a prominent role in funding mixed methods studies through its Research Methods Program (Creswell & Plano Clark, 2011). The international Mixed Methods Conference, hosted by Leeds University in the United Kingdom, has been conducted annually since 2005 (http://www.healthcareconferences.leeds.ac.uk/conferences/) with worldwide representation of presenters and attendees. Globally, the international mixed methods research community is united through the Special Interest Group "Mixed Methods Research" within the American Educational Research Association (http://www.aera.net/Default.aspx?menu_id=524&id=10668), the Topical Interest Group "Mixed Methods Evaluation" within the American Evaluation Association (http://www.eval.org/p/cm/ld/fid=11), and the Mixed Methods International Research Association, which is a new professional association created to promote the development of an international and interdisciplinary mixed methods research community (http://mmira.wildapricot.org/). Online courses in mixed methods research now are offered by a number of U.S. universities, including the University of Alabama at

Birmingham and the University of Nebraska–Lincoln, and often enroll students from non-U.S. schools and universities. Additionally, mixed methods workshops and courses are now being conducted on-site in different countries throughout the world.

This account leaves no doubt that mixed methods has been successfully adopted around the world. So, what is the underlying philosophy that makes mixed methods so applicable in different disciplines and so appealing to novice and seasoned researchers?

PHILOSOPHICAL FOUNDATION OF MIXED METHODS RESEARCH

Similar to any form of scientific inquiry, mixed methods research has a set of underlying **philosophical assumptions** or beliefs that influence how mixed methods is applied in practice. Mixed methods research is commonly associated with the philosophy of **pragmatism** that helps justify the combination of quantitative and qualitative methods within one study (Datta, 1994; Howe, 1988). Pragmatism is a philosophical position that underscores the idea that what has practical and functional value is ultimately important and valid (Johnson & Christensen, 2012). A major argument of pragmatism whose origin is traced back to the ideas of American scholars John Dewey, Richard Rorty, and Donald Davidson, is that quantitative and qualitative methods are compatible because they have enough similarities in fundamental values (Howe, 1988; Reichardt & Rallis, 1994). Specifically, both quantitative and qualitative researchers follow the same methodological steps in designing and conducting studies, both use empirical data to draw study conclusions, and both use validation techniques to safeguard the study conclusions. Pragmatists reject the dogmatic either/or choice between quantitative and qualitative approaches and believe that the truth is "what works" best for understanding a particular research problem (Johnson & Onwuegbuzie, 2004; Patton, 2002; Rossman & Wilson, 1985; Tashakkori & Teddlie, 1998). The research questions that a study aims to answer are considered to be more important than the methods used or the philosophical views underlying each method (Maxcy, 2003). Johnson and Gray (2010) presented seven major principles of pragmatism, summarized in Box 1.4. These principles shape mixed methods researchers' philosophical assumptions and influence the choice of the methods for the study (Maxwell & Mittapalli, 2010).

In the first edition of the *Handbook of Mixed Methods in Social & Behavioral Research,* Tashakkori and Teddlie (2003) formally introduced pragmatism as a philosophical foundation for mixed methods and discussed how pragmatism guides mixed methods research. They argued that pragmatism makes it possible for researchers to collect and analyze both quantitative and qualitative data within a single study to address different aspects of the same general research problem with the aim of providing its more complete understanding. See Box 1.5 for how Tashakkori and Teddlie related pragmatism and mixed methods research.

Being shaped by the philosophy of pragmatism and aimed at reaching comprehensive solutions to the studied problems, mixed methods research has developed its own unique methodological features. Although by definition mixed methods incorporates quantitative and qualitative methods, mixed methods research has methodological features that make it distinct from quantitative and qualitative research approaches.

So, what are the key characteristics of mixed methods research?

BOX 1.4

Principles of Pragmatism

- Rejects dichotomous either-or thinking
- Agrees with Dewey that knowledge comes from person-environment interaction (dissolving subject-object dualism)
- Views knowledge as both constructed *and* resulting from empirical discovery (emphasis in original)
- Takes the ontological position of pluralism (i.e., reality is complex and multiple)
- Takes the epistemological position that there are multiple routes to knowledge and that researchers should make "warranted assertions" rather than claims of unvarying Truth
- Views theories instrumentally (i.e., theories are not viewed as fully True or false, but as more or less useful for predicting, explaining, influencing desired change)
- Incorporates values directly into inquiry and endorsees equality, freedom, and democracy.

Reprinted from Johnson and Gray (2010, p. 88), with permission of SAGE Publications, Inc.

BOX 1.5

Tashakkori and Teddlie on Relating Pragmatism and Mixed Methods Research

- Pragmatism supports the use of both quantitative and qualitative research methods in the same research study and within multistage research programs.
- Pragmatist researchers consider the research question to be more important than either the method they use or the paradigm that underlines the method.
- Pragmatists also reject the forced choice between postpositivism and constructivism with regard to logic, epistemology, and so on. In each case, pragmatism rejects the either/or of the incompatibility thesis and embraces both points of view.
- Specific decisions regarding the use of mixed methods or qualitative methods or quantitative methods depend on the research question as it is currently posed and the stage of the research cycle that is ongoing.
- Pragmatism avoids the use of metaphysical concepts (e.g., "truth," "reality").
- Pragmatism presents a very practical and applied research philosophy.

Reprinted from Tashakkori and Teddlie (2003, p. 21), with permission of SAGE Publications, Inc.

METHODOLOGICAL CHARACTERISTICS OF MIXED METHODS RESEARCH

Like any research approach, mixed methods has its methodological characteristics that distinguish it from quantitative and qualitative approaches. These characteristics relate to the design and implementation procedures of mixed methods studies and include (1) the number of quantitative and qualitative strands, (2) the sequence of quantitative and qualitative data collection and analysis procedures, (3) the emphasis

> Application of these methodological characteristics to specific mixed methods designs used in action research are discussed and illustrated in Chapter 5.

given to either or both of the quantitative and qualitative methods, and (4) the process of integration of the quantitative and qualitative methods used in the study (Creswell & Plano Clark, 2011; Teddlie & Tashakkori, 2009). These characteristics play an important role in guiding the researchers to decide what mixed methods design to select and how to implement the study so that it produces meaningful meta-inferences. Creswell and Plano Clark (2011) referred to these characteristics as "key decisions" that researchers should consider while choosing an appropriate mixed methods design for the study (p. 63). Depending on the purpose of the study, mixed methods researchers select and implement these procedures within specific mixed methods designs. These methodological characteristics are summarized in Box 1.6 and are explained and illustrated in the following sections.

Number of Study Strands

A mixed methods study can consist of one or more strands. A **strand** is a component of a mixed methods study that encompasses the basic process of conducting quantitative or qualitative research. In other words, it is a phase of a mixed methods study that includes three stages—the conceptualization stage (posing the study question), the experiential phase (collecting and analyzing the data), and the inferential stage (interpreting results based on the data; Creswell & Plano Clark, 2011; Teddlie & Tashakkori, 2009). A typical mixed methods study will include two different strands: a quantitative and a qualitative. However, a mixed methods study may also consist of one strand during which both quantitative and qualitative data will be collected—

> The decisions on the number of the study strands in mixed methods designs used in action research are discussed in more detail in Chapter 5.

for example, via a survey that includes both close-ended (multiple choice) and open-ended (narrative) questions. Sometimes a mixed methods study targeting a large-scope project may present a sequence of multiple quantitative and qualitative strands or phases where each strand builds on the previous strand and informs the next strand (Creswell & Plano Clark, 2011). The decision on the number of the study strands to include in a mixed methods study depends on the study purpose and some other factors. For example, Ivankova and Stick's (2007) study discussed in Box 1.2 utilized two strands: the quantitative strand during which the Web survey data were collected and analyzed and the qualitative strand that encompassed a multiple-case study and used different text and

BOX 1.6

Key Methodological Characteristics of Mixed Methods Research

- *Strand*—Component of a mixed methods study that encompasses the basic process of conducting quantitative or qualitative research: posing a question, collecting and analyzing data, and interpreting results.

  o A mixed methods study includes at least one quantitative and one qualitative strand and may consist of two or more varied strands.

- *Sequence or timing*—Temporal relationship between the quantitative and qualitative strands within a study:

  o *Concurrent:* Collecting and analyzing both quantitative and qualitative data at the same point in time or independently.
  o *Sequential:* Collecting and analyzing quantitative data first, followed by qualitative data collection, or collecting and analyzing qualitative data first, followed by quantitative data collection.
  o *Multistrand combination:* Combining concurrent and sequential data collection and analysis in a study consisting of more than two strands.

- *Priority or weighting*—Relative importance or weighting of quantitative and qualitative methods for answering the study's questions:

  o *Equal priority:* Equal emphasis is placed on quantitative and qualitative methods.
  o *Quantitative priority:* Greater emphasis is placed on quantitative methods; qualitative methods perform a secondary role.
  o *Qualitative priority*: Greater emphasis is placed on qualitative methods; quantitative methods perform a secondary role.

- *Integration or mixing*—Explicit interrelating of the quantitative and qualitative methods in a study:

  o *Combining:* Integrating quantitative and qualitative methods during the interpretation of both quantitative and qualitative results
  o *Connecting:* Integrating quantitative and qualitative methods during data collection; that is, quantitative or qualitative data are collected based on the results of data analysis in the previous qualitative strand or quantitative strand.
  o *Merging:* Integrating quantitative and qualitative methods during data analysis; that is, quantitative and qualitative data from different study strands are analyzed together.

Adapted from Creswell and Plano Clark (2011); Teddlie and Tashakkori (2009).

image data. Each of these strands consisted of posing research questions, collecting and analyzing the data, and interpreting the results.

Timing or Type of Implementation Process

The implementation of quantitative and qualitative data collection and analysis can occur either concurrently or sequentially in a mixed methods study. This is often referred to as **timing** (Creswell & Plano Clark, 2011). *Concurrent timing* implies that both quantitative and qualitative data are collected independent from each other, sometimes at the same time. *Sequential timing* refers to the situations when quantitative and qualitative data are collected in sequence, one following another (Morse, 1991). For example, a researcher can collect and analyze the quantitative data first and then collect and analyze the qualitative data, but the decisions related to what qualitative data to collect will be determined by the quantitative results, because the qualitative data will be used to help understand the initial statistical findings. Alternatively, a researcher may decide to collect both quantitative and qualitative data at the same time or independent from each other. For example, a researcher may collect the data from a quantitative survey and from qualitative individual interviews. In this case, the researcher will compare the quantitative and the qualitative results only after each strand is completed. The decision on the concurrent or sequential timing for quantitative and qualitative data collection in a mixed methods study is linked to the purpose of the study. If the purpose of the study calls for comparisons of quantitative and qualitative findings to form more validated conclusions, a researcher may choose a concurrent timing. If the purpose of the study necessitates informing one data set by first collecting and analyzing another data set, a researcher may choose a sequential timing (Creswell & Plano Clark, 2011).

> The decisions on the timing of the study strands in mixed methods designs used in action research are discussed in more detail in Chapters 5 and 6.

In Ivankova and Stick's (2007) study the quantitative and qualitative data were collected sequentially because the researchers wanted first to identify the significant predictors of students' persistence in an online doctoral program and then to follow up on these significant results and some unexpected insignificant findings using four qualitative case studies. The four cases were selected based on the typical response to the Web survey in each matriculation group. The researchers could have collected the quantitative and qualitative data concurrently if the purpose of the study called for comparisons of quantitative and qualitative findings to form more validated conclusions and not to build one data collection on another.

Priority or Weighting of the Methods

Quantitative and qualitative methods can vary in their relative importance to answer the research questions in a mixed methods study (Creswell & Plano Clark, 2011). The study can have either a quantitative **priority or weighting** when more emphasis is placed on the quantitative data collection and analysis, a qualitative priority when more emphasis is placed on the qualitative data collection and analysis, or equal priority where both types of data play an equally important part in answering the study research questions. Teddlie and Tashakkori (2009) argued that priority of the method cannot be completely determined before the study is implemented. Often the priority can shift from one method to another based on the need to better understand the studied phenomenon. The choice of the quantitative or qualitative method priory can also be influenced by a researcher's training, comfort level with either of the methods, the intended audience for the study results, the available funding, and access to participants and data. For example, in their study, Ivankova and Stick (2007) gave more priority to the qualitative strand because the goal of this strand was to provide in-depth explanations of the statistical results obtained in the quantitative strand. Besides, for the qualitative study strand, the researchers used a multiple case study design that required more time to complete and involved substantial data collection and analysis from different sources.

Integration or Mixing of Methods

Integration or mixing of the quantitative and qualitative methods is an essential component of a mixed methods study (Creswell & Plano Clark, 2011; Greene et al., 1989; Morse & Niehaus, 2009; Teddlie & Tashakkori, 2009). Stated simply, there is no true mixed methods study without methods integration or mixing. Teddlie and Tashakkori (2009) pointed out, "Recent conceptualizations of MM [mixed methods] research recognize that a study is truly mixed only if there is an *integration* of approaches across the stages of the study" (p. 142; emphasis in original). According to Yin (2006), integration of the quantitative and qualitative methods can occur at different stages in the research process from the study conceptualization to posting research questions, to data collection and analysis, and to interpretation of the study results. The decision on how to integrate the methods depends on the purpose of the study, its design, and the strategies used for data collection and analysis. Most common approaches to methods integration include combining quantitative and qualitative results during their joint interpretation, merging quantitative and qualitative data during the analysis and connecting quantitative and qualitative methods during data collection.

> A detailed discussion of quantitative and qualitative methods' integration in mixed methods designs used in action research is provided in Chapter 6.

For example, in Ivankova and Stick's (2007) study, integration of the methods occurred at three primary stages: at the study conceptualization, when connecting the two study strands, and at the completion of the study during the discussion of the results from the entire study. The researchers conceptualized their study as mixed methods because the study research questions called for obtaining the information that would both confirm and explain the role of different factors in predicting students' persistence in an online doctoral program. Besides separate research questions for the quantitative and qualitative study strands, the researchers developed two overarching mixed methods questions that guided the whole study (Plano Clark & Badiee, 2010): How did the selected factors (internal and external) identified in Phase I contribute to and/or impede students' persistence in the ELHE-DE program? How can the statistical results obtained in the quantitative phase be explained? The quantitative and qualitative strands of the study were connected by selecting four participants for the qualitative follow-up multiple case study after the responses to the survey questions were analyzed. These purposefully selected participants represented typical responses from each matriculation group that were calculated using rigorous statistical procedures. The two study strands were also connected by developing the qualitative interview questions grounded in the quantitative results from the first study strand (Ivankova, Creswell, & Stick, 2006). Finally, the findings from the quantitative and qualitative study strands were integrated while the quantitative and qualitative results from the entire study were discussed to create the meta-inferences or conclusions about students' persistence in an online doctoral program.

Visual presentation of mixed methods procedures in action research studies is further discussed and illustrated in Chapter 6.

To better understand how the discussed methodological characteristics of mixed methods research were reflected in Ivankova and Stick's (2007) mixed methods study, consider Figure 1.2 that visually presents the sequence of quantitative and qualitative study strands, the flow of the procedures within each strand, and the points of methods integration in the study. Note that the priority of the qualitative method is expressed in capital letters in the name of the strand.

These methodological characteristics of mixed methods research (number of study strands, timing or type of implementation, priority of the methods, and methods integration) are discussed in greater detail in Chapters 5 and 6 with reference to MMAR studies because these characteristics are embedded in mixed methods designs and help researchers decide on how to plan the study procedures.

FIGURE 1.2 **Visual Diagram of Ivankova and Stick's Mixed Methods Study Research Activities**

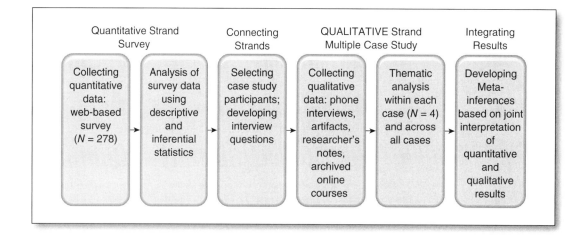

SUMMARY

Mixed methods research is growing in its applications across social, behavioral, and health sciences due to its ability to address the research problem more comprehensively. By conducting a mixed methods study, researchers can obtain answers to confirmatory and exploratory questions within a single study. This may be appealing to practitioner-researchers, who encounter the need for comprehensive solutions while addressing complex practical issues in their professional settings. Mixed methods is defined as research in which the investigator collects and analyzes data, integrates the findings, and draws inferences using both qualitative and quantitative approaches or methods in a single study or program of inquiry. The mixed methods approach is seen as advantageous over mono-method approaches, such as quantitative or qualitative because it can produce much stronger and more credible results by integrating multiple data sources.

In spite of receiving recent recognition as a research approach, mixed methods has a long history with different stages of its acceptance and adoption within the U.S. and international research communities. This is evident from the emergence of numerous books and methodological articles devoted to conceptual and procedural issues of mixed methods research, as well as increasing mixed methods empirical studies. Currently mixed methods research is applied in more than 70 disciplines and is crossing the boundaries of many traditionally quantitative fields. Additionally, mixed methods studies receive increasing support from major funding agencies. The philosophy of pragmatism that underlies mixed methods research justifies this integration of quantitative and qualitative methods within one study to provide a more complete understanding of the research problem. As a research approach, mixed methods has its unique methodological characteristics that relate to the number of quantitative and qualitative study strands, sequence or timing of quantitative and qualitative data collection and analysis procedures, the emphasis or priority given to one or both methods, and the integration or mixing of the quantitative and qualitative methods used in the study. Depending on the purpose of the study, mixed methods researchers select and implement these procedures within specific mixed methods designs. The discussion of mixed methods research is illustrated in this chapter by a mixed methods study of students' persistence in an online doctoral program in higher educational administration.

REFLECTIVE QUESTIONS AND EXERCISES

1. Locate a mixed methods published study in your area of interest. What makes this study a mixed methods study? Discuss how well this study reflects the definitions of mixed methods research discussed in this chapter.

2. Reflect on different reasons for conducting mixed methods research. What reasons do you think may be the most important for using mixed methods in your discipline? What were the reasons for applying mixed methods research in the published mixed methods study that you found? Do you think the authors justified the use of mixed methods research well enough? What might be additional reasons for the use of mixed methods research that the authors did not mention?

3. Conduct a quick search of the library databases for mixed methods empirical studies in your discipline. Use the key words "mixed methods" and the name of your discipline. Record the number of mixed

methods studies found for each year of publication. What trends do you see in the use of mixed methods research in your discipline across the years?

4. Consider the trends of mixed methods research applications across disciplines discussed in Ivankova and Kawamura (2010). What factors do you think affect the use of mixed methods research in your discipline and in your area of interest?

5. Reflect on the seven principles of pragmatism as discussed by Johnson and Gray (2010). How do these principles help justify the need for mixed methods research? How do your philosophical views align with pragmatism?

6. Explore the key methodological characteristics of mixed methods research. Discuss how these characteristics are reflected in the mixed methods studies that you found in your area of interest. Did the authors discuss these characteristics in these articles? If you were to report a mixed methods study, how would you explain these characteristics? Write a few sentences for each characteristic to illustrate your thinking.

FURTHER READINGS

To learn more about mixed methods research as a "third research paradigm" or the "third research community," examine the following sources:

Johnson, B., & Onwuegbuzie, A. (2004). Mixed methods research: A research paradigm whose time has come. *Educational Researcher, 33*(7), 14–26.

Teddlie, C., & Tashakkori, A. (2009). *Foundations of mixed methods research: Integrating quantitative and qualitative approaches in the social and behavioral sciences.* Thousand Oaks, CA: Sage, Ch. 1, pp. 3–18.

To learn more about the purposes of mixed methods research, examine the following sources:

Creswell, J. W., & Plano Clark, V. L. (2011). *Designing and conducting mixed methods research* (2nd ed.). Thousand Oaks, CA: Sage, Ch. 1, pp. 1–18.

Greene, J. C., Caracelli, V. J., & Graham, W. F. (1989). Toward a conceptual framework for mixed-method evaluation designs. *Educational Evaluation and Policy Analysis, 11*(3), 255–274.

To learn more about the history of mixed methods research, examine the following sources:

Creswell, J. W., & Plano Clark, V. L. (2011). *Designing and conducting mixed methods research* (2nd ed.). Thousand Oaks, CA: Sage, Ch. 2, pp. 19–52.

Teddlie, C., & Tashakkori, A. (2009). *Foundations of mixed methods research: Integrating quantitative and qualitative approaches in the social and behavioral sciences.* Thousand Oaks, CA: Sage, Ch. 3–4, pp. 40–82.

To learn more about the current status of mixed methods research, examine the following sources:

Creswell, J. W. (2010). Mapping the developing landscape of mixed methods research. In A. Tashakkori & C. Teddlie (Eds.), *SAGE handbook of mixed methods in social & behavioral research* (2nd ed., pp. 45–68). Thousand Oaks, CA: Sage.

Ivankova, N., & Kawamura, Y. (2010). Emerging trends in the utilization of integrated designs in social, behavioral, and health sciences. In A. Tashakkori & C. Teddlie (Eds.), *SAGE handbook of mixed methods in social & behavioral research* (2nd ed., pp. 581–611). Thousand Oaks, CA: Sage.

To learn more about pragmatism as a philosophical foundation for mixed methods research, examine the following sources:

Johnson, B., & Gray, R. (2010). A history of philosophical and theoretical issues for mixed methods research. In A. Tashakkori & C. Teddlie (Eds.), *SAGE handbook of mixed methods in social & behavioral research* (2nd ed., pp. 69–94). Thousand Oaks, CA: Sage.

Maxcy, S. J. (2003). Pragmatic threads in mixed methods research in the social sciences: The search for multiple modes of inquiry and the end of the philosophy of formalism. In A. Tashakkori & C. Teddlie (Eds.), *Handbook of mixed methods in social & behavioral research* (pp. 51–89). Thousand Oaks, CA: Sage.

2

Introducing Action Research

INTRODUCTION

While mixed methods research has been formally established as a research approach fairly recently, **action research** has been known and applied since the beginning of the 20th century (Greenwood & Levin, 2007; Hinchey, 2008). Similar to mixed methods research, action research is increasingly being used in many fields including education, health care, nursing, social work, organizational development, and criminology. Action research is also gaining a growing international recognition (Herbert, Stephen, Robin, & Ortrun, 2002; Koshy, Koshy, & Waterman, 2011; Lingard, Albert, & Levinson, 2008). Traditionally, action research has been associated with disciplined inquiry done by teachers with the intent of informing and changing their classroom practices. However, a pragmatic focus and flexibility of action research has attracted practitioners from different fields who express concerns over the ever-important questions, "What am I doing?" and "How can I improve what I am doing?" (Koshy et al., 2011). Reportedly, the popularity of action research is growing due to (1) its focus on the solution of practical issues that require immediate attention, (2) its goal of improving practice or developing individuals, and (3) its emphasis on empowerment and emancipation with the focus on social change (Brown & Tandon, 1983; Herbert et al., 2002; Herr & Anderson, 2005). As Kemmis and McTaggart (2007) observed, action research is "directed towards studying, reframing and reconstructing social practices" (p. 277).

According to Stringer (2014), action research is "a systematic approach to investigation that enables people to find effective solutions to problems they confront in their everyday lives" (p. 1). Action or intervention is central to the idea of action research and requires a spiral of action cycles aimed at developing, implementing, and evaluating action or intervention plan to improve the practice (Kemmis, 1982). By observing and reflecting on the effects of intervention, and using this information for planning subsequent action cycles, practitioner-researchers, like teachers, nurses, health care workers, managers, or community dwellers, get empowered to make improvements to their working and living environments and to bring about social change. Therefore, the primary purpose of action research is to produce practical knowledge that will contribute to the increased economic, political, psychological, health, and spiritual well-being of persons and communities, and will help promote a more equitable and a more sustainable relationship with the wider ecologic context of the society.

So, what is action research as a methodological approach? How is it defined and described?

DEFINITIONS OF ACTION RESEARCH

The popularity of action research and its applicability in many settings have brought variations in how researchers and practitioners from multiple disciplines understand and define this research approach. Indeed, Herr and Anderson (2005) referred to "the plethora of terms coined to describe this research" (p. 3), while Carboni, Wynn, and McGuire (2007) argued, "action research is a term that is anything but unanimously and clearly defined" (p. 51). Different views on what constitutes action research can be attributed to differences in researchers' **worldviews** and philosophical beliefs, the goals of action research, its expected outcomes, and the ownership of the action research process and its consequences (Cochran-Smith & Lytle, 1993). The most common terms for action research as a research approach include *action research, participatory action research, collaborative action research, community-based action research, community action research, practitioner research, community-based participatory research, teacher research, teacher inquiry, cooperative inquiry, emancipatory praxis,* and *critical action research*. In spite of this variety, all these terms underscore the important features of action research that are discussed further in the chapter—that is, its practical focus, community-based orientation, participatory and collaborative nature, emphasis on empowerment, and value of reflection.

What is important for this book is that *action research* has been used as a cover term and has embraced several approaches that emerged from different forms of inquiry (Herr & Anderson, 2005). In the most recent edition of the *SAGE Handbook of Action Research,* Reason and Bradbury (2008) described action research as "a family of practices of living inquiry that aims, in a great variety of ways, to link practice and ideas in the service of human flourishing" (p. 1). Those authors also provided a comprehensive definition of action research that emphasizes its universal character and practical focus, its emergent nature and connection between theory and practice, its collaboration and community aspects, and the focus on social change:

> Action research is a participatory process concerned with developing practical knowing in the pursuit of worthwhile human purposes. It seeks to bring together action and reflection, theory and practice, in participation with others, in the pursuit of practical solutions to issues of pressing concern to people, and more generally, the flourishing of individual persons and their communities. (p. 4)

As seen, this definition of action research includes many components. Each component of this definition reflects a specific feature of action research. Box 2.1 summarizes these features, as described by Reason and Bradbury (2008).

Kurt Lewin, a German psychologist and originator of **change theory** (Burnes, 2004) was the first to introduce the term *action research* in his famous paper "Action Research and Minority Problems" in 1946 (Lewin, 1948a). Lewin viewed action research as a tool to understanding social systems or organizational learning that would lead to social action and change in the status quo. In describing action research, he emphasized the connection between theory and practice and their reciprocal relationship: "No action without research; no

---

BOX 2.1

Features of Action Research

- Action research is a set of practices that respond to people's desire to act creatively in the face of practical and often pressing issues in their lives in organizations and communities.
- Action research calls for an engagement with people in collaborative relationship, opening new "communicative spaces" in which dialogue and development can flourish.
- Action research draws on many ways of knowing, both in the evidence that is generated in inquiry and its expression in diverse forms of presentation as we share our learning with wider audiences.
- Action research is value oriented, seeking to address issues of significance concerning the flourishing of human persons, their communities, and the wider ecology in which we participate.
- Action research is a living, emergent process that cannot be pre-determined but changes and develops as those engaged deepen their understanding of the issues to be addressed and develop their capacity as co-inquirers both individually and collectively.

From Reason and Bradbury (2008, pp. 3–4).

research without action" (Lewin, as cited in Adelman, 1993, p. 8). Lewin believed that as a form of active inquiry, action research has the capacity to empower ordinary people through collaborative reflection, discussion, and action about the issues in common. He described the action research process as a spiral of cyclical steps consisting of planning, action, and fact finding about the result of the action leading to social change.

Building on Lewin's ideas, Carr and Kemmis (1986), who are known for their significant contribution to the methodological development of action research, provided what is now considered to be the classic definition of action research:

> Action research is simply a form of self-reflective enquiry undertaken by participants in social situations in order to improve the rationality and justice of their own practices, their understanding of these practices, and the situations in which the practices are carried out (p. 162).

Carr and Kemmis's definition captures the essential features of action research—focus on practice, real-world settings, practitioners' active role, collaboration, disciplined self-evaluation, reflection, and social change. In these authors' view, action research is about the improvement of practice, the improvement of the understanding of practice, and the improvement of the situation in which the practice takes place.

McKernan (1988) provided another description of action research, putting more emphasis on its problem-solving capacity. He defined action research as "a form of self-reflective problem solving, which enables practitioners to better understand and solve pressing problems in social settings" (p. 6). Recently, Hinchey (2008) combined multiple viewpoints on action research and suggested its more comprehensive definition. This definition is inclusive of all the other views on action research and is adopted in this book:

> Action research is a process of systematic inquiry, usually cyclical, conducted by those inside a community rather than outside experts; its goal is to identify action that will generate improvement the researchers believe important. (p. 7)

In spite of different existing definitions and views on action research, Herr and Anderson (2005) concluded that "most agree on the following: action research is inquiry that is done *by* or *with* insiders to an organization or community, but never *to* or *on* them" (p. 3, emphasis in original). This essential feature of action research sets it apart from other scientific forms of inquiry and safeguards consensus among action researchers about the peculiarities of the action research process.

So, how do the key features of action research shape this research approach and make it distinct from traditional forms of scientific inquiry?

ESSENTIAL FEATURES OF ACTION RESEARCH

In contrast to traditional scientific research that aims at generating credible knowledge to add to a knowledge base in a particular field, action research has a local focus and addresses specific practical issues that

The role of these features in applying mixed methods in action research is also discussed in Chapters 5 through 10.

have value for a specific **community** and a professional setting. Participation in action research projects enables the community members and practitioner-researchers to work in a collaborative and reflective manner to generate practical knowledge that can be applied to benefit a community or increase the effectiveness of a professional practice. Therefore, the essential and unique features of action research that are further discussed in this chapter include community orientation, practical focus, participation and collaboration, reflection, and empowerment.

Community Orientation

The idea of community is central in action research and is emphasized through creating collaborative knowledge within what Stringer (2014) referred to as the "community of interest" (p. 6). All **stakeholders** who have a stake in the issue engage in the process of investigation to find effective solutions to resolve the problem. These stakeholders may include anybody who is or may be affected by the issue. They collaboratively participate in the action research process within their professional or social communities working as a team that is often facilitated by practitioner-researchers. As stated in the Preface to this book, community is defined broadly as inclusive of all types of communities from educational to professional to public. Community in this context includes any professional (e.g., an educational institution, a business firm, a hospital), charitable (e.g., a shelter for homeless people), or religious (e.g., a church) organization; neighborhoods made up of area residents (e.g., city, region, street, subdivision); or groups of people who share cultural, political, social, economic, and other interests (e.g., skin-heads, gays, and lesbians). This definition of community is reflective of the connection between action research and community made by Lewin (1951) when he described action research as a reflective process of progressive problem solving led by individuals working with others in teams or as part of a "community of practice" to improve the way those individuals address issues and solve problems.

This emphasis on community in action research has introduced community-based variations within an action research approach, such as *community-based action research* and *community-based participatory research.* According to Senge and Scharmer (2001), **community-based action research** "builds on the tradition of action research by embedding change oriented projects within a larger community of practitioners, consultants, and researchers" (p. 238). While outside experts can and often do participate in the action research project, professional practitioners, such as educators, social workers, health-care professionals, office workers, and administrators, serve as research facilitators. These practitioners engage their communities of interest in the systematic exploration of the issue to equip them with knowledge on how to improve the situation and to help them design effective strategies to implement and evaluate the needed changes. In community-based participatory action research, community is viewed as "a social and cultural entity with the active engagement and influence of community members in all aspects of the research process" (Israel, Schulz, Parker, & Becker, 2001, p. 184). For example, in public health, community-level models provide frameworks for promoting healthy behaviors (National Cancer Institute, 2005), whereas in education, community involvement is viewed as an important factor in school improvement (Mills, 2011).

Eisinger and Senturia (2001) suggested three key principles that form the foundation of community-based participatory action research: participation, equal power, and joint planning. Participation emphasizes the involvement of community members in specific projects with shared ownership, from setting project objectives to disseminating project outcomes. Equal power builds on the respect of values, perspectives, contributions, rewards, and confidentiality of people in the community. Joint planning implies community involvement and commitment to the project from the beginning and maintaining the **sustainability** and livelihood of projects with long-term benefits. Schulz, Israel, Selig, Bayer, and Griffin (1998), who discussed applications of community-based participatory action research in public health, provided nine guiding principles of this approach that are explained in Box 2.2. These principles have been applied in numerous ways by practitioner-researchers in different fields beyond public health and health care in general.

BOX 2.2

Nine Principles of Community-Based Participatory Action Research

1. *Recognizes community as a unit of identity.* Units of identity in this principle refer to socially created entities in which people have membership. Communities of identities may be geographically bounded or geographically dispersed, but members should hold a sense of common identity and shared fate.

2. *Builds on strengths and resources within the community.* This principle implies identification, support, and reinforcement of social structures, processes, and knowledge that already exist in the community. These may include individual skills, social networks, and organizations.

3. *Facilitates collaborative partnerships in all phases of the research, involving empowering and power sharing process that attends to social inequalities.* In this principle, all partners should participate in the decision-making and control over all stages of the research process from the problem definition, data collection and analysis, interpretation of results, and application of the results to address community concerns. This may utilize skills from outside the community, but should focus on the issues identified by the community.

4. *Fosters colearning and capacity building among all partners.* This principle involves a reciprocal exchange of skills, knowledge, and capacity among all partners, recognizing that partners bring diverse skills, expertise, perspectives, and experiences to the partnership process.

5. *Integrates and achieves a balance between knowledge generation and intervention for the mutual benefit of all partners.* This principle implies a reasonable balance between contributions to science and addressing issues and concerns identified by the community. All parties must have a commitment to translate the research results to action strategies that are intended to benefit all partners.

(Continued)

(Continued)

6. *Focuses on the local relevance of public health problems and on ecological perspectives that attend to multiple determinants of health.* This principle emphasizes an ecological approach to health that focuses on individuals, their immediate context (e.g., family or social network) and larger contexts within which these smaller entities exist (e.g., community and society). Although originally developed for public health, this principle is applicable to many other social phenomena that are influenced and shaped by multiple factors at different levels.

7. *Involves systems development using a cyclical and iterative process.* This principle draws on the skills and expertise of each partner to fully engage in all research cycles from problem definition and initial assessment of the situation, to intervention planning, implementation, and evaluation. It implies trust-building, partnership development, and maintenance at all stages of research.

8. *Disseminates results to all partners and involves them in wider dissemination of the results.* This principle states that research findings should be regularly disseminated to all stakeholders in a respectful and understandable language acknowledging all partners' contribution to the process. Community members should also be involved in the broader dissemination of the results.

9. *Involves a long-term process and commitment to sustainability.* In this principle, all partners should be ready to monitor the positive social change and ensure its sustainability to produce long-term effects. This long-term commitment may extend beyond one research cycle and one project.

From Schulz et al. (1998).

Practical Focus

In action research, a practitioner's own practice is often the focus of research and a researcher-practitioner's insider perspective informs the inquiry. According to Herr and Anderson (2005), a major goal of action research is to "generate local knowledge that is fed back into the setting" (p. xv). For that reason, inclusion of practitioners in the research process allows for the development of knowledge that is relevant and can be utilized by the professional community to improve its practices (Teram, Schachter, & Stalker, 2005). The emphasis is on studying one's own professional or personal situation, clarifying what the organization or community is trying to achieve, and creating conditions to remove the obstacles (Kemmis & McTaggart, 2007).

In addition, Kemmis and McTaggart (2007) argued that action research is practical because it targets the practices of social organizations and represents the process through which people explore "their practices of communication, production, and social organization" and try to find ways "how to improve their interactions by changing the acts that constitute them" (p. 282). An effective solution to these practical problems is expected to have an immediate positive effect on the community and its members. The examples can include teachers working together or with students to improve the processes of teaching and learning in the classroom, health educators collaborating with the residents of low-income rural communities to help them develop healthy eating habits and promote healthier lifestyles, or prison staff working together with community college leaders to help incarcerated young males obtain associate degrees. In every scenario, the solution to practical issues will involve examination and improvement of social interactions that are viewed as "irrational, unproductive (or inefficient), unjust, and/or unsatisfying (alienating)" (Kemmis & McTaggart, 2007, p. 282).

Participation and Collaboration

Action research is participatory by nature because it involves multiple stakeholders and is a social process (Hinchey, 2008; Kemmis & McTaggart, 2007). The word *participatory* is often added to the term *action research* to stress the importance of participation of the community members in the process of generating knowledge and promoting social change. Kemmis and McTaggart (2007) emphasized the fact that participatory action research "engages people in examining the *social practices* that link them with others in social interaction" (p. 280, emphasis in original). Herr and Anderson (2005) also argued that action research is best done in collaboration with the stakeholders who have a stake in the issue under investigation. Specifically, collaboration with "outsiders," such as a local university or agency partners, is important when community members experience the need to bring in relevant skills or resources (Herr & Anderson, 2005, p. 4). Performing research in collaboration with those affected by the issue for the purpose of taking action and making change increases the likelihood that targeted communities will accept and use research findings (Royal Society of Canada, 1995).

During the action research process, participants collaboratively explore how their own understandings, skills, values, and knowledge shape their actions and practices. Mills (2011) referred to this process as "building the community of learners" (p. 7). These can include professional learning communities, work groups, panels, and task forces made up of university, school, hospital, agency, and community members. Multidisciplinary teams can often be formed to address complex problems (Koshy et al., 2011), such as medical workers working in teams with social workers and religious organizations to address HIV/AIDS prevention and treatment, or school educators collaborating with public health professionals to decrease tobacco smoking among high school and middle school students. It is also important that everybody with a vested interest in the project participates in all stages of the research cycle to provide the needed input and ensure the stakeholders' interests are represented. Oftentimes, participatory research requires a considerable amount of time and effort to establish rapport among the project's participants (Herr & Anderson, 2005); establishing such rapport is a key for ensuring the mutual benefit of all involved and for securing the project's success.

Reflection

Action research is reflexive or dialectical and occurs through spirals of reflection and action (Stringer, 2014). Herr and Anderson (2005) pointed out, "intense self-reflection . . . is the hallmark of good practitioner research" (p. 47). In action research, reflection is part of the research process and is done systematically and purposefully at all stages. According to Kemmis and McTaggart (2007), reflection is a deliberate process in which the participants who want to transform their practices engage by going through a spiral of cycles of critical and self-critical action and reflection. As practitioner-researchers study their own practices, they reflect on what they learn from the assessment of current situations, what actions or interventions should be taken to improve the situations, and how the results of the taken actions affect their practices. Creswell (2012) described this process as the following:

> Action researchers deliberately experiment with their own practices, monitor the actions and circumstances in which they occur, and then retrospectively reconstruct an interpretation of the action as a basis for future action. In this reflection, action researchers weight different solutions to their problems and learn from testing ideas. (p. 586)

Mills (2011) recommended that practitioners who are willing to critically examine their own practices in order to improve or enhance them should assume a reflective stance that will help their self-development and will give them the power to take risks and make changes they believe are important and necessary.

Empowerment

Like all forms of inquiry, action research is value laden (Herr & Anderson, 2005). Participation in action research projects raises practitioner-researchers' awareness of their right to a voice in reframing and reconstructing social practices, and informs and empowers them to take actions they perceive important. Greenwood and Levin (2007) argued that action research creates social change because of the involvement and engagement of the participants in researching and solving a problem. For example, when discussing action research for teachers, Fueyo and Koorland (1997) indicated that through action research, teachers are empowered to (1) make informed decisions about what to change and what not to change, (2) link prior knowledge to new information, (3) learn from experience (even from failures), and (4) ask questions and systematically find answers. These empowering results of action research can occur in all situations where practitioners are empowered to study and change their own practices, both professional and social. By empowering action researchers it is anticipated that change started at a specific workplace or in a local setting, may help bring change to a larger community and may ultimately have a more global effect.

Empowering action research is emancipatory. According to Kemmis and McTaggart (2007), through action research

> people explore the ways in which their practices are shaped and constrained by wider social (cultural, economic, and political) structures and consider whether they can intervene to release themselves from these constraints—or, if they cannot, how best to work within and around them to minimize the extent to which they contribute to irrationality, lack of productivity (inefficiency), injustice, and dissatisfactions (alienation) as people whose work and lives contribute to the structuring of a shared social life. (p. 282)

So, action research empowers practitioner-researchers to take an active role and question every aspect of a situation that they may have overlooked, underestimated, or taken for granted. Because action research takes place in the settings that reflect a society characterized by conflicting values and an unequal distribution of resources and power, the question of who ultimately benefits from the action or intervention taken becomes equally important (Herr & Anderson, 2005). Therefore, considering the issues of power and predominance of interests is essential when evaluating the results of the action taken and informing further action steps.

The discussed unique characteristics of action research—community orientation, practical focus, participation and collaboration, reflection, and empowerment—make it an effective approach for practitioner-researchers to explore and utilize when addressing the need for change in their professional and community settings. So, how is action research applied in practice?

EXAMPLE OF AN ACTION RESEARCH STUDY

A study by Giachello and colleagues (2003) summarized in Box 2.3 presents a good example of a community-based participatory action research study addressing a public health problem.

BOX 2.3

Example of an Action Research Study

Giachello and colleagues (2003) described how a group of community residents, medical and social service providers, and representatives from a local university established the Chicago Southeast Diabetes Community Action Coalition to address high rates of diabetes morbidity and mortality in Chicago's medically underserved minority communities through the Racial and Ethnic Approaches to Community Health (REACH) 2010 Initiative. The development and activities of the coalition were guided by the principles of community-based participatory action research. The process started with the community dialogue to explain the purposes of the REACH 2010 Initiative and explore the interest of local leaders from six communities in becoming partners. About 15 community representatives agreed to participate and worked closely with the Latino Health Research Center to help secure the project funding to identify the community needs related to the impact of diabetes on community members and the local health-care delivery system.

Once the coalition was formed and task forces consisting of community members, health-care professionals, university employees, and Latino Health Research Center leaders were convened, Phase I of the study began. The objectives of this phase were (1) identify key social, medical, environmental, cultural, institutional, and behavioral factors that may be associated with racial/ethnic disparities in diabetes risk, prevalence, and quality of care among minority groups in six identified communities; (2) identify effective strategies for diabetes prevention and control through community action planning; (3) engage in analysis and dissemination of results to promote replication and adaptation of the project to other communities. Phase I task forces planned and implemented numerous data collection activities including focus groups with health-care providers and with diabetic and at-risk community residents, a household telephone survey, community inventory of health and human services, and epidemiologic data from publicly available sources.

(Continued)

(Continued)

Based on the data analysis and interpretation, the action plan was developed, implemented, and evaluated during Phase II. Task forces were reorganized in to working committees to assist with the implementation of the intervention in four areas: (1) community awareness education, (2) diabetes health-care quality improvement, (3) diabetes self-management and control, and (4) policy development. A rigorous evaluation using multiple levels was designed to measure the progress with the plan implementation and its impact on community residents, and on health and human services providers. An evaluation committee was formed following the participatory process and included all community stakeholders and outside consultants. Evaluation activities consisted of multiple community-based focus groups, a community telephone survey, analysis of client data, and coalition surveys. Each intervention component was evaluated separately with multiple data sources to help monitor the intervention progress.

From Giachello et al. (2003).

 Check Box 2.2 for the nine principles of community-based participatory action research as presented by Schulz and colleagues (1998).

Giachello and colleagues' (2003) study reflects all major features of the action research approach. The study was community oriented and followed the nine principles of community-based action research outlined by Schulz and colleagues (1998). The researchers recognized community as a unit of identity. The study was carried out within six geographically bounded minority neighborhoods with known disproportionately high rates of diabetes morbidity and mortality in southeastern Chicago. The study built on the strengths and resources within the community by inviting interested community residents and health-care and human services professionals to be partners in the research process. These stakeholders were involved in the community needs assessment, the development and implementation of the intervention, and the evaluation of the intervention progress and its impact. Collaborative partnerships with the stakeholders were facilitated in all phases of the study through a coalition steering committee, task forces, and working and evaluation committees.

The study action research approach helped foster colearning and capacity building among all partners. During Phase I of the study, community capacity building included training for community agency staff and concerned community residents on diabetes, coalition building, and research methods to be employed in the study. The project balanced knowledge generation through needs assessment and intervention development and implementation for the mutual benefit of all stakeholders. The taskforces were committed to collecting the necessary information and translating the research results to action strategies in order to benefit the residents of six participating southeastern Chicago neighborhoods, and potentially other communities. An ecological approach to health was emphasized through identifying key social, medical, environmental, cultural, institutional, and behavioral factors that may be associated with racial disparities in diabetes risk, prevalence, and quality of care among minority groups in the six identified communities and addressing these multiple determinants of health in developing the intervention. The study followed a cyclical and iterative process by fully engaging the stakeholders in all research cycles from the initial assessment of the situation, obtaining funding, and Phase I research activities to intervention planning, implementation, and evaluation. Research findings from each preceding phase were regularly disseminated to all stakeholders and to the coalition members. The project started in 1999 and was conducted over several years. At the time of the article publication in 2003 (Giachello et al., 2003) the study was in the intervention evaluation and monitoring phase. Commitment to ensuring the project sustainability and readiness to monitor the positive social change was demonstrated through active partnership between and among coalition members, health and human services providers, university representatives, and community partners.

Additionally, consistent with Kemmis and McTaggart's (2007) point about the emphasis on studying one's own situation and creating conditions to remove existing obstacles, the study addressed a practical problem of reducing diabetes health disparities in minority neighborhoods in southeastern Chicago. The study was participatory because it involved multiple stakeholders at every stage during the research process. Community residents collaborated with health and human services providers, coalition members, and university partners at all stages of the project, from assessing the community needs to implementing and evaluating the action plan. All participants had "a stake in the problem under investigation," which ensured that community members would accept and use the intervention activities (Herr & Anderson, 2005, p. 4). Reflection was part of the process and occurred deliberately at each study cycle, first while exploring the community needs with regard to diabetes management by community leaders, then through collecting and analyzing the data to develop an action plan or intervention by task forces, subsequently through implementing the intervention by working committees, and finally during evaluation, monitoring, and revision of the intervention by the evaluation committee. Last, this action research project was aimed at creating social change by reducing diabetes health disparities and calling for reform in health care due to the involvement and engagement of all community partners in researching and solving an important health problem (Greenwood & Levin, 2007).

Analysis of Giachello and colleagues' (2003) study makes it clear that action research is not linear and involves multiple steps. So, what is the process of action research? How can it be conceptually presented?

CONCEPTUAL MODELS OF ACTION RESEARCH

Multiple views of action research are reflected through different conceptual models that are important to discuss so as to better understand the methodological features of this research approach. These models, despite differences in contextual details and suggested activities, have a general framework. In other words, they promote the same cyclical or spiral approach to action and reflection, and present action research as a series of cyclical steps aimed at identifying action that will generate some desired change in the current situation. With some variation, these steps will include identifying the problem, developing a plan of action, implementing and evaluating the action, and monitoring the action. Any practitioner-researchers who become engaged in the action research process will follow these steps regardless of their professional or philosophical orientation; examples are social workers who seek to improve the living conditions in transient shelters for homeless women with children, or school administrators who strive to get parents to be more involved in school activities, or health-care professionals who try to increase people's awareness of the negative consequences of avoiding screening for colorectal cancer.

Select Models of Action Research

Kurt Lewin, who is credited with coining the term *action research,* suggested the first action research model (Tomal, 2010). Lewin (1948b) conceptually viewed action research as a cyclical process of four iterative stages of reflecting, planning, acting, and observing (see Figure 2.1). The cycle begins when practitioner-researchers encounter a problem that requires solution in the workplace or other community setting. Then they reflect on the situation trying to identify what is known about the problem and what could be some potential solutions. Next practitioner-researchers develop a plan on how to proceed and take an action or carry out the plan. Finally, they observe the results that the action brings and reflect on the outcomes and what needs to be improved or changed. The process is repeated as many times as needed until the issue is resolved.

| **FIGURE 2.1** | **Basic Four-Stage Action Research Model** |

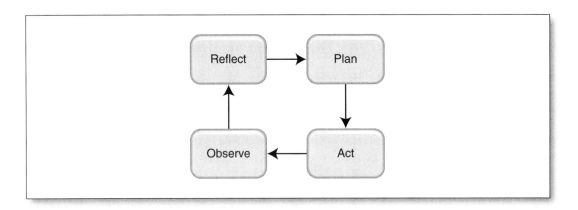

Based on Lewin (1948b).

Lewin's (1948b) conceptual view of action research informed the development of a more detailed model that outlines specific action research methodological steps (see Figure 2.2). According to Lewin, the first step is to identify a general idea and then "to examine the idea carefully in the light of the means available" (p. 205). This step involves **reconnaissance** or fact finding about the situation, planning action, or intervention, and testing it through the first action step. "The result of the action" (p. 206) is then evaluated and the initial plan or intervention is revised or modified for the next action step. In Lewin's words, this "circle of planning, executing, and reconnaissance or fact finding" is repeated "for the purpose of evaluating the results of the second step, and preparing the rational basis for planning the third step, and for perhaps modifying again the overall plan" (1948b, p. 206).

Lewin's (1948b) views on action research inspired many action researchers in different disciplines to propose their conceptual models of the action research process building on Lewin's conceptual four-stage model and the methodological steps action research model. For instance, Kemmis and McTaggart (2007) presented action research as a spiral consisting of self-reflective cycles starting with planning a change,

FIGURE 2.2	**Methodological Steps Action Research Model**

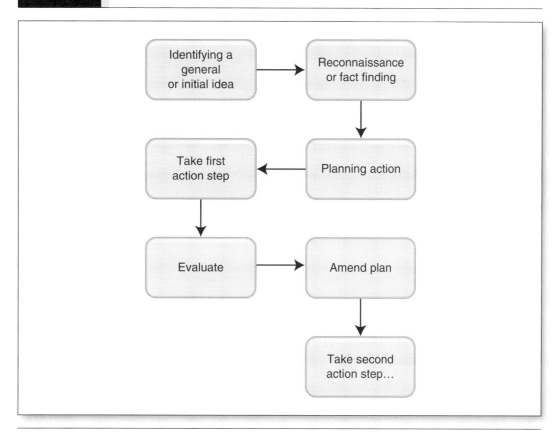

Based on Lewin (1948b).

acting on that plan and observing the process and consequences of the change, then reflecting on these processes, and replanning, and again acting, observing, and reflecting (see Figure 2.3). This process can continue and the cycles of activity may overlap, making the plan obsolete. The plan may be revised or changed multiple times under the new circumstances.

Another model, this one created by Elliott (1991), presents a more elaborate version of Lewin's methodological steps model (see Figure 2.4). Elliot's model also includes the cycles consisting of identifying a general idea, reconnaissance or fact finding, planning, acting, monitoring, and revising the plan. However, Elliott's model emphasizes constant evolution and redefinition of the original goal through a series of reconnaissance steps recurring every cycle. Elliott referred to this model as "the study of a social situation with a view to improving the quality of the action within it" (p. 69). Elliott's vision of action research permits greater flexibility with the research process, as later cycles reflect changes in the action goals as determined through reflection and evaluation of earlier iterations of the action research process.

FIGURE 2.3 **Action Research Spiral**

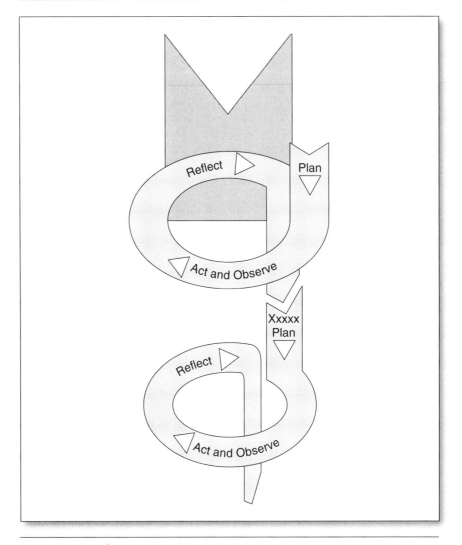

From Kemmis and McTaggart (2007, p. 596).

Stringer (2014) approached action research from a position of a framework for basic action research routine—Look, Think, and Act, presented as cycles (see Figure 2.5). These cycles may also correspond to the three phases of planning, implementing, and evaluating. Stringer referred to this framework as an action research interacting spiral that "enables people to commence their inquiries in a straightforward manner and build greater detail into procedures as the complexity of issues increases" (p. 8). The purpose of the "Look" cycle of the action research process is to build a picture of the problem. This is done through gathering information

FIGURE 2.4 **Action Research Model**

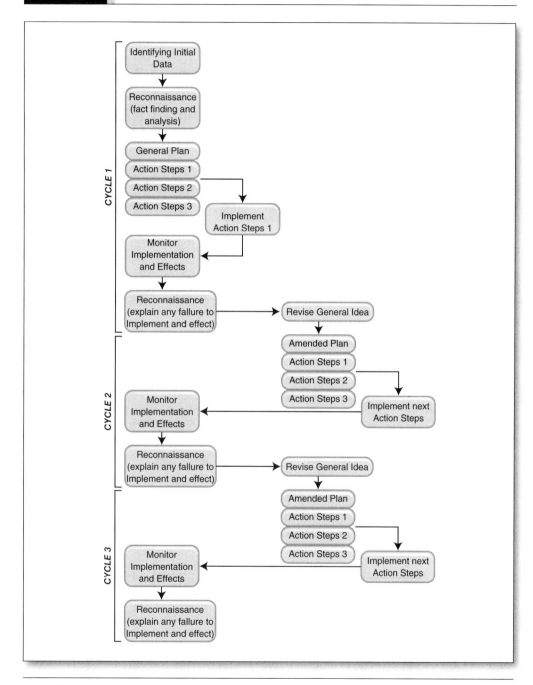

From Elliott (1991, p. 71).

| FIGURE 2.5 | **Action Research Interacting Spiral** |

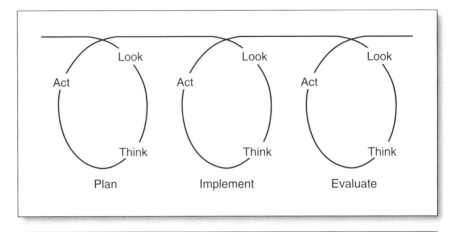

From Stringer (2014, p. 9).

that will allow practitioner-researchers to extend their understanding of the issue, their current experiences related to the problem, and the views of the stakeholders involved. The "Think" cycle includes analysis and interpretation of the information collected during the "Look" cycle. It involves identifying the pieces of information that will help practitioner-researchers understand the nature of the activities and events that they are researching. Finally, during the "Act" cycle, practitioner-researchers develop and implement the plan for taking action based on the results of the analysis and interpretation of the information that occurred during the "Think" cycle.

Mills (2011) analyzed major conceptual models of action research and suggested a dialectic action research spiral model that consists of four stages: identifying an area of focus, collecting data, analyzing and interpreting the data, and developing an action plan (see Figure 2.6). Designed for teachers, this model reflects the methodological steps that practitioner-researchers take when conducting an action research project. Researchers cycle back and forth between the problem and data collection and analysis, and data collection and analysis and interpretation. Mills (2011) termed his model dialectic because it is dynamic and responsive and can be adapted to different situations. According to Wolcott (1989), this model provides practitioner-researchers with "provocative and constructive ways" of reflecting about and evaluating their work (p. 137).

Steps in the Action Research Process

As it is clear from the discussion of select action research models, conceptually the action research process involves the following iterative steps: diagnosing an issue (identifying a problem), reconnaissance (collecting, analyzing, and interpreting data about a problem), planning (developing plan for action/intervention),

FIGURE 2.6	**Dialectic Action Research Spiral**

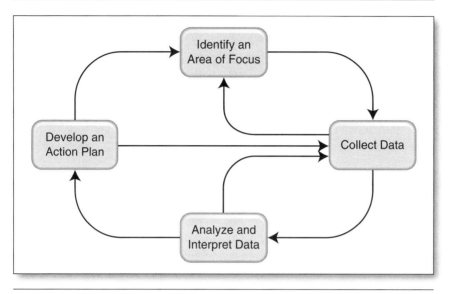

From Mills (2011, p. 19).

acting (implementing action/intervention plan), evaluation (collecting, analyzing, and interpreting data about action/intervention), and monitoring (revising and testing action/intervention). These steps are captured in the comprehensive conceptual model of action research steps developed for this book based on the discussed action research models. This model is presented in Figure 2.7. The six steps outlined in this model can be repeated in a cycle, depending on the needs of the situation. The linear progression of the steps may not be always observed. Dashed arrows show the possible interactions of the steps within an action research cycle. For instance, the development of the action plan may require collecting and analyzing additional data, thus prompting practitioner-researchers to go back to the reconnaissance phase. The action/intervention can be continually revised and improved during the monitoring phase, based on its continuous evaluation. Replanning of the action/intervention or additional needs assessment may be necessary based on the evaluation results or during the intervention monitoring process. In case intervention has been found ineffective, further diagnosing of the problem may be necessary and the new plan of action may be developed and implemented. Sometimes evaluation of the action may require practitioner-researchers to abandon the original plan and to develop a new plan, which is further evaluated and tested. This conceptual model of action research steps is used to guide the discussion of the applications of mixed methods in action research and the related methodological procedures.

Types and levels of integration of quantitative and qualitative methods are further discussed in Chapter 6 in relation to study designs.

So, what are the methodological characteristics of action research?

METHODOLOGICAL CHARACTERISTICS OF ACTION RESEARCH

The role of these methodological characteristics in applying mixed methods in action research is also discussed in Chapters 5 through 10.

Action research, like any other research approach, has a set of methodological characteristics that inform the design and implementation of an action research study. These methodological or procedural characteristics of action research are closely related to its dynamic character and cyclical nature as discussed above. Many action research authors agree on the following methodological features of action research: action research is systematic, cyclical, and flexible; it involves collection of multiple data sources and generation of a plan of action or intervention.

Systematic

As is true of any form of inquiry, action research occurs in a systematic manner. Stringer (2014) emphasized the systematic nature of action research as enabling practitioner-researchers to engage in an organized and methodologically sound process of investigation to achieve a desired outcome and to evaluate its effectiveness. Using systematic research procedures allows for producing knowledge that is credible and has a potential to be replicated in other settings. This knowledge is not only used to inform action/intervention, but also is refined and improved as a result of the action implementation and evaluation. To support this point, O'Leary (2004) stated that "[a]ction research is more than just change implementation and relies heavily on both the production of knowledge to produce change and the enacting of change to produce knowledge" (p. 139). So, action research is about both taking action to improve practice, and creating new knowledge about how and why improvement has happened (McNiff & Whitehead, 2011). Similarly, Creswell (2012) indicated, that high-quality action research follows the systematic procedures of problem identification, data collection, analysis, and interpretation, thus generating reliable knowledge to inform improvement of practice. The process is repeated in cycles of research and action, and involves constant evaluation of the actions taken.

For instance, Giachello and colleagues' (2003) action research study of reducing high rates of diabetes morbidity and mortality in Chicago's medically underserved minority communities, described in Box 2.3, is an example of a systematic inquiry that was carried out following the standards of good research practice. The study was guided by the purpose and research objectives that were implemented in two study phases: the reconnaissance phase (Phase I) and the evaluation phase (Phase II). In Phase I a comprehensive needs assessment of the situation was conducted to inform the development of the intervention. The data were collected by trained staff from multiple qualitative and quantitative data sources and analyzed using qualitative and quantitative analytic techniques. A rigorous evaluation plan was developed for Phase II to assess the results of the intervention activities. The process was guided by task forces, committees, collation members, and university consultants.

Cyclical

Action research occurs in cycles. In action research, one step leads to another and is repeated multiple times in "a continual improvement process" (Hinchey, 2008, p. 5). The end of the cycle generally initiates the beginning

FIGURE 2.7   **Steps in Action Research Process**

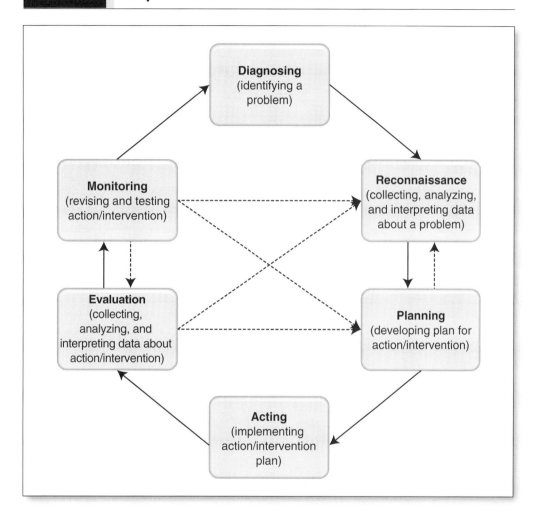

of another cycle. The cycle of activities forms an action research spiral in which each cycle is aimed at increasing practitioner-researchers' knowledge of the original problem (Herr & Anderson, 2005). Hinchey (2008) pointed out that "[i]t is not enough to plan and implement an action: its results must be systematically analyzed to determine whether desired improvements have occurred and whether unintended consequences, good or bad, turn up as well" (p. 4). Therefore, each cycle includes problem identification, data collection, analysis and interpretation, action implementation, and evaluation. According to O'Leary (2004), the goal is to continually refine the methods, the data collection, and their interpretation based on the knowledge gained in earlier cycles.

For example, Giachello and colleagues' (2003) study consisted of several cycles. They started with establishing community dialogue to inform the coalition formation. Coalition building involved capacity building through training of community members and stakeholders who volunteered to serve on the coalition. Then, the researchers together with community representatives collected, analyzed, and interpreted the community needs assessment data. The dissemination of the findings and consultations with the community followed, and resulted in the development and implementation of the action/intervention plan. The coalition evaluation committee, coalition staff, and a research consultant evaluated the results of the intervention. This process was ongoing and led to more cycles of data collection and analysis and refinement of the action plan.

Flexible

Action research takes shape as the knowledge emerges (O'Leary, 2004). Practitioner-researchers go back and forth between reflection about the problem, data collection, interpretation, and action. The process is not always linear and the next step is often influenced by what understanding action researchers develop about the problem and the actions taken to resolve the problem. Hinchey (2008) explained this process: "researchers commonly move back and forth among various activities, for the simple reason that later work often produces ideas for useful changes to original plans" (p. 52). This flexibility of the action research process is tied to its cyclical nature that allows practitioner-researchers to increase their knowledge about the complex situations and to learn how to find effective solutions. Consequently, although action research follows a series of systematic steps, the process is often "a flexible tool for the researcher's purposes—not a rigid and restrictive regimen" (Hinchey, 2008, p. 53).

For example, in their study Giachello and colleagues (2003) noted that the process that they have gone through with the coalition formation and development, and the implementation of the intervention, was ongoing and flexible. As such, once the task forces had analyzed the needs assessment data, they shared the preliminary findings with the coalition and drafted an action plan. The coalition conducted two community forums to present the findings and a preliminary plan to the community. Based on the feedback received, the coalition finalized the action plan and the study moved into the implementation phase.

Multiple Data Sources

In action research, practitioner-researchers often make use of all data that are available from both quantitative and qualitative sources. The purpose of using different types of data is to develop "a rigorous, cohesive set of conclusions about their topic" to inform the action planning and the evaluation of the outcomes (James, Milenkiewicz, & Bucknam, 2008). Many authors who write about action research agree that data should be collected from many sources to better understand the problem and to identify more viable solutions (Creswell, 2012; Mills, 2011). Sagor (2005) argued that **triangulation** or combination of multiple data sources enhances the credibility of research findings, and results in developing more feasible and more reliable action plans. These data sources can include both quantitative, or numeric data (e.g., responses to surveys, test scores, or health indicators) and qualitative, or text data (e.g., individual or focus group interviews, naturalistic observations, participants' narratives, and analysis of documents or pictures).

For example, Giachello and colleagues' (2003) study employed multiple sources of quantitative and qualitative data in both the reconnaissance (Phase I) and the evaluation (Phase II) study phases. In Phase I, qualitative data were collected from focus groups with health-care providers and diabetic and at-risk community residents. The quantitative data were collected through community inventory, and a telephone survey. Additionally, one of the coalition task forces obtained epidemiologic data about diabetes prevalence and rates in the community. During Phase II, more focus groups were conducted with community residents. The coalition evaluation committee also launched the plan to survey multiple stakeholders, including the coalition members, about the intervention effectiveness and fidelity. Additionally, the evaluation committee planned to compile hospitalization data at several stages to measure the intervention progress.

Plan of Action or Intervention

In action research, each cycle concludes with either developing and implementing, or refining the plan of action. According to Stringer (2014), the **action plan** consists of a series of tasks that would help practitioner-researchers achieve a resolution of the problem they are investigating. An action plan may target both the process of action research when the focus is more on activities and steps to be taken, and the outcomes of the process when the focus is on intervention development. Herr and Anderson (2005) observed that "[a]ction research is oriented to some action or cycle of actions that organizational or community members have taken, are taking, or wish to take to address a particular problematic situation" (pp. 3–4). An action plan may take the form of a presentation of the needs assessment or research results to the community, or developing a series of interventions to address the problem, or just implementing an ongoing research agenda to explore new practices. Once developed and implemented, the action plan frequently generates a new cycle of the process aimed at evaluating and monitoring the action or intervention (Hinchey, 2008).

The action plan is discussed in more detail in Chapter 10.

For example, in Giachello and colleagues' (2003) study, an action plan or intervention that targeted diabetic and at-risk people, as well as a broader community, was developed as a result of a comprehensive assessment of the community needs in addressing high rates of diabetes morbidity and mortality. The goals of the intervention plan were "to change community norms by working not only with community residents and health and human service providers but also with the school system, business (e.g., food industry), and labor unions" (p. 321). The plan included multiple intervention activities; the coalition further evaluated the intervention plan to assess its effectiveness and sustainability in this community with potential transferability to other similar communities.

SUMMARY

Action research is a popular approach and is increasingly being used in many fields. The popularity of action research is growing due to its focus on the solution of practical issues that require immediate attention, its goal at improving practice or developing individuals, and its emphasis on empowerment and emancipation with the focus on social change. Action research is viewed as a process of systematic inquiry, usually cyclical, conducted by those inside a community rather than by outside experts; its goal is to identify action that will generate improvement that practitioner-researchers believe is important. A practitioner's own practice is often the focus of research, and practitioner-researchers' insider perspectives inform the inquiry. Action or intervention is central to the idea of action research and requires a spiral of action cycles aimed at developing, implementing, and evaluating action or intervention plan to improve the practice.

The term *action research* was introduced by Kurt Lewin. It embraces different approaches influenced by how researchers and practitioners from multiple disciplines understand and define action research. Action research is participatory in that it involves multiple stakeholders and is a social process. It is reflexive and occurs through spirals of reflection and action. The idea of community is central in action research and is emphasized through a collaborative knowledge creation within a "community of interest" that includes all stakeholders with a vested interest in the issue. Participation in action research projects raises practitioner-researchers' awareness of their right to a voice in reframing and reconstructing social practices, and informs and empowers them to take actions they perceive important.

A variety of conceptual models of action research exist, however, they all present action research as a series of cyclical steps aimed at identifying action that will generate improvement that practitioner-researchers believe is important. The chapter discusses major action research models developed by Lewin, Kemmis and McTaggart and Elliot, Stringer, and Mills. The chapter advances a comprehensive conceptual model of the iterative steps involved in the action research process: diagnosing an issue (identifying a problem), reconnaissance (collecting, analyzing, and interpreting data about a problem), planning (developing plan for action/intervention), acting (implementing action/intervention plan), evaluation (collecting, analyzing, and interpreting data about action/intervention), and monitoring (revising and testing action/intervention). Methodological characteristics of action research are closely related to its dynamic character and cyclical nature. Action research is systematic, cyclical, and flexible; it involves collection of multiple data sources and generation of a plan of action or intervention.

REFLECTIVE QUESTIONS AND EXERCISES

1. Locate an action research published study in your area of interest. What characteristics of action research can you identify in this study? Discuss how well this study reflects the definitions of action research discussed in this chapter.

2. What features make action research a unique inquiry approach? Explain each feature and provide an illustrative example from your discipline.

3. Reflect on the role of community in action research. Why is the focus on community important? Discuss the nine principles of community-based action research. How do these principles shape action research?

4. Conduct a quick search of the library databases for action research studies in your discipline. Use the key words "action research," or "community-based action research" and the name of your discipline. Limit your search to the past 10 years. Record the number of action research studies found. What trends do you see in the application of action research in your discipline across the years?

5. Reflect on different models of action research. What similarities and differences do you find across these models? If you were to design an action research study, which model would you follow and why? Outline the steps in the research process and explain the goal of each step.

6. Explore the key methodological characteristics of action research. Discuss how these characteristics are reflected in action research studies that you found in your area of interest. Did the authors discuss these characteristics in these articles? If you were to report an action research study, how would you explain these characteristics? Write a few sentences for each characteristic to illustrate your thinking.

FURTHER READINGS

To learn more about a history of action research, examine the following sources:

Adelman, C. (1993). Kurt Lewin and the origins of action research. *Educational Action Research, 1*(1), 7–25.

Greenwood, D., & Levin, M. (2007). *Introduction to action research: Social research for social change* (2nd ed.). Thousand Oaks, CA: Sage, Ch. 2, pp. 13–34.

Hinchey, P. H. (2008). *Action research: Primer.* New York: Peter Lang, Ch. 1, pp. 1–17.

To learn more about the characteristics of action research, examine the following sources:

Kemmis, S., & McTaggart, R. (2007). Participatory action research: Communicative action and the public sphere. In N. Denzin & Y. Lincoln (Eds.), *Strategies of qualitative inquiry* (3rd ed., pp. 271–330). Thousand Oaks, CA: Sage.

McKernan, J. (1988). The countenance of curriculum action research: Traditional, collaborative, and emancipatory-critical conceptions. *Journal of Curriculum and Supervision, 3*(3), 173–200.

Schulz, A. J., Israel, B. A., Selig, S. M., Bayer, I. S. & Griffin, C. B. (1998). Development and implementation of principles for community-based research in public health. In R. H. MacNair (Ed.), *Research strategies for community practice* (pp. 83–110). New York: Haworth Press.

Senge, P., & Scharmer, O. (2001). Community action research: Learning as a community of practitioners, consultants and researchers. In P. Reason & H. Bradbury, *SAGE handbook of action research: Participative inquiry and practice* (pp. 238–249). Thousand Oaks, CA: Sage.

To learn more about the models of action research, examine the following sources:

Koshy, E., Koshy, V., & Waterman, H. (2011). *Action research in healthcare.* Thousand Oaks, CA: Sage, Ch. 1, pp. 1–10.

Mills, G. E. (2011). *Action research: A guide for the teacher researcher* (4th ed.). Boston: Pearson Education, Ch. 1, pp. 14–19.

Stringer, E. T. (2014). *Action research* (4th ed.). Thousand Oaks, CA: Sage, Ch. 1, pp. 5–10.

To learn more about the applications of action research in different disciplines, examine the following sources:

James, E. A., Milenkiewicz, M. T., & Bucknam, A. (2008). *Participatory action research for educational leadership: Using data-driven decision making to improve schools.* Thousand Oaks, CA: Sage.

Koshy, E., Koshy, V., & Waterman, H. (2011). *Action research in healthcare.* Thousand Oaks, CA: Sage.

Mills, G. E. (2011). *Action research: A guide for the teacher researcher* (4th ed.). Boston: Pearson Education.

3

Applying Mixed Methods in Action Research

OBJECTIVES

By the end of this chapter, the reader should be able to

- Understand different viewpoints on integrating mixed methods and action research,
- Describe features that are common in both mixed methods and action research,
- Explain the advantages of applying mixed methods in action research,
- Understand how mixed methods can inform each step in the cycle of the action research process,
- Describe the mixed methods methodological framework for action research,
- Discuss the trends in application of mixed methods in action research studies across disciplines, and
- Discuss in detail select examples of MMAR studies.

INTRODUCTION

The idea of applying mixed methods in action research is not novel. Action research and mixed methods methodologists have discussed the growing use of both quantitative and qualitative data in action research projects.

For example, Creswell (2012) drew a parallel between mixed methods and action research because in both research approaches quantitative and qualitative data are collected within one study. Mills (2011) indicated that in spite of the fact that qualitative methods seem to fit action research efforts more appropriately, study research questions may necessitate action researchers to use both quantitative and qualitative data sources, particularly when teacher-researches have to include student achievement data to augment classroom observations and qualitative narratives. Similarly, Koshy and colleagues (2011) referred to a frequent combination of the quantitative and qualitative data in action research studies in health care. In fact, Richardson and Reid (2006) in their action research evaluation study of a group cognitive behavioral therapy program for older adults with depression noted that,

> The triangulation or synthesis of multiple sources of data is a core element of action research and serves to integrate apparently disparate sources of sometimes gross, quantitative data with finer, qualitative data to titrate their combined contribution to global variable change. (pp. 62–63)

Finally, James and colleagues (2008) argued that in participatory action research, practitioners "make use of all available data (both qualitative and quantitative) in order to build a rigorous, cohesive set of conclusions" (p. 81). These assertions are supported by the growing number of empirical action research studies in different disciplines in which both quantitative and qualitative data were collected either at some or all stages of the research process—that is, the stages of reconnaissance or fact finding and evaluation of the action/intervention.

Recognition of mixed methods as a research approach promoted further discussions of a possible connection between mixed methods and action research. Recent action research texts (e.g., James et al., 2008; McNiff & Whitehead, 2011; Mills, 2011) have included some explanation of mixed methods as a potential design or method within action research. In their editorial to one of the first issues of the *Journal of Mixed Methods Research,* Creswell and Tashakkori (2007b) pointed out how the practice perspective or "bottom-up" approach to conducting research influences investigators to apply mixed methods in "traditional" research approaches, including action research (p. 306). The editors argued that researchers tend to adopt new methodological ideas "when they can attach them, in some way, to their current forms of and preferences for research" (p. 306). McNiff and Whitehead (2011) extended Creswell and Tashakkori's (2007b) view on mixed methods and traditional forms of research, suggesting that action research is a broad methodological approach and therefore "can and should incorporate a range of methods from other approaches" (p. 49).

Alternatively, Christ (2009, 2010) argued that action research should be viewed as "a form of mixed methods research," because action research shares the same philosophy, methodologies, and design characteristics as mixed methods research (p. 293). While Christ's observations about **epistemological** and methodological similarities between mixed methods and action research are correct, there is widespread recognition of action research as a methodology and not a single method (McNiff & Whitehead, 2011), which makes it difficult to position action research within a mixed methods approach. Similarities and differences between mixed methods and action research were also explored by Wisniewska (2011). She compared mixed methods and action research empirical studies in the English Language Teaching field and concluded that the two approaches may be similar

Refer to Chapter 2 and Figure 2.6 for the discussion and illustration of the stages or steps in the action research process.

in terms of stating goals for data collection and integrating methods, although they may differ in data analysis, results presentation, and how qualitative and quantitative methods are combined within a study.

So, what common features do mixed methods and action research share? What makes researchers integrate mixed methods into action research studies?

CONNECTING MIXED METHODS AND ACTION RESEARCH

There are a number of features that make the integration of mixed methods and action research justifiable and realistic. These features should not be interpreted as providing complete and absolute similarity between the two approaches, but rather as offering common ground for connecting mixed methods and action research to produce scientifically sound and effective plans for action and evaluation of the action results. These features relate to the overarching goals of mixed methods and action research; their philosophical foundations, social justice perspective, and certain methodological and procedural characteristics. Box 3.1 summarizes these features, which are further discussed in the following sections.

BOX 3.1

Common Features of Mixed Methods and Action Research

- Mixed methods and action research follow the principles of systematic inquiry in designing and implementing research endeavors.
- Mixed methods and action research are aimed at providing comprehensive information: mixed methods seeks to provide comprehensive answers to study research questions, whereas action research seeks to provide comprehensive solutions to practical problems.
- Mixed methods and action research have an underlying pragmatic philosophical foundation of rejecting the quantitative and qualitative incompatibility thesis.
- Mixed methods and action research are dialectical in nature, moving from exploratory to explanatory, and then to confirmatory, through identifiable study phases.
- Mixed methods and action research use reflective practice, because both require reflection about the next step that is grounded in the results from the previous step.
- Mixed methods and action research apply a transformative/advocacy lens aimed at seeking social justice.
- Mixed methods and action research use quantitative and qualitative information sources; they both collect and analyze quantitative and qualitative data.
- Mixed methods and action research are cyclical in nature, and both follow clearly defined study phases.
- Mixed methods and action research apply a collaborative approach to research because they seek knowledge about "what works" in practice.
- Mixed methods and action research combine *insider–outsider* perspectives: in mixed methods due to a changing researcher's role and in action research due to its participatory nature.

Following Principles of Systematic Inquiry

As research approaches, both mixed methods and action research are designed and conducted following a set of systematic procedures or steps, from the identification of the research problem and formulation of research questions to data collection, analysis, interpretation, and evaluation. Specifically, Maxwell and Loomis (2003) suggested that mixed methods researchers should consider five interconnected research components while designing a mixed methods study: (1) the study purpose, (2) its conceptual framework, (3) research questions, (4) methods for data collection and analysis, and (5) validity or credibility issues. Writing about action research, Stringer (2014) emphasized its systematic character by describing action research as a mechanism for practitioners to engage in a systematic inquiry "to design an appropriate way of accomplishing a desired goal and to evaluate its effectiveness" (p. 6). By providing the means to systematically investigate the issue in diverse contexts, action research enables practitioner-researchers to find more effective solutions and their efficient applications. Indeed, Kurt Lewin's (1948b) original idea of action research, as discussed in Chapter 2, is grounded in the systematic cycle of information gathering, analysis, and reflection.

Providing Comprehensive Information

Mixed methods research seeks to provide more comprehensive answers to study research questions through the integration of quantitative and qualitative methods with the purpose of examining an issue from different aspects. Speaking about the advantages of mixed methods, Yin (2006) wrote that "Implicit in the prominent role played by a single study is the valuing of mixed methods in producing converging evidence, presumably more compelling than might have been produced by any single method alone" (p. 41). Mixed methods studies tend to be more informative than mono-method studies, because they follow a fundamental principle of mixed methods research—that of building on the strengths of different methods (Johnson & Onwuegbuzie, 2004; Johnson & Turner, 2003).

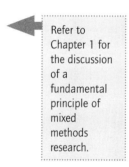

Refer to Chapter 1 for the discussion of a fundamental principle of mixed methods research.

While mixed methods seeks to provide more comprehensive answers to study research questions, action research seeks to provide more comprehensive solutions to practical problems. As discussed in Chapter 2, an overall purpose of action research is to enable practitioner-researchers to better understand and solve imperative problems in their social settings (McKernan, 1988). Herr and Anderson (2005) insightfully observed, "Solid action research leads to a deepened understanding of the question posed as well as to more sophisticated questions" (p. 86). By going through a spiral of cycles of critical action and reflection, practitioner-researchers gain a more robust understanding of the issue and thus are able to design action plans grounded in more weighted solutions.

Being Pragmatic

As discussed in Chapter 1, pragmatism serves as a philosophical foundation for mixed methods research. Pragmatism rejects the quantitative and qualitative incompatibility thesis and helps justify the

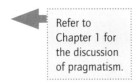

Refer to Chapter 1 for the discussion of pragmatism.

combination of quantitative and qualitative methods within one study in order to seek the best answers to the posed research questions (Maxcy, 2003). Johnson and Onwuegbuzie (2004) suggested that the basic pragmatic research method applied in a mixed methods approach should consist of choosing "the combination or mixture of methods and procedures that works best for answering your research questions" (p. 17).

Although action research is sometimes associated with a **constructivist** worldview because of its exploratory nature and reliance on qualitative methods (Stringer, 2014), a practical focus of action research and the need to design and implement effective action plans often calls for a "what works" approach. Importantly, considering their own experiences of conducting action research, Greenwood and Levin (2007) referred to it as pragmatic because they rejected the assumption that action research cannot be scientific. They also believed that "action researchers are obligated to be competent in all major forms of social inquiry" (p. 6). Indeed, as discussed in Chapter 2, action research is viewed as a combination of empirical (knowledge derived from experience) and rational (knowledge derived from scientific reasoning) procedures that require multiple sources of evidence; therefore, pragmatic epistemological principles provide a useful philosophical rationale for action research studies that use both quantitative and qualitative data. Christ (2010) also argued that action research is influenced by Dewey's view of pragmatism, because knowledge is created through action.

Being Dialectical

The fact that mixed methods research is grounded in the philosophy of pragmatism makes mixed methods acceptable to other philosophical paradigms underlying quantitative and qualitative research approaches (Johnson et al., 2007; Teddlie &Tashakkori, 2009). A complex nature of mixed methods research aimed at addressing exploratory and confirmatory questions within a study requires an effective combination of available methods, diverse viewpoints, and creative ideas. Greene (2007) suggested that mixed methods researchers should adopt the "**dialectic stance**" (p. 79). In other words, researchers need to think dialectically and incorporate multiple **mental models** with their distinctive epistemological characteristics and research traditions when designing and conducting mixed methods studies. Thinking dialectially implies critically selecting the best available methods and their combinations to address the complexity of the modern society and to better understand the studied phenomena.

Refer to Chapter 2 and Figure 2.5 for the discussion and illustration of Stringer's (2014) action research interacting spiral.

A practical focus of action research also necessitates using a dialectical approach to seeking effective solutions. For example, Winter (1987) argued that any attempt to understand practice must be dialectical because any social practice consists of an intertwined network of complex and contradictory elements and relationships, including individual and organizational knowledge, skills, values, and ethics. Winter indicated that these relationships are "experienced in almost instantaneous succession as a single essence and a plurality of qualities, as universal and specific, as self-defined and as defined-in-relation-to-another" (p. 12). The dialectical nature of action research is reflected through the spiral of action research cycles consisting of reflecting, planning, acting, and observing

(Lewin, 1948b). Stringer's (2014) representation of the action research process as an interacting spiral of look-ing, thinking, and acting, perhaps, best captures the dialectical essence of action research.

Using Reflective Practice

Reflexivity in mixed methods and action research is closely related to the dialectical nature of these research approaches (Greene, 2007). When conceptualizing a mixed methods study, the researchers critically consider the choice of the epistemological strategies that best match the research problem they intend to investigate. Designing and conducting a mixed methods study requires reflection about a range of theoretical and practical issues, including the choice of a research focus, a study design, quantitative and qualitative methods to collect and analyze the data, and the strategies for integrating the quantitative and qualitative methods. A team approach, which is often used in mixed methods projects due to complexity of the research problems addressed, establishes the need for reflection and exchange among the members of the team (Curry et al., 2012; Hemmings, Beckett, Kennerly, & Yap, 2013).

As noted in Chapter 2, reflection is an essential feature of action research. Reflection is "deliberately and systematically undertaken and generally requires that some form of evidence be presented to support assertions" (Herr & Anderson, 2005, p. 3). Reflection is embedded in action research cycles, as is evident from all conceptual models of action research. According to Mills (2011), action research-ers incorporate a reflective stance into their daily practices to critically examine and improve them. Researchers critically reflect on the assessment of the identi-fied problem, they use reflection to make a decision about the needed action or intervention, and they reflect on the action outcomes and further steps to take.

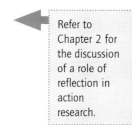

Refer to Chapter 2 for the discussion of a role of reflection in action research.

Applying Transformative/Advocacy Lens

Mixed methods research is frequently cited as lending itself to a **transformative-emancipatory framework** (Mertens, 2003), or as applying an **advocacy lens** (Creswell, 2003). For example, Johnson and colleagues (2007), who analyzed 19 definitions of mixed methods research, quoted Mertens (2003) when defin-ing mixed methods research within a transformative-emancipatory framework as the following:

> Mixed methods research, when undertaken from a transformative stance, is the use of qualitative and quantitative methods that allow for the collection of data about historical and contextual factors, with special emphasis on issues of power that can influence the achievement of social justice and avoidance of oppression. (Mertens, 2003, as cited in Johnson et al., 2007, p. 120)

In fact, transformative mixed methods approach is often viewed as embedded in participatory action research. According to Mertens, Bledsoe, Sullivan, and Wilson (2010), transformative mixed methods "suggests the need for community involvement, as well as the cyclical use of data to inform decisions for next steps, whether those steps related to additional research or to program changes" (p. 199). The argument for such assertions is that mixed methods produces knowledge that reflects the power and social relationships in society, thus giving people the tools to improve it.

As discussed in Chapter 2, action research is always value laden. For instance, Herr and Anderson (2005) wrote that "[a]ction research takes place in settings that reflect a society characterized by conflicting values and an unequal distribution of resources and power. . . . Action researchers must interrogate received notions of improvement or solutions in terms of who ultimately benefits from the actions undertaken" (p. 4). In action research, practitioner-researchers cocreate knowledge, policy, and practice through an iterative process of action and learning. This process often includes reappraisal of the existing norms, values, and assumptions and developing an understanding of how they are shaped by power, raising an awareness of a social change (Pettit, 2010).

Using Quantitative and Qualitative Information Sources

As discussed in Chapter 1, one of the characteristic features of mixed methods research is the integration of both quantitative and qualitative methods within a study; such methods' integration has its unique advantages (Creswell & Plano Clark, 2011; Teddlie & Tashakkori, 2009). In mixed methods studies, researchers combine quantitative and qualitative data to reach more validated and more complete answers to the posed research questions. Both types of data are particularly required when there is a need to address confirmatory (verifying knowledge) and exploratory (generating knowledge) questions within a single study (Teddlie & Tashakkori, 2009).

The ability to address both confirmatory and exploratory questions is also appealing to action researchers, who look for more comprehensive solutions to complex practical issues in professional settings. Many action research texts emphasize the need for including multiple sources of evidence, and discuss collection and analysis of different types of quantitative and qualitative data (Hinchey, 2008; Koshy et al., 2011; Tomal, 2010). Some authors mention the use of mixed methods designs (James et al., 2008; McNiff & Whitehead, 2011; Mills, 2011). As Greenwood and Levin (2007) indicated, the need for addressing complex social problems makes it necessary for action researchers to be knowledgeable about major quantitative and qualitative data collection strategies and to be able to use them effectively when engaged in action research studies.

Being Cyclical

A mixed methods study may often consist of multiple quantitative and qualitative strands that researchers implement sequentially. As discussed in Chapter 1, these strands often build on each other, with one strand informing the next strand. Creswell and Plano Clark (2011) referred to such mixed methods designs as multiphase—that is, consisting of multiple phases. Teddlie and Tashakkori (2009) suggested that sequential mixed methods designs consisting of more than two strands have an iterative nature, meaning that researchers can move from the initial strand of quantitative or qualitative data collection and analysis to the next strand of alternative data collection and analysis, and then to the next quantitative or qualitative strand seeking more credible answers to the research questions. Additionally, Bryman (2006) noted that a mixed methods study "frequently brings more to researchers' understanding than they anticipate at the outset" (p. 111). A new focus on the studied problem may prompt refining research questions and/or changing the study direction.

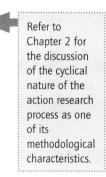

Refer to Chapter 2 for the discussion of the cyclical nature of the action research process as one of its methodological characteristics.

The cyclical nature is one of the characteristic features of action research. The cycle of activities forms a research spiral in which "each cycle increases the researcher's knowledge of the original question, puzzle, or problem" (Herr & Anderson, 2005, p. 5). In action research, one step leads to another and is repeated multiple times to form a continual improvement process. During these steps the methods and the understanding of the problem are refined based on the knowledge gained in earlier steps (O'Leary, 2004).

Adopting a Collaborative Approach to Research

The breadth and scope of mixed methods studies often require a collaborative team approach. An integrative use of quantitative and qualitative methods in a mixed methods study calls for the utilization of different research strategies and approaches, and requires different forms of expertise. Shulha and Wilson (2003) described collaborative mixed methods research as "the purposeful application of a multiple person, multiple perspective approach to questions of research and evaluation" (p. 640). They argued that collaborative mixed methods is different from traditional forms of inquiry in its ability to produce results that are reflective not only of certain levels of expertise in quantitative and qualitative data collection and analysis, but also of the researchers' capacity to learn though collaboration and to construct joint meanings of the data. Moreover, Nastasi, Hitchcock, and Brown (2010) proposed a *synergistic partnership-based fully integrated mixed methods research framework* that implies collaboration and partnership with all interested stakeholders in a mixed methods research project. The authors claimed that inclusion of professional collaboration and stakeholder participatory approaches in mixed methods research is necessary to achieve its pragmatic and transformative goals. Other mixed methods researchers also discussed the need and advantages of a collaborative, team-based, and often multidisciplinary mixed methods approach (Creswell et al., 2011; Padgett, 2012; Tritter, 2007).

Collaboration is one of the principles of action research because through action research people engage in examining the social practices that connect them with other people in their social network through social interactions over the studied issue (Kemmis & McTaggart, 2007). Knowledge generation is a collaborative process and requires collegial interactions, active participation, and joint problem solving by all stakeholders and at all stages in the study process (McNiff & Whitehead, 2011). As noted in Chapter 2, action research is best done in collaboration with others who are affected by the issue under investigation. Collaboration takes multiple forms and may involve not only collaboration among practitioner-researchers in their professional settings but also partnerships between "insiders" with outside experts, such as university consultants, other professionals, and/or representatives from a larger community.

Combining Insider–Outsider Perspectives

The use of both quantitative and qualitative methods that have different underlying philosophical assumptions and epistemological strategies often requires mixed methods researchers to balance insider and outsider perspectives on the problem they study. For example, in the quantitative strand of the study, mixed methods researchers take an outsider (or observer) role and collect numeric data, often referred to as *etic* data (Currall & Towler, 2003), using quantitative measurement instruments. In the qualitative strand of the mixed methods study, researchers explore and interpret the perspectives and experiences of the individuals who are insiders to the system or organization; this type of data is often referred to as *emic* data. The challenge mixed methods researchers face is to balance etic and emic views in accurately utilizing and presenting the insider's view and the outsider's view (Johnson & Onwuegbuzie, 2006).

Action research is believed to have a focus on the insider because it is originated by practitioners in their communities. However, Herr and Anderson (2005) argued that since action research often involves multiple stakeholders and collaborative partnerships, it "leaves the positionality (insider or outsider) of the researcher open" and may create challenges associated with the balance of power, ownership of the data, and accuracy of the problem rep-

Refer to Chapter 2 for the discussion of the nine principles of community-based participatory action research.

resentation (p. 3). To overcome this "insider-outsider conundrum" (p. 53) and bring both the insider and outsider perspectives into the inquiry process, action research should always be collaborative and participatory, regardless of whether a researcher is an outsider or an insider to the study setting. As discussed in Chapter 2, fostering colearning and capacity building among all partners in an action research project is one of the principles of community-based action research (Schulz et al., 1998).

So, these common features between mixed methods and action research seem to provide enough support for integrating the two approaches within a study. This leads to an important question related to the application of mixed methods in action research: How can mixed methods inform and enhance action research?

ADVANTAGES OF APPLYING MIXED METHODS IN ACTION RESEARCH

As explained in the introduction to this chapter, the argument for connecting or integrating mixed methods and action research is not new. Many mixed methods and action research authors recognize the need for and advantages of applying mixed methods in action research studies. First and foremost, an increased utility of the mixed methods approach across social, behavioral, and health sciences in the recent decade (Alise & Teddlie, 2010; Creswell, 2010; Ivankova & Kawamura, 2010) produces evidence to conclude that mixed methods can provide a sound methodological framework for action research due to its ability to produce conclusions about the research issue that are more rigorous and more consistent. Moreover, in times of evidence-based and data-driven calls for improvement, there is a need for action research that meets rigorous standards to generate scientifically sound and effective plans for action or interventions (James et al., 2008; Lyons & DeFranco, 2010; McNiff & Whitehead, 2011; Mills, 2011). For example, McNiff and Whitehead (2011) argued that without a solid research and knowledge base, action research often turns into "a form of personal-professional development" (p. 11). Applying mixed methods in action research may help provide a comprehensive initial assessment of the problem, develop a more solid plan of action, and conduct a more rigorous evaluation of the action/ intervention implementation through informed integration of multiple quantitative and qualitative data sources. When combined with mixed methods, action research can assist practitioner-researchers and stakeholders in developing what Lyons and DeFranco (2010) referred to "a new appreciation for a data-driven decision-making process" to inform the improvement of their current practices (p. 149).

Rigorous action research goes beyond simply solving a problem. It compels practitioner-researchers to reconsider the problem in a more complex way, often leading to a new set of questions or problems (Anderson & Herr, 1999). Incorporating mixed methods procedures into each action research cycle may help practitioner-researchers secure a more systematic approach to action/intervention monitoring, thus providing a solid ground for promoting sustainability of change. Additionally, by capitalizing on the strengths of both quantitative and qualitative methods (Johnson & Turner, 2003), mixed methods can help ensure better transferability of the action research study results to other contexts and community settings. As Young and Higgins (2010) indicated with reference to public health and health care, action research that "frames mixed method research has potential to bring contextualized clinically relevant findings into program planning and policy-making arenas toward developing meaningful health and social policies relevant to primary prevention" (p. 346).

Besides, action research is seen "as producing not only conceptual knowledge but also as exploring *new ways of knowing*" (Herr & Anderson, 2005, p. 58, emphasis in original). Mixed methods, as an established research approach, builds on the meaningful integration of quantitative and qualitative methods, thus creating new and more enhanced ways of learning about the problem of interest. The ability of mixed methods research to provide opportunities to think creatively and to theorize beyond a traditional quantitative-qualitative divide helps generate more valid meta-inferences to inform the need and direction for social change (Greene & Caracelli, 1997; Mason, 2006). Furthermore, a pragmatic nature of mixed methods research makes it advantageous over a single method approach, such as quantitative or qualitative, in illuminating and assessing change over time without sacrificing the credibility and validity standards (Perry, 2009).

Box 3.2 summarizes the advantages of applying mixed methods in action research. These observations are grounded in the literature about these two research approaches and in published action research studies that applied mixed methods in one or several stages in the research process. Refer to Box 3.3 for an illustration of how Phillips and Davidson (2009) explained the advantages of applying mixed methods in their Residential-Palliative Approach Competency (R-PAC) action research project.

So, mixed methods, as a sound and pragmatic research approach, is viewed as being advantageous for supporting action research and providing a solid scientific methodological framework for it. This leads to another question: At what stages or steps in the action research process can practitioner-researchers apply mixed methods?

APPLICATION OF MIXED METHODS IN ACTION RESEARCH

Mixed Methods Methodological Framework for Action Research

A new mixed methods methodological framework for action research is proposed to guide further discussion of how mixed methods can be applied in action research. This mixed methods methodological framework for action research is graphically presented in Figure 3.1 and conceptually follows the model of action research steps discussed in Chapter 2. Each step is treated as an individual phase in the research process because it has clearly defined boundaries with the starting and ending points. Figure 3.1 shows how mixed methods can inform and enhance each phase in the cycle of the action research process. Solid arrows indicate the

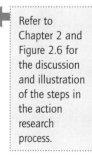

Refer to Chapter 2 and Figure 2.6 for the discussion and illustration of the steps in the action research process.

BOX 3.2

Advantages of Applying Mixed Methods in Action Research

- Mixed methods research helps establish a scientific methodological framework for action research.
- Mixed methods research helps enhance a systematic approach to research through informed and consistent utilization of quantitative and qualitative methods.
- Mixed methods research helps create new and more enhanced ways of learning about a practical problem/issue.
- Mixed methods research helps provide a comprehensive assessment of the problem through informed integration of multiple quantitative and qualitative data sources.
- Mixed methods research helps generate a more reliable and more valid action/intervention plan, which is scientifically designed and tested.
- Mixed methods research helps enrich credibility and validity of the study results through informed integration of multiple quantitative and qualitative data sources.
- Mixed methods research helps provide a more rigorous evaluation of the action/intervention implementation through informed integration of multiple quantitative and qualitative data sources.
- Mixed methods research helps provide a more systematic approach to action/intervention monitoring and promoting sustainability of change.
- Mixed methods research helps ensure better transferability of the study results to other contexts and settings.

BOX 3.3

Advantages of Using Mixed Methods in an Action Research Study to Investigate a Palliative Approach in Residential Aged Care

The expansive scope of these research questions suggested that neither purely qualitative nor quantitative methods of data collection would be adequate to provide comprehensive insight into this complex care issue (Mertens 2004). Using mixed methods allowed the researcher to draw from the strengths and minimize the weaknesses of the quantitative and qualitative paradigms across the R-PAC Project's eight sub-studies (Johnson and Onwuegbuzie 2004).

It was also anticipated that conducting a mixed methods research design within an action research framework would help to hasten the teams' understanding of the area of enquiry and achieve the R-PAC Project's research goals in a timely manner (Winter and Munn-Giddings 2001). This occurred because mixed methods offered a practical and outcome-oriented method of enquiry and complemented the action research cycle of reflection, assessment, planning, action and observation.

From Phillips and Davidson (2009, p. 202).

FIGURE 3.1	Mixed Methods Methodological Framework for Action Research

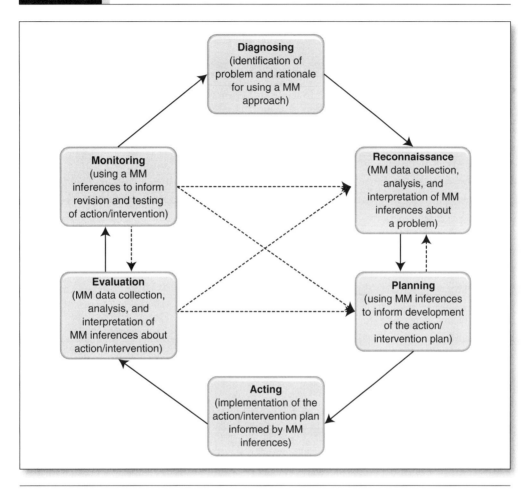

Note: MM = mixed methods.

sequence of the phases in the action research process, while dashed arrows show other possible iterations of the research activities within an action research cycle.

According to the suggested mixed methods methodological framework for action research, mixed methods or some procedural and conceptual aspects of it can be applied at each phase within an action research cycle. During the **diagnosing phase**, when practitioner-researchers identify the problem or issue in the workplace or other community setting that requires a solution, mixed methods can help conceptualize the problem and identify the rationale for investigating it by using both quantitative and qualitative methods. The **reconnaissance, or fact finding, phase** in Kurt Lewin's (1948b) terminology, is when a preliminary assessment of the identified problem or issue is conducted in order to develop a plan of action/intervention. A systematic and integrative collection and analysis of quantitative and qualitative data during this phase helps generate more thorough interpretations of the assessment results, and create meta-inferences that inform the development of the plan of action/intervention. During the **planning phase**, practitioner-researchers critically reflect on the meta-inferences that were generated as a result of conducting a mixed methods preliminary assessment of the issue; they set the action objectives or expected outcomes and design an action/intervention based on these interpretations and reflections.

The next step in the action research cycle is to act. During the **acting phase**, an action/intervention plan, which was informed by mixed methods inferences, is implemented. Then it is necessary to conduct a rigorous evaluation of the action/intervention to see whether it has produced the desired outcomes. The use of mixed methods during the **evaluation phase** involves collection and analysis of quantitative and qualitative data and interpretation of the integrated quantitative and qualitative results. During the **monitoring phase**, based on the new set of mixed methods inferences that were generated during the action/intervention evaluation, practitioner-researchers make decisions about whether the revisions or further testing of the action/intervention plan is needed. The decision may be to continue with the planned intervention and subsequently conduct more mixed methods evaluation of the intervention outcomes, which may lead to further refinement of the action/intervention plan. Alternatively, a decision may be to return to the reconnaissance phase and conduct more needs assessment or more in-depth investigation of the problem and change the action plan based on the new mixed methods inferences.

The results of mixed methods evaluation can also help practitioner-researchers recognize that the problem or issue is not well identified or focused and that further diagnosing of the problem is needed. In this situation, practitioner-researchers may return to the initial diagnosing phase to further conceptualize the problem and assess the current situation; based on this assessment, practitioner-researchers will make a decision about how to best proceed and develop a revised plan of action/intervention using informed integration of multiple quantitative and qualitative data sources. If the action/intervention is successful, continuous mixed methods evaluation of its progress can help promote sustainability of the action/intervention and enable transferability of the action research study results to other contexts and community settings.

The mixed methods methodological framework for action research is further discussed and illustrated in this chapter using examples of published action research studies that applied mixed methods in different disciplines. One example includes a published research protocol for an action research study in health care to illustrate how the study has been conceptualized during the diagnosing phase. But before moving to this discussion it is worthwhile to look at the trends in the application of mixed methods in published action research studies across disciplines.

So, how do action researchers use mixed methods, and what reasons do they provide for integrating mixed methods into the action research process?

Application of Mixed Methods in Published Action Research Studies

To assess the scope and level of use of mixed methods in action research studies, six library databases (Academic One File, Academic Search Premier, ERIC, PsycINFO, PubMed, and Social Sciences Full Text) were searched for empirical studies using combinations of the following search terms: "action research," "practitioner research," "participatory research," "community-based research," "mixed method(s)," and "mixed-method(s)." The search was limited to articles in the English language published in peer-reviewed journals. No limit on the year of publication was set, but the search was limited to inclusion of articles up to December 2012. The goal was to identify action research studies that intentionally used mixed methods as part of the study design, data collection, or analysis. Only completed action research studies or those that were in progress were considered. Both quantitative and qualitative data collection had to be reported to meet an accepted definition of mixed methods research (Tashakkori & Creswell, 2007). Methodological discussions, meta-analysis, and reviews of the literature were excluded from analysis. After eliminating over-lapping studies across the databases, 108 action research studies that had both quantitative and qualitative components reported in one paper were considered eligible for further analysis. These studies were termed **mixed methods action research (MMAR)** studies and are referred to as such in this book hereafter. Being embedded into the mixed methods methodological framework for action research, a MMAR study includes the methodological and procedural steps that characterize a traditional mixed methods research study, but differs from it in the specific purposes of the reconnaissance or evaluation phases of the action research cycle.

Refer to Chapter 1 for Tashakkori and Creswell's (2007) definition of mixed methods research.

Each article was obtained in full text and coded for the following eight indicators: (1) subject area or discipline, (2) indication of the use of mixed methods, (3) phase in the action research process where mixed methods was used (reconnaissance, evaluation, or both), (4) rationale for using mixed methods, (5) study purpose and research questions/objectives/aims, (6) sequence or timing of the quantitative and qualitative data collection and analysis during each phase, (7) indication of the mixed methods design used, and (8) types of quantitative and qualitative data collected. Since the coded information was explicitly presented or not presented in the reviewed articles, there was no need for an inter-coder agreement procedure to verify the credibility of this information (Babbie, 2005).

Year of Publication and Discipline

The selected 108 MMAR studies were published between 1999 and 2012, with the majority of the studies (80, or 74%) published between 2009 and 2012 (see Figure 3.2). Such an increase in the reported studies that applied mixed methods in action research is not surprising, if we take into account a dramatic increase in published mixed methods methodological discussions, publication of some major mixed methods books, and adoption of mixed methods in the disciplines that previously favored a mono-method approach (Ivankova & Kawamura, 2010). The MMAR studies covered 10 subject areas or disciplines with the predominance of them in health and education (87, or 76%): health care (42), higher education (21), kindergarten through 12th grade, or K–12 education, (17), nursing (7); other disciplines included psychology (6), social work (5), sociology (4), environmental science (2), management (2), and organizational learning (2; see Figure 3.3). The historical receptivity to using action research in education and the increasing utilization of participatory and community-based research in health can account for the prevalence of MMAR studies in health and education.

| FIGURE 3.2 | **MMAR Studies by Year of Publication** |

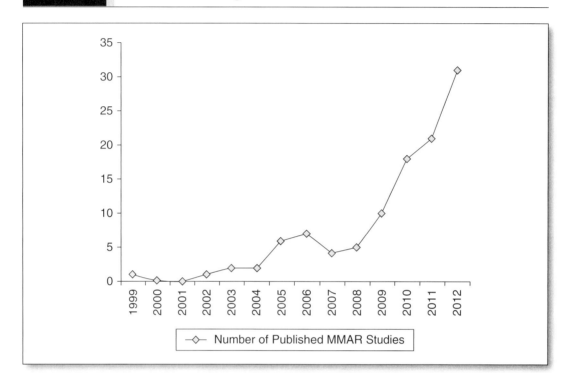

Indication of the Use of Mixed Methods

In more than half of the studies (56%) reviewed, the authors explicitly indicated the use of mixed methods either in the article title, or abstract, or the methods section, or both in the abstract and the methods section. The observed tendency is for the authors in recent years (2010–2012) to more frequently mention employing a mixed methods approach or design in addition to action research. In the earlier years, the authors tended to discuss the use of both quantitative and qualitative methods as part of the action research process without specifically referring to mixed methods.

It is interesting that in less than half of the reviewed studies (47%) in which the use of mixed methods was indicated the authors did not elaborate on mixed methods in the body of the article after referring to it in the title or abstract. No observable trends per year or per discipline were noticed for the articles that reported but did not explain the use of mixed methods, or for those that did not refer to mixed methods but utilized both quantitative and qualitative data. This lack of consistency in explaining a mixed methods study design in addition to using an action research approach may be attributed to the fact that not all action researchers had enough information on how to integrate mixed methods and action research at the time of the article publication or, alternatively, that they considered the use of multiple quantitative and qualitative methods as part of the action research design.

| FIGURE 3.3 | MMAR Studies by Subject Area or Discipline and Year of Publication |

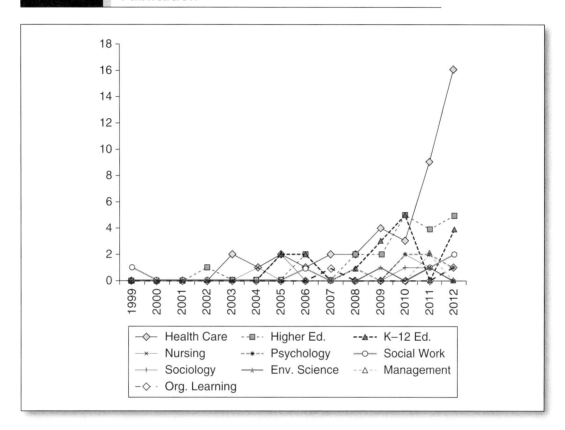

Rationale for Using Mixed Methods

More than half of the articles (53%) that indicated the use of mixed methods included the rationale for using this approach as part of the action research study. The most common rationale was triangulation of quantitative and qualitative data sources to ensure the breadth and depth of the study and to enhance the study validity. Another argument provided for combining quantitative and qualitative methods was the fact that such integration gives researchers an opportunity to view the studied phenomenon from multiple perspectives and to draw more enriched conclusions about the problem/issue. Authors also mentioned that using mixed methods allowed for capturing perspectives of multiple stakeholders to better inform the policymakers and to ensure the right direction for a change action. Additionally, a systematic collection and analysis of information from multiple data sources was seen as providing a necessary foundation for monitoring the processes and outcomes of change over time. Table 3.1 presents select examples of the reasons for applying mixed methods in action research studies in different subject areas.

Stage in the Action Research Process

A mixed methods approach was more frequently used during the evaluation phase (62%) in the action research cycle to evaluate a program, educational activity, organization of practice, intervention, or public health initiative (e.g., Akintobi et al., 2012; Arnold et al., 2012; Davidson et al., 2008; Kostos & Shin, 2010; Shattuck, Dubins, & Zilberman, 2011; Strang, 2011). Application of mixed methods during this phase was more common in action research studies in education, including higher education and K through 12. In 29% of the studies, both quantitative and qualitative methods were used during the reconnaissance phase in the action research cycle, when the assessment of the situation, the problem, and the needs was conducted (e.g., Greysen, Allen, Lucas, Wang, & Rosenthal, 2012; Krueger, 2010; Maritz, Pretorius, & Plant, 2011; Pickard, 2006; Thornewill, Dowling, Cox, & Esterhay, 2011). Such use of mixed methods during this phase was common for MMAR studies across all disciplines. In only 9 % of the reported studies, quantitative and qualitative methods were applied during both reconnaissance and evaluation phases. The articles typically reported either a completed action research study or the first complete action research cycle (e.g., McKellar, Pincombe, & Henderson, 2009; Taut, 2007; White & Wafra, 2011; Williamson, Webb, & Abelson-Mitchell, 2004). In such instances the predominance of MMAR studies was obvious in health care and nursing.

Mixed Methods Design

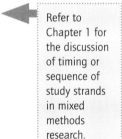

Refer to Chapter 1 for the discussion of timing or sequence of study strands in mixed methods research.

A majority of the reviewed articles (73%) used concurrent sequence or timing of quantitative and qualitative data collection and analysis, which means that both quantitative and qualitative data were collected and analyzed independently from each other, sometimes at the same time or parallel. Several studies used different timing during the reconnaissance and evaluation phases. For example, Sampson's (2010) study (discussed further in this chapter) used different timing of quantitative and qualitative data collection and analysis during the reconnaissance (concurrent timing) and evaluating action (sequential timing) phases.

The qualitative-quantitative sequence—that is, collecting qualitative data via individual interviews or focus groups and then using these results to develop an instrument to collect further quantitative information—was more frequently used during the reconnaissance or fact finding phase (e.g., Craig, 2011; Vecchiarelli, Prelip, Slusser, Weightman, & Neumann, 2005). This focus on exploration and an increased use of qualitative data in action research studies was emphasized by many action researchers (Koshy et al., 2011; Mills, 2011; Stringer, 2014). In several MMAR studies (e.g., Pickard, 2006; Seymour, Almack, Kennedy, & Froggatt, 2011), the authors started with collecting data via quantitative surveys; after the analysis of the quantitative data, they conducted focus groups and/or individual interviews to explore the survey results in more depth. In only a small number of studies (7%) the authors labeled the mixed methods design they used as, for example, dominant/less dominant (Reutzel, Fawson, & Smith, 2006), two-phase (Buck & Cordes, 2005), triangulation (Glasson et al., 2006), and parallel (Zoellner, Zanko, Price, Bonner, & Hill, 2012).

Refer to Box 1.2 in Chapter 1 for the example of Ivankova and Stick's (2007) mixed methods study that used a similar design.

TABLE 3.1   **Reasons for Applying Mixed Methods in Select Action Research Studies**

Article Citation	Subject Area	Article Purpose	Reason
Clark, Lee, Goodman, & Yacco (2008)	K–12 Education	To report on the action research study that examined male underachievement in public education in one school district	"The purpose of this mixed design was 'to obtain different but complementary data on the same topic rather than to replicate results' (Morse, 1991, p. 121). Using both approaches can also add new perspective and meaning because of the different philosophical assumptions underlying qualitative and quantitative methods (Lawrenz & Huffman, 2002)" (p. 115).
Galini & Efthymia (2010)	K–12 Education	To report on a collaborative action research project carried out to explore the introduction of internal evaluation processes in kindergarten	"A combination of quantitative and qualitative methods and different methodological tools such as questionnaires, interview, observation protocols, journals, were used as it is advisable to have at least two or three different data resources or/and methods (Cohen, Manion & Morrison, 2007. McFee, 1992)" (p. 22).
Blanco, Pino, & Rodriguez (2010)	Higher Education	To report on a collaborative action research study carried out on three groups of beginning Spanish learners during the implementation of a strategy awareness raising program	"The study can be broadly classified as an action research project. It also involved the use of mixed methods combining self-report and observational data. The advantage of combining these methods is that it 'can broaden the scope of the investigation, and enrich the researcher's ability to draw conclusions' (Dornyei 2007, 186)" (p. 56).
Medves et al. (2008)	Higher Education	To report on the community-based action research study of a new inter-professional course preparing learners for life in rural communities	"The evaluation of this course included a mixed methods approach in order to enhance the breadth and depth of the study, and to enable method triangulation to ensure validity" (p. 4).

(Continued)

TABLE 3.1 **Continued**

Article Citation	Subject Area	Article Purpose	Reason
King (2010)	Higher Education	To report on a cross case study of three different educational podcast series to provide a grounded research model based on a macro perspective of these needs and opportunities	"Examining the literature of instructional technology research among diverse populations, action research (Hinchey, 2008) and mixed-methods research (Glaser & Strauss, 1967; Tashakkori & Teddlie, 1998) have served as effective strategies for numerous studies (Jonassen et al., 2003; King & Griggs, 2006) because of the ability to view the experience and data from multiple perspectives" (p. 146).
Davidson et al. (2008)	Health Care	To describe the development of a nurse-directed cardiac rehabilitation program tailored to the needs of women following an acute cardiac event to address their psychological and social needs	"The mixed methods approach uses multiple data sources and approaches. . . . The use of this approach was not only elucidating in the pilot process of intervention development but also increased the depth and scope of exploring women's recovery and adjustment processes" (p. 125).
Kilbride, Meyer, Flatley, & Perry (2005)	Health Care	To report on selected findings from an action research study that addressed the lessons learned from setting up a new inpatient stroke service in a London teaching hospital	"A variety of quantitative and qualitative data were used to systematically generate data, and monitor the processes and outcomes of change over time" (p. 29).
Westhues et al. (2008)	Nursing	To report on the participatory action research project to explore, develop, pilot, and evaluate how best to provide community-based mental health services and support that are effective for people from culturally diverse backgrounds	"The research design can be described as mixed method because it draws on both qualitative and quantitative data, though it is qualitatively driven (Tashakkori & Teddlie, 1998). It can also be described as multimethod because it included 'the conduct of two or more research methods, each conduce rigorously and complete in itself, in one project. The results are then triangulated to form a comprehensive whole' (Morse, 2003, p. 190)" (p. 703).

Article Citation	Subject Area	Article Purpose	Reason
Young & Higgins (2010)	Nursing	To report on a participatory research program aimed at challenging the status quo for women's cardiovascular health	"We reasoned that a mixed method research program, one in which qualitative and quantitative studies informed each other, had the potential to provide 'numbers' for policy-makers and program planners while acting as a vehicle for bringing marginalized women's voices into policy-making and program-planning arenas" (p. 347).
Aylward, Murphy, Colmer, & O'Neill (2010)	Psychology	To report on the intervention, evaluation and specific findings for the mothers and children who participated in the project targeting Australian parents of young children with attachment issues	"By triangulating quantitative and qualitative approaches and varying data sources to obtain a range of stakeholder perspectives (Denzin, 1989), the evaluation established the intervention's impact and acceptability using objective standardized tools, complemented by the participants' subjective and personally articulated experiences" (p. 15).
White & Wafra (2011)	Psychology	To report on an action research mixed methods case study to investigate what impact character education has on school climate and pupil behavior within a primary school in England	"[W]e used Tashakkori and Teddlie's cycle of scientific research design with a qualitative-quantitative-qualitative sequence of investigation to develop a thick description of the human experience underpinning the quantitative finding" (p. 49).
Mirza, Anandan, Madnick, & Hammel (2006)	Social Work	To report on pilot testing and evaluation of an innovative program providing information technology access to people with disabilities that transition out of nursing homes into the community using a participatory approach	"Triangulation of methods and investigators was used to capture a more complete and holistic picture of the phenomenon of IT access for the target population" (p. 1189).

This overview of 108 MMAR studies gives a snapshot of how a mixed methods approach is currently applied in action research. The observed trends provide enough evidence to expect further integration of mixed methods into action research as a way to enhance its effectiveness through the use of many methodological features that mixed methods offers. These MMAR studies are used to support the discussion about the application of mixed methods in action research in Chapters 4 through 9 that focus on the process of conceptualizing, designing, and conducting MMAR studies. The rest of Chapter 3 illustrates how a mixed methods approach was used in select examples of MMAR studies.

EXAMPLES OF FIVE MMAR STUDIES

Five examples of MMAR studies were selected from different disciplines to illustrate how a mixed methods approach is utilized or can be utilized in action research: in the fields of K–12 education (Kostos & Shin, 2010), nursing (Glasson et al., 2006), social work (Craig, 2011), higher education (Sampson, 2010), and health care (Montgomery et al., 2008). These studies differ in how and when mixed methods was used in the action research process, the study design, and other related methodological characteristics. To facilitate the current discussion and to further illustrate the study details in other chapters of the book, full texts of these articles are included in the Appendix (Examples A–E). *Note:* All page numbers in citations to these illustrative articles throughout the book refer to the original publications.

Example A: MMAR Study in the Field of K–12 Education (Kostos & Shin, 2010)

Kostos and Shin (2010) used mixed methods in an action research study to investigate how the use of math journals affected second-grade students' communication of mathematical thinking. Since journaling was found to be an effective math teaching and learning strategy in previous studies, the teacher-researcher decided to try it in her classroom to enhance the students' learning of mathematics. The purpose of the study was to design, implement, and evaluate the new instructional approach to teaching math. An action research approach was chosen because the study was conducted by the teacher in her classroom. This enabled the teacher-researcher "to utilize the insight that can only be obtained as an insider to the setting" (p. 226); specifically, it allowed the teacher-researcher to capture the students' thinking process more closely and to collect and analyze the information in more depth.

While conceptualizing and designing the study, Kostos and Shin (2010) decided to employ mixed methods because they wanted "to provide a more in-depth look at how the students communicated their mathematical thinking when using math journals" (p. 226). They stated the following rationale for using mixed methods: "The benefit of using a mixed methodology is triangulation of the findings and adding scope and breadth to a study" (p. 226). Based on the review of the previous studies about math journaling, Kostos and Shin developed an intervention—math journaling instruction that consisted of students writing in math journals three times a week using 16 different prompts. These prompts related to basic and newly learned mathematical concepts. The first three prompts were modeled by the teacher-researcher during the classroom instruction using different strategies on how to solve math problems. Students were required to provide step-by-step explanations of how they solved the posted math problem in their journals.

The study was conducted in a second-grade mixed-ability classroom in a suburban school in Chicago. Sixteen students, eight girls and eight boys, participated in the study. Math journaling instruction was carried out during a 5-week period. To evaluate the effectiveness of the instruction, both quantitative and qualitative data were collected concurrently or independent from each other. The quantitative data consisted of an identical math assessment administered to students before and after the intervention using the Illinois State Board of Education Mathematics Scoring Rubric. The qualitative data included students' math journal entries, interviews with eight randomly selected students, and the teacher-researcher's reflective journal.

The analysis of the quantitative and qualitative information demonstrated an overall improvement of students' mathematical thinking through math communication. The students' postassessment scores of mathematical knowledge, strategic knowledge, and reasoning were significantly better after than they were before the math journaling intervention. The qualitative results revealed that the use of math journals positively influenced the students' communication of mathematical thinking and the use of math vocabulary. Based on these findings and personal reflections about the instructional intervention process, the teacher-researcher began to use math journaling in daily math lessons: "The use of math journals has become an important part of my classroom" (Kostos & Shin, 2010, p. 230).

In Kostos and Shin's study, mixed methods was used at several phases in the action research cycle. Specifically, an intentional choice of a mixed methods approach initially helped with conceptualizing and designing the study. Then mixed methods was employed to evaluate math journaling instruction through the collection and analysis of the quantitative and qualitative data. The integrated quantitative and qualitative findings provided evidence that math journaling enhanced student learning. The positive study conclusions helped the teacher-researcher make a decision to continue using math journaling in teaching mathematics. Using the mixed methods methodological framework for action research (Figure 3.1) presented earlier in this chapter, a visual diagram was developed to capture the flow of the research activities in Kostos and Shin's (2010) MMAR study (Figure 3.4). Solid arrows show the actual flow of the research activities in the study, while dashed arrows highlight potential future activities related to further evaluation of the instruction or the need to conduct a more detailed literature review in order to inform more effective changes in the current instruction.

Example B: MMAR Study in the Field of Nursing (Glasson et al., 2006)

Glasson and colleagues (2006) applied mixed methods in a participatory action research study to improve the quality of nursing care for older acutely ill hospitalized medical patients through developing, implementing, and evaluating a new model of care. The study sought to address one of the challenges for nursing practice to better meet the health-care needs of the growing older population. Participatory action research was chosen as an appropriate approach for "re-evaluating and changing nursing practice not only because of its reflecting process during the stages of planning, taking action in practice, observing, reflecting, and replanning, but also for its similarity to the nursing process through the steps of assessment, planning, implementation, evaluation, and replanning (Nolan & Hazelton 1996)" (p. 590). A mixed methods triangulation approach was used "to establish an evidence-base for an evolving model of care" (p. 588). The authors also stated that "[t]he advantages

| FIGURE 3.4 | **Research Activities in Kostos and Shin's (2010) MMAR Study (Example A)** |

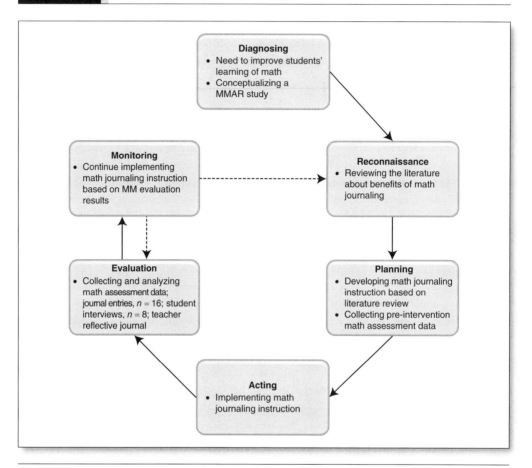

Note: MM = mixed methods.

of using several methods to examine the same phenomenon are that it provides more in-depth information on the participants' experiences and feelings (Morse & Field 1996)" (p. 590).

The study was conducted in an acute medical ward in a public hospital in Sydney, Australia. During the first phase of the study (the reconnaissance phase), the aspects of nursing care that acutely ill older patients perceived as being important but found unsatisfactory were identified. The quantitative data were collected from 41 male and female patients (mean age 78 years) using the Barthel Activity of Daily Living Index questionnaire to determine patients' functional capacity and medication regime assessment and to determine patients' knowledge level of their medications. Another quantitative instrument included the Caregiving Activities Scale questionnaire that researchers administered to both patients and nursing staff to identify their levels of satisfaction with nursing care in that medical ward. The Caregiving Activities Scale questionnaire combined both close-ended (quantitative) and open-ended (qualitative) items. Additional qualitative data included the researchers' field notes taken during the observations of the nursing staff discussions about the need for the model grounded in the analysis of patients' responses, the process of the model development, and ways to implement and evaluate the model. During those meetings, the nurses collaboratively chose a model of care that emphasized addressing two major identified concerns, "encouraging self care and increasing medication knowledge in patients" (Glasson et al., 2006, p. 590).

Based on the findings from the reconnaissance phase, the model was implemented in the medical ward and its outcomes were evaluated with 60 acutely ill patients of both genders (mean age 76 years) and 13 nurses working in the ward (the evaluation phase). The patients' functional activities were assessed on hospital admission and prior to discharge using the Barthel Activity of Daily Living Index. The patients' knowledge level about medication administration was also assessed on admission, during the hospital stay, and prior to discharge. Finally, when leaving the hospital patients completed the Caregiving Activities Scale satisfaction questionnaire "to determine whether the implementation of the model of care that was considered to address older patients' identified nursing care issues had resulted in increased patient satisfaction and improved patient care" (Glasson et al., 2006, p. 593). During the last 2 weeks of the model implementation process, the nurses in the ward also completed the Caregiving Activities Scale satisfaction questionnaire that included quantitative items and open-ended questions. The analysis of the quantitative and qualitative evaluation data provided evidence about the efficacy of the new model of nursing care in improving the quality of care for older patients in an acute medical ward setting. The qualitative findings from nurses' comments added understanding of the key concepts related to the process of model development and implementation: barriers to change, enthusiasm to change, collaboration in planning, empowerment in planning, expanding knowledge, and empowerment to change process. Glasson and colleagues (2006) reported that further monitoring and improvement of the model was planned during the re-planning stage.

In Glasson and colleagues' (2006) study, mixed methods was used to inform the data collection and analysis during both the reconnaissance and the evaluation phases in the action research cycle. During the reconnaissance phase, quantitative and qualitative data from questionnaires and focus group discussions were collected and analyzed concurrently to assess the situation in the ward and identify patients' concerns with received nursing care. The results of the analysis informed further discussions among nurses to help choose an appropriate new model of nursing care. The evaluation of the model was conducted through a concurrent collection and analysis of quantitative and qualitative data using the same instruments. The integrated quantitative and qualitative findings confirmed the efficacy of the new model of nursing care and provided directions for its further implementation and monitoring. Figure 3.5 presents the flow of the research activities in Glasson and colleagues' MMAR study. Solid arrows show the actual flow of the research activities in the study, while the dashed arrow suggests potential replanning and revisions of the model to increase its efficacy.

Example C: MMAR Study in the Field of Social Work (Craig, 2011)

Craig (2011) applied mixed methods in a community-based participatory research project aimed at creating a system of care for gay, lesbian, bisexual, transgender, and questioning (GLBTQ) youths in an urban

FIGURE 3.5 **Research Activities in Glasson et al.'s (2006) MMAR Study (Example B)**

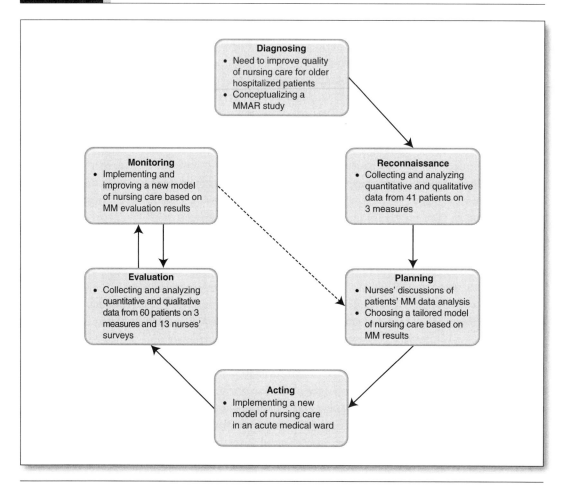

Note: MM = mixed methods.

area. Reportedly, GLBTQ youths are considered a population at risk because they have more predispositions for psychiatric disorders, substance abuse, and suicide. The article reports on the first phase in the project—conducting community needs assessment (the reconnaissance phase). A community-based participatory research approach was necessary to create collaborative partnerships with local agencies. Such partnerships with stakeholders were needed to effectively assess existing health and mental health service delivery systems for GLBTQ young people in the community in order to inform the development of an effective system of care. In Craig's (2011) words, "Successful initiatives require research and collaboration between stakeholders" (p. 275). A mixed methods approach was used to inform a sequential collection and analysis of qualitative and quantitative information to secure the credibility of the findings from the entire study: "The entire research process was designed to elicit rich qualitative data to contextualize and develop a comprehensive quantitative survey tool (Creswell, 2009; Denzin & Lincoln, 2008) from which to design an evidence-informed system of care. Such heterogeneous sources and approaches to data collection ensure trustworthiness (Clark, Creswell, Green, & Shope, 2008)" (p. 278).

The study was conducted in Miami Dade County, Florida, in collaboration with six agencies that had programs for GLBTQ young people. The needs assessment included five stages that followed a sequential mixed methods approach. During the first stage, the researcher reviewed national and local GLBTQ programs for young people and arranged for visiting select programs to obtain a broad perspective on the creation of a system of care. The analysis of this information helped identify the key informants for qualitative individual interviews to get more in-depth understanding of the desired program components. Forty-five interviews were conducted with local service providers, community leaders, and other stakeholders at different sites during the second stage. The analysis of the interview data informed 10 subsequent focus groups discussions with 180 GLBTQ youths during the third stage of the study. The purpose of the focus groups was "to deepen relationships with the population of interest and to provide a richer understanding of the true needs of the population" (p. 281). During the fourth stage of the study, a quantitative survey instrument for GLBTQ youths, "Youth Speak Out," was collaboratively developed that was grounded in the qualitative results from the interviews and focus groups. Each draft of the survey was reviewed by a Youth Advisory Board that consisted of 10 youth representatives from the target population. The survey was administered to a nonrandom sample of an additional 273 GLBTQ youths in Miami Dade County. Finally, during the fifth stage, the findings from the survey were presented to the community members to solicit their feedback as well as to identify and implement particular services for GLBTQ young people.

In Craig's (2011) study, mixed methods was used during the reconnaissance phase to inform a systematic large-scale assessment of the community needs to identify and develop an appropriate intervention for the GLBTQ young people. The qualitative and quantitative data collection and analysis was conducted sequentially: First, the environmental scan was done to inform the selection of the key informants; then qualitative data from key informant individual interviews and youth focus groups were collected and analyzed. The results of the qualitative analysis were used to develop a quantitative survey instrument, "Youth Speak Out," to get the perspectives of GLBTQ youths in the community. Thus, a systematic mixed methods approach to the survey development helped capture the views of multiple stakeholders and design an intervention consisting of numerous programs and services tailored to GLBTQ youths. Figure 3.6 presents the flow of the research activities in Craig's (2011) MMAR study. Solid arrows show the actual flow of the research activities in the study, while dashed arrows suggest potential evaluation and monitoring of the system of care for GLBTQ youths with the possibility for conducting more community needs assessment if it becomes necessary.

Example D: MMAR Study in the Field of Higher Education (Sampson, 2010)

Sampson (2010) applied mixed methods in a semester-long action research study that reported on how students' feedback was used to guide the choice of a lesson style in a college-level class in which English was the language of instruction. Specifically, the project focused on "identifying the problems and needs felt by the

| FIGURE 3.6 | Research Activities in Craig's (2011) MMAR Study (Example C) |

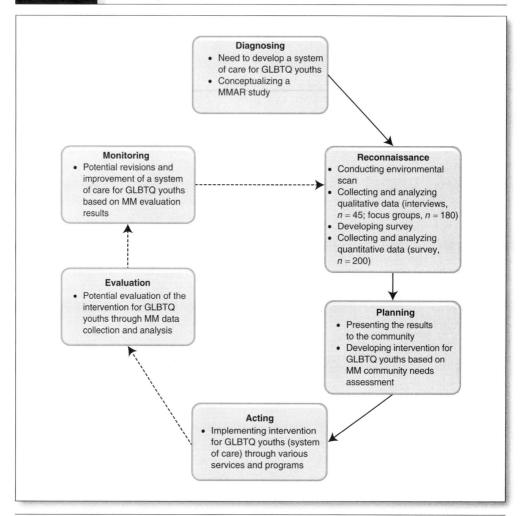

Note: MM = mixed methods.

learners after previous learning experiences, exploring a change-action in methodology from the start of the class and follow-up change-actions throughout the semester, to try to address these recognized problems as a group" (p. 284). Action research was chosen for its participatory and collaborative nature and the fact that "the subjective views of learners are of most importance in enacting change" (p. 286). Mixed methods was used for data collection and analysis during both the reconnaissance and evaluation phases for triangulation purposes: "From a practical perspective, quantitative data elicitation methods were employed to provide triangulation, but kept relatively simple so as to most effectively inform the change-action without interfering with student learning" (p. 286).

The study was conducted at a women's university in Japan in Interpersonal Communication classes that were taught in English. Twenty-two first-year students in two classes took part in the study. During the reconnaissance phase (Cycle 1—Sampson, 2010), the students completed both a quantitative survey (the Lesson Style Questionnaire) and a narrative exercise (the Language Learning Autobiography) to identify the preferred lesson style. Based on the analysis of these data, task-based oriented lessons were developed to shape the instruction during Cycle 2 (the planning phase) and to introduce more opportunities for a practical use of English in the classroom. The instruction was refocused to have students "using language in context to complete a variety of tasks, individually or in small groups" (p. 287). Students were required to keep a learning journal to reflect on the activities and learning during each class. During Cycle 3 (the action implementing and evaluation phases), students participated in goal-setting activities for the subsequent lessons to increase their motivation to speak English. The qualitative data from students' journals were analyzed for themes; the emergent themes informed the development of the quantitative Learning Experience Questionnaire that was completed by the students at the end of the course. The purpose of the questionnaire development was to obtain quantitative indicators of students' experiences with learning in the course to compare with journal entries "in attempt at triangulating results" (p. 287).

In Sampson's (2010) study, mixed methods was employed during several phases in the action research process. Initially it was used in the reconnaissance phase to explore students' preferences for the lesson style to facilitate the use of English during the course. Subsequently it was used during the development of task-based-oriented lessons instruction based on the integrated quantitative and qualitative findings, and then when evaluating the effectiveness of the new lesson style and students' perceptions of their speaking and communication abilities in English. Of note is that quantitative and qualitative data collection and analysis used different timing during the reconnaissance phase (i.e., concurrent timing when the data from the survey and a narrative exercise were collected and analyzed at the same time), and in the evaluation phase (i.e., sequential timing when the themes from learning journal entries were used to inform the development of the quantitative Learning Experience Questionnaire). Figure 3.7 presents the flow of the research activities in Sampson's (2010) MMAR study. Solid arrows show the actual flow of the research activities in the study, while dashed arrows suggest potential further evaluation and monitoring of the task-based-oriented lessons intervention with the possibility for conducting more assessment of new students' preferences for English as a Foreign Language (EFL) lesson style instruction.

Example E: MMAR Study in the Field of Health Care (Montgomery et al., 2008)

Montgomery and colleagues' (2008) article presents an example of a published research protocol that describes the research problem, the research goals and questions, and methodological aspects of the study design for a proposed MMAR study. The authors intended to apply mixed methods in an action research study to "describe and evaluate the processes and outcomes" of supported housing programs for persons with serious mental illness in rural communities in northeastern Ontario, Canada, "from the perspective of clients,

| FIGURE 3.7 | **Research Activities in Sampson's (2010) MMAR Study (Example D)** |

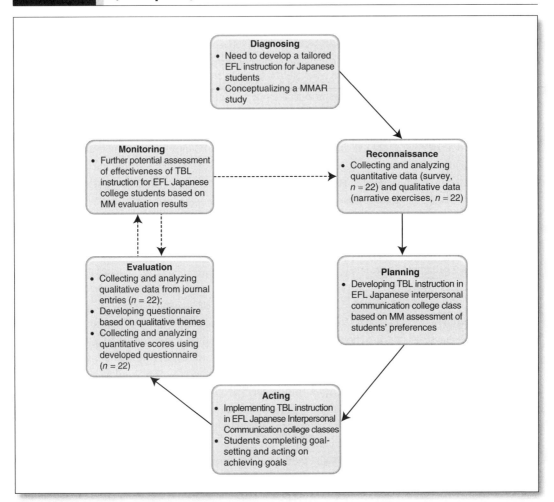

Note: MM = mixed methods.

their families, and community workers" (p. 3). To address this issue, the researchers proposed to use "a mixed methods design guided by participatory action research" (p. 1). The researchers believed that the use of an action research approach would allow for including various stakeholders to explore the issue from multiple perspectives—housing residents, their families, and health-care providers. Specifically, a participatory research approach was deemed necessary for several reasons: to create a collaborative research partnership at each of the four identified research sites, to involve the residents in collecting the qualitative data through photo-voice, and to disseminate the findings among community members to implement them into practice. The researchers considered combining quantitative and qualitative methods within a mixed methods design to be a rigorous research approach that would "allow a more robust analysis and provide multidimensional answers of maximum relevance to the research questions" (p. 3). The researchers explained that the quantitative data would be necessary to describe the study sample, and to measure the residents' quality of life, housing stability, and housing preference. Qualitative data would help to further explore and understand the patterns and relationships in the collected and analyzed quantitative data.

Montgomery and colleagues' (2008) study was planned to be conducted over a 2-year period in four iterative stages, including the first stage of planning the research activities, two consecutive stages of quantitative and qualitative data collection and analysis, and the fourth stage of synthesizing the findings and translating them into practice. During Stage 1 the researchers proposed to form research partnerships at four research sites so that they could introduce the study and organize the research activities. During Stage 2 the researchers planned to survey 172 residents with serious mental illness at four research sites using four quantitative survey instruments to obtain information about their quality-of-life experiences, subjective feelings about these experiences, housing history, and housing preferences. During Stage 3 the researchers proposed to select eight clients from each site based on the analysis of the survey data to further explore the residents' perceptions of supported housing services using photo-voice and focus groups. The researchers also planned to include clients' families and community health workers in the focus group discussions. During Stage 4 the researchers proposed to conduct a community forum including all stakeholder groups to discuss the study findings and how they might be used to inform the changes in current practices. A focus group discussion strategy was proposed to guide the community forum.

In Montgomery and colleagues' (2008) study proposal, mixed methods will be used to evaluate the existing supporting housing programs for persons with serious mental illness and to use these results to inform health services planning. The qualitative and quantitative data collection and analysis will be conducted sequentially. First, the survey data will be collected and analyzed to address the first three research questions related to housing residents' quality of life, housing stability, and housing preferences. Second, the qualitative data from photo-voice and focus groups will be subsequently collected and analyzed to explore the stakeholders' perceptions of supported housing services in more depth and to address the rest of the study research questions. According to the authors, the results from the initial quantitative data analysis phase "will serve as the basis for discussion in the project's subsequent stages" using qualitative methods (p. 6).

The researchers included a visual diagram of the study design to better communicate a sequential flow of the research activities to their community partners. Montgomery and colleagues believed that blending the two research approaches—mixed methods and action research—would allow them to generate the results that would reflect the perspectives of both the housing residents and housing service providers. Figure 3.8 presents the flow of the research activities in Montgomery and colleagues' (2008) MMAR study. Solid arrows show the actual flow of the research activities in the study leading from the reconnaissance phase immediately to evaluating the existing supporting housing intervention and then to the planning action and acting phases. Dashed arrows suggest further potential evaluation and monitoring of the improved supported housing services for persons with serious mental illness in rural areas with the possibility for further refinement of the existing policies and the development of the new policies.

| FIGURE 3.8 | Research Activities in Montgomery et al.'s (2008) MMAR Study (Example E) |

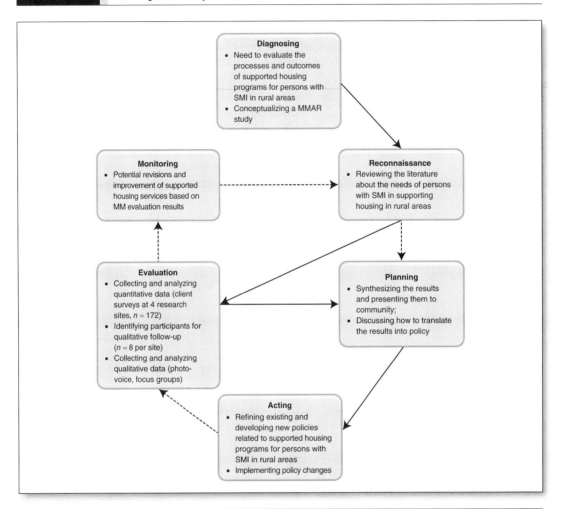

Note: MM = mixed methods.

SUMMARY

The advantages of using quantitative and qualitative methods in action research studies have long been the focus of attention for action and mixed methods researchers. The increasing utilization of mixed methods as a research approach promoted further discussions of the connection between mixed methods and action research. A number of features that action research and mixed methods share make the integration of the two approaches justifiable and realistic. Both approaches follow the principles of systematic inquiry in designing and implementing studies, both are aimed at providing more comprehensive information, both have an underlying pragmatic philosophical foundation, both have a dialectical nature, both use reflective practice, both apply a transformative/advocacy lens, both use quantitative and qualitative information sources, both are cyclical, both apply a collaborative approach to research, and both combine insider–outsider perspectives. The chapter further discusses the advantages of applying mixed methods in action research. The mixed methods methodological framework for action research is proposed that was developed based on the model of action research steps discussed in Chapter 2. This framework details how mixed methods can inform each step or phase in the cycle of the action research process.

Application of mixed methods in action research is further discussed and illustrated using 108 empirical MMAR studies from 10 subject areas or disciplines. The results of this analysis show a predominance of MMAR studies in health and education, an increased number of published MMAR studies in recent years (2009–2012), an intentional and recognized use of mixed methods in the action research process, and application of mixed methods concurrently or sequentially at different phases in the action research process. Five examples of MMAR studies in the fields of K–12 education, nursing, social work, higher education, and health care are discussed in detail to illustrate the concepts presented in the chapter.

REFLECTIVE QUESTIONS AND EXERCISES

1. Conduct a quick search of the library databases for MMAR studies in your discipline. Use the combination of the following search terms: "action research," "practitioner research," "participatory research," "community-based research," "mixed method(s)," "mixed-method(s)," and the name of your discipline. Record the number of MMAR studies found during each year of publication. What trends do you see in the use of mixed methods in action research studies in your discipline across the years?

2. Reflect on different reasons for applying mixed methods in action research. What reasons do you think may be the most important for using mixed methods in action research studies in your discipline? What reasons have the authors provided for applying mixed methods in the action research published studies that you located? Do you think the authors justified the use of mixed methods in action research well? What may be some additional reasons that the authors did not mention?

3. Reflect on the advantages of using mixed methods in action research studies. Choose several MMAR studies from those that you located and identify at least three benefits of applying mixed methods in these studies. Try to explain how the use of mixed methods has enhanced these studies.

4. Examine the mixed methods methodological framework for action research. In your own words, explain how mixed methods can inform and enhance action research at each phase in the action research cycle.

5. Read MMAR studies (Examples A through E) and reflect on the discussion about these studies in this chapter. Consider how mixed methods and action research approaches were combined or integrated in these studies. Examine Figures 3.4 through 3.8 that reflect the flow of the research activities in the studies.

Discuss what further action research steps may be taken if you were asked to continue implementing these projects.

6.   Locate an MMAR published study in your discipline. Carefully read the study report and identify when and how mixed methods was used in the action research process. Specifically, at what phase or phases in the action research cycle was mixed methods used? What quantitative and qualitative data were collected and analyzed? How did the use of mixed methods help inform the development and implementation, or evaluation of the action/intervention in the study? Draw a diagram that reflects the flow of the research activities in these studies.

FURTHER READINGS

To learn more about a pragmatic nature of action research, examine the following source:

Greenwood, D., & Levin, M. (2007). *Introduction to action research: Social research for social change* (2nd ed.). Thousand Oaks, CA: Sage, Ch. 9, pp. 133–150.

To learn more about mixed methods as a collaborative research approach, examine the following source:

Shulha, L. M., & Wilson, R. J. (2003). Collaborative mixed methods research. In A. Tashakkori & C. Teddlie (Eds.), *Handbook of mixed methods in social & behavioral research* (pp. 639–669). Thousand Oaks, CA: Sage.

To learn more about transformative mixed methods research, examine the following source:

Mertens, D. M., Bledsoe, K. L., Sullivan, M., & Wilson, A. (2010). Utilization of mixed methods for transformative purposes. In A. Tashakkori & C. Teddlie (Eds.), *SAGE handbook of mixed methods in social & behavioral research* (2nd ed., pp. 193–214). Thousand Oaks, CA: Sage.

To learn more about a synergistic partnership-based fully integrated mixed methods research framework, examine the following source:

Nastasi, B. K., Hitchcock, J. H., & Brown, L. M. (2010). An inclusive framework for conceptualizing mixed methods design typologies: Moving toward fully integrated synergistic research models. In A. Tashakkori & C. Teddlie (Eds.), *SAGE handbook of mixed methods in social & behavioral research* (2nd ed., pp. 305–338). Thousand Oaks, CA: Sage.

To learn more about Wisniewska's (2011) comparison of the use of mixed methods and action research in English Language Teaching, examine the following source:

Wisniewska, D. (2011). Mixed methods and action research: Similar or different? *Glottodidactica, 37,* 59–72.

To learn more about how mixed methods was applied in action research studies in education, examine the following sources:

Blanco, M., Pino, M., & Rodriguez, B. (2010). Implementing a strategy awareness raising programme: Strategy changes and feedback. *Language Learning Journal, 38*(1), 51–65.

Buck, G. A., & Cordes, J. G. (2005). An action research project on preparing teachers to meet the needs of underserved student population. *Journal of Science Teacher Education, 16,* 43–64.

Lyons, A., & DeFranco, J. (2010). A mixed-methods model for educational evaluation. *The Humanistic Psychologist, 38,* 146–158.

To learn more about how mixed methods was applied in action research studies in health care and nursing, examine the following sources:

Davidson, P., Digiacomo, M., Zecchin, R., Clarke, M., Paul, G., Lamb, K., . . . Daly, J. (2008). A cardiac rehabilitation program to improve psychosocial outcomes of women with heart disease. *Journal of Women's Health, 17*(1), 123–134.

Kilbride, C., Meyer, J., Flatley, M, & Perry, L. (2005). Stroke units: The implementation of a complex intervention. *Educational Action Research, 13*(4), 479–504.

Williamson, G. R., Webb, C., & Abelson-Mitchell, N. (2004). Developing lecturer practitioner roles using action research. *Journal of Advanced Nursing, 47*(2), 153–164.

To learn more about how mixed methods was applied in action research studies in psychology, sociology, and social work, examine the following sources:

Aylward, P., Murphy, P., Colmer, K., & O'Neill, M. (2010). Findings from an evaluation of an intervention targeting Australian parents of young children with attachment issues: The "Through the Looking Glass" (TtLG) project. *Australian Journal of Early Childhood, 35*(3), 13–23.

Krueger, P. (2010). It's not just a method! The epistemic and political work of young people's lifeworlds at the school-prison nexus. *Race, Ethnicity and Education, 13*(3), 383–408.

Mirza, M., Anandan, N., Madnick, F., & Hammel, J. (2006). A participatory program evaluation of a systems change program to improve access to information technology by people with disabilities. *Disability and Rehabilitation, 28*(19), 1185–1199.

To learn more about how mixed methods was applied in action research studies in management, environmental science, and organization learning, examine the following sources:

Downs, T. J., Ross, L., Patton, S., Rulnick, S., Sinha, D., Mucciarone, D., & Goble, R. (2009). Complexities of holistic community-based participatory research for a low income, multi-ethnic population exposed to multiple built-environment stressors in Worcester, Massachusetts. *Environmental Research, 109,* 1028–1040.

Strang, K. D. (2011). Radioactive manufacturing projects and politics: Scientist and politician normalized risk decision process. *International Journal of Management and Decision Making, 11*(3/4), 231–248.

Taut, S. (2007). Studying self-evaluation capacity building in a large international development organization. *American Journal of Evaluation, 28*(1), 45–59.

PART II

Designing and Conducting a Mixed Methods Action Research Study

4

Conceptualizing a Mixed Methods Action Research Study

OBJECTIVES

By the end of this chapter, the reader should be able to

- Understand and describe each step in an MMAR study process,
- Describe the steps in conceptualizing an MMAR study,
- Explain how to identify a problem area in an MMAR study,
- Understand the role of the literature review in an MMAR study,
- Identify steps in conducting a literature review for an MMAR study,
- Describe the flow of ideas in an MMAR study research problem statement,
- Understand the components of an MMAR general research plan,
- Learn how to develop an MMAR study purpose statement and research questions, and
- Explain ethical considerations in an MMAR study.

INTRODUCTION

Chapters 1 through 3 discussed methodological characteristics of mixed methods and action research, some common features between these two research approaches, and the advantages of applying mixed methods in the action research process. The utility of mixed methods in action research was illustrated using the examples of MMAR studies from different disciplines that applied mixed methods during different phases in the action research cycle. Decisions to use mixed methods made by action researchers were part of an overall study plan and were dictated by different reasons, which included the purpose of the study, the specific aims of the phase in the action research cycle, and the need to produce more credible solutions that are grounded in the perspectives of all stakeholders.

As discussed in Chapter 3, a systematic nature inherent to both mixed methods and action research approaches implies that an MMAR study is designed and conducted following a set of research procedures that are common to any form of scientific inquiry. These procedures include, in the logical order, identification of the research problem, formulation of the study purpose and research questions, selection of the study sample, collection and analysis of the data, and interpretation and evaluation of the study results. Importantly, these research procedures correspond to specific steps in conceptualizing, designing, and conducting a study. These steps are further discussed as they apply to the development and implementation of an MMAR study. Following these research steps is critical because adherence to systematic procedures adds scientific rigor to the study, and "allows researchers to reveal valid empirical findings" (Edmonds & Kennedy, 2013, p. 1). Adherence to these steps also enables practitioner-researchers to identify scientific means to effectively address the practical problems or issues and produce useful and meaningful data-driven solutions.

So, what are the steps in the development and implementation of an MMAR study? How can practitioner-researchers apply the mixed methods procedures in the action research process?

STEPS IN AN MMAR STUDY PROCESS

Refer to Chapter 3 and Figure 3.1 for the discussion and illustration of the mixed methods methodological framework for action research.

To better understand the steps in the development and implementation of an MMAR study, revisit the mixed methods methodological framework for action research presented in Chapter 3. This framework, developed based on both Kurt Lewin's (1948b) model of action research and a model of steps in the action research process, illustrates how mixed methods can inform each phase in the cycle of the action research process: beginning with the phase of diagnosing the problem; moving through the phases of reconnaissance, planning action, and implementing action; and finishing the cycle with the phases of evaluating and monitoring the action/intervention. The framework also emphasizes the iterative nature of the steps in the action research process and the cyclical character of the development, implementation, and monitoring of the action/ intervention. These methodological characteristics of action research make it possible to use mixed methods in different timing variations for different purposes during the reconnaissance and evaluation phases within an action research project (e.g., collect and analyze quantitative and qualitative data concurrently or sequentially to assess the issue during the reconnaissance phase and/or to evaluate the impact of the action/intervention).

To help practitioner-researchers apply this methodological framework when conceptualizing, designing, and conducting an MMAR study, an MMAR Study Process Model is presented to show the important methodological and procedural steps for each phase in an MMAR study (see Figure 4.1). This model reflects the six phases in the action research cycle delineated in the mixed methods methodological framework (diagnosing, reconnaissance, planning, acting, evaluation, monitoring), and outlines the specific procedural and action steps within each phase. These procedures are discussed and illustrated further in the chapter using the previously reviewed MMAR study Examples A through E.

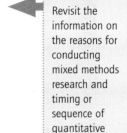

Revisit the information on the reasons for conducting mixed methods research and timing or sequence of quantitative and qualitative data collection and analysis in Chapter 1.

Diagnosing Phase

The process of designing an MMAR study begins during the first, diagnosing phase, when the conceptualization of an MMAR study occurs. This process involves a sequence of logical but often iterative steps:

- Identifying a problem area that requires improvement
- Reviewing the literature on the topic and existing theories and practices
- Developing a study general plan
- Considering potential ethical issues
- Specifying an overall study purpose, the expected outcomes, study objectives, and research questions

In Sampson's (2010) MMAR study (Example D) about student-negotiated lesson style, the practical problem that required a solution was lack of apparent motivation to use the English language for "free expression" by Japanese college students enrolled in an Interpersonal Communication course (p. 283). The review of the literature about Asian students' language learning style preferences prompted Sampson to combine action research and mixed methods approaches to explore the effects of a student-negotiated lesson style on their ability to use English for communication. A general plan for the study was developed that incorporated all six phases of an action research cycle and that included "identifying the problems and needs felt by the learners after previous learning experiences, exploring a change-action in methodology from the start of classes and follow-up change-actions throughout the semester, to try to address these recognized problems as a group" (p. 284). The study was initially guided by the following research question: "In what ways will information about students' past English learning experiences and hopes for college English lesson style guide design of motivating lessons?" (p. 286). Three other research questions evolved during the progression of the study: (1) "What elements of task-based lessons might students perceive as motivating?" (p. 286; the reconnaissance phase), (2) "In what ways will students' perception of speaking ability be affected through introduction of TBL [task-based] lessons?" (p. 286), and (3) "In what ways will students' awareness of goal-motivated behavior be affected through introduction to a goal-setting framework?" (p. 286; the evaluation phase). The major expected outcome of the action/intervention was students' obvious willingness to reflect on their English learning actions, thus enhancing their learning process.

FIGURE 4.1 **MMAR Study Process Model**

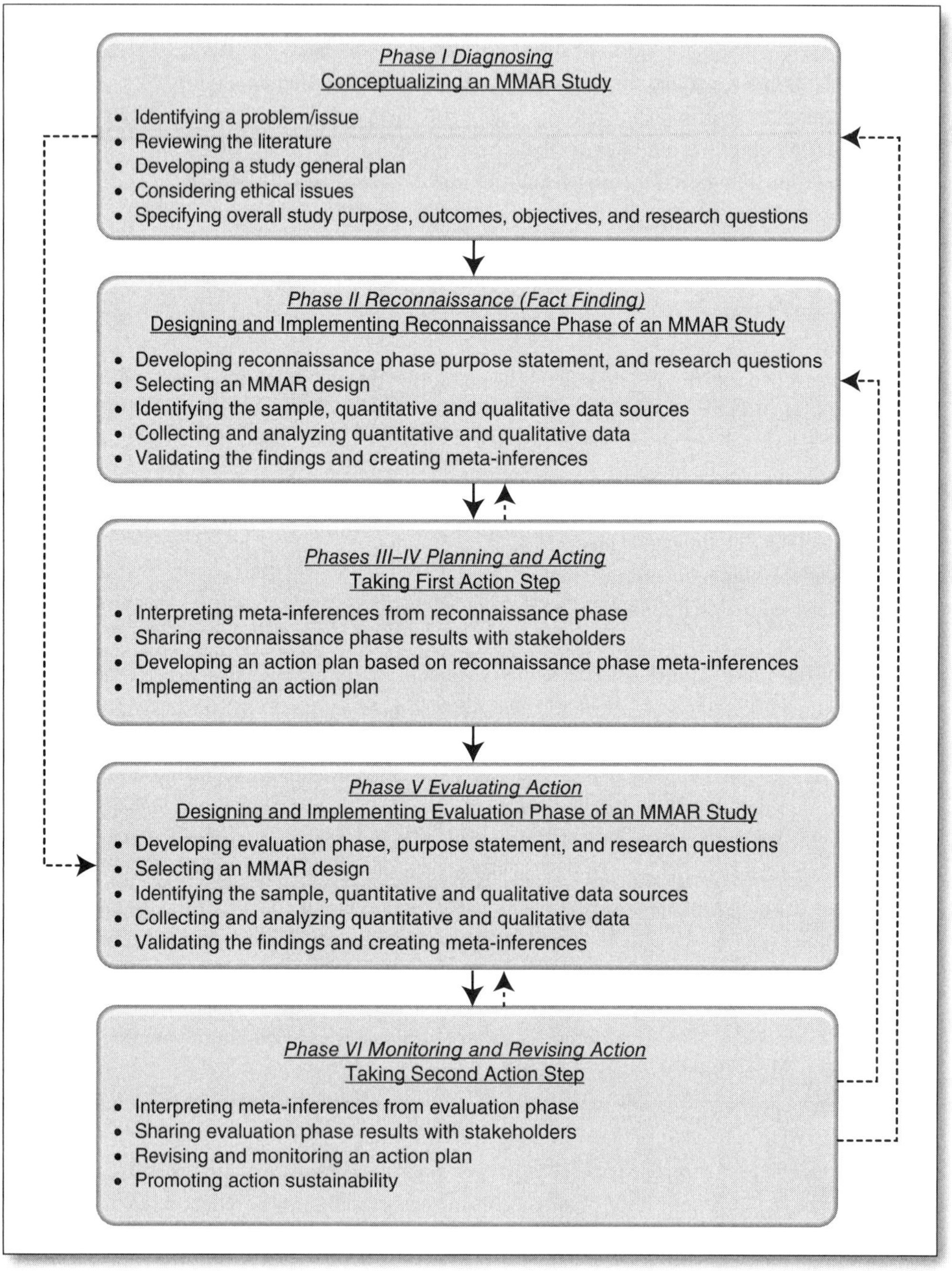

Phase I Diagnosing
Conceptualizing an MMAR Study

- Identifying a problem/issue
- Reviewing the literature
- Developing a study general plan
- Considering ethical issues
- Specifying overall study purpose, outcomes, objectives, and research questions

Phase II Reconnaissance (Fact Finding)
Designing and Implementing Reconnaissance Phase of an MMAR Study

- Developing reconnaissance phase purpose statement, and research questions
- Selecting an MMAR design
- Identifying the sample, quantitative and qualitative data sources
- Collecting and analyzing quantitative and qualitative data
- Validating the findings and creating meta-inferences

Phases III–IV Planning and Acting
Taking First Action Step

- Interpreting meta-inferences from reconnaissance phase
- Sharing reconnaissance phase results with stakeholders
- Developing an action plan based on reconnaissance phase meta-inferences
- Implementing an action plan

Phase V Evaluating Action
Designing and Implementing Evaluation Phase of an MMAR Study

- Developing evaluation phase, purpose statement, and research questions
- Selecting an MMAR design
- Identifying the sample, quantitative and qualitative data sources
- Collecting and analyzing quantitative and qualitative data
- Validating the findings and creating meta-inferences

Phase VI Monitoring and Revising Action
Taking Second Action Step

- Interpreting meta-inferences from evaluation phase
- Sharing evaluation phase results with stakeholders
- Revising and monitoring an action plan
- Promoting action sustainability

An MMAR study conducted by Glasson and colleagues (2006; Example B) addressed the problem of meeting the health-care needs of the growing older population and providing quality nursing care for acutely ill hospitalized older patients. The review of the literature focused on identifying a guiding model of patient-centered care in a hospital setting. The major aim of the study was "to improve the quality of nursing care for older acutely ill hospitalized medical patients through developing, implementing and evaluating a new model of care" (p. 590). Specific expected outcomes of using a new model of care included the improvement of older patients' functional activities of daily living and their medication knowledge and management.

The focus of Montgomery and colleagues' (2008) research protocol for an MMAR study (Example E) is on evaluating the existing supporting housing programs for persons with serious mental illness to inform further health service planning for this population. Based on an extensive literature review, the researchers concluded that an evaluation of supporting housing in rural areas was needed to identify the effective elements and "their relationship to outcomes to such as mental status, social functioning and quality of life" (p. 3). The study listed five broad research questions to guide the proposed evaluation processes from the perspective of clients, their families, and community workers.

Reconnaissance Phase

During the second phase in the cycle, the reconnaissance (fact-finding) phase of an MMAR study is designed and implemented to assess the problem or situation revealed during the diagnosing phase, to identify the areas for change or improvement, and to inform the development of the action/intervention plan to address the problem/issue. The specific procedural steps include the following:

- Developing the reconnaissance phase study purpose and research questions
- Selecting a mixed methods design to best address this purpose and answer the posted research questions
- Identifying the study sample and quantitative and qualitative types of data to be collected
- Collecting and analyzing the data
- Validating the findings and creating meta-inferences

Craig's (2011) MMAR study (Example C) reported on the community needs assessment as the first phase of the project that was aimed at developing a system of care for GLBTQ young people. Mixed methods data collection and analysis was used sequentially, and included an environmental scan of other existing GLBTQ programs for young people, key informant individual interviews with local service providers and community leaders, and focus groups with GLBTQ youths to inform the development of a quantitative survey that was administered to a large sample of GLBTQ youths in the community. The Youth Advisory Board and community representatives assisted with validating and interpreting the findings from the qualitative and quantitative strands (meta-inferences). In Sampson's (2010) MMAR study (Example D), assessment of students' preferences for a lesson style included concurrent completion of the quantitative Lesson Style Questionnaire

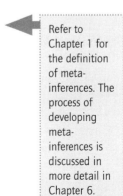

Refer to Chapter 1 for the definition of meta-inferences. The process of developing meta-inferences is discussed in more detail in Chapter 6.

and a qualitative language learning narrative exercise. Descriptive statistics and content analysis were used, respectively, to analyze the questionnaire and the narrative exercise data to develop meta-inferences that guided a new lesson structure.

Planning and Acting Phases

During the next two phases, planning and implementation of action/intervention takes place. Lewin (1948b) referred to this as taking the first action step. Meta-inferences that were created during the reconnaissance phase of the study, based on the integrated quantitative and qualitative data collection and analysis, are interpreted and shared with all stakeholders from the community of interest. Based on these meta-inferences and input from stakeholders a plan for action/intervention is developed. Sometimes the stakeholders' insight and feedback may suggest the need for conducting additional assessment of the problem to develop a more tailored action/intervention. This may prompt practitioner-researchers to return to the reconnaissance phase in order to collect and analyze more data, or to completely redesign this phase (as shown by a dashed arrow from this phase to the reconnaissance phase in the MMAR Study Process Model in Figure 4.1). During the acting phase an action/intervention plan that was systematically designed and informed by the meta-inferences from the reconnaissance phase is carried out.

In Craig's (2011) MMAR study (Example C) the findings from the survey, that was constructed using the themes from the qualitative interviews and focus groups during the reconnaissance phase, were presented to the community members. The purpose of this presentation was to solicit the community stakeholders' feedback and identify specific services that can be developed for GLBTQ young people using the available community resources. Based on the community input, an intervention consisting of numerous programs and services tailored to GLBTQ youths was designed and implemented. In Example B, Glasson and colleagues (2006) described how the quantitative survey data that had been collected from patients and nurses and the qualitative data that had been compiled from observing and recording the nursing staff discussions about the need for the new model that was grounded in the analysis of patients' responses helped the nurses identify and implement a new model of care for older patients in an acute medical ward. In Sampson's (2010) MMAR study (Example D), the analysis of the quantitative data from the Lesson Style Questionnaire and the qualitative data from a language learning narrative exercise completed by the students helped modify the class instruction to include task-based lessons.

Evaluating Action Phase

During this phase in the research cycle the evaluation phase of an MMAR study is designed and implemented. The goal of this phase is to collect evidence about the action/intervention effectiveness, to understand how it is viewed and if it has been embraced by interested stakeholders, what needs to be changed in the initial action plan, or whether the action/intervention should be completely revised. The same methodological steps that were used during the reconnaissance phase of an MMAR study are repeated. These steps are the following:

- Developing the study purpose and research questions for the evaluation phase
- Selecting an appropriate mixed methods design to address this purpose and answer the research questions

- Identifying the study sample and quantitative and qualitative types of data to be collected
- Collecting and analyzing the data
- Validating the findings and creating meta-inferences

In Glasson and colleagues' (2006) MMAR study (Example B) the implementation of a model of nursing care for older patients in an acute care setting was evaluated using mixed methods. The research questions that guided the evaluation phase of this MMAR study were "Is the implementation of a model of care tailored to the nursing needs of older patients effective in enhancing outcomes such as functional activities of daily living and medication knowledge and management? Were older patients who were admitted during model implementation more satisfied with the nursing care they received than premodel patients?" (p. 590). The quantitative and qualitative data from patients and nurses were collected and analyzed concurrently and compared to the results from similar data collected from patients and nurses before the model implementation. The interpretation of the integrated quantitative and qualitative findings (meta-inferences) confirmed the efficacy of the new model of nursing care.

In Kostos and Shin's (2010) MMAR study (Example A), the teacher-researcher used a math journaling approach, identified through a literature review, to enhance second-grade students' communication of mathematical thinking. The purpose of the study was "to examine how using a math journal affected in building a necessary foundation for second grade students to communicate mathematical thinking" (p. 225). After 5 weeks of implementing this teaching and learning strategy, quantitative data (math assessments) and qualitative data (students' math journal entries, student interviews, and the teacher-researcher's reflective journal) were collected and analyzed concurrently to evaluate the effectiveness of the new instruction.

Monitoring and Revising Action Phase

During this final phase, monitoring and revising of the action/intervention are undertaken based on the meta-inferences from the interpretation of the integrated quantitative and qualitative results from the evaluation phase. Lewin (1948b) referred to this process as taking the second action step. The results from the evaluation of the action/intervention are presented to all stakeholders with the goal of soliciting their feedback about any needed changes or adjustments to the action/intervention plan.

In Kostos and Shin (2010) MMAR study (Example A), the teacher-researcher began to use the journaling approach in daily math lessons. Although the authors of the article did not explain further steps, it was implied that more evaluation of that math teaching and learning strategy for second-grade students would be conducted to inform potential revisions or adjustments in the instructional intervention. In Glasson and colleagues' (2006) MMAR study (Example B), "replanning" of the action was discussed as part of the participatory action research process (p. 590). So it is likely that the new model of nursing care for older patients in the acute medical ward will be further evaluated and revised to better meet the needs of these patients.

When the action/intervention is successful, Phase V (evaluating action) and Phase VI (monitoring and revising action) can be repeated iteratively to continue with the action/intervention monitoring (as shown by a dashed arrow between these phases in Figure 4.1). Ongoing evaluation of the action/intervention outcomes following the procedural steps outlined in Phase V and sharing the results with the community stakeholders help promote project sustainability, viability, and relevancy. If the action/intervention is not successful and does not lead to desired outcomes, a reconceptualization of the entire study may be needed and further identification of the problem or issue may be necessary. So practitioner-researchers may decide to return to Phase I (the diagnosing phase) of the cycle and start all over (as shown by a dashed arrow leading from Phase VI to Phase I in Figure 4.1). Alternatively, additional needs assessment and further exploration of the problem may be required; in this situation practitioner-researchers return to Phase II (as shown by a dashed arrow in Figure 4.1) and conduct another reconnaissance phase of an MMAR study. This is a critically import-ant aspect of the action research process because it allows for recycling of the action/intervention plan based on the new data and additional reflection. The revised action/intervention plan is implemented in Phase IV and is evaluated through designing and conducting another evaluation phase (Phase V). For example, in Sampson's (2010) MMAR study (Example D), it is likely that the researcher will return to the reconnaissance phase when teaching another course to identify the lesson style preferences of a different cohort of Japanese college students. This cohort may be different from the one used in the study, and the previously developed intervention consisting of task-based lessons may not meet the needs of these students.

It is important to keep in mind that, due to an iterative nature of action research, practitioner-researchers do not proceed in a linear manner and can skip certain phases in an action research cycle. For example, if an intervention or a new program is already in place in an organization or community (for instance, established professional learning communities in schools or school districts, an existing human papillomavirus (HPV) vaccination program in the local health department for female teenagers, or a substance abuse prevention curriculum in urban high schools), practitioner-researchers may want to first evaluate the effectiveness of the existing intervention by designing and conducting the evaluation phase of an MMAR study (Phase V). Evaluation results will provide information on whether to make changes to further enhance the effectiveness of the existing action/intervention, or to revise it and significantly change the nature and direction of the inter-vention. In any case, practitioner-researchers may need to start with the diagnosing phase (Phase I) to better conceptualize an MMAR study (as shown by a dashed arrow leading from Phase VI to Phase I in Figure 4.1). For example, in Kostos and Shin's (2010) MMAR study (Example A), the researchers implemented and evaluated the math journaling instruction previously reported in the literature, but they had to conceptualize an overall MMAR study and provide the rationale for using mixed methods "to provide a more in-depth look at how the students communicated their mathematical thinking when using math journals" (p. 226).

The remainder of this chapter focuses on the first, diagnosing phase in an MMAR study process and dis-cusses the specifics of conceptualizing an MMAR study. So, what does conceptualizing an MMAR study exactly involve? How can practitioner-researchers implement these procedures?

CONCEPTUALIZING AN MMAR STUDY

The process of conceptualizing an MMAR study typically includes the following steps or procedures: identify-ing the problem or issue, reviewing the literature, writing a research problem statement, developing a general plan for the study, considering ethical issues, and formulating an overall study purpose, expected outcomes, objectives, and research questions. Although these steps are presented in a sequential order, in practice they often overlap: practitioner-researchers may need to revisit prior steps to make adjustments in the study focus, add additional literature, provide more justification for the study, refine a study plan, or revise the study purpose and research questions. The following sections discuss and illustrate each step in conceptualizing an MMAR study.

Identifying the Problem/Issue

As in any research study, the first step that practitioner-researchers need to take is to identify a problem area requiring investigation in their professional or community settings. This step is critical because the degree of the problem exposure may have implications for the whole study. According to Mills (2011), making a problem or issue explicit helps practitioner-researchers define an area of focus and ensure that the study will be meaningful and engaging for them. As previously discussed, in action research the focus is on the practical problem or issue. If the problem is successfully resolved, it will result in the improvement of practice, improvement of the understanding of practice, or improvement of the situation in which the practice takes place (Carr & Kemmis, 1986). In other words, identifying and addressing a pressing issue or problem that can have immediate benefits for practitioners, organizations, and communities is important for conceptualizing an action research study.

Speaking about the practical nature of action research, Mills (2011) identified several important criteria that should be applied by practitioner-researchers when selecting an area of focus: addressing an issue within one's own practice or within one's own locus of control, focusing on something one feels passionate about, or focusing on something one would like to change or improve. These criteria should help practitioner-researchers to better focus the study to be able to generate knowledge that is relevant, useful, and beneficial for those involved. As Koshy and colleagues (2011) observed, when practitioner-researchers are involved in a research endeavor that informs practice, the knowledge is generated from practice.

To illustrate this point, Glasson and colleagues' (2006) MMAR study (Example B) addressed the practical issue of improving the quality of nursing care for older acutely ill hospitalized medical patients through development of a new model of care. The area of focus was on the nurse practice in an acute medical ward in a public hospital in Sydney, Australia. Nursing staff were anxious to improve their practice and volunteered to participate in the study. The identified problem was within the nurses' loci of control, and they willingly participated in the development, implementation, and evaluation of a new model of nursing care through participatory action research process.

The focus of Craig's (2011) MMAR study (Example C) was to conduct a community needs assessment that would lead to creation of a system of care for GLBTQ youths in an urban area. Although the study was initiated by a university faculty member, it was conducted in close partnership with local agencies and representatives of GLBTQ youths within the geographic community. Active collaboration of all identified community stakeholders in the study process was indicative of their concern about the problem and the need for change, as GLBTQ youths were considered a population at risk that had more predispositions for psychiatric disorders, substance abuse, and suicide.

In Sampson's (2010) MMAR study (Example D), the apparent absence of Japanese college students' motivation to use English for communication in class prompted the researcher to try to solve this problem in his own classroom. Developing a new lesson style based on students' feedback was within the researcher's locus of control. The researcher showed his passion about the problem by allowing his class to become an experimental zone and by involving students as active participants in the action research process.

Reviewing the Literature

According to Herr and Anderson (2005), when conceptualizing an action research study, "one way to begin is to ask what is already known about the question or puzzle that is the focus of the inquiry" (p. 78). Literature review is an important component of conceptualizing a research study as it represents what is already known about the topic or the problem in question. Fink (2005) provided the following comprehensive definition of a literature review:

A research literature review is a systematic, explicit and reproducible method of identifying, evaluating and synthesizing the existing body of completed and recorded work produced by researchers, scholars and practitioners (p. 3).

Researchers conduct literature reviews for different purposes depending on the goal of the study, which may be adding to existing knowledge base in general, or adding knowledge to a specific practice (Creswell, 2012). In action research, reviewing available literature may help practitioner-researchers better understand the problem or the situation, and, thus, may better focus the study. A major purpose is to identify the reported best practices of other practitioner-researchers, organizations, and communities, and to justify the need for a planned change or improvement. A distinctive feature of the literature review in action research is that it may be ongoing, and practitioner-researchers may refer to other research studies and published materials to make adjustments to the study general plan or to revise an initial action/intervention plan based on its evaluation results and findings from reported studies.

Learning how other practitioner-researchers have addressed a similar or closely related problem may help reveal the strategies that have been found effective and ready to be tested in other practical situations. Mills (2011) explained that reviewing the literature may allow teacher-researchers to reflect on their problem by referring to other researchers' views, and may help them save time in their endeavors by better focusing the study. Koshy and colleagues (2011), with reference to conducting action research in health care, noted that through a literature review practitioner-researchers can gain insights into the topic, consider different perspectives on the issue, and thus ground their ideas within available research literature and have greater confidence when conducting the study and disseminating its results. Additionally, Hinchey (2008) discussed how conducting a preliminary literature review and sharing similar studies with local authorities and other stakeholders may help elicit their cooperation and secure their buy-in into the project.

Besides identifying previous research on the topic and determining a range of possible solutions to the problem or issue in question, a literature review can reinforce development of the conceptual or theoretical framework for how to best address or solve a particular issue in the study. According to McNiff and Whitehead (2011), the conceptual or theoretical framework is a set of ideas within which a researcher locates his or her thinking and writing. As discussed in Chapter 2, action research is always value laden, and raises an awareness of a need for improvement and a social change. For example, Craig's (2011) MMAR study

(Example C) about creating a system of care for GLBTQ youths was guided by critical and gender theories that advanced an advocacy perspective for young people of alternative sexual orientation. Although this theoretical perspective was not stated explicitly in the study, the researcher argued that developing a new system of care for GLBTQ youths would help address health and mental problems of that reportedly vulnerable population. Montgomery and colleagues (2008; Example E) cited the known theoretical framework of Getting, Losing, and Keeping Housing, previously developed based on housing experiences of persons with serious mental illness (Forchuk, Ward-Griffin, Csiernik, & Turner, 2006, as cited in Montgomery et al., 2008). That knowledge guided the conceptualization of their proposed MMAR study.

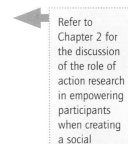

Refer to Chapter 2 for the discussion of the role of action research in empowering participants when creating a social change.

When conceptualizing an MMAR study, reviewing existing studies on a topic of interest may also help identify an appropriate research approach and provide the rationale for using mixed methods to solve the known problem or issue. Understanding how mixed methods was applied by other researchers to conduct a needs assessment of a similar problem, or how it was used to evaluate the action/intervention, may help practitioner-researchers make an informed decision to integrate quantitative and qualitative methods in seeking solutions to their practical problems. It can also provide practitioner-researchers with the appropriate research terminology, reveal potential quantitative and qualitative data sources and means of their analysis, and demonstrate how mixed methods inferences can inform the development, implementation, and evaluation of the action/intervention plan. For example, conducting a literature review on barriers in health vaccination for their MMAR study helped Baker and colleagues (2010) locate and use a previously reported universalistic translation process model to measure hardships and obstacles to vaccination within the Hmong community in the United States. This model combined mixed methods data collection and analysis and process-oriented language translation, and was found to be an effective method for translating health surveys and promoting culturally responsive health care. Box 4.1 summarizes how a literature review can enhance and inform the conceptualization of an MMAR study.

Many research methods books and chapters in associated textbooks discuss how to conduct a literature review and what sources of reference it is useful to consider. A number of authors (Creswell, 2012; Fink, 2005; Koshy et al., 2011; Mills, 2011) describe the steps that researchers need to take when undertaking a literature review. With some variation, these steps include the following:

Refer to Further Readings at the end of this chapter, which includes a number of useful resources about conducting literature reviews.

- Selecting bibliographic databases and Web sites to conduct the search
- Identifying key terms reflective of the topic/problem of interest to use in the search for literature
- Locating suitable sources for review (books, articles, reports, conference papers, dissertations)
- Reading through and critically evaluating the identified sources for quality and suitability to the topic/problem of interest
- Organizing the selected sources by abstracting them, taking notes, and developing a literature review map
- Producing a descriptive review of the literature for the topic/problem of interest

BOX 4.1

Role of Literature Review in an MMAR Study

- It helps assess the body of available knowledge relating to the problem/issue.
- It helps evaluate the existing body of knowledge about the problem/issue.
- It helps understand the problem/issue through reflection on the existing literature.
- It helps understand existing different perspectives on the problem/issue.
- It helps connect to practitioner-researchers' personal experiences with the problem/issue.
- It helps position the study within a context of existing literature about the problem/issue.
- It helps develop the conceptual/theoretical framework to address the problem/issue.
- It helps identify a range of possible solutions to the problem/issue.
- It helps identify the best practices relating to the problem/issue as discovered by others.
- It helps identify gaps in knowledge about how to best address the problem/issue.
- It helps justify the need for a planned change or improvement.
- It helps elicit cooperation and participation by community stakeholders.
- It helps make adjustments and revisions to the initial action/intervention plan.
- It helps identify the appropriate methodological approaches to research the problem/issue.
- It helps provide the rationale for applying mixed methods in an action research study.
- It helps identify appropriate mixed methods terminology as well as data sources, and their analytical means.
- It helps understand how mixed methods inferences can inform the development, implementation, and evaluation of the action/intervention plan.

Searching for the literature to inform an MMAR study, in addition to the terms reflective of the topic/problem of interest, practitioner-researchers may include such search terms as "action research," "practitioner research," "participatory research," "community-based research," "mixed method(s)," and "mixed-method(s)." Adding these search terms will help locate action research studies that used a mixed methods approach and integrated quantitative and qualitative methods to address a similar problem or issue.

Another helpful tool is to create a visual diagram or a concept map of the literature reviewed on the topic (Creswell, 2012). A **literature review map** may help organize the selected sources by emergent themes and subthemes to determine how a conceptualized study may add to the existing body of the literature on the same problem/issue. Visually organizing all available sources may also help practitioner-researchers construct a conceptual framework for understanding the problem/issue under investigation (Koshy et al., 2011).

When writing a descriptive summary of the literature review, it is recommended to arrange the reviewed published sources by themes or concept areas following the literature review map, and to do a study-by-study review within themes and related subthemes. It is important to organize the reviewed sources in the chronological order within a certain theme because it is common for more recent studies to be informed by previous research. The concluding part of the literature review should tie everything together, building the connection with the MMAR study that is being conceptualized.

Writing a Research Problem Statement

A problem or issue that leads to a research study is generally referred to as a **research problem** (Creswell, 2012; Johnson & Christensen, 2012). It establishes the need for conducting a study; it sets the stage for the entire study and justifies the importance of the identified problem/issue that is the study focus. In action research, this problem is related to the situation that practitioner-researchers want to change or improve, thus connecting a conceptual idea to a concrete action (Elliott, 1991). Developing or writing a statement of the research problem is part of the process of conceptualizing the study. Creswell (2012) outlined a logical model of the flow of the ideas in a research problem statement that includes five components: (1) the research topic, (2) the research problem, (3) a justification of the importance of the problem based on the literature review, (4) the deficiencies or gaps in existing knowledge about the problem, and (5) the audiences that may benefit from the completed study. In conceptualizing an MMAR study, it is also necessary to consider the advantages of using a mixed methods approach to help find a more effective and more reliable solution to the problem.

Creswell's (2012) logical model for a research problem statement was adapted to reflect the practical nature of the research problem in action research and the methodological advantages of using mixed methods in the action research process. A research problem statement for an MMAR study includes five logically sequenced components that are summarized in Box 4.2. Figure 4.2 organizes these five components in a visual diagram that depicts a logical flow of ideas in an MMAR study research problem statement.

To better understand how these components were applied in the statement of the research problem in an MMAR study, refer to the introduction and the subsequent two sections in Kostos and Shin's (2010) MMAR study (Example A) on the use of math journals to enhance second graders' communication of mathematical thinking. The authors introduced their practical problem in the opening paragraph of the article, summing it up with the following sentence: "The students' response does not demonstrate the mathematical thinking

BOX 4.2

Five Components of a Research Problem Statement in an MMAR Study

1. Identifying a practical problem/issue that requires solution, and justifying the need for the situation change or improvement

2. Identifying available solutions for the problem/issue and explaining strategies used to address the problem/issue identified through the review of existing literature or other credible sources

3. Identifying gaps in knowledge about the problem/issue and recognizing missing information or knowledge that may help solve the problem/issue

4. Explaining how the current study may help solve the problem/issue and specifying how the problem/issue can be solved by conducting an MMAR study

5. Explaining who may benefit from solving the problem/issue and specifying how solving the problem/issue may be helpful to study participants, practitioners, and other stakeholders

| FIGURE 4.2 | **Logical Flow of Ideas in an MMAR Study Research Problem Statement** |

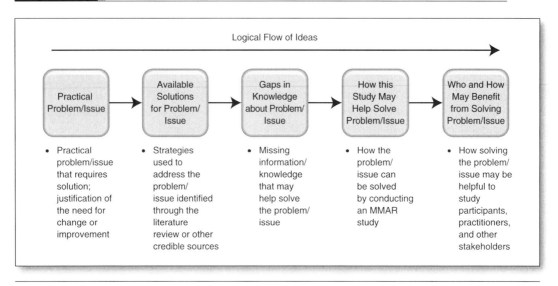

Adapted from Creswell (2012, p. 71).

process; rather it merely demonstrates the students' ability to memorize and recall a method of solving a problem to find a correct answer" (p. 223). In the next paragraph, the authors emphasized the importance of the problem: "It is important for students to be able to demonstrate their mathematical thinking as well as their method of solving a problem" (p. 223). They further connected the development of mathematical thinking with mathematical communication grounding this observation in previous research on this topic.

In the following paragraph, Kostos and Shin (2010) provided additional justification for the need of developing mathematical communication in elementary students by relating to professional standards in the field, such as the National Council of Teachers of Mathematics. Further justification of the need to improve this current math learning deficiency in students stems from the requirement for students "to demonstrate their ability to communicate their mathematical thinking on high stakes testing," such as the Illinois Standards Assessment Test (p. 224). The authors described how the teacher-researcher tried different strategies to teach her students how to communicate their mathematical thinking, but "the results were not satisfactory" (p. 224). The teacher-researcher realized that she needed an innovative approach to solve this problem and tried math journaling with her second-grade students: "I believe allowing my students to demonstrate their mathematical thinking through writing and drawing in a math journal would be a comfortable, non-threatening, and effective way to express their mathematical thinking" (p. 224). An extensive literature review that was summarized in two sections—"The Importance of Math Communication" and "Writing and Journaling to Communicate Mathematical Thinking"—explained the known benefits and disadvantages of math journaling for developing and communicating mathematical thinking. In spite of the fact that much research has been completed on writing and communicating mathematical thinking, it seemed that the benefits of math journaling was not explored for elementary students.

By conducting an MMAR study in a teacher-researcher's own classroom, Kostos and Shin (2010) wanted to provide an effective solution to this problem. They discussed how using math journaling may help students to better learn mathematics, thus identifying the benefiting audience for the study: "Math journals would allow students to convey their knowledge about math concepts in their own words and/or illustrations. They would also give students opportunities to demonstrate their knowledge or ask questions without fear of embarrassment" (p. 224). By the end of the literature review section, the authors addressed how using math journaling may also benefit the teachers.

Although Kostos and Shin (2010) discussed the benefits of using mixed methods within an action research approach in the methods section of the article, it may be beneficial for readers to have this information earlier in the research problem statement. It was obvious that the following reasons for applying mixed methods were helpful in advancing an overall study; therefore, these reasons could have played a role in the study conceptualization process too: "to triangulate findings and to provide a more in-depth look at how the students communicated their mathematical thinking when using math journals" (p. 226). Kostos and Shin (2010) concluded the research problem statement by stating the purpose of their study that provided the direction for the entire investigation: "This research was to examine how using a math journal affected in building a necessary foundation for second grade students to communicate mathematical thinking" (p. 225).

Developing a Study General Research Plan

To quote Hinchey (2008), "[a]ny purposeful journey has a planned route to a specific destination" (p. 53). As in any research study, action researchers need to have a research plan that will guide and direct the study. Developing such a plan is part of the study conceptualization process too, and may evolve along with conducting a literature review and elaborating a research problem statement for the study. A research plan will typically include a study purpose, research questions and/or hypotheses, methods, and a timeline (Hinchey, 2008). However, a research plan for an action research study may deviate from a standard research plan. Since action research follows a research spiral and consists of cycles, the study methods may evolve and change as the study progresses (Herr & Anderson, 2005). Therefore, in an MMAR study that includes one complete cycle of six phases, a research plan will take a more general character. This is because the purpose of conducting the needs assessment related to the problem/issue during the reconnaissance phase may require a different design and may call for the need to collect and analyze different types of data than the purpose of evaluating the effects of the implemented action/intervention during a later phase.

Developing a general research plan for an MMAR study will help keep the study focused on the problem or issue in question, will provide the direction for the overall study, and will list the goals the practitioner-researches want to accomplish. Accordingly, this plan should include the following important components: the purpose of the overall study, the expected outcomes, the study objectives, and the research questions. These are discussed later in the chapter. Additionally, the action research literature suggests that the general plan should include the discussion of the study timeline, the investigators' research skills, available or anticipated resources, stakeholders' involvement, project feasibility, and the venues for disseminating the study findings (Hinchey, 2008; Koshy et al., 2011; McNiff & Whitehead, 2011; Mertler, 2012; Mills, 2011; Stringer, 2014).

Timeline

When conceptualizing a research study it is important to realistically assess the time it will take to conduct the study. Setting and meeting the deadlines for various stages of the project helps improve the study quality and ensure that it proceeds smoothly (Hinchey, 2008; Koshy et al., 2011). It also helps estimate the resources needed for each stage and researchers' involvement and time commitment. However, it may be difficult to accurately estimate the time needed to complete an action research study due to the cyclical nature of the action research process. The same holds true for an MMAR study that may consist of multiple phases and may require adjustments in specific goals and the amount and type of data needed at each phase. In spite of this versatility of an MMAR study, it is important to make a best estimate on the time frame for at least the first study phases (reconnaissance and action planning) to stay within the study assigned time. As a helpful toolkit, Mills (2011) suggested developing a timeline specifying "who will be doing *what* and *when*" (p. 62; emphasis in original) and at which stage in the research process, while James and colleagues (2008) recommended having all participating co-researchers and stakeholders "hold each other accountable to time lines and plans, acting as critical friends to ensure that everyone stays on task" (p. 81). Additionally, practitioner-researchers need to realize that it might require more time to conduct the reconnaissance or evaluation phases of an MMAR study because each phase involves collection and analysis of multiple quantitative and qualitative data. The process for designing and conducting mixed methods studies benefits from a team approach and makes mixed methods data collection and analysis more manageable (Creswell & Plano Clark, 2011). Additionally, it supports the participatory and collaborative nature of action research that encourages involvement of study participants and stakeholders as coresearchers.

Research Skills

To make an MMAR study realistic and to ensure that it will produce credible outcomes, it is necessary to assess the available research expertise that may be required to design and conduct the study. Because an MMAR study involves collecting and analyzing both quantitative and qualitative data, practitioner-researchers should be familiar with these procedural strategies, and the general principles of conducting mixed methods research (Creswell & Plano Clark, 2011). It may be useful to create a research team consisting of practitioner-researchers with a range of different research skills and also to form partnerships with experts from professional communities and local higher educational establishments. Community members and academic consultants with requisite expertise may also be invited to form a project advisory board in order to provide oversight for the study design and implementation (Herr & Anderson, 2005).

Resources

Conceptualizing an MMAR study will also require consideration of the needed resources. Practitioner-researchers should reflect on whether they have enough means—such as monetary funds, equipment, and physical material—to carry out the project (Koshy et al., 2011). Conducting an MMAR study may require equipment for collecting numeric information, such as measuring tools, validated questionnaires, and survey administration programs (e.g., SurveyMonkey), and for collecting qualitative information, such as voice and video recorders, cameras, and qualitative data transcribing tools. Software programs may be needed for data analysis, such as Excel and Statistical Package for the Social Sciences (SPSS) for quantitative data analysis, and NVivo or MAXQDA for qualitative data analysis. Obtaining money through research grants has become a standard procedure in MMAR studies, particularly in large-scale projects.

Revisit the description of Giachello and colleagues' (2003) MMAR study summarized in Box 2.3 in Chapter 2. Also, refer to Chapter 10 for the discussion on how to develop a proposal for an MMAR study.

Stakeholders' Involvement

Planning for inclusion of all interested stakeholders into an MMAR study process is critical for the project success and buy-in in the community. Support from community members will help gain access to quantitative and qualitative information and will also help with recruitment of the study participants. According to Stringer (2014), action research creates opportunities to involve diverse groups of people with various interests to work collaboratively toward effective solutions to problems that may be of interest or concern to them. Assigning project roles to everybody who wishes to participate in the study should be part of the general research plan and may include other practitioners in the field, community leaders, study participants, academic consultants, and representatives from governing bodies. Project roles may range from serving on the study advisory board to participating in data collection and analysis. Building community capacity is an integral component of the process of active involvement of all stakeholders in action research (Grant, Nelson, & Mitchell, 2008). In an MMAR study, **capacity building** activities may include providing training in quantitative, qualitative, and mixed methods research, conducting literature reviews, and performing action planning and evaluation to interested community members. Koshy and colleagues (2011) also suggested establishing the ground rules for participation in project activities and project-related meetings as part of the study planning.

Feasibility

Assessing the feasibility of an MMAR study should also be part of the general research plan. How viable a study seems will depend on many factors: allotted time, research expertise of the project team, monetary and physical resources, support and collaboration of stakeholder groups, access to quantitative and qualitative information, and acceptance of the study by the community. Conceptualizing an MMAR study should also include the discussion of how communication among the members of the research team and the stakeholders will be achieved and sustained. Stringer (2014) argued that involvement in an action research study "requires all participants to engage in communication that facilitates the development of harmonious relationships and the effective attainment of group or organizational objectives" (p. 26). Additionally, it is important to have everybody understand the logistics of an MMAR study process, characteristics of quantitative and qualitative methods, the role of mixed methods in different phases in an action research cycle, and how to use mixed methods inferences to inform the development and evaluation of the action/intervention plan. Understanding of the study methodology will help decrease potential errors in designing the study, eliminate unnecessary delays in information processing, and ultimately enhance the study implementation. Moreover, such careful preplanning potentially can provide valuable educational experiences for the members of the team.

Dissemination of Findings

Refer to Chapter 2 and Box 2.2 for the discussion of the nine principles of community-based participatory action research.

It is important to consider the venues for the dissemination of the project results when conceptualizing the study and developing the study research plan (Koshy et al., 2011). In an MMAR study, identification of effective communication channels for the dissemination of the results during each study phase is critical for obtaining feedback from the community and stakeholders regarding the relevance of the suggested steps in the action/intervention and interpretation of the results of the action/intervention evaluation. Dissemination of the research findings to all partners is one of the principles of community-based action research, as discussed earlier in Chapter 2. According to Schulz and colleagues (1998), research findings should be regularly disseminated to all stakeholders using a respectful and understandable language. It is also important to acknowledge all partners' contributions to the research process. Active engagement with the study process will promote broader acceptance and subsequent dissemination of the results by the community representatives.

Specifying Overall Study Purpose, Expected Outcomes, Objectives, and Research Questions

Developing an overall study purpose statement, listing the study research objectives, and outlining research questions that practitioner-researchers want to answer by conducting the project is also part of the process of conceptualizing an MMAR study. Because an action research project has a practical focus and aims at solving some pertinent problem or issue, it is also important to specify the expected study outcomes early in the research process.

Study Purpose and Expected Outcomes

The specific problem area that practitioner-researchers choose to focus on, as discussed earlier in the chapter, helps identify the study purpose (Mills, 2011). This purpose is expressed in a succinct statement that conveys the overall intent of the study and advances its overall direction (Creswell, 2012, 2014; Johnson & Christensen, 2012). The study **purpose statement** is important because it is grounded in the research problem and is further refined into specific study objectives and research questions.

Creswell and Plano Clark (2011) suggested that an effective mixed methods purpose statement should include an overall intent or the content aim of the study, indicate a mixed methods design, specify participants, sites, and data to be collected for each quantitative and qualitative study strand, and provide a rationale for using a mixed methods approach. However, specific characteristics of an MMAR study require some adjustments to what should be included in an MMAR purpose statement. Because an MMAR study is cyclical and consists of several phases in which a mixed methods approach can be applied (e.g., reconnaissance and evaluation phases, as shown in Figure 4.1), its purpose statement may include specific goals for each phase in addition to an overall study intent. Taking into account the evolving nature of action research and the fact that all study design details may not yet be known during the diagnosing phase, it is reasonable to state these goals in general terms. This will enable practitioner-researchers to provide a broad methodological framework for the planned study phases within the action research cycle and decide on the details later as the study unfolds.

Additionally, specifying a mixed methods design for the reconnaissance and evaluation phases may not yet be necessary, unless practitioner-researchers want to make a commitment to a specific design up front and to inform the direction of the overall study. Explicitly expressing the goals of reconnaissance and evaluation phases of the study in an MMAR purpose statement may help practitioner-researchers better understand, design, and implement these components of the action research cycle. As stated earlier, an MMAR study purpose statement should also include the expected outcomes of the planned action/intervention. Specifying what the study plans to achieve in terms of solving the problem or improving the practice is important because an overall goal of action research is to influence practice and promote a desired change in the existing situation. Clearly identifying the study outcomes may also help with the study's acceptance by the community and by the stakeholders during the study conceptualization phase.

To make it easier for practitioner-researchers to write a purpose statement for an overall MMAR study including all the suggested components, an MMAR study general purpose statement script is provided in Box 4.3. The script is followed by an example of how this script was used to develop a purpose statement for a hypothetical MMAR study about changes in existing school policies related to the use of Dynamic Indicators of Basic Early Literacy Skills (DIBELS) reading assessment test to improve third-grade students' reading self-efficacy. To use the script, practitioner-researchers should fill in the information that applies to their study in the spaces between the parentheses.

After an overall MMAR study purpose is explicitly stated and the goals of the reconnaissance and evaluation study phases are identified, practitioner-researchers need to think about developing more specific purpose statements for each of these phases to guide their design and implementation. However, these purpose statements should be completed when practitioner-researchers are ready to move on to these phases and when they have more details about the particular goals of these steps in the action research cycle. The development of the purpose statements for the reconnaissance and evaluation phases of an MMAR study are further discussed in Chapter 6 in the context of specific MMAR study designs.

Research Objectives and Research Questions

Once the purpose statement of the study is developed, it is narrowed down to specific research objectives and research questions. **Research objectives** are statements of intent that identify the goals researchers plan to achieve by undertaking the study (Creswell, 2012). They are more frequently found in the studies conducted in health and behavioral science fields rather than in social sciences. For example, in Giachello and

---

BOX 4.3

MMAR Study General Purpose Statement Script and Example

MMAR Study General Purpose Statement Script

The purpose of this MMAR study is to (<u>investigate/transform/explore the</u> <u>issue/practice</u>) in order to (<u>state the action expected outcomes</u>) for (<u>state participants</u> <u>and site</u>). The goal of the reconnaissance phase is to (<u>state the content aim</u>) by using a (<u>concurrent/sequential/multistrand</u>) mixed methods design to collect and analyze (<u>state quantitative and qualitative data</u>) to inform the development of (<u>state the purpose of the action plan</u>). The goal of the evaluation phase of the study is to (<u>state the purpose of evaluation</u>) by using a (<u>concurrent/sequential/multistrand</u>) mixed methods design to collect and analyze (<u>state quantitative and qualitative data</u>). The rationale for applying mixed methods in the study is to gain more insight into (<u>state the problem/issue</u>) so that it may lead to a more effective problem solution.

MMAR Study General Purpose Statement Script Example

The purpose of this MMAR study is to <u>transform the existing school policies related to the DIBELS reading test administration</u> in order to <u>enhance reading self-efficacy for third grade students in school X.</u> The goal of the reconnaissance phase is to <u>identify the reasons for students' failure to meet DIBELS standards</u> by using a <u>concurrent</u> mixed methods design to collect and analyze <u>students' DIBELS test scores, reading self-efficacy scores, and data from individual interviews with teachers and parents</u> to inform the development of <u>more effective test administration policies.</u> The goal of the evaluation phase of the study is to <u>identify the effectiveness of the new DIBELS test administration policies as they relate to students' reading self-efficacy</u> by using a <u>sequential</u> mixed methods design to collect and analyze <u>students' test scores, teacher and parent survey responses, and focus group interviews with teachers, parents, and students.</u> The rationale for applying mixed methods in the study is to gain more insight into <u>how the DIBELS reading test administration affects third-grade students' reading self-efficacy</u> so that it may lead to a more effective problem solution.

---

colleagues' (2003) MMAR study discussed in Chapter 2, the following objectives guided the research activities in Phase 1 of the study:

- Identify key social, medical, environmental, cultural, institutional, and behavioral factors that may be associated with racial/ethnic disparities in diabetes risk, prevalence, and quality of care among Latinos and African Americans and other groups in specific community areas on Chicago's Southeast Side.
- Identify effective strategies for diabetes prevention and control through community action planning.
- Engage in analysis and dissemination so as to allow replication and adaptation of the project to other communities (p. 315).

Research questions stated in the question format narrow the study purpose to specific questions that researchers seek to answer in the research project (Creswell, 2012). Mills (2011) described research questions as "questions that breathe life into the area-of-focus statement and help provide a focus for your data collection plan" (p. 61). Research questions are important because they set boundaries to the study, clarify its specific directions, and influence the selection of the research methods (Plano Clark & Badiee, 2010; Teddlie & Tashakkori, 2009). According to Plano Clark and Badiee (2010), research questions "provide a direct link from the study's purpose to its design and methods" (p. 278).

Consistent with the recommendations for the type of research questions to be included in a mixed methods study, in an MMAR study that aims at integrating quantitative and qualitative methods three types of research questions may be asked. First, an overarching integrated question (Teddlie & Tashakkori, 2009), also referred to as a **mixed methods research question** (Creswell & Plano Clark, 2011), should be developed that addresses an overall intent of the study. According to Onwuegbuzie and Leech (2006), this is a research question that "embeds both a quantitative research question and a qualitative research question within the same question" (p. 483). An integrated/mixed methods question is necessary because it addresses integration of the quantitative and qualitative methods in the process of the study implementation (Creswell & Plano Clark, 2011). Posting only separate quantitative and qualitative research questions may keep the methods separate, resulting in lack of their integration in the study (Yin, 2006). Plano Clark and Badiee (2010) indicated that mixed or integrated questions should convey the need for quantitative and qualitative methods' integration or foreshadow an integrated approach, or both. The authors suggested five pertinent characteristics of mixed methods research questions; these are presented in Box 4.4.

BOX 4.4

Five Characteristics of Mixed Methods Research Questions

1. *Mixed questions should be researchable.* Mixed methods research questions should be able to generate answers using a combination of quantitative and qualitative methods and their integration strategies.

2. *Mixed questions should be important.* Mixed methods research questions should be relevant to the study purpose and contribute to the generation of knowledge about the studied phenomena.

3. *Mixed questions should have conceptual clarity.* Mixed methods research questions should clearly convey what researchers plan to achieve in the study and how they interpret the questions in the context of quantitative/qualitative/mixed continuum.

4. *There should be congruence among the mixed questions, overall mixed methods design, and results.* Mixed methods research questions should correspond to the methods employed in the study and to the study results.

5. *Mixed questions should convey the need for integration or foreshadow an integrated approach, or both.* Mixed methods research questions should support meaningful integration of the quantitative and qualitative methods in the study.

Adapted from Plano Clark and Badiee (2010, p. 299).

Besides a focus on quantitative and qualitative methods' integration, an integrated/mixed methods question for an MMAR study should also reflect a practical nature of research questions in action research aiming at finding effective solutions to pertinent practical issues. According to Mills (2011), in an action research project research questions also help practitioner-researchers validate if the chosen research strategies are effective, and help obtain all the information practitioner-researchers need in the process of conducting the study. Therefore, in an MMAR study an **integrated mixed methods action research (MMAR) question** will address an overall practical intent of an MMAR study, as well as foreshadow an integrated or a mixed methods approach to exploring the issue.

For example, an overall practical purpose for a hypothetical MMAR study about the DIBELS reading test administration policies presented in Box 4.3 can be addressed by an integrated MMAR question that will be answered by developing meta-inferences based on the collection and analysis of multiple forms of quantitative and qualitative data in the process of the whole study:

- How can changes in the existing school policies related to the DIBELS reading test administration for third-grade students enhance students' reading self-efficacy in school X, as measured by test and reading efficacy scores and as described through perceptions of teachers, parents, and students?

In addition to an integrated MMAR question, quantitative and qualitative research questions should be developed that will be answered by collecting and analyzing numerical and narrative information, respectively. Quantitative research questions may also be presented in the hypotheses format. **Research hypotheses** are statements that contain predictions about the outcomes of a relationship among variables and are a type of research questions that are used in a quantitative approach (Creswell, 2012; Plano Clark & Badiee, 2010). Research hypotheses are less common in action research because of their confirmatory nature and the need for more advanced statistical analysis, which often requires specific research skills. According to Mertler (2012), a research question format is appropriate for both quantitative and qualitative questions in action research. Quantitative research questions tend to be more close-ended and narrow, and are focused on revealing the relationships among variables, whereas qualitative research questions tend to be more open-ended and holistic in nature (Mertler, 2012), and are aimed at exploring the phenomenon or concept from participants' perspectives (Creswell, 2012). Following is an illustration of a quantitative research question for the reconnaissance phase of a hypothetical MMAR study about DIBELS reading test administration policies:

- What is the relationship between third-grade students' DIBELS test scores and reading self-efficacy scores in school X?

A qualitative research question for the same study phase can be written as follows:

- How do teachers and parents explain third-grade students' failure to meet the DIBELS reading test standards in school X?

Box 4.5 contains the research questions (integrated, quantitative, and qualitative) that were developed for a hypothetical MMAR study about the DIBELS reading test administration policies. Each set of questions

BOX 4.5

Examples of Integrated MMAR, Quantitative, and Qualitative Research Questions Matching Study Purpose

- *The purpose* of this MMAR study is to transform the existing school policies related to the DIBELS reading test administration in order to enhance reading self-efficacy for third grade students in school X.

- *Overall Content Aim*—Integrated MMAR Question:

  ○ How can changes in the existing school policies related to the DIBELS reading test administration enhance third-grade students' reading self-efficacy in school X, as measured by test and reading efficacy scores and as described through perceptions of teachers, parents, and students?

- *The goal* of the reconnaissance phase is to identify the reasons for students' failure to meet DIBELS standards by using a concurrent mixed methods design to collect and analyze students' DIBELS test scores, reading self-efficacy scores, and data from individual interviews with teachers and parents to inform the development of more effective test administration policies.

- *Reconnaissance Phase*—Quantitative Research Questions:

  ○ What is the relationship between the DIBELS test scores and reading self-efficacy scores for third-grade students' in school X?
  ○ How do third-grade students with high and low reading self-efficacy scores perform on the DIBELS test in school X?

- *Reconnaissance Phase*—Qualitative Research Questions:

  ○ How do teachers and parents explain third-grade students' failure to meet the DIBELS reading test standards in school X?
  ○ What factors may contribute to third-grade students' failure to meet the DIBELS reading test standards in school X?
  ○ How can the reading self-efficacy scores be improved for third-grade students in school X?

- *The goal* of the evaluation phase of the study is to identify the effectiveness of the new DIBELS test administration policies as they relate to students' reading self-efficacy by using a sequential mixed methods design to collect and analyze students' test scores, teacher and parent survey responses, and focus group interviews with teachers, parents, and students.

- *Evaluation Phase*—Quantitative Research Questions:

  ○ Have the reading self-efficacy scores for third-grade students changed after the new DIBELS test administration policies were introduced in school X?

(Continued)

(Continued)

- ○ What is the relationship between the DIBELS test scores and reading self-efficacy scores for third-grade students after the new DIBELS test administration policies were introduced in school X?
- ○ How do third-grade students with high and low reading self-efficacy scores perform on the DIBELS test after the new DIBELS test administration policies were introduced in school X?
- ○ What are teachers' and parents' attitudes about the effectiveness of the new DIBELS test administration policies that were introduced for third-grade students in school X?

- *Evaluation Phase*—Qualitative Research Questions:

- ○ How do teachers and parents explain the effects of the new DIBELS test administration policies on reading self-efficacy for third-grade students in school X?
- ○ What are teachers' and parents' perceptions of the new DIBELS test administration policies for third-grade students introduced in school X?
- ○ How comfortable are third-grade students with taking the DIBELS test after the new DIBELS test administration policies were introduced in school X?
- ○ How do third-grade students describe their experiences with taking the DIBELS test before and after the new DIBELS test administration policies were introduced in school X?

addresses a related part in the purpose statement initially presented in Box 4.3. Research questions are further discussed in the context of specific MMAR study phases and designs in Chapter 6.

Considering Ethical Issues

Although ethical issues should be addressed at each stage in the research process, it is important to carefully consider **research ethics** when initially conceptualizing the study. Referring to ethics in social science research, Hesse-Biber and Leavy (2011) argued that consideration of ethical issues should not be done as an afterthought, but that it should become a critical component of the whole research process, from its inception to dissemination of research findings. Research ethics is a set of moral principles that are aimed at assisting researchers in conducting research ethically, particularly research involving human beings (Mertler, 2012). Conducting ethical research implies ensuring the well-being of the study participants and preventing any potential abuse. It also involves delineating all researchers' responsibilities and ensuring that they abide by appropriate codes of professional conduct. In an MMAR study, due to its methodological specificity ethical issues should be considered in three contexts: research in general, action research, and mixed methods research.

General Research Ethics

Many national and international professional organizations in different fields have developed codes of research ethics: the American Psychological Association (APA), the American Educational Research

Association (AERA), the American Evaluation Association (AEA), the American Counseling Association, the American Nurses Association, the American Medical Association, the World Medical Association, the World Health Organization (WHO), the British Psychological Society, the British Sociological Association, and others. These codes address ethical standards of conducting research in general and particular ethical considerations specific for each field. In the United States, research ethical principles are aligned with the federal government's guidelines for conducting research with humans and ethical standards of NIH (2009). These general research ethical principles include the following:

- *Veracity.* Telling the truth; having full disclosure before participating
- *Justice.* Being fair to all participants; recognizing participants' needs first; avoiding discrimination based on sex, age, religion, age, SES, or sexual orientation
- *Beneficence.* Benefiting both participants and society; preventing any harm; protecting the weak and vulnerable; performing an advocacy role
- *Fidelity and respect.* Building trust; respecting participants' rights, dignity, and autonomy; promoting participants' well-being; recognizing participants' right for self-determination; ensuring privacy and respect; securing anonymity and confidentiality

Federal government guidelines related to conducting research with humans require that an Institutional Review Board (IRB) approve of any research study before its inception. IRBs are committees that are located at most postsecondary institutions, medical centers, and other organizations. When employing people as study participants, the researchers are required to obtain a signed and dated informed consent from each participant. An informed consent discloses the study procedures; ensures that participation in the study is voluntary; protects participants from physical, emotional, and mental harm; and safeguards participants' privacy and confidentiality.

Research Ethics Related to Action Research

In addition to the need for complying with general research ethical principles, practitioner-researchers have to consider ethical issues that are specific to action research. Due to the participatory nature of action research, it is important that all participants stay informed about the project activities, thus making the research process "inherently transparent to all" (Stringer, 2014, p. 89). In action research, study participants often have dual roles because they are also engaged in the process of the study design and implementation as co-researchers. Despite this dual status, informed consent is required from all persons serving as study participants. Importantly, Stringer (2014) also addressed possible exceptions from an informed consent requirement. These exceptions occur when participants perform routine activities as part of their regular professional practice and no additional legal authorization is necessary; examples are educators engaging their students in some form of assessment or project work that is part of instruction, or store managers conducting customer satisfaction surveys as part of their regular duties, or health-care professionals discussing options and preferences for a patient to quit smoking while performing a regular physical exam. In such cases this information can be used as part of the data collection process during the reconnaissance phase of the study when conducting an initial assessment of the problem or situation.

Another ethical issue that action researchers face is related to having special provisions about preserving anonymity of the study participants and settings when collecting the data and disseminating the study results (Koshy et al., 2011). As discussed in Chapter 2, action research studies are often small-scale projects conducted in work settings, so it may become easy to recognize people and events if their anonymity is not protected well. Mills (2011) also discussed how the "intimate" nature of action research in an educational setting created by "little distance between teacher researchers and their subjects, the students in their classrooms and schools" can impose additional ethical challenges that should be considered by IRBs (p. 29).

This brings into focus the issues of power and authority in action research when practitioner-researchers study their own practices (Herr & Anderson, 2005), such as teachers conducting research with their students, physicians using patients as participants in clinical trials, or social workers engaging clients in discussions about their problems and needs. As indicated by Nolen and Vander Putten (2007), these potentially conflicting roles can confound researchers' primary professional objectives and interfere with the expected outcomes. Additionally, it may raise legitimate concerns about coercing the study participants to provide the information without due process. To avoid potential issues of coercion in action research it is important to ensure voluntary participation and to make study participants feel empowered with regard to their own change processes (Herr & Anderson, 2005). Additional suggestions include having a mediator administer the informed consent to study participants (Tanke & Tanke, 1982), and asking potential participants about creating specific conditions that would allow them to freely consent to participating in research (Herr & Anderson, 2005). Considering the issues of power becomes important when reporting the action research study results. If research is done in active collaboration with community stakeholders, the following questions may arise: "Who owns the data? Are all the stakeholders comfortable with public dissemination of the data?" (Herr & Anderson, 2005, p. 74). Reaching agreement about these issues is an ethical dilemma that needs to be seriously considered while conceptualizing the study.

The evolving nature of action research studies and a potential need for additional data collection and recruitment of new study participants when developing a plan of action/intervention based on the assessment of the problem or situation may require obtaining additional permissions and submitting amendments to an initially approved IRB application. Involving new study participants may also lead to potential new ethical issues that practitioner-researchers need to foresee and be ready to deal with (Koshy et al., 2011). Finally, the purposes of action research are fundamentally different from traditional forms of inquiry where researchers are outsiders and do not wish to influence the conduct of the study, as in quantitative experiments or clinical trials. Because action researchers are committed to working toward change, they must acknowledge the effects of their presence on the community where the study is being conducted (Herr & Anderson, 2005). This issue is equally important in situations where practitioner-researchers study their own practices and contexts or when they are involved as invited co-investigators.

Research Ethics Related to Mixed Methods Research

Although the same general principles of research ethics apply in mixed methods research (Teddlie & Tashakkori, 2009), there are several additional ethical considerations that may be imposed by the procedural logistics of conducting mixed methods research. In particular, researchers who engage in mixed methods studies should address the context and demands of both quantitative and qualitative research procedures and settings within one IRB application. Because collecting quantitative and qualitative data entails different levels of data sensitivity, an IRB may require explanations of different details related to these processes. For example, individual interviews or focus group discussions typically reveal information that is more personal, and sometimes more sensitive, than do surveys sent to an electronic mailing list or to a random list of informants. In such instances, more precautions should be taken when developing the procedures for preserving anonymity of the settings in the qualitative strand of the mixed methods study. Qualitative research is conducted in natural settings (Creswell, 2013), and a research site potentially can be easily recognized, if measures are not taken to conceal its identity.

Another issue to consider is a cyclical nature of an IRB application for mixed methods designs in which quantitative and qualitative data are collected and analyzed sequentially—that is, when one data set informs another data set. These may include examples of deciding who to interview for a qualitative follow-up explanation of certain trends that emerged in the analysis of the initial quantitative survey responses, or deciding what sample to choose for collecting quantitative data using an instrument that was developed based on the findings from the initial qualitative focus groups. In such cases an IRB application for approval to conduct a study should be submitted with an explanation that an amendment to the initial IRB application will be filed based on the results from the first study strand, and further approval will be sought based on the new study details.

An important ethical issue specific to mixed methods research is related to the need to have survey responses linked to study participants to be able to follow up with them in some sequential mixed methods designs. Because it is important that the same individuals participate in both quantitative and qualitative strands for the credibility of the study results (Creswell & Plano Clark, 2011), knowing who responded and how they responded to the survey questions is critical. Potential respondents may be intimidated by the fact that their anonymity is not preserved and may elect either not to participate in the study or to skip answering some important questions, or even to provide socially desirable responses—that is, the responses they think are expected from them. In such cases it is the responsibility of the researchers to ensure that the anonymity and confidentiality of the survey respondents is preserved and that they are informed of the planned ethical security measures. Box 4.6 summarizes the ethical issues that should be considered by practitioner-researchers when conceptualizing, designing, and implementing an MMAR study.

BOX 4.6

Ethical Issues in an MMAR Study

- General research ethical issues:

    o Obtaining IRB approval for the study
    o Securing informed consent from the study participants
    o Disclosing the study procedures to participants
    o Ensuring that participation in the study is voluntary
    o Protecting participants from physical, emotional, and mental harm
    o Preserving participants' anonymity and confidentiality

(Continued)

- Ethical issues related to action research:

  o Considering participatory nature of action research:
  o Keeping all participants informed about the study activities
  o Involving all participants in the process of the study design and implementation
  o Getting a waiver of an informed consent for routine activities viewed as part of regular practice
  o Having special provisions about preserving anonymity of the study participants and settings in small-scale studies conducted in work settings
  o Considering the issues of power and authority when studying one's own practice
  o Recognizing the evolving nature of the action research study and the need for additional data collection and recruitment of new study participants
  o Acknowledging the effects of researchers' presence on the community where the study is being conducted

- Ethical issues related to mixed methods research:

  o Addressing context and demands of both quantitative and qualitative research procedures and settings within one IRB application
  o Submitting IRB protocol amendments for each sequential mixed methods design study strand that is informed by the results from the previous strand
  o Considering the need to have survey responses linked to study participants to enable following up with them in certain sequential mixed methods designs

SUMMARY

The design and implementation of an MMAR study follows the research principles that are common for any form of scientific inquiry: identification of the research problem, formulation of the study purpose and research questions, selection of the study sample, collection and analysis of the data, and interpretation and evaluation of the study results. An MMAR Study Process Model that was developed grounded in a mixed methods methodological framework for action research is proposed to help practitioner-researchers apply this methodological framework to the process of conceptualizing, designing, and conducting an MMAR study.

An MMAR Study Process Model reflects six phases in the action research cycle (diagnosing, reconnaissance, planning, acting, evaluation, monitoring) and delineates important methodological and procedural steps for each phase in an MMAR study. During the first, diagnosing phase, the conceptualization of an MMAR study occurs. This involves identifying the problem area that requires improvement, reviewing the literature on the topic and existing theories and practices, developing a study general plan, specifying the overall study purpose, identifying expected outcomes, clarifying the study objectives, formulating the research questions, and considering ethical issues. The chapter discusses the criteria that practitioner-researchers should apply in selecting an area of focus, and presents and explains the diagram depicting a logical flow of ideas in an MMAR study research problem statement. The role of the literature review in an MMAR study is examined and the steps for conducting a literature review are listed.

A general research plan for an MMAR study should include the purpose of an overall study, expected outcomes, study objectives, research questions, timeline, research skills, resources, stakeholders' involvement, feasibility, and plans for the dissemination of findings. The development of an MMAR study purpose statement is described that suggests the inclusion of the following components: an overall intent of the study or content aim, the specific goals of the reconnaissance and evaluation phases, and a rationale for using a mixed methods approach. A purpose statement script for an MMAR study with a supporting example is provided. In an MMAR study that integrates quantitative and qualitative methods, three types of research questions should be considered: an integrated MMAR question that addresses an overall practical intent of the study and the integration of the quantitative and qualitative methods in the process of the study implementation, and quantitative and qualitative research questions that are answered by collecting and analyzing numerical and narrative information, respectively, to address specific goals of these study strands. The chapter provides examples of each type of research questions in the context of an MMAR purpose statement. Finally, research ethics of an MMAR study is discussed in three contexts: ethical issues related to research in general, specific ethical issues related to action research, and specific ethical issues related to a mixed methods approach.

REFLECTIVE QUESTIONS AND EXERCISES

1. Select an MMAR study in your discipline or area of interest. Identify a practical problem or issue that was the focus of the study. Reflect on how the researchers addressed this problem/issue and what steps they took in the study process.

2. Carefully read the introduction part to the article you selected. Reflect on the logical flow of ideas in the research problem statement. Develop a diagram of how the ideas are presented and of how the need for the study is justified and explained.

3. Reflect on the role of the literature review in an MMAR study. What components listed in Box 4.1 does the literature review presented in this article reflect?

4. Identify the practical problem or issue in your work setting that requires improvement. Reflect on how you would apply the steps outlined in an MMAR Study Process Model to address this problem/issue. Briefly describe what actions you would take during each study phase.

5. Revisit the components of an MMAR general research plan. Reflect on how you would address these components when you develop a general plan for an MMAR study to solve the problem/issue you identified in your work setting. What potential ethical issues would you have to consider and why?

6. Using the purpose statement script for an MMAR study, develop a purpose statement for the study you have conceptualized in Questions 4 and 5. Write an integrated MMAR question to address the content aim of the study and at least one quantitative and qualitative research question for the reconnaissance and evaluation study phases.

FURTHER READINGS

To learn more about the statement of the research problem, examine the following source:

Creswell, J. W. (2012). *Educational research: Planning, conducting, and evaluating quantitative and qualitative research* (4th ed.). Upper Saddle River, NJ: Merrill Prentice Hall, Ch. 2, pp. 58–78.

To learn more about conducting a literature review, examine the following sources:

Creswell, J. W. (2012). *Educational research: Planning, conducting, and evaluating quantitative and qualitative research* (4th ed.). Upper Saddle River, NJ: Merrill Prentice Hall, Ch. 3, pp. 79–108.

Fink, A. (2005). *Conducting research literature reviews: From the Internet to paper.* London: Sage.

Koshy, E., Koshy, V., & Waterman, H. (2011). *Action research in healthcare.* Thousand Oaks, CA: Sage, Ch. 3, pp. 50–67.

To learn more about research ethics in general and in action research, examine the following sources:

Creswell, J. W. (2014). *Research design: Qualitative, quantitative, and mixed methods approaches* (4th ed.). Thousand Oaks, CA: Sage, Ch. 4, pp. 92–101.

Herr, K., & Anderson, G. L. (2005). *The action research dissertation: A guide for students and faculty.* Thousand Oaks, CA: Sage, Ch. 7, pp. 112–126.

Koshy, E., Koshy, V., & Waterman, H. (2011). *Action research in healthcare.* Thousand Oaks, CA: Sage, pp. 102–107.

Mills, G. E. (2011). *Action research: A guide for the teacher researcher* (4th ed.). Boston: Pearson Education, Ch. 2, pp. 22–37.

To learn more about study purpose statement and research questions, examine the following sources:

Creswell, J. W. (2014). *Research design: Qualitative, quantitative, and mixed methods approaches* (4th ed.). Thousand Oaks, CA: Sage, Ch. 6–7, pp. 123–152.

Mertler, C. A. (2012). *Action research: Improving schools and empowering educators.* Thousand Oaks, CA: Sage, pp. 84–89.

Plano Clark, V., & Badiee, M. (2010). Research questions in mixed methods research. In A. Tashakkori & C. Teddlie (Eds.), *SAGE handbook of mixed methods in social & behavioral research* (2nd ed., pp. 275–304). Thousand Oaks, CA: Sage.

5

Designing a Mixed Methods Action Research Study

OBJECTIVES

By the end of this chapter, the reader should be able to

- Describe current mixed methods design typologies and their relevance to an MMAR study design,
- Understand and explain key methodological dimensions of mixed methods designs and how they guide an MMAR study design,
- Explain MMAR designs and their methodological characteristics,
- Understand how MMAR designs can be applied in an MMAR study process,
- Understand strengths and challenges associated with the use of each MMAR design, and
- Be able to use the flowcharts to make informed decisions in applying MMAR designs to research problems addressing practical issues.

INTRODUCTION

In Chapter 4, an MMAR Study Process Model was introduced and explained. This model reflects six phases in the action research cycle (diagnosing, reconnaissance, planning, acting, evaluation, monitoring) and outlines important methodological and procedural steps for each phase in an MMAR study. Conceptualization of

Refer to Chapter 4 and Figure 4.1 for the discussion and illustration of an MMAR Study Process Model and of procedural and action steps within each study phase.

Refer to Chapter 4 for the discussion of the first, diagnosing phase in an MMAR study process and the specifics of conceptualizing an MMAR study.

an MMAR study is the first step in the process and occurs during the diagnosing phase. As discussed in Chapter 4, this involves identification of the problem area that requires improvement, reviewing the literature on the topic and existing theories and practices, developing a study general research plan, specifying an overall study purpose, expected outcomes, objectives, and research questions, and addressing ethical issues.

Once a practical problem or issue is identified and the conceptualization process of an MMAR study is complete, practitioner-researchers move to the next, reconnaissance phase. During this phase a mixed methods study is designed and implemented to assess the problem or situation, identify the areas for improvement, and inform the development of the action/intervention plan. After the action/intervention is developed and implemented, an evaluation phase of an MMAR study is designed and conducted. The purpose of this phase is to collect evidence about the effectiveness of the action/intervention and to learn whether the action/intervention targets the identified problem areas, how the action/intervention is viewed and adopted by interested stakeholders, what needs to be changed in the initial plan to reach more effective outcomes, or whether the plan needs to be completely revised. In spite of the fact that the design of the reconnaissance and evaluation phases in an MMAR study is guided by a different perspective, the research process in both phases follows the same procedural steps. These steps include the following:

- Developing the purpose statement and research questions for the reconnaissance study phase
- Selecting a mixed methods design to best address the purpose and answer the posted research questions
- Identifying the study sample and quantitative and qualitative types of data to be collected
- Collecting and analyzing the data
- Establishing credibility or validating the findings

Designing a study is a key methodological step in the study process because the study design guides other methodological procedures aimed at answering the posted research questions (Creswell, 2014). Selecting an appropriate study design does not only help researchers choose appropriate methods, but also helps "set the logic by which they [researchers] make interpretations at the end of their studies" (Creswell & Plano Clark, 2011, p. 53).

So, what mixed methods designs can be used to guide an MMAR study process, and how can they be informed by existing mixed methods designs and their typologies?

CURRENT MIXED METHODS DESIGN TYPOLOGIES

To better understand how existing mixed methods designs can be adapted to an MMAR study process, it is necessary to acknowledge the existence of different mixed methods design typologies. Authors writing about mixed methods research have always tried to classify the designs based on some common methodological characteristics and procedural features. Teddlie and Tashakkori (2009) underscored the relative usefulness of such classifications, and argued that mixed methods design typologies help researchers choose the right direction for designing a study. They explained that typologies "provide a variety of paths, or ideal design types, that may be chosen to accomplish the goals of the study" (p. 139). Typologies also help with establishing a methodological structure of a mixed methods research approach, and with identifying the design features common to a group of mixed methods studies. Conversely, Creswell and Plano Clark (2011) considered mixed methods design typologies to be useful because they help select and adapt an existing design to a specific study purpose and research questions. Mixed methods design typologies can also be important for understanding the mechanism of combining quantitative and qualitative methods in a variety of ways within one study or program of inquiry.

At the same time, no typology can capture all possible variations in designing and conducting mixed methods studies (Greene, 2007; Guest, 2013; Maxwell & Loomis, 2003). This is mostly due to the fact that a study design is driven by a unique research problem that requires exploration, and by the need to gather information to answer the posted research questions within the parameters of this problem. Consistent with Greene's (2007) insightful observation that "methodology is ever the servant of purpose" (p. 97), complexity of a research situation may often lead to changes in the study design direction and blending of the research components in new and sometimes unexpected ways. Acknowledging the continuous evolution of mixed methods designs and a diversity of approaches to classifying mixed methods designs, Teddlie and Tashakkori (2009) proposed the term "families" with reference to mixed methods design groupings and types that researchers can creatively employ while addressing complex research problems. Alternatively, Creswell and Plano Clark (2011) referred to major mixed methods designs as prototypes.

Table 5.1 presents four recent mixed methods design typologies. Despite the observed differences in the designs' names and the methodological characteristics used to classify these designs, these typologies have many common features and highlight common design elements that make mixed methods designs distinct and different from other quantitative and qualitative designs. For example, Teddlie and Tashakkori (2009) differentiated five families of mixed methods designs based on how quantitative and qualitative methods are mixed or integrated within a study. These designs typically consist of at least two study strands. Mixing or integrating the methods may occur at any or all these stages.

 Revisit the discussion about the study strands in mixed methods research in Chapter 1.

Creswell and Plano Clark (2011) proposed six prototypes of mixed methods designs based on four methodological decisions: level of interaction of quantitative and qualitative methods in the study, priority of the quantitative or qualitative method, timing or implementation of the quantitative and qualitative study strands, and mixing or integration of the quantitative and qualitative methods. They also suggested taking into account a theoretical framework, which may include a transformative lens and a "substantive framework" that inform the study design, or a "program-objective framework" that guides the integration of the quantitative and qualitative study components consistent with an overall program objective (p. 68).

Morse and Niehaus (2009) developed their mixed method design typology based on the role the two main components, quantitative and qualitative, play in the study. Depending on which role, core or supplementary, the researcher assigns to quantitative and qualitative study components, Morse and Niehaus suggested two major

TABLE 5.1 Recent Typologies of Mixed Methods Designs

Typology	Design	Description
Five Families of Mixed Methods Designs (Teddlie & Tashakkori, 2009)	• Parallel Mixed Designs	• Mixing of quantitative and qualitative methods occurs in a parallel manner, either simultaneously or with some time lapse.
	• Sequential Mixed Designs	• Mixing of quantitative and qualitative methods occurs across chronological quantitative and qualitative study phases; questions or procedures of one strand emerge from or depend on the previous strand.
	• Conversion Mixed Designs	• Mixing of quantitative and qualitative methods occurs when one type of data is transformed and analyzed both quantitatively and qualitatively.
	• Multilevel Mixed Designs	• Mixing of quantitative and qualitative methods occurs in a parallel or chronological manner across multiple levels of analysis, as quantitative and qualitative data from these levels is analyzed and integrated.
	• Fully Integrated Mixed Designs	• Mixing of quantitative and qualitative methods occurs in an interactive manner at all stages of the study; at each stage, one approach affects the formulation of the other.
Prototypes of Mixed Methods Designs (Creswell & Plano Clark, 2011)	• Convergent Parallel Mixed Methods Design	• Concurrent timing is used to implement quantitative and qualitative strands during the same phase of the research process; two methods are equally prioritized; the strands are kept independent during analysis; quantitative and qualitative results are mixed during the overall interpretation.

(Continued)

Typology	Design	Description
	• Explanatory Sequential Mixed Methods Design	• Sequential timing is used to implement quantitative and qualitative strands or phases; quantitative data collection and analysis occurs first and is prioritized; qualitative data collection and analysis occurs next and follows from the quantitative results; qualitative findings are interpreted to help explain the initial quantitative results.
	• Exploratory Sequential Mixed Methods Design	• Sequential timing is used to implement quantitative and qualitative strands or phases; qualitative data collection and analysis occurs first and is prioritized; quantitative data collection and analysis occurs next to test or generalize the initial qualitative findings; quantitative results are interpreted to show how they build on the initial qualitative findings.
	• Embedded Mixed Methods Design	• Both quantitative and qualitative data are collected and analyzed concurrently or sequentially within a traditional quantitative or qualitative design; the supplemental data strand is added to enhance the overall design.
	• Transformative Mixed Methods Design	• A transformative theoretical framework shapes timing, interaction, priority, and mixing decisions.
	• Multiphase Mixed Methods Design	• Concurrent and sequential strands are combined over a period of time within an overall program-objective framework.
Mixed Method Design Typology (Morse & Niehaus, 2009)	• Qualitatively Driven Mixed Method Designs ○ Qualitatively Driven Simultaneous Designs	• Quantitative supplemental component is added simultaneously during the qualitative core component implementation or on the completion of the core component data analysis to compensate for its information inadequacy.

TABLE 5.1 Continued

Typology	Design	Description
	○ Qualitatively Driven Sequential Designs	
	• Quantitatively Driven Mixed Method Designs ○ Quantitatively Driven Simultaneous Designs ○ Quantitatively Driven Sequential Designs	• Qualitative supplemental component is added simultaneously during the quantitative core component implementation or on the completion of the core component data analysis to compensate for its information inadequacy.
	• Complex Mixed and Multiple Method Designs ○ Qualitatively Driven ○ Quantitatively Driven	• Multiple supplemental quantitative and qualitative components are added in different combinations to the theoretical core project to form a series of linked mixed methods studies.
Interactive-Independent Dimension Design Clusters (Greene, 2007)	• Component Mixed Methods Designs	
	○ Convergence	• Quantitative and qualitative methods are used to measure the same phenomenon; methods are of equal weight; implementation is concurrent; linking or connection of the methods is through comparison of quantitative and qualitative results.
	○ Extension	• Quantitative and qualitative methods are used to measure different phenomena; methods are of varied weight; implementation is variable; linking of the methods is either

Typology	Design	Description
		absent, or through connection of quantitative and qualitative results.
	• Integrated Mixed Methods Designs	
	○ Iteration	• The results of one method, quantitative or qualitative, are used to inform the development of another method; methods are preferably of equal weight; implementation is sequential; methods are integrated through quantitative and qualitative data representation.
	○ Blending	• Quantitative and qualitative methods are used to assess varied facets of the same phenomenon; methods are of equal weight; implementation is concurrent; methods are integrated through joint analysis or connection between quantitative and qualitative data during analysis.
	○ Nesting or Embedding	• A supplementary quantitative or qualitative method is embedded or nested in the study's primary methodology; methods are of unequal weight; implementation is concurrent; methods are integrated through joint analysis or connection between quantitative and qualitative data during analysis.
	○ Mixing for Reasons of Substance or Values	• Quantitative and qualitative methods are directly tied to the substantive or ideological framework employed in the study; methods are preferably of equal weight; implementation is variable; methods are integrated through joint analysis, comparison, or connection between quantitative and qualitative data during analysis.

Refer to Chapter 1 and Table 1.1 for the discussion of Greene and colleagues' (1989) reasons for conducting mixed methods studies.

groups of designs: qualitatively driven and qualitatively driven. Additionally, the authors set aside complex mixed and multiple method designs consisting of multiple supplemental components added to the theoretical core project to form a series of linked mixed methods studies.

Finally, building on a typology of reasons or purposes for conducting mixed methods studies (Greene et al., 1989), Greene (2007) presented two groups or clusters of mixed methods designs characterized by differences in their "most salient and critical dimensions," such as (1) implementation of quantitative and qualitative methods in the study—independent or interactive, and (2) weight of quantitative and qualitative methods in the study—relatively equal or not (pp. 120–121). Greene (2007) argued that an exhaustive listing of all designs within these clusters is not possible because of a potential variation of mixed methods designs observed in research practice.

TYPOLOGY OF MMAR STUDY DESIGNS

Practitioner-researchers who wish to design and conduct an MMAR study can choose a suitable mixed methods design from the existing mixed methods design typologies. However, to stay consistent with a practical focus of action research and to make the application of mixed methods in action research conceptually easier for practitioner-researchers, a more generic typology of MMAR study designs is suggested. This typology of MMAR study designs builds on the mixed methods design typologies discussed earlier and incorporates their major common design elements. An important consideration is also the longitudinal and interactive nature of MMAR studies in which all phases are conceptually linked in the pursuit of an effective solution to a practical problem/issue. Thus, each complete MMAR study, including all six phases of the action research cycle, may be viewed as a multilevel or fully integrated mixed design (Teddlie & Tashakkori, 2009), multiphase design (Creswell & Plano Clark, 2011), or complex mixed and multiple method design (Morse & Niehaus, 2009) study. Specifically, a complete MMAR study that includes all the six phases from at least one action research cycle may consist of multiple concurrent and/or sequential strands. These strands may be combined in different ways to address various goals of each phase by encompassing evidence from multiple quantitative and qualitative data sources within an overall action research project framework.

Refer to Chapter 2 for the discussion of empowerment as an essential feature of action research. Also refer to Chapter 3 for the explanation of transformative/advocacy lens used in mixed methods and action research.

Additionally, Creswell and Plano Clark (2011) distinguished a transformative mixed methods design, in which a researcher's theoretical or ideological perspective, such as transformative orientation or advocacy lens, guides all methodological decisions in the study. Although important, this feature may not be essential for shaping an MMAR design because a transformative orientation reflected in the pursuit of social justice and empowerment is inherent to action research and its purposes. Following this criterion, all action research is transformative and an

MMAR study is designed to adhere to transformation goals. Furthermore, an ideological perspective provides reasons for conducting the study, a perspective that "supersedes design choices" (Teddlie & Tashakkori, 2009, p. 140). Thus, a suggested typology of MMAR designs includes basic mixed methods designs that can be used in different combinations in the reconnaissance and evaluation phases in an MMAR study process to inform other phases in the action research cycle.

So, what are MMAR study designs and how can they be adapted and applied to address the purposes of action research?

Key Methodological Dimensions of MMAR Study Designs

A proposed typology of MMAR study designs incorporates the key methodological characteristics or dimensions specific to mixed methods designs that have been well described and established in the mixed methods literature. Those dimensions include a number of study strands, sequence or timing of the strand implementation, priority or weighting of quantitative or qualitative methods, and integration or mixing of the quantitative and qualitative methods discussed in Chapter 1 (Creswell & Plano Clark, 2011; Teddlie & Tashakkori, 2009). These methodological dimensions are important to consider when designing an MMAR study because they guide practitioner-researchers in selecting a study design that will best address the posted research questions within a specific MMAR study phase. Additionally, knowledge of these design dimensions will help practitioner-researchers understand how to implement the study so that it will produce meaningful meta-inferences to inform the next step in an MMAR study process. Importantly, having a practical grasp of MMAR study design elements will also provide practitioner-researchers with relative flexibility in making adjustments to the study design in response to the cyclical and dialectical nature of action research.

Revisit the explanation of the key methodological characteristics of mixed methods research in Chapter 1. Refer to Box 1.6, which summarizes the major aspects of these mixed methods characteristics.

To better understand the role of the key methodological dimensions in guiding the design of an MMAR study, consider how these characteristics were addressed and explained in two MMAR study proposals in the fields of K–12 education and health promotion. Davis's (2011) MMAR study (Box 5.1) focused on identifying the technological needs of parents to increase their school involvement through an after-school technology use program at an elementary school in northern Alabama employing a concurrent MMAR design. Cunningham's (2011) MMAR study (Box 5.2) focused on identifying factors related to intent for vaccination against HPV among college males in Alabama and thus to increase their vaccination rates at one southeastern Research I university. Cunningham proposed to use a sequential MMAR design.

Both studies consist of two strands, during which quantitative and qualitative data will be collected and analyzed. In Davis's study, the strands will be implemented concurrently because quantitative survey and qualitative interview data from a sample of parents in a specific elementary school will be collected and analyzed independently during the same period to assess their technological needs. Cunningham proposes to use the strands sequentially because she plans first to survey male students at a southeastern Research I university to identify factors associated with their uptake of HPV vaccination. Once the analysis of the

---

BOX 5.1

Parent Involvement Technology Use Program: A Concurrent MMAR Study

Study Purpose: The purpose of this MMAR study is to identify the technological needs of parents to increase their school involvement through an after-school technology use program at an elementary school in north Alabama by using a concurrent MMAR design.

Study Strands: The study will consist of two strands: quantitative and qualitative. The goal of the quantitative strand of the study is to identify specific needs in a parenting technology use program by conducting and analyzing surveys administered to parents at an elementary school. The goal of the qualitative strand of the study is to explore specific technological support services that may enhance parental involvement in the school program through conducting interviews with participating parents at the end of each semester during one school year.

Sequence or Timing: Concurrent—quantitative survey and qualitative interview data will be collected and analyzed independently. The results from both study strands will be compared at the conclusion of quantitative and qualitative analysis.

Priority or Weighting: Priority will be given to qualitative data. The quantitative survey data will focus on identifying parents' specific technological needs. The qualitative data, however, will provide information on how best to get parents to participate in the program; the study emphasis on exploring ways for parent involvement leads to the premise of the study being qualitatively driven.

Integration or Mixing: The rationale for integrating quantitative and qualitative methods in the study is to gain a deeper understanding of parental technological needs to inform the development of an after-school technology use program. Integration of the data will occur at the stage of data analysis where meta-inferences are developed based on the results of the qualitative and quantitative analysis. Survey and individual interview results will be compared to produce well-validated conclusions about how to stimulate parents' involvement in the program.

Adapted from Davis (2011) with the author's permission.

---

quantitative survey data is completed, the researcher will further explore these factors through individual interviews with select survey respondents to better understand the role of these factors in shaping vaccination uptake. Davis assigns priority to the qualitative data because she believes they will provide information on how to best get parents involved in participating in the school-based technology use program. On the other side, Cunningham proposes to weight quantitative data more because the study's focus tends to be more on the prediction of HPV vaccination intention among males rather than on the explanation of the role of promoting and impeding factors.

In Davis's study, the results from concurrently implemented quantitative and qualitative study strands will be combined and compared at the completion of both strands to develop meta-inferences and produce

BOX 5.2

A Sequential MMAR Study to Examine Factors Related to Intent for HPV Vaccination among Collegiate Males in Alabama

Study Purpose: The purpose of this MMAR study is to investigate factors associated with the HPV vaccination uptake among male college students to increase HPV vaccination rates for college males at a southeastern Research I university by using a sequential mixed methods design.

Study Strands: The study will consist of two strands: quantitative and qualitative. The goal of the quantitative strand is to identify prevalence of factors associated with intention of HPV vaccination among college males using survey data. The goal of the qualitative strand is to better understand and explain the factors influencing HPV vaccination intention, as revealed by the analysis of the survey data, using semistructured interviews with eight to ten purposefully selected survey respondents. The first, quantitative strand provides a scope of the research, while the second, qualitative strand will explain the scope of the research problem.

Sequence or Timing: The study will use a sequential timing—quantitative strand will be followed by the qualitative strand that builds on the results from the initial quantitative strand. In the first strand, quantitative data will be collected and analyzed to describe the sample and to identify prevalence of factors associated with the intention of HPV vaccination among college males. In the second strand, qualitative data will be collected and analyzed to explain the factors toward HPV vaccination intention identified in the first strand.

Priority or Weighting: Priority will be given to quantitative data due to the study focus on the prediction of outcomes with regard to HPV vaccination intention among males. The quantitative strand will be emphasized because it will guide the data collection in the qualitative strand.

Integration or Mixing: The rationale for integrating quantitative and qualitative methods in this study is to obtain validated meta-inferences to inform the development of HPV prevention education programs for males. The quantitative and qualitative study strands will be connected by selecting the participants for qualitative interviews from those who completed the survey and by developing interview questions addressing significant factors identified in the first strand. Additionally, the results from the quantitative and qualitative study strands will be combined when discussing the meta-inferences resulting from the findings from both strands related to promoting HPV vaccination among the students at a southeastern Research I university.

Adapted from Cunningham (2011) with the author's permission.

well-validated conclusions about how to stimulate parents' involvement. In Cunningham's study, due to the sequential nature of quantitative and qualitative data collection and analysis, integration of the quantitative and qualitative methods will occur while connecting the two study strands: first, by selecting the participants for qualitative interviews from those college students who completed the survey and, second, by developing the interview questions addressing the factors that were identified as statistically significant in the first, quantitative study strand. Additionally, integration will occur when discussing the meta-inferences resulting from the findings from both study strands to enhance understanding of how to promote HPV vaccination among the students at that university.

BASIC MMAR STUDY DESIGNS

Based on the variation of the key methodological dimensions discussed above, four basic types of MMAR study designs are suggested to address the purposes and needs of the action research process:

- Concurrent Quan + Qual MMAR design
- Sequential Quan → Qual MMAR design
- Sequential Qual → Quan MMAR design
- Multistrand MMAR design

While the first three designs consist of two concurrent (Quan + Qual) or sequential (Quan → Qual or Qual → Quan) quantitative and qualitative strands, a multistrand MMAR design may consist of multiple concurrent and sequential strands. These designs are distinguished based on how quantitative and qualitative methods are jointly used to create meta-inferences to enhance practitioner-researchers' understanding of practical issues and to develop and implement action/intervention plans aimed at providing effective solutions to practical problems/issues. Being generic, functional, and conceptually easier for practitioner-researchers to implement, these designs allow for a wider application when addressing different purposes of the reconnaissance and evaluation phases in an MMAR study process. Box 5.3 summarizes MMAR designs and the purposes of their application in action research projects. The rest of the chapter describes the methodological characteristics of each design, illustrates their applications in published MMAR studies, and discusses the pros and cons of using these designs in the action research process.

> Specific sampling, data collection, and data analysis strategies used in these MMAR designs are discussed in more detail in Chapters 7 and 8.

Concurrent Quan + Qual MMAR Study Design

Methodological Characteristics

A concurrent Quan + Qual MMAR design typically includes two strands, during which quantitative and qualitative data are collected and analyzed separately or independently of each other (see Figure 5.1 for a conceptual model of this design).

The primary purpose of this design is to compare quantitative and qualitative results to obtain complementary evidence in different types of data and produce well-validated conclusions. The major advantage of this design is that it allows exploring a range of confirmatory (verifying knowledge) and exploratory (generating knowledge) research questions concurrently or simultaneously within the same study phase (Teddlie &

BOX 5.3

Typology of MMAR Study Designs

- *Concurrent Quan + Qual MMAR design,* consisting of two parallel or independent strands:

  o Purpose: To compare or merge quantitative and qualitative results to produce well-validated conclusions

- *Sequential Quan → Qual MMAR design,* consisting of two chronological strands with a quantitative strand first in sequence:

  o Purpose: To use follow-up qualitative data to elaborate, explain, or confirm initial quantitative results

- *Sequential Qual → Quan MMAR design,* consisting of two chronological strands with a qualitative strand first in sequence:

  o Purpose: To use initial qualitative data to develop new measures, and to identify unknown variables and relationships

- *Multistrand MMAR design,* consisting of multiple consecutive quantitative and qualitative concurrent and sequential strands:

  o Purpose: To combine and address the study goals consecutively in multiple strands by using the results from a previous sequential strand or two concurrent strands to inform the next consecutive combination of strands.

Tashakkori, 2009). For example, using a concurrent Quan + Qual MMAR design, an educational administrator who is seeking ways to effectively address the problem of high school students' truancy can concurrently explore the following research questions:

- Quantitative strand: What are the trends of students' absenteeism across the grades and school year in high school X? How do these trends correlate with reported students' absenteeism trends across the school district?
- Qualitative strand: What factors from the perspective of students, parents, and teachers can explain the reported students' absenteeism trends in high school X?

A concurrent design is well established in mixed methods literature, but it is referred to using different names: convergent parallel design (Creswell & Plano Clark, 2011), parallel mixed design (Teddlie & Tashakkori, 2009), concurrent triangulation design (Creswell, 2009), simultaneous design (Morse & Niehaus, 2009), convergent design (Greene, 2007), triangulation design (Creswell & Plano Clark, 2007), and simultaneous triangulation design (Morse, 1991). As all these names suggest, in this design the two study strands, quantitative and

FIGURE 5.1	Conceptual Model of a Concurrent Quan + Qual MMAR Study Design

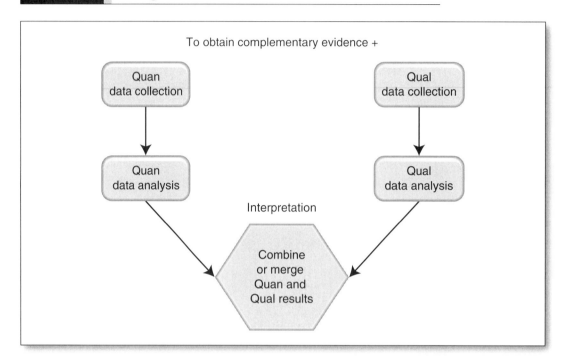

qualitative, are conducted independently from each other, either at the same time or with some time lapse within the same phase in the study process.

For example, in a high school student's truancy situation, numeric absenteeism data can be obtained from the school records and compared with absenteeism indicators across the school district to address quantitative research questions. At the same time, individual interviews can be conducted with select students who missed school at a higher rate than average and with those students' parents and teachers to answer a qualitative research question. Two other examples of concurrent timing include administration of a quantitative survey to a large group of people while simultaneously conducting individual or focus group interviews with a few individuals; or using a survey instrument that contains both close-ended and open-ended questions, thus allowing for collecting both types of data—quantitative and qualitative—within one survey administration.

> Refer to Chapter 4 for the discussion of research questions in an MMAR study.

The priority or weight in a concurrent Quan + Qual MMAR design is typically given to both study strands because each study strand addresses related aspects of the same overarching mixed methods or integrated MMAR question in a complementary way. Integration of the quantitative and qualitative methods occurs after the analysis of the data in both study strands is completed; then the results are interpreted together. The most typical integration strategy is to compare or synthesize quantitative and qualitative results to find corroborating evidence and to produce a more complete understanding of the research problem (Creswell & Plano Clark, 2011). For example, the numeric absenteeism trends from the school records and their correlations with overall school district trends can be compared with the themes about absenteeism influencing factors from the interviews to find explanations for variations in the trends across the grades and different time periods during the school year. Another strategy is to merge both set of results for further quantitative or qualitative analysis; this strategy involves transformation of one type of results, such as quantitative counts, into another type, such as qualitative categories and themes, or vice versa, and then conducting the joint analysis of the transformed data. Merged data analysis through data transformation is discussed in more detail in Chapter 8. Integration of quantitative and qualitative methods in this design is further discussed in Chapter 6.

Examples of Application in Action Research

A concurrent Quan + Qual MMAR design is commonly used in action research. The review of the 108 MMAR studies discussed in Chapter 3 revealed that it was the design of choice in about 73% of all studies. In the process of conducting an MMAR study, a concurrent Quan + Qual MMAR design can be applied in both reconnaissance and evaluation phases, however it was more frequently used to evaluate the effects of the action/intervention than to conduct the needs assessment. In both instances, practitioner-researchers can use this design to compare or triangulate quantitative results from statistical tests with qualitative findings from thematic analysis of text data by comparing or merging them to obtain more complete evidence for the studied issue.

In the reconnaissance phase, using a concurrent Quan + Qual MMAR design can help conduct a more thorough initial analysis of a practical problem or lead to a more comprehensive needs assessment by collecting data from multiple data sources, for example, using quantitative surveys and tests, and qualitative interviews and observations of multiple stakeholders at the same time. In the evaluation phase, a concurrent Quan + Qual MMAR design can help provide more validated conclusions about the effectiveness of the employed action/intervention plan by triangulating multiple quantitative and qualitative data sources to seek corroborating evidence and input from those involved in the action research process.

For example, in Glasson and colleagues' (2006) MMAR study (Example B) of nursing care for older acutely ill hospitalized patients, a concurrent Quan + Qual MMAR design was applied in both the reconnaissance and evaluation phases. During the reconnaissance phase, the aspects of nursing care that acutely ill older patients perceived as being important but found unsatisfactory were identified by triangulating the results from patient and nurse quantitative questionnaires and the researcher's observation notes of the nursing staff discussions about a new model of care grounded in patients' needs. The purpose of quantitative and qualitative data triangulation at this stage was "to establish an evidence-base for an evolving model of care" (p. 588). A concurrent Quan + Qual MMAR design was also employed to evaluate the effectiveness of the implemented new model. The quantitative and qualitative data from 60 acutely ill patients, of both genders, and from 13 nurses working in the ward were collected and analyzed concurrently using the same instruments and strategies. The integrated survey and focus group findings confirmed the efficacy of the new model of nursing care and provided directions for its further implementation and monitoring in the ward. In both applications of a concurrent Quan + Qual MMAR design in this study, the priority was given to both survey and narrative data, because both were seen equally important in providing insight related to improving the quality of nursing care for older acutely ill hospitalized patients.

Similarly, in the field of management Maritz and colleagues (2011) used a concurrent Quan + Qual MMAR design in the reconnaissance phase of their MMAR study to explore the interface between strategy-making and responsible leadership within organizations in South Africa. The use of this design was emphasized through the combination of qualitative and quantitative data collection and analysis procedures. To capture multiple views on strategy-making modes, different types of data were collected from participants at different organizational levels, including top- and lower-level management and nonmanagerial employees. The researchers conducted in-depth interviews with 17 CEOs and managers involved in strategy-making, and surveyed 210 managerial and nonmanagerial employees across different organizations. The weight that the quantitative and qualitative methods carried in the study seemed equal as both types of data were perceived "instrumental in providing knowledgeable information through interviews as well as distribute questionnaires to respondents within their organizations" (p. 106). Comparison of the survey and interview findings allowed the researchers to identify two types of strategy-making in organizations—deliberate and emergent—and to provide recommendations for specific training in strategy making for organizational leaders.

Alternatively, in Kostos and Shin's (2010) MMAR study (Example A) of the effectiveness of journaling as a math teaching and learning strategy, a concurrent Quan + Qual MMAR design was applied in the evaluation phase to assess whether the use of math journals had improved the second graders' communication of mathematical thinking. The researchers chose a design that allowed for the concurrent analysis of multiple forms of quantitative and qualitative data—students' math assessments, math journals, and interviews, along with the teacher's reflective journal because they viewed triangulation of quantitative and qualitative methods and findings as beneficial and allowing to add "scope and breadth to a study" (p. 226). Qualitative data such as journals and interviews seemed to receive more priority in the study because the researchers' focus was on how the students communicated their mathematical thinking when using math journals before and prior to this instructional intervention. Comparison of students' pre- and posttest scores, with qualitative themes from students' math journals and interviews and the teacher's reflections, allowed the researchers to obtain corroborating evidence that the use of math journals positively influenced the students' communication of mathematical thinking and use of math vocabulary. Based on these findings, the teacher-researcher decided to more systematically incorporate math journaling in daily math lessons.

Procedural Pros and Cons

Practitioner-researchers who decide to use a concurrent Quan + Qual MMAR design in the reconnaissance and/or evaluation phases in an MMAR study should consider the pros and cons of this design. On the one hand, this design is advantageous because it allows for collecting both quantitative and qualitative data within a short period of time, thus helping save time and the associated cost for conducting the study (Creswell & Plano Clark, 2011; Morse & Niehaus, 2009). Being cost- and time-efficient is an important consideration for action research projects that are often initiated to address immediate problems within a short time-frame. Another major strength of this design is that it allows for obtaining "different but complementary data on the same topic" (Morse, 1991). Implementing quantitative and qualitative strands of this design within the same time frame often calls for a team approach (Creswell & Plano Clark, 2011), which aligns well with a collaborative and inclusive nature of action research. The necessity to simultaneously handle different data collection and analysis procedures may require different research skills, as well as active involvement of community members.

Alternatively, a concurrent Quan + Qual MMAR design is associated with a number of challenges that also should be considered when weighting the pros and cons of using this design. As a downside to the advantage discussed above, implementing this design may be challenging for a sole practitioner-researcher because of the need to concurrently implement quantitative and qualitative strands of equal priority that often require different sets of research skills (Creswell & Plano Clark, 2011; Teddlie & Tashakkori, 2009). However, the collaborative nature of action research and partnerships with other practitioner-researchers, community members, and college faculty may help overcome this challenge. Additional challenges may be associated with the integration of quantitative and qualitative results that may not produce supporting or corroborating evidence, but rather show divergent and even conflicting outcomes. In this situation, practitioner-researchers may find it difficult to explain or resolve these inconsistencies and produce meaningful conclusions (Teddlie & Tashakkori, 2009). Carefully selecting the study participants and the most relevant data sources may help reduce this threat, although practitioner-researchers should always be ready to face this particular challenge because of different underlying epistemological approaches to quantitative and qualitative data collection and analysis. Finally, merging the two sets of results in order to produce one quantitative or qualitative data set and to use that data set in further analysis may be challenging, particularly if the collected data do not explore the same concepts (Creswell & Plano Clark, 2011).

Figure 5.2 presents a flow of ideas and methodological steps in a concurrent Quan + Qual MMAR design that may help practitioner-researchers make informed decisions in applying this design to their MMAR projects.

Sequential Quan → Qual MMAR Study Design

Methodological Characteristics

A sequential Quan → Qual MMAR design consists of two chronological strands, during which quantitative data are collected and analyzed first in the sequence, and qualitative data are collected and analyzed second and follows up on the meaning of specific quantitative results (see Figure 5.3 for a conceptual model of this design).

The primary purpose of this design is to use subsequent qualitative data to elaborate, explain, or confirm initial quantitative results to obtain a more complete understanding of the emergent trends and relationships in the data. The study strands are connected and address confirmatory and exploratory questions in chronological order (Teddlie & Tashakkori, 2009). For example, using a sequential Quan → Qual MMAR design, an educational administrator who is seeking ways to effectively address the problem of high school students' truancy can sequentially explore the following research questions:

- Quantitative strand: What is the relationship between students' absenteeism across grades and school climate in high school X?
- Qualitative strand: How does school climate promote or impede students' absenteeism across grades in high school X?

FIGURE 5.2 **Concurrent Quan + Qual MMAR Study Design Decision Flowchart**

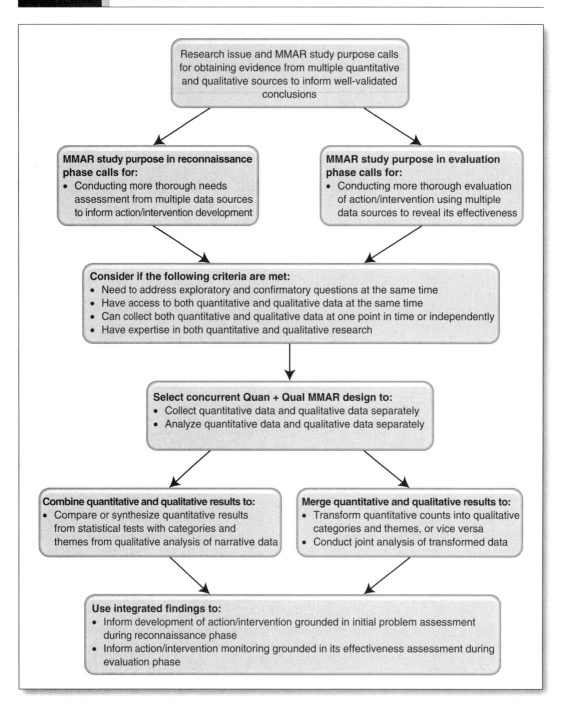

FIGURE 5.3	**Conceptual Model of a Sequential Quan → Qual MMAR Study Design**

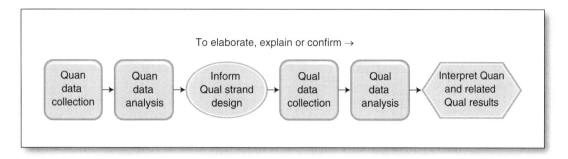

A sequential Quan → Qual design is popular among mixed methods researchers and is known under different names: sequential explanatory design (Creswell & Plano Clark, 2011), sequential mixed design (Teddlie & Tashakkori, 2009), two-phase design (Creswell, 1994), sequential quantitatively driven design (Morse & Niehaus, 2009), iteration design (Greene, 2007), and sequential triangulation (Morse, 1991). A sequential implementation of the quantitative and qualitative strands makes the design more straightforward and easier to organize and implement: first conducting a quantitative strand and obtaining the quantitative results, and then conducting a qualitative strand to explain or elaborate on these quantitative results.

For example, in a high school student's truancy situation, teachers, students, and parents can be surveyed to obtain their assessment of school climate and its potential relationship with students' absenteeism to address a quantitative research question. Once the quantitative analysis of the survey data and absenteeism indicators is complete, a subset of teachers, students, and parents who responded to the survey can be selected for individual or focus group interviews to better understand the revealed relationships in the quantitative data and thus to address a qualitative research question. In this design the study research questions and specific quantitative findings predetermine the particular individuals or groups of individuals who are selected for qualitative follow-up. These may include typical cases—that is, individuals who represent how the dominant majority responded to survey questions (Ivankova et al., 2006; Morgan, 1998), or extreme, outlier, or unique cases—that is, individuals who hold a different opinion or experience from the dominant majority (Caracelli & Greene, 1993; Ivankova, 2014; Morse, 1991).

The priority or weight in a sequential Quan → Qual MMAR design is typically given to the first, quantitative study strand because this design is typically used when the research problem and related study purpose require exploration using quantitative methods (Creswell & Plano Clark, 2011). Similarly, Morse and Niehaus (2009) considered quantitative to be a core, or a primary, component in this design and qualitative to perform a supplemental role. However, sometimes the study research focus may shift toward in-depth understanding of the issue versus assessment of trends and relationships, and the qualitative component takes more weight in the study (Ivankova et al., 2006). This often happens in action research; for example, during an initial assessment of a practical problem/issue, practitioner-researchers may decide to conduct more qualitative interviews and review more relevant documents than they had initially planned, because exploration of the views of additional stakeholders becomes important for the development of an effective action/intervention plan. In this design integration of the quantitative and qualitative methods typically occurs chronologically at the completion of the first, quantitative strand and beginning of the second, qualitative strand—that is, "questions or procedures of one strand emerge from or depend on the previous strand" (Teddlie & Tashakkori, 2009, p. 151). Additionally, the results from both study strands are interpreted together so that the qualitative findings can provide a better understanding of the initial quantitative results.

For example, the results from quantitative survey data analysis about a potential relationship of school climate with students' absenteeism will inform the selection of a sample of teachers, students, and parents for individual follow-up interviews and what quantitative results to further elaborate on qualitatively. The researcher may proportionally select participants who responded similarly to survey questions representing each grade or may decide to follow up on unique or outstanding responses. Once the second, qualitative study strand is completed, the results from both study strands will be interpreted together to provide an in-depth explanation of the studied problem. Integration of quantitative and qualitative methods in this design is further discussed in Chapter 6.

Examples of Application in Action Research

Although a sequential Quan → Qual design is very popular in mixed methods studies in social and health sciences (Ivankova et al., 2006; Morse & Niehaus, 2009), the analysis of the 108 MMAR studies discussed in Chapter 3 revealed that this design was used in a small number of studies. The review of these studies and additional published MMAR research proposals in health care showed that a sequential Quan → Qual MMAR design can be equally applied in the reconnaissance and evaluation phases to elaborate, explain, or confirm initial quantitative results with follow-up qualitative data to obtain a better understanding of the situation or problem. Practitioner-researchers can employ a sequential Quan → Qual MMAR design to conduct an initial quantitative assessment of the problem using surveys and tests, and then to explore these results through in-depth individual interviews or focus group discussions with key stakeholders or select community members who can provide additional insight into the issue. In the evaluation phase, a sequential Quan → Qual MMAR design can help practitioner-researchers perform a more effective evaluation of the employed action/intervention plan, first by collecting numeric indicators and then by following up with select stakeholders to explain what these indicators mean to them and how the initial action/intervention plan can be revised based on this evaluation. In both phases, the use of a sequential Quan → Qual MMAR design can help first obtain a broad assessment of the problem and then secure understanding of its specific aspects that is more in-depth.

For example, Pickard (2006) applied a sequential Quan → Qual MMAR design in the reconnaissance phase to explore faculty and college students' attitudes to plagiarism at University College Northampton (UCN) in the United Kingdom. The overall aim of this study was "to contextualize the problem at UCN [University College Northampton]; to produce evidence, raise awareness of the issues and encourage debate about the pedagogical issues associates with it" (p. 215). During the first strand, quantitative survey data were collected from 53 faculty and 509 students from a range of disciplines to assess the extent of the problem; during the second strand, individual unstructured and semistructured interviews were planned to be conducted with faculty and students to follow up on the major findings from the survey related to students' behavior and staff's experiences with plagiarism. To justify the use of a sequential Quan → Qual MMAR design, Pickard pointed out that quantitative survey "was valuable in contextualizing the issue and allowed some scope for empirical generalizations but was not considered to be an appropriate methodology to explore the more complex human behaviors" (pp. 218–219). Qualitative follow-up individual interviews allowed "the voices of those involved to he heard and to develop explanations based on analysis of their narratives" (p. 219).

In a published research protocol for a proposed MMAR study (Montgomery et al., 2008; Example E), the researchers chose a sequential Quan → Qual MMAR design to evaluate "the processes and outcomes of supported housing programs for persons living with a serious mental illness in northeastern Ontario from the perspective of clients, their families and community workers" (p. 3). During the first study strand, the quantitative data collected from a series of surveys with housing residents will provide baseline data about their demographic characteristics, quality of life, housing stability, and housing preferences. These results will inform qualitative focus groups and photo-voice data collection strategies to further explore perceptions of the supported housing services from multiple stakeholders' perspectives in the second, qualitative study strand. One of the research questions that this proposed study aims to answer using the integrated findings is, "What supported housing services need to be changed in order to make the most difference in the day-to-day lives of clients?" (p. 3)

Similarly, Seymour and colleagues (2011) applied a sequential Quan → Qual MMAR design to evaluate a three-day community-based peer education training program aimed at preparing volunteers for advance care planning and associated end-of-life care issues. The researchers first collected quantitative data via a mail questionnaire sent to 24 participants four months after the completion of the training. The questionnaire results were used to inform the development of the qualitative interview protocol created to guide a focus group discussion with 20 peer educators six months after the training, and individual and group interviews with 25 volunteers over a period of 12 to 18 months. These follow-up focus groups and interviews addressed peer educators' perceptions of and experiences with peer education and related activities. The qualitative findings helped understand the initial quantitative results of why certain individuals in the community were more likely to take on the role of a peer educator and ultimately helped enhance this training program effectiveness.

Procedural Pros and Cons

Practitioner-researchers who decide to use a sequential Quan → Qual MMAR design in the reconnaissance and/or evaluation phases in an MMAR study should consider the pros and cons of this design. On one hand, the sequential nature of the quantitative and qualitative data collection and analysis makes this design more straightforward and easier to implement by one researcher (Creswell & Plano Clark, 2011; Ivankova et al., 2006; Morse & Niehaus, 2009). Because a study using a sequential Quan → Qual MMAR design typically progresses in "a slower, more predictable manner," it is less complicated methodologically (Teddlie & Tashakkori, 2009, p. 153). A strong quantitative orientation of this design makes it attractive in disciplines where quantitative is the dominant research approach. Other advantages of this design include the opportunities for the exploration of the initial quantitative results in more detail, especially when unexpected results arise from a quantitative strand (Morse, 1991). Besides, an emergent nature of a sequential Quan → Qual MMAR design (Morse & Niehaus, 2009) allows for a certain methodological flexibility because the design components of the follow-up qualitative strand are shaped by the outcomes of the first quantitative strand.

Despite obvious advantages inherent to a sequential Quan → Qual MMAR design, its implementation is associated with a number of challenges that should also be considered in weighting the pros and cons for using this design. The limitations of this design are related to the length of time and feasibility of resources to collect and analyze both sets of data. Using this design may be especially challenging in small-scale action research projects that need to address immediate practical problems, but that have limited resources at hand. Another challenge for practitioner-researchers is related to a wait time that is associated with having first to complete quantitative data collection and analysis before making a decision about what stakeholders to approach to further explore the emerged quantitative results and what additional permissions may be needed. This is particularly important when obtaining an approval for a sequential Quan → Qual MMAR study by the IRB (Creswell & Plano Clark, 2011). Because many of the research aspects of the second qualitative strand are yet unknown at the study design stage—for example, what participants will be selected for follow-up interviews, or what questions will be discussed during the follow-up focus groups—practitioner-researchers have to submit an IRB amendment once the first quantitative strand is completed, which ultimately extends the time of the study. This can potentially make this design less attractive in addressing immediate practical problems or in responding to urgent situations.

Additional challenges may be associated with deciding what quantitative results to follow up and what stakeholders' views and opinions to further explore. Choosing less important quantitative results and selecting wrong individuals for follow-up may produce inconsistencies in the quantitative and qualitative conclusions (Creswell & Plano Clark, 2011) and result in an erroneous and incomplete assessment of a practical problem leading to the development of a less effective action/intervention plan, or making flawed conclusions about the effectiveness of the action/intervention during its evaluation and monitoring.

Figure 5.4 presents a flow of ideas and methodological steps in a sequential Quan → Qual MMAR design that may help practitioner-researchers make informed decisions when applying this design to their MMAR projects.

Sequential Qual → Quan MMAR Study Design

Methodological Characteristics

A sequential Qual → Quan MMAR design also consists of two chronological strands. However, this design starts with qualitative data collection and analysis to first explore the problem using qualitative methods. Quantitative data collection builds on the findings from the first, qualitative strand, and occurs during the second study strand (see Figure 5.5 for a conceptual model of this design).

The primary purpose of this design is to initially explore the phenomenon of interest using qualitative methods and then to test the revealed variables and relationships quantitatively. This design is often used to inform the development of quantitative measurement instruments, to identify variables to study quantitatively, to reveal patterns in behavior, to test the emergent theory, and to determine the distribution of a phenomenon within a chosen population (Creswell & Plano Clark, 2011; Greene, 2007; Morgan, 1998; Morse, 1991; Morse & Niehaus, 2009). Similar to a sequential Quan → Qual MMAR design, in Qual → Quan MMAR design the study strands are connected and address both exploratory and confirmatory questions in chronological order (Teddlie & Tashakkori, 2009). For example, using a sequential Qual → Quan MMAR design, an educational

| **FIGURE 5.4** | **Sequential Quan → Qual MMAR Design Decision Flowchart** |

Research issue and MMAR study purpose calls for an initial quantitative examination of the problem and then elaborating, explaining, or confirming quantitative results through qualitative follow-up to obtain a more complete understanding of the emergent trends and relationships

MMAR study purposein reconnaissance phase calls for:
- Conducting an initial quantitative assessment of the problem and then further exploring these results using qualitative data from select stakeholders

MMAR study purpose in evaluation phase calls for:
- Conducting a thorough evaluation of action/intervention effectiveness by first collecting numeric indicators and then following up with select stakeholders to explain what these indicators mean to them

Consider if the following criteria are met:
- Need to sequentially address both confirmatory and exploratory questions
- Need to conduct quantitative assessment first to better understand trends and patterns and then to follow up on individual aspects
- Have sufficient time to collect quantitative and qualitative data chronologically building one on another
- Have expertise in both quantitative and qualitative research

Select sequential Quan → Qual MMAR design:
- Collect and analyze quantitative data first
- Use quantitative results to inform the design of qualitative follow up
- Collect and analyze qualitative data second

Integrate quantitative and qualitative results:
- Use categories and themes from qualitative analysis of text data to elaborate, explain, or confirm quantitative results from statistical tests

Use integrated findings to:
- Inform development of action/intervention grounded in initial problem assessment during reconnaissance phase
- Inform action/intervention monitoring grounded in its effectiveness assessment during evaluation phase

| FIGURE 5.5 | **Conceptual Model of a Sequential Qual → Quan MMAR Study Design** |

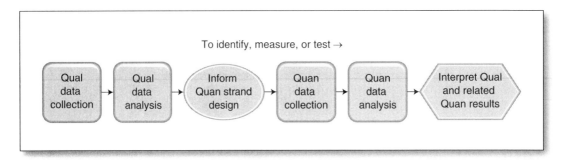

administrator who is seeking ways to effectively address the problem of high school students' truancy can sequentially explore the following research questions:

- Quantitative strand: What school-, home-, and community-related factors, as perceived by students, parents, and educators, influence students' absenteeism across grades in high school X?
- Qualitative strand: How do these factors correlate with the number of days missed for different reasons by students in high school X?

A sequential Qual → Quan design is frequently used in mixed methods research. It is most often used to inform the development of a new measurement instrument when a needed tool is not available. Therefore, this design is often referred to as instrument-development design (Creswell, Fetters, & Ivankova, 2004), but in the mixed methods literature it is also known as sequential exploratory design (Creswell & Plano Clark, 2011), sequential mixed design (Teddlie & Tashakkori, 2009), iteration design (Greene, 2007), sequential qualitatively driven design (Morse & Niehaus, 2009), and quantitative follow-up design (Morgan, 1998). Similar to a sequential Quan → Qual MMAR design, a consecutive implementation of the qualitative and quantitative strands makes Qual → Quan MMAR design easier to implement in separate strands: first, conducting a qualitative strand to obtain an in-depth understanding of the studied phenomenon or issue and, then, developing a quantitative strand to measure and test the revealed variables, patterns, and relationships.

For example, individual or focus group interviews can be conducted with selected individuals first to explore the phenomenon of interest (e.g., student absenteeism) and to identify important factors or variables to further study quantitatively (Creswell & Plano Clark, 2011). In many cases, themes, categories, and quotes from the qualitative analysis of interview and focus group data inform the development of the quantitative instrument to measure the identified variables or to test an emergent theory (Palcanis et al., 2012). Once the instrument is created and tested, a larger group of individuals who have not participated in the first, qualitative study strand is selected to complete a quantitative survey in the second, quantitative strand. Thus, the use of a sequential Qual → Quan MMAR design allows researchers to systematically explore the phenomenon of interest and to test and generalize the qualitative exploratory findings to a larger population.

To refer to a high school students' truancy situation, focus groups can be conducted with select students, parents, and educators to reveal the role that school-, home-, and community-related factors may play in influencing students' absenteeism in this school, thus addressing a qualitative research question. Based on the analysis of the focus group data, a new questionnaire that will include qualitatively identified factors/variables can be developed to survey all school personnel, students, and parents in order to identify the relationships between these factors and students' absenteeism, thus addressing a quantitative research question.

The priority or weight in a sequential Qual → Quan MMAR design is typically given to the first, qualitative study strand because in this design "the researcher starts by qualitatively exploring a topic before building to a second, quantitative phase" (Creswell & Plano Clark, 2011, p. 86). Similarly, Morse and Niehaus (2009) considered qualitative to be a core, or a primary, component in this design, while the qualitative component is performing a supplemental role.

For example, practitioner-researchers may extensively use qualitative methods to conduct an in-depth exploration of the practical problem; then they may use these findings to inform a focused assessment of the views of multiple stakeholders to verify the issue and identify its effective solution. In this design, integration of the qualitative and quantitative methods typically occurs chronologically at the completion of the first, qualitative strand and beginning of the second, quantitative strand. As in a sequential Qual → Quan MMAR design, "questions or procedures of one strand emerge from or depend on the previous strand" (Teddlie & Tashakkori, 2009, p. 151). Additionally, the results from both study strands are interpreted together so that the quantitative results can verify, confirm, or generalize the initial exploratory qualitative findings.

To illustrate, in a high school student's truancy situation, qualitative themes and categories from the analysis of the focus groups with students, parents, and educators will inform the development of a new survey instrument that will be administered to all school personnel, students, and parents in this school. Once the second, quantitative study strand is completed and the survey data are analyzed, the results from both study strands will be interpreted together to confirm and generalize the focus group qualitative findings, thus providing a more complete understanding of the studied problem. Integration of qualitative and quantitative methods in this design is further discussed in Chapter 6.

Examples of Application in Action Research

A sequential Qual → Quan MMAR design is a more frequently used sequential design. The analysis of the 108 MMAR studies discussed in Chapter 3 showed that this design is more often applied in the reconnaissance phase of an MMAR study because the intent is to obtain a more complete exploration of a practical problem and thus to better inform the development of the action/intervention plan. Practitioner-researchers can employ a sequential Qual → Quan MMAR design to conduct an initial qualitative exploration of the problem/issue using naturalistic observations of the settings and employing individual and focus group interviews with key informants to identify and subsequently test important variables and relationships with a larger group of stakeholders. A sequential Qual → Quan MMAR design can also help practitioner-researchers perform a more effective evaluation of the implemented action/intervention by first exploring select stakeholders' perceptions about the action/intervention effects so that to inform further quantitative examination of its effectiveness among multiple stakeholders. In both of these phases in the action research process, the use of a sequential Qual → Quan MMAR design can help initially explore the phenomenon or issue of interest, and then assess it by using quantitative methods.

For example, in Craig's (2011) MMAR study (Example C), a sequential Qual → Quan MMAR design was applied during the reconnaissance phase to conduct "a mixed-methods community needs assessment with the intent of creating a system of care for gay, lesbian, bisexual, transgender, and questioning (GLBTQ) youths in an urban area" (p. 274). During the first, qualitative strand, documented evidence about existing national and local GLBTQ programs was collected to identify the key informants. Then, the researcher interviewed 45 key informants from the community consisting of local service providers, community leaders, and other stakeholders. In addition, 10 focus groups with GLBTQ youths were conducted "to deepen relationships with the population of interest and to provide a richer understanding of the true needs of the population by building upon the perspective of the providers" (p. 281). During the second, quantitative strand, "based on the domains articulated in the qualitative research," the researcher identified and modified a survey instrument that was completed by 273 GLBTQ youths (p. 282). Such a deliberate approach to needs assessment and exploration of the issue from multiple perspectives ensured that all stakeholders' views were represented in the recommendations for developing a system of care for GLBTQ youths. It has also supported the effectiveness of the approach as a means "of community empowerment and decision-making in the development of a plan for a system of care" (p. 283).

In Reese, Ahern, Nair, O'Faire, and Warren's (1999) MMAR study exploring cultural and institutional barriers to access and use of hospices by African Americans, a sequential Qual → Quan MMAR design was also applied in the reconnaissance phase "to explore unexpected reasons for the lack of participation of African Americans in hospice" (p. 552). During the first study strand, qualitative interviews were conducted with six African American pastors to identify major themes "to develop a quantitative measure, which was used in the subsequent quantitative strand of the study" (p. 553). Additionally, several hypotheses were generated based on the emergent qualitative findings that were further tested in the quantitative strand. During the second strand, 127 hospice patients, churchgoers, and nonchurchgoers completed the developed questionnaire. Besides testing those research hypotheses, the quantitative findings were also used to explore the credibility of the qualitative findings.

Similarly, in a study of transitions in care from hospital to homeless shelter, Greysen and colleagues (2012) used a sequential Qual → Quan MMAR design in the reconnaissance phase to accomplish two objectives: "to understand patients' experiences of transitions from hospital to a homeless shelter, and to determine aspects of these experiences associated with perceived quality of these transitions" (p. 1485). During the first strand, consistent with the community-based participatory research approach, the researchers explored the key stakeholders' perspectives by conducting several focus groups with case managers, social workers, and executive staff, and by conducting 10 individual interviews and one focus group with homeless individuals at one shelter. The purpose of the qualitative data collection was to identify improvement priority areas and to design a survey instrument to explore the views and experiences of all shelter residents. Based on the analysis of those qualitative data, Greysen and colleagues determined that their "first research priority would be to generate patient-centered data about transitions in hospital care from individuals actively seeking shelter in our community" (p. 1486). To collect the data from a large sample of homeless individuals, they designed a 20-item multiple choice survey with two open-ended questions grounded in the results from the qualitative analysis. During the second study strand, a new instrument was pilot tested and administered to 98 eligible shelter residents.

Procedural Pros and Cons

Practitioner-researchers who decide to use a sequential Qual → Quan MMAR design in the reconnaissance and/or evaluation phases in an MMAR study should consider the pros and cons of this design. Similar to a sequential Quan → Qual MMAR design, the sequential nature of the qualitative and quantitative data collection and analysis makes Qual → Quan MMAR design more straightforward methodologically and thus easier to implement by a single researcher (Creswell & Plano Clark, 2011; Morse & Niehaus, 2009; Teddlie & Tashakkori, 2009). The strong qualitative orientation of this design makes it particularly appropriate for action research because qualitative methods allow for in-depth input from the study participants as key informants. In their justification of the use of qualitative methods to inform the subsequent quantitative data collection, Reese and colleagues (1999) stated, "Thus, we see qualitative methodology as an important component of participatory action research" (p. 552). A sequential Qual → Quan MMAR design is specifically advantageous for those researcher-practitioners who want first to explore the phenomenon of interest in depth with a few stakeholders, and then to expand these findings to multiple stakeholders. Similar to a sequential Quan → Qual MMAR design, the emergent nature of Qual → Quan MMAR design (Morse & Niehaus, 2009) allows for methodological flexibility because the design components of the subsequent quantitative strand are shaped by the initial qualitative findings about the studied problem.

As with any MMAR design, a sequential Qual → Quan MMAR design is not void of challenges that should be considered when weighting the pros and cons of this design. Similar to a sequential Quan → Qual MMAR design, this design requires lengthy time and resources to collect and analyze both sets of data (Creswell & Plano Clark, 2011). This may have negative implications for small-scale action research projects that need to promptly address immediate practical issues with sometimes limited resources. Additionally, developing a measurement instrument is a lengthy and complex process that requires adherence to special psychometric procedures (DeVellis, 2011). Partnerships with local university or professional agency consultants may help practitioner-researchers acquire the expertise needed to ensure the new instrument is reliable and valid and correctly reflects the views of large groups of stakeholders.

Another challenge is related to the need for practitioner-researchers to wait until the completion of the initial qualitative exploration of the studied phenomenon to be able to identify the variables, patterns, and relationships that will be examined further with large groups of stakeholders. Similar to a sequential Quan → Qual MMAR design, adhering to Qual → Quan MMAR design requires practitioner-researchers to submit an amendment to an original IRB approval after the instrument is developed and thus to secure additional permissions to use it to survey large groups of stakeholders. Additional challenges may be associated with deciding what qualitative results to choose to inform the development of the instrument (Creswell & Plano Clark, 2011), what hypotheses generated from the qualitative strand might be used to further test quantitatively, what groups of stakeholders to survey, how many individuals to include, and how to gain access to these individuals. Creswell and Plano Clark (2011) warned that choosing weak qualitative findings, focusing on testing hypotheses that are less important, and selecting wrong individuals to survey may produce inconsistencies in the qualitative and quantitative conclusions. Such inconsistent and unreliable results may lead to an erroneous and incomplete assessment of the practical problem, development of a less effective action/intervention plan, or flawed conclusions about the effectiveness of the plan during its implementation and evaluation.

Figure 5.6 presents a flow of ideas and methodological steps in a sequential Qual → Quan MMAR design that may help practitioner-researchers make informed decisions in applying this design to their MMAR projects.

Multistrand MMAR Study Design

Methodological Characteristics

A multistrand MMAR design typically consists of more than two concurrent or sequential strands and is considered to be a more complex design (Teddlie & Tashakkori, 2009). For example, this design can begin as a concurrent Quan + Qual MMAR design and have quantitative and qualitative data collected and analyzed independently. Then it can be followed by a strand of a different method (Quan + Qual → Quan, or Quan + Qual → Qual). Similarly, it can start as a sequential Quan → Qual or Qual → Quan MMAR design and can be followed by a concurrent Quan + Qual (Quan → Qual → Quan + Qual, or Qual → Quan → Quan + Qual) or another sequential strand (Quan → Qual → Quan, or Qual → Quan → Qual) of data collection and analysis. Variations are numerous and are evident from the review of published MMAR studies. The sequence and number of the quantitative and qualitative concurrent and sequential strands depend on the project purpose and specific goals of each study strand (see Figure 5.7 for a conceptual model of this design). As stated earlier in this chapter, the longitudinal and interactive nature of action research makes it easy to align it with a multistrand MMAR design, generating evidence from multiple differently sequenced quantitative and qualitative study strands within an overall action research project framework.

Consistent with a sequential implementation of different forms of data collection and analysis, the results from one method, quantitative or qualitative, are used to inform the development of another method, quantitative or qualitative. This design is particularly useful when the project has multiple exploratory and confirmatory questions that need to be addressed chronologically. The priority or weight of quantitative and qualitative methods may be equal because one method meaningfully informs the development of the other and builds on the previous method (Greene, 2007). The integration of the quantitative and qualitative methods in a multistrand MMAR design is done in accordance with the integration procedures specific to the concurrent or sequential designs. However, because in this design each strand often leads to another, integration may occur chronologically at the completion of one strand and beginning of the next strand when research questions and procedures of one strand emerge from or depend on the results from the previous strand (Teddlie & Tashakkori, 2009).

Examples of Application in Action Research

Applying a multistrand MMAR design during the reconnaissance phase of an MMAR study can be advantageous because an additional chronological or concurrent exploration of a practical problem or issue may be important to capture all aspects of the issue from multiple stakeholders' viewpoint. In the evaluation phase, inclusion of multiple chronological or concurrent quantitative and qualitative strands may be necessary to ensure that the conclusions made about the effectiveness of the action/intervention are thorough and consistent with the views of everybody involved in the action research process.

To illustrate, in Sampson's (2010) MMAR study (Example D), a multistrand MMAR design was applied to inform the development and implementation of the English language instruction in the EFL Japanese Interpersonal Communication college class that was based on the assessment of students' preferences. The study consisted of the following multiple strands: Quan + Qual → Qual → Quan. First, a concurrent Quan + Qual data collection and analysis was applied to identify students' preferred lesson style by triangulating the results from a quantitative survey, the Lesson Style Questionnaire, and students' stories from a narrative exercise, the Language Learning Autobiography. The author explicitly discussed the purpose of data triangulation at this stage "to most effectively inform the change-action without interfering with student learning" (p. 286). The priority was given to qualitative data, because they were seen as being more important in providing insight into the students' lesson style preferences. Based on the analysis of the quantitative and qualitative

FIGURE 5.6   **Sequential Qual → Quan MMAR Design Decision Flowchart**

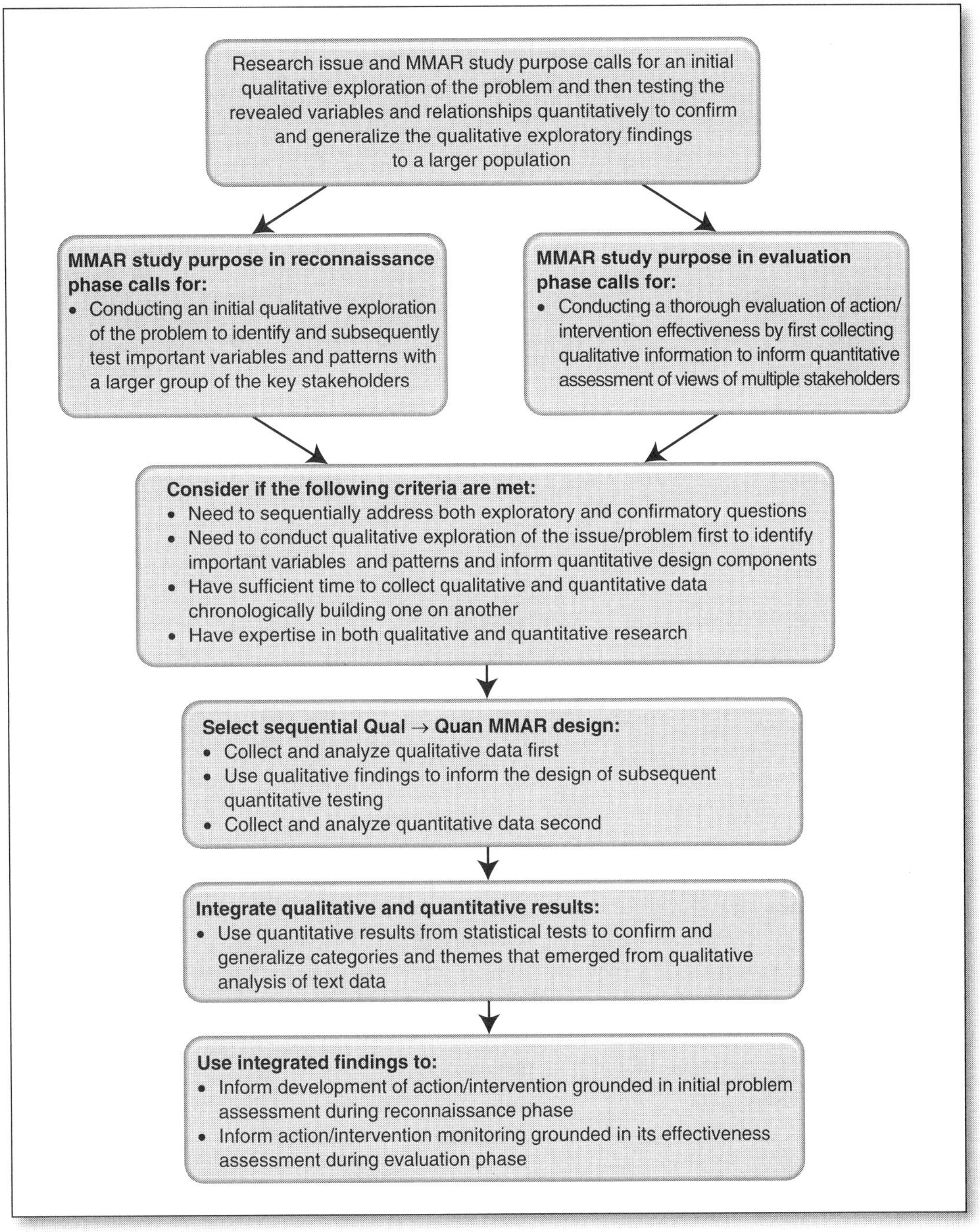

Research issue and MMAR study purpose calls for an initial qualitative exploration of the problem and then testing the revealed variables and relationships quantitatively to confirm and generalize the qualitative exploratory findings to a larger population

MMAR study purpose in reconnaissance phase calls for:
- Conducting an initial qualitative exploration of the problem to identify and subsequently test important variables and patterns with a larger group of the key stakeholders

MMAR study purpose in evaluation phase calls for:
- Conducting a thorough evaluation of action/intervention effectiveness by first collecting qualitative information to inform quantitative assessment of views of multiple stakeholders

Consider if the following criteria are met:
- Need to sequentially address both exploratory and confirmatory questions
- Need to conduct qualitative exploration of the issue/problem first to identify important variables and patterns and inform quantitative design components
- Have sufficient time to collect qualitative and quantitative data chronologically building one on another
- Have expertise in both qualitative and quantitative research

Select sequential Qual → Quan MMAR design:
- Collect and analyze qualitative data first
- Use qualitative findings to inform the design of subsequent quantitative testing
- Collect and analyze quantitative data second

Integrate qualitative and quantitative results:
- Use quantitative results from statistical tests to confirm and generalize categories and themes that emerged from qualitative analysis of text data

Use integrated findings to:
- Inform development of action/intervention grounded in initial problem assessment during reconnaissance phase
- Inform action/intervention monitoring grounded in its effectiveness assessment during evaluation phase

| FIGURE 5.7 | Conceptual Model of a Multistrand MMAR Study Design |

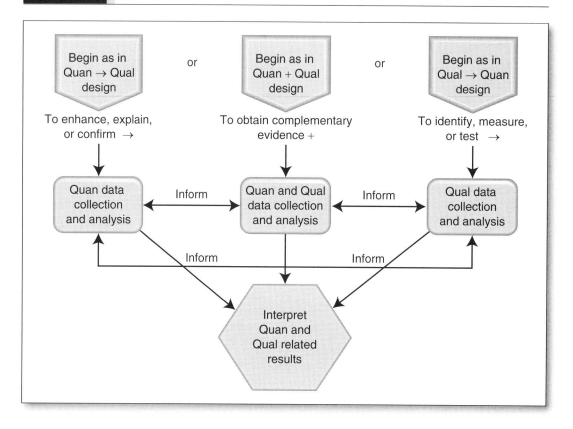

data, task-based-oriented lessons were developed to refocus the instruction and introduce more opportunities for practical use of English by the students during the class time.

By obtaining and comparing evidence from students' surveys and narratives, the instructor-researcher was able to better understand the needs of the students in his class and a preferred mode for classroom instruction. Subsequently, a sequential Qual → Quan data collection and analysis was applied to inform the development of the quantitative Learning Experience Questionnaire that was completed by the students at the end of the course with the purpose of evaluating the new task-based oriented language instruction. Qualitative narrative data from the journals that the students kept to reflect on the learning activities during each class were analyzed for themes that made the basis of the quantitative questionnaire. The survey yielded quantitative indicators of students' experiences with learning in the course that were compared with respective narrative journal entries and served to confirm the students' positive perceptions of their learning experiences.

In another example, Vecchiarelli and colleagues (2005) used a multistrand MMAR design in the reconnaissance phase to inform the development of a school-based environmental intervention to support healthy eating and physical activity among students. The study consisted of the following multiple strands: Qual → Quan → Quan. During the first, qualitative strand, participating community stakeholders used a Delphi process to identify the top 15 benchmark criteria for each of eight components to include in a Nutrition Friendly School program. During the next, quantitative strand, all participating stakeholders rank ordered these 15 criteria for each of the eight components. In a subsequent quantitative strand, based on the selected criteria, the researchers developed a user-friendly self-evaluation tool so that the schools could assess their nutrition environment and determine specific actions that they should take to reach all 15 benchmarks.

In their MMAR study, Akintobi and colleagues (2012) employed a multistrand MMAR design to evaluate a community-based training program aimed at helping 20 community-based organizations conducting HIV prevention in the southern United States. The project was funded by The Pfizer Foundation Southern HIV/AIDS Prevention Initiative. The study consisted of the following multiple strands: Quan → Qual→ Quan + Qual. During the program implementation, a cross-site quantitative program assessment survey was conducted to determine changes in participants' knowledge, skills, abilities, and technical needs based on the participation in the program. It was followed by one-on-one semistructured qualitative teleconferences with participating community-based organizations to gain better insight into their training needs based on the quantitative assessment. At the completion of all evaluation-capacity-building activities, another quantitative assessment survey was conducted concurrently with qualitative semistructured interviews with the representatives from each community-based organization to gather additional feedback on the evaluation-capacity-building partnerships. According to Akintobi and colleagues (2012), each step in the evaluability assessment was systematically staged to build upon each other in preparation for evaluation capacity-building through understanding of each community-based organization's program and evaluation context" (p. 36).

Procedural Pros and Cons

Practitioner-researchers who decide to use a multistrand MMAR design in the reconnaissance and/or evaluation phases in an MMAR study should consider the same pros and cons discussed earlier for a concurrent Quan + Qual and sequential Quan → Qual and Qual → Quan MMAR designs. Additional challenges may be associated with the need to submit more than one IRB amendment and request additional permissions for each study strand as the study progresses. Additional time and resources may be needed as the project grows, and a team approach may be advantageous for implementing each study strand due to the complexity of the design. Specific considerations should be given to ensure the quality of quantitative and qualitative data collection and analysis, as faulty decisions made at one strand may threaten the chosen methodological procedures and related outcomes of the next study strand (Ivankova, 2014). Practitioner-researchers may refer to Figures 5.2, 5.4, and 5.6 for the flow of ideas and methodological steps in concurrent Quan + Qual and sequential Quan → Qual and Qual → Quan MMAR designs to guide their decisions in sequencing concurrent and chronological strands when applying a multistrand MMAR design to their MMAR projects.

Box 5.4 summarizes the essential features of MMAR designs to assist practitioner-researchers in their design considerations when conceptualizing and designing an MMAR study.

BOX 5.4

Essential Features of MMAR Study Designs

- MMAR designs consist of two or more concurrent or sequential quantitative and qualitative strands, and can include one or several chronological strands.
- MMAR designs can be applied in both reconnaissance and evaluation phases in an MMAR study.
- Different or similar MMAR designs can be applied in different phases in an MMAR study process.
- A concurrent Quan + Qual MMAR design is the most commonly used MMAR design; its purpose is to help seek corroborating evidence and produce more-validated conclusions to inform the development, implementation, and evaluation of the action/intervention plan.
- A concurrent Quan + Qual MMAR design is more frequently used in the evaluation phase of an MMAR study with the purpose of data triangulation.
- A sequential Quan → Qual MMAR design can be used both in the reconnaissance and evaluation phases of an MMAR study with the purpose of elaborating, explaining, or confirming initial quantitative results with follow-up qualitative data so as to obtain a better understanding of the problem or evaluate the effectiveness of the action/intervention.
- A sequential Qual → Quan MMAR design is more frequently used in the reconnaissance phase of an MMAR study with the purpose of obtaining a more complete assessment of a practical problem and informing the development of the action/intervention plan.
- A multistrand MMAR design can begin as a concurrent Quan + Qual, sequential Quan → Qual or Qual → Quan MMAR design, but can include additional sequential or concurrent quantitative and qualitative strands to inform data collection and analysis during a subsequent study strand.
- A multistrand MMAR design is reflective of a longitudinal and interactive nature of action research allowing for generating evidence from multiple differently sequenced quantitative and qualitative study strands within an overall action research project framework.
- Priority or weighting is often placed on qualitative methods, such as interviews, focus groups, and naturalistic observations in the reconnaissance phase of an MMAR study to understand the issue and inform action/intervention plan, while the evaluation phase may include more quantitative methods, such as surveys and hypothesis testing to assess effectiveness of the action/intervention plan.

SUMMARY

The chapter begins with the discussion of four recent mixed methods design typologies. To stay consistent with a practical focus of action research and to make the application of mixed methods in action research conceptually easier for practitioner-researchers, a more generic typology of MMAR study designs is suggested. The typology of MMAR study designs builds on major mixed methods design typologies and incorporates their common design elements. This typology includes basic MMAR designs that can be used in different combinations during the reconnaissance and evaluation phases in an MMAR study process to inform other phases in the action research cycles. Importantly, due to the longitudinal and interactive nature of MMAR projects in which all phases are conceptually linked in the pursuit of an effective solution to a practical problem/issue, each completed study including all six phases of the action research cycle may be viewed as a multilevel or multiphase integrated design.

Based on the variation of the key methodological dimensions specific to mixed methods designs (number of study strands, priority or weighting of quantitative or qualitative method, sequence or timing of the study strands, and mixing or integration of the quantitative and qualitative methods) four basic types of MMAR designs can be distinguished: a concurrent Quan + Qual design, a sequential Quan → Qual design, a sequential Qual → Quan design, and a multistrand design. Methodological characteristics, application in the action research process, and procedural pros and cons of each design are discussed and illustrated using examples from published MMAR studies. A conceptual visual model and a design decision flowchart for each design are presented to help practitioner-researchers make informed decisions in applying these designs to their MMAR projects.

REFLECTIVE QUESTIONS AND EXERCISES

1. Reflect on the purposes and key methodological dimensions of MMAR study designs (number of study strands, priority or weighting of quantitative or qualitative method, sequence or timing of the study strands, and mixing or integration of the quantitative and qualitative methods). Discuss how each methodological characteristic shapes a specific MMAR design.

2. Select a published MMAR study in your discipline or area of interest. Identify the type of MMAR design and in what phase—reconnaissance or evaluation, or both—it was used in the action research process. Discuss the methodological dimensions of the design. Reflect on how well the chosen MMAR design helped address the study purpose and research questions.

3. Carefully examine Figures 5.2, 5.4, and 5.6 for the flow of ideas and methodological steps in concurrent Quan + Qual, sequential Quan → Qual, and sequential Qual → Quan MMAR designs. Identify the flow of the procedures and discuss the guiding decisions made by the researchers when selecting the MMAR design used in the article.

4. Discuss pros and cons of the MMAR design used. Could the researchers have applied a different MMAR design to address the same research problem? How would a choice of a different design change the study procedures?

5. Draw a conceptual model of the MMAR design used in the article you selected. Compare your model with the suggested conceptual model for this MMAR design.

6. Identify a practical problem or issue in your work or community setting that requires improvement. Reflect on how you will design an MMAR study and what MMAR design you will use to address this problem/issue. Describe the methodological characteristics of the proposed design and how they will guide your decisions. Draw a conceptual model of the proposed MMAR design.

FURTHER READINGS

To learn more about recent mixed methods design typologies, examine the following sources:

Creswell, J. W., & Plano Clark, V. L. (2011). *Designing and conducting mixed methods research* (2nd ed.). Thousand Oaks, CA: Sage, Ch. 3–4, pp. 68–142.

Greene, J. C. (2007). *Mixed methods in social inquiry.* San Francisco, CA: Jossey-Bass, Ch. 7, pp. 112–141.

Morse, J. M., & Niehaus, L. (2009). *Mixed method design: Principles and procedures.* Walnut Creek, CA: Left Coast Press, Ch. 8–10, pp. 85–155.

Teddlie, C., & Tashakkori, A. (2009). *Foundations of mixed methods research: Integrating quantitative and qualitative approaches in the social and behavioral sciences.* Thousand Oaks, CA: Sage, Ch. 7, pp. 137–167.

To learn more about key methodological dimensions of mixed methods designs examine the following sources:

Creswell, J. W., & Plano Clark, V. L. (2011). *Designing and conducting mixed methods research* (2nd ed.). Thousand Oaks, CA: Sage, Ch. 3, pp. 63–68.

Greene, J. C. (2007). *Mixed methods in social inquiry.* San Francisco, CA: Jossey-Bass, Ch. 7, pp. 118–120.

Morse, J. M., & Niehaus, L. (2009). *Mixed method design: Principles and procedures.* Walnut Creek, CA: Left Coast Press, Ch. 1, pp. 16–22.

Teddlie, C., & Tashakkori, A. (2009). *Foundations of mixed methods research: Integrating quantitative and qualitative approaches in the social and behavioral sciences.* Thousand Oaks, CA: Sage, Ch. 7, pp. 142–147.

6

Planning Integration of Quantitative and Qualitative Methods in a Mixed Methods Action Research Study

OBJECTIVES

By the end of this chapter, the reader should be able to

- Understand the role and importance of mixing or integrating quantitative and qualitative methods,
- Explain the concept of meta-inferences and their role in an MMAR study process,
- Describe the levels and strategies of quantitative and qualitative methods' integration in MMAR study designs,
- Develop a study purpose and research questions for reconnaissance and evaluation phases in an MMAR study,
- Understand a notation system for a visual presentation of MMAR study procedures, and
- Be able to draw a visual diagram of the study procedures for different MMAR study designs.

INTRODUCTION

Chapter 5 introduced four basic MMAR study designs that differ along the key methodological dimensions: number of study strands, sequence or timing of their implementation, priority or weighting of quantitative or qualitative methods, and integration or mixing of the quantitative and qualitative methods in the study process. Each design has a specific purpose that shapes how quantitative and qualitative methods are jointly used or mixed to produce study conclusions that are more robust, and that are grounded in the integrated results from the quantitative and qualitative study strands. Such integrated study conclusions are often referred to as meta-inferences, because they are generated from the interpretations or inferences that are "drawn from the separate quantitative and qualitative strands of a study as well as across the quantitative and qualitative strands" (Teddlie & Tashakkori, 2009, p. 412). Importantly, meta-inferences permeate every phase in the MMAR Study Process Model: They enhance practitioner-researchers' understanding of the critical issue or situation, inform the development of the plan for action/intervention, support an effective evaluation of the implemented action/intervention, and show the direction for the action/intervention monitoring.

> Revisit the discussion of an MMAR Study Process Model in Chapter 4; refer to Figure 4.1 that visually presents the Model.

As was briefly discussed in Chapter 1, integration of the quantitative and qualitative methods is viewed as a critical component of a mixed methods study (Creswell & Plano Clark, 2011; Greene et al., 1989; Morse & Niehaus, 2009; Teddlie & Tashakkori, 2009). Deciding on how and when the integration between the quantitative and qualitative strands will occur in the study process is one of the key decisions in choosing a mixed methods design (Creswell & Plano Clark, 2011). Additionally, making the right decisions on methods' integration in a mixed methods study has implications for the study outcomes and shapes the answers to the research questions. Importantly, in action research, where the outcomes of each phase inform the next step in the research cycle, planning integration of the quantitative and qualitative strands should occur early in the research process—when conceptualizing the whole study and when choosing an MMAR design for the reconnaissance and evaluation phases. Therefore, addressing the issues of quantitative and qualitative methods' integration in relation to the study's expected or desired outcomes should help practitioner-researchers choose an MMAR design and strategies of data collection and analysis that will ensure a systematic and comprehensive exploration of a studied problem/issue.

So, what is a methodological role of integrating or mixing quantitative and qualitative methods in a study, and what implications does it have for creating the meta-inferences to guide the development and evaluation of the action/intervention in an MMAR study?

INTEGRATION OR MIXING OF QUANTITATIVE AND QUALITATIVE METHODS

Integration or Mixing in Mixed Methods Research

The idea of the integration of quantitative and qualitative methods in a mixed methods study is emphasized in many definitions of mixed methods research. According to Teddlie and Tashakkori (2009), the focus

on methods' integration or mixing is a prominent feature of the current conceptualizations of mixed methods research. For a mixed methods study to be "truly
mixed" there should be an integration of quantitative and qualitative approaches
at different stages in the study process (p. 142). Based on this assumption, Teddlie
and Tashakkori (2009) suggested differentiating **quasi-mixed designs** from
true mixed methods designs to separate the designs where quantitative and
qualitative data were collected and analyzed with no or little attempt for mean-

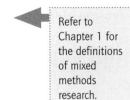

Refer to
Chapter 1 for
the definitions
of mixed
methods
research.

ingful integration of results. To illustrate this point, Teddlie and Tashakkori (2009) discussed an example of a
quasi-mixed design study where a social psychologist would use a quantitative survey and some open-ended
interviews to test a theory but would not integrate the results from both data sets to generate the study conclusions grounded in the findings from all data. In a true mixed methods design study a researcher would jointly
interpret the quantitative and qualitative results and use the integrated conclusions in answering the research
questions.

To underscore the importance of integrating quantitative and qualitative methods in producing joint conclusions, Morse and Niehaus (2009) introduced the term **point of interface,** which describes "the position
in which the two methods join" in the process of the study implementation (p. 25). According to these authors,
the point of interface can occur either at the analytic stage when the quantitative and qualitative data are
analyzed together (e.g., qualitative themes are transformed into quantitative scores and are incorporated into
the quantitative analysis), or at the results interpretation stage when the findings from the quantitative and
qualitative study strands are discussed together in a complimentary manner. Thus, the point of interface, or
how and when the two methods are integrated, shapes a mixed methods study design and the relationships
between the study strands.

Integration in a mixed methods study is also viewed as an important tool to tighten the relationship
between the quantitative and qualitative methods and to ensure all study components fit together in jointly
addressing the study purpose. Yin (2006) argued that integration in a mixed methods study should occur
through the interrelationship of the research components and procedures related to (1) research questions,
(2) units under analysis, (3) study samples, (4) study instruments and methods
of data collection, and (5) analytic strategies. The more the two methods are
integrated across these five research components and procedures, the more
integrated a mixed methods study will be. Similar to Teddlie and Tashakkori
(2009), Yin (2006) differentiated between the mixed methods studies that integrate or mix the methods across all five components and separate or parallel
studies that use the methods in isolation.

Refer to
Chapter 1 for
the discussion
of a
fundamental
principle of
mixed
methods
research in the
context of
reasons and
rationales for
conducting
mixed
methods
research.

The idea of quantitative and qualitative methods' integration is reflected in
what Johnson and Turner (2003) referred to as a fundamental principle of mixed
methods research. According to this principle, integration of quantitative and qualitative methods in the study should draw on their complementary strengths rather
than on "nonoverlapping weaknesses" (p. 299) to produce quality meta-inferences.
Integration is a critical stage in a mixed methods study process, and the choice of
levels and strategies of methods' integration across the quantitative and qualitative
strands has implications for the value of the meta-inferences and the overall study
outcomes.

Creating Meta-Inferences

Teddlie and Tashakkori (2009) defined meta-inference as "a conclusion generated through an integration of the inferences that have been obtained from the results of the QUAL and QUAN strands of a MM study" (p. 152). As such, meta-inferences are the product of the integration processes that occur in a mixed methods study. According to the authors, during a mixed methods study process each quantitative and qualitative study strand produces inferences that are referred to as "the outcome of the process of meaning making" (Teddlie & Tashakkori, 2003, p. 27). A mixed methods study design shapes the process of making inferences because it influences their point of interface (how and when the methods are integrated) and aligns it with the overall intent of the study. For example, in a concurrent mixed methods design, inferences from the quantitative and qualitative study strands are combined or synthesized to create meta-inferences aimed at providing corroborating evidence. In sequential designs, inferences from the follow-up strand depend on and are shaped by the inferences produced in the first study strand and are aimed at yielding complementary information. So, both the way inferences are derived using different quantitative and qualitative methods and the way they are integrated in the study process have strong implications for creating meta-inferences resulting from an overall study (Yin, 2006).

Meta-inferences play an important role in an MMAR study process. Adopting the role of reflection, they guide practitioner-researchers' decisions about the important steps in the action research process and inform the study direction and cycles. Since they relate to the expected or desired study outcomes, they are embedded in the purposes of the reconnaissance and evaluation phases of an MMAR study and help shape the study process. For example, the meta-inferences produced during the reconnaissance phase of an MMAR study help with generating comprehensive conclusions about the assessment of the problem or critical situation; these conclusions are then used to inform the development and implementation of the action/intervention plan. Similarly, the meta-inferences generated during the evaluation phase of an MMAR study provide evidence about the effectiveness of the implemented action/intervention, help inform its monitoring, and support action/intervention sustainability and fidelity.

Refer to Figure 4.1 MMAR Study Process Model to see how meta-inferences inform each phase in an action research cycle.

To illustrate these points, consider Kostos and Shin's (2010) MMAR study (Example A) that employed a concurrent Quan + Qual MMAR design to evaluate math journaling instruction for second-grade students. The researchers collected quantitative data from students' pre- and post-math skills assessments and qualitative data from students' math journal entries and interviews, and teacher-researcher's reflective journaling. Both quantitative and qualitative data sets were analyzed, and the results were jointly interpreted to imply that math journaling instructional intervention resulted in the improvement of students' mathematical thinking through math communication. The positive meta-inferences generated through informed and planned integration of the quantitative and qualitative methods in the study confirmed the teacher-researcher's intention to continue using students' journaling in teaching math.

In Craig (2011) MMAR study (Example C), a sequential Qual → Quan design was used to conduct a systematic large-scale assessment of the community needs to identify and develop an appropriate intervention for GLBTQ young people. The qualitative and quantitative data collection and analysis were conducted sequentially. The inferences generated from the documented evidence about existing national and local GLBTQ programs, key informant individual interviews, and focus groups with GLBTQ youths informed the development of a quantitative survey instrument that reflected the community views about the needs of GLBTQ youths. During the next step the survey was administered to a large group of GLBTQ youths to obtain their perspective about what needed to be included in the community-based system of care. The meta-inferences created based on the inferences from both study strands informed the design of an intervention consisting of numerous programs and services tailored to GLBTQ youths.

Points and Strategies of Methods' Integration

Similar to other mixed methods authors, Creswell and Plano Clark (2011) viewed integration in a mixed methods study as the relationships that develop between its quantitative and qualitative components. They referred to integration or mixing as "the explicit interrelating of the study's quantitative and qualitative strands" (p. 66). Picking up on Morse and Niehaus's (2009) term "point of interface" (p. 25), Creswell and Plano Clark (2011) identified four possible points (or levels) in the study process where the integration of quantitative and qualitative strands may occur:

- *During the results' interpretation,* when the results from the quantitative and qualitative study strands are combined and are interpreted together to develop overall study conclusions
- *During the data collection,* when the results from the previous strand (quantitative or qualitative) inform the data collection in the next strand, so that the two study strands are connected
- *During the data analysis,* when one type of collected data (quantitative or qualitative) is transformed into a different type (qualitative or quantitative) and both data sets are analyzed together
- *During the study design,* when quantitative and qualitative study strands are integrated during the larger design stage guided by an overall program objective, as in a multistrand design

They also suggested a number of integration or mixing strategies associated with each of these points and discussed their potential application in mixed methods designs.

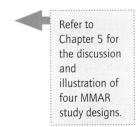

Refer to Chapter 5 for the discussion and illustration of four MMAR study designs.

The four points of quantitative and qualitative methods' integration and the associated integration strategies identified by Creswell and Plano Clark (2011) are well-suited for the purposes of methods' integration in an MMAR study. Table 6.1 summarizes these points and strategies of methods' integration as they can be adjusted to MMAR study designs introduced in Chapter 5. The description and application of these integration strategies is further discussed in this chapter in the context of each MMAR study design.

So, how can practitioner-researchers integrate quantitative and qualitative methods in MMAR study designs?

TABLE 6.1	**Points and Strategies of Quantitative and Qualitative Methods' Integration in MMAR Study Designs**

Point of Integration	Integration Strategy	Description of Integration Strategy	Application in an MMAR Design
Interpretation of results	Combining	Comparing or synthesizing quantitative and qualitative results and their interpretations.	Concurrent Quan + Qual Sequential Quan → Qual Sequential Qual → Quan
Data collection	Connecting	Using quantitative and qualitative results from the first study strand to inform the type and means of data collection in the subsequent qualitative or quantitative strand.	Sequential Quan → Qual Sequential Qual → Quan
Data analysis	Merging	Transforming one data set (quantitative or qualitative) into an alternative data set for further joint analysis.	Concurrent Quan + Qual
Design	Combining Connecting Merging	Using integrating strategies from other levels consistent with the purposes of each strand combination.	Multistrand

INTEGRATING QUANTITATIVE AND QUALITATIVE METHODS IN MMAR STUDY DESIGNS

Integrating Methods in a Concurrent Quan + Qual MMAR Study Design

The purpose of a concurrent Quan + Qual MMAR study design is to compare or merge quantitative and qualitative results to produce well-validated conclusions. Consistent with this design purpose, quantitative and qualitative methods' integration often occurs at the level of the results interpretation during the final stage of the study when the analysis and the interpretation of the data from both quantitative and qualitative study strands are completed. The most common integration strategy is *combining* the inferences from the interpretation of both quantitative and qualitative results to generate meta-inferences based on what was learned in the overall study process. To achieve this purpose, the results from the quantitative and qualitative study strands and their interpretations are compared side by side or synthesized to find corroborating evidence or to reveal discrepancies that may require further exploration. Identifying inconsistencies in quantitative and qualitative inferences may be particularly important in informing the next cycle in the action research process to avoid inaccurate conclusions about the problem assessment or action/intervention effectiveness. Figure 6.1 presents a conceptual model of a combining integration strategy in a concurrent Quan + Qual MMAR study design.

For example, in Glasson and colleagues' (2006) MMAR study (Example B) that used a concurrent Quan + Qual design, the results from patients' quantitative questionnaires and the findings from the researcher's qualitative reflective notes from the observations of nurses' discussions were combined "to establish an evidence-base for an evolving model of care" (p. 588). Specifically, information about the patients' knowledge of medication regime and their satisfaction with the nursing care from the quantitative instruments was compared with the themes that emerged from the nursing staff discussions about the need for a new model of nursing care and its important aspects. Similarly, during the evaluation phase, the meta-inferences created through the synthesis of the patient and nursing staff responses to the quantitative items and open-ended questions on the survey were used to evaluate the efficacy of a new model of nursing care in an acute medical ward setting.

FIGURE 6.1 **Conceptual Model of Combining Integration Strategy in a Concurrent Quan + Qual MMAR Study Design**

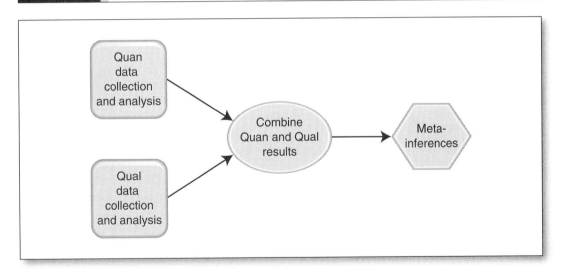

Merging is another integration strategy associated with a concurrent Quan + Qual MMAR study design; it occurs during the data analysis. This integration strategy is more difficult to implement, which may account for its relatively rare use in action research. Merging involves a joint analysis of the quantitative and qualitative data but, prior to analysis, data from one type (e.g., quantitative or qualitative) are converted or transformed into the data of a different type (e.g., qualitative or quantitative), so that both data sets can be analyzed together using either quantitative or qualitative methods. For example, quantitative scores can be stratified to form qualitative themes and categories and analyzed using qualitative methods together with other collected qualitative data from interviews or observations; alternatively, qualitative themes and categories can be assigned numeric scores and added to the quantitative data set for further joint analysis. Meta-inferences are created based on the merged analysis of the two data sets. Figure 6.2 presents a conceptual model of a merging integration strategy in a concurrent Quan + Qual MMAR study design.

For example, Blanco and colleagues (2010) used a merging integration strategy in a concurrent Quan + Qual MMAR study that evaluated a Spanish learning program for college students. Data from qualitative interviews with 11 students and the lecturer's observation journal were first categorized and subjected to content analysis. Data transformation occurred when frequencies and percentages were assigned to the qualitative categories and merged with the quantitative survey data collected from 24 students. The authors referred to this process as data triangulation; they believed it "can broaden the scope of the investigation, and enrich the researcher's ability to draw conclusions" (Dornyei, 2007, as cited in Blanco et al., 2010, p. 56).

| FIGURE 6.2 | **Conceptual Model of Merging Integration Strategy in a Concurrent Quan + Qual MMAR Study Design** |

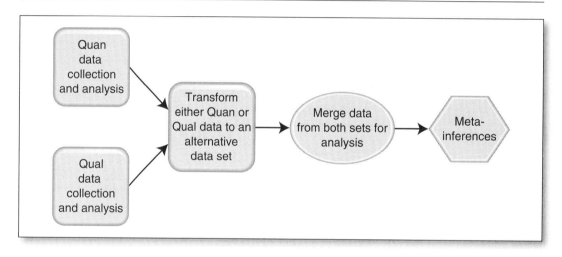

Integrating Methods in a Sequential Quan → Qual MMAR Study Design

The purpose of a sequential Quan → Qual MMAR study design is to use follow-up qualitative data to elaborate, explain, or confirm initial quantitative results. Consistent with the purpose of this design, integration occurs during the data collection when the analysis of the quantitative data from the first strand is completed and the results are used to inform the types and strategies for subsequent qualitative data collection. The integration strategy is *connecting* the two study strands based on the inferences that emerged from the quantitative results. For example, quantitative results can inform the selection of the participants for qualitative follow-up interviews and/or observations based on their test scores, their responses to the quantitative survey, or other quantitative indicators depending on the study purpose. Quantitative results also can guide the development of qualitative data collection protocols and shape the emergent qualitative research subquestions (Ivankova et al., 2006). Practitioner-researchers may find this integration strategy useful when trying to identify important stakeholders or to follow up on important information in order to produce more credible solutions to the studied problem/issue.

Additionally, at the completion of the qualitative data analysis, the inferences from the two study strands are *combined* and interpreted together to produce the overall study conclusions. The quantitative and qualitative results are compared and the qualitative findings are used to explain or confirm the quantitative results. Thus, the meta-inferences are developed based on the connected and combined results from the two study strands. Figure 6.3 presents a conceptual model of a connecting integration strategy in a sequential Quan → Qual MMAR study design.

For example, in Pickard's (2006) sequential Quan → Qual MMAR study the two study strands were connected to explore in depth the faculty and college students' attitudes to plagiarism with the purpose of raising awareness of this issue among the university administration and faculty. The analysis of the quantitative survey data from 53 faculty and 509 students from a range of disciplines informed the questions to explore in the follow-up individual interviews with faculty and students. These interviews were aimed at obtaining more insight into the major findings from the survey related to students' behaviors and staff/faculty experiences with plagiarism. While Pickard's (2006) article focused on reporting the results from the first, quantitative strand of the study, the author explained that a sequential addition of qualitative interviews would add explanation of the participants' survey responses and give them "some degree of empowerment with the process of institutional change" (p. 219). Reportedly, the meta-inferences generated from the combined results from the two study strands allowed for contextualizing the problem of plagiarism and producing evidence of the issue at that university.

| **FIGURE 6.3** | **Conceptual Model of Connecting Integration Strategy in a Sequential Quan → Qual MMAR Study Design** |

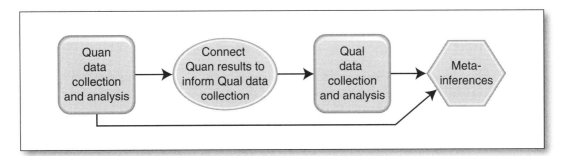

Integrating Methods in a Sequential Qual → Quan MMAR Study Design

The purpose of a sequential Qual → Quan MMAR study design is to use initial qualitative data to develop new measures, or to identify unknown variables and relationships. Similar to a sequential Quan → Qual MMAR design, the integration strategy is *connecting* the two study strands based on the inferences that emerged from the qualitative results to inform the types and strategies for subsequent quantitative data collection. For example, the themes from an initial qualitative exploration of the problem or situation can be used to inform the development of a quantitative measurement instrument, help identify the variables to study quantitatively, or reveal an emergent theory to be tested further in the quantitative strand. Such an integration strategy may be particularly useful in action research when the key informants' views need to be compared with the views of a large group of stakeholders.

Similar to a sequential Quan → Qual MMAR design, the inferences from the two study strands are also *combined* during the interpretation of the overall study conclusions, and the quantitative results are used to help confirm or generalize the qualitative results that provided an initial exploration of the problem. The meta-inferences are developed based on the connected and combined results from the two study strands. Figure 6.4 presents a conceptual model of a connecting integration strategy in a sequential Qual → Quan MMAR study design.

For example, in Reese and colleagues' (1999) sequential Qual → Quan MMAR study exploring cultural and institutional barriers to access and use of hospices by African Americans, the two study strands were connected to achieve two purposes. First, the themes from individual interviews with six African American pastors led the researchers to generate and subsequently test the following hypothesis: "Barriers to hospice access and use exist to a greater degree in the African American population than in the European American population" (p. 554). The analysis of the qualitative interview data also informed the development of the two quantitative questionnaires about hospice barriers and values to statistically test that hypothesis and "to examine the credibility of the qualitative findings" (p. 553). The questionnaires were administered to a sample of 127 hospice patients, churchgoers, and nonchurchgoers in the second, quantitative strand. The meta-inferences created from the combined results from the two study strands provided an understanding of the existing barriers to enable the researchers, pastors, and community leaders to collaboratively develop "a plan for solutions to the barriers" (p. 552).

| **FIGURE 6.4** | **Conceptual Model of a Connecting Integration Strategy in a Sequential Qual → Quan MMAR Study Design** |

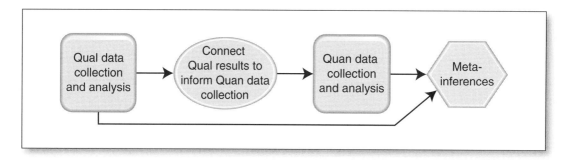

Integrating Methods in a Multistrand MMAR Study Design

The purpose of a multistrand MMAR study design is to combine and address the study goals consecutively via multiple quantitative and qualitative concurrent and sequential strands by using the results from a previous sequential strand or two concurrent strands to inform the next consecutive combination of strands. In this design, quantitative and qualitative methods' integration occurs at the overall study design level because it is guided by an overall study purpose or program objective, like a purpose for an MMAR study that includes multiple phases in an action research cycle. Because this design may consist of a different number and combination of concurrent and sequential strands, all integration strategies associated with a specific combination and integration purposes of the two strands (combining, connecting, merging) can be applied. The meta-inferences are developed based on the combined, merged, and connected inferences from all study strands.

> Revisit the discussion of an MMAR Study Process Model in Chapter 4.

For example, Akintobi and colleagues' (2012) multistrand MMAR study that evaluated a community-based training program aimed at building evaluation capacity for community-based organizations conducting HIV prevention consisted of two sequential strands and two concurrent strands. All study strands were connected by using the inferences derived from a previous strand to inform the development of the next study strand. During the first, quantitative strand, a cross-site quantitative program assessment survey was conducted to determine changes in participants' knowledge, skills, abilities, and technical needs. The results of the survey informed a follow-up qualitative strand that consisted of one-on-one, semistructured qualitative teleconferences with 20 project grantees to gain a better insight into the community-based organizations' training needs based on the information gleaned from the quantitative assessment. The interpretation of these results informed the direction for an additional round of the evaluation of the program. During the next study phase, when all evaluation-capacity-building activities were completed, quantitative assessment survey data and qualitative data from the interviews with the community-based organizations' representatives were collected and analyzed concurrently to gather additional feedback on the evaluation-capacity-building partnerships. Thus, the inferences from the three sequential and concurrently employed study strands contributed to the development of the meta-inferences that informed a systematic evaluation of the effectiveness of the community-based training program.

So, how can this knowledge of quantitative and qualitative methods' integration help practitioner-researchers formulate a study purpose and research questions to reflect the methodological features of specific MMAR study designs that are used to guide the implementation of the reconnaissance and evaluation phases of an MMAR study?

DEVELOPING STUDY PURPOSE AND RESEARCH QUESTIONS FOR RECONNAISSANCE AND EVALUATION PHASES IN AN MMAR STUDY

Since the generation of meta-inferences has implications for how the expected or desired outcomes are addressed during each phase in the action research process, it is important to consider the reasons for integrating quantitative and qualitative methods when designing the reconnaissance and evaluation phases of an MMAR study. Explaining the rationale for integrating quantitative and qualitative methods within the reconnaissance and evaluation study phases will help emphasize the reasons for choosing an MMAR design and will communicate the expected outcomes of these study phases. Greene (2007) argued that one of the integrative tasks mixed methods researchers face is to "represent the results of one method in ways that meaningfully inform the desired development of another" (p. 126). Besides the obvious advantages of planning for quantitative and qualitative methods' integration when conceptualizing and designing the needs assessment or action/intervention evaluation, communicating how the conclusions about the outcomes of a specific action step are planned to be achieved in the study process may enhance the study's comprehension by stakeholders and secure their support for the study implementation. Therefore, it is important to include specific reasons for quantitative and qualitative methods' integration that are consistent with an MMAR study design in the purpose statement and in the research questions for the reconnaissance and evaluation phases of an MMAR study.

Study Purpose and Research Questions for Reconnaissance and Evaluation Phases

Refer to an MMAR Study Process Model and the components of the first diagnosing phase in the action research cycle in Box 4.1 in Chapter 4.

Refer to Chapter 4 for a discussion of the recommended components of an MMAR study purpose statement.

Before learning about what components to include in a specific purpose statement for the reconnaissance and evaluation phases of an MMAR study, revisit the discussion of how an MMAR study is conceptualized during the first diagnosing phase in the action research process in Chapter 4. During this phase, practitioner-researchers develop a general purpose statement for an overall MMAR study and outline the research questions that they want to answer by conducting the project. This purpose statement includes an overall intent of the study and the goals of the reconnaissance and evaluation study phases. Once an overall MMAR study purpose is formulated and the goals of the reconnaissance and evaluation phases are identified and agreed on, practitioner-researchers are ready to move to the next phase in an MMAR study process and reflect on a specific purpose and design for each study phase. By this time, practitioner-researchers should have a better understanding of the particular needs of each phase in the action research cycle and that will enable them to develop clearer purpose statements to guide the design and implementation of the reconnaissance and evaluation phases. Importantly, Newman, Ridenour, Newman, and DeMarco (2003) suggested that researchers should choose a methodological approach and a design for the study only after fully contemplating potential complexities of its research purpose.

Following the recommendations for writing an MMAR study purpose statement discussed in Chapter 4, a purpose statement for the reconnaissance and evaluation phases should include the following components:

- The intent of the reconnaissance or evaluation phase
- An MMAR study design
- The goals of each quantitative and qualitative study strand, including the content aim, data collection tools, participants, and site(s)
- A specific reason for integrating quantitative and qualitative methods in this study phase

Box 6.1 offers a purpose statement script for the reconnaissance and evaluation phases of an MMAR study to assist practitioner-researchers with writing a purpose statement that includes all suggested components. To use the script, practitioner-researchers should fill in the information that applies to their study in the spaces between

BOX 6.1

MMAR Study Reconnaissance/Evaluation Phase Purpose Statement Script

The purpose of the (reconnaissance/evaluation) phase of this MMAR study is to (state the overall intent of this study phase, participants, and site) by using a (concurrent/sequential/multistrand) mixed methods design. The goal of the quantitative strand of the study is to (state the content aim of the quantitative strand; indicate independent and dependent variables, instruments, and participants). The goal of the qualitative strand of the study is to (state the content aim of the qualitative strand; indicate the central phenomenon, type of data, and participants). The rationale for integrating quantitative and qualitative methods in this study phase is to (state the reason for using a mixed methods design) to inform (state the purpose of this action step).

MMAR Study Reconnaissance Phase Purpose Statement Script Example

The purpose of the reconnaissance phase of this MMAR study is to identify the reasons for third-grade students' failure to meet the DIBELS reading test standards in school X by using a concurrent mixed methods design. The goal of the quantitative strand of the study is to compare the DIBELS test performance with reading self-efficacy scores for third-grade students by using available DIBELS indicators and reading self-efficacy scale. The goal of the qualitative strand of the study is to understand the factors affecting third-grade students' reading self-efficacy scores by using the data from individual interviews with teachers, parents, and students. The rationale for integrating quantitative and qualitative methods in this study phase is to obtain validated meta-inferences to inform the development of the new DIBELS test administration policies.

MMAR Study Evaluation Phase Purpose Statement Script Example

The purpose of the evaluation phase of this MMAR study is to identify the effectiveness of the new DIBELS test administration policies as they relate to third-grade students' reading self-efficacy in school X by using a sequential mixed methods design. The goal of the quantitative strand of the study is to (1) identify if students have improved their DIBELS test performance and reading self-efficacy by comparing students' new and previous DIBELS test scores and reading self-efficacy scores and (2) assess teachers and parents' opinions on the new DIBELS test administration policies via a survey. The goal of the qualitative strand of the study is to better understand how the new test administration policies have affected select students' DIBELS test performance and reading self-efficacy scores by conducting focus group interviews with purposefully selected teachers, parents, and students. The rationale for integrating quantitative and qualitative methods at this study phase is to provide a more complete evaluation of the new DIBELS test administration policies and identify areas for further improvement.

the parentheses. The script is followed by the examples of its application in developing purpose statements for the reconnaissance and evaluation phases of a hypothetical MMAR study about the changes in existing school policies related to the DIBELS reading test administration to improve third-grade students' reading self-efficacy that was used for illustration in Chapter 4.

Refer to Chapter 4 and Box 4.4 for an MMAR study general purpose statement script and an example of its application to a hypothetical MMAR study about changes in existing school policies related to the use of the DIBELS reading assessment test to improve third-grade students' reading self-efficacy.

Because research questions help narrow the study purpose and clarify the study direction, they should also highlight the reasons for quantitative and qualitative methods' integration within the reconnaissance and evaluation study phases. Consistent with the discussion of research questions for an MMAR study in Chapter 4, research questions for the reconnaissance and evaluation study phases may include three types of questions. The first type of a research question includes an integrated MMAR question that addresses an overall practical intent of the reconnaissance and evaluation study phases and guides their implementation. The other two types of questions include quantitative and qualitative research questions that address the specific purposes of the quantitative and qualitative study strands within a particular MMAR design and guide the methodological procedures to help fulfill an overall intent of this study phase. Therefore, an integrated MMAR question for the reconnaissance and evaluation phases of an MMAR study should emphasize the reason for integrating quantitative and qualitative methods in addressing a practical problem/issue during this study phase, in addition to stating the purpose for choosing a specific MMAR design. Depending on whether practitioner-researchers are using a concurrent or a sequential MMAR design, the content and format of an integrated MMAR question will reflect the manner and process of integrating quantitative and qualitative strands within the context of the selected design (Onwuegbuzie & Leech, 2006; Plano Clark & Badiee, 2010).

Examples of Study Purpose and Research Questions for MMAR Study Designs in Reconnaissance and Evaluation Phases

Revisit the discussion of research questions for an MMAR study in Chapter 4.

Consider the examples of purpose statements and related research questions from the research proposals for MMAR studies developed to explore practical issues in the fields of health promotion, K–12 education, and higher education. These examples, presented in Boxes 6.2 through 6.5, address different MMAR designs used in the reconnaissance and evaluation phases of an MMAR study. Each set of research questions consists of integrated MMAR questions addressing an overall practical intent of the reconnaissance or evaluation MMAR study phase, and research questions specific to quantitative and qualitative strands of the respective study.

In Example 1 (Box 6.2), Hales (2011) proposes the evaluation phase of an MMAR study to investigate the effectiveness of the Early Interventions in Reading (EIR) Tier 3 program with the purpose of increasing literacy skills for English learner first-grade students in an elementary school in north Alabama by using a concurrent Quan + Qual design. She plans to conduct the quantitative (measuring students' reading skills) and qualitative (conducting interviews with teachers) strands of the study independently in a concurrent manner and then combine the results from the two strands and interpret them together. Hales's integrated MMAR questions reflect this integration point because they seek to obtain both confirmatory evidence related to whether the

BOX 6.2

Example 1: A Concurrent Quan + Qual MMAR Study Design Applied in the Evaluation Phase to Explore a Reading Program's Effectiveness

Practical Problem

With a growing number of students with limited English entering America's public schools, we must find a way to increase the capacity of first-grade students to acquire the English system of phonics and reading comprehension.

Purpose Statement

The purpose of the evaluation phase of this MMAR study is to investigate the effectiveness of the Early Interventions in Reading (EIR) Tier 3 program with the purpose of increasing literacy skills for English learner first-grade students in an elementary school in northern Alabama by using a concurrent mixed methods design. The goal of the quantitative strand of the study is to measure the effectiveness of the EIR Tier 3 program using the DIBELS data from English learner first-grade students. The goal of the qualitative strand of the study is to explore how the EIR Tier 3 program may have affected students' DIBELS scores and literacy skills by conducting interviews with purposefully selected teachers. The rationale for integrating quantitative and qualitative methods in this study is to measure the level of literacy skills along with the understanding of the teachers' perspectives of the program's effect on the development of students' English literacy skills in order to determine the next steps for reading intervention.

Integrated MMAR Questions

How does the EIR Tier 3 program impact reading achievement of English learner first-grade students? How can the quantitative test scores and interview themes jointly explain the EIR Tier 3 program's impact on reading achievement of English learner first-grade students?

Quantitative Strand Research Questions

What is the relationship between small group instruction and English learner first-grade students' reading achievement? What is the relationship between scripted/explicit instruction and English learner first-grade students' reading achievements?

Qualitative Strand Research Questions

What are the teacher's views of the effect of the EIR Tier 3 program on the number of words read correctly by English learner first-grade students? What are the teacher's views of the effect of the EIR Tier 3 program on reading comprehension of English learner first-grade students?

Adapted from Hales (2011) with the author's permission.

students have improved their reading test scores through participation in the program, and an explanation of the effects of the program on students' achievement: How does the EIR Tier 3 program impact reading achievement of English learner first-grade students? How can the quantitative test scores and interview themes jointly explain the EIR Tier 3 program's impact on reading achievement of English learner first-grade students?

In Example 2 (Box 6.3), Cunningham proposes the reconnaissance Quan → Qual phase of an MMAR study to investigate factors associated with HPV vaccination uptake among male college students with the purpose of increasing HPV vaccination rates for college males at a southeastern Research I university. Consistent with this sequential design, Cunningham plans to integrate quantitative and qualitative methods at two stages in the study process: (1) when connecting quantitative (student survey) and qualitative (student interviews) study strands through selecting the participants for qualitative interviews from those who completed the survey, and by developing interview questions addressing significant factors identified in the first, quantitative study strand; and (2) when combining quantitative and qualitative methods during the interpretation of the results from both quantitative and qualitative strands. Cunningham's integrated MMAR questions reflect these methods' integration points because they target both identifying the critical factors and explaining their potential effects: What factors influence HPV vaccination among college males? How do interviews with male college students explain the factors identified in the survey about students' attitudes toward HPV vaccination?

BOX 6.3

Example 2: A Sequential Quan → Qual MMAR Study Design Applied in the Reconnaissance Phase to Explore HPV Vaccination Uptake among College Students

Practical Problem

While traditionally less affected by HPV, males play an important role in HPV acquisition, increasing the cervical cancer risk among women. However, there is low HPV vaccination uptake among young college males. A need exists to educate these men on preventative measures against HPV to increase vaccination uptake.

Purpose Statement

The purpose of the reconnaissance phase of this MMAR study is to investigate factors associated with HPV vaccination uptake among male college students to increase HPV vaccination rates for college males at a southeastern Research I university by using a sequential mixed methods design. The goal of the quantitative strand of the study is to identify the prevalence of factors associated with intention of HPV vaccination among college males using survey data. The goal of the qualitative strand of the study is to better understand the factors influencing HPV vaccination intention by conducting semistructured interviews with eight to ten purposefully selected survey respondents. The rationale for integrating quantitative and qualitative methods in this study phase is to obtain validated meta-inferences to inform the development of HPV prevention education programs for college males.

Integrated MMAR Questions

What factors influence HPV vaccination among college males at a southeastern Research I university? How do interviews with male college students explain the factors identified in the survey about students' attitudes toward HPV vaccination?

Quantitative Strand Research Questions

What is the level of knowledge about HPV for male college students? What factors are attributable to level of knowledge? What are college male attitudes toward HPV vaccination? What are college male intentions to get HPV vaccinated? What factors contribute to HPV vaccination intention among male college students? How do these factors compare to other male ethnicities?

Qualitative Strand Research Questions

How do factors identified through the quantitative survey influence the intentions to get HPV vaccinated among male college students? What role do attitudes toward HPV play in uptake of the vaccine? What factors are viewed as barriers to HPV vaccination? What factors are viewed as facilitators for HPV vaccination? What role does level of knowledge about HPV play in college males' intentions to get vaccinated against HPV?

Adapted from Cunningham (2011) with the author's permission.

In Example 3 (Box 6.4), Stripling (2011) proposes the reconnaissance phase of an MMAR study aimed at exploring the role of parental involvement in improving students' behavior and academic achievement in one school district by using a sequential Qual → Quan design. Stripling plans to integrate quantitative and qualitative methods when connecting the two study strands by developing a survey instrument based on the results from the interviews with students and parents from the first strand and then administering the survey to a larger group of parents. The second integration point will occur during the interpretation of the results that will be obtained from both quantitative and qualitative strands. Stripling's integrated MMAR questions reflect this integration point because they focus on exploring the issue of parental school involvement and on confirming the relationship between parents' involvement and students' behavior and academic performance: What is the role of parental involvement in secondary schools in explaining students' academic achievement? How can the results from parents' and students' interviews inform the development of a survey instrument grounded in the participants' views?

BOX 6.4

Example 3: A Sequential Qual → Quan MMAR Study Design Applied in the Reconnaissance Phase to Explore Parental Involvement in Secondary School

Practical Problem

A student's success in school is measured by his or her academic achievement and behavior. An education is unattainable if the student's behavior is a hindrance to students' performance. One of the most effective ways to increase students' achievement is for parents to be actively involved in the education of their children. Parental involvement is a major ingredient in reducing the occurrences of unacceptable behavior in schools.

Purpose Statement

The purpose of the reconnaissance phase of this MMAR study is to explore parental involvement in secondary schools in Jefferson County School System in order to improve students' behavior and academic achievement by using a sequential mixed methods design. The goal of the first, qualitative strand is to explore parents' and students' views of parent–school involvement through individual interviews with the purpose of developing a survey instrument grounded in partici- pant's views. The goal of the subsequent quantitative strand is to identify the relationship between students' behavior and academic achievement and different levels of their parents' involvement in the school by using students' discipline and attendance records, term grades, and parents' survey data. The rationale for integrating quantitative and qualitative methods in the study is to obtain validated meta-inferences to inform the development of an effective parental involvement program for student behavioral and academic achievement success.

Integrated MMAR Questions

What is the role of parental involvement in secondary schools in explaining students' behavior and academic achievement? How can the results from parents' and students' interviews inform the development of a survey instrument grounded in the participants' views?

Qualitative Strand Research Question

What are the students' and parents' views of parental involvement in the school?

Quantitative Strand Research Question

What relationship exists between parental involvement and students' behavior and academic achievement in secondary school?

Adapted from Stripling (2011) with the author's permission.

In Example 4 (Box 6.5), Blackstone (2011) proposes the evaluation phase of an MMAR study to assess the effectiveness of the university support structures in assisting community college transfer students at a 4-year public Research I institution in the southeastern United States by using a multistrand Quan → Qual → Quan design. The proposed study consists of three sequential strands. Blackstone plans several stages of quantitative and qualitative methods' integration in the study. First, a quantitative strand and a follow-up qualitative strand will be connected through selecting the students with low and high GPAs and having varied experiences with the university support structures for follow-up focus group interviews based on the quantitative results from the first study strand. Next, the qualitative and subsequent quantitative strands will be connected by developing a survey instrument based on the themes that will emerge from the focus group interviews with students to determine the effectiveness of the university support structures. Finally, Blackstone plans to combine the results from all study strands during the interpretation of the results at the conclusion of the study. Blackstone's integrated MMAR questions reflect the requisite integration points because they focus on understanding both the university support system for transfer students and students' experiences with securing support during the transfer process, as well as on measuring the effectiveness of the support services in assisting the students with their transition: How effective are university support structures that are designed to assist community college transfer students at a 4-year public Research I institution in the southeastern United States? What findings emerge from comparing the quantitative results regarding the effectiveness of the university support structures for these community college transfer students with the qualitative data reported by the students regarding their experiences with these support structures?

BOX 6.5

Example 4: A Multistrand Quan → Qual → Quan MMAR Study Design Applied in the Evaluation Phase to Examine Institutional Support Structure for Community College Transfer Students

Practical Problem

Transition from a community college to a 4-year institution is not always smooth. Without an effective university support system designed to assist them, community college transfer students may be subjected to failure, resulting in poor achievement, absenteeism, and dropout.

Purpose Statement

The purpose of the evaluation phase of this MMAR study is to assess the effectiveness of the university support structures designed to assist community college transfer students at a 4-year public Research I institution in the southeastern United States by using a multistrand mixed methods design. The goal of the quantitative strand of the study is to identify whether differences in GPAs

(Continued)

(Continued)

exist between students who utilized such support structures and those who did not. The goal of the follow-up qualitative strand is to understand how these new support structures assisted students during the course of the semester by conducting focus group interviews with purposefully selected students. The goal of the next quantitative strand is to determine the effectiveness of the university support structures by surveying all community college transfer students at that university by using an instrument grounded in the themes from the student focus groups that were conducted in the preceding qualitative strand. The rationale for integrating quantitative and qualitative methods in this study phase is to provide a more complete evaluation of the new university support structures for community college transfer students to facilitate their smoother transition to the university.

Integrated MMAR Questions

How effective are university support structures designed to assist community college transfer students at a 4-year public Research I institution in the southeastern United States? What findings emerge from comparing the quantitative results regarding the effectiveness of the university support structures for these community college transfer students with the qualitative data reported by the students about their experiences with these support structures?

Quantitative Strand Research Question

What is the relationship between the use of the university support structures designed to assist community college transfer students and these students' GPAs?

Qualitative Strand Research Question

What are community college transfer students' experiences with the university support structures that are designed to assist them?

Quantitative Strand Research Question

How effective are the university support structures that are designed to assist community college transfer students?

Adapted from Blackstone (2011) with the author's permission.

These four examples illustrate different ways of addressing integration of quantitative and qualitative methods in the study purpose and research questions within four designs during the reconnaissance and evaluation phases in an MMAR study. As shown with the four examples, types and strategies of quantitative and qualitative methods' integration may vary across the designs, thus introducing another layer of complexity when designing and implementing an MMAR study. This may create some difficulties in understanding the purposes and procedures of an MMAR study and introduce some obstacles to collaboration with other practitioner-researchers and stakeholders who are not familiar with mixed methods research.

So, how can practitioner-researchers effectively communicate their MMAR study designs to other stakeholders? What are the ways to visually present MMAR study procedures?

VISUAL PRESENTATION OF MMAR STUDY PROCEDURES

Because mixed methods studies tend to be more complex than studies that employ one method—quantitative or qualitative—mixed methods researchers have always sought ways to visually represent a study's procedures in a visual diagram. This diagram is like a flowchart showing the study strands and stages, the quantitative and qualitative procedures within each stage, and the outcomes of each study stage. A visual representation of the mixed methods procedures in a study helps a researcher visualize the sequence of the quantitative and qualitative study strands, the weighting of the quantitative and qualitative methods, and specific methodological details of each stage within a strand. Importantly, a visual diagram allows a researcher to model the connecting and other integrating points of the quantitative and qualitative study components and plan respective data integration procedures. As such, it helps specify the place or places where the integration of the quantitative and qualitative methods occurs in the study process. Developing a visual diagram of an MMAR study is particularly important because it can facilitate comprehending a study design by interested stakeholders, including prospective funding agencies, community partners, and other practitioner-researchers. Additionally, it may help them to visually capture the complex cyclical nature of the action research process and how it is enhanced by the integration of mixed methods procedures into one or more of its steps.

Notation System for Visual Presentation of MMAR Study Procedures

Morse (1991) developed the first notation system to document and explain the mixed methods procedures in a study, and suggested a terminology that has become part of the typology for mixed methods designs. Since then, Morse's (1991) notation system has been expanded to include more notations and symbols to capture a variety of relationships between quantitative and qualitative components in a mixed methods study (Creswell & Plano Clark, 2011). Based on descriptions in mixed methods texts (Creswell & Plano Clark, 2011; Morse & Niehaus, 2009; Teddlie & Tashakkori, 2009), Box 6.6 presents the most frequently used notations to communicate the flow of the study procedures in a visual diagram for an MMAR study.

Using Morse's (1991) notation system and the related discussions in mixed methods literature (Creswell, Plano Clark, Gutmann, & Hanson, 2003; Tashakkori & Teddlie, 1998), Ivankova and colleagues (2006) developed 10 guidelines for drawing a visual diagram for the mixed methods procedures in the study presented in Box 6.7. These guidelines include the steps to follow when drawing a visual diagram of the study design, as well as specific guidelines related to its content and format.

BOX 6.6

A Notation System for Visual Presentation of MMAR Study Procedures

- QUAN, QUAL—Uppercase letters indicate higher priority or increased weight for either quantitative or qualitative method.
- quan, qual—Lowercase letters indicate lesser priority or decreased weight for either quantitative or qualitative method.
- Plus sign (+)—indicates that quantitative and qualitative data are collected and analyzed concurrently.
- Arrow (→)—indicates that quantitative and qualitative data are collected and analyzed in a sequence.
- Rectangle (▭)—indicates a stage in quantitative and qualitative data collection and analysis.
- Oval (◯)—indicates a stage in quantitative and qualitative methods' integration and results' interpretation.
- Hexagon (⬡)—indicates a stage where meta-inferences from the quantitative and qualitative inferences are created.

BOX 6.7

Ten Rules for Drawing a Visual Diagram of Mixed Methods Procedures in an MMAR Study

1. Give a title to the visual diagram.

2. Choose either a horizontal or a vertical layout for the diagram.

3. Draw boxes for the quantitative and qualitative stages of data collection, data analysis, and interpretation of the study results.

4. Use uppercase or lowercase letters to designate the priority of quantitative and qualitative data collection and analysis.

5. Use single-headed arrows to show the flow of procedures in the study.

6. Specify procedures for each quantitative and qualitative data collection and analysis stage.

7. Specify expected products or outcomes for each quantitative and qualitative data collection and analysis procedure.

8. Use concise language for describing the procedures and products.

9. Make your diagram simple.

10. Size your diagram to a single page.

Adapted from Ivankova et al. (2006, p. 15).

EXAMPLES OF VISUAL DIAGRAMS IN MMAR STUDY DESIGNS

The following sections provide the visual diagrams for four MMAR studies that used different MMAR designs introduced in Chapter 5: concurrent Quan + Qual, sequential Quan → Qual, sequential Qual → Quan, and multistrand MMAR study designs. To enhance understanding, these visual diagrams were developed for the MMAR studies included in appendix (Examples A, C, D, E).

Visual Diagram of a Concurrent Quan + Qual MMAR Study Design (Example A: Kostos & Shin, 2010)

Kostos and Shin (2010) utilized a concurrent Quan + Qual MMAR study design that consisted of two concurrent strands—quantitative and qualitative—to evaluate how the use of math journals affected second-grade students' communication of mathematical thinking. The quantitative data consisted of an identical math assessment administered before and after the intervention using the Illinois State Board of Education Mathematics Scoring Rubric. The qualitative data included students' math journal entries, interviews with eight randomly selected students, and the teacher-researcher's reflective journal. Both sets of data were collected and analyzed concurrently. The priority or weighting was equally distributed between the quantitative and qualitative methods. The two study strands were integrated in the final stage when the results from the quantitative and qualitative strands were combined and compared to better understand the effectiveness of using math journaling in teaching mathematics. Figure 6.5 presents a visual diagram of the concurrent Quan + Qual MMAR design procedures in Kostos and Shin's (2010) study.

Visual Diagram of a Sequential Quan → Qual MMAR Study Design (Example E: Montgomery et al., 2008)

Montgomery and colleagues (2008) proposed to use a sequential Quan → Qual MMAR study design to evaluate the existing supported housing programs for persons living with a serious mental illness from the perspective of clients, their families, and community workers. The study will consist of two strands—a quantitative strand followed by a qualitative strand. During the first, quantitative study strand, the survey data, including demographic characteristics, quality of life, housing stability, and housing preferences, will be collected from all stakeholders. During the second, qualitative strand focus groups and photo-voice will be used to explore stakeholders' perceptions of supported housing services. The priority or weighting will be given to the quantitative methods, which is typical in this design because the quantitative results inform the design of the subsequent qualitative strand. The two study strands will be connected when the quantitative results from the first strand will inform the development of the focus groups and photo-voice data collection protocols in the second, qualitative study phase. The findings from both strands will also be integrated in the final study stage when the survey, focus group, and photo-voice results will be combined to inform policy changes related to supported housing programs for this population. Figure 6.6 presents a visual diagram of the sequential Quan → Qual MMAR design procedures in Montgomery and colleagues' (2008) proposed study.

| FIGURE 6.5 | **Visual Diagram of a Concurrent Quan + Qual MMAR Study Design** |

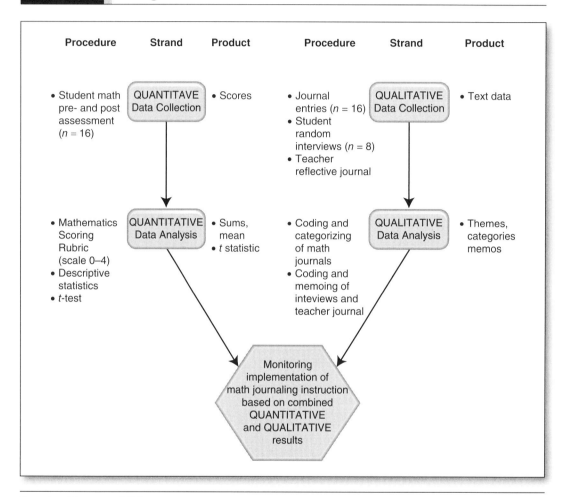

Based on Kostos and Shin (2010).

Visual Diagram of a Sequential Qual → Quan MMAR Study Design (Example C: Craig, 2011)

Craig (2011) utilized a sequential Qual → Quan MMAR study design that consisted of two sequential strands—a qualitative strand followed by a quantitative strand—to conduct a community needs assessment to inform the development of an effective system of care for GLBTQ young people in an urban area. During the first, qualitative strand, documented evidence about existing national and local GLBTQ programs was

| **Figure 6.6** | **Visual Diagram of a Sequential Quan → Qual MMAR Study Design** |

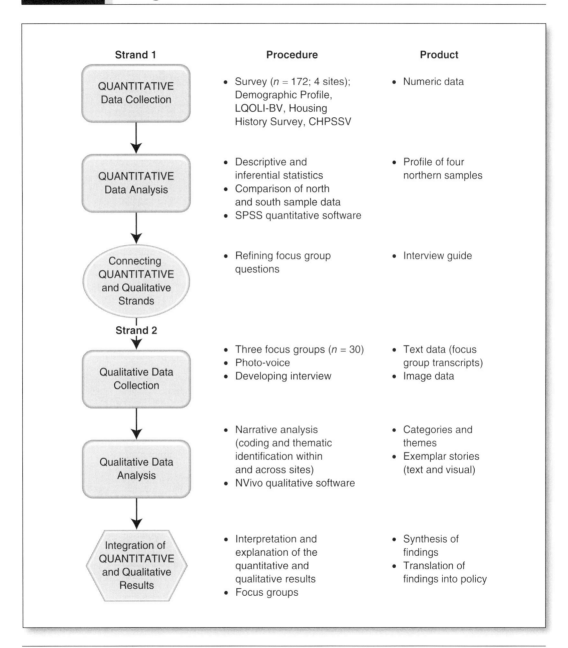

Strand 1	Procedure	Product
QUANTITATIVE Data Collection	• Survey ($n = 172$; 4 sites); Demographic Profile, LQOLI-BV, Housing History Survey, CHPSSV	• Numeric data
QUANTITATIVE Data Analysis	• Descriptive and inferential statistics • Comparison of north and south sample data • SPSS quantitative software	• Profile of four northern samples
Connecting **QUANTITATIVE** and Qualitative Strands	• Refining focus group questions	• Interview guide
Strand 2		
Qualitative Data Collection	• Three focus groups ($n = 30$) • Photo-voice • Developing interview	• Text data (focus group transcripts) • Image data
Qualitative Data Analysis	• Narrative analysis (coding and thematic identification within and across sites) • NVivo qualitative software	• Categories and themes • Exemplar stories (text and visual)
Integration of **QUANTITATIVE** and Qualitative Results	• Interpretation and explanation of the quantitative and qualitative results • Focus groups	• Synthesis of findings • Translation of findings into policy

Based on Montgomery et al. (2008, Figure 2, p. 4).

FIGURE 6.7 | **Visual Diagram of a Sequential Qual → Quan MMAR Study Design**

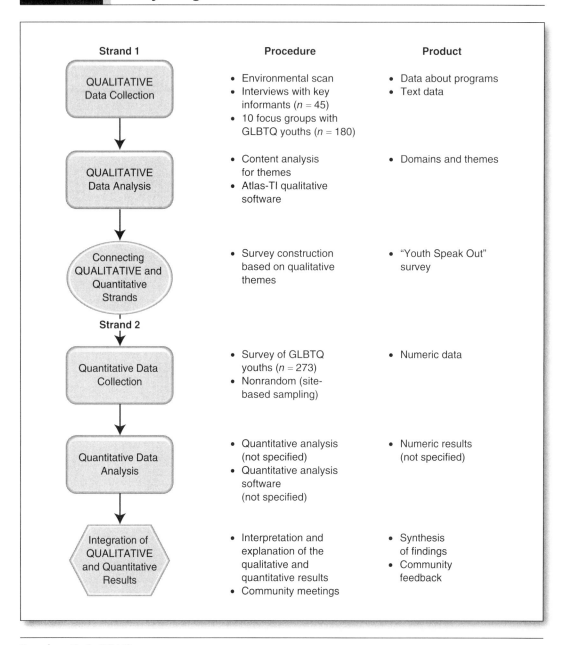

Based on Craig (2011).

FIGURE 6.8   **Visual Diagram of a Multistrand MMAR Study Design**

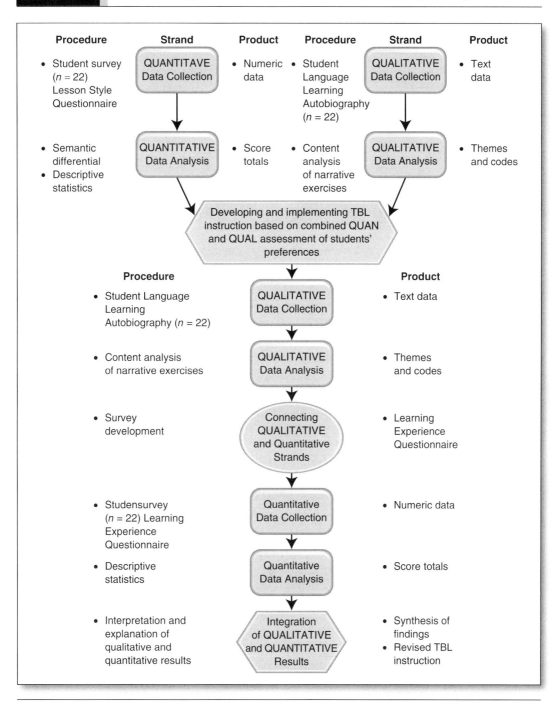

collected to identify the key informants. Individual interviews were then conducted with 45 key informants from the community. In addition, 10 focus groups with GLBTQ youths were organized to provide a richer understanding of the true needs of this population. Interview and focus group data were analyzed for themes, which subsequently were used to create the questionnaire that was administered to 273 GLBTQ youths during the second, quantitative strand. The priority or weighting was given to the qualitative methods, which is typical in this design because the qualitative results inform the design of the subsequent quantitative strand. The two study strands were connected when the questionnaire was developed from the themes generated in the first, qualitative study strand. The findings from both study strands were also integrated in the final study stage when the views of multiple stakeholders were combined to inform the design of an intervention consisting of numerous programs and services tailored to GLBTQ youths. Figure 6.7 presents a visual diagram of the sequential Qual → Quan MMAR design procedures in Craig's (2011) study.

Visual Diagram of a Multistrand MMAR Study Design (Example D: Sampson, 2010)

Sampson (2010) utilized a multistrand MMAR study design to inform the development of the English language instruction in the EFL Japanese Interpersonal Communication college class based on the assessment of students' preferences. The study consisted of two concurrent Qual + Quan and two sequential Qual → Quan strands. During the two concurrent strands, the quantitative data (consisting of students' responses to the survey) and the qualitative data (including students' narrative exercises) were collected and analyzed independently. The combined findings from the analysis of the two data sets informed the development of task-based oriented lessons to introduce more opportunities for practical use of English in the classroom setting. During the next, qualitative strand, the students participated in goal-setting activities for the upcoming lessons and continued writing in their learning journal to reflect on their learning during each class. The students' journals were analyzed for themes that were subsequently used to create the quantitative Learning Experience Questionnaire the students completed during the next, quantitative phase. These two sequential study strands were connected when the quantitative questionnaire was developed from the themes generated in the qualitative study strand. The priority or weighting was given to the qualitative methods due to their role in informing the development and evaluation of the language instruction. The findings from all strands were also integrated in the final study stage when the quantitative indicators of students' experiences with learning in the course obtained from the questionnaire were compared with qualitative journal entries to confirm students' positive views of their learning experiences. Figure 6.8 presents a visual diagram of the multistrand MMAR design procedures in Sampson's study.

SUMMARY

Integration or mixing of quantitative and qualitative methods is a critical component of an MMAR study. Deciding on how and when the integration between the quantitative and qualitative strands will occur in the study process is one of the key decisions when choosing an MMAR design and should be a part of a study's conceptualization, design, and implementation process. This chapter discusses the importance and implications of quantitative and qualitative methods' integration, quasi-mixed designs versus true mixed methods designs, the point of methods' interface in the process of the study implementation, and the role of integration for ensuring the study's cohesiveness. The notion of meta-inferences as the product of the integration processes that occur in a mixed methods study is introduced and the role that meta-inferences perform in an MMAR study is discussed. Four points of methods integration (results interpretation, data collection, data analysis, and design) and related strategies (combining, merging, and connecting) are explained and illustrated for each MMAR study design. The chapter provides suggestions for developing a study purpose and research questions to reflect the methodological features of specific MMAR study designs and offers a purpose statement script for the reconnaissance and evaluation phases of an MMAR study. The use of the script is illustrated with the examples of purpose statements and research questions from MMAR study research proposals in three disciplines that used different MMAR study designs. The chapter further discusses the advantages of developing a visual diagram of procedures in an MMAR study and provides common notations and guidelines for drawing such diagrams. Finally, the chapter gives illustrations of the visual diagrams in four MMAR study designs developed for four MMAR studies included in the appendix (Examples A, C, D, E).

REFLECTIVE QUESTIONS AND EXERCISES

1. Reflect on the importance of integration of quantitative and qualitative methods. Explain the concept of meta-inferences and how it is related to quantitative and qualitative methods' integration in mixed methods research. Revisit Figure 4.1 MMAR Study Process Model in Chapter 4. Discuss the role that meta-inferences play in an MMAR study process.

2. Reflect on the points and strategies of quantitative and qualitative methods' integration in MMAR study designs. Describe the purpose of each strategy and its role in MMAR study designs. Explain how each strategy contributes to the development of meta-inferences in these designs.

3. Select a published MMAR study in your discipline or area of interest. Identify the study design, and the point and strategies of quantitative and qualitative methods' integration in the study. Explain what meta-inferences were created in this study process. Using the provided conceptual models of the integration strategies, draw the process of the development of meta-inferences in this study.

4. Using the purpose statement script for the reconnaissance and evaluation phases of an MMAR study, develop a purpose statement for the published MMAR study that you located. In addition, write an integrated MMAR question addressing the intent of the reconnaissance or evaluation MMAR study phase, and write research questions specific to each quantitative and qualitative strand of the study.

5. Using the notation system and guidelines for drawing a visual diagram of the mixed methods procedures in an MMAR study, draw a visual diagram of the design used in the published study you reviewed in Questions 3 and 4. Compare your diagram with the example of the diagram for the MMAR study design provided in the chapter.

6. Identify a practical problem or issue at your workplace or in a community setting that requires improvement. Reflect on how you would design the reconnaissance and evaluation phases of an MMAR study and what design you will use to address this problem/issue. Develop a purpose statement for this study, and write an integrated MMAR question addressing the intent of the reconnaissance and evaluation phases and research questions specific to the quantitative and qualitative strands of this study.

FURTHER READINGS

To learn more about quantitative and qualitative methods integration in mixed methods research, examine the following sources:

Creswell, J. W., & Plano Clark, V. L. (2011). *Designing and conducting mixed methods research* (2nd ed.). Thousand Oaks, CA: Sage, Ch. 3, pp. 66–68.

Morse, J. M., & Niehaus, L. (2009). *Mixed method design: Principles and procedures.* Walnut Creek, CA: Left Coast Press, Ch. 2, pp. 25–26.

Teddlie, C., & Tashakkori, A. (2009). *Foundations of mixed methods research: Integrating quantitative and qualitative approaches in the social and behavioral sciences.* Thousand Oaks, CA: Sage, Ch. 7, p. 142.

Yin, R. K. (2006). Mixed methods research: Are the methods genuinely integrated or merely parallel? *Research in the Schools, 13*(1), 41–47.

To learn more about developing the purpose statement and research questions in mixed methods research, examine the following sources:

Creswell, J. W., & Plano Clark, V. L. (2011). *Designing and conducting mixed methods research* (2nd ed.). Thousand Oaks, CA: Sage, Ch. 5, pp. 151–168.

Plano Clark, V., & Badiee, M. (2010). Research questions in mixed methods research. In A. Tashakkori & C. Teddlie (Eds.), *SAGE handbook of mixed methods in social & behavioral research* (pp. 275–304). Thousand Oaks, CA: Sage.

Teddlie, C., & Tashakkori, A. (2009). *Foundations of mixed methods research: Integrating quantitative and qualitative approaches in the social and behavioral sciences.* Thousand Oaks, CA: Sage, Ch. 6, pp. 129–134.

To learn more about visual presentation of procedures in an MMAR study, examine the following sources:

Creswell, J. W., & Plano Clark, V. L. (2011). *Designing and conducting mixed methods research* (2nd ed.). Thousand Oaks, CA: Sage, Ch. 4, pp. 108–111.

Ivankova, N. V., Creswell, J. W., & Stick, S. (2006). Using mixed methods sequential explanatory design: From theory to practice. *Field Methods, 18*(1), 3–20.

Morse, J. M. (1991). Approaches to qualitative-quantitative methodological triangulation. *Nursing Research, 40*(1), 120–123.

7

Sampling and Collecting Data in a Mixed Methods Action Research Study

OBJECTIVES

By the end of this chapter, the reader should be able to

- Understand and apply the steps in the data collection process in an MMAR study,
- Describe major sample types and general sampling strategies used in research,
- Explain sampling issues that should be considered in an MMAR study,
- Describe approaches to sampling in mixed methods research,
- Understand and apply sampling schemes for MMAR study designs,
- Describe major sources of quantitative and qualitative data and their relevance in an MMAR study,
- Explain data collection issues that should be considered in an MMAR study, and
- Understand quantitative and qualitative data integration strategies in an MMAR study.

INTRODUCTION

Revisit the discussion of an MMAR Study Process Model in Chapter 4; refer to Figure 4.1 that visually presents the Model.

Revisit the discussions in Chapters 4 and 6 of the study purpose and research questions in an MMAR study.

Chapters 5 and 6 introduced four basic MMAR study designs and described how quantitative and qualitative methods can be integrated within one study to create strong meta-inferences to guide the steps in the action research process, as reflected in an MMAR Study Process Model. As was discussed in Chapter 6, planning integration of the quantitative and qualitative methods early in an MMAR study process is essential because it helps practitioner-researchers make an informed decision about the choice of an MMAR design and strategies of data collection and analysis that will lead to generating information about finding an effective solution to the practical problem/issue. The way practitioner-researchers plan to integrate quantitative and qualitative research components in an MMAR study process is predetermined by the study purpose and research questions that practitioner-researchers seek to answer to find effective solutions.

The study purpose and research questions guide all methodological decisions in the research process, including the procedures for data collection. Data collection typically includes five research steps. Following these steps systematically helps ensure that the collected information is reliable and credible (Creswell, 2012):

- Selecting the study site and participants
- Obtaining the permissions for conducting research at the chosen site and consent from the participants
- Identifying the types of data to collect
- Locating or developing the data collection tools
- Administering the data collection procedures

A community-based orientation and the practical focus of action research often predetermine the selection of the research site. Since practitioner-researchers tend to study their own practices or conduct research within a specified community, the research site is identified in advance, most often at the study conceptualization stage. The process of data collection begins with the selection and recruitment of the study participants, who will best represent a "community of interest" and will have a stake in the issue that requires investigation (Stringer, 2014, p. 6).

So, how do practitioner-researchers decide who to include as participants in an MMAR study and what sampling strategies to use to ensure that the study sample is inclusive of all the stakeholders who have a vested interest in the study outcomes?

SAMPLING IN AN MMAR STUDY

Overview of Major Sampling Strategies and Sample Types in Research

The concept of **sampling** in a research study has been widely discussed in the research methods texts. In the first edition of the *Handbook of Mixed Methods in Social & Behavioral Research,* Tashakkori and Teddlie

(2003) defined sampling as "selecting units (e.g., events, people, groups, settings, artifacts) in a manner that maximizes the researcher's ability to answer research questions that are set forth in a study" (p. 715). Sampling is an important component of a research study because it helps generate the information about the population of interest (Babbie, 2005). Because it is not possible to always include all people or collect all relevant pieces of information that may be important for the study, a smaller group of people or a selected sample of artifacts is chosen that "might potentially inform the research process" (Stringer & Genat, 2004, p. 41). The purpose of sampling is to ensure that the selected people and informational sources adequately reflect the characteristics of the population for whom the study results are intended and may be relevant. The decisions on the type of sample and criteria for the sample selection have strong implications for the quality of the data collected and the inferences or conclusions that are generated based on these data (Mertens, 2005).

There are two major types of samples: **probability/nonprobability** samples and **purposeful** samples, which are associated with the quantitative and qualitative research approaches, respectively. The difference between these two types of samples lies in whether the study participants are selected randomly, providing an equal opportunity or probability for each individual to be chosen or are selected intentionally or purposefully, choosing only those who have experience with or knowledge about the studied phenomenon or issue. An alternative type of probability sampling is nonprobability or convenience sampling; that is when the study participants are selected from those who are available and who volunteer to participate.

Probability and purposeful samples also differ in the size or number of participants and the extent to which the findings from the sample are generalizable or transferrable to other groups and individuals (Babbie, 2005; Creswell, 2013). Quantitative probability samples tend to include many individuals who represent the studied population, because the goal is to generalize the study results to a much larger group. Qualitative purposeful samples tend to be small, because the purpose is to understand the individuals' experiences about a phenomenon or an issue in more depth (Creswell, 2012). Such individual experiences may be transferrable only to individuals who have similar demographic characteristics. The size of a quantitative sample is calculated, taking into account the degree of the statistical power and effect sizes for determining the significant effect. The size of a qualitative purposeful sample is determined based on whether a researcher has achieved **saturation**—that is, the point in data collection and analysis at which additional individuals or cases do not provide new information (Guest, Bunce, & Johnson, 2006). Each major sample type has a number of varied sampling strategies used to select the research participants. Box 7.1 summarizes the most common probability/nonprobability and purposeful sampling strategies, their purposes, and their specific approaches; it also gives some examples of each strategy.

> Refer to the Further Readings at the end of this chapter for detailed information about major sample types and sampling strategies used in research.

These sampling strategies can be applied in different combinations in an MMAR study, depending on the study purpose, the scope of the project, type of an MMAR study design, and the phase (reconnaissance or evaluation) in the MMAR study process. Combining probability and nonprobability sampling strategies to collect quantitative and qualitative data is advantageous because it allows practitioner-researchers to simultaneously achieve the purposes of generalizability and transferability of the results within the same study, thus obtaining the information about the scope and depth of the participants' views and experiences. Table 7.1 provides the examples of the application of some of these strategies in published MMAR studies in the fields of education, nursing, health care, and psychology. These examples illustrate how

BOX 7.1

Major Sample Types and Sampling Strategies

- *Probability Sample*—Selecting a large number of individuals from the population in a manner that provides equal opportunity for each individual to be chosen; the focus is on selecting study participants who are representative of the studied population (Babbie, 2005; Creswell, 2012; Leman, 2010; Teddlie & Tashakkori, 2009):

  - *Simple random sampling:* Randomly selecting individuals using strategies that ensure equal and independent chance of being selected (e.g., selecting engineering college students using a random numbers table)
  - *Cluster sampling:* Randomly selecting individuals from subgroups or clusters when there is no access to a particular population (e.g., randomly selecting an equal number of orthopedic patients from each hospital in an urban health system)
  - *Stratified sampling:* Randomly selecting individuals from homogenous subgroups or strata proportionally to defined characteristics (e.g., proportionally selecting community residents based on joint household income)
  - *Systematic sampling:* Selecting every preset individual from the list until the needed sample size is reached (e.g., selecting every fifth member of the senior community center)

- *Nonprobability Sample*—Selecting large numbers of individuals in a nonrandom manner from those who are easily accessible; the focus is on potential study participants' accessibility and availability, although they may not be well representative of the studied population (Babbie, 2005; Creswell, 2012; Leman, 2010; Teddlie & Tashakkori, 2009):

  - *Convenience sampling:* Selecting individuals who are available and are willing to participate in the study (e.g., a teacher using his or her own class of students, or a health science researcher recruiting individuals who responded to the study promotion flyer)
  - *Quota sampling:* Selecting individuals based on the required numbers or quotas from the individuals with varying characteristics (e.g., controlling for age, gender, and race when recruiting individuals for large-scale surveys to assess healthy eating habits)

- *Purposeful Sample*—Intentionally selecting a small number of "information rich" participants from those who have knowledge of or experience with the studied phenomenon; the focus is on generating in-depth information and understanding of individual experiences (Creswell, 2012; Davies, 2010; Patton, 2002; Teddlie & Tashakkori, 2009):

  - *Maximal variation sampling:* Purposefully selecting individuals or cases that differ on some demographic or other characteristic (e.g., age, gender, education, work experience, role in the community, etc.)
  - *Typical case sampling:* Purposefully selecting individuals or cases that are the most typical or representative of the studied participant group (e.g., being of the same gender, age, or having the same work experience, etc.)
  - *Extreme case sampling:* Purposefully selecting individuals or cases that are extremely different from each other and the rest in the studied participant group, often referred to as *outlier*

cases (e.g., having extremely opposite experiences with the studied phenomenon/issue in question, etc.)

o *Homogeneous case sampling:* Purposefully selecting individuals or cases that are the members of the same group with defining characteristics (e.g., being residents of the same community or employees of the same organization, etc.)

o *Theoretical (theory-based) sampling:* Purposefully selecting individuals or cases that can help generate a theory about a particular experience or phenomenon (e.g., having experience of maintaining weight loss and healthy eating habits)

o *Snowballing sampling:* Purposefully selecting individuals or cases that are being recommended by other study participants after the study has started (e.g., using innovative science teaching strategy in the fifth grade and referring the researcher to other teachers who use the same strategy)

practitioner-researchers approached and explained the choice of the sampling strategies used in the reconnaissance or evaluation phases of their MMAR studies. The sections that follow discuss specific sampling issues related to mixed methods application in action research and different sampling schemes that can be used in an MMAR study to achieve a desired research goal.

Sampling Considerations in an MMAR Study

Selecting a sample of participants is an important step in a research study because a sample helps generate information about the population of interest (Babbie, 2005). The focus on generalizability of the quantitative results or, alternatively, on in-depth understanding of the qualitative findings, dictates the approaches to sampling and the choice of sampling strategies to be used in the study. When selecting the sampling strategies in an MMAR study, practitioner-researchers also have to decide whether the same sample of individuals should be used for collecting both quantitative and qualitative data, or whether different sampling strategies should be applied to select participants for the quantitative and qualitative study strands. These methodological considerations are related to specific MMAR designs and are further discussed in the chapter. Additionally, practitioner-researchers have to take into account several issues specifically related to action research—that is, the need to represent the views of all potential stakeholders, the practicability of the sample size for solving an issue, the trade-offs of using the nonprobability sampling strategies, use of multiple recruitment venues, and use of incentives.

Stakeholder Representation

In action research a specific focus on addressing a practical problem or issue that affects a group of people and assisting these people with finding an effective solution to this problem influences how practitioner-researchers approach the selection of potential study participants. According to Stringer (2014), a major guiding criterion in identifying a sample in an action research study is "the extent to which a group

TABLE 7.1 Examples of Descriptions of Select Sampling Strategies from Published MMAR Studies

---

Example of simple random sampling strategy used in the reconnaissance phase in Giachello et al. (2003) MMAR study addressing diabetes health disparities

"The specific aim of the telephone survey was to obtain quantitative data on key access, medical, environmental, and behavioral factors that may be associated with racial/ethnic disparities in diabetes risk, prevalence, and quality of care. . . . The telephone survey was based on a probability sample using random digit dialing in pre-selected SIP Code areas (60617, 60633, 60649). Respondents were ≥ 18 years of age. In households with more than one eligible member, the one with the most recent birthday was selected. A total of 411 interviews were completed. Of these, 394 were included in the analysis; individuals who did not self-identify as non-Hispanic black, Hispanic/Latino, or non-Hispanic white were excluded" (p. 316).

Example of convenience sampling strategy used in the evaluation phase in Buck and Cordes (2005) MMAR study addressing preparation of preservice science teachers

"Since this program was in the trial stages and was the focus of a research project, student participation was voluntary. The students were recruited from the science methods courses that occurred in the semester prior to this program. For their participation, the participants received 2 h of graduate credit and $150 worth of diversity materials at the completion of the seminar.

Overall, 22 preservice teachers responded to the advertisement for this field experience and seminar. Two of the students decided not to participate after the initial meeting, leaving 20 participants. All but one of the students completed the program ($N = 19$). This population included 17 females and 2 males. Ten of the participants were seeking certification in grades K–6 and nine were seeking certification in grades 4–9" (pp. 48–49).

Example of quota sampling strategy used in the evaluation phase in Montgomery et al. (2008) MMAR study (Example E) addressing housing services for individuals with mental health problems

"Stage II will address the first three research questions related to clients' quality of life, housing stability, and housing preference. A descriptive cross-sectional survey design and quota-sampling will be used. To be eligible for inclusion in this study, participants must be using or waiting for supported housing services, understand English, and be willing to provide informed consent. To be eligible for CMHA [Canadian Mental Health Association] housing services, a client must have a SMI [serious mental illness] as defined by diagnosis, duration and disability. A minimum sample size is 43 persons per site using the standard deviations and mean scores from the CURA data related to the Lehman Quality of Life scale with a power of .80 and an alpha of .05" (p. 4).

Example of purposeful sampling strategy used in the reconnaissance phase in Thomas-Maclean, Hamoline, Quinlan, Ramsden, and Kuzmicz (2010) MMAR study addressing mentorship program for primary care physicians

"An invitation to participate was sent to 170 physicians with faculty appointments in the Department of Medicine at the University of Saskatchewan. Forty-nine physicians responded to the invitation, and 25 of them were purposefully sampled based on location, sex, and years of experience. Fourteen were urban physicians and 11 were rural; 11 were men and 14 were women; and 10 were junior faculty and 15 were senior. Senior physicians were defined as those who graduated from medical school before 1980, and junior physicians were those who graduated after 1995" (p. e266).

Example of maximal variation sampling strategy used in the evaluation phase in Bond, Cole, Fletcher, Noble, and O'Connell (2011) MMAR study addressing a school-based program for children with motor skills difficulties

"An initial evaluation phase focused on eight schools from the 39 schools that had been trained since 2006, when the project begin. A selected sample of schools was approached in order to represent different localities; schools where different members of the research team had been involved and schools who had been implementing the programme for different lengths of time and therefore might have different views on implementation or sustainability issues. This sample was purposefully selected in order to explore the experiences of a potentially diverse group of schools. Schools selected included; schools which had been part of the first cohort in 2006 who were still running targeted motor)-skills interventions, schools trained in 2006 who had ceased to run interventions and schools that had been trained in 2008 and were beginning to embed the programme" (p. 341).

Example of homogenous case sampling strategy used in the evaluation phase in Blackford and Street (2012) MMAR study addressing community palliative care services

"Three Victorian-based community palliative care services, two metropolitan (Site A and B) and one regional site (Site C), were recruited through their prior involvement with the Respecting Patient Choices® programme described earlier. They became collaborative partners and participated in the design of the study and the implementation of the Model. In feasibility studies, it is suggested that it is important to maintain homogenous samples in the early stage of the study (Burns & Grove, 2009). Homogeneity existed because all community services were from Victoria and managed by the State government and therefore they had similar client populations, reporting mechanisms, funding and service profiles (see Tables 1 and 2). Differences existed in the size of the services, which is reflected in the staff (see Table 2) and client profile and organizational configuration (see Table 1)" (p. 2023).

Example of snowballing sampling strategy used in the reconnaissance phase in Zoellner et al. (2012) MMAR study addressing community garden program

"The qualitative phase consisted of key informant interviews with community stakeholders who were external to the obesity task force at the time of the interview. At a monthly CBPR [community-based participatory research] obesity task force meeting, the nutrition subcommittee members informed attendees of the goals of the qualitative interviews and encouraged members to suggest relevant stakeholders representing a variety of community sectors. Through snowball sampling procedures, a total of 52 community stakeholders from a variety of sectors (e.g., education, church, community, recreation, health care, farming) were identified. Of these 52 stakeholders, 10 agreed to participate in the study" (pp. 155–156).

or individual is affected by or has an effect on the problem or issue of interest" (p. 77). Therefore, it becomes important to identify and include the representatives of all potential stakeholders who have a stake in the problem and may provide a critical insight into it. To achieve this purpose, Stringer (2014) recommended conducting a preliminary social analysis of the community setting to ensure that the representatives of all stakeholder groups across ages, genders, races, community roles, and so on are included in the study, whereas Hacker (2013) suggested asking community partners to help with participant recruitment.

For example, in her MMAR study (Example C), Craig (2011) explored the views of multiple stakeholders to inform the development of an effective system of care for GLBTQ young people. These stakeholders included local and national service providers, community leaders, educators, and young people identified as GLBTQ. In another MMAR study, Torre and Fine (2005) selected inmate women, correctional administrators and officers, and college faculty because the researchers considered the perspectives and experiences of those stakeholders important in understanding the impact of a higher education program in prison. Similarly, in their research protocol for an MMAR study, Hinchcliff and colleagues (2012) suggested recruiting multiple stakeholders to evaluate current Australian health service accreditation processes, including representatives from the accreditation agencies, federal and state government departments, professional colleges and associations, consumer advocates, and staff of acute, primary, and aged care services.

Sample Size

Deciding on the size of the sample is another critical component that practitioner-researchers have to consider when designing an MMAR study. Often the need to promptly address a practical problem within a community or a professional setting necessitates the use of a small number of participants confined by a specified intact group. For example, Kostos and Shin (2010; Example A) used a single second-grade classroom to explore the use of math journals to enhance students' communication of mathematical thinking. Sixteen second graders from a classroom of 20 participated in the study. Likewise, the setting for Glasson and colleagues' (2006) MMAR study (Example B) was one acute medical ward located in a public hospital in Sydney. The researchers used 60 patients hospitalized in the same medical ward and 15 nurses who were registered permanent staff members in this ward to test a new model of nursing care for older patients. In another MMAR study conducted by Richardson and Reid (2006), the researchers used only five participants to develop and evaluate a group cognitive–behavioral therapy program for older adults with depression. However, a small sample size was outweighed by the use of mixed methods, which, in the authors' words, "encourages the synthesis, or triangulation of both qualitative and quantitative types of data from multiple sources" and helps transform a weakness of a small sample size into a "design strength" (p. 62).

At the same time, large-scale MMAR projects that address global educational, social, or health issues may involve large numbers of participants at multiple sites. Such studies are typically conducted in close collaboration with multiple stakeholders and community members "to address a mutually agreed-on challenge or goal" (Thornewill et al., 2011, p. S125). For example, in their MMAR study Thornewill and colleagues (2011) investigated health information exchange needs for 12 health-care stakeholder groups and the consumers they served in a large metropolitan area in the United States. A total of 1,182 individuals representing health-care providers and community dwellers participated in different forms of surveys (phone-, paper-, and Web-based) in the quantitative study strand and focus group discussions in a qualitative strand. Similarly, in another MMAR study a team of educational psychologists and school teachers from the United Kingdom used a large sample to evaluate an intervention program designed to improve provision for children with motor skills difficulties (Bond et al., 2011). This 3-year action research project was conducted in 39 schools in one inner-city local community and involved quantitative surveys and qualitative interviews with the school personnel.

Sample Type

Another consideration for practitioner-researchers is to decide whether to employ a probability or a non-probability sampling strategy when designing an MMAR study. In spite of the fact that a probability random sample is viewed as the "gold standard" in research (Wright & London, 2009, p. 62), a focus on a local community in most action research projects calls for the use of a convenience sample selected from small, intact groups of people with predefined characteristics, such as a classroom, hospital ward, or a residential area. Convenience sampling allows practitioner-researchers to quickly select the study participants affected by the problem that requires an immediate solution. Although nonprobability sampling introduces limitations on generalizing the study results to a larger population, a convenience sampling strategy seems appropriate when conducting needs assessment and collecting background information for the problem during the study reconnaissance phase (James et al., 2008), or when seeking more in-depth information about the action/intervention results (Stringer & Genat, 2004).

For example, Buck and Cordes (2005) used a convenience sampling strategy to recruit 22 preservice teachers to evaluate a program designed to prepare science teachers to meet the needs of the underserved student population. This selection strategy was justified because the researchers evaluated the program that was designed for this group of students in a specific college major. However, a random sampling strategy may be used when an MMAR project is aimed at addressing an issue within a larger community. For example, in Giachello and colleagues' (2003) MMAR study discussed in Chapter 2, a random digit dialing was used to select residential households for a telephone survey with the purpose of obtaining representative quantitative data on the primary access, medical, environmental, and behavioral factors that may be associated with racial/ethnic disparities in diabetes risk, prevalence, and quality of care.

Refer to Chapter 2 and Box 2.3 for the example and discussion of Giachello and colleagues' (2003) MMAR study.

Recruitment Venues and Use of Incentives

Obtaining a representative sample of participants is an important consideration in any research study. Since a sample in an MMAR study should be inclusive of all potential stakeholder groups, practitioner-researchers often use multiple venues to recruit study participants. Conducting research within a researcher's own organization or professional practice usually provides an easy access to participants. For example, Kostos and Shin (2010; Example A) studied Kostos's second-grade classroom, Buck and Cordes (2005) recruited preservice science teachers from the program they taught in, while Glasson and colleagues (2006; Example B) engaged patients and nurses in one acute medical ward.

However, when conducting research in a larger community setting, practitioner-researchers often seek help of "opinion leaders" or "gatekeepers" to help obtain access to potential study participants (Stringer, 2014). Securing community access requires establishing good rapport with community gatekeepers and engaging them as collaborators according to the principles of action research. Strand, Marullo, Cutforth, Stoecker, and Donohue (2003) observed, "When community members know about and support a research project, they are far more likely to be

Refer to Chapter 2 for the discussion of collaboration and participation as essential features of action research.

willing participants and may even seek out researchers to volunteer their participation as respondents or even as researchers" (p. 108). They also recommended using incentives—such as gift cards, money, meals, and other tokens of appreciation—to facilitate people's involvement in the study. Additionally, providing incentives may become an important recruitment strategy in an MMAR study that requires extensive participation of the same individuals in several study strands—for example, in both survey and focus groups.

To illustrate, in an MMAR study aimed at identifying health problems for American Indians in the Tulsa area of Oklahoma, Johnson, Bartgis, Worley, Hellman, and Burkhart (2010) recruited the study participants in a variety of ways: sending letters to students' parents, publishing advertisements in local newspapers, posting flyers in churches, distributing project information at community events, and making in-person requests. Eligible participants were offered $20 gift cards to Wal-Mart. The goal of this recruitment strategy was "to obtain a representative sample from different regions (by zip code) in the Tulsa area" (p. 54). Similarly, to understand perception of health in African American communities in Arizona, Hussaini, Hamm, and Means (2013) combined the efforts of the Arizona Department of Health and community-based partners to recruit potential participants for focus group interviews using recruitment flyers. Focus group participants were given monetary incentives of $55 for participation. This incentive was increased to $65 and $75 to encourage the same individuals to participate in the subsequent second and third focus groups. Box 7.2 summarizes sampling considerations that practitioner-researchers should take into account when designing an MMAR study.

So, how can practitioner-researchers select the participants for an MMAR study? What are the sampling schemes that practitioner-researchers can apply in different MMAR study designs?

BOX 7.2

Sampling Considerations in an MMAR Study

- Probability and nonprobability sampling strategies can be combined within the same MMAR study to achieve both the purposes of generalizability and transferability of participants' views and experiences.
- More emphasis may be given to nonprobability (convenience) and purposeful sampling strategies due to the confined nature of MMAR projects and focus on intact groups.
- The focus on generalizability of the study results to a larger population may be shifted toward the need to address a practical problem/issue.
- Representatives of all potential stakeholder groups who may have an interest in the problem/issue should be included in the sample.
- Smaller sample sizes may be more efficient when there is a need to promptly address a practical problem/issue within a professional or community setting.
- A variety of recruitment methods and access to the community can help secure a representative sample of all stakeholder groups.
- Incentives may help enhance recruitment and participation of the same individuals in several study strands.

Approaches to Sampling in Mixed Methods Research

Different combinations of probability and nonprobability sampling strategies in mixed methods studies have been addressed by several authors, however no agreed-on typology of mixed methods sampling strategies is readily available (Collins, 2010; Teddlie & Tashakkori, 2009). Onwuegbuzie and Leech (2007) identified 24 sampling schemes that are associated with quantitative and qualitative research approaches—5 probabilistic or random and 19 nonprobabilistic or nonrandom—that can be used in mixed methods studies. Collins, Onwuegbuzie, and Jiao (2007) analyzed how sampling was conducted in mixed methods studies according to the timing of the implementation of the quantitative and qualitative strands (concurrent and sequential) and the relationship between the quantitative and qualitative samples within the study. Based on the review of 121 empirical studies in nine disciplines, the authors reported that two thirds of the studies used concurrent sampling. In a later work, Collins (2010) emphasized the connection between mixed methods sampling decisions and other study research components, such as the study goals, objectives, purpose, research questions, design, sampling, and sample size.

Teddlie and Yu (2007) and Teddlie and Tashakkori (2009) proposed a provisional typology of mixed methods sampling strategies that included five groups of strategies: (1) basic mixed methods sampling strategies, (2) sequential mixed methods sampling, (3) parallel mixed methods sampling, (4) multilevel mixed methods sampling, and (5) multiple mixed methods sampling strategies. In this typology, concurrent and sequential mixed methods sampling strategies are based on the characteristics of the established concurrent and sequential mixed methods designs. Similarly, Creswell and Plano Clark (2011) related the choice of sampling strategies to specific mixed methods design considerations, such as timing or the sequence of the quantitative and qualitative data collection, and the priority or weighting of each data set in a study.

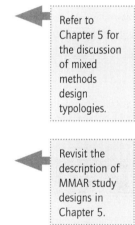

Refer to Chapter 5 for the discussion of mixed methods design typologies.

Revisit the description of MMAR study designs in Chapter 5.

Following the discussion of sampling in mixed methods literature (Creswell & Plano Clark, 2011; Teddlie & Tashakkori, 2009; Teddlie & Yu, 2007) sampling schemes for an MMAR study are grounded in the methodological characteristics of MMAR designs. These sampling schemes offer different combinations of probability, nonprobability, and purposeful sampling strategies presented in the context of sampling concerns that practitioner-researchers have to consider when designing and implementing MMAR studies.

SAMPLING SCHEMES FOR MMAR STUDY DESIGNS

Sampling Scheme for a Concurrent Quan + Qual MMAR Study Design

Concurrent Quan + Qual sampling involves selecting different or the same individuals or cases for quantitative and qualitative strands by independently combining probability/nonprobability and purposeful sampling strategies. Selecting the same participants for both study strands may be consistent with a practical purpose of an MMAR study because it is easier to get access to potential participants within one's own practice or community. Additionally, the need to address the problem/issue quickly may necessitate selecting the same individuals. However, when practitioner-researchers want to explore the problem or evaluate the action/intervention from different stakeholder perspectives, it may be more appropriate to select different samples of individuals or cases for the quantitative and qualitative study strands. Figure 7.1 presents a conceptual diagram of a concurrent sampling scheme for Quan + Qual MMAR study design.

For example, Kostos and Shin (2010; Example A) used one sample of second-grade students in Kostos's classroom to collect quantitative and qualitative data in two study strands. The researchers applied a nonprobability convenience sampling strategy when they administered a math assessment to all students in the class and asked all students to complete math journals. The researchers also used a probability random sampling when they selected 8 students out of 16 to participate in the interviews at the end of the study. Similarly, Blanco and colleagues (2010) used one sample of college students to collect the quantitative survey and qualitative interview data when exploring the impact of the strategy awareness–raising program on students' learning process. A convenience sample of 24 students recruited from three beginning-level Spanish courses completed the survey. Concurrently, 11 students were purposefully selected from the same group of students to participate in individual interviews to better explore the impact of the program. Thornewill and colleagues (2011) approached sampling differently in their MMAR study. They used various sampling strategies to select different groups of individuals to investigate health information exchange needs for 12 health-care stakeholders. Thus, they randomly selected 386 community residents to complete a phone quantitative survey. Additionally, they used a convenience sample of respondents when they distributed the same survey in the area physician offices and at state fair booths. In the qualitative strand, they used a purposeful sampling strategy to select 191 community leaders to take part in focus group interviews.

| FIGURE 7.1 | **Conceptual Diagram of a Concurrent Sampling Scheme for Quan + Qual MMAR Study Design** |

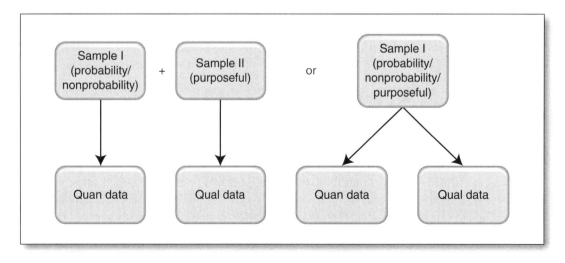

Sampling Scheme for a Sequential Quan → Qual MMAR Study Design

Sequential sampling for Quan → Qual MMAR design involves selecting individuals or cases for quantitative and qualitative strands sequentially or chronologically by applying probability/nonprobability and purposeful sampling strategies. Following a sequential implementation of the study strands in this design, the results from the initial quantitative strand are used to inform the selection of participants for the following qualitative strand. Because the purpose of a sequential Quan → Qual design is to elaborate, explain, or confirm the initial quantitative results to obtain a more complete understanding of the emergent trends and relationships in the data, it is recommended to select the participants for the follow-up qualitative strand from those who participated in the initial quantitative study strand (Creswell & Plano Clark, 2011). Using the same participants for the quantitative and qualitative study strands meets the practical purposes of an MMAR study as discussed above. Often fewer individuals are selected for a qualitative follow-up because the focus is on an in-depth exploration of the problem. Such participants can represent either typical responses to an initial quantitative survey, extreme or outlier cases, or unexpected or contradicting viewpoints (Ivankova, 2014; Ivankova et al., 2006; Morse & Niehaus, 2009). However, in an MMAR study, different participants for the qualitative follow-up also may be selected in an attempt to explore a broader range of stakeholders' perspectives on the studied issue. Figure 7.2 presents a conceptual diagram of a sequential sampling scheme for Quan → Qual MMAR study design.

For example, in a published research protocol for an MMAR study, Montgomery and colleagues (2008; Example E) proposed to use a nonprobability quota sampling strategy to initially select the clients from four supported housing units for individuals with serious mental illness in order to complete several quantitative questionnaires. Building on these quantitative results in the follow-up qualitative strand, the researchers planned to purposefully select the representatives from three stakeholder groups—clients, their families, and community health workers—to get a broader perspective on a supported housing program to inform the requisite policy changes. In another MMAR study, Aldridge, Fraser, Bell, and Dorman (2012) used a convenience sampling strategy to select a large sample of 2,043 students from nine coeducational schools in Western Australia to complete the newly developed quantitative questionnaire aimed at assessing students' perceptions of a classroom learning environment. In the qualitative strand, eight teachers were purposefully selected

---

FIGURE 7.2 **Conceptual Diagram of a Sequential Sampling Scheme for Quan → Qual MMAR Study Design**

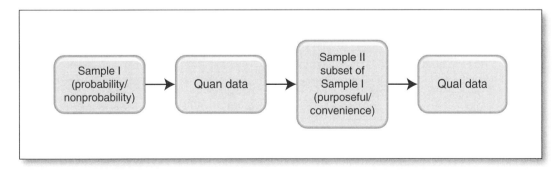

for individual interviews to further explore the teaching strategies they implemented in the classroom in order to better understand the students' survey responses related to the impact of the instructional strategies on their learning.

Sampling Scheme for a Sequential Qual → Quan MMAR Study Design

Similar to sequential sampling for Quan → Qual MMAR design, sequential sampling for Qual → Quan MMAR design involves selecting individuals or cases sequentially. In this design, purposeful sampling strategies are applied in the first, qualitative study strand to explore select participants' experiences with the studied situation or issue. Probability/nonprobability sampling strategies are used in the second, quantitative strand to select a larger sample for the quantitative examination of these experiences. Following a sequential implementation of the study strands in this design, the results from the initial qualitative strand are used to inform the selection of the participants for the following quantitative strand. Since the primary goal of this design is, first to explore the phenomenon of interest and then to test the revealed variables and relationships quantitatively with the purpose of trying to generalize the results to a larger population, a different and a larger sample is needed for the quantitative strand. Ideally, the individuals in the quantitative sample should be similar in major demographic characteristics to those in the qualitative sample to avoid potential inconsistencies in the interpretation of the qualitative and quantitative results (Creswell & Plano Clark, 2011). Employing this sampling scheme may fit the inclusive and collaborative nature of action research well because it allows for exploring the issue or the situation with a few key informants, and then using this information to develop a culturally relevant instrument for surveying larger groups of stakeholders about the same problem/issue. Figure 7.3 presents a conceptual diagram of a sequential sampling scheme for Qual → Quan MMAR study design.

For example, Craig (2011; Example C) used documented evidence about existing national and local GLBTQ programs for young people to purposefully select 45 local service providers, community leaders, and other stakeholders for initial individual interviews. In addition, 180 youths were selected using a convenience sampling strategy to participate in 10 focus groups. During the second, quantitative strand, the researcher used a nonprobability venue-based sampling strategy to select 273 GLBTQ youths to complete a survey instrument that was developed based on the qualitative domains revealed through interviews and focus groups in the

FIGURE 7.3   **Conceptual Diagram of a Sequential Sampling Scheme for Qual → Quan MMAR Study Design**

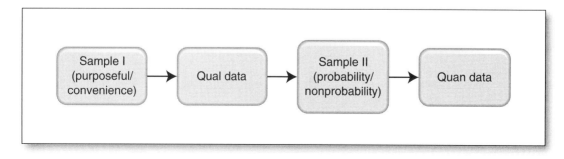

first, qualitative study strand. Similarly, in Reese and colleagues' (1999) MMAR study that explored cultural and institutional barriers to access and use of hospices by African Americans, six African American pastors were purposefully selected from six different congregation churches to participate in individual interviews in order to inform the development of the survey instrument. The selection of the pastors for this study strand was particularly important because it took into account the significant role that a church plays in African American culture. During the second study strand, a convenience sample of 98 shelter residents completed the instrument to test the hypothesis generated based on the initial qualitative findings.

Sampling Scheme for a Multistrand MMAR Study Design

As discussed in Chapter 5, a multistrand MMAR design may include more than two concurrent or sequential strands. So, a sampling scheme for this design will reflect its complex nature and combine probability/nonprobability and purposeful sampling strategies applied concurrently and sequentially in different study strands. Depending on the number of concurrent and sequential strands planned for a multistrand MMAR study, practitioner-researchers can select individuals or cases using MMAR sampling schemes for two sequential or concurrent study strands, as described in earlier sections. To decide on a specific sampling scheme, practitioner-researchers should consider the purposes of the quantitative and qualitative study strands and the timing (concurrent or sequential) of their implementation in a multistrand MMAR study.

For example, Akintobi and colleagues (2012) employed a multistrand Quan → Qual → Quan + Qual sampling scheme to select the participants for the three strands of their MMAR study. The researchers first selected a convenience sampling of 20 organizational designees to respond to the quantitative questionnaire during the program implementation, and then used the same sample of participating organizations for follow-up, one-on-one, semistructured qualitative teleconferences to gain a better insight into their training needs as based on the quantitative assessment. At the completion of all evaluation-capacity-building activities, the researchers concurrently collected additional quantitative assessment and qualitative interview data from a larger group of representatives of the same organizations on the evaluation-capacity-building partnerships.

Refer to Chapter 5 for a more detailed description of Akintobi and colleagues' (2012) multistrand MMAR study.

In another MMAR study, Vecchiarelli and colleagues (2005) used a sequential Qual → Quan → Quan sampling scheme when they selected a convenience sample of 100 school community stakeholders for a Delphi process to identify the criteria to include in a Nutrition Friendly School program, and then used the same sample to quantitatively assess the identified criteria. In a subsequent quantitative study strand, the new self-evaluation tool informed by the Delphi process analysis was pilot tested with a large nonprobability convenience sample of teachers, administrators, food service staff, and nurses.

Refer to Chapter 5 for a more detailed description of Vecchiarelli and colleagues' (2005) multistrand MMAR study.

Sampling decisions are closely related to decisions about the types of information to collect from the selected participants in the study. The rest of the chapter discusses common sources of quantitative and qualitative data and their applications in different MMAR study designs. So, what are the sources of quantitative and qualitative data that are commonly used in an MMAR study, and how do practitioner-researchers decide on their relevance for the practical purposes pursued in the study?

DATA COLLECTION IN AN MMAR STUDY

Refer to Chapter 4 for the discussion of the ethical issues that should be taken into consideration in an MMAR study.

Once a sampling scheme for an MMAR study is selected and the site and potential study participants are identified, the next step is to decide what quantitative and qualitative data should be collected to best address the problem or issue, and what permissions should be obtained for conducting the study. Tomal (2010) argued that selecting the best method of data collection is "a crucial aspect in ensuring the acquisition of relevant and valid information" in an action research study (p. 35). As the first step in deciding what information to select, it may be useful to explore what data are already available that may have relevance to the proposed study and that may provide insight into how to address the issue (Herr & Anderson, 2005). For example, Downs and colleagues (2009) described how they used the available secondary data about the environmental stressors of violent crime and asthma rates along with containment effects of average time spent indoors to determine what components should be included in the intervention targeting adverse health outcomes for residents of a low-income multiethnic urban community in England.

Revisit the review in Chapter 3 of the application of mixed methods in published action research studies.

In an MMAR study, different types of quantitative and qualitative data and in various combinations can be collected during the reconnaissance and evaluation phases, first to provide a comprehensive initial assessment of the practical problem/issue, and then to conduct a thorough evaluation of the developed and implemented action/intervention. Similar to making decisions about what sampling strategies to employ, the choice and combination of the quantitative and qualitative data sources depend on an MMAR study purpose, the scope of research project, the type of MMAR study design, and the phase (reconnaissance or evaluation) in an MMAR study process.

Quantitative Data Sources

Refer to the Further Readings at the end of this chapter for detailed information about quantitative data sources.

Quantitative data provide numerical information and involve measuring variables. The purpose is to compare individuals or groups of individuals on a certain measure or measures, or to test the relationship between the variables. In action research, quantitative data are useful for conducting the initial needs assessment using numeric indicators, providing evidence for the problem or issue, obtaining the attitudes about the issue from large groups of stakeholders, and identifying a potential direction for the action/intervention. Quantitative data also play an important role when it is necessary to evaluate the effectiveness of the action/intervention, survey the views of stakeholders' about its impact, identify the critical barriers and facilitators, and inform the future direction of the change implementation. Although their value and importance is recognized (Koshy et al., 2011; Mills, 2011; Tomal, 2010), quantitative data are reportedly less represented in action research. At the same time, a growing number of MMAR studies across the disciplines provide supporting evidence that quantitative data in combination with qualitative data are necessary for a comprehensive assessment of the problem and for a more complete evaluation of the action/intervention outcomes.

Based on the review of published MMAR studies, the most common sources of quantitative data are surveys, different forms of assessment, and observation checklists. Box 7.3 summarizes each quantitative data source, lists the advantages for its use in an MMAR study along with the issues to consider, and provides an illustration of its application in published MMAR studies.

BOX 7.3

Common Quantitative Data Sources in an MMAR Study

- *Survey* is a process of gathering data employing questionnaires consisting of items with fixed response options aimed to collect attitudes and opinions on the studied issue from a large group of people; open-ended questions often are also included to help clarify the selected responses or solicit additional information. Surveys help collect large amounts of data to show the trends in different stakeholders' views and opinions about the problem or issue, the needed action/intervention, and the effectiveness of the taken action; in combination with qualitative data, surveys can generate more complete assessment of the issue and provide data about the intervention effectiveness. Surveys can be adminsitered personally (door to door), via mail, phone, e-mail, Internet, or in a mixed (combined) mode; surveys also require adherence to systematic follow-up procedures (Creswell, 2012; Dillman, Smythe, & Christian, 2009; Hinchey, 2008; Koshy et al., 2011; Teddlie & Tashakkori, 2009).

  o Advantages for an MMAR study:

   - It is an effective method to collect background information about the issue and stakeholders' opinions in a short period of time, and can be used both in the reconnaisance phase to help assess the situation and in the evaluation phase to help measure the effect of the change effort and inform the needed modifications in the action/intervention plan.
   - It is an effective means to identify potential participants to follow up with individual interviews, focus groups, or observations.
   - It can be used as a primary or supplemental data source in all concurrent and sequential MMAR study designs consistent with the study purpose.

  o Issues to consider:

   - It can be time-consuming and may require additional training to locate or develop and test a survey instrument that will elicit credible and honest responses.

(Continued)

(Continued)

- It is necessary to follow systematic procedures in the survey administration and correctly identify a target population.
- It can be difficult to get compliance from all stakeholders to complete the survey, which may introduce a bias in the presentation of the results.
- It can be difficult to get community members and other stakeholders to assist with the survey administration without ensuring they have proper training and education.

o Illustration:

- In a concurrent Quan + Qual MMAR study, Giachello et al. (2003) conducted a telephone survey of 441 randomly selected community residents to obtain quantitative assessment data about the critical factors that may be associated with racial disparities in diabetes risk, prevalence, and quality of care (the reconnaissance phase).
- In a multistrand MMAR study, Sampson (2010; Example D) used surveys first to obtain the information about students' learning and teaching style preferences, and then to evaluate their learning experiences in a new instructional format; the second questionnaire was informed by the findings from the students' qualitative learning journal (the reconnaissance and evaluation phases).

- *Assessment* is a process of gathering data employing instruments consisting of close-ended questions or fixed categories aimed at evaluating an individual's performance, ability, or health condition. An assessment often takes the form of a test, rubric, record, report card, portfolio, etc. that yields numeric indicators to inform the studied issue; it may also contain open-ended items that are assigned a score on a numeric scale. Assessment tools are often used to collect benchmark data before the action/intervention implementation (baseline or pretest) and post-intervention (posttest) data for evaluating purposes and measuring a potential change. Teacher-made and standardized aptitude and achievement tests are widely used in educational action research; the first help monitor and adjust instruction, while the latter inform administrators and policymakers of students' relative standing (Creswell, 2012; Mills, 2011; Teddlie & Tashakkori, 2009; Tomal, 2010):

o Advantages for an MMAR study:

- It is an effective tool for collecting benchmark indicators or baseline data to inform the action and for testing the effectiveness of the intervention because it allows for noting change over time. It can be used both in the reconnaisance phase to help conduct the needs assessment, and in the evaluation phase to help measure the effect of the change effort and inform the needed modifications in the action/intervention plan.
- It may be used in a large-scale MMAR project involving a randomized controlled trial to assess the effects of the intervention.
- It is an effective means to identify individuals to follow up with semistructured or focus group interviews or observations in Quan → Qual MMAR design.
- It can be used as a primary or supplemental data source in all concurrent and sequential MMAR study designs, consistent with the study purpose.

o Issues to consider:

  - It can be difficult to develop a self-made test or assessment with sound psychometric properties to produce credible information.
  - It is necessary to follow standardized systematic procedures when collecting assessment data to avoid bias and error.
  - It may be difficult to involve community residents and other stakeholders in assisting with collecting assessment data because the procedures may require professional skills and training.
  - It is important to consider a potential presence of cultural bias in educational and cognitive ability tests and its effect on the resulting scores for minority groups.

o Illustration:

  - In a concurrent Quan + Qual MMAR study, Bradley and Puoane (2007) collected anthropometric measurements (height, weight, and blood pressure) from 43 community health workers as part of an overall assessment to gain an understanding of local factors contributing to increased risk of hypertension and diabetes among community residents, and to inform culturally appropriate prevention and treatment interventions. Community health workers were later trained by a professional nurse to assist with subsequent anthropometric measurements (the reconnaissance phase).
  - In a concurrent Quan + Qual MMAR study, Kostos and Shin (2010; Example A) collected math assessment scores before and after the instructional (math journaling) intervention as part of the evaluation process to measure the effects of math journals on enhancing second graders' communication of mathematical thinking (the evaluation phase).

- *Observation checklist* is a process of gathering data employing a list of indicators that guides the observation and recording of a prespecified behavior at predetermined intervals or during the observation interval (continuous recording); this checklist is often referred to as a *quantitative structured observation*. The focus is on specific incidents or behaviors as they are monitored in a group over time. Observation checklists serve to help with the needs assessment or evaluation of the people's responses to action/intervention; the observer has to select the most appropriate response for each demonstrated or not demonstrated behavior. When used as a *critical* or *significant incident log,* it also includes a brief description of the incident (James et al., 2008; Koshy et al., 2011; Teddlie & Tashakkori, 2009; Tomal, 2010).

o Advantages for an MMAR study:

  - It is an effective tool for testing interventions and allows for noting change over time. It can be used both in the reconnaisance phase to help assess the individuals' needs and in the evaluation phase to help measure the effect of the change effort and inform the needed modifications in the action/intervention plan.
  - It can provide the foundation for reflective discussions of the studied issue over time.

(Continued)

(Continued)

- It can be used as a complementary data source and supplement other forms of data to develop a holistic and convincing view of the situation and to measure a response to action/intervention.
- It can be used as a supplemental data source in all concurrent and sequential MMAR study designs, consistent with the study purpose.

○ Issues to consider:

- It can be time-consuming and require additional training to develop and pilot test the checklist that will accurately capture the targeted behaviors.
- It is necessary to develop a precise definition of each behavior so that a specific behavior becomes easily recognizable.
- It requires training of stakeholders in the use of checklists.
- It is important to enage multiple observers to rate the same behavior during the same period to produce consisent results.

○ Illustration:

- In a multistrand MMAR study, Phillips and Davidson (2009) used a chart audit to examine the level and type of care provided to aged residents during their last 72 hours of life and to identify priorities for the needed action/intervention. Two clinicians conducted the audit using selected outcome criteria specified in the best practice guidelines (the reconnaissance phase).
- In a concurrent Quan + Qual MMAR study, Galini and Efthymia (2010) employed observation checklists when they observed teachers for 4.5 hours in 15 daily programs during a set of 15 free-play and 56 organized activities with the goal of evaluating a new model of formative assessments in the kindergarten. Teachers' behaviors were recorded every three minutes during every cycle of the program activities (the evaluation phase).

Qualitative Data Sources

Qualitative data produce narrative information about individuals' experiences, behaviors, and feelings in the natural environments. The purpose is to gain insight into individuals' perceptions of and their experiences with reality (Creswell, 2013). In action research, qualitative data are useful in helping identify the problem or issue, present it in stakeholders' words, and develop understandings and potential solutions to the problem (Stringer, 2014). Qualitative data can be equally useful in helping practitioner-researchers to explore stakeholders' perceptions of the impact of the action/intervention, to understand the barriers and facilitators to change, and to inform the future direction of the change action. Therefore, qualitative data are viewed as an important component of participatory action research by many action research authors (Koshy et al., 2011; McNiff & Whitehead, 2011; Stringer, 2014).

The most common sources of qualitative data used in MMAR studies are individual or one-on-one interviews, focus group interviews, naturalistic observations, documents, and audiovisual materials and photo-voice. Box 7.4 summarizes each qualitative data source, lists the advantages for its use in an MMAR study, details the issues to consider, and provides an illustration of the application of qualitative data in published MMAR studies.

 Refer to the Further Readings at the end of this chapter for detailed information about qualitative data sources.

BOX 7.4

Common Qualitative Data Sources in an MMAR Study

- *Individual or one-on-one interview* is a one-on-one conversation between an interviewee and an interviewer to collect rich in-depth information about an interviewee's experiences with and views on the studied issue. An interview is the most common data source in action research and is often referred to as a *key informant interview.* Semistructured interviews are guided by an interviews protocol that consitsts of 10 to 15 open-ended questions with probing or stimulating questions. Interviews may be elicited by using supporting materials to help uncover unarticulated knowledge. The conversation is typically recorded and then transcribed verbatim. Interviews can be conducted face-to-face, or via phone, e-mail, Skype, and social networking venues, such as Facebook, and may involve several sessions with the same interviewee (Creswell, 2013; Johnson & Weller, 2001; Koshy et al., 2011; Teddlie & Tashakkori, 2009).

  o Advantages for an MMAR study:

    - It provides a firsthand account of the experiences with the issue and can be used both in the reconnaisance phase to help explore stakeholders' individual needs and in the evaluation phase to help explore the relevance and usefulness of the action/intervention and inform the needed modifications.

    - It is an effective method of exploring the experiences and views of community members and other stakeholders who may not be comfortable speaking in a group, particularly on sensitive topics.

    - It is an effective venue to get community members and other stakeholders actively involved with the data collection process.

    - It can be used as a primary or supplemental data source in all concurrent and sequential MMAR study designs, consistent with the study purpose.

  o Issues to consider:

    - It can be time-consuming, and transcribing a recorded interview verbatim may be labor intensive.

(Continued)

(Continued)

- It may not be an effective data collection strategy for individuals with limited language proficiency, limited social skills, and other disorders.
- It may be intimidating for some individuals to have their interview recorded and they may refuse to allow a recording to be made, thus leaving it for the interviewer to rely on written notes.
- It requires training of stakeholders in qualitative interviewing and transcribing techniques.

○ Illustration:

- In a sequential Quan → Qual MMAR study, Pickard (2006) planned to conduct semistructured interviews with university faculty and students to follow up on the major findings from the quantitative survey related to students' behavior and staff experiences with plagiarism (the reconnaissance phase).
- In a concurrent Quan + Qual MMAR study, Blackford and Street (2012) conducted nine key informant interviews with service managers, senior nursing staff, and allied health staff to explore the feasibility of the developed advanced care planning model in community palliative care services (the evaluation phase).

- *Focus group interview* is a type of a group interview or discussion in which a representative group of key informants is brought together to explore their perceptions of a problem of interest or experiences with the studied issue. A group discussion format can stimulate participants to exchange their views, motives, and feelings and is particularly useful for exploring controversial viewpoints. A focus group typically includes 5–10 participants. The discussion is facilitated by a moderator and one or two co-moderators. The questions are stated broadly and are aimed at facilitating an honest and open discussion of the issue (Creswell, 2013; Koshy et al., 2011; Kreuger & Casey, 2008; Teddlie & Tashakkori, 2009).

○ Advantages for an MMAR study:

- It is an efficient method for exploring the experiences and views of different stakeholders within one session.
- It can be used both in the reconnaisance phase to help assess the scope and depth of the problem, and in the evaluation phase to help explore the relevance and usefulness of the action/intervention and to inform the needed modifications.
- It can be used as a primary or supplemental data source in all MMAR study designs, consistent with the study purpose. It usually plays a major role in a sequential Qual → Qual MMAR design, however, due to its suitability for the initial exploration of the issue from multiple stakeholders' perspectives.

○ Issues to consider:

- It can be difficult to get stakeholders' compliance to attend and participate in a focus group.
- It may require financial resources to provide incentives for participation, such as food and gift cards.

- It is important to observe the issues of power within a focus group and ensure the participants have equal opportunities to contribute to the discussion.
- It requires training of community members and other stakeholders in focus group facilitating and recording techniques.

o Illustration:

- In a sequential Qual → Quan MMAR study, Craig (2011; Example C) conducted 10 focus groups with 180 GLBTQ young people to obtain their perspectives about the needed system of care and to inform the development of the survey instrument to assess the views of a large group of GLBTQ youths (the reconnaissance phase).
- In a concurrent Quan + Qual MMAR study, Aubel, Toure, and Diagne (2004) utilized focus group interviews with grandmothers, men, nurses, health workers, and schoolteachers in 13 villages to evaluate the intervention aimed at promoting improved nutritional practices related to pregnant women and infant feeding in Senegal (the evaluation phase).

- *Observation* is the process of observing and recording events, situations, behaviors, and interactions of people in natural settings to explore individuals' experiences with the studied issue. It can take the form of participant observation when the observer is a researcher or a member of the community, or the form of a nonparticipant observation when the observer is an outsider. Observation process requires careful planning and is guided by a protocol where the observer records the field notes consisting of descriptions and reflections; multiple observations of the same event or behavior may be required to produce credible inferences (Creswell, 2013; Koshy et al., 2011; Stringer, 2014).

o Advantages for an MMAR study:

- It is an efficient method for exploring firsthand experiences of people in natural settings and can be used both in the reconnaisance phase to help explore stakeholders' individual needs and in the evaluation phase to help explore the relevance and usefulness of the action/intervention and to inform the needed modifications.
- It can help reveal the details that may not be easily captured through other data collection methods.
- It can help identify the gatekeepers to the community and the key informants for individual and focus group interviews.
- It can be used as a supplemental data source in all concurrent and sequential MMAR study designs, consistent with the study purpose.

o Issues to consider:

- It can cause disruption of routine activities in a setting.
- It requires good listening skills and attention to visual detail.
- It can affect natural behavior and interactions of those who are being observed.
- It requires training of community members and other stakeholders in qualitative observation and recording techniques.

(Continued)

(Continued)

- ○ Illustration:

  - In a concurrent Quan + Qual MMAR study, Glasson et al. (2006; Example B) conducted nonparticipant observations of staff discussing the need for a new model of nursing care for older patients, the details of its implementation, and directions for its evaluation (the reconnaissance phase).
  - In a sequential Quan → Qual MMAR study, Blanco et al. (2010) used reflective notes from the lecturer's participant observation journal along with other data to evaluate the implementation of a strategy awareness raising program for teaching in a beginning level Spanish college course (the evaluation phase).

- *Document* is a public or private record that may provide objective information about an issue of interest. A document is often referred to as an *environmental scan* in action research. Documents may include reports; policy statements; minutes; organizational records; procedural manuals; patient, student, and employee files; public relations materials; and other relevant organizational and community documents (Creswell, 2013; Koshy et al., 2011; Stringer, 2014; Stringer & Genat, 2004).

  - ○ Advantages for an MMAR study:

    - It is a reliable and unobtrusive source of information that exists independent of researchers and participants.
    - It is an efficient method of exploring the background information and evidence for the issue when conducting the needs assessment in the reconnaissance phase.
    - It can help reveal potential solutions to similar problems that have been reported in published sources.
    - It can help identify the gatekeepers to the community and the key informants for individual and focus group interviews.
    - It can be used as a supplemental data source in all concurrent and sequential MMAR study designs, consistent with the study purpose.

  - ○ Issues to consider:

    - It may require careful consideration of ethical principles because documents often contain private and sensitive information.
    - It can be time-consuming to review available documents. Researchers need to be selective in identifying relevant information.
    - It is important to be aware of potential issues of power within an organization and community that may have influenced the production of a report or a policy statement.

  - ○ Illustration:

    - In a sequential Qual → Quan MMAR study, Craig (2011; Example C) conducted an environmental scan of existing national and local GLBTQ programs for young people that informed the logistics of the new program and helped identify potential community leaders to interview (the reconnaissance phase).

- In a concurrent Quan + Qual MMAR study, Blackford and Street (2012) conducted the analysis of the relevant documents that consisted of client records, policies, procedures, and quality improvement strategies before and after the implementation of the palliative care community program to inform the intervention and to evaluate its effects (the reconnaissance and evaluation phases).

- *Audiovisual material and photo-voice* is image and sound data that may provide both objective information and stakeholders' perceptions about an issue of interest; they include photos, videos, DVDs, paintings, pictures, and so on. Photos and video recordings are used to stimulate individual and focus group interviews; they help capture important details about participants' behaviors and interactions that may be overlooked during observations or focus group discussions. *Photo-voice* is increasingly used in action research as a means to document community assets and concerns through photographs taken by study participants and other stakeholders to stimulate critical discussions of the needed action/intervention (Berg, 2004; Creswell, 2013; Koshy et al., 2011; Stringer & Genat, 2004; Wang, 1997).

  o Advantages for an MMAR study:

    - It is an efficient method of collecting evidence for the issue when conducting the needs assessment in the reconnaissance phase.
    - It is an effective venue to get study participants, community members, and other stakeholders involved with the data collection process.
    - It is a means of empowering community members, particularly marginalized groups, through photo-voice to commnicate and seek solution to their needs.
    - It can be used to enhance reporting of the study findings to interested stakeholders and policy advocate groups.
    - It can be used as a supplemental data source in all concurrent and sequential MMAR study designs, consistent with the study purpose.

  o Issues to consider:

    - It can be expensive to purchase video equipment and digital cameras for all study participants and stakeholders.
    - It can affect natural behavior and interactions of people being recorded.
    - It can introduce a bias in the selection of the images to capture and conversations to record.

  o Illustration:

    - In a concurrent Quan + Qual MMAR study, Krieger, Rabkin, Sharify, and Song (2009) used photo-voice to have the community members document the features in their neighborhood

(Continued)

that promoted or inhibited walking. This information and other data were used to inform the development and implementation of the program in a public housing community to support walking (the reconnaissance phase).

- In a concurrent Quan + Qual MMAR study, Bradley and Puoane (2007) took pictures of cooking methods and food portions served when community members demonstrated how they cooked for their families. These pictures, along with the community surveys and focus groups, were used to identify the factors contributing to hypertension and diabetes in the community with the purpose of developing a community-based intervention (the reconnaissance phase).

Data Collection Considerations in an MMAR Study

Besides having general knowledge of and skills in collecting quantitative and qualitative data, practitioner-researchers have to consider additional issues related to collecting data in an MMAR study. For example, practitioner-researchers should decide what quantitative and qualitative data to give more weight in the context of the needed action, what data may be more useful during the reconnaissance and evaluation study phases, how to decide which quantitative and qualitative data sources to combine or triangulate within a study, and what data may be more feasible to collect taking into account the availability of financial resources and time. As was previously discussed, a participatory and collaborative nature of both mixed methods and action research calls for an active involvement of stakeholders, who often are also the study participants, into the data collection process. Engaging community members with research procedures is part of the community capacity building and should be included in the study general research plan. It is also important to consider how to ensure quality of the collected data to generate creditable inferences that will inform the development, implementation, and evaluation of the action/intervention plan.

Refer to Chapter 4 for the discussion of the components of an MMAR study general research plan.

Prioritizing Data Sources

Decisions about what data—quantitative, qualitative, or both—to prioritize in an MMAR study may not always be possible at the study planning stage due to the emergent nature of action research. Although there tends to be a faulty perception that only qualitative data from small samples are collected in the action research studies (Koshy et al., 2011), qualitative data seem to be more weighted in action research. For example, Stringer (2014) prioritized the use of qualitative data in action research. He emphasized that the information gathered by practitioner-researchers in the first cycle of the study is qualitative in nature because it helps capture participants' perspectives and "define the problem/issue in terms that 'make sense' in their own terms" (p. 101). James and colleagues (2008) also assigned the major role to qualitative information in action research because, reportedly, it enables practitioner-researchers to be more responsive to the needs of the community where the study is being conducted. Moreover, soliciting information through interviews and observations with the key informants helps engage the stakeholders in the action research process and promote the feeling of empowerment in addressing the change. Additionally, it may also be easier for practitioners to learn qualitative data-gathering techniques than to learn quantitative terms and experimental research methods. Hacker (2013) argued that qualitative, nonexperimental methods can be more easily adapted to action research, thus making it more appealing for stakeholders to engage in the data collection process.

The tendency to give more priority to qualitative data has also been reflected in many reviewed MMAR studies. For example, Kostos and Shin (2010; Example A) assigned more priority to qualitative data, such as students' math journals, students' interviews, and the teacher's reflective journal to get in-depth understanding of the process of students' math communication skills development during the evaluation of the math journaling instructional intervention. Quantitative pre- and post-math assessment scores were used before and after the intervention, respectively, to compare the students' math knowledge and reasoning. To get firsthand accounts of the students' learning experiences, however, qualitative data were needed. Similarly, Krieger and colleagues (2009) employed extensive qualitative data collection including interviews, focus groups, and photo-voice in addition to the survey when conducting community assessment of the barriers to physical activity. In this study, community action team members were involved in collecting the data through photo-voice, interviews, and surveys.

While qualitative data are often assigned more priority in MMAR studies, quantitative data from surveys, assessments, and observation checklists can also be extensively collected to provide a comprehensive assessment of the problem/issue and to ensure a more robust evaluation of the implemented action/intervention. Priority on the quantitative data is often placed in large-scale MMAR studies when there is a need to address global educational, social, or health issues. Qualitative data can either play a supplemental role or can be also collected in large numbers from many study participants. Sometimes a pre- and post-experimental design, which is often associated with traditional quantitative research, can also be utilized in the evaluation phase of an MMAR study.

For example, Thornewill and colleagues' (2011) MMAR study about health information exchange needs discussed earlier in the chapter involved phone, paper, and Web quantitative surveys of nearly 1,000 healthcare providers and community dwellers. Twenty-three focus groups that included 191 participants were also conducted to get more in-depth stakeholders' perspectives. Similarly, Aldridge and colleagues (2012) surveyed 2,043 students in nine coeducational schools from Western Australia to pilot test their newly developed quantitative questionnaire aimed at assessing students' perceptions of a classroom learning environment. Qualitative reflective journaling data from eight teachers played a supplemental role and helped further explore the teaching strategies they implemented in the classroom. Lustick (2009) used a pre- and posttest design to conduct an evaluation of 15 college students' experiences, knowledge, beliefs, and attitudes of scientific inquiry as a result of the implementation of a new curriculum. Qualitative data consisting of students' reflections, assignments, and discussions in class were collected "to supplement the pre- and postassessment tools" (p. 590).

Triangulation of Data Sources

Another consideration is related to combining or triangulating different quantitative and qualitative data sources in an MMAR study. Triangulation is an important concept in research: combining different types of data and individual perspectives helps enhance the credibility of the data and their interpretation (Creswell, 2013; Lincoln & Guba, 1985). Moreover, triangulation is an inherent feature of mixed methods research. As discussed in Chapter 1, triangulation is viewed as one of the underlying purposes or reasons for combining quantitative and qualitative methods within one study (Greene et al., 1989). In action research, triangulation of multiple data sources is particularly important because it helps minimize ambiguity when developing an action/intervention plan and helps increase confidence in the research findings (Hinchey, 2008). In addition, the emergent and iterative nature of action research cycles often calls for the need to collect additional data (Stringer, 2014) to create "a deeper and wider picture" of the issue (Koshy et al., 2011, p. 121).

Revisit the discussion of the reasons or rationales for mixed methods research in Chapter 1.

In an MMAR study, triangulation is achieved by integrating the inferences that are generated through the collection and analysis of multiple forms of quantitative and qualitative data from different stakeholder groups. Various sources of quantitative and qualitative data may be used concurrently or sequentially to address the posed research questions. Getting evidence from different groups of individuals and different forms of information enables practitioner-researchers to develop a more holistic view of the problem, provides them with a more accurate assessment of the situation, and helps them conduct more complete and exhaustive evaluation of the impact of the action/intervention.

For example, in the reconnaissance phase of her MMAR study, Craig (2011; Example C) used multiple sources to conduct a community assessment to inform the development of a system of care for GLBTQ youths: environmental scan of GLBTQ programs, key informant interviews with local service providers and community leaders, focus groups with GLBTQ young people, and a survey of GLBTQ youths. Likewise, multiple quantitative and qualitative data were collected in Kilbride and colleagues' (2005) MMAR study, such as audit of stroke patient admissions, focus groups with the hospital staff, individual interviews with select staff members, a staff quantitative survey, observations, researchers' field notes, and examination of documents, policies, and minutes from the meetings, in order to evaluate the stroke intervention and "to monitor the process and outcomes of change over time" (p. 482). Torre and Fine (2005) also triangulated multiple data sources in a study that evaluated the impact of the college-in-prison educational program on inmate women and their children.

Triangulation as the means of establishing credibility in an MMAR study is further discussed in Chapter 9.

The researchers collected data from eight quantitative and qualitative sources during a 4-year period: archival analysis of the college program records, review of recidivism rates, college faculty surveys, participant observation of the activities in the learning center, focus groups with inmates, and individual interviews with current and former inmates, prison administrators, corrections officers, and inmates' children. The collected information allowed for reporting a positive transformational effect of a higher education program on incarcerated women's lives.

Building Capacity and Engaging Community Partners

As discussed in Chapter 2, action research is often done in collaboration with those whose interests are represented in the study. A reciprocal effect of conducting action research in professional and community settings is enhanced through engaging community members and other stakeholders, who oftentimes are the study participants themselves, in the research process (Robertson, 2000). Besides being gatekeepers to the community, community partners can often help identify "novel and more applicable methods" for data collection (Hacker, 2013, p. 48). Hacker also argued that community is a living and changing entity, and may require constant adjustments in the study methodology. Decisions about data sources and methods of data collection should be made jointly with those who have the insight and the firsthand experience with the studied problem. Additionally, due to the cyclical nature of action research, the need for inclusion of additional data sources may emerge during the study process (Stringer, 2014).

Involvement of stakeholders in the data collection process is particularly important in an MMAR study that employs multiple forms of quantitative and qualitative data, and oftentimes simultaneously as it is done in a concurrent Quan + Qual MMAR design. Members of the community and other stakeholders can be trained to assist practitioner-researchers with administering the surveys and conducting interviews, focus groups, and observations. They can also help refine research protocols by providing their knowledge and expertise with local issues (Macaulay et al., 1999). Therefore, building community capacity through training and educating community partners about the strengths and limitations of different data collection tools and their relevance to the study research questions is one of the issues that practitioner-researchers have to consider and attend to at the data collection stage. Of note, Nastasi and colleagues (2010) described the inclusion of community members in the data collection process as one of the aspects of their synergistic partnership-based fully integrated mixed methods research model. The authors emphasized the importance of establishing collaborative teams between researchers and community representatives in enhancing the quality of the mixed methods research and in achieving the transformative goals.

> Revisit the discussion in Chapter 3 about a transformative or advocacy perspective as a characteristic of mixed methods and action research.

For example, Giachello and colleagues (2003) described how the Chicago Southeast Diabetes Community Action Coalition engaged in building community capacity by training the agency staff, local providers, and residents to conduct community surveys in English and Spanish, to collect publicly available health indicators, and to facilitate focus group discussions. Similarly, Kilbride and colleagues (2005) described the formation of the project team consisting of researchers and hospital staff members as one of the first cycles in their MMAR study. Hospital staff helped facilitate the focus groups with other staff members and helped administer the survey in their unit. In Krieger and colleagues' (2009) MMAR study, community members were trained in collecting the data through photo-voice to document what supported or inhibited walking in their neighborhood. Galini and Efthymia (2010) reported on an MMAR study that involved a team of teachers, parents, and the university researcher to collaboratively evaluate the kindergarten practices in two public schools in Greece.

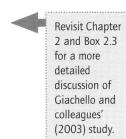

> Revisit Chapter 2 and Box 2.3 for a more detailed discussion of Giachello and colleagues' (2003) study.

Ensuring Data Quality, Utility, and Feasibility

Quality of the collected data is an important aspect of any research study because it is directly related to the quality of the findings and the generated conclusions. In action research, data quality is also determined by the usefulness and relevance of the study results for those whose interests are represented in the study (Mertler, 2012). Eliminating the researcher's bias in selecting the data sources through collaboration with the stakeholders becomes very important because it helps ensure that the collected data truly represent stakeholders' views. Collaboration with community partners and other practitioner-researchers may also help provide access to data that are germane to the study purpose. It may also help decide what data may be available and may be feasible to gather. For example, Johnson, Bartgis, Worley, Hellman, and Burkhart (2010) described how, consistent with the community-based participatory approach, they assembled a community advisory board that included tribal elders and leaders, parents, youths, and other community members to guide the study implementation. The board members provided regular feedback on every research aspect of the study, including the research purpose, design, methodology, development of the survey instrument, and discussion of the results.

At the same time, Stringer (2014) warned that active participation and collaboration of all interested parties in the study design and implementation should not preclude practitioner-researchers from using "the

> Assessing quality of data and their interpretation is discussed in more detail in Chapter 9.

systematic and rigorous processes that are the hallmark of good research" (p. 93). In an MMAR study, collecting extensive data from quantitative and qualitative sources may help decrease the bias that researchers bring into the study. Triangulating information from multiple data sources provides corroborating evidence that secures quality in the data interpretation. Additionally, since the ultimate goal in an MMAR study is to generate creditable meta-inferences to inform the development, implementation, and evaluation of the action/intervention plan, consideration of the relevance of the selected quantitative and qualitative sources for the specific MMAR study design and the data integration strategies are of particular importance. Box 7.5 summarizes data collection considerations that practitioner-researchers should take into account when designing and conducting an MMAR study.

So, how do practitioner researchers integrate quantitative and qualitative data in an MMAR study?

BOX 7.5

Data Collection Considerations in an MMAR Study

- Extensive data from both quantitative and qualitative data sources are collected for the purposes of triangulation to generate credible meta-inferences.
- More emphasis may be given to qualitative data due to the need to study professional and community settings, the need to use intact groups, and the need to secure participants' perspectives on the issue of interest.

- Qualitative data may be easier to collect and analyze for researcher-practitioners, and may be more easily adapted to an MMAR study, making it more appealing for stakeholders to engage in the data collection process.
- More emphasis may be given to quantitative data in large-scale MMAR studies when there is a need to address global educational, social, or health issues.
- Consideration should be given to data that naturally occur in the environment of the study and that yield the most efficient and useful information to inform the development, implementation, and evaluation of the action/intervention plan.
- Members of the community can be engaged in collecting quantitative and qualitative data, and can be trained to assist with administering surveys and conducting interviews, focus groups, and observations.
- Community capacity should be built through training and educating community partners and other stakeholders about the strengths and limitations of different quantitative and qualitative data collection tools and their relevance in an MMAR study.

Integrating Quantitative and Qualitative Data in an MMAR Study

Data collection procedures and related data integration strategies is one of the least addressed topics in mixed methods literature (Creswell & Plano Clark, 2011). However, the available discussions may offer some useful tips for integrating quantitative and qualitative data during the data collection process in an MMAR. For example, Teddlie and Tashakkori (2009) defined mixed methods data collection as "gathering of both QUAN and QUAL data in a single study" (p. 218). These authors suggested two basic data collection strategies related to mixed methods, **within-strategy mixed methods data collection** and **between-strategies mixed methods data collection**. As the name suggests, within-strategy mixed methods data collection implies collecting both quantitative and qualitative data employing one strategy—for example, using a survey instrument that includes both close- and open-ended questions. A between-strategies mixed methods data collection involves collecting quantitative and qualitative data using different methods—for example, combining survey and focus groups, or combining individual interviews, document analysis, and achievement scores in one study. Teddlie and Tashakkori (2009) identified 30 possible combinations of a between-strategies mixed methods data collection that can range from the combination of two strategies—one quantitative and one qualitative—to many more. For example, Kostos and Shin (2010; Example A) utilized a between-strategies mixed methods data collection consisting of one quantitative data source—pre- and post-math assessment, and three qualitative data sources—students' journals, interviews, and teacher-researcher's reflective notes. In Torre and Fine's (2005) MMAR study, the researchers applied between-strategies data collection that included three quantitative strategies (analysis of archival college program records, review of recidivism rates, and college faculty surveys) and three qualitative strategies (participant observation of the activities in the learning center, focus groups with inmates, and individual interviews with current and former inmates, prison administrators, corrections officers, and inmates' children).

Earlier, Johnson and Turner (2003) discussed similar approaches to data collection in mixed methods studies referring to them as **intramethod mixing** (using one method) and **intermethod mixing** (using different methods). They emphasized the integrative nature of combining different quantitative and qualitative data collection methods at different points in time within one study. Yin (2006) also underscored the importance of integration at the data collection level in addition to other integrating points in the study. Recognizing that "each method's preferred instrumentation is central to the method itself," he suggested trying to align quantitative and qualitative data collection tools in the study as much as possible (p. 44)—for example, through selecting or developing survey quantitative items and qualitative interview questions that overlap or complement each other in the content focus.

When planning and implementing data collection in MMAR studies, practitioner-researchers may find it useful to differentiate between within-strategy or between-strategies approaches, because it may enhance their understanding of the quantitative and qualitative data integration procedures. Additionally, thinking about the data collection process in the study as intramethod or intermethod mixing may help researchers decide what data collection strategies to use to be able to generate creditable meta-inferences needed to inform the development, implementation, and evaluation of the action/intervention. As was previously discussed, many factors may play a role in shaping the data collection process in an MMAR study. However, it is important to select the types of data and the strategies of their collection within a specific study design that will serve the purpose of the study and yield the needed information. Table 7.2 summarizes how mixed methods data collection strategies can be used in MMAR study designs.

A within-strategy mixed methods data collection can be a cost- and time-effective way to collect both quantitative and qualitative information using one instrument with close- and open-ended items in both reconnaissance and evaluation phases of a concurrent Quan + Qual MMAR study design. This strategy utilizes one sample of individuals who respond to both quantitative and qualitative questions at one point in time. For example, to identify the community strengths and the needs for a comprehensive model of health care, Johnson and colleagues (2010) concurrently collected both quantitative and qualitative data from 650 urban American Indians using a "mixed-methods survey" (p. 49). Two parallel survey forms for adults and young people were developed to address physical health, behavioral health, wellness, demographics, community services, and support structures, using both Likert-type and open-ended questions. In Glasson and colleagues' (2006) MMAR study (Example B), the same survey instruments were administered to patients and nurses in the same acute medical ward in both reconnaissance (before the implementation of a model of nursing care) and evaluation (after the model implementation) phases of the study. The survey component measuring satisfaction with nursing care consisted of 50 five-point Likert items. Each quantitative item had a follow-up qualitative prompt question, which asked, "If not provided, then why do you think this was the case?" (p. 592).

A between-strategies mixed methods data collection can be employed in both concurrent and sequential MMAR design studies. A between-strategies approach in a concurrent Quan + Qual MMAR design often uses different samples of individuals to collect quantitative and qualitative data for the purpose of triangulating stakeholders' views, as evident from Kilbride and colleagues' (2005) stroke intervention evaluation study and Torre and Fine's (2005) college-in-prison program study discussed earlier. Emphasis may be given to any or all quantitative and qualitative data, depending on the study purpose and the scope of the problem addressed.

Application of a between-strategies approach in sequential MMAR designs is different from a concurrent Quan + Qual MMAR design and reflects a chronological sequence of the study design strands. In a sequential

TABLE 7.2	**Mixed Methods Data Collection in MMAR Study Designs**

MMAR Study Design	Mixed Methods Data Collection Strategy	Samples for Quantitative and Qualitative Strands	Data Sources
Concurrent Quan + Qual	• Within-strategy (intramethod mixing) • Between-strategies (intermethod mixing)	• Same • Same or different	• One instrument with close- and open-ended items • Concurrent combination of quantitative and qualitative data sources
Sequential Quan → Qual	• Between-strategies (intermethod mixing)	• Same (often with a subset) or different	• Sequential combination of quantitative and qualitative data sources
Sequential Qual → Quan	• Between-strategies (intermethod mixing)	• Different	• Sequential combination of qualitative and quantitative data sources
Multistrand	• Combination of within-strategy (intramethod mixing) and between-strategies (intermethod mixing)	• Same or different	• Combination of one instrument (with close- and open-ended items) and concurrent and sequential combination of quantitative and qualitative data sources

Quan → Qual MMAR design, both sets of data are often collected from the same study participants, but quantitative data are collected first in the sequence and then qualitative data are collected from a subset of the original sample. Quantitative data may be given more priority because the emphasis is on the quantitative examination of the issue, and qualitative data may play a supporting but an important explanatory role. For example, in a reported research protocol for a sequential Quan → Qual MMAR design study, Montgomery and colleagues (2008; Example E) planned to first survey 172 individuals with serious mental illness who were using or waiting for supported housing services, and then to conduct three focus groups with 10 participants in each to get additional perspectives of supported housing clients. They also planned to explore the perspectives of clients' families and community mental-health workers that were not included in the original quantitative sample. In another sequential Quan → Qual MMAR study, Seymour and colleagues (2011) emphasized qualitative data. They first collected the quantitative survey data from 24 participants 4 months after the completion of a community-based peer education training aimed at preparing volunteers for advance care planning and associated end-of-life care issues. Based on the survey results, the researchers developed a protocol to guide focus group discussions with 20 peer educators and also individual and group interviews with 25 trainees who completed the training.

Alternatively, in a sequential Qual → Quan MMAR design, both sets of data are often collected from differ-ent study participants, but the samples may be similar in demographic characteristics to enable potential gen-eralizations of the initial qualitative findings. Qualitative data are collected first in the sequence to explore the issue and quantitative data are collected next from a much larger sample. Qualitative data are often given more priority and can be very extensive as the emphasis is on the qualitative exploration of the issue and understand-ing of stakeholders' views so that to inform further quantitative assessment of the problem and identification of the areas for action/intervention. For example, Craig (2011; Example C) used key-informant interviews with 45 community leaders and 10 focus groups with 180 GLBTQ young people to develop the "Youth Speak Out Survey" that was later administered to 273 GLBTQ youths. Sampson (2010; Example D) employed a sequential Qual → Quan data collection as part of a multistrand MMAR study design. Narrative data from 22 students' reflective journals were used to inform the development of the quantitative Learning Experience Questionnaire that was completed by the same students at the end of the course. Box 7.6 provides some useful tips for practi-tioner-researchers to consider when integrating quantitative and qualitative data in an MMAR study.

BOX 7.6

Tips for Integrating Quantitative and Qualitative Data in an MMAR Study

- Consider data integration strategies early in the research process when conceptualizing and designing an MMAR study.
- Consider selecting data sources and data collection strategies that will serve the purpose of the study and yield the needed information for the development and evaluation of the action/intervention.
- Consider the input of the study participants and community stakeholders regarding relevance and feasibility of the data to be included in the study.
- Consider collecting data from multiple quantitative and qualitative data sources for the purpose of triangulating stakeholders' views.
- Consider the purposes of MMAR study designs in deciding on the sequence of data collection and types of data sources.
- Consider tailoring within-strategy and between-strategies mixed methods data collection approaches to MMAR study designs.
- Consider the study purpose and research questions when deciding which data to prioritize in the study.

SUMMARY

In an MMAR study, a research site is identified early, at the study conceptualization stage, because practi-tioner-researchers tend to study their own practices or conduct research within a specified community. The process of data collection begins with selection and recruitment of the study participants, who will represent a community of interest and will have a stake in the issue that requires investigation. Probability/nonprobability and purposeful sampling strategies can be applied in different combinations in an MMAR study, depending on the study purpose, the scope of the project, type of an MMAR study design, and the phase (reconnaissance or evaluation) in the MMAR study process. Excerpts from published MMAR studies in different fields are used to illustrate how practitioner-researchers approached and explained different sampling strategies used in the reconnaissance and evaluation phases of their MMAR studies. The following issues should be taken into consideration when selecting the sampling strategies in an MMAR study: the decision whether to use the same or different samples of participants for the quantitative and qualitative study strands, the need to represent the views of all potential stakeholders, the practicability of the sample size for solving an issue, the trade-offs of using the nonprobability sampling strategies, and utilization of multiple recruitment venues and incentives. Four MMAR sampling schemes that are grounded in the methodological characteristics of concurrent, sequential, and multistrand MMAR designs are presented, supported by their conceptual diagrams.

Next, common sources of quantitative and qualitative data used in an MMAR study are discussed with the focus on their relevance for the practical purposes of action research and the issues to consider. Application of each data source in different MMAR designs and phases is illustrated using published MMAR studies. Special considerations that practitioner-researchers have to take into account when collecting data in an MMAR study include decisions on what quantitative and qualitative data to give more weight, what data may be more useful during the reconnaissance and evaluation phases, how to decide which quantitative and qualitative data sources to triangulate within a study, what data may be more feasible to collect, how to involve stakeholders in the data collection process, how to build community capacity, and how to ensure the quality of the gathered data. When planning and implementing data collection in MMAR studies, practitioner-researchers may find it useful to differentiate between within-strategy and between-strategies approaches. This may enhance their understanding of the quantitative and qualitative data integration procedures and what data collection strategies to use to generate creditable meta-inferences that will inform the development, implementation, and evaluation of the action/intervention plan.

REFLECTIVE QUESTIONS AND EXERCISES

1. Reflect on probability/nonprobability and purposeful sampling strategies that can be applied in an MMAR study. Describe the purpose of each strategy and its role in MMAR study designs. Explain the issues that should be taken into consideration when selecting the sampling strategies in an MMAR study.

2. Describe four MMAR sampling schemes and explain how they reflect the methodological characteristics of concurrent, sequential, and multistrand MMAR designs. Draw a conceptual diagram for each MMAR sampling scheme and illustrate it with a hypothetical MMAR study.

3. Select a published MMAR study in your discipline or area of interest. Identify an MMAR study design and an MMAR sampling scheme used in the study. Using a conceptual model of this sampling scheme, draw a detailed diagram of the study participants' selection process indicating the study strands, type of a sampling strategy used in each strand, number of samples, and sample sizes.

4. Describe the common sources of quantitative and qualitative data used in an MMAR study. Describe each quantitative and qualitative data source and discuss its relevance for the practical purposes of the action

research process. Explain the issues that should be taken into consideration when selecting data sources in an MMAR study.

5. For the study that you discussed in Question 2, identify what quantitative and qualitative data were collected, explain what data were weighted in the study, and discuss the relevance of the collected data for the study purpose. Explain how the collaborative nature of an MMAR study was addressed and what quality control of the gathered data was implemented.

6. Explain how the within-strategy or between-strategies mixed methods data collection approaches can be applied in an MMAR study and the importance of those approaches for data integration purposes. Identify whether the researchers used a within-strategy or between-strategies data collection in the study discussed in Question 2. Describe in detail the steps the researchers had to take to achieve quantitative and qualitative data integration in the study.

FURTHER READINGS

To learn more about major sample types and sampling strategies used in research, examine the following sources:

Creswell, J. W. (2012). *Educational research: Planning, conducting, and evaluating quantitative and qualitative research* (4th ed.). Upper Saddle River, NJ: Merrill Prentice Hall, Ch. 5, pp. 142–146, Ch. 7, pp. 206–209.

Davies, J. (2010). Preparation and process of qualitative interviews and focus groups. In L. Dahlberg & C. McCaig (Eds.), *Practical research and evaluation: A start-to-finish guide for practitioners* (pp. 126–144). Thousand Oaks, CA: Sage.

Leman, J. (2010). Different kinds of quantitative data collection methods. In L. Dahlberg & C. McCaig (Eds.), *Practical research and evaluation: A start-to-finish guide for practitioners* (pp. 159–171). Thousand Oaks, CA: Sage.

Teddlie, C., & Tashakkori, A. (2009). *Foundations of mixed methods research: Integrating quantitative and qualitative approaches in the social and behavioral sciences.* Thousand Oaks, CA: Sage, Ch. 8, pp. 169–178.

To learn more about approaches to sampling in mixed methods research, examine the following sources:

Collins, K. (2010). Advanced sampling designs in mixed research: Current practices and emerging trends in the social and behavioral sciences. In A. Tashakkori & C. Teddlie (Eds.), *SAGE handbook of mixed methods in social & behavioral research* (2nd ed., pp. 353–377). Thousand Oaks, CA: Sage.

Morse, J. M., & Niehaus, L. (2009). *Mixed method design: Principles and procedures.* Walnut Creek, CA: Left Coast Press, Ch. 6.

Teddlie, C., & Tashakkori, A. (2009). *Foundations of mixed methods research: Integrating quantitative and qualitative approaches in the social and behavioral sciences.* Thousand Oaks, CA: Sage, Ch. 8, pp. 178–196.

To learn more about methods of data collection and procedures in action research, examine the following sources:

Koshy, E., Koshy, V., & Waterman, H. (2011). *Action research in healthcare.* Thousand Oaks, CA: Sage, Ch. 5, pp. 107–123.

Mills, G. E. (2011). *Action research: A guide for the teacher researcher* (4th ed.). Boston: Pearson Education, Ch. 4, pp. 68–98.

Stringer, E. T. (2014). *Action research* (4th ed.). Thousand Oaks, CA: Sage, Ch. 4, pp. 99–134.

Wang, C. (1997). Photovoice: Concept, methodology, and use for participatory needs assessment. *Health Education and Behavior, 24*(3), 369–387.

To learn more about methods of data collection in mixed methods research, examine the following sources:

Creswell, J. W., & Plano Clark, V. L. (2011). *Designing and conducting mixed methods research* (2nd ed.). Thousand Oaks, CA: Sage, Ch. 6, pp. 171–201.

Johnson, B., & Turner, L. (2003). Data collection strategies in mixed methods research. In A. Tashakkori & C. Teddlie (Eds.), *Handbook of mixed methods in social & behavioral research* (pp. 297–320). Thousand Oaks, CA: Sage.

Teddlie, C., & Tashakkori, A. (2009). *Foundations of mixed methods research: Integrating quantitative and qualitative approaches in the social and behavioral sciences.* Thousand Oaks, CA: Sage, Ch. 9, pp. 197–248.

8

Analyzing Data in a Mixed Methods Action Research Study

OBJECTIVES

By the end of this chapter, the reader should be able to

- Understand and apply the steps in the data analysis process in an MMAR study,
- Describe common descriptive and inferential statistics analytical methods used in an MMAR study,
- Understand and describe the process of qualitative data analysis and how it is used in an MMAR study,
- Understand and describe mixed methods data analysis for MMAR study designs, and
- Apply the steps in mixed methods data analysis in MMAR study designs.

INTRODUCTION

Chapter 7 discussed the strategies for selecting the sample and collecting the data in an MMAR study. The process of selecting the study participants and relevant data sources is guided by many factors, but the most important are the study purpose and the research questions that practitioner-researchers seek to answer to address the pertinent problem/issue. Considerations on how to analyze the collected quantitative and qualitative data and on how to ensure that the results and subsequent interpretations are legitimate and credible are other important steps in an MMAR study process.

Hinchey (2008) argued that data analysis is both the most exciting and "the most frustrating" aspect of the action research process (p. 86). Data analysis is a critical step that should be carefully considered in an MMAR study because it serves as a link between raw data collected from different stakeholders and the results and interpretations, or meta-inferences. Being the product of data collection and analysis, meta-inferences inform each phase in an MMAR Study Process Model. So, the choice of the analytical strategies has direct implications for how action/intervention is designed, implemented, and evaluated.

> Revisit the discussion about an MMAR Study Process Model in Chapter 4; refer to Figure 4.1 that visually presents the model.

Similar to data collection considerations in an MMAR study, the choice of the analytical strategies is determined by several factors, such as posted research questions, an MMAR study design, the goals of a specific phase (reconnaissance or evaluation) in the MMAR process, and types of data collected in the quantitative and qualitative study strands. The analytical process involves using existing methods for quantitative and qualitative data analysis, and also considering mixed methods data analysis strategies specific for MMAR study designs. Additionally, the analytical skills of practitioner-researchers and availability of academic partnerships may influence the decisions in selecting statistical methods and the decision of which method, quantitative or qualitative, to emphasize.

Similar to the data-collection process, data analysis in an MMAR study is complicated by the very fact that practitioner-researchers have to apply different sets of analytical strategies to analyze quantitative and qualitative data within one study. This requires different sets of skills and mind-sets, which is best addressed when research is conducted in teams. On the other hand, the inherently collaborative nature of action research provides a fertile ground for securing the needed analytical expertise and resources through forming partnerships with local higher education institutions, community agencies, and other stakeholders. Outside expertise may also be helpful when addressing the specific types of mixed methods data analysis employed in an MMAR study.

So, how do practitioner-researchers approach data analysis in an MMAR study, and what analytical strategies do they select in different quantitative and qualitative study strands to produce quality conclusions about the issue of interest?

ANALYZING QUANTITATIVE DATA IN AN MMAR STUDY

When dealing with quantitative information, statistics is one of the tools that can help practitioner-researchers understand the relationships in the data and communicate the results efficiently (Mills, 2011). Gay, Mills, and Airasian (2006) defined **statistics** as "a set of procedures for describing, synthesizing, analyzing, and interpreting quantitative data" (p. 301). A quantitative analysis begins with a set of procedures aimed at preparing and organizing data for analysis. The suggested steps include the following (Creswell, 2012):

- Create a codebook or a list of response categories with assigned values for each item on a survey instrument or a checklist.

- Score each response category for each item on a survey instrument or a checklist using the codebook.
- Select a statistical computer program that meets the requirements of the chosen analytical strategy or test.
- Enter data into the computer program for analysis.
- Clean or check the data file for any errors and missing data (blank responses).

These steps are important to follow to ensure quality control over data analysis and accuracy in the interpretation of the statistical results. Assessing quality of data and their interpretation is discussed in more detail in Chapter 9.

Depending on the nature of the study purpose, research questions, specific objectives, and the weight assigned to the quantitative data in an MMAR study, practitioner-researchers may select either descriptive or inferential statistics analytical methods, or combine them within the same study strand. Using a statistical computer program will make quantitative data analysis less complex and less time-consuming. Although numerous software programs are available, practitioner-researchers may consider using SPSS (www.spss.com) or JMP (www.jmp.com). These programs may be easier to use because they allow entering data and conducting statistical tests using built-in commands and prompts versus having to construct the commands for each analysis using a special statistical syntax, as in SAS (www.sas.com).

Descriptive Statistics Analytical Methods

Descriptive statistics is the most common approach to analyze and present quantitative data in action research studies (Tomal, 2010). As discussed in Chapter 7, quantitative data often play a supplemental role in action research due to the fact action research studies address practically oriented questions for a specific sample and give less emphasis to generalizing the results to a larger population. The main focus of descriptive statistics is to describe and summarize quantitative information with the purpose of identifying trends and patterns in the data and uncovering potential relationships among the **variables** (defined as something that can change or vary; Vogt, 2005). Use of descriptive statistics is an effective means for presenting general or initial information of the problem/issue in one's professional setting or about the community needs (e.g., students' test scores, health indicators, crime rates, etc.) that may inform the development of the action/intervention during the reconnaissance phase of an MMAR study.

The simplest way to get an initial sense of quantitative data importance is to organize numeric values in summary displays, such as tables, graphs, and charts, and to calculate their frequencies of occurrence. Frequencies are often reported as percentages of the total and are used to describe the sample characteristics, such as participants' age, gender, ethnicity, and so on, and the distribution of numeric scores. Summary displays can be very helpful for practitioner-researchers to understand the information from the collected quantitative data and to communicate this information to community members and other stakeholders. The next step would be to explore the data using descriptive statistics analytical methods to detect meaningful patterns and relationships.

Based on the review of published MMAR studies, the most common descriptive statistics analytical methods used in action research are measures of central tendency, measures of variability, and measures of association or relationship. These are relatively simple mathematical procedures and can be easily applied by practitioner-researchers to analyze different amounts of numeric information. Measures of relative standing are also frequently used in action research studies, particularly in education, when there is a need to compare students' progress on several dimensions or tasks (Creswell, 2012; Vogt, 2005); no examples of their use in published MMAR studies were found, however. Most common measures of relative standing include percentile rank (the percent of scores that fall at or below a specific score in a set of scores) and the *z* score (a type of a calculated score with a mean of 0 and a standard deviation of 1 that allows comparing scores across different scales). Box 8.1 summarizes each descriptive statistics analytical method, lists advantages for its use in an MMAR study along with the issues to consider, and provides illustration of its application in published MMAR studies.

BOX 8.1

Common Descriptive Statistics Analytical Methods in an MMAR Study

- *Measures of central tendency*—are statistical procedures that yield a summary score of what is standard or typical about a group of individuals in the study. These measures are the *mean* (the arithmetic average of a set of scores), the *mode* (the most frequently occurring score or scores in a set of scores), and the *median* (the score that differentiates the top half from the lower half in a set of data). The mode and the median are usually reported when the data are represented in categories. Scores on all or select measures are typically reported to describe the study sample and general trends in the collected data (Creswell, 2012; Mills, 2011; Tomal, 2010; Vogt, 2005):

  o Advantages for an MMAR study:

    - It is a relatively simple set of statistical procedures that can be easily applied by practitioner-researchers to obtain a sense of numerical data in all concurrent and sequential MMAR study designs, consistent with the study purpose.

(Continued)

Inferential Statistics Analytical Methods

Inferential statistics analytical methods are less frequently used in action research than descriptive statistics analytical methods. The main focus of inferential statistics is on making predictions or drawing conclusions about a larger population based on the data collected from a sample of a given population (Vogt, 2005). These involve testing hypotheses about whether the observed differences among the groups or the relationships among the variables can be expected in a larger population. Action research, on the opposite, tends to be more exploratory in nature, focusing on the issue that has relevance for a specific group of people affected by this issue (Hacker, 2013; Koshy et al., 2011; Mills, 2011; Stringer & Genat, 2004). At the same time, an observed tendency to expand the scope of the

Refer to the Further Readings at the end of this chapter for detailed information about the illustrated descriptive statistics analytical methods.

(Continued)

- It is an effective venue to get stakeholders involved with the data analysis process, because it does not require extensive training.
- It is a means to provide general information about the issue both in the reconnaisance phase to help explore the individual needs and in the evaluation phase to help explore the relevance and usefulness of the action/intervention and inform the needed modifications.

o Issues to consider:

- It is not possible to make general claims about a larger population affected by the issue due to a descriptive nature of the measures.
- It requires consideration of the distribution of scores before deciding what measure to use, because the mean is greatly affected by extreme scores; in such cases, the median may be a more accurate descriptor of the set of scores.
- It requires educating community members and other stakeholders on how to interpret the measures of central tendency scores.

o Illustration:

- In a sequential Qual → Quan MMAR study, Johnson and colleagues (2010) used descriptive statistics to analyze the survey responses of adults and youths as part of the assessment of the strengths, needs, and limitations in the community to inform the development of a comprehensive service system model. The authors reported the mean, standard deviation, skewness, and kurtosis (shape of charts) scores for each survey item for adults and youths and the two groups together (the reconnaissance phase).
- In a concurrent Quan + Qual MMAR study, Akintobi and colleagues (2012) used descriptive statistics to assess organization leaders' skills, knowledge, and ability developed through their participation in a new community capacity-building training program. They reported the mean and the median for composite scores measured across each administration of the program (the evaluation phase).

- *Measures of variability*—are statistical procedures that provide information on how the individual scores vary or are different from each other within a set of scores. These measures include the *range* (the difference between the highest and the lowest scores in a set of scores), the *variance* (the dispersion or spread of the scores around the mean in a set of scores), and the *standard deviation* (the average distance of scores away from the mean). The use of these measures is typically associated with the data that follow a normal (bell-shaped, symmetrical) curve distribution. Measures of variability provide a foundation for more advanced statistical analysis, such as univariate analytical methods. Standard deviation is commonly reported along with the mean to describe the study sample and general trends in the collected data (Creswell, 2012; Mertler, 2012; Tomal, 2010; Vogt, 2005).

○ Advantages for an MMAR study:

- It is a relatively simple set of statistical procedures that can be easily applied by practitioner-researchers to understand the variability in the numerical data in all concurrent and sequential MMAR study designs, consistent with the study purpose.
- It is an effective means for comparing the data from the study sample to normative scores from regional or national databases, for example, standardized tests in education, or national registry of health indicators.
- It is an effective venue to get stakeholders involved with the data analysis process because it requires some, but not extensive, training.
- It is a means to provide general information about the issue both in the reconnaisance phase to help explore the individual needs and in the evaluation phase to help explore the relevance and usefulness of the action/intervention and to inform the needed modifications.

○ Issues to consider:

- It is not possible to make general claims about a larger population affected by the issue due to the descriptive nature of the measures.
- It requires consideration of the distribution of scores because deviations from the normal distribution (having extreme scores) may significantly affect the range of scores.
- It requires educating community members and other stakeholders on how to interpret the scores produced by measures of variability.

○ Illustration:

- In a concurrent Quan + Qual MMAR study, Glasson et al. (2006; Example B) used descriptive statistics to analyze the survey results as part of the evaluation of the efficacy of the new model of nursing care. They reported the range and standard deviation for four categories of patient satisfaction before and after the new model implementation (the evaluation phase).
- In a concurrent Quan + Qual MMAR study, Davidson et al. (2008) used descriptive statistics to analyze pre- and posttest scores as part of the evaluation of a new cardiac rehabilitation program to improve psychological outcomes of women with heart diseases. In addition to the mean, they reported minimum and maximum scores and the standard deviation for each pre- and postmeasure of psychological outcomes (the evaluation phase).

- *Measures of association or relationship*—are statistical procedures that provide information on how two sets of scores are related to each other. These measures include *correlation* coefficients expressing the direction and degree of relationship between two variables between +1.00 and −1.00. The most frequently used are *Pearson correlation* for normally distributed data and *Spearman correlation* for ranked or categorical data (Creswell, 2012; Gay et al., 2006; Mertler, 2012; Teddlie & Tashakkori, 2009; Vogt, 2005).

(Continued)

(Continued)

○ Advantages for an MMAR study:

- It is a set of statistical procedures that can be applied by practitioner-researchers with some training or assistance from academic partners to relate the variables in all concurrent and sequential MMAR study designs, consistent with the study purpose.
- It is an effective means to identify connections between certain factors to inform direction for action/intervention and communicate the need for change to community members and stakeholders.
- It is a means to provide general information about the issue both in the reconnaisance phase to help explore the individual needs and in the evaluation phase to help explore the relevance and usefulness of the action/intervention and to inform the needed modifications.

○ Issues to consider:

- It is important to keep in mind that correlation does not imply causal relationship between the variables; this is why correlation results should be interpreted with caution.
- It may be difficult to meaningfully communicate correlation results that have negative values.
- It requires educating community members and other stakeholders on how to interpret the correlation coefficients.
- It may be difficult to get community members and stakeholders involved with the data analysis process because it requires understanding and training.

○ Illustration:

- In a concurrent Quan + Qual MMAR study, Williamson et al. (2004) used correlations to examine the relationship between lecturer-practitioners' biographical data and aspects of occupational stress and burnout as part of the assessment of lecturer-practitioners' work roles and its effects on individuals (the reconnaissance phase).
- In a sequential Quan → Qual MMAR study, Montgomery et al. (2008; Example E) planned to use correlations to identify the relationship between the quality of life, housing stability, and housing preferences and selected demographic characteristics among a sample of housing residents from four northern Canada sites and a matched comparison group drawn from a different location in the country as part of the evaluation process of the existing supported housing programs for persons with serious mental illness in rural areas (the evaluation phase).

addressed problem beyond the conventional local boundaries, for example, of a single classroom, a hospital unit, or a specific locale, to a larger community sometimes necessitates the need for inferential statistical analysis and understanding of tests of significance both at the conceptual and the practical levels. For example, Tomal (2010) argued that understanding inferential statistics may be helpful to practitioner-researchers in interpreting published research studies because such knowledge can guide and support the decisions in the action research process. Similarly, Stringer and Genat (2004) emphasized usefulness of understanding inferential statistics results of survey and epidemiological studies to better inform the stakeholders about specific health issues.

Additionally, a growing application of mixed methods in action research studies supports the ability of action research projects to address both exploratory and confirmatory questions. Inferential statistics analytical methods are helpful when there is a need to compare groups of students on test scores, or categories of patients on some health-related outcomes before and after the intervention, or to relate certain factors to identify a predictable change in the given situation or condition (James et al., 2008; Koshy et al., 2011; Mertler, 2012). In an MMAR study, inferential statistics can be particularly useful to examine the impact of action/intervention, to inform the needed changes in the action plan, and to provide the foundation for further monitoring of the implemented action/intervention.

Inferential statistical methods are categorized into *parametric* and *nonparametric* methods based on the type of data collected. Parametric tests require that data are measured on continuous scales (interval and ratio), whereas nonparametric tests are used when data are measured using categories (nominal or ordinal). The most common parametric and nonparametric inferential statistical tests used in MMAR studies seem to be *t*-tests, analysis of variances (ANOVA), regression, and Chi-square, but other inferential statistical tests occasionally are applied in action research. For example, Reutzel and colleagues (2006) conducted pretest and posttest comparisons for a large-scale education-based MMAR project. The purpose of the project was to design, implement, and evaluate "The Words to Go" parent involvement program as part of a larger effort aimed at enhancing children's literacy development. The researchers used analysis of covariance (ANCOVA) and factor analysis tests to evaluate the impact of the program on the first-grade students' reading and writing scores as compared with first-grade students in a matched school. In another MMAR study, Arnold and colleagues (2012) applied logistic regression to identify the relationship between gender, school, grade level, and students' sexual experiences as part of their evaluation of the impact of a school- and community-based HIV prevention interventions in rural Nigeria.

> Revisit the discussion in Chapter 1 about exploratory and confirmatory questions in mixed methods research.

Practitioner-researchers should consult available texts in statistics for discussion of these tests or seek help from partnerships with trained statisticians. For example, Galini and Efthymia (2010) described how a university researcher helped analyze the data in their MMAR study aimed at examining the results of implementing internal evaluation process in a kindergarten in northeastern Greece. The university partner performed a dual role—serving as a research consultant for the project and also assisting with the data collection and analysis.

For brief guidance on how to choose an appropriate statistical test, refer to Table 8.1. This table highlights the statistical considerations that practitioner-researchers should make when selecting an appropriate inferential statistical analytical method. These considerations include the focus of hypothesis or research question on group comparison or relating variables; number and type (continuous or categorical) of independent, dependent, and covariate variables in the test; whether the distribution of scores follows a normal curve; and whether the test is categorized as parametric or non-parametric.

> Refer to the Further Readings at the end of this chapter for detailed information about the illustrated inferential statistics analytical methods.

Box 8.2 summarizes select inferential statistics analytical methods used in an MMAR study, lists advantages for their use in an MMAR study along with the issues to consider, and provides illustration of their application in published MMAR studies.

TABLE 8.1 Statistical Tests and Criteria for Choosing the Statistics for Hypothesis Testing

Statistical Test	Focus of Hypothesis/Research Question	Number and Type of Independent Variables	Number and Type of Dependent Variables	Number of Covariates	Distribution of Scores	Type of Test
Simple *t*-test	Compares one group to a known population	0	1 Continuous	0	Normal	Parametric
Independent measures *t*-test	Compares two groups under the same condition	1 Categorical	1 Continuous	0	Normal	Parametric
Paired *t*-test	Compares the same group under two different conditions	1 Categorical	1 Continuous	0	Normal	Parametric
Pearson correlation	Measures relationship between two variables	1 Continuous	1 Continuous	0	Normal	Parametric
Spearman correlation	Measures relationship between two variables	1 Categorical	1 Categorical	0	Nonnormal	Nonparametric
One-way analysis of variance (ANOVA)	Compares three or more groups under the same condition	1 Categorical	1 Continuous	0	Normal	Parametric
Two-way ANOVA	Compares two or more groups under two different conditions condition	2 Categorical	1 Continuous	0	Normal	Parametric
Repeated-measures ANOVA	Compares the same group under three or more different conditions	1 Categorical	1 Continuous	0	Normal	Parametric

Test	Description					
Analysis of covariance (ANCOVA)	Compares two or more groups under the same condition controlling for one other variable	≥ 1 Categorical	1 Continuous	1	Normal	Parametric
Multiple analysis of variance (MANOVA)	Compares two or more groups under different conditions	≥ 1 Categorical	≥ 2 Continuous	0	Normal	Parametric
Chi-square test	Compares categories within a group	≥ 1 Categorical	≥ 1 Categorical	0	Nonnormal	Nonparametric
Mann-Whitney U test	Compares two groups under the same condition	1 Categorical	1 Continuous or categorical	0	Nonnormal	Nonparametric
Kruskall-Wallis test	Compares three or more groups under the same condition	≥ 1 Categorical	≥ 1 Continuous or categorical	0	Nonnormal	Nonparametric
Simple regression	Predicts relationship between two variables	1 Continuous	1 Continuous	0	Normal	Parametric
Multiple regression	Predicts relationship between more than two variables	≥ 2 Continuous	1 Continuous	0	Normal	Parametric
Logistic regression	Predicts relationship between more than two variables	≥ 2 Continuous or categorical	1 Categorical	0	Normal	Parametric
Discriminant function analysis	Predicts relationship between more than two variables (category membership)	≥ 2 Continuous	1 Categorical	0	Normal	Parametric

Source: Adapted from Creswell, J. W. (2012). *Educational research: Planning, conducting, and evaluating quantitative and qualitative research* (4th ed.). Upper Saddle River, NJ: Merrill Prentice Hall. Used with permission.

BOX 8.2

Common Inferential Statistics Analytical Methods in an MMAR Study

- *T-test*—a parametric statistical procedure for continuous data. It involves testing the difference between the two groups using the group means. There are three types of *t*-tests: a *simple t-test* that compares one group to a known population; *independent-measures t-test* that compares two groups under the same condition; and *paired t-test* that compares the same group under two different conditions. The tests yield a *t*-statistic that is used to draw conclusions about whether the difference between the two group means is statistically significant (Mertler, 2012; Mills, 2011; Tomal, 2010; Vogt, 2005).

  o Advantages for an MMAR study:

    - It is a relatively simple set of statistical procedures that can be easily applied by practitioner-researchers to obtain information about two group differences in all concurrent and sequential MMAR study designs, consistent with the study purpose.
    - It is an effective venue to get stakeholders involved with the data analysis process because it does not require extensive training.
    - It is a means to help explore the relevance and usefulness of the action/intervention and inform the needed modifications in the evaluation phase of an MMAR study.

  o Issues to consider:

    - It requires caution to make definitive assumptions about the effectiveness of the taken action/intervention based on the statistical significance of the test because significance determined statistically may not reflect practical significance that implies subjective judgment.
    - Smaller samples tend to yield nonsignificant results, whereas large sample sizes may yield statistical significance but not practical significance.
    - It requires educating community members and other stakeholders on how to interpret the results of *t*-tests.

  o Illustration:

    - In a concurrent Quan + Qual MMAR study, Kostos and Shin (2010; Example A) used a paired *t*-test to analyze the pre- and postinstructional math assessment scores of the students before and after the instructional intervention as part of the evaluation process to measure the effects of math journals on enhancing second graders' communication of mathematical thinking (the evaluation phase).
    - In a sequential Quan → Qual MMAR study, Montgomery et al. (2008; Example E) proposed to use independent-measures *t*-test to examine the outcome differences between the group of housing residents from four northern sites and a matched comparison group drawn from a different location in Canada as part of the evaluation process of the existing supported housing programs for persons with serious mental illness in rural areas (the evaluation phase).

- *ANOVA (analysis of variances)*—a parametric statistical procedure for continuous data. It involves testing the difference between three or more groups using the group means. It is similar to *independent-measures t-test* but it is used when two or more groups need to be compared. There are several types *of ANOVA* tests. The most commonly used in action research are: (1) *one-way ANOVA* which tests differences between different groups to determine whether at least one group is statistically significantly different from other groups; (2) *two-way ANOVA*, which tests differences between the groups on two variables to determine whether at least one group is statistically significantly different from other groups based on the effect of each variable and their interaction; and (3) *repeated-measures ANOVA,* which tests the same group of individuals at several points in time to determine whether a statistically significant change has occurred. ANOVA tests yield an *F*-ratio (variance between groups compared to variance within groups) that is used to draw conclusions about whether the difference between the group means is statistically significant. Follow-up post hoc tests are used to find out which specific group or groups are different from the others (Gay et al., 2006; Mertler, 2012; Tomal, 2010; Vogt, 2005).

  ○ Advantages for an MMAR study:

    - It is not a complex set of statistical procedures that can be applied by practitioner-researchers with some training and assistance to learn if three or more groups differ from each other in all concurrent and sequential MMAR study designs, consistent with the study purpose.
    - It may be an effective venue to get community members and other stakeholders involved with the data analysis process, although it requires some training.
    - It is a means to help explore the relevance and usefulness of the action/intervention, particularly if there is a control group for comparison, and to inform the needed modifications of the planned action/intervention in the evaluation phase of an MMAR study.
    - Repeated-measures ANOVA is useful in pretest–posttest designs to determine the change between the baseline and outcome data to measure change.

  ○ Issues to consider:

    - It requires caution to make definitive assumptions about the effectiveness of the action/intervention taken based on statistical significance of the test because any significance determined statistically may not reflect practical significance or usefulness of the change that implies subjective judgment.
    - Smaller samples tend to yield nonsignificant results, whereas large sample sizes may yield statistical significance but not practical significance.
    - It requires educating community members and other stakeholders on how to interpret the results of ANOVA tests, particularly the interaction effect in two-way ANOVA.
    - It requires advanced knowledge of conducting and interpreting follow-up post hoc tests, which may necessitate seeking help from partnerships with trained statisticians.

(Continued)

(Continued)

o Illustration:

- In a concurrent Quan + Qual MMAR study, Glasson et al. (2006; Example B) used a two-way ANOVA to compare satisfaction scores on physical and psychological care, doctors' orders, and discharge planning between the premodel and model patients' groups to evaluate the new model of nursing care for older acutely ill hospitalized medical patients (the evaluation phase).
- In a sequential Qual → Quan MMAR study, Johnson et al. (2010) used a one-way ANOVA to compare the survey responses of adults and youths as part of the assessment of the strengths, needs, and limitations in the community to inform the development of a comprehensive service system model (the reconnaissance phase).

- *Regression*—a parametric statistical procedure for continuous data. It involves testing what factors (independent variables) may predict some outcome (dependent variable). There are two primary types of regression: *simple regression* in which an effect of one independent variable is tested, and *multiple regression* that tests an effect of several independent variables. *Multiple regression* is effective when there is a need to identify a degree of influence of each potential factor. Regression tests yield a regression coefficient that is used to draw conclusions about the association between the variables and how much change in the dependent variable can be predicted based on the change in the independent variable or variables (Gay et al., 2006; Johnson & Christensen, 2012; Vogt, 2005).

o Advantages for an MMAR study:

- It is not a very complex set of statistical procedures, and can be applied by practitioner-researchers with some training and assistance for the purpose of gaining information about the association between the factors and an outcome in all concurrent and sequential MMAR study designs, consistent with the study purpose.
- It may be an effective venue to get university partners involved with the data analysis and interpretation process.
- It is an effective means to help with the needs assessment by identifying influencing factors, and to inform the action/intervention during the reconnaissance phase. It can also help explore the relevance and usefulness of the action/intervention and inform the needed modifications in the evaluation phase of an MMAR study.

o Issues to consider:

- It requires caution to make definitive assumptions about the effectiveness of the taken action/intervention based on statistical significance of the test because significance determined statistically may not reflect practical significance that implies subjective judgment about the usefulness of the change action.
- Smaller samples tend to yield nonsignificant results, whereas large sample sizes may yield statistical significance but not practical significance.

- It requires educating community members and other stakeholders on how to interpret the results of regression tests, particularly multiple regression, that involves several analytical steps.
- Quality of collected data is of particular importance because it can affect the strength of association.

○ Illustration:

- In a sequential Qual → Quan MMAR study, Reese et al. (1999) used multiple regression to test if ethnicity was a barrier to hospice access and use among African Americans and European Americans as part of the problem assessment and attempts to advance social change in the community (the reconnaissance phase).
- In a concurrent Quan + Qual MMAR study, Zoellner et al. (2012) used multiple regression to identify the predicting factors, such as parent gardening attitudes, beliefs, and intentions for gardening engagement and thus to inform the development and implementation of the community garden program (the reconnaissance phase).

- *Chi-square test*—a nonparametric statistical procedure for categorical data. It is used when data are categorized based on some characteristic (e.g., gender, age group, education levels, soft drink preferences, etc.). It involves testing the difference between the groups comparing the proportions actually observed in a study (observed frequencies) to the expected or hypothesized proportions (expected frequencies; what would be expected if the groups were equal). The test yields an χ^2 statistic that is used to draw conclusions about whether the difference between the groups is statistically significant. The χ^2 value increases as the difference between observed and expected frequencies increases (Gay et al., 2006; Mertler, 2012; Vogt, 2005).

○ Advantages for an MMAR study:

- It is not a very complex set of statistical procedures, and can be applied by practitioner-researchers with some training and assistance to obtain information if the groups are different in all concurrent and sequential MMAR study designs, consistent with the study purpose.
- It is an effective test in research situations when it is easier to collect categorical data and continuous data are not available.
- It may be an effective venue to get university partners involved with the data analysis and interpretation process.
- It is a means to help explore the relevance and usefulness of the action/intervention, particularly if there is a control group for comparison, and to inform the needed modifications in the evaluation phase of an MMAR study.

○ Issues to consider:

- It requires caution to make definitive assumptions about the effectiveness of the taken action/intervention based on statistical significance of the test because significance determined statistically may not reflect practical significance that implies subjective judgment.

(Continued)

(Continued)

- Smaller samples tend to yield nonsignificant results, whereas large sample sizes may yield statistical significance but not practical significance.
- It requires educating community members and other stakeholders on how to interpret the results of Chi-square tests.
- It has limitations related to sample size and strength of the relationship that may affect the interpretation of the Chi-square test results and their substantive significance.

  o Illustration:

- In a sequential Quan → Qual MMAR study, Reutzel and colleagues (2006) used a Chi-square test to compare the responses of parents and students on the survey as part of evaluating the efficacy of the parents' involvement program in school (the evaluation phase).
- In a concurrent Quan + Qual MMAR study, Phillips and Davidson (2009) used a Chi-square test to compare the views and attitudes of aged care nurses and care assistants in a variety of aged care nurse practice settings to identify priorities for action and inform the development of the intervention—sustainable model of palliative care (the reconnaissance phase).

ANALYZING QUALITATIVE DATA IN AN MMAR STUDY

As discussed in Chapter 7, qualitative data often receives more emphasis than does quantitative data in an MMAR study due to the focus on a specific problem in a professional context and the need to explore all stakeholders' perspectives, including their attitudes, beliefs, and feelings about the issue of interest. Importantly, the analysis of qualitative information reflecting participants' experiences and views on the existing problem may help practitioner-researchers to achieve an in-depth understanding of the studied problem, and to gain insight into the social reality of situations through the interpretations that stakeholders offer (Koshy et al., 2011). According to Tesch (1990), the purpose of qualitative data analysis is to generate a larger, consolidated picture of the studied phenomenon. Combined with the results of the descriptive and inferential statistical analysis in an MMAR study, qualitative findings help create a holistic perspective on the studied problem and inform the direction of the change action.

Reportedly, there is no single accepted approach to qualitative data analysis (Miles & Huberman, 1994). The approaches vary across the disciplines and within research communities from being mostly interpretative in clarifying the meaning of the data (Denzin & Lincoln, 2011) to taking the form of frequency counts of the generated codes and categories, which is often referred to as content analysis (Schwandt, 2001). No matter what approach is employed, for the analysis to generate credible results it needs to be performed in a systematic and consistent way. It is also important to remember that effective qualitative data analysis typically is performed in a zigzag or iterative manner; that is, data analysis occurs simultaneously with data collection (Creswell, 2012). A zigzag process implies collecting some of the data (e.g., several interviews), conducting their preliminary analysis, and then proceeding with the data collection looking for additional information that may have been missed. Analyzing the data early in the data collection process may give practitioner-researchers a general sense of the collected information to decide whether it has relevance for the study research questions, what aspects need to be elaborated more during subsequent data collection (e.g., probing more during the interview), and whether additional study participants should be recruited to explore new information. It may also help decide whether saturation in the data is reached—that is, the point in data collection and analysis when adding new individuals or cases does not provide any new information. Herr and Anderson (2005) observed that in action research the data analysis process begins immediately and guides further data collection and subsequent decision making. Starting data analysis early also has advantages, as it prompts when it is necessary to follow up with the study participants on some important information that is emerging from the analysis while the participants are still available and their memory of what has been discussed during the recent interview or focus group is still fresh. Consider how Thomas-MacLean and colleagues (2010) described this aspect of qualitative data analysis in their MMAR study quoted in Table 8.3.

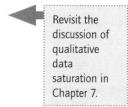

Revisit the discussion of qualitative data saturation in Chapter 7.

So, what is the process of qualitative data analysis and how do practitioner-researchers apply qualitative analytical strategies in an MMAR study?

Process of Qualitative Data Analysis

The process of qualitative data analysis involves an **inductive** approach that aims at reducing the volume of information by systematically organizing the data into categories and themes from specific to general (Creswell, 2014; Mertler, 2012; Miles & Huberman, 1994). Boeije (2009) described qualitative analytic process as the following:

> Qualitative analysis is the segmenting of data into relevant categories and the naming of these categories with codes while simultaneously generating the categories from the data. In the reassembling phase the categories are related to one another to generate theoretical understanding of the social phenomenon under study in terms of the research questions. (p. 76)

The aim of segmenting and reassembling the data again is to transform the data into findings. This transformation is achieved through a researcher's interpretation of the data (sorting, naming, categorizing, and connecting) and by researcher's reflecting on what the data means and how a researcher believes it should be understood.

In action research, qualitative data analysis is often referred to as theorizing or "making meaning" of the data (Hinchey, 2008, p. 94). It involves organizing, describing, and interpreting perspectives of multiple groups of stakeholders to facilitate an overall understanding of the studied problem/issue, while preserving the complexity of unique experiences and their pragmatic and personally relevant explanations. The outcome of the analytical process is often a set of themes and categories with related codes and descriptions that provide an effective and easy-to-follow framework for communicating the findings to interested stakeholders for further action (Koshy et al., 2011; Mertler, 2012; Mills, 2011; Stringer, 2014). Using an inductive thematic approach to qualitative data analysis is in line with the methodological characteristics of MMAR study designs because it allows practitioner-researchers to combine or connect the qualitative findings in the form of themes, categories, or even codes, to the quantitative test results, thus making the integration of the quantitative and qualitative results procedurally more manageable.

For example, in Glasson and colleagues' (2006) MMAR study (Example B), the following themes or "key concepts" emerged from the analysis of the nurses' responses to the open-ended items on the questionnaire: barriers to change, enthusiasm to change, collaboration in planning, empowerment in planning, expanding knowledge, and empowerment to change practice (p. 594). These themes with related categories were used to inform the evaluation of the new model of nursing care implementation in that medical ward. Consider Table 8.2, which provides an example of some of the themes that emerged from the interviews with 10 stakeholders in Zoellner and colleagues' (2012) MMAR study on community gardening. The researchers organized the three themes (community cohesion,

TABLE 8.2 **Example of Themes and Supporting Quotes in Zoellner et al. (2012, p. 158) MMAR Study**

Social-Ecological Level	Theme	Example Quote(s)
Community/ Environmental	Community cohesion	"I think when the community is working together and is cohesive they begin addressing not just their food issues, but other issues they may be facing as a community." "I think that the primary function of the community garden would be to bring the community together."
	Nutrition	"The benefits of a community garden would be local produce that perhaps would be certainly traveling less distance and would be available to those who need it to supplement their diet with healthier foods to eat." "[Community gardens] would definitely potentially increase [fruit and vegetables consumption] and this would be beneficial because it would definitely help out a lot of these neighborhoods which are basically low income, not low-middle class and it's a good way for them to benefit not only by increasing their [fruit and vegetables] but by decreasing the money they had spent on food." "Access to vegetables and fruits and making them aware of what's out there and what is available in the city even though it's limited at this point . . ."
	Physical activity	"We don't have very many places where you can do physical fitness such as gyms and the city parks are not as well distributed as they should be for exercise." "I think if there were more opportunities and convenience and easy ways to be physically active that would help."

nutrition, and physical activity) with supporting stakeholders' quotes within a community/environmental level of a socioecological framework. The goal was to provide evidence for the potentially beneficial effects of a community garden initiative that would inform the action/intervention.

As was mentioned earlier in the chapter, any data analysis should follow a sequence of steps to produce credible and reliable results. Creswell's (2009) step-by-step approach to qualitative data analysis and interpretation presented in Box 8.3 was previously suggested as an efficient framework to guide practitioner-researchers in this process (Koshy et al., 2011). Accordingly, a researcher starts with raw text data, such as interview and focus group transcripts, observation field notes, photos, and images, and finishes with interpreting the meaning of the generated themes and descriptions. The steps in between include organizing and preparing the data for analysis, reading and getting familiar with the data, coding the data manually or with the help of a computer-based program, synthesizing the codes to generate descriptions and themes, and organizing the themes to produce an exhaustive explanation or description of the studied phenomenon. In spite of being presented in a linear order, Creswell (2009) viewed these analytical steps occurring as an interactive process. During the analytical process, the steps may be often interrelated, and the same steps may be repeated cyclically until the level of data interpretation sufficient to answer the posted research questions is reached, or a new question surfaces.

BOX 8.3

Steps in Qualitative Data Analysis

1. Organize, transcribe, sort, and prepare the data for analysis.

2. Review all data files to get a general sense of the collected information and to reflect on its overall meaning.

3. Start coding the data and developing a qualitative codebook.

4. Use the coding process to generate a description of the setting or people and categories and themes for analysis.

5. Decide on the way to represent the qualitative findings in narrative reports organized by themes, visual diagrams, tables, and figures.

6. Interpret the meaning of the findings focusing on the lessons learned in the context of existing research and theories about the studied issue.

From Cresswell (2009).

Consider how the process of qualitative data analysis is described in the nine selected published MMAR studies presented in Table 8.3. The various authors approached this analytical task differently, but they all followed the steps outlined in Box 8.3, although with some variation. In their descriptions of qualitative data analysis, the authors highlighted an inductive approach, an iterative nature of the analytical process, immersion into the text data, coding, synthesizing, and interpreting the data.

| TABLE 8.3 | Examples of Descriptions of Qualitative Data Analysis from Published MMAR Studies |

Example of qualitative data analysis of students' autobiographical narratives used in the reconnaissance phase to inform the type of a lesson style of students' choice in Sampson's (2010) MMAR study (Example D)[1]

"The Language Learning Autobiography underwent qualitative content analysis—that is, the teacher-researcher read over the written texts a number of times, highlighting different phrases across the texts that reflected categories of interest to the change-action. These were allocated codes, and further refined into groupings to represent the main themes emergent from the texts" (p. 287).

Example of qualitative data analysis of individual interviews with family physicians used in the reconnaissance phase to inform the development of a mentorship program for primary care physicians in Saskatchewan in Thomas-MacLean's et al. (2010) MMAR study[2]

"Thematic codes and a standardized coding structure were created using NVivo 8. Categories, or themes, were identified via thorough reading of transcripts. The coding structure was initially developed by the research assistant who conducted the interviews. The interview guide was adapted during interview analysis in order to refine interview questions and create 'novel questions' based on 'constant comparison' of participant views. Discussion between 2 researcher team members and the research assistant provided additional verification and trustworthiness of the coding structure, codes, and categories (or themes)" (p. e267).

Example of qualitative data analysis of shelter residents' responses to the open-ended survey questions used in the reconnaissance phase to understand homeless individuals' needs when transitioning from hospital to homeless shelter in Greysen's et al. (2012) MMAR study[3]

"Using qualitative survey data from open-ended questions, we employed the constant comparative method of qualitative data analysis. A multidisciplinary team of four study authors with expertise in homelessness, hospital discharge planning, community-based participatory research, and qualitative methods independently coded the open-ended responses and met as a group to resolve discrepancies through negotiation. We developed codes iteratively, and refined them to identify conceptual segments of the data. The team reviewed the code structure throughout the analytic process, and revised the scope and content of codes as needed. The final code structure contains 15 codes, which we subsequently integrated into one overarching theme and three recurring themes on recommendations for improvement" (p. 1486).

Example of qualitative data analysis of individual interviews with nurses used in the evaluation phase to explore the effectiveness of the new appreciative inquiry intervention strategy in inpatient pediatric care in Kavanagh, Stevens, Seers, Sidani, and Watt-Watson's (2010) MMAR study[4]

"Qualitative content analysis was conducted in verbatim transcripts of the semistructured interview by the lead author to determine the acceptability and fidelity of the AI intervention. Concepts were derived inductively from the data using open coding and assimilated into a conceptual index of main themes and subthemes. NVivo 8 was used to manage the data. Memos were written to maintain a record of concept development and analytic decisions, and a reflexive journal was kept to record reactions to the data and examine biases. A second analyst independently coded two transcripts using the conceptual index" (p. 4).

Example of qualitative data analysis of individual interviews with second-grade students and the teacher's reflective journal used in the evaluation phase to explore the effectiveness of math journal instructional strategy in Kostos and Shin's (2010) MMAR study (Example A)[5]

"Third, the interviews with eight randomly selected students were analyzed by coding and memoing (Dana and Yendol-Silva 2003). The students' answers to the interview questions were read several times. The emerging themes focusing on consistencies and changes in the students' responses as well as relationships and connections between the responses were recorded and then placed in categories. These categories were reviewed carefully to establish patterns. Lastly, the teacher's reflective journal was also analyzed qualitatively using coding and memoing techniques. The teacher's reflective journal entries were read and re-read several times to look for emerging themes and patterns that informed how the use of math journals affected the second-grade students' communication of mathematical thinking" (p. 227).

Example of qualitative data analysis of individual interviews with stakeholders from each partner accreditation agency to be used in the evaluation phase to examine strengths and weaknesses of Australian health service accreditation processes in Hinchcliff's et al. (2012) MMAR study[6]

"Thematic analysis of interview transcriptions will be undertaken inductively, supported by the use of the textual grouping software, NVivo V. 9 (Doncaster, Australia). Such programmes are used to facilitate systematic classification of the data. . . . Preliminary development of thematic categories (ie, key topics discussed by respondents) and initial coding will be conducted by the first author, who has extensive qualitative data analysis experience. After discussion among the research team to cross-check the validity and relevance of developed themes, categories will be refined and adjusted until a coherent scheme is developed that admits all instances and is applied to all interview data. To determine the reliability of categorization by the first author, 50 randomly selected coded sentences will be assessed by a second researcher issued with category definitions. The level of inter-rater reliability will be assessed using Cohen's Kappa statistic, which measures the inter-rater agreement, accounting for that expected by chance. A result less than 0.7 will necessitate further refinement of categories until a higher level of agreement is achieved" (p. 4).

Example of qualitative data analysis of reflective observation field notes, individual interviews, and focus groups with doctors, staff, and students used in both reconnaissance and evaluation phases to inform the development and assessment of the community of practice model to promote quality of stroke care in Kilbride, Perry, Flatley, Turner, and Meyer's (2011) MMAR study[7]

"Qualitative data were analyzed thematically using a process of Immersion/Crystallization. In this systematic, iterative process the researcher read and re-read to immerse herself in the texts, created notes and coded text with intuitive interpretations. Each re-reading sought evidence for congruent and different perspectives (Borkan, 1999). Progress was regularly presented and discussed with co-authors who also examined selected transcripts. Textual interpretation was by consensus" (p. 92).

(Continued)

TABLE 8.3   **Continued**

Example of qualitative data analysis of baseline and follow-up individual interviews used in the evaluation phase to explore the effectiveness of a community–academic partnership created to address hepatitis health disparities in Asian American and Pacific Islander communities in VanDevanter, Kwon, Sim, Chun, and Trinh-Shevrin's (2011) MMAR study[8]

"All baseline interviews were transcribed verbatim. After an initial review of transcripts, using an iterative process, the evaluator and a graduate research assistant developed a preliminary coding scheme that included primary themes related to the evaluation foci and themes that emerged from the data. Content analysis using a constant comparison approach was used to examine variations in the data to further refine the coding scheme. Coded data was entered into Atlas.ti qualitative software for data analysis. Inter-rater reliability was high (<0.85). For the follow-up interviews, the evaluator and a graduate research assistant independently reviewed and took detailed notes from the interviews and audiotapes. A content analysis of the data was performed to identify themes related to core domains and new themes related to the expanded scope of the follow-up study. Coding differences were resolved through discussion" (p. 226).

Example of qualitative data analysis of individual interviews and document audit used in the evaluation phase to determine the feasibility of an advance care planning model developed with Australian community palliative care services in Blackford and Street's (2012) MMAR study[9]

"The interview data were imported into NVivo (Ver8.0) (QSR International 2009) for coding. A directed content analysis (Ezzy 2002, Hsieh & Shannon 2005, Grbich 2007) using the categories from preexisting literature (Street & Ottmann 2006) was undertaken to build a profile of each service. Line-by-line coding was used to identify implementation issues for services and the strategies used to embed ACP [advance care planning] into the service structure. In the final stage of analysis, the different services were compared and contrasted to identify the key components of a feasible Model for community palliative care (see Table 4). The analysis from the document audit added a further dimension to the directed content analysis. The document audit analysis was combined with the directed content analysis to identify evidence of the changes implemented and provide verification of the interview data (see Table 3)" (p. 2024).

[1]From Sampson (2010).

[2]From Thomas-MacLean et al. (2010).

[3]From Greysen et al. (2012).

[4]From Kavanagh et al. (2010).

[5]From Kostos and Shin (2010).

[6]Reprinted from Hinchcliff et al. (2012) with permission of BMJ Group.

[7]From Kilbride et al. (2011).

[8]From VanDevanter et al. (2011).

[9]From Blackford & Street (2012).

To facilitate practitioner-researchers' application of the described analytical steps when analyzing qualitative data in an MMAR study, Figure 8.1 presents a visual model of qualitative data analysis process that was adapted to an MMAR study based on Creswell's (2012) original diagram. It shows how the synthesized themes about the studied phenomenon are generated from multiple pieces of individual text data using an inductive approach. The process involves segmenting or dividing the data into semantic segments, labeling the segments with codes that capture the meaning of the segments, examining the codes for overlap and redundancy, reassembling or aggregating these codes into broader categories and themes, and interpreting the meaning of the themes. Creswell (2014) advised having five to seven themes with subthemes or categories as major findings of the analysis.

Coding and Theme Development

> Refer to the Further Readings at the end of this chapter for detailed information about qualitative data analytical methods used in action research.

The following sections discuss some aspects of the process of coding and theme development in an MMAR study. While it is not possible to discuss all the nuances of qualitative data analysis in action research in this text, it is important to highlight several procedural components, such as the process of coding, development of a codebook, using constant comparative method, conducting inter-coder agreement, and employing computer programs for qualitative analysis.

Coding and Types of Codes

Coding is a central strategy used in inductive qualitative data analysis that helps to distill units of meaning and then to combine them in a new way into groups or categories, thus recreating participants' common experience with the studied phenomenon. Craig (2009) pointed out that "it is the coding that truly creates the picture of events" (p. 189). Coding is part of the data-segmenting process. It aims to reduce large amounts of text data into a system of hierarchically organized categories and themes based on similar types of information for identifying and presenting the findings. Practically speaking, the purpose of coding is to conceptualize and reduce the data to fit it into a format that will allow generating substantive conclusions (Koshy et al., 2011; Strauss & Corbin, 1998). Guest, MacQueen, and Namey (2012) defined coding as "identifying a meaningful segment of text [that] calls for some minimal representation of that meaning" (p. 52). Some researchers refer to such coding as *open coding*, emphasizing an initial inductive approach of capturing and segmenting information in the given text data (Strauss & Corbin, 1998). Oftentimes participants' actual words, which are referred to as in vivo codes, are used for code labels. An **in vivo coding** strategy is particularly useful in action research because it helps illuminate participants' experiences and preserve their voices to inform future action. Stringer (2014) advised that explanations and interpretations produced in an action research study "should be framed in terms that participants use in their everyday lives" (p. 137).

There are three types of codes that practitioner-researchers can use during the coding process: (1) emergent codes that are developed inductively from the text data in the study, (2) predetermined codes that are derived deductively from the literature and theory and are applied to code the text data in the study, and (3) combination of the emergent (inductive) and predetermined (deductive) codes (Creswell, 2014). A number of factors—such as a dominating epistemological tradition within the discipline, a researcher's skills

| FIGURE 8.1 | **Visual Model of Qualitative Data Analysis Process in an MMAR Study** |

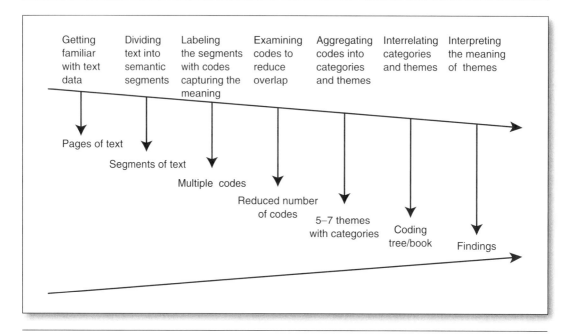

Adapted from Creswell (2012).

with inductive coding, and the absence or presence of a solid theoretical framework guiding the study—influence the choice of a coding strategy and types of codes selected. In social sciences, inductive coding is more frequently used, whereas in health and behavioral sciences, predetermined or a priori developed codes, or a combination of the inductive and deductive coding, is more applicable. For example, Greysen and colleagues (2012) employed an inductive coding strategy to code the responses to the open-ended survey questions by homeless shelter residents, whereas Blackford and Street (2012) used deductive coding by applying the categories from preexisting literature to interview transcripts to build a profile of each community palliative care service (see Table 8.3).

Qualitative Codebook

The process of coding involves developing a qualitative **codebook** that presents a list of codes and their groupings into emergent categories and themes. Guest and colleagues (2012) considered a codebook development as one of the most critical components of inductive qualitative analysis. A codebook helps to systematically sort the coded text into "categories, types, and relationships of meaning" (p. 52). In addition to codes, a codebook may include a working definition of a code, an illustrative example of its use in the analyzed text, or a verbatim text segment that was coded by this code, that is a participant's quote. A codebook evolves as the data analysis continues and new codes are added to it.

Having a developed codebook to guide further analysis is advantageous because it enhances the process of coding and makes it more manageable for practitioner-researchers; it helps ensure consistency in the coding, particularly when several coders are involved in coding the data for the same project. Using a codebook can also help promote collaboration with stakeholders and involve them in the data analysis process. Hacker (2013) indicated that by integrating community partners into the qualitative data analysis process, practitioner-researchers may not only facilitate the process of stakeholder engagement with the study's findings, but also seek continuous refinement of the codebook. For example, in their proposal for an MMAR study, Hinchcliff and colleagues (2012) discussed how they planned to develop a codebook, which they called a coherent scheme of categories and themes, to guide their analysis of the interview data with stakeholders from each partner accreditation agency as part of the evaluation of Australian health service accreditation processes. Similarly, Kavanagh and colleagues (2010) reported on using a conceptual index of main themes and subthemes to guide the analysis of the nurse interview data by another independent analyst in their MMAR study (see Table 8.3).

Constant Comparative Method

The process of coding and theme development is enhanced by the use of the **constant comparative method,** which supports inductive coding and is iterative in nature. It involves comparing the data from all data sources in a given study segment by segment during the coding process (Strauss & Corbin, 1998). More specifically, it involves comparing each new segment of data to other segments of data similarly categorized or labeled before creating a new code. As segments are compared, new analytic categories and new relationships between the categories may be discovered in the data. This ongoing search for comparison cases continues until no new insights are gained from them for further development of the categories (Schwandt, 2001). While there are other analytical strategies that can be effectively used when coding the data, applying the constant comparison method may have some practical implications for practitioner-researchers because it will signal reaching saturation in the data—that is, the point in data collection and analysis when additional individuals or cases do not provide new information (Guest et al., 2006). Check how the use of the constant comparison method is described in the two MMAR studies by Greysen and colleagues (2012) and Thomas-MacLean and colleagues (2010) presented in Table 8.3.

Inter-coder Agreement

The quality of coding also can be promoted by coding data in teams for the purposes of establishing consistency in coding and engaging stakeholders in the data analysis process. Two or more research team members can participate in coding the same data, thus enhancing agreement for the developed codes, categories, and themes. This process is referred to as an **inter-coder agreement,** and consists of the team members independently coding select pieces of text data, and then comparing the codes and emergent themes to resolve discrepancies. During each discussion session, the percent of agreement among the coders is calculated and reported. Sometimes, this process is termed as inter-rater reliability to underscore the notion of consistency in qualitative data interpretations (Miles & Huberman, 1994). Miles and Huberman (1994) suggested that inter-coder reliability should be calculated based on the following formula and should be considered acceptable in the 90% range:

reliability = # of agreements / total # of agreements + total # of disagreements

Alternatively, a statistical procedure of Cohen's Kappa that measures the inter-rater agreement and accounts for what might occur by chance may be calculated (Fleiss, 1981). An acceptable statistic for inter-rater reliability when using Cohen's Kappa is higher than 0.7. For example, Payne (2008) described the process of establishing inter-rater reliability of the focus group data during the reconnaissance phase of his MMAR study that was aimed at understanding the relationship between attitudes toward opportunity and life-street orientation in black men with the purpose of informing a culturally relevant intervention. Three students were recruited to analyze two different transcripts, highlighting in color all text passages about men's use of the streets for economic survival. Then Payne scored each transcript according to a master copy and calculated the inter-rater alpha coefficient of 0.82, which indicated a high level of consistency among the student coders.

Approaches to establishing inter-coder agreement vary across qualitative research authors. Some argue that there are more chances to have consensus on the themes among different researchers than on the "packaging" of these themes (Armstrong, Gosling, Weinman, & Marteau, 1997, p. 3), while Miles and Huberman (1994) suggested that team members should compare all codes and related text segments. Opinions also vary on how much of the data should be subjected to inter-coder agreement process, ranging from the first few pages to an entire transcript, and on how to select the specific data to compare—for example, at random from all transcripts or the first available transcripts.

It seems more effective for practitioner-researchers to compare both the codes and the themes on select pieces of data (e.g., select interview or focus group transcripts or observation notes) to ensure all stakeholders' views are being captured and are categorized appropriately. This approach should help the community partners and other stakeholders get immersed in the data and better understand the coding process because they will have a voice in determining these critical components. Importantly, starting with the first available text data (e.g., the first interview transcripts) will help develop a codebook to guide further analysis. Other randomly selected pieces of text data can be added later to verify consistency in the analysis and the presentation of findings. Check how the inter-coder agreement procedure is described in four MMAR studies presented in Table 8.3 (Greysen et al., 2012; Hinchcliff et al., 2012; Kavanagh et al., 2010; VanDevanter et al., 2011).

Computer-based Programs for Qualitative Analysis

Data coding and analysis process can be enhanced by the use of computer programs for qualitative analysis. These programs operate differently from how quantitative software for statistical analysis does because the process of inductive coding cannot be performed automatically; however, computer-based programs for qualitative analysis can assist practitioner-researchers with data organization, management, and display. Computer-based programs are particularly helpful when the project contains large qualitative data sets that may be difficult to manage manually. For example, Hinchcliff and colleagues (2012), Kavanagh and colleagues (2010), and Thomas-MacLean and colleagues (2010) applied NVivo program, and VanDevanter and colleagues (2011) used ATLAS.ti to analyze text data in their MMAR studies (see Table 8.3). Some of the most popular qualitative computer-based programs are described in Table 8.4. Of note is that many of these programs now offer features that assist with mixed methods data analysis and may help practitioner-researchers in the analysis of the data for their MMAR studies.

| **TABLE 8.4** | **Computer-Based Programs for Qualitative and Mixed Methods Data Analysis** |

ATLAS.ti for Windows PC

(http://www.atlasti.com/index.html)

The program helps organize, code, and annotate textual, visual, and audio data. It helps facilitate the data categorization process and organize the evolving categories in a (causal) network. It allows exporting the coded data for further analyses to other programs, particularly SPSS, for which it has a syntax-generating interface.

HyperRESEARCH for Windows PC and Mac

(http://www.researchware.com/products/hyperresearch.html)

The program assists with coding and analyzing textual data, retrieving information, and building theories. It allows working with text, graphic, audio, and video data. A built-in hypothesis tester feature enhances building and testing theories.

MAXQDA for Windows PC

(http://www.maxqda.com/qualitative-data-analysis-software)

The program supports qualitative and mixed methods data analysis. Besides assisting with qualitative analysis of text, graphic, audio, and video data, it has the features to support combined quantitative and qualitative analysis. It allows for including variables or quantifying the results of the qualitative analysis. Data matrices can be exported to statistical programs, such as SPSS and SAS (Statistical Analysis System), for further analyses.

NVivo for Windows PC

(http://www.qsrinternational.com/products_nvivo.aspx)

The program supports qualitative and mixed methods data analysis. It facilitates the process of collecting, organizing, and analyzing the content from interviews, focus group discussions, surveys, audio and social media data, YouTube videos, and Web pages. It also offers features for quantifying the coded text and audio data and visually organizing the data in charts and diagrams. It allows creating and exporting data reports in different formats to Excel, pdf, and Word. Data can be easily exchanged between NVivo and quantitative programs such as SPSS.

QDA Miner for Windows PC

(http://provalisresearch.com/products/qualitative-data-analysis-software/)

The program is a qualitative data analysis software package for coding, annotating, retrieving and analyzing small and large collections of documents and images. It may be used to analyze interview or focus group transcripts, legal documents, journal articles, books, as well as image data. The program has SimStat, a statistical data analysis tool, and WordStat, a quantitative content analysis and text mining module that allows for analyzing text and converting its content to numerical and categorical data.

Box 8.4 summarizes data analysis considerations that practitioner-researchers should take into account when analyzing quantitative and qualitative data in an MMAR study.

BOX 8.4

Quantitative and Qualitative Data Analysis Considerations in an MMAR Study

- The choice and use of data analytical strategies is predetermined by the study purpose, the research questions, and a practical focus of an MMAR study.
- More emphasis may be given to qualitative data and analysis due to the need to address a practical problem/issue and to understand stakeholders' perspectives on the issue of interest.
- In small-scale studies, descriptive statistics (measures of central tendencies, variability, and association) and basic inferential statistics (t-test, one- and two-way ANOVA, regression, and Chi-square) may be more frequently used than complex multivariate analysis.
- Descriptive statistical methods may be more frequently used than inferential statistics due to the focus on the issue that has relevance for a specific group of people affected by this issue rather than on the generalizability of the results to a larger population.
- Descriptive and inferential statistics analytical methods can be used in all MMAR study designs and in both phases of the MMAR process (reconnaissance and evaluation); however, descriptive statistics may be more emphasized during the reconnaissance phase to provide an initial assessment of the problem and describe the needs of the community.
- Analysis of qualitative data should be done in a systematic way and follow a sequence of logical but interactive steps.
- The process of qualitative data analysis follows an iterative, zigzag process of data collection and analysis; it employs constant comparative method in coding and theme development; it involves the development of a codebook to guide the analysis; it includes the establishment of an inter-coder agreement; and it uses computer-based qualitative analysis programs.
- Practitioner-researchers are encouraged to collaborate with university partners who have necessary expertise when conducting complex quantitative and qualitative data analysis using computer programs.
- Community partners can be engaged in data analysis and can be trained to assist with simple sets of statistical procedures and the basic processes of qualitative analysis, although the process of qualitative data analysis may be easier to understand and master.
- Community capacity should be built through training and educating stakeholders and community partners about the ways for interpreting the results from quantitative and qualitative data analysis and how combining, merging, and connecting these results may help generate meta-inferences relevant to an MMAR study purpose.

In addition to considering appropriate analytical strategies for quantitative and qualitative study strands, practitioner-researchers need to decide on the mixed methods data analysis approach that is specific to the MMAR design chosen for the study. So, what is mixed methods data analysis and how can it be applied in an MMAR study?

MIXED METHODS DATA ANALYSIS IN AN MMAR STUDY

Mixed methods authors define **mixed methods data analysis** as the methodological procedures referring to how quantitative and qualitative analytical strategies are integrated in a mixed methods study (Creswell & Plano Clark, 2011; Greene, 2007; Onwuegbuzie & Combs, 2010; Teddlie & Tashakkori, 2009). Mixed methods data analysis builds on traditional analytic methods applied in quantitative and qualitative data analysis and interpretation, which are integrated in different ways, depending on the type of the study design and the timing of quantitative and qualitative data collection (concurrent or sequential). Specifically, mixed methods data analysis implies analyzing quantitative and qualitative data using the available statistical and inductive analysis procedures along with applying an integrated analysis that focuses on the goals and research questions of each study strand, and the purposes of mixing quantitative and qualitative methods in the study.

Teddlie and Tashakkori (2009) and Creswell and Plano Clark (2011) proposed types and strategies of mixed methods data analysis that are connected to their respective typologies of mixed methods designs. Specifically, Teddlie and Tashakkori (2009) suggested six "mixed data analysis techniques" aligned with the design implementation processes in their mixed methods design typology (p. 264): parallel, sequential, conversion, multilevel, fully integrated, and application of analytical techniques from one research approach within another research approach. Creswell and Plano Clark (2011) considered two types of mixed methods analysis—merging and connecting—based on how quantitative and qualitative data are analyzed to meet the specific purposes of mixed methods designs. Greene (2007) connected mixed methods data analysis strategies to four analytical phases that occur within the proposed interactive-independent dimension design clusters: data transformation, data correlation and comparison, data analysis for inquiry conclusions and inferences, and data analysis that utilizes "the analytic framework of one methodological tradition within the analysis of data from another tradition [for] a broad analytic concept" (p. 152).

Mixed methods data analysis has received relatively little attention in action research literature. Craig (2009) referred to creating a triangulation matrix to help an action researcher "decide how to organize the data before beginning the analysis process" (p. 171). The triangulation matrix serves as an organizational framework and helps align the collected data with the study research questions. Mills (2011) provided three examples of data analysis and interpretation techniques related to the mixed methods designs reported in mixed methods literature: triangulation, explanatory, and exploratory. While these are valuable insights that help support and advance mixed methods application in action research, they may not address all variations in integrated mixed methods data analysis that practitioner-researchers may encounter when conducting MMAR studies in different disciplines.

Refer to Chapter 5 and Table 5.1 for Teddlie and Tashakkori's (2009) and Creswell and Plano Clark's (2011) typologies of mixed methods designs.

Refer to the Further Readings at the end of this chapter to learn more about mixed methods analytical methods discussed in mixed methods texts.

> Revisit the discussion in Chapter 5 of the purposes of MMAR designs and the discussion in Chapter 6 of the goals of quantitative and qualitative methods' integration.

The approaches to mixed methods data analysis suggested by Creswell and Plano Clark (2011) and Teddlie and Tashakkori (2009) were adapted to the purposes of mixed methods data analysis in an MMAR study. Aligning with the practical focus of action research, this process is matched with the specific purposes of MMAR designs and the goals of quantitative and qualitative methods' integration (combining, connecting, merging) within these designs for producing credible and meaningful meta-inferences. Thus, the process of mixed methods data analysis in an MMAR study refers to the procedures of combining, merging, and connecting data analysis within and across the quantitative and qualitative study strands. The following sections discuss the procedures and steps in mixed methods data analysis in MMAR study designs.

Mixed Methods Data Analysis in a Concurrent Quan + Qual MMAR Study Design

In a concurrent Quan + Qual MMAR study design, practitioner-researchers can employ two procedures of mixed methods data analysis: *combined* data analysis for the purpose of comparing quantitative and qualitative results and *merged* data analysis for the purpose of conducting further data transformation. Consistent with the purpose of this MMAR design, the goal of combined and merged mixed methods data analysis is to provide more credibility to the overall study conclusions and to achieve valid meta-inferences to inform the action/intervention or its evaluation.

Combined mixed methods data analysis is implemented to assess whether the results from the quantitative and qualitative study strands converge or diverge when addressing the posed research questions, and whether any further analysis should be conducted to decrease the discrepancies in the joint data interpretation. To apply this procedure, practitioner-researchers should first conduct separate analysis of the quantitative and qualitative data and then compare the quantitative and qualitative results side by side in a summary table or a joint data display (Creswell & Plano Clark, 2011). In each case, practitioner-researchers should identify the dimensions along which they plan to compare the quantitative and qualitative results. Specific goals of the reconnaissance and evaluation phases of an MMAR study and the research questions for each study strand should help practitioner-researchers in choosing the dimensions for comparing the results.

For example, in their MMAR study, Davidson and colleagues (2008) compared the themes that emerged from the qualitative focus group and telephone interviews with the quantitative survey results during the final stage of analysis as part of the evaluation of the impact of a cardiac rehabilitation program for women with heart diseases. The results from two concurrent strands were compared along each program aspect to assess the positive changes in behavior and related psychological and social needs, and to inform further action. Similarly, Arnold and colleagues (2012) coded the transcripts of focus group discussions for "themes that paralleled the outcomes tested in the statistical models" from student survey data during the evaluation of school- and community-based HIV prevention interventions in Nigeria

(p. 107). Systematically comparing the quantitative test results with related qualitative findings allowed the researchers to claim the positive effects of the intervention on students' attitudes related to abstinence, use of condoms, and sexual activity.

Merged mixed methods data analysis through data transformation implies transforming one type of data into another type for further analysis (Creswell & Plano Clark, 2011; Teddlie & Tashakkori, 2009). This can be done by either quantitizing qualitative or text/narrative data, or qualitizing quantitative or numeric data. Teddlie and Tashakkori (2009) referred to this process as conversion; it can also be done on a single data set in the study when no other type of data is available—for example, a quantitative survey or qualitative interviews.

In the case of **quantitizing**, qualitative data from interviews, focus group discussions, or observations are first analyzed inductively for codes, categories, and themes; then, depending on the level of data transformation, codes, categories, and/or themes are assigned numeric values or frequency counts—for example, how many times a specific code, category, or theme is used (often referred to as content analysis). Then these counts, representing a quantitized data set, are merged with the original quantitative data set and are analyzed together using a statistical strategy. For example, in Blanco and colleagues' (2010) MMAR study, discussed in Chapter 6, the researchers calculated frequencies and percentages on the themes that emerged from the analysis of 11 students' questionnaires, interviews, and the teacher's observation journal. Those data were merged with the quantitative survey data collected from 24 students in order to provide a comprehensive evaluation of the instructional strategies for teaching beginning Spanish in a 4-year college.

In the case of **qualitizing**, quantitative data are first analyzed using statistical methods to identify trends and relationships; then narrative categories are identified within each variable based on the distribution of scores (Teddlie & Tashakkori, 2009). These narrative categories are then compared with the themes and categories that emerged from the analysis of the original qualitative data set, or merged with the qualitative data for further joint analysis. Another example of qualitizing is to perform factor analysis on the quantitative data set to identify significant factors, and then compare these factors with the themes and categories from the qualitative data analysis (Punch, 1998). Maritz and colleagues' (2011) MMAR study illustrates how exploratory factor analysis can be used to identify critical constructs or themes based on survey responses to help reveal strategy-making modes within organizations. Qualitizing quantitative data may be less frequently used in an MMAR study due to complexity of factor analysis procedures. Figure 8.2 presents a conceptual diagram of a concurrent Quan + Qual mixed methods data analysis in an MMAR study.

Mixed Methods Data Analysis in a Sequential Quan → Qual MMAR Study Design

In a sequential Quan → Qual MMAR study design, practitioner-researchers can conduct mixed methods data analysis by sequentially connecting or interlinking the results from the two chronological study strands with the purpose of explaining the joint results and creating a more in-depth understanding of the studied issue. Creswell and Plano Clark (2011) referred to it as **connected mixed methods data analysis**, in

FIGURE 8.2	**Conceptual Diagram of a Concurrent Quan + Qual Mixed Methods Data Analysis in an MMAR Study**

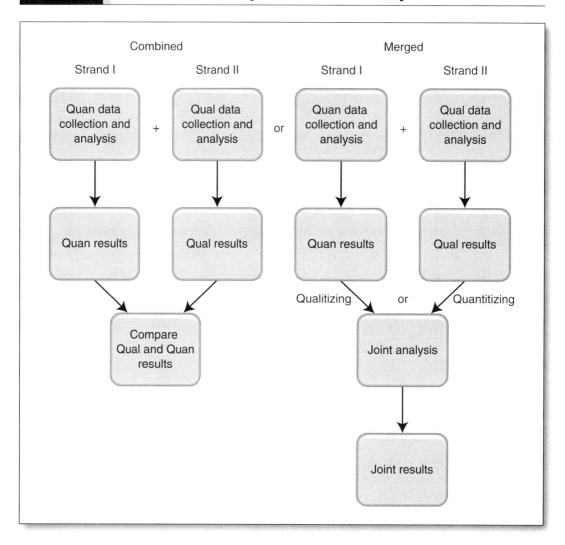

which "the analysis of the first data set is connected to data collection in the second data set" (p. 234). Part of this process is consideration of how to build the analysis of the follow-up qualitative study strand based on the results from the initial quantitative strand. Teddlie and Tashakkori (2009) pointed out that such connection is critical for mixed methods integration to occur in a sequential design.

Specifically, mixed methods data analysis in a sequential Quan → Qual MMAR study design may occur when the quantitative results from the first strand are used to guide the choice of the participants for qualitative follow-up; it may also occur when specific quantitative attributes, relationships, and trends identified in the quantitative strand are chosen for further qualitative exploration. Practitioner-researchers should be aware that selecting wrong participants for qualitative follow-up may create a bias in the interpretation of the overall study results and may have implications for informing the next step in the action research process. Similarly, choosing unimportant quantitative findings may result in superficial study conclusions and can incorrectly inform the direction and target of the action/intervention. Therefore, the application of this mixed methods data analysis strategy should be guided by an MMAR study purpose, research questions, and the specific goals of the reconnaissance and evaluation phases.

To implement connected mixed methods data analysis, practitioner-researchers should first analyze the quantitative data and then decide how these results may inform the direction of the next, qualitative strand, so that the qualitative results can help explain or elaborate on the initial quantitative findings. For example, practitioner-researchers may select a few typical respondents from those who completed quantitative measures to obtain a general sense of the problem, or, alternatively, may choose respondents with extreme scores on the survey who may provide divergent views on the issue. In action research studies in education, Mills (2011) discussed the relevance of following up with outlier cases using qualitative methods for further understanding of critical situations. Results from the statistical tests may also indicate what aspects of these findings should be explored during the subsequent qualitative interviews or focus group discussions. Ivankova and colleagues (2006) discussed the procedures related to systematically selecting participants for a follow-up qualitative analysis using a typical response to the initial quantitative survey, and also provided guidance to developing an interview protocol grounded in the results from the statistical tests. Additionally, Ivankova (2014) suggested another systematic procedure aimed at identifying extreme, unique, and typical cases for qualitative follow-up based on the consistency of the respondents' scores on the initial quantitative survey.

Reutzel and colleagues' (2006) MMAR study illustrates the use of connected mixed methods data analysis in a sequential Quan → Qual MMAR design. The researchers first collected survey data from first-grade students, their parents, and their teachers for the purpose of evaluating the efficacy of the existing parent–school involvement program. Then they randomly selected a number of students, parents, and teachers from those who completed the survey to participate in the focus group discussions in order to understand the survey results and to capture more in-depth participants' perspectives on the program. Random selection of the qualitative follow-up participants helped secure varied perspectives on the program's effectiveness for improving children's literacy.

The research questions may sometimes dictate the need to use a different and broader sample for the qualitative follow-up strand. This may be particularly important in an MMAR study because of the need to capture the views of all stakeholders. For example, in a research protocol for an MMAR study, Montgomery and colleagues (2008; Example E) described how they planned first to survey the clients in four supported housing units for individuals with serious mental illness to understand their needs, and then to purposefully select clients, their families, and community health workers based on the analysis of the survey results in order to explore the perspectives of all key informants on a supported housing program. Figure 8.3 presents a conceptual diagram of a sequential Quan → Qual mixed methods data analysis in an MMAR study.

| FIGURE 8.3 | **Conceptual Diagram of a Sequential Quan → Qual Mixed Methods Data Analysis in an MMAR Study** |

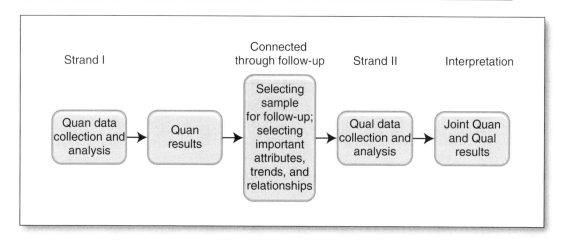

Mixed Methods Data Analysis in a Sequential Qual → Quan MMAR Study Design

Similar to data analysis in a sequential Quan → Qual MMAR study design, in a sequential Qual → Quan design, mixed methods data analysis is conducted sequentially by connecting or interlinking the results from the two chronological study strands. Practitioner-researchers should first conduct the analysis of the qualitative data and then decide how these results may inform the development of the next, quantitative strand. This implies reflecting on how the subsequent quantitative results may confirm, extend, or generalize the initial qualitative findings from the first study strand. Therefore, a subsequent quantitative strand "builds on" the first qualitative strand. This type of sequential mixed methods data analysis can be particularly useful in designing an intervention or planning the next phase of the quantitative data collection in a longitudinal MMAR study. The two purposes of connecting qualitative and subsequent quantitative results are (1) to generalize the findings of the first, qualitative strand by identifying a typology of variables for further testing and (2) to develop and test a measurement instrument (Creswell & Plano Clark, 2011; Teddlie & Tashakkori, 2009).

Specifically, in a sequential Qual → Quan MMAR study design, the qualitative results from the first study strand may be used to identify the variables to be further examined in the next, quantitative strand. Practitioner-researchers can use this approach when the problem or issue requires initial qualitative exploration because potentially important aspects or influencing factors that need to be investigated with a large group of stakeholders are unknown. For example, in the reconnaissance phase of their MMAR study, Young and Higgins (2010) conducted seven focus groups and two individual interviews with low-income single mothers to understand their perceptions of risk factors for cardiovascular diseases. The analysis of the qualitative data informed the researchers of the type of variables to look for in large quantitative databases; in their words, those were the variables "that had potential to resonate with the women's perspectives on their risk for CVD [cardiovascular diseases] advanced in the qualitative data" (p. 349). Teddlie and Tashakkori (2009) also suggested using a sequential Qual → Quan data analysis to identify the critical groups of people based on qualitative observations or interviews and then comparing the groups statistically. In an MMAR study, this may help identify the key stakeholders to be further surveyed using quantitative instruments.

Another way of conducting Qual → Quan mixed methods data analysis is to use the qualitative results from the first study strand to help identify or design a reliable quantitative instrument to be further administered to a larger group of people. This is a helpful approach when a needed measurement instrument does not exist or is not readily available. Mills (2011) considered this as an example of a useful application of mixed methods in action research studies in education. The mixed methods analytical process includes analyzing the qualitative data to identify useful codes, themes, and participants' quotes to inform the design of the items and scales on an instrument (Palcanis et al., 2012). Then the developed instrument can be administered to collect quantitative information from a larger group of people to measure the themes and categories that emerged during the analysis of qualitative data in the first study strand.

Practitioner-researchers should be aware that the process of an instrument development may not be easy and should involve pilot testing of the new instrument for reliability and validity prior to its administration to a large group of stakeholders. Low reliability and lack of validity of an instrument has important implications for the instrument's ability to generate the data that can truly reflect the studied phenomenon and that can be generalized to a larger population. When it is important for an MMAR study goals to develop a new measurement instrument, it may be beneficial for practitioner-researchers to seek partnerships with trained statisticians from local colleges, as well as secure input from key stakeholders in the interpretation of the qualitative information and the development of the survey items. Following correct psychometric procedures for developing an instrument grounded in the views and experiences of stakeholders will result in a more accurate assessment of the problem or the action/intervention taken to address this problem.

For example, in their MMAR study aimed at understanding patients' experiences with transitioning from hospital to a homeless shelter, Greysen and colleagues (2012) used qualitative information from individual interviews and focus group discussions with homeless individuals and key community stakeholders to develop an initial survey instrument. The survey consisted of 20 multiple-choice questions assessing "basic demographic information, frequency of acute care visits, transportation to and from the hospital, ED [emergency department], or hospital course, assessment of housing status by hospital staff, hospital discharge and disposition" (p. 1486). In another MMAR study, Hicks and colleagues (2012) reported using a literature review on effective community-academic partnerships in communities with health disparities to create a variable matrix to locate and then evaluate the available instruments for surveying academic researchers and community members about the role of partnerships when researching community health. They also conducted case studies of two partnerships to inform the development of their final instrument. Figure 8.4 presents a conceptual diagram of a sequential Qual → Quan mixed methods data analysis in an MMAR study.

FIGURE 8.4	**Conceptual Diagram of a Sequential Qual → Quan Mixed Methods Data Analysis in an MMAR Study**

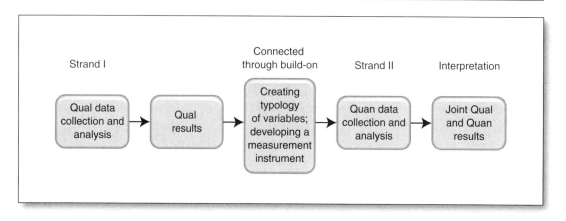

Mixed Methods Data Analysis in a Multistrand MMAR Study Design

In a multistrand MMAR design that consists of more than two concurrent or sequential strands, mixed methods data analysis can occur through a combination of combined, merged, and connected data analysis. Teddlie and Tashakkori (2009) referred to an *iterative sequential mixed analysis* when the study consists of more than two sequential strands. For example, in their MMAR study, Vecchiarelli and colleagues (2005) used an iterative sequential mixed analysis, Qual → Quan → Quan, when they first asked school community stakeholders to qualitatively identify self-evaluated criteria to include in a Nutrition Friendly School program and then to quantitatively rank the identified criteria using the Delphi process techniques to select the top 10 criteria in each specific area. In a subsequent quantitative study strand, they used these criteria to develop a self-evaluation tool that was administered to a large sample of teachers, administrators, food service staff, and nurses to detect the areas for improvement in school nutrition programs. Similarly, Blackstone (2011) proposed to employ an iterative sequential mixed analysis, Quan→ Qual → Quan, to evaluate the new university support structures for

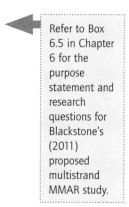

Refer to Box 6.5 in Chapter 6 for the purpose statement and research questions for Blackstone's (2011) proposed multistrand MMAR study.

community college transfer students. The researcher will first examine if a relationship exists between students' use of these university support structures and these students' GPAs. Then based on the results of this analysis she will select students with low and high GPAs and varied experiences with the university support structures to participate in follow-up focus group interviews to inform the development of the new survey instrument. The qualitative themes, subthemes, and quotes from the focus group discussions will provide the foundation for the new survey scales and items. In the final study strand, the survey instrument will be administered to all university transfer students to determine the effectiveness of the university support structures.

The choice of the mixed methods data analysis approach depends on whether the quantitative and qualitative data collection and analysis in two contiguous study strands is concurrent or sequential, and if the purpose of mixed methods data analysis is to combine, merge, or connect the data. It is also critical to consider the purposes of the joint analysis of the quantitative and qualitative results as a foundation for data collection and analysis in the next study strand. For example, in Sampson's (2010) multistrand MMAR design study (Example D), concurrent Quan + Qual mixed methods data analysis was applied by combining the analysis of a quantitative survey, the Lesson Style Questionnaire, and the narrative data from the Language Learning Autobiography completed by the students to identify their preferred lesson style. Subsequently, a sequential Qual → Quan mixed methods data analysis was applied to inform the development of the quantitative Learning Experience Questionnaire that was based on the qualitative data from the journals that the students had to keep to reflect on the activities and learning that occurred during each class. The surveys were completed by the students at the end of the course and the quantitative results were compared with the journal entries to confirm the students' views of their learning experiences. Box 8.5 summarizes the steps in mixed methods data analysis as applied in MMAR study designs.

BOX 8.5

Steps in Mixed Methods Data Analysis in MMAR Study Designs

Concurrent Quan + Qual MMAR Study Design

Combined and Merged Mixed Methods Data Analysis

1. Collect and analyze quantitative and qualitative data concurrently.

2. Decide on the purpose of mixed methods data analysis:

    a. Combined mixed methods data analysis to compare quantitative and qualitative results; or

    b. Merged mixed methods data analysis to conduct further data transformation (quantitizing or qualitizing).

3. Identify the dimensions by which to compare the results or the variables that will be quantitized or qualitized.

4. Conduct selected combined or merged data analysis.

5. Interpret joint quantitative and qualitative results specifying how the combined or merged results produce more rigorous conclusions.

Sequential Quan → Qual MMAR Study Design

Connected Mixed Methods Data Analysis

1. Collect and analyze quantitative data first.

(Continued)

2. Decide on the purpose of connected mixed methods data analysis:

   a. Select sample for follow-up; and/or

   b. Select important attributes, trends, and relationships.

3. Design the qualitative follow-up strand based on the purpose of connected data analysis.

4. Collect and analyze qualitative data.

5. Interpret joint quantitative and qualitative results specifying how qualitative findings help explain initial quantitative results.

Sequential Qual → Quan MMAR Study Design

Connected Mixed Methods Data Analysis

1. Collect and analyze qualitative data first.

2. Decide on the purpose of connected mixed methods data analysis:

   a. Create typology of variables, and/or

   b. Develop a measurement instrument.

3. Design the consecutive quantitative strand based on the purpose of connected data analysis.

4. Collect and analyze quantitative data.

5. Interpret joint qualitative and quantitative results specifying how quantitative results help confirm or generalize initial qualitative findings.

Multistrand MMAR Study Design

Combination of Combined, Merged, and Connected Mixed Methods Data Analysis

1. Decide on the concurrent or sequential nature of the study strands.

2. Identify the purpose of each combined, merged, or connected mixed methods data analysis.

3. Conduct selected combined, merged, or connected data analysis.

4. Interpret joint qualitative and quantitative results.

SUMMARY

In an MMAR study the analytical process involves the use of traditional methods for quantitative and qualitative data analysis, and also the consideration of mixed methods data analysis strategies specific for MMAR study designs. Data analysis in an MMAR study is complicated by the very fact that practitioner-researchers have to apply different sets of analytical strategies to analyze quantitative and qualitative data within one study. Action research provides a fertile ground for securing the needed analytical expertise and resources through forming partnerships with local higher education institutions, community agencies, and other stakeholders. Depending on the nature of the study purpose, the posed research questions, specific objectives, and the scope of the quantitative strand, descriptive and inferential statistics can be used in different combinations within the same study strand in an MMAR study. Descriptive statistics can be particularly useful to gain an initial insight into the problem, to get information about the community needs, and to inform the development of the action/intervention during the reconnaissance phase of an MMAR study. Inferential statistics can be particularly useful to determine the impact of action/intervention, to inform the needed changes in the action/intervention plan, and to provide the foundation for further monitoring of the action/intervention. Some of the more commonly used descriptive and inferential statistics in an MMAR study are discussed, focusing on their relevance for the practical purposes of the action research process and on the issues to consider. Application of each analytical strategy is illustrated by its use in published MMAR design studies.

Next the chapter discusses the role and the process of qualitative data analysis. In an MMAR study, qualitative data and analysis may be given more emphasis due to the need to address a practical problem/issue and understand related stakeholders' perspectives. Qualitative data should be done in a systematic way and follow a sequence of logical but interactive steps. The chapter addresses the issues of an iterative or zigzag process of data collection and analysis, and some procedural components of data coding and theme development, such as types of codes, development of a codebook, using constant comparative method, conducting inter-coder agreement, and employing computer programs for qualitative analysis. Excerpts from published MMAR studies in different fields illustrate how practitioner-researchers approached qualitative data analysis in the reconnaissance and evaluation phases of their MMAR studies. Finally, mixed methods data analysis with the focus on the processes of combining, merging, and connecting data analysis within and across quantitative and qualitative study strands in four MMAR study designs is explained and illustrated. A conceptual diagram of the application of mixed methods data analysis strategies for each MMAR design is presented.

REFLECTIVE QUESTIONS AND EXERCISES

1. Describe common descriptive and inferential statistics analytical methods used in an MMAR study. Discuss their relevance for the practical purposes of an MMAR study. Explain the issues that should be taken into consideration when selecting and applying quantitative analytical strategies in an MMAR study.

2. Describe the process of qualitative data analysis. Discuss the steps in qualitative data analysis and their relevance for the practical purposes of an MMAR study. Explain how community members and other stakeholders can be engaged in the process of qualitative data analysis.

3. Explain the concept of mixed methods data analysis and how this analysis can be applied in an MMAR study. Discuss the steps in mixed methods data analysis in an MMAR study. Illustrate the steps with an example of a hypothetical MMAR study in your area of interest.

4. Explain the procedures of mixed methods data analysis. Discuss how they reflect the methodological characteristics of concurrent, sequential, and multistrand MMAR designs. Draw a conceptual diagram of mixed methods data analysis for each MMAR study design. Compare your diagrams with the diagrams provided in this chapter.

5. Select a published MMAR study in your discipline or area of interest. Identify an MMAR study design. Describe what quantitative and qualitative data were collected and how those data were analyzed. Explain the purpose of mixed methods data analysis and the specific procedures that were used to achieve this purpose.

6. Draw a detailed diagram of the mixed methods data analysis process used in this study. Compare your diagram with the suggested conceptual diagram of mixed methods data analysis for this MMAR design.

FURTHER READINGS

To learn more about the steps in quantitative data analysis, examine the following sources:

Creswell, J. W. (2012). *Educational research: Planning, conducting, and evaluating quantitative and qualitative research* (4th ed.). Upper Saddle River, NJ: Merrill Prentice Hall, Ch. 6, pp. 175–182.

To learn more about descriptive and inferential statistics analytical methods used in action research, examine the following sources:

Creswell, J. W. (2012). *Educational research: Planning, conducting, and evaluating quantitative and qualitative research* (4th ed.). Upper Saddle River, NJ: Merrill Prentice Hall, Ch. 6, pp. 182–186.
Gay, L. R., Mills, G. E., & Airasian, P. (2006). *Educational research: Competencies for analysis and applications* (8th ed.). Upper Saddle River, NJ: Merrill Prentice Hall, Chs. 11–12, pp. 300–382.
Mertler, C. A. (2012). *Action research: Improving schools and empowering educators.* Thousand Oaks, CA: Sage, Ch. 6, pp. 163–193.
Mills, G. E. (2011). *Action research: A guide for the teacher researcher* (4th ed.). Boston: Pearson Education, Ch. 6, pp. 139–143.
Tomal, D. R. (2010). *Action research for educators* (2nd ed.). Lanham, MD: Rowman & Littlefield, Ch. 4, pp. 96–117.

To learn more about qualitative data analytical methods used in action research, examine the following sources:

Creswell, J. W. (2014). *Research design: Qualitative, quantitative, and mixed methods approaches* (4th ed.). Thousand Oaks, CA: Sage, Ch. 9, pp. 194–201.
Guest, G., MacQueen, K. M., & Namey, E. E. (2012). *Applied thematic analysis.* Thousand Oaks, CA: Sage, Ch. 3, pp. 49–78.
Koshy, E., Koshy, V., & Waterman, H. (2011). *Action research in healthcare.* Thousand Oaks, CA: Sage, Ch. 6, pp. 132–141.
Mills, G. E. (2011). *Action research: A guide for the teacher researcher* (4th ed.). Boston: Pearson Education, Ch. 6, pp. 126–139.

To learn more about mixed methods analytical methods, examine the following sources:

Bazeley, P., & Kemp, L. (2012). Mosaics, triangles, and DNA: Metaphors for integrated analysis in mixed methods research. *Journal of Mixed Methods Research, 6*(1), 55–72.

Creswell, J. W., & Plano Clark, V. L. (2011). *Designing and conducting mixed methods research* (2nd ed.). Thousand Oaks, CA: Sage, Ch. 7, pp. 212–238.

Greene, J. C. (2007). *Mixed methods in social inquiry.* San Francisco, CA: Jossey-Bass, Ch. 8, pp. 142–163.

Mills, G. E. (2011). *Action research: A guide for the teacher researcher* (4th ed.). Boston: Pearson Education, Ch. 6, p. 144.

Teddlie, C., & Tashakkori, A. (2009). *Foundations of mixed methods research: Integrating quantitative and qualitative approaches in the social and behavioral sciences.* Thousand Oaks, CA: Sage, Ch. 11, pp. 263–283.

Assessing Quality of a Mixed Methods Action Research Study

INTRODUCTION

Chapter 8 discussed the strategies and issues of analyzing data in an MMAR study. The process of data analysis goes hand in hand with the process of assessing the quality of the interpretations and making accurate inferences from the data. This process is often referred to as **validation** and implies assessing the rigor of the methodological procedures used in the study. Validation is an important aspect of the research process because it makes the knowledge claims from the study more powerful and more representative of the problem under investigation (Koshy et al., 2011). Validating the findings and creating meta-inferences is a final methodological step in the reconnaissance and evaluation phases in an MMAR study. The quality of meta-inferences produced during these study phases has implications for how action/intervention is designed, implemented, and evaluated during the phases in an MMAR Study Process Model.

> Revisit the discussion in Chapter 4 about an MMAR Study Process Model; refer to Figure 4.1 that visually presents the Model.

In action research, practitioner-researchers should be concerned not only if the knowledge produced in the study is scientifically valid and credible but also if the study's practical outcomes stimulate change and empowerment of all stakeholders (Herr & Anderson, 2005). With regard to assessing quality of an action research study, McNiff and Whitehead (2011) suggested differentiating validity as "establishing the truth value of a claim" from legitimacy of "establishing its acceptance in the public sphere" (p. 171), while Jacobson (1998) recommended considering the study integrity as a criterion for good action research. The study integrity implies "the quality of action which emerges from it, and the quality of data on which the action is based" (p. 130). The collaborative nature of action research enhances the study validation process allowing for developing common understandings and interpretations of the findings, thus making them more representative of stakeholders' views.

In mixed methods research, ensuring quality of the overall study can be especially challenging because of the intended integration of quantitative and qualitative results to produce credible meta-inferences (Teddlie & Tashakkori, 2009). The quality or legitimacy of meta-inferences, in its turn, is determined by the quality of the collected data and their interpretation in each quantitative and qualitative study strand, as well as the methods of data integration (Bryman, Becker, & Semptik, 2008; Creswell & Plano Clark, 2011; Dellinger & Leech, 2007; Greene, 2007; Onwuegbuzie & Johnson, 2006; Teddlie & Tashakkori, 2009). It is also important to consider how specific mixed methods design features, such as different timing (concurrent or sequential) of quantitative and qualitative data collection and analysis and the order of quantitative and qualitative strands in sequential designs (quantitative or qualitative first), may

> Revisit the discussion in Chapter 6 about integration of quantitative and qualitative methods and its role in creating meta-inferences.

influence the quality of the study's conclusions (Ivankova, 2014). Therefore, in assessing quality of an MMAR study, practitioner-researchers have to (1) evaluate the methodological rigor of each quantitative and qualitative study strand, (2) observe specific quality considerations of the action research process, and (3) consider the legitimacy and quality of the integrated study conclusions or meta-inferences.

So, how do practitioner-researchers assess the methodological rigor of the quantitative and qualitative data and their interpretation in an MMAR study?

ASSESSING VALIDITY AND RELIABILITY OF QUANTITATIVE DATA AND THEIR INTERPRETATION IN AN MMAR STUDY

To establish the truth-value of the knowledge claims, practitioner-researchers should be certain that the tools they use to collect quantitative data produce consistent and accurate results. Despite a local and practical focus of action research, it is important that the quantitative evidence results in the correct assessment of the problem or situation and the accurate evaluation of the effects of the action/intervention. Regardless of the type of quantitative data collected (e.g., test scores, attitude scores, health indicators), employed instruments (e.g., educational tests, attitudinal surveys, or observation checklists), and research settings (e.g., schools and colleges, communities, agencies, hospitals), practitioner-researchers should be able to assess the methodological quality of these data.

Means of Assessing Quantitative Validity and Reliability

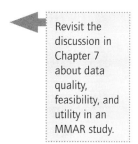

Revisit the discussion in Chapter 7 about data quality, feasibility, and utility in an MMAR study.

Data quality, feasibility, and utility have been discussed briefly as part of data collection considerations in an MMAR study. Traditional means for evaluating methodological quality of quantitative data is to assess its validity and reliability. While some authors expressed concerns that validity and reliability may not be considered important in an action research study (Herr & Anderson, 2005; Stringer & Genat, 2004; Tomal, 2010), Koshy and colleagues (2011) argued that it is important for practitioner-researchers to use reliable instruments to ensure the results are consistent with other applications of the same measurement tools. Additionally, despite a limited generalizability of action research studies, practitioner-researchers should be concerned about how valid their results are and if they can be applicable or relevant to other but similar settings and situations. Mills (2011) argued that when the study involves intervention and its evaluation, validity should be discussed from the perspective of how well the study conclusions reflect the relationships observed in the data (internal validity) and how much the study results can be generalized to other situations, settings, and people (external validity).

Validity is defined as "the degree to which a test measures what it is supposed to measure, and, consequently, permits appropriate interpretation of the scores" (Gay et al., 2006, p. 134). There are three major types of validity that are inter-related and inter-connected in the process of the overall validity assessment: *content, criterion,* and *construct* validity (Thorndike & Thorndike-Christ, 2011). Typically, all sources of validity evidence are considered to establish the validity of the quantitative data in a study. For example, in the quantitative strand of their MMAR study, Maritz and colleagues (2011) conducted factor analysis to assess construct validity of the questionnaire they developed to explore strategy-making modes within organizations. The exploratory factor analysis revealed three factors related to the construct of strategy-making. These factors reflected the critical themes that "could clearly be identified in the research" (p. 107). In another MMAR study, this one evaluating a first-grade parent involvement program to increase children's early literacy learning, Reutzel and colleagues (2006) assessed discriminant validity of the developed questionnaires in addition to their construct validity. They used a discriminant validity index that showed "the mean correlation of a scale with other scales" to prove that each scale on the survey measured "a separate dimension that is distinct from the other scales in this questionnaire" (p. 274).

Reliability is referred to as "the degree to which a test consistently measures whatever it is measuring" (Gay et al., 2006, p. 139). The three most common types of reliability assessment are *internal consistency reliability, test–retest reliability,* and *equivalent forms reliability* (Thorndike & Thorndike-Christ, 2011). They are calculated using statistical analytical procedures and produce a coefficient ranging from 0 to 1, with 1 indicating a very high reliability. For example, in the quantitative strand of their MMAR study, Baker and colleagues (2010) discussed the issues of assessing reliability of the Searching for Hardships and Obstacles to Shots immunization survey instrument that was translated into the Hmong language. The researchers tested for the internal consistency reliability of the survey items in the translated language and reported high reliability (as measured by Cronbach's alpha coefficient of above .9) for two tested groups: those who completed the survey in English, and those who completed the survey in Hmong. Similarly, in Maritz and colleagues' (2011) MMAR study discussed in the previous paragraph, internal consistency reliability was also performed for each scale in the developed questionnaire. Cronbach's Alpha coefficient ranged from .73 to .89 and indicated high reliability of the instrument. Based on the results of validity and reliability assessments, the researchers concluded, "the questionnaire was both valid in terms of accuracy and reliable in terms of consistency" (p. 107).

Validity and reliability are connected in many ways. Validity is the key factor in assessing the relevance and the fit of the data for the study purpose and research questions, while reliability provides confidence that the same data will be obtained through the administration of the same instruments in similar research situations (Mertler, 2012). Importantly, not all reliable instruments produce valid data; a valid instrument should always yield reliable data, however (Gay et al., 2006).

> Refer to Further Readings at the end of this chapter for detailed information about validity and reliability in quantitative research.

Teddlie and Tashakkori (2009) suggested two major questions for the researchers to answer when addressing validity and reliability of the quantitative data: (1) Am I truly measuring what I intend to measure, rather than something else? and (2) Assuming that I am measuring what I intend to measure, is my measurement consistent and accurate? Although these questions provide a helpful approach to testing for validity and reliability, assessing methodological quality of the quantitative data often involves advanced statistical procedures. If necessary, practitioner-researchers may secure the requisite analytical expertise from partnerships with statisticians at local postsecondary institutions or private consulting groups. Box 9.1 summarizes the information about the types of validity and reliability of quantitative data and the strategies used to address them. A guiding procedural question is included for each validity and reliability type to assist practitioner-researchers in choosing the right assessment type and strategy.

Box 9.2 presents an example of how Cunningham (2011) plans to address reliability and validity of the quantitative data in her proposed sequential Quan → Qual MMAR study to examine factors leading to intent for HPV vaccination discussed in Chapter 5.

> Refer to Box 5.2 in Chapter 5 for the description of Cunningham's (2011) proposed sequential Quan → Qual MMAR study design.

ASSESSING TRUSTWORTHINESS OF QUALITATIVE DATA AND THEIR INTERPRETATION IN AN MMAR STUDY

Validation of qualitative data is achieved through different means. As was previously discussed, qualitative data and their interpretation are subjective in nature and reflect the views and experiences of different individuals that are shaped by local and temporary contexts. Therefore, assessing quality of the data expressed in participants' words and through a researcher's interpretation has different underlying assumptions and requires a different set of procedures than those that are used to assess reliability and

BOX 9.1

Means of Assessing Validity and Reliability in Quantitative Research

- *Validity*—The degree to which an instrument measures what it is supposed to measure.

  o Question to ask: Does the instrument truly measure what it claims to measure?

- *Content validity*—The degree to which the instrument measures the intended subject matter of the content and takes into account all aspects of a particular situation.

  o Question to ask: Do the questions on the instrument represent all possible questions about this subject matter or this particular situation?
  o Strategies:

    - *Expert panel* on the intended content of the instrument are asked to assess the relevance of the questions and the response options.
    - *Cognitive interviews* are conducted with those who completed the instrument to seek how they understand and interpret the questions and construct their answers.

- *Criterion* (also *discriminant validity*—the degree to which the scores on the instrument correlate with the scores on a similar instrument measuring the same or similar concept.

  o Question to ask: Does the performance on this instrument show expected correlations with the performance on another instrument measuring the same or similar concept?
  o Strategies:

    - *Correlation coefficient* (*r* value) is calculated on the scores from the same instrument completed by the same respondents at two different points in time.

- *Construct validity*—The degree to which the instrument actually measures an intended concept or construct.

  o Question to ask: Does the instrument truly measure the concept or construct it claims to measure?
  o Strategies:

    - *Factor analysis* is conducted to analyze the relationship among the instrument questions to determine if all measure the same construct.
    - *Correlation coefficient* (*r* value) is calculated on the scores from the tested instrument and another instrument that measures another construct to determine if the construct is correlated with another construct in ways that are expected and shown by previous research.

- *Reliability*—The degree to which an instrument consistently and accurately measures the concept or construct it claims to measure.

  o Question to ask: Does the instrument consistently and accurately measure what it claims to measure over time?

- *Internal consistency reliability*—The degree to which the questions on the test are consistent among themselves and the overall instrument.

  o Question to ask: Does the instrument consistently and accurately measure what it claims to measure over time?
  o Strategies:
    - *Coefficient alpha* (*Cronbach's alpha*) is calculated on continuous variables at one instrument administration to provide an estimate of the consistency of scores on the instrument.
    - *Kuder-Richardson 20* (*KR-20*) estimate is calculated on categorical variables when instrument questions have dichotomous response options.

- *Test–retest reliability*—The degree to which the scores on the same instrument are consistent over time.

  o Question to ask: Does the instrument provide evidence that the scores that are obtained on it the first time will be consistent with the scores obtained during its next administration to the same respondents?
  o Strategies:
    - *Coefficient of stability* is calculated on two administrations of the same instrument.

- *Equivalent forms reliability*—The degree to which the scores on the equivalent forms of the same instrument are consistent over time.

  o Question to ask: Does the instrument provide evidence that the scores that are obtained from its equivalent forms administered to the same respondents will be consistent?
  o Strategies:
    - *Coefficient of equivalence* is calculated on two equivalent forms of the same instrument.

BOX 9.2

Example of Quantitative Data Reliability and Validity Assessment in a Sequential Quan → Qual MMAR Study Examining Factors Related to Intent for HPV Vaccination among College Males in Alabama

Reliability. Reliability is defined as the ability of an instrument to produce consistent and accurate results over time (Thorndike, 1997). In this study, internal consistency reliability will be used to access how well the items of the HPV survey measured on a Likert-type scale correlate with each other and the scale in general (Thorndike, 1997). The following three indicators of internal consistency reliability will be considered: (a) inter-item correlation, (b) item total correlation, and (c) Cronbach's coefficient alpha;

(Continued)

(Continued)

they will be used to identify how accurately the items measure the students' intention to get vaccinated against HPV. This reliability test will be conducted on the results of the pilot testing of the modified survey and it will determine which items should be reworded or removed, if necessary.

Validity. Validity is defined as the ability of an instrument to measure the concept of interest it intends to measure (Thorndike, 1997). A valid instrument allows for removing other possible explanations of the results (Thorndike, 1997). In this study, content, construct, and face validity will be assessed. For content validity, content experts who have specialized knowledge of HPV and survey development will review the modified instrument (Dillman et al., 2009). The reviewers' feedback will help ensure that the essential variables critical for understanding factors influencing HPV vaccination intent among college males are included in the measurement instrument. Dillman et al. (2009) indicated that the choice of the survey mode influences the construction of the questions and how they are understood by potential respondents. The questions should mean the same thing to every respondent, be communicated consistently to all respondents, and should be scripted to prepare a respondent to answer the questions (Fowler, 2009). The content reviewers will generate new ideas, concerns, and challenges in reaching the population of interest.

Construct validity will be established by conducting an exploratory factor analysis of Likert-type survey items if a large enough sample is available. The factor analysis will be performed on the data collected for the major survey administration. It will be used to identify the important questions on the scale and will reveal how each item relates to the overall factor (Creswell, 2009).

In terms of face validity, regular meetings will be held over a 3-month period by the content reviewers, the researcher, and other key stakeholders to develop a survey instrument to identify the risk factors that contribute to HPV acquisition among this high-risk group, that is male college students. Additionally, trained interviewers will conduct individual face-to-face cognitive interviews with 8 to 10 survey participants probing into every survey item to help the researcher understand whether the intent for each question is realized (Dillman et al., 2009). Willis (2005) defined cognitive interviewing as a "process of identifying how participants comprehend, process, and/or detect any problems" (p. 3). Cognitive interviews will provide information on how the survey respondents comprehend and interpret the questions and how consistently the participants respond to the same set of questions. Cognitive interviews will also help detect if the questions are worded correctly, if the directions for the survey are clear and if the format for the survey is reasonable.

Adapted from Cunningham (2011) with the author's permission.

validity of quantitative data. According to Creswell (2014), judging the rigor of the qualitative study is based on "determining whether the findings are accurate from the standpoint of the researcher, the participant, or the readers of an account" (p. 201).

Criteria for Assessing Trustworthiness in Qualitative Research

To capture the interpretative nature of qualitative research, Lincoln and Guba (1985) suggested assessing the **trustworthiness** of the findings of a qualitative study instead of testing for conventional validity and reliability used in quantitative research. They proposed to consider the following criteria as indicators of the rigor of a qualitative study: credibility, transferability, dependability, and confirmability.

Credibility refers to the extent to which the study findings are believable and promote confidence in their "truth." In Lincoln and Guba's (1985) view, credibility is one of most important factors in establishing trustworthiness because it addresses the question, How congruent are the findings with reality? (Merriam, 1998; Shenton, 2004). Stringer (2014) argued that credibility in action research is imperative because of the direct connection between the study integrity and stakeholders' engagement with the research outcomes.

Transferability refers to the extent to which the study findings are applicable to other contexts. In contrast to generalizability of the quantitative results, transferability aims at drawing similarities based on the detailed description of a research situation. Transferability in action research is important because the consumers of research can identify with the study setting by noting the specific details of the research situation and methods and comparing them to their own situation (Mills, 2011). Despite a local focus of an action research study, its outcomes may be applicable to other people and places (Stringer, 2014)—that is, "transferred from a sending context to a receiving context" (Herr & Anderson, 2005, p. 61).

Dependability refers to the extent to which the study findings are consistent and could be repeated. Dependability is critical because it assesses the methodological rigor of the study and the adherence to a systematic research process in how the data were collected and analyzed. Lincoln and Guba (1985) believe that dependability and credibility are interrelated because systematic methodological procedures generate confidence in the "truth" of the findings.

Confirmability refers to the extent to which the study findings are shaped by participants' views and not a researcher's bias. Confirmability helps assess the neutrality and objectivity of the collected data; it questions how the research findings are supported by the data. Herr and Anderson (2005) indicated that although bias and subjectivity are natural and acceptable in action research, practitioner-researchers need to critically examine them so that they do not influence the study outcomes. In action research, it is critical to demonstrate that the study findings are the result of the experiences and views of the informants so as to ensure stakeholders' buy-in to the problem and thus engage them with the action/intervention planning and implementation.

Each of these quality criteria has a set of associated strategies that are summarized in Box 9.3. These strategies can be applied in different combinations in the study, depending on the time and resources, access to study participants, availability of external reviewers, and other project related considerations. Lincoln and Guba's (1985) approach to assessing trustworthiness has been adopted by many researchers across disciplines, including action research, due to its conceptual comprehensiveness and applicability in different research settings (Herr & Anderson, 2005; Mills, 2011; Stringer, 2014). The following section describes and illustrates the common strategies for assessing trustworthiness of qualitative data and their interpretations that are used in an MMAR study.

BOX 9.3

Criteria and Strategies for Assessing Trustworthiness in Qualitative Research

- *Credibility*—The extent to which the findings are believable and promote confidence in their "truth."

  - Strategies:
    - *Triangulating* different methods, different types of informants, different participants, and different sites to obtain converging evidence.
    - *Spending prolonged time* at the research site with study participants to develop in-depth understanding and test for biases.
    - *Engaging in persistent observation* to identify patterns and consistency in the data.
    - *Using member checking* by engaging study participants in reviewing data and findings to check for accuracy of recording and interpretation.
    - *Using peer debriefing* by engaging individuals not involved in the study to quiz about the study procedures and findings to ensure accuracy of the account.
    - *Using negative case analysis* by revealing and discussing disconfirming evidence to incorporate all stakeholders' perspectives.

- *Transferability*—The extent to which the findings are applicable to other contexts.

  - Strategies:
    - *Collecting detailed descriptive data and providing detailed description* of the study setting and participants—"rich, thick description"—to enable possible comparison with other research contexts.

- *Dependability*—The extent to which the findings are consistent and could be repeated.

  - Strategies:
    - *Triangulating* different methods, different types of informants, different participants, and different sites to obtain converging evidence.
    - *Keeping an audit trail* of the study procedures to provide documentary evidence of the process of data collection, analysis, and interpretation.
    - *Using an external audit* by an individual not involved in the study to review the study procedures and findings to ensure accuracy of the account.

- *Confirmability*—The extent to which the findings are shaped by participants' views and not a researcher's bias.

  - Strategies:
    - *Triangulating* different methods, different types of informants, different participants, and different sites to obtain converging evidence.
    - *Keeping an audit trail* of the study procedures to provide documentary evidence of the process of data collection, analysis, and interpretation.
    - *Clarifying a researcher's bias* by practicing reflexivity to reveal underlying assumptions and biases.

Strategies for Assessing Trustworthiness of Qualitative Data and Their Interpretation in an MMAR Study

The review of the published MMAR studies showed that strategies for assessing trustworthiness of the data used in the qualitative study strand are not always reported. However, among the strategies discussed most often are member checking, triangulation, and clarifying the researcher's bias or bracketing. The participatory and collaborative nature of action research, as well as its practical focus and community orientation, means that other strategies listed in Box 9.3 can be effectively employed in the qualitative strand of an MMAR study. For example, by studying their own practices, practitioner-researchers typically spend prolonged time at the research site and with the study participants; for the same reason, they become engaged in persistent observation that helps reveal and assess any disconfirming evidence in the data. By virtue of their constant and immediate involvement with the study, practitioner-researchers have access to rich descriptive data and may document the study procedures for the purpose of sharing and reporting the findings. They may not use an external audit on a regular basis due to ethical considerations and IRB's regulations about data sharing; they may, however, rigorously employ peer debriefing, engaging community members and other stakeholders in providing input into the study procedures and interpretation of the conclusions. Additionally, advisory groups, boards, or councils that are often formed to assist with the study design and implementation in community-based participatory action research can perform the role of an external audit (Newman et al., 2011). For example, in their MMAR study Greysen and colleagues (2012) shared the data and the findings with community stakeholders seeking their input on the accuracy of the interpretations when conducting the needs assessment of patients' transition from hospital to a homeless shelter.

Refer to the Further Readings at the end of this chapter for detailed information about assessing trustworthiness in qualitative research.

Member Checking

Lincoln and Guba (1985) described member checking as "the most critical technique for establishing credibility," because engaging study participants in reviewing data and findings can help ensure their perspectives are captured accurately (p. 314). With regard to action research, Hinchey (2008) argued that only direct and active involvement of the study participants in the review of the findings and that their interpretation can render an accurate account of their views and experiences. Importantly, member checking fits well with the collaborative and participatory nature of the action research process.

To perform member checking, practitioner-researchers can use several approaches. They can ask the study participants to review the verbatim transcripts or the summaries of their interviews or focus group discussions; they can share the results of data analysis, such as the list of codes and themes, with the study participants or other stakeholders to get their views on the accuracy of the data interpretation; or they can seek the participants' input in developing the study conclusions by providing them with the synopsis of the findings. For example, in their MMAR study examining male underachievement in public education, Clark and colleagues (2008) conducted individual interviews with 15 teachers, school counselors, and administrators. The interview summaries that were developed based on the notes taken during the interviews were sent to each interviewee "for review and approval so as to corroborate the content of the report" (p. 116). Alternatively, in the research protocol for an MMAR study aimed at evaluating the implementation of an evidence-based nursing model in oncohematology, Abad-Corpa and colleagues (2010) planned to involve the study participants at a later stage to discuss the findings from the team meetings with registered nurses.

Triangulation

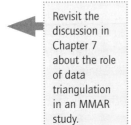
Revisit the discussion in Chapter 7 about the role of data triangulation in an MMAR study.

Triangulation of quantitative and qualitative data sources has already been discussed as one of the considerations of data collection in an MMAR study. Triangulation is also a powerful technique for establishing qualitative data credibility because by combining and comparing different forms of text data, such as interviews, observations, and focus groups, it is possible to "cross-check," or verify, the data (Mills, 2011, p. 104). For example, in their MMAR study, Warren, Noftle, Ganley, and Quintanar (2011) used the evidence from three qualitative data sources, including individual and small group interviews, course evaluations, and analysis of student asset maps, in the process of evaluating the impact of the graduate coursework on urban teacher's knowledge, skills, and dispositions about family and community involvement.

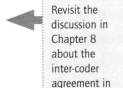
Revisit the discussion in Chapter 8 about the inter-coder agreement in the qualitative data analysis.

Triangulation also implies involving different categories of informants so that their views and experiences can be compared, and thus verified against each other, to create a rich picture of their attitudes, needs and behaviors (Shenton, 2004). Additionally, the process of establishing an inter-coder agreement, as discussed in Chapter 8, can help with assessing the study trustworthiness when researchers reach similar conclusions by independently analyzing the same data (Creswell, 2014; Hinchey, 2008). Hinchey (2008) observed that triangulation, "is simply a sophisticated way of naming the common sense principle that the more evidence there is to support a finding, the more credible the finding" (p. 96). For example, Thornewill and colleagues (2011) conducted 23 focus groups with 12 groups of community stakeholders in the reconnaissance phase of their MMAR study. The goal was to explore their attitudes toward an effective health information exchange so as to inform the needed changes in the existing system. Several researchers independently analyzed the data from the focus groups to identify the key themes and to reach consensus in the interpretation of stakeholders' views.

Clarifying the Researcher's Bias or Bracketing

Revisit the discussion in Chapter 2 about reflexivity as an important feature of action research.

In action research, reflection is part of the research process and is done systematically and purposefully at all stages. Reflexivity about one's role in the research process is an essential feature of action research (Herr & Anderson, 2005). Practicing reflexivity and bracketing personal views, assumptions, and biases is also important for assessing confirmability of the qualitative findings. Even though practitioner-researchers often focus on studying their own practices and communities, it is important to ensure that their biases do not have an impact on the way the qualitative data are collected, analyzed, and interpreted in the study (Merriam, 1998). To clarify a researcher's bias, practitioner-researchers should keep a research journal where they can reflect on the emergent themes in the data and check these observations against their own perceptions of the studied issue (Mills, 2011). For example, King (2010) described how she bracketed her biases when conducting an MMAR study to develop a podcasting education model for K–12 schools. Specifically, she kept a journal where she reflected on her educational philosophy and her experiences with podcasting, and documented all aspects of the research process. She also engaged in analytic bracketing "to work back and forth between what was happening among the data, its meaning and effect on the larger podcasting community" (p. 147).

 Refer to Box 5.2 in Chapter 5 for the description of Cunningham's (2011) proposed sequential Quan → Qual MMAR study design.

As it is evident from the research literature and the reviewed MMAR studies, strategies for assessing trustworthiness of the qualitative data and their interpretation should be planned in advance and should be part of a research plan. Box 9.4 presents an example of how Cunningham (2011) plans to assess trustworthiness of the qualitative data and their interpretation in her proposed sequential Quan → Qual MMAR study to examine factors leading to intent for HPV vaccination discussed in Chapter 5.

BOX 9.4

Example of Qualitative Data Trustworthiness Assessment in a Sequential Quan → Qual MMAR Study Examining Factors Related to Intent for HPV Vaccination among College Males in Alabama

Assessing credibility and trustworthiness. To secure methodological rigor of the qualitative component of this study, multiple verification procedures will be employed to validate the qualitative findings and to determine the credibility and trustworthiness of the researcher's interpretation and explanation of the meaning of the data. Eight verification methods or strategies are mainly used to validate qualitative findings. It is recommended to utilize at least two such strategies in any study (Creswell, 2009). For this study, member checking; rich, thick description; peer debriefing; intercoder agreement; and identification of researchers' assumptions, beliefs, and biases will be utilized (Creswell, 2009).

Member checking implies using the individuals that are closest to the situation to validate the findings and interpretations of the researcher (Creswell, 2009; Lincoln & Guba, 1985). In this study, the transcripts created at the completion of each interview will be shared with the interviewees to ensure the accuracy of the participants' words. Additionally, the researcher will send the summary of the qualitative findings to each participant to seek their input into the accuracy of the interpretation of their interviews.

Peer debriefing is defined as a process that promotes honesty among the researcher(s) via the usage of peer debriefer(s) to question the researchers on methods, meanings, and interpretations

(Continued)

(Continued)

(Creswell & Miller, 2000). In this study, the stakeholders (i.e., physicians, teachers, public health practitioners) will serve continuously as peer debriefer(s) throughout the research process. They will provide feedback on the study research design and implementation.

Rich, thick description will include the researcher providing a description of the findings in detail (Creswell, 2009; Onwuegbuzie & Johnson, 2006). A detailed narrative of the themes and sub-themes that will emerge from the analysis of the interviews will be included in the study report. The readers will receive a firsthand account of the factors that may influence HPV vaccination among college males.

Inter-coder agreement, also known as cross-checking, involves the process of multiple coders viewing and analyzing the data from the transcripts. The purpose is to ensure stability of responses across the data among the coders (Creswell, 2009). For this study, data analysis will be performed by the members of the research team and will target 80% or higher of inter-coder reliability on the codes and themes from the participants' interviews.

Disclosing the researcher's assumptions, beliefs, and biases involves identifying the researcher's beliefs toward HPV vaccination among college males. This disclosure will allow the reader to understand the preconceived positioning of the principal investigator regarding the problem explored in this study (Creswell & Miller, 2000). Clarification of the researcher's bias will be addressed by disclosing the researcher's experiences, orientations, and preconceptions that may have affected the research approach and the interpretation of the data in this study (Creswell, 2009).

Adapted from Cunningham (2011) with the author's permission.

ADDRESSING QUALITY CONSIDERATIONS RELATED TO ACTION RESEARCH

While preserving the methodological rigor of the quantitative and qualitative strands in an MMAR study is important, practitioner-researchers should also observe quality considerations specific to action research. Herr and Anderson (2005) argued that neither the term *validity* accepted in quantitative research, nor the term *trustworthiness* accepted in qualitative research is adequate for action research because neither term acknowledges its "action-oriented outcomes" (p. 49). Consequently, they suggested that rigor of action research should not be evaluated using the traditional criteria for quantitative and qualitative research, warning against a potential "narrow insider or outsider view of the problematic situation under study" (p. 54). Rather, Herr and Anderson proposed to "democratize action research" (p. 54) and aligned the validity criteria with the five goals of action research listed in Box 9.5. These criteria may also serve as the indicators of quality for action research studies.

Mertler (2012) also addressed the issue of quality assessment in action research, stating that action researchers focus more on the quality of the entire action research process and whether the action/intervention results resonate with the intended audience whose interests are presented in the study. For example, when

BOX 9.5

Validity Criteria for Action Research

- *Outcome validity*—The extent to which action occurs, which leads to a resolution of the problem that led to the study.

  o Action research goal:

    - The achievement of action-oriented outcomes.

  o Quality indicators:

    - The action emerging from the study led to a successful resolution of the problem.
    - The action emerging from the study forced the researcher to reframe the problem in a more complex way.

- *Process validity*—The extent to which problems are framed and solved in a manner that permits ongoing learning of the individual or system.

  o Action research goal:

    - Use of sound and appropriate research methodology.

  o Quality indicators:

    - The research is conducted in "dependable" and "competent" manner.
    - The research findings are the result of a series of reflective cycles.

- *Democratic validity*—The extent to which research is done in collaboration with all parties who have a stake in the problem under investigation.

  o Action research goal:

    - Generation of results that are relevant to the local setting.

  o Quality indicators:

    - Multiple perspectives and material interests of all stakeholders are taken into account.
    - The research is inclusive of all stakeholders as collaborators in the process.

- *Catalytic validity*—The extent to which the research process empowers participants to transform the reality.

  o Action research goal:

    - Education of both researcher and participants.

  o Quality indicators:

    - The research results serve as a "catalyst" for action.
    - All involved in the study get empowered for social change.

(Continued)

(Continued)

- *Dialogic validity*—The extent to which the research undergoes peer review.
  - ○ Action research goal:
    - Generation of new knowledge.
  - ○ Quality indicators:
    - The research findings and procedures are peer reviewed.
    - The researcher participates in critical and reflective dialogue with other action researchers.

Adapted from Herr and Anderson (2005) with permission of Sage Publications, Inc.

conducting action research in health care, it is particularly important for other health-care professionals to understand and interpret the study results with relevance to their own practices and their professional tasks of meeting specific patients' needs (Morton-Cooper, 2000; Stringer & Genat, 2004). The focus on rigor and relevance of action/intervention outcomes brings additional quality considerations into action research, such as balancing the insider-outsider status of practitioner-researchers, achieving objectivity when studying their own practice, and deciding on the extent of the generalizability of the study outcomes.

These issues are discussed in more detail in the following sections and are illustrated using Arcidiacono and colleagues' (2009) concurrent Quan + Qual MMAR design study that reported on the reconnaissance phase in the development of the five-step intervention for families coping with substance misuse and treatment. The study was conducted at three research sites in Italy using a cross-cultural framework and involved more than 70 researchers and professionals. Survey and semistructured interview data were collected from each member of 113 families to explore the impact of drinking or drug misuse by a close relative on other family members. The researchers devoted considerable attention to the discussion of establishing trustworthiness of their research when reporting on their study.

Insider versus Outsider Status of Practitioner-Researchers

Revisit the discussion in Chapter 2 about the essential features of action research.

As discussed in Chapter 2, action research is practically oriented, and practitioner-researchers tend to focus on studying their own professional or community settings. As such, practitioner-researchers often have to consider "multiple positionalities" and balance insiders' and outsiders' views on the research process (Herr & Anderson, 2005, p. 43). This has implications for assessing the study quality because, being insiders to their setting, practitioner-researchers have to take an outsider stance "to see the taken-for-granted aspects of their practice from an outsider perspective" (p. 51). Using traditional quality assessment criteria, such as prolonged engagement in the field, persistent observation, or a reflective journal, may not help reach objectivity in the data interpretation, and may fail to address "the unique dilemmas of practitioners studying their own sites" (p. 47).

Two strategies—using "critical friends" and involving collaborators from different stakeholder groups—have been recommended to address the dual positionality stance of practitioner-researchers when conducting action research (Herr & Anderson, 2005; Koshy et al., 2011; McNiff & Whitehead, 2011). The concept of using "critical friends" is similar to peer debriefing that is employed to assess credibility in qualitative research. McNiff and Whitehead (2011) also suggested organizing validation groups, consisting of three to ten people, from a practitioner-researcher's professional circle, but who are not directly involved in the project. A validation group meets regularly to review the study process and provide input to all its critical aspects.

Collaborating with stakeholders may also help secure both the insider and outsider perspectives on the research findings (Herr & Anderson, 2005). Koshy and colleagues (2011) discussed using action research groups or communities of enquiry that make it easier for practitioner-researchers to reach a common ground in interpreting the meaning of the data. Involving community members and other stakeholders in the data analysis and interpretation process also helps to make the findings more representative of stakeholders' views. For example, in their MMAR study, Arcidiacono and colleagues (2009) addressed the issue of balancing insiders' and outsiders' views by conducting regular research group meetings with all partners who helped improve and standardize the data collection procedures, interpret the interview findings, and evaluate the results of the subsequent interventions. According to the researchers, these meetings "fostered a systematic reflection by the researchers and practitioners, drawing on their different interpretations of the social situation and the quality and relevance of the results of the research" (p. 101).

Objectivity versus Subjectivity When Studying One's Own Practice

Achieving objectivity when studying one's own practice is closely related to the issue of balancing insider-outsider status of practitioner-researchers. Studying one's own practice or one's own community is embedded in action research, but also has important implications for the rigor of an action research study. Practitioner-researchers not only bring their own biases and unique perspectives into research, but also it may be difficult for them to disengage themselves from what they believe the purpose of inquiry is and what the truth value of the knowledge claims is within the study context (Lincoln & Guba, 1985). To control for subjectivity when interpreting the meaning of the qualitative data, practitioner-researchers may use a number of strategies, many of which have already been discussed in this chapter.

It is important that practitioner-researchers engage in the process of self-reflexivity from the beginning of the study and acknowledge their own values and epistemological stances prior to the data collection process. Herr and Anderson (2005) pointed out that "developing the skills and habits of self-reflexivity is necessary for any action researcher" (p. 60). The process of self-reflexivity includes clarifying a researcher's bias and bracketing used to assess confirmability in qualitative research. Disclosing the nature of a research setting and a studied situation, in addition to keeping an audit trail, may help decrease potential biases and ensure accuracy of the data interpretation. Mills (2011) also suggested developing a list of propositions for potential or expected findings and testing them through "critical friends" and peer debriefers to seek desired objectivity. Similarly, collecting data from multiple sources and comparing stakeholders' perspectives while considering alternative hypothesis, meanings, conclusions, and disagreement in the data can be particularly helpful in achieving objectivity (James et al., 2008). Importantly, the collaborative nature of action research and the opportunity to involve other practitioners, research participants, and stakeholders in the research process or for peer-debriefing purposes can enhance the quality of the study conclusions. Hinchey (2008) indicated that "action research does not involve studies *on* participants. . . . Instead, it involves studies *with* participants" (p. 97, emphasis in original). In Arcidiacono and colleagues' (2009) MMAR study, the researchers addressed the issue of balancing objectivity and subjectivity by triangulating three research sites, quantitative (questionnaire) and qualitative (semistructured interviews) data sources, and multiple researchers' perspectives, and by using peer discussion groups to control for researchers' interpretation biases.

Generalizability versus Transferability of Study Results

Generalizability of the study results, which is a hallmark of good quantitative research, does not apply to action research (Stringer, 2014). In action research, any generalizations are contextual because action research findings can be generalizable or transferable only within specific research situations and specific professional contexts. Herr and Anderson (2005) suggested thinking about generalizability of action research studies in terms of naturalistic generalizations as advanced by Stake (1986), which is similar to transferability as suggested by Lincoln and Guba (1985) and discussed earlier. Therefore, the outcomes of an action research study may be applicable to other settings, if enough detail is provided for the consumers of research to identify with in the study context.

Lincoln and Guba (1985) argued that it is the responsibility of the consumers to decide about the extent of the findings' transferability based on the specific details about the study setting and the problem addressed. So, to enhance the transferability of a study's outcomes and to make the findings more representative of the studied situation, practitioner-researchers have to provide a detailed description of the study setting, the practical problem addressed, and the research participants to enable possible comparisons with other research contexts and similar situations. For example, in their MMAR study, Arcidiacono and colleagues (2009) addressed the transferability issues by providing a detailed description of the study context, by explaining the methodological procedures employed in the quantitative and qualitative study strands, and by using a critical peer-group and professional focus group discussions of the study outcomes.

While it is important to apply appropriate strategies to address the issues of quality assessment related to an action research process, practitioner-researchers should also consider how using a mixed methods approach can help overcome some of these challenges. For example, a meaningful integration of the quantitative and qualitative methods in the study can help achieve more rigorous study outcomes to inform the action/intervention, thus increasing the outcome validity of the study. Triangulating multiple forms of quantitative and qualitative data from different stakeholder groups in a concurrent Quan + Qual MMAR study design can help practitioner-researchers make more objective conclusions when studying their own practices and address the process and democratic validity. The issue of insider–outsider status of a researcher can be specifically addressed by employing sequential Quan → Qual and Qual → Quan MMAR study designs, in which these two perspectives get explored through first employing one method (quantitative or qualitative) and then an alternative method. Additionally, by collecting and analyzing qualitative data to inform the development and administration of the quantitative questionnaire in a sequential Qual → Quan MMAR study design, the issue of the generalizability and transferability of the study findings to other situations and contexts can be addressed.

At the same time, mixed methods research has its own quality considerations that have to be taken into account when assessing quality of the knowledge claims in an MMAR study. These are legitimate concerns because they have implications for generating valid and credible meta-inferences from quantitative and qualitative methods' integration. So, what are the criteria of quality in mixed methods research and how can practitioner-researchers employ these quality criteria in an MMAR study?

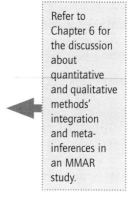

Refer to Chapter 6 for the discussion about quantitative and qualitative methods' integration and meta-inferences in an MMAR study.

ASSESSING QUALITY IN AN MMAR STUDY

Quality Considerations in Mixed Methods Research

Despite a rapid adoption and utilization of mixed methods research across disciplines, assessment of quality or validity in mixed methods studies remains a provocative methodological issue and one of the most debatable topics in the mixed methods field (Creswell, 2010; Ivankova & Kawamura, 2010; Teddlie &Tashakkori, 2010). Tashakkori and Teddlie (2003, 2010) referred to drawing quality conclusions or inferences in mixed methods studies as being among the major controversies of mixed methods research in the two editions of the *SAGE Handbook of Mixed Methods in Social & Behavioral Research.* Recognizing the complex nature of quality assessment in mixed methods research, Teddlie and Tashakkori (2003) introduced the term **inference quality** as a criterion to use when considering validity and transferability of the generated meta-inferences in a mixed methods study. The authors defined inference quality as "standards for evaluating the quality of conclusions that are made on the basis of research findings" in a mixed methods study (p. 287). As such, integration of the inferences derived from the quantitative and qualitative data is a critical stage in a mixed methods process, and researchers are encouraged to adhere to rigorous standards for assessing inference quality to ensure their validity and trustworthiness.

A number of mixed methods authors emphasized that the complexity of mixed methods validity can be traced to different conceptualizations of quality in mixed methods research (Creswell, 2010; Maxwell & Mittapalli, 2010; O'Cathain, 2010; Onwuegbuzie & Johnson, 2006). Importantly, there is a consensus that ensuring quality in mixed methods studies is particularly challenging because of the intended integration of the quantitative and qualitative results to produce credible meta-inferences. Moreover, unique mixed methods design features—such as a different chronology of quantitative and qualitative data collection and analysis in concurrent and sequential mixed methods designs, the order of quantitative and qualitative strands in sequential designs (quantitative or qualitative first), and the way quantitative and qualitative methods are integrated within the designs—have special implications for the quality of the generated meta-inferences (Ivankova, 2014). For example, in sequential mixed methods designs, in which one study strand is connected to another, the quality of the inferences produced in the first study strand may significantly impact the quality of the inferences generated in another strand, and ultimately affect the quality of the meta-inferences from the overall study (Creswell & Plano Clark, 2011; Teddlie & Tashakkori, 2009). The following sections describe major approaches to assessing quality in mixed methods research.

Approaches to Assessing Quality in Mixed Methods Research

Conceptual Models and Frameworks of Quality Assessment

Several conceptual models and frameworks have been proposed to assess the methodological quality of mixed methods research and the resulted meta-inferences. Teddlie and Tashakkori (2009) suggested the *integrative framework for inference quality*, which includes ten aspects of quality, the first four of which are related to a mixed methods study design and address suitability to answer the research questions, fidelity of the study procedures and methodological rigor, consistency of all research aspects of the study, and adequacy of analytic procedures. The other six are related to the interpretive rigor of meta-inferences that are produced as overall study outcomes and target; consistency of meta-inferences with findings, theory, previous research, study purpose, and inferences from each study strand; other possible interpretations by scholars and study participants; and distinctiveness of credible conclusions. The focus of the integrative framework for inference quality is to help researchers first reduce any inconsistencies by assessing quantitative and qualitative inferences from separate study strands by using respective quality criteria and standards, and then by assessing the degree to which meta-inferences resulting from the entire study are valid or credible.

Onwuegbuzie and Johnson (2006) proposed to assess the quality of meta-inferences using the *legitimation model* that addresses nine types of establishing legitimation or validity in mixed methods research. The authors referred to the problem of legitimation in a mixed methods study as "the difficulty in obtaining findings and/or making inferences that are credible, trustworthy, dependable, transferable, and/or confirmable" (p. 52). These legitimation types permeate all research aspects of a mixed methods study from a researcher's philosophical beliefs to a study design and implementation (sample integration, inside-outside, weakness minimization, sequential, conversion, paradigmatic mixing, commensurability, multiple validities, and political). The authors viewed legitimation as a continuous process of evaluating the study design, the procedures for data collection and analysis, and the interpretation of the results. The advantage of the legitimation model is that it connects the process of establishing validity in a mixed methods study with the stages in its implementation, thus giving researchers conceptual knowledge of the potential legitimation threats to anticipate and address during the study process. Therefore, it is important to consider potential legitimation types at the study design stage to ensure that integration of the inferences derived from the quantitative and qualitative results meets rigorous quality standards.

Refer to Box 5.2 in Chapter 5 for the description of Cunningham's (2011) proposed sequential Quan → Qual MMAR study design.

Box 9.6 presents an example of how Cunningham (2011) plans to address the issues of quality using Onwuegbuzie and Johnson's (2006) legitimation model in her proposed sequential Quan → Qual MMAR study to examine factors leading to intent for HPV vaccination discussed in Chapter 5.

BOX 9.6

Example of the Discussion of Mixed Methods Inference Assessment in a Sequential MMAR Study Examining Factors Related to Intent for HPV Vaccination among College Males in Alabama

Legitimation. The term *legitimation* has been used by quantitative and qualitative researchers to represent validity assessment in mixed methods research. Legitimation is a process of continuous evaluation throughout a mixed methods study to demonstrate the quality of produced meta-inferences. Legitimation checks should occur at the end of each study strand (Onwuegbuzie & Johnson, 2006). Onwuegbuzie and Johnson (2006) developed the legitimation model, which consists of nine types of legitimation and includes sample integration, inside–outside, weakness minimization, sequential, conversion, paradigmatic, commensurability, multiple validities, and political legitimation. In this sequential explanatory study, legitimation will be assessed during the data interpretation prior to results' generalization. This study will address five types of legitimation, which will be used to ensure the quality of the inferences consistent with this mixed methods study design. These five legitimation types are sequential, inside–outside, weakness minimization, paradigmatic mixing, and multiple validities. Each type will be described below along with an explanation of how the procedures relate to the sequential mixed methods design used in this study.

Sequential legitimation refers to the minimization of problems associated with the order of the quantitative and qualitative mixed methods study strands (Onwuegbuzie & Johnson, 2006). This study is designed to consist of two sequential strands: a quantitative strand that focuses on identifying the factors that influence HPV vaccination among college males and a subsequent qualitative strand aimed to provide a better understanding of those factors. The sequential explanatory design will be used to assist in finding similarities and differences in categories and themes in factors associated with HPV vaccination in college males. In order to reduce a potential threat of generating inconsistent inferences, the same participants will be selected for the qualitative and quantitative strands in this study.

Inside–outside legitimation refers to how accurately the researcher presents the insider's and observer's view within the description or explanation of the study integrated results. The insider view is reflected in the qualitative data collection and analysis, whereas the outsider view is present in the quantitative data collection and analysis. It is pertinent that the researcher justifies the conclusions and minimizes bias of quantitative and qualitative data interpretation and integration. In this study this will be achieved via member checking, peer review, and external auditing in the qualitative strand (Onwuegbuzie & Johnson, 2006). The use of the standardized survey instrument and a statistical computer program will help secure a researcher's objective stance when collecting and analyzing the data in the quantitative strand.

Weakness minimization legitimation refers to how the weakness of one method (quantitative/qualitative) is strengthened by the other approach (qualitative/quantitative). The weakness of each method should be assessed, and the researcher should identify the means of using the strength of one method to overcome the weakness of another method to create high-quality meta-inferences

(Continued)

(Continued)

(Onwuegbuzie & Johnson, 2006). The researcher adopts this perspective to guide the quantitative and qualitative methods' integration in the study when combining, weighing, and interpreting both sets of results. In this sequential mixed methods study, the weaknesses of the two approaches will be counterbalanced: The quantitative approach will help determine the type and prevalence of the factors associated with intention of HPV vaccination among college males; the use of the qualitative approach will enable the researcher to better understand the factors influencing HPV vaccination. Together the two methods will provide a richer explanation of what influences HPV vaccination among college males.

Paradigmatic mixing legitimation refers to the degree the researcher's philosophical beliefs related to the integration of quantitative and qualitative methods are intertwined and blended in a mixed methods study. These underlying beliefs are competing in nature and include epistemological, ontological, axiological, methodological, and rhetorical dualisms. Within paradigmatic mixing, the researcher should view the combination of these dual beliefs as complementary rather than separate (Onwuegbuzie & Johnson, 2006). In this study, feedback to the quantitative and qualitative data analysis and interpretation will be solicited from the study participants and other stakeholders to avoid potential threats associated with the mixing of the paradigms.

Multiple validities legitimation refers to yielding higher-quality meta-inferences via mixing of quantitative, qualitative, and mixed validity types. All validity types should be addressed and minimized in a mixed methods study (Onwuegbuzie & Johnson, 2006). In this study, in the quantitative strand, students will be administered surveys in a group setting with adequate space to ensure accuracy and independence of the data. Additionally, the survey instrument will be tested for reliability and validity. In the qualitative strand, minimizing bias using rich, thick descriptions, peer debriefing, inter-coder agreement, and member checking, and disclosing of the researcher's beliefs and biases is essential to produce accurate results. During the integration of quantitative and qualitative data, meta-inferences will be drawn relevant to the population of interest.

Issues to affect quality of meta-inferences. Due to the action research nature of the study, a few legitimation issues may arise and affect the quality of the produced meta-inferences. First, the researcher may be unable to view the underlying beliefs of quantitative and qualitative approaches as complementary, and will rather view them as separate, which could affect the degree of the integration of the quantitative and qualitative results. Second, if the inferences produced in one of the strands are not valid, then high-quality meta-inferences will not be generated. Third, the sequence of quantitative and qualitative study strands could pose a legitimation threat. Finally, the researcher might fail to utilize the strengths of each approach to compensate for the methods' weaknesses resulting in poor-quality meta-inferences (Onwuegbuzie & Johnson, 2006).

Adapted from Cunningham (2011) with the author's permission.

Dellinger and Leech (2007) proposed the *validation framework* and discussed mixed methods validity from the perspective of construct validity in quantitative research that embraces all validity evidence in a study. They viewed construct validation as "a continuous process of negotiation of meaning" that is created during the conduct of a mixed methods research study (p. 320). The validation framework is structured to guide the exploration of the meaning of the measures used in a mixed methods study and how these measures contribute to the quality and stability of the generated meta-inferences. The validation framework includes four elements (foundational, inferential consistency, utilization, and consequential) that are present at all phases of the research process, from the review of the literature, to the study design, implementation, and evaluation, and to the generation and application of inferences.

O'Cathain (2010) advanced a comprehensive *quality framework for mixed methods research* by synthesizing various approaches to mixed methods validity. This framework attempts to provide researchers with a common language and with guidance on how to access the quality of meta-inferences. The framework consists of eight domains corresponding to the stages of the study design, implementation, and dissemination (quality of planning, design, data, interpretive rigor, inference transferability, reporting, synthesizability, and utility). Each domain has a number of specific criteria for assessing quality related to a particular stage in the study process. Table 9.1 summarizes the four discussed conceptual models and frameworks for assessing quality in mixed methods research along with the proposed criteria for quality assessment and the related quality indicators.

While the models and frameworks of assessing quality in mixed methods research presented in Table 9.1 have different assessment criteria, they all are closely connected to the process of the study design and implementation; in addition, they all emphasize the fact that the purpose of integrating quantitative and qualitative methods is to produce quality meta-inferences. Such an approach to quality assessment is aligned with the fundamental principle of mixed methods research (Johnson & Turner, 2003) that suggests that the integration of quantitative and qualitative methods should take advantage of their strengths, but not their weaknesses.

Refer to Chapter 1 for the discussion of a fundamental principle of mixed methods research in the context of reasons and rationales for conducting mixed methods research.

Threats to Validity

Creswell and Plano Clark (2011) approached mixed methods validity from a study design perspective and the purposes of data integration within mixed methods designs. They defined validity in mixed methods research as "employing strategies that address potential issues in data collection, data analysis, and the interpretations that might compromise the merging or connecting of the quantitative and qualitative strands of the study and the conclusions drawn from the combination" (p. 239). Employing this practical focus, the authors outlined specific threats that can compromise the validity of resulting meta-inferences at different levels of mixed methods design implementation:

- At the level of data collection, threats can be caused by sample selection and size, research bias, faulty procedures, and wrong data sources in quantitative and qualitative study strands.
- At the level of data analysis, threats to validity may arise from inadequate quantitative and qualitative data representation, inappropriate statistical analytical techniques, and choice of weak results for qualitative follow-up.
- At the level of data interpretation, quality of inferences may be threatened by failing to address contradictions or divergent findings, attending to one set of results at the expense of the other, switching the order of results interpretation in sequential designs, using the wrong integration strategy, and not discussing the results in the context of the mixed methods research questions.

TABLE 9.1 Conceptual Models and Frameworks of Assessing Quality in Mixed Methods Research

Conceptual Model of Quality Assessment in Mixed Methods Research	Aspect/Type/Element/Domain	Quality Indicators
Integrative Framework for Inference Quality (Teddlie & Tashakkori, 2009)	• Design Quality ○ Design Suitability	• The extent to which the study design matches the research questions and the study strands address the same or closely related research questions
	○ Design Fidelity	• The extent to which the study design components (sampling, data collection, analysis) were implemented adequately
	○ Within-design Consistency ○ Analytic Adequacy	• The extent to which the study design components fit together in a logical and seamless manner • The extent to which the data analysis techniques are appropriate and adequate for answering the research questions
	• Interpretive Rigor ○ Interpretive Consistency	• The extent to which the study inferences follow the findings and multiple inferences based on the same findings are consistent with each other
	○ Theoretical Consistency ○ Interpretive Agreement	• The extent to which each inference is consistent with theory and empirical knowledge • The extent to which other researchers' and study participants' agree with the study inferences
	○ Interpretive Distinctiveness ○ Integrative Efficacy	• The extent to which each study inference provides the most credible explanation of the results • The extent to which each quantitative and qualitative inference is integrated into the meta-inferences

Conceptual Model of Quality Assessment in Mixed Methods Research	Aspect/Type/Element/Domain	Quality Indicators
	○ Interpretive Correspondence	• The extent to which the meta-inferences reflect the study purpose and research questions
Legitimation Model (Onwuegbuzie & Johnson, 2006)	• Sample Integration	• The extent to which the relationship between quantitative and qualitative sampling produces quality meta-inferences
	• Inside-Outside	• The extent to which a researcher accurately presents and appropriately utilizes the insider's view and the observer's views for description and explanation
	• Weakness Minimization	• The extent to which the weakness from one approach is compensated by the strengths from the other approach
	• Sequential	• The extent to which one has minimized the potential problem that the sequence of the quantitative and qualitative strands may have on the quality of the meta-inferences
	• Conversion	• The extent to which quantitizing or qualitizing of data produces quality meta-inferences
	• Paradigmatic Mixing	• The extent to which the researcher's philosophical beliefs that underlie quantitative and qualitative approaches are mixed
	• Commensurability	• The extent to which the meta-inferences produced reflect a mixed worldview

(Continued)

TABLE 9.1 Continued

Conceptual Model of Quality Assessment in Mixed Methods Research	Aspect/Type/Element/Domain	Quality Indicators
	• Multiple validities	• The extent to which quantitative, qualitative, and mixed methods used produce valid and quality meta-inferences
	• Political	• The extent to which the consumers of mixed methods research value the meta-inferences generated from both quantitative and qualitative study components
Validation Framework (Dellinger & Leech, 2007)	• Foundational element	• The extent of researchers' prior understanding of a construct and/or phenomenon under study to control for bias
	• Inferential consistency	• The extent to which the inferences in a study are grounded in the study design, measurement, and analysis
	• Utilization/historical element	• The extent to which multiple uses of the measures add to credibility of the meta-inferences
	• Consequential element	• The extent to which a study's findings, measures, or inferences contribute to the social acceptability of generated consequences
(O'Cathain, 2010)	• Planning quality	• The extent to which the study is situated in a comprehensive literature review, provides justification for the use of mixed methods, has detailed description of all research aspects (design, data collection and analysis), and is feasible

Conceptual Model of Quality Assessment in Mixed Methods Research	Aspect/Type/Element/Domain	Quality Indicators
	• Design quality	• The extent to which the study design is described in detail, is appropriate for addressing the research questions, minimizes shared bias, and optimizes the study depth and breadth
	• Data quality	• The extent to which each method is described in detail and is implemented with rigor and the extent to which analytical methods are appropriate for research questions
	• Interpretive rigor	• The extent to which inferences are consistent with related results and current knowledge or theory, are integrated to produce meta-inferences, and have a potential to be replicated in similar research scenarios
	• Inference transferability	• The extent to which inferences are transferable to other contexts and settings, people, and methods and have temporal value
	• Reporting quality	• The extent to which the study is reported in a timely and adequate manner
	• Synthesizability	• The extent to which the study quality is sufficient for inclusion in systematic reviews
	• Utility	• The extent to which the findings are used by consumers and policymakers

Refer to the Further Readings at the end of this chapter for detailed information about approaches to quality assessment in mixed methods research.

Creswell and Plano Clark (2011) emphasized the importance of observing these validity threats in designing and implementing a mixed methods study and offered practical strategies for minimizing validity threats at each level of design and implementation. These strategies are aimed at helping researchers avoid inconsistent and wrongful conclusions caused by inadequate integration of the quantitative and qualitative components within a mixed methods study.

Process of Assessing Quality in an MMAR Study

As discussed at the beginning of the chapter, assessing quality in an MMAR study is a multilevel process and should include quality checks consistent with each methodological approach and with the process of quantitative and qualitative methods' integration. Specifically, in assessing quality of an MMAR study, practitioner-researchers have to address three sets of issues related to three quality assessment domains:

- Quality issues related to the methodological rigor of quantitative and qualitative methods used in each quantitative and qualitative study strand
- Quality issues related to specific quality considerations of action research used in the action research cycle
- Quality issues related to the legitimacy and quality of the study conclusions or meta-inferences resulting from the integration of quantitative and qualitative methods

Since the methodological purpose of an MMAR study is to produce quality meta-inferences about the practical problem/issue that are grounded in the inferences from the quantitative and qualitative strands, practitioner-researchers should make efforts to ensure the quantitative and qualitative results are valid and credible. Therefore, they should use the discussed strategies to test for reliability and validity of the collected survey and quantitative assessment data and conduct recommended procedures to verify credibility and trustworthiness of the qualitative interview and observation data and their interpretation. Besides, taking into consideration an action research focus of the study, practitioner-researchers should address specific quality considerations related to the nature of action research and employ the validity criteria consistent with its goals. Finally, threats to validity related to the planned integration of quantitative and qualitative methods in the study should be considered and addressed during the study design and implementation stages.

Refer to Chapter 4 and Figure 4.1 for the discussion and illustration of an MMAR Study Process Model, and procedural and action steps within each study phase.

In addition to addressing the issues within the three quality assessment domains (quantitative and qualitative methods, action research, meta-inferences), the assessment of an MMAR study quality should be guided by specific goals of the six phases in an MMAR Study Process Model. As previously discussed, this model reflects six phases in the action research cycle (diagnosing, reconnaissance, planning, acting, evaluation, monitoring) and outlines important methodological and procedural steps for each phase in an MMAR study process. Importantly, the purpose of an MMAR study is to produce an effective change action that is informed by the entire study process. Preserving methodological rigor of each phase in the study cycle has implications for the quality of the generated meta-inferences because meta-inferences in an MMAR study enhance practitioner-researchers' understanding of the critical issue or situation: (1) They inform the development of the plan for action/intervention, (2) they support an effective evaluation of the implemented action/intervention, and (3) they show the direction for the action/intervention monitoring. Figure 9.1 provides a conceptual diagram of the relationship among the three quality assessment domains for an MMAR study within an MMAR Study Process Model framework. The diagram shows how the process of an MMAR study is embedded into the quality assessment criteria that are shaped

FIGURE 9.1 **Quality Assessment Domains within an MMAR Study Process Model**

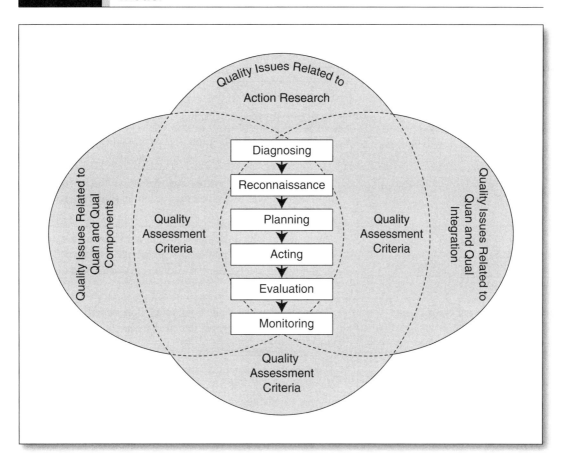

Refer to Box 5.1 in Chapter 5 for the description of Davis's (2011) proposed concurrent Quan + Qual MMAR study design.

by the three quality assessment domains related to action research, quantitative and qualitative study components, and quantitative and qualitative methods' integration.

To help practitioner-researchers apply an MMAR Study Process Model as a framework for assessing quality of an MMAR study process and its outcomes, Table 9.2 presents quality assessment criteria for each component within the six phases of the action research cycle. These criteria reflect specific indicators of quality related to a certain stage in the study planning, design, implementation, and dissemination, and can be used as helpful quality checks in addition to validation strategies related to methodological considerations of an MMAR study.

Box 9.7 illustrates how Davis (2011) described the planned procedures for addressing quality issues in a research proposal for a concurrent Quan + Qual MMAR study in the field of K–12 education.

TABLE 9.2 | **Quality Assessment Criteria for Six Phases in an MMAR Study Process Model**

Study Component	Quality Assessment Criteria
Phase I Diagnosing Conceptualizing an MMAR Study	
• Identifying a problem/issue	• The extent to which the problem has a practical focus and addresses professional or community needs
• Reviewing the literature	• The extent to which a comprehensive literature review has been conducted to identify a potential solution to the problem
• Developing a study general plan	• The extent to which the study general plan adequately addresses the study timeline, research skills, resources, stakeholders' involvement, feasibility, and dissemination of findings
• Considering ethical issues	• The extent to which ethical issues are considered in three contexts: research in general, action research, and mixed methods research
• Specifying overall study purpose, outcomes, objectives, and research questions	• The extent to which an overall study purpose is explicitly stated, the goals of the reconnaissance and evaluation study phases are identified, the expected study outcomes are stated, and research questions including each study strand are specified

Study Component	Quality Assessment Criteria
Phase II Reconnaissance (Fact Finding) Designing and Implementing Reconnaissance Phase of an MMAR Study	
• Developing the reconnaissance phase purpose statement and research questions	• The extent to which the purpose and research questions aim at assessing the problem or situation and identifying the areas for improvement
• Selecting an MMAR design	• The extent to which the selected MMAR design is appropriate for addressing the reconnaissance phase study purpose and research questions
• Identifying the sample, quantitative and qualitative data sources	• The extent to which the chosen sample and quantitative and qualitative data match the reconnaissance phase study purpose and research questions
• Collecting and analyzing quantitative and qualitative data	• The extent to which quantitative and qualitative data collection and analysis follow the scientific standards adopted in each approach
• Validating the findings and meta-inferences	• The extent to which the methodological rigor of each quantitative and qualitative study strand, quality considerations of the action research process, and the legitimacy and quality of the integrated study conclusions or meta-inferences are established
Phases III–IV Planning and Acting Taking First Action Step	
• Interpreting the meta-inferences from the reconnaissance phase	• The extent to which the meta-inferences from the reconnaissance phase are interpreted to inform an effective action/intervention development
• Sharing the reconnaissance phase results with the stakeholders	• The extent to which the results of assessing the problem or situation and identifying the areas for improvement are shared with all the stakeholders, and their input is sought
• Developing an action plan based on the reconnaissance phase meta-inferences	• The extent to which the development of the action/intervention is grounded in the valid meta-inferences from the reconnaissance phase
• Implementing an action/intervention plan	• The extent to which the action plan/intervention is implemented in a consistent, collaborative, and ethical manner

| **TABLE 9.2** | **Continued** |

Study Component	Quality Assessment Criteria
Phase V Evaluating Action	
Designing and Implementing Evaluation Phase of an MMAR Study	
• Developing the evaluation phase purpose statement and research questions	• The extent to which the purpose and research questions aim at evaluating the action/intervention and informing further action
• Selecting an MMAR design	• The extent to which the selected MMAR design is appropriate for addressing the evaluation phase study purpose and research questions
• Identifying the sample, quantitative, and qualitative data sources	• The extent to which the chosen sample and quantitative and qualitative data match the evaluation phase study purpose and research questions
• Collecting and analyzing quantitative and qualitative data	• The extent to which quantitative and qualitative data collection and analysis follow the scientific standards adopted in each approach
• Validating the findings and meta-inferences	• The extent to which the methodological rigor of each quantitative and qualitative study strand, quality considerations of the action research process, and the legitimacy and quality of the integrated study conclusions or meta-inferences are established
Phase VI Monitoring and Revising Action	
Taking Second Action Step	
• Interpreting meta-inferences from the evaluation phase	• The extent to which the meta-inferences from the evaluation phase are interpreted to inform the revisions or adoption of the action/intervention
• Sharing the evaluation phase results with the stakeholders	• The extent to which the results of action/intervention evaluation are shared with all the stakeholders and their input is sought
• Revising and monitoring the action/intervention plan	• The extent to which revising and monitoring of the action/ intervention is implemented in a consistent, collaborative, and ethical manner
• Sustaining the action/ intervention sustainability	• The extent to which the sustainability of the action/ intervention promotes change, social acceptability, and empowerment

BOX 9.7

Example of Assessing Quality in a Concurrent Quan + Qual MMAR Study Exploring Parent Involvement Technology Use Program

Creswell and Plano Clark (2011) identify validity in mixed methods research as "employing strategies that address potential issues in data collection, data analysis, and the interpretations that might compromise the merging or connecting of the quantitative and qualitative strands of the study and the conclusions drawn from the combination" (p. 239). Specific data quality and interpretation threats for this study could include obtaining unequal sample sizes for quantitative and qualitative data collection, collecting two types of data that do not address the same topics, giving more weight to one form of data, and choosing participants who cannot help explain significant results.

The researchers will use a large sample size ($n = 100$) for the quantitative strand of the study and will employ the inferential statistical tests for assessing the significance of the relationships in the data. Choosing the qualitative participants ($n = 15$) from the initial quantitative sample will help address the threats related to producing credible study conclusions. Credibility of the qualitative data will be achieved through maintaining the confidentiality of the study participants and creating a trustworthy relationship between the participants and the researchers. Member checking with the study participants' will be utilized in verifying the accuracy of the emerged themes, interpretations, and conclusions. Researchers will also use thick, rich descriptions in the qualitative strand, which "involves making detailed descriptions of the context and other aspects of the research setting so that other researchers can make comparisons with other contexts in which they are working" (Teddlie & Tashakkori, 2009, p. 296).

Onwuegbuzie and Johnson (2006) identify nine types of legitimation for mixed methods research. For the purpose of this study, sample integration and inside-outside legitimation will be used for assessing the quality of the quantitative and qualitative data. Onwuegbuzie and Johnson (2006) described sample integration as "the extent to which the relationship between quantitative and qualitative sampling designs yields quality meta-inferences" (p. 56). Fifteen participants will be recruited from the original 100 quantitative sample for the qualitative follow-up strand to ensure the researchers will gain explanations to the quantitative results from the same individuals in the study. Inside-outside legitimation is described as "the extent to which the researcher accurately presents and appropriately utilizes the insider's view and the observer's views for the purposes such as description and explanation" (p. 57). The researchers will use an outside consultant to examine the interpretations and conclusions in the study. The research team will also consistently review the data and their integration to address other legitimation issues.

To secure the stakeholders' input in the study validation process, study participants and other parents will be invited to assist with the data analysis and interpretation to ensure the researchers are consistent and accurate in presenting the results of the overall study.

Adapted from Davis (2011) with the author's permission.

Box 9.8 provides some useful tips for practitioner-researchers to consider when assessing quality in an MMAR study.

BOX 9.8

Useful Tips for Assessing Quality in an MMAR Study

- Use rigorous and systematic procedures for data collection and analysis in quantitative and qualitative study strands to address weakness minimization and to ensure process validity.
- Apply validation strategies recommended for quantitative and qualitative research approaches in quantitative and qualitative study strands.
- Consider and address potential quality issues related to conducting action research to ensure dialogic and democratic validity.
- Consider and address potential quality issues related to mixed methods research and integration of quantitative and qualitative methods.
- Address potential threats related to MMAR study designs and the purposes and procedures of quantitative and qualitative methods' integration.
- Employ collaborative strategies to ensure democratic validity and involvement of all parties who have a stake in the problem.
- Create meta-inferences grounded in both quantitative and qualitative results and related inferences.
- Assess the extent to which meta-inferences meet quality indicators related to mixed methods research.
- Evaluate how the generated meta-inferences address the study purpose and the posed research questions.
- Apply quality assessment criteria consistent with the specific phase in an MMAR Study Process Model.
- Determine the extent to which meta-inferences are transferable to other contexts, settings, communities, individuals, and stakeholder groups to ensure catalytic validity.
- Assess the extent to which the action/intervention taken leads to a resolution of the problem to ensure outcome validity.

SUMMARY

When assessing the quality of an MMAR study, practitioner-researchers have to address three sets of issues related to (1) the methodological rigor of each quantitative and qualitative study strand, (2) the specific quality considerations of the action research process, and (3) the legitimacy and quality of the integrated study conclusions or meta-inferences. Despite a local and practical focus of action research, it is important that the quantitative evidence results in the correct assessment of the problem or situation and the accurate evaluation of the effects of the action/intervention. It is also critical that the qualitative findings and their interpretation accurately reflect stakeholders' views and experiences with the problem under investigation. Traditional means for evaluating methodological quality of the quantitative data are to assess its validity (the degree to which an instrument measures the concept or construct it is supposed to measure) and reliability (the degree to which an instrument consistently measures the concept or construct it claims to measure). Trustworthiness of qualitative data and their interpretation is assessed using the following criteria: credibility, transferability, dependability, and confirmability. Application examples of quality assessment for the quantitative and qualitative strands in an MMAR study are provided.

Quality considerations related to action research, such as addressing the issues of insider versus outsider status of practitioner-researchers, objectivity versus subjectivity when studying one's own practice, and generalizability versus transferability of the study results are discussed. The chapter also addresses Herr and Anderson's (2005) validity criteria (outcome, process, democratic, catalytic, dialogic) related to five goals of action research. Ensuring quality in an MMAR study can be especially challenging because of the intended integration of quantitative and qualitative results to produce credible meta-inferences. Unique mixed methods design features related to different chronology of quantitative and qualitative data collection and analysis procedures, the order of quantitative and qualitative strands in sequential designs, and the way quantitative and qualitative methods are integrated have special implications for the quality of the generated meta-inferences. Several approaches for assessing the methodological quality of mixed methods research and the produced meta-inferences are presented and illustrated.

In addition to addressing the issues within the three quality assessment domains (quantitative and qualitative methods, action research, meta-inferences), the assessment of an overall quality of an MMAR study should be guided by specific goals of the six phases (diagnosing, reconnaissance, planning, acting, evaluation, monitoring) in an MMAR Study Process Model. To apply this model as a framework for assessing quality of the study process and its outcomes, quality assessment criteria for each component within six phases of the action research cycle are presented. These criteria reflect specific indicators of quality related to a certain stage in the study planning, design, implementation, and dissemination, and can be used as quality checks in addition to validation strategies related to methodological considerations of an MMAR study. Finally, some useful tips for practitioner-researchers to consider when establishing quality in an MMAR study are provided.

REFLECTIVE QUESTIONS AND EXERCISES

1. Describe the issues that practitioner-researchers have to address in assessing the quality of an MMAR study. Explain why it is important to approach the process of assessing the quality of an MMAR study with these issues in mind.

2. Describe common ways of assessing validity and reliability in quantitative research. Discuss their relevance for the practical purposes of an MMAR study.

3. Describe the criteria and strategies for assessing trustworthiness of qualitative data and their interpretation. Discuss their relevance for the practical purposes of an MMAR study. Explain how stakeholders can be engaged in the process of assessing trustworthiness of an MMAR study.

4. Explain why and how practitioner-researchers should address quality considerations specific to action research. Using an example of a hypothetical MMAR study in your area of interest, describe how you plan to address these quality considerations and what specific strategies you will use.

5. Describe approaches to quality assessment used in mixed methods research. Choose one framework or model presented in Table 9.1. Using an example of a hypothetical MMAR study in your area of interest, describe how you will apply the listed quality indicators for this framework to assess the methodological quality of this study.

6. Select a published MMAR study in your discipline or area of interest. Determine what phase or phases in an MMAR Study Process Model are reported in the article. Identify an MMAR study design. Describe what quantitative and qualitative data were collected, how these data were analyzed, during what stages in the research process quantitative and qualitative methods were integrated, and how the meta-inferences were generated. Using the quality assessment criteria for six phases in an MMAR Study Process Model presented in Table 9.2, explain how you will apply these criteria to assess the quality of each study component within a corresponding phase in the model.

FURTHER READINGS

To learn more about the process of assessing validity and reliability of quantitative data in their interpretation, examine the following sources:

Gay, L. R., Mills, G. E., & Airasian, P. (2006). *Educational research: Competencies for analysis and applications* (8th ed.). Upper Saddle River, NJ: Merrill Prentice Hall, Ch. 5, pp. 134–145.

Mills, G. E. (2011). *Action research: A guide for the teacher researcher* (4th ed.). Boston: Pearson Education, Ch. 5, pp. 102–103, 112–114.

Thorndike, R. M., & Thorndike-Christ, T. M. (2011). *Measurement and evaluation in psychology and education* (8th ed.). Upper Saddle River, NJ: Pearson Education, Chs. 4–5 pp. 118–199.

To learn more about the criteria and strategies for assessing trustworthiness of qualitative data and their interpretation, examine the following sources:

Creswell, J. W. (2014). *Research design: Qualitative, quantitative, and mixed methods approaches* (4th ed.). Thousand Oaks, CA: Sage, Ch. 9, pp. 201–204.

Mills, G. E. (2011). *Action research: A guide for the teacher researcher* (4th ed.). Boston: Pearson Education, Ch. 5, p. 103–108.

Stringer, E. T. (2014). *Action research* (4th ed.). Thousand Oaks, CA: Sage, Ch. 3, pp. 91–94.

To learn more about quality considerations in action research, examine the following sources:

Herr, K., & Anderson, G. L. (2005). *The action research dissertation: A guide for students and faculty.* Thousand Oaks, CA: Sage, Chs. 4–5, pp. 49–82.

Koshy, E., Koshy, V., & Waterman, H. (2011). *Action research in healthcare.* Thousand Oaks, CA: Sage, Ch. 6, pp. 143–144.

McNiff, J., & Whitehead, J. (2011). *All you need to know about action research* (2nd ed.). London, UK: Sage, Chs. 15–16, pp. 161–179.

Mills, G. E. (2011). *Action research: A guide for the teacher researcher* (4th ed.). Boston: Pearson Education, Ch. 5, p. 108–112.

To learn more about approaches to quality assessment in mixed methods research, examine the following sources:

Creswell, J. W., & Plano Clark, V. L. (2011). *Designing and conducting mixed methods research* (2nd ed.). Thousand Oaks, CA: Sage, Ch. 7, pp. 238–249.

Leech, N. L., Dellinger, A. B., Brannagan, K. B., & Tanaka, H. (2010). Evaluating mixed research studies: A mixed methods approach. *Journal of Mixed Methods Research, 4*(1), 17–31.

O'Cathain, A. (2010). Assessing the quality of mixed methods research: Toward a comprehensive framework. In A. Tashakkori & C. Teddlie (Eds.), *SAGE handbook of mixed methods in social & behavioral research* (2nd ed., pp. 531–555). Thousand Oaks, CA: Sage.

Onwuegbuzie, A. J., & Johnson, R. B. (2006). The validity issue in mixed research. *Research in the Schools, 13*(1), 48–63.

Teddlie, C., & Tashakkori, A. (2009). *Foundations of mixed methods research: Integrating quantitative and qualitative approaches in the social and behavioral sciences.* Thousand Oaks, CA: Sage, Ch. 12, pp. 300–313.

PART III

Using Mixed Methods Inferences to Inform Community Action

10

Planning and Implementing Action Using Mixed Methods Action Research Study Inferences

OBJECTIVES

By the end of this chapter, the reader should be able to

- Understand how to use meta-inferences from an MMAR study to inform community action/intervention,
- Explain the advantages of sharing the results of an MMAR study with stakeholders,
- Understand the logistics of developing and implementing action/intervention in an MMAR study,
- Describe the components of an action plan and levels of action planning in an MMAR study,
- Understand potential challenges and possible solutions when implementing action/intervention in an MMAR study,
- Describe the role of evaluation and monitoring of action/intervention in an MMAR study,
- Understand how to report the findings from an MMAR study, and
- Describe the structure of the proposal for an MMAR study.

INTRODUCTION

Revisit Figure 2.2 in Chapter 2, which illustrates Lewin's (1948b) model of the methodological steps in action research.

Planning and implementing action are the integral components of the action research process. According to Lewin (1948b), they conceptually follow the step of reconnaissance or fact finding about the problem or situation during which the evidence for the issue is collected, analyzed, and interpreted. This is done through critical reflection about the presented evidence and in collaboration with interested stakeholders. Developing an action/intervention grounded in a systematic and comprehensive assessment of the problem from stakeholders' perspectives helps to efficiently reveal critical areas for targeted intervention and identify effective strategies for improvement. Once the action/intervention is planned and implemented, it undergoes evaluation and further revisions during the next action step. In an MMAR study, practitioner-researchers take the advantage of using the integrated conclusions or meta-inferences from the quantitative and qualitative study strands to inform action planning, evaluation, and monitoring.

Revisit Figure 4.1 and the discussion in Chapter 4 about an MMAR Study Process Model.

Chapters 4 and 9 discussed the process of conceptualizing, designing, and conducting an MMAR study following the methodological and procedural steps within the six phases (diagnosing, reconnaissance, planning, acting, evaluation, and monitoring) outlined in an MMAR Study Process Model. Each phase in the model performs a vital role in the action research cycle and is uniquely informed and enhanced by the use of the mixed methods approach that contributes to the development of meta-inferences. Being the product of systematic collection, analysis, and integration of quantitative and qualitative data, meta-inferences help generate more consistent and thus credible conclusions about the studied issue (Teddlie & Tashakkori, 2009). Adherence to meta-inferences is important because it promotes cohesiveness and integrity of an MMAR study; it also equips practitioner-researchers with the necessary knowledge and strategies to address the next step in the problem-solving cycle when seeking a desired solution for the issue. Ultimately, it facilitates the process of data-driven decision-making and provides strong support for developing evidence-based and data-driven plans for improvement (Tomal, 2010).

So, how can practitioner-researchers use the meta-inferences from an MMAR study to inform the design, implementation, evaluation, and monitoring of the action/intervention in order to promote the sustainability of change?

USING META-INFERENCES TO INFORM ACTION/INTERVENTION IN AN MMAR STUDY

Consistent with an MMAR Study Process Model, planning and implementing of the action/intervention requires practitioner-researchers to carefully consider and accurately interpret the findings from the reconnaissance phase where the problem was initially explored using mixed methods. Likewise, monitoring of the implemented action is based on a thorough examination of the quantitative and qualitative results from the evaluation phase in order to more completely understand the effect of the change effort. During each phase, the generated meta-inferences are shared with stakeholders and their feedback is used to help develop or improve the action/intervention plan. This process is more iterative than linear because oftentimes the steps leading from results' interpretation to action inform and refine each other and redirect future actions. For example, stakeholders' feedback to the conclusions from the reconnaissance and evaluation phases may change the initial interpretation of the reported results. Similarly, the development and implementation of the action/intervention plan requires consistent input from stakeholders. Their feedback is compared with practitioner-researchers' interpretations of the integrated quantitative and qualitative results and is incorporated into the action/intervention plan.

So, how do practitioner-researchers interpret the meta-inferences from an MMAR study?

Interpreting Meta-Inferences from an MMAR Study

Creswell and Plano Clark (2011) defined interpretation of results as the process of "stepping back from the detailed results and advancing their larger meaning in view of the research problems, questions in a study, the existing literature, and perhaps personal experiences" (p. 209). Thus, interpretation of the study results is the clarification of the meaning that is generated in the process of data analysis (Denzin, 1978); how the meaning of the data is interpreted and what conclusions are perceived to be credible and of value to the interested individuals have implications for how the study results may be used to advance knowledge and inform practice.

In an MMAR study, the results from the quantitative and qualitative study strands are interpreted to jointly produce meta-inferences that inform the subsequent phases in the action research cycle. Teddlie and Tashakkori (2009) referred to this process as **interpretive consistency** that indicates the extent to which each conclusion follows the results obtained from the quantitative and qualitative study strands. Additionally, interpretive consistency reveals if multiple conclusions generated on the basis of the same results are consistent with each other. For example, the conclusions from the interviews conducted with participants selected from all stakeholder groups should reflect multiple perspectives on the problem/issue, whereas the interpretation of the photo-voice data reported by participants should depict the real situation. Likewise, the analysis of the quantitative data from surveying a sample of community residents should be representative of the views of the entire community. Thus, drawing consistent conclusions from multiple pieces of evidence result in meta-inferences that provide a realistic depiction of the problem and identify direction for its possible solution. Greene (2007) observed that "[i]nference and interpretation are fundamentally human cognitive processes" (p. 142). So, reaching interpretive consistency for quantitative and qualitative conclusions should yield meta-inferences that are scientifically credible and provide a reliable explanation of the research situation.

In an MMAR study, the process of interpreting meta-inferences involves a number of systematic but interactive actions, such as determining how the results address the study purpose and posted research questions and thus meet the expected outcomes; critically reflecting on the meaning of the results in the context of the studied issue, reported solutions, and personal experiences; and sharing the results with stakeholders to ensure their views are integrated with researchers' interpretations. Figure 10.1 conceptually presents multiple entities and their iterative relationships that play a role in shaping the meta-inferences that emerge in a MMAR study process to inform action/intervention. The practical problem/issue that requires solution guides the whole

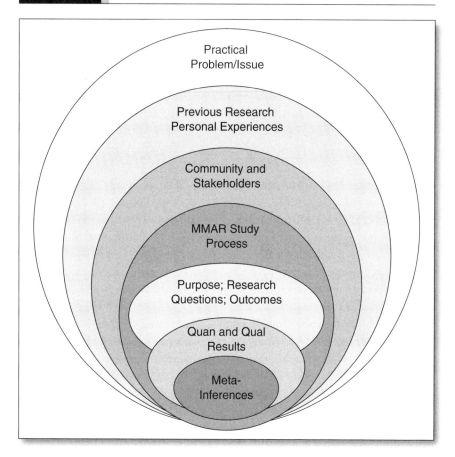

FIGURE 10.1 **Multiple Entities that Shape Meta-inferences in an MMAR Study**

research process and embeds other influencing factors: previous research and personal experiences, community and stakeholders, and an MMAR study process from research questions to quantitative and qualitative results and meta-inferences.

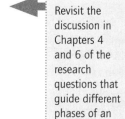

Revisit the discussion in Chapters 4 and 6 of the research questions that guide different phases of an MMAR study.

Revisiting Study Purpose, Research Questions, and Study Outcomes

As was discussed in Chapter 4, the study purpose renders the intent and an overall direction of the study, while research questions help focus the study and determine the choice of the methodological procedures. Therefore, revisiting the study purpose and research questions and determining how well or how completely the results from the quantitative and qualitative study strands answer these questions is important for making correct inferences about the generated knowledge claims. Additionally, it serves the purposes of validating the chosen methodology and the credibility of the collected information. Furthermore, consideration should be given to whether the integration of the quantitative and qualitative results produces meta-inferences that fully address the integrated MMAR questions from the reconnaissance and evaluation phases and the integrated MMAR question for the entire MMAR study.

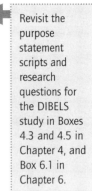

Revisit the purpose statement scripts and research questions for the DIBELS study in Boxes 4.3 and 4.5 in Chapter 4, and Box 6.1 in Chapter 6.

Consider the previously discussed hypothetical MMAR study about the changes in existing school policies related to the administration of the DIBELS reading assessment test with the purpose of improving third-grade students' reading self-efficacy. The purpose of the reconnaissance phase is to identify the reasons for third-grade students' failure to meet the DIBELS reading test standards in school X. At the conclusion of the data collection and analysis, each set of the quantitative and qualitative results is reviewed within their requisite research questions to determine if the questions have been fully addressed. Furthermore, the statistical results about the relationship between students' performance on the DIBELS test and their reading self-efficacy are compared with the qualitative findings from individual interviews with teachers, parents, and students about their perceptions of factors that may affect students' reading self-efficacy. Combining the inferences from the quantitative and qualitative study strands provides a more complete understanding of how the DIBELS test performance and reading self-efficacy may be related, and what factors may aggravate or improve this relationship. These meta-inferences are then used to inform the development and implementation of the new DIBELS test administration policies in school X.

The purpose of the evaluation phase of the study is to identify the effectiveness of the new DIBELS test administration policies as they relate to third-grade students' reading self-efficacy in school X. During this phase, the effectiveness of the new DIBELS test administration policies is examined by combining the inferences from the quantitative and qualitative results, such as differences in the students' performance scores on the DIBELS test and reading self-efficacy before and after the new policies administration, quantitative survey responses about teachers and parents' opinions on the new DIBELS test administration policies, and the themes from focus group interviews with purposefully selected teachers, parents, and students. Each set of results is evaluated on how well they answer the posted quantitative and qualitative research questions. The joint interpretation of these results creates meta-inferences that provide evidence about the effectiveness of the new DIBELS test administration policies and guide their further implementation and monitoring in school X.

Finally, creating meta-inferences based on all the inferences generated from the reconnaissance and evaluation study phases will help answer an integrated MMAR question that addresses the practical intent of the study, which is to change the existing school policies related to the DIBELS reading test administration so as to enhance third-grade students' reading self-efficacy in school X:

- How can changes in the existing school policies related to the DIBELS reading test administration for third-grade students enhance their reading self-efficacy, as measured by test and reading efficacy scores and as described through the interpretation of teachers, parents and students' views?

Importantly, practitioner-researchers should also consider the extent to which the study conclusions support the expected outcomes of the study phase specified in its purpose statement. As discussed in Chapter 4,

Revisit the discussion in Chapter 4 about the importance of including expected outcomes of the planned action/ intervention in a study purpose for an MMAR study.

Refer to Chapter 2 for the discussion about the role of reflection in the action research process.

an overall goal of action research is to influence practice and promote a desired change in the existing situation; therefore, generated meta-inferences should be aimed at providing the means for solving the problem specified in the expected outcomes. Aligning the study results with the expected outcomes may also help with the study being more readily accepted in the community and by the stakeholders.

Critically Reflecting on the Meaning of Results

As previously discussed, reflection is an important part of the action research process and is done systematically and purposefully at all stages. For practitioner-researchers to assume a reflective stance toward the study outcomes is consistent with the goals of action research. Mills (2011) indicated that critical reflection about the study outcomes helps practitioner-researchers position themselves "to act responsively" with regard to the study results (p. 161), particularly when communicating with stakeholders and initiating and monitoring action/intervention.

In an MMAR study, interpretation of the integrated study results and creating meta-inferences to inform action/intervention or its evaluation involves consistent reflection on the part of practitioner-researchers. As practitioner-researchers study their own practices, they reflect on what they learn from the initial exploration of the issue or evaluation of actions/interventions taken to improve the current situation. Importantly, a critical reflection on the meaning of the results from the reconnaissance and evaluation phases may indicate when it is needed to repeat a certain step in the action research process. For example, practitioner-researchers may decide that more data are needed to explore the nature and extent of the problem during the reconnaissance phase or that more stakeholder groups should be included in the evaluation of the impact of the implemented action/ intervention. It is also advisable to compare the ongoing study outcomes with the available literature that addressed a similar problem and to reflect on possible explanations of their meaning in the context of the reported solutions and personal experiences with the problem/issue. Comparing the study results with the best practices of other practitioner-researchers and professional organizations may provide additional insight into the interpretation of specific results, particularly if these results emerged as unexpected, or prompted inconsistent interpretations.

Craig (2009) provided five questions that may guide critical reflection in action research. These questions were adjusted to the purposes of an MMAR study, taking into account the role of meta-inferences for informing action/intervention planning and evaluation, and are presented in Box 10.1.

Shortt's (2002) MMAR study that evaluated the redesign of a first-year undergraduate research methods course module based on the students' suggestions offers an excellent example of a practitioner-researcher's reflection about the study outcomes. After comparing the assessment results of the learning intervention between the two groups of students, those who received an original and those who received a redesigned course instruction, with their narrative feedback, Shortt provided "reflections upon the action"

BOX 10.1

Questions to Guide Reflection about Meta-Inferences in an MMAR Study

- How can the meta-inferences from the quantitative and qualitative strands be applied to the design of the action/intervention in a way that promotes further examination?
- What possible solutions can these meta-inferences help generate?
- What do these meta-inferences convey regarding improving practice?
- What strategies may be integrated into the action/intervention plan based on these meta-inferences?
- What may be the goals and expected outcomes of the action/intervention based on these meta-inferences?

Adapted from Craig (2009, p. 220).

(p. 65). He connected the study outcomes with his personal experiences of being a relatively new college instructor. The author discussed the action outcomes from the perspective of allowing students more control over learning, emphasizing the mutual benefits of reflective practice. Shortt concluded,

> This learning may not just be for the students' benefit, but also for the staff involved—especially where the staff member is relatively new. I now feel more comfortable relinquishing some of my previously precious control in many other sessions I take. Additionally I realised that students really do learn differently from how I imagined they learn, in terms of both content and time taken to learn (p. 66).

Sharing Results with Stakeholders

Besides an obvious importance for practitioner-researchers to accurately interpret meta-inferences from the reconnaissance and evaluation phases, it is also critical to share the results from each study phase with stakeholders in order to solicit their input into the action planning, implementation, and evaluation. Koshy and colleagues (2011) argued that the way "the emerging findings are shared with all the participants and used to refine any action" differentiates action research from other forms of scientific inquiry (pp. 97–98). Vecchiarelli and colleagues (2005) emphasized this distinct feature of action research when they

Revisit the discussion about the importance of stakeholders' involvement in action research in Chapters 2 and 4.

reported on the results of their multistrand MMAR study about the development of a school-based environmental intervention to support students' healthy eating and physical activity. They wrote, "Through participatory research, the school community members and research team shared in the decision-making process as opposed to the researchers making all decisions and asking the school community members for input after decisions have already been made" (p. 36).

Involving the study participants and stakeholders in the interpretation of the results maximizes democratic and catalytic validity of an MMAR study and creates their "emancipatory knowledge interest" in the study outcomes (Herr & Anderson, 2005, p. 90). In conjunction with mixed methods, developing an action/intervention grounded in the systematic and comprehensive assessment of the problem from stakeholders' perspectives helps practitioner-researchers efficiently reveal critical areas for targeted intervention and identify effective strategies for improvement. Additionally, soliciting continuous stakeholders' feedback ensures that their perspectives are not lost or are not dominated by original researchers. Hinchey (2008) contended that stakeholders who believe their views are encouraged and valued may be more willing to engage in action/intervention planning and implementation and help facilitate the change process.

For example, when reporting their MMAR study aimed at understanding patients' experiences with transitioning from hospital to a homeless shelter, Greysen and colleagues (2012) described how they presented the outcomes of each data collection step to the study participants and key stakeholders in the community with the purpose of seeking their input on the accuracy of the results' interpretation and their recommendations for changes in the care for homeless people in hospitals and shelters in that area. The researchers explained: "This feedback process was critical for shaping our interpretation and presentation of data collected from study participants in the context of the community to which they belong" (p. 1486). Similarly, Phillips and Davidson (2009) discussed how they consistently shared the data and results with the key sponsors and stakeholders from the Critical Reference Group that guided the development and implementation of the Residential-Palliative Approach Competency MMAR project. Such sharing provided "opportunities for a creative period of transformation which enabled new and improved action to be tested" (p. 202).

Sharing the results with stakeholders can be done using different informal and formal venues, such as engaging study participants as co-researchers, having discussions with other practitioner-researchers; participating in professional learning communities; regularly reporting to project advisory boards, steering committees, and community groups; providing formal reports to sponsoring agencies, professional boards, and community organizations; presenting at professional conferences; and publishing in professional journals. In the Residential-Palliative Approach Competency MMAR project, Phillips and Davidson (2009) regularly reported to the Critical Reference Group of stakeholders. Sharing the needs assessment results with the Group helped the researchers design the action research phase and inform the data collection methods; at a later stage, the Group helped inform the redesign of the planned intervention and its subsequent testing and evaluation. Likewise, Hesselink, Verhoeff, and Stronks (2009) reported using multiple approaches to sharing their MMAR study results during the evaluation of the new health-care advisor program for ethnic population in four districts in the Netherlands. Each district formed a steering committee consisting of stakeholders from health-care, welfare, and migrant organizations to supervise health-care advisors and the program activities. During the 2 years of pilot testing the project, the researchers sent two interim evaluation reports and a final report to each district. They also conducted interim presentations and consultations with the representatives from each district. The goal of this information sharing was to enable the districts "to adapt the function based on the research results during the pilot period" (p. 420).

In their MMAR study aimed at exploring the existing community-based mental health services for people from culturally diverse backgrounds, Westhues and colleagues (2008) created a project-governing partnership committee consisting of representatives from all community organizations that supported the project. In addition, they formed two steering committees to oversee the project at two participating sites. These committees included stakeholders from five local cultural-linguistic communities, practitioners, and researchers at a given site. During the study, Westhues and colleagues presented the results from the initial and advanced analysis of the focus group and survey data to the committee members for their input in the results' interpretation. They also conducted a one-day conference with all project stakeholders to finalize a conceptual analytical framework to inform the intervention development. Stakeholders represented various groups and included academics, policymakers, consumers, community members, and service providers, many of whom were also the study participants. Working in groups, conference participants brainstormed about potential intervention types and helped prioritize those they considered the most important to be implemented in the community.

Importantly, Herr and Anderson (2005) recommended taking into account the audience and a presentation style that "speaks to those being addressed" (p. 86) when reporting an action research study results to stakeholders. For example, Downs and colleagues (2009) described how they communicated the household environmental testing results to community members in their MMAR study that explored built-environment stressors in a low-income multiethnic residential area. Each report was tailored to each household in format and content. According to the researchers, the goal of those reports was "to present residents with an accurate report that provided adequate resources without being overwhelming" (p. 1033). Follow-up meetings were conducted with the residents to discuss the study results and explain the strategies to reduce potential risks.

Box 10.2 provides useful tips for practitioner-researchers to consider when interpreting meta-inferences generated in an MMAR study in order to help inform the design, implementation, and evaluation of the action/intervention.

So, how do practitioner-researchers interpret meta-inferences in different MMAR study designs?

Examples of Interpreting Meta-Inferences in Different MMAR Design Studies

Consider how meta-inferences generated from the quantitative and qualitative integrated results were interpreted and helped inform action/intervention planning, implementation, evaluation, and monitoring in different MMAR design studies included in the Appendix (Examples A–E). In Kostos and Shin's (2010) concurrent Quan + Qual MMAR design study (Example A), the researchers evaluated an instructional intervention—math journaling instruction—that required students to write in their math journals three times a week using 16 different prompts. The researchers separately analyzed and interpreted the students' math assessment scores from before and after the intervention, the data from the interviews with eight randomly selected students, and the comments from the teacher-researcher's reflective journal. Meta-inferences that emerged from the comparison of the improved math test results with students' positive qualitative feedback about writing in math journals and teacher-researchers' reflections allowed Kostos and Shin to conclude that math journaling instructions enhanced students' mathematical thinking.

In Glasson and colleagues' (2006) MMAR study (Example B), meta-inferences guided both the development and evaluation of the new model of nursing care for older patients that was implemented in an acute medical ward. During the study reconnaissance phase, the interpretation of the results from concurrently collected and analyzed quantitative surveys of patients and nursing staff and qualitative observations of the activities in the medical ward helped reveal the aspects of nursing care that required improvement. Based on these

---

BOX 10.2

Tips for Interpreting Meta-Inferences in an MMAR Study

- Revisit the research questions that guided the study and determine how well or how fully the results from the quantitative and qualitative study strands answer these questions.
- Consider whether the integration of the quantitative and qualitative results produce meta-inferences that fully address the integrated MMAR question rendering the intent of the reconnaissance or evaluation phases and an overall intent of an MMAR study.
- Check if the study conclusions support the expected outcomes of this study phase as specified in the purpose statement.
- Compare the study results with the available literature about the best practices dealing with a similar problem or issue and reflect on possible explanations of their meaning in the context of the reported solutions, particularly if the results emerged as unexpected, or prompted inconsistent interpretations.
- Critically reflect on the integrated quantitative and qualitative results and the study outcomes: What was learned from the assessment of the current situation and evaluation of the action/intervention taken to improve practice?
- Regularly share the study progress and the results with stakeholders to solicit their input in the results' interpretation so as to inform action/intervention design, implementation, and evaluation.
- Use appropriate and effective venues for sharing the results from an MMAR study; regularly share the results and other project steps.
- Use meta-inferences from the reconnaissance and evaluation phases of an MMAR study created in collaboration with stakeholders to inform the next step in the action research process.

---

meta-inferences, a new model of nursing was selected by the ward staff. After the model implementation, it was evaluated using a concurrent Quan + Qual MMAR design. Integrated quantitative and qualitative findings from surveying patients and nurses about their experiences and satisfaction with the new model of nursing care confirmed the model efficacy and provided direction for its further implementation and monitoring.

In Craig's (2011) sequential Qual → Quan MMAR design study (Example C), meta-inferences from conducting community needs assessment during the reconnaissance phase were used to inform the development of an effective system of care for GLBTQ young people in the community. First, the inferences drawn from the content analysis of the individual interviews with the key informants and focus group discussions with GLBTQ youths were used to guide the development of the survey instrument that was administered to a large sample of GLBTQ young people in the community. Subsequently, the inferences from the quantitative survey results were combined with the inferences from the interviews and focus groups, that had been generated in the initial qualitative strand, to help identify and implement the appropriate services for GLBTQ young people.

In Sampson's (2010) multistrand MMAR design study (Example D), different sets of meta-inferences were used to guide the development and evaluation of the instructional intervention consisting of task-based-oriented lessons in a college-level Interpersonal Communication course. During the reconnaissance phase, the interpretation of the results from concurrently collected and analyzed students' quantitative survey and qualitative journaling data informed the design and implementation of task-based-oriented lessons intervention in the course. During the evaluation phase, data collection, analysis, and interpretation followed a sequential Qual → Quan pattern, and the themes from qualitative students' journals were used to guide the development of the quantitative Learning Experience Questionnaire. This questionnaire was completed by the students at the end of the course. Meta-inferences that were generated based on the interpretation of the positive quantitative indicators of students' learning experiences and the description of these experiences in students' journal entries supported the effectiveness of the new lesson style for enhancing students' speaking and communication abilities in English.

In Example D, Montgomery and colleagues (2008) proposed to use a sequential Quan → Qual MMAR study design to evaluate the existing supporting housing programs for persons with serious mental illness in rural communities. The researchers planned to use meta-inferences from a sequential integration of quantitative and qualitative inferences to identify potential improvements in health service planning for individuals with serious mental illness in rural communities. The researchers planned first to use the inferences from the quantitative survey of housing program residents about their quality of life and housing preferences to inform the direction of the subsequent qualitative data collection. The purpose of the qualitative data, consisting of photo-voice and focus groups, is to get a broader perspective on supported housing services for people with serious mental illness from three stakeholder groups (clients, their families, and community mental health workers). The sequentially generated meta-inferences will be presented during a planned community forum with all stakeholder groups to discuss how the study findings can be used to guide the changes in the current practices of running housing programs for persons with serious mental illness.

So, what is involved in the development and implementation of an action/intervention plan in an MMAR study?

DEVELOPING AND IMPLEMENTING ACTION/INTERVENTION IN AN MMAR STUDY

Once the diagnosing and reconnaissance phases of an MMAR study are over and a preliminary assessment of the identified problem or situation is completed, practitioner-researchers can proceed to the planning and acting phases in an MMAR study process. Kurt Lewin observed that "no action without research, no research without action" (Lewin, 1946, as cited in Adelman, 1993, p. 8), so it is at this stage that practitioner-researchers need to decide how to use the evidence collected through researching the issue to develop an appropriate action plan that will help identify a solution to the problem at stake. Craig (2009) argued that an action plan is the integral and distinct component of the action research process and should not be taken for an action research study itself or an action research report. Craig considered the action plan to be "a direct result of the inquiry" (p. 220) and thus to serve as a guide for action/intervention design and implementation. Therefore, the effectiveness of the action/intervention designed to find a solution to the problem often depends on the scientific quality of an action plan, and the degree the plan reflects the research evidence obtained during the initial assessment of the problem/issue.

Action Plan

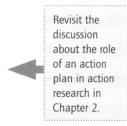

Revisit the discussion about the role of an action plan in action research in Chapter 2.

Craig (2009) defined an action plan as "a framework or blueprint that is implemented to improve practice, conditions, or the environment in general" (p. 237), while another definition of action plan emphasizes an organized program of measures to be taken in order to achieve a goal (Oxford Dictionaries, n.d.). In action research, the purpose of an action plan is "to target information gleaned from the action research study findings in order to set goals and establish a plan for meeting the goals" (Craig, 2009, p. 221). Stringer (2014) suggested that an action plan should consist of a series of tasks that would help practitioner-researchers achieve a resolution of the problem or situation they investigate.

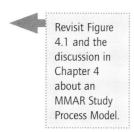

Revisit Figure 4.1 and the discussion in Chapter 4 about an MMAR Study Process Model.

In an MMAR study, the process of developing an action/intervention plan is guided by meta-inferences generated from the interpretation of the quantitative and qualitative results obtained during the reconnaissance phase of the study. However, as discussed in Chapter 4, consistent with the cyclical process of action research reflected in an MMAR Study Process Model, practitioner-researchers may sometimes skip the reconnaissance phase and proceed directly to an action planning phase using the results from the evaluation of the existing practice to determine its usefulness and effectiveness and the needed changes. Bypassing the reconnaissance phase might occur when a program, practice, policy, or intervention is already in place and there is a need to first evaluate the existing outcomes before developing an action to inform its modification or redesign. In either case, it is recommended that practitioner-researchers should start with the diagnosing phase to conceptualize an overall MMAR study and approach the investigation of an issue in a systematic and scientifically credible manner. Building on the advantages of a systematic integration of quantitative and qualitative methods to collect and analyze multiple forms of data from different stakeholders, practitioner-researchers can design action plans that are more rigorous and better tailored to the needs of those involved.

Seeking a potential solution to a problem/issue is at the heart of the action research process, so it is important to have clearly identified outcomes and to develop an action plan that is consistent with the expected outcomes and an overall intent of an MMAR study. Moreover, an action plan should be realistic and should promote an intervention that is appropriate for the specific group of people or practice and that can be sustained in a particular community. Having stakeholders' support for the action and making them empowered in the decision-making process is critical for ensuring the intervention success. Hinchey (2008) observed that "the more input all stakeholders have into design of a specific action, the more likely it is to be successful" (p. 104). Making an action plan grounded in the study research inferences with the input from stakeholders should help practitioner-researchers prioritize the areas for targeted intervention and gain the necessary community support.

Action research authors have provided various suggestions about what to include in an action plan; however, many agree that a plan should specify the following basic components (Craig, 2009; Mertler, 2012; Mills, 2011; Stringer, 2014):

- The purpose of the intervention
- A set of objectives

- Specific tasks and activities for each objective
- Individuals or groups responsible for each objective
- A site for each task and activity
- Timeline for each task with start and end points
- The needed resources

Stringer (2014) also suggested including outcome statements that describe the outcome sought for each activity. Although the listed components are essential to any action plan, the uniqueness of the addressed problem/issue will shape the specific format of the plan and the resources needed to achieve it. Additionally, practitioner-researchers should provide some background information about the project in an action plan when they present its initial draft to community members and other stakeholders for their feedback. Including such details will enhance stakeholders' understanding of the issue and the need for its successful resolution. For example, in Giachello and colleagues' (2003) MMAR study discussed in Chapter 2, the researchers reported on the following content

Refer to Chapter 2 and Box 2.3 for the example and discussion of Giachello and colleagues' (2003) MMAR study.

of the action plan that the coalition members developed and presented to the community to address high rates of diabetes morbidity and mortality in Chicago's medically underserved minority communities:

> This action plan included a brief story of the coalition, its vision, mission, collective values, and principles; stated the coalition's broader overall goals and objectives; outlined major areas of work with specific measurable goals and objectives; suggested strategies for targeted action; set deadlines; and determined resources needed to implement the plan. (p. 321)

Box 10.3 summarizes the action plan components for an MMAR study. Each component is described and illustrated using Buck and Cordes's (2005) MMAR study that reported on the development and implementation of the intervention aimed at reforming elementary- and middle-level science teacher preparation programs so as to better meet the needs of underserved children.

Levels of Action Planning

Mills (2011) argued that action planning in education can occur at several levels, depending on the scope of the project and the impact of the proposed intervention: individual, team, and single school or school district. These levels may often intersect, and the same action/intervention can be carried out at multiple levels and at the same time. Differentiating the levels of the planned action/intervention impact is also critical in an MMAR study because such considerations at the action planning stage may have important implications for the intervention effect and the achievement of the planned outcomes. It is of particular importance when the resources are limited or when not all stakeholder groups may be ready or willing to participate in the proposed intervention and accept the needed change. Additionally, in an MMAR study, where action planning is influenced by meta-inferences from the integrated quantitative and qualitative

BOX 10.3

Components of an Action Plan in an MMAR Study

- *Purpose*—A practical goal that is desirable to achieve through the planned intervention; this goal is informed through conceptualization of the problem during the diagnosing phase and meta-inferences generated from the integrated results of the quantitative and qualitative study strands during the reconnaissance or evaluation phases.

  - o Illustration:

    - Purpose: "How to better prepare science teachers to meet the needs of youth from underserved populations" (Buck & Cordes, 2005, p. 47).
    - Conceptual framework: "The conceptual framework of our plan of action predicted that providing teachers with experiences in teaching science to diverse learners in a nonformal educational setting and exploring these experiences in a seminar setting will increase the teachers' confidence and knowledge in regard to teaching science to children from diverse populations and backgrounds" (Buck & Cordes, 2005, p. 45).

- *Objectives*—A set of objectives that are planned to be achieved as the study outcomes; these objectives are informed by specific reconnaissance or evaluation phase meta-inferences, and are shaped by the purpose of the planned intervention.

  - o Illustration:

    - Three major outcomes:

      1. Increase preservice teachers' level of confidence in teaching science to underrepresented populations in education. . . .

      2. Increase knowledge of pedagogical strategies that foster or impede success for underserved populations. . . .

      3. Increase teachers' preparedness to teach students from diverse backgrounds. (Buck & Cordes, 2005, p. 49)

- *Tasks and activities*—A sequence of specific tasks and activities for each objective, also referred to as strategies; these strategies are developed for each objective and are informed by the reported "best practices" in the field.

  - o Illustration:

    - A cohort of 20 preservice teachers participated "in a seminar that focused on helping them develop the confidence and knowledge that would enable them to successfully educate children who are traditionally left out of science education" (Buck & Cordes, 2005, p. 48).
    - In this seminar, students (1) completed 12 hours of teaching in nonprofit organizations that work with at-risk youths, (2) took part in five 2-hour seminar meetings, and (3) participated in a distance-delivered reflection and discussion group.

- *Those responsible for objectives*—Individuals or groups responsible for the attainment of each objective; these may include anyone who has a stake in the problem/issue, from practitioner-researchers studying their own practices, to professional groups, community stakeholders, partners, administrators, and organizations.

  - ○ Illustration:

    - • The project was a collaborative effort between a university college of education and nonprofit community organizations "whose mission is to help children, youth, and their families grow to live safe, healthy, and productive lives" (Buck & Cordes, 2005, p. 46). University faculty conducted training seminars with preservice teachers, while community organization partners assisted with youths' behavior issues during the sessions. "Employees of the youth organizations accompanied all groups of children. These employees were responsible for any behavior that can pose a threat to the other children or to the preservice teachers. . . . The preservice teachers were responsible for teaching a coherent and accurate science concept to the youth" (Buck & Cordes, 2005, p. 51).

- *Site*—A site for each task and activity outlined in the plan; depending on the purpose and objectives of the plan, the number of specific sites for intervention implementation may vary.

  - ○ Illustration:

    - • The action site: a university college of education and nonprofit community organizations working with at-risk youths. "The facilities served either elementary- or middle-level-aged children. The children were in temporary residence at these facilities and, in most cases, were attending a local school" (Buck & Cordes, 2005, p. 51). Seminar meetings were held at the university premises, while field experiences consisting of inquiry-based science teaching sessions took place in the community organizations.

- *Timeline*—Timeline for each task and activity indicating when they should start and be completed; specific time periods are identified based on the intervention goals, professional and scientific standards accepted in the field, and available resources.

  - ○ Illustration:

    - • The intervention took place during an academic semester over 4 months. Five seminars took place during the semester; field experiences occurred once a month within each seminar;. Students also participated in online discussions over the duration of the semester.

- *Resources*—The resources that are needed to accomplish the tasks and activities to meet the intervention objectives; these include financial and material resources, and availability of specific services.

  - ○ Illustration:

    - • The study was funded by an external grant.

findings, it is critical to consider how the results from the initial assessment of the issue or the evaluation of the current situation may be comprehended and trusted by stakeholders at different targeted levels. Furthermore, knowing the level of the targeted intervention effect may help other practitioner-researchers adapt the existing intervention to their own professional and community settings.

Review of published MMAR studies across disciplines demonstrated that action planning may occur at the following levels: individual, group, organization, community/district, and regional. Kostos and Shin's (2010; Example A) and Sampson's (2010; Example D) MMAR studies exemplify action planning at *an individual level,* because both studies reported on the intervention conducted to improve a researcher's professional practice. In Kostos and Shin's (2010) study, a teacher-researcher planned an intervention to be implemented in her own classroom when she decided to explore if math journaling could enhance second-grade students' communication of mathematical thinking and the use of math vocabulary. Based on the positive study outcomes, Kostos planned to use the intervention results to further inform her math instructional strategies to improve students' mathematical thinking. Sampson (2010) used his college course as a site for designing and testing an instructional intervention of task-based oriented lessons. He solicited initial quantitative and qualitative feedback from the students in the course and used that information to tailor the instruction with the purpose of promoting students' English-speaking and communication abilities. Based on the positive results from this study, Sampson planned to apply this MMAR study approach to shape his instructional strategy in every subsequent offering of the course.

Glasson and colleagues' (2006) MMAR study (Example B) illustrates *a group-level* action planning because the intervention was conducted to improve the situation for a group of affected people. The researchers' action plan included the development and evaluation of a new model of nursing care for older patients in a particular acute medical ward in an Australian hospital. Glasson and colleagues planned to monitor the implementation of the model of nursing care in that medical ward using the integrated findings from the quantitative and qualitative survey responses provided by the ward patients and nurses. Similarly, in Galini and Efthymia's (2010) MMAR study, a university researcher, several kindergarten teachers, and parents from two kindergarten classes in a Greek school formed a team to plan and implement an internal system of self-evaluation for kindergarten teachers. A combination of multiple quantitative and qualitative methods, including parents' questionnaires, children's testing, classroom observations, and teacher interviews, were used to inform the development of the action plan.

Pickard's (2006) MMAR study that reported on the results of students' and faculty's attitudes toward plagiarism in a UK university illustrated action planning at *an organization level,* because the problem called for changes in existing policies affecting an entire organization. In this study, the conclusions based on the interpretation of the quantitative survey and qualitative interview responses from faculty, staff, and students informed an action effort aimed at promoting changes in the existing plagiarism policies at the university. Crilly and Plant (2007) also used action planning at an organization level that involved an entire hospital system. The purpose of their MMAR project was to explore the process of patient flow from triage to discharge or admission to hospital in order to use this information to redesign the entire emergency care system. The researchers used the integrated findings from patient tracking, observations, and interviews to inform the action plan that targeted reduction in patients' admissions, delayed discharges, and diagnostic waits in the emergency hospital system.

In Craig's (2011) MMAR study (Example C), action planning occurred at *the level of community/district,* because the issue called for developing an intervention that would result in improving the welfare of an entire community. The purpose of the action plan was to develop an effective system of care for GLBTQ young people in the county based on the initial needs assessment. The intervention was informed by the analysis of multiple forms of quantitative and qualitative data collected from the key informants and young GLBTQ people in the community. It was planned to identify and implement the services for GLBTQ young people that could be tailored to their specific needs and that could be supported by the community members. Giachello and colleagues' (2003) MMAR study presents another example of action planning at a community/district level. In this study, the Chicago Southeast Diabetes Community Action Coalition (including community residents, medical and social service providers, and representatives from a local university) was established to develop and evaluate an intervention that would address high rates of diabetes morbidity and mortality in Chicago's medically underserved minority communities. Members of the coalition developed and implemented the action plan based on the analysis and interpretation of the residents' telephone survey, focus group, and available epidemiologic data. Involvement of community stakeholders into action planning was important "to allow replication and adaptation of the project to other communities" (p. 315).

Montgomery and colleagues' (2008) proposed MMAR study (Example D) illustrates action planning at *a regional level*, because the problem called for changes in existing policies affecting a geographically and culturally bounded region. Their action plan focused on evaluating the existing supporting housing programs for persons with serious mental illness and to use the findings to inform health service planning in rural communities in northeastern Ontario. The researchers proposed to include quantitative and qualitative data collected from multiple stakeholders, such as housing program residents, their families, and community health workers within the region, and to organize a community forum with all stakeholder groups to discuss how the study findings could be used to guide changes to existing practices of operating such housing programs. Krueger's (2010) MMAR study of criminal-justice-oriented school safety practices in New York City offers another example of action planning at a regional level. In this study, quantitative and qualitative data collected by adolescent coresearchers from public high schools in various districts in New York City provided an initial exploration of students' perceived lived experiences with space in schools in order to promote potential changes in school safety rules and security measures in this metropolitan area.

Sometimes the impact of the planned action/intervention may extend beyond individual, local, or regional boundaries, and may affect an entire *country*. As discussed in the previous chapters, the number of large-scale MMAR projects that address global educational, social, or health issues is growing. Such projects are often funded through extramural sources and involve large numbers of participants and multiple sites. For example, Aubel and colleagues' (2004) MMAR study reported on a country-wide initiative in Senegal to promote improved maternal and child nutrition practices among grandmothers due to their influential role in household maternal and child matters. The project was supported by an international nongovernmental organization, the Christian Children's Fund, and by the Ministry of Health in Senegal. The community informed intervention plan that consisted of educational sessions for grandmothers on nutrition and health topics, was developed and implemented during 9 months in 13 villages around the country. The intervention was evaluated using pre- and postintervention quantitative surveys, and qualitative interview data with grandmothers in intervention villages and female adolescents and women of reproductive age in both intervention and control villages to document the effect of the intervention.

Hinchcliff and colleagues' (2012) research protocol for an MMAR study provides another example of action planning at a country level. The researchers proposed an action plan for the evaluation of a system of accreditation processes used in acute, primary, and aged care health services across Australia. The research project was funded by the Australian Research Council through a program that aimed "to promote collaboration between researchers and industry groups to generate rigorous research with practical implications for Australian society" (p. 2). The action plan included extensive quantitative and qualitative data collection from multiple stakeholders, such as individual interviews with the representatives of partner accreditation agencies, Web-based surveys of staff from accreditation agency member organizations, and from accredited health services, focus groups with agency stakeholders, jurisdictional health department representatives and staff from accredited acute, and primary and aged care services; it also included quantitative organizational performance data. The researchers planned to disseminate the evaluation results to Australian and international health-care stakeholders with the purpose of improvement of health services accreditation processes.

Success and Challenges of Implementing Action/Intervention in an MMAR Study

Implementing an action/intervention plan in an MMAR study is not void of challenges that have been discussed in action research texts. These challenges are related to numerous factors and may include availability of resources and limited time for action implementation (Hacker, 2013; Mills, 2011); building community capacity and forming partnerships (Hacker, 2013); the issue of data ownership and protection (Hacker, 2013; Herr & Anderson, 2005); engaging stakeholders into action/intervention, lack of stakeholders' understanding of the plan, and the need to adjust the plan details to avoid complexity (Hinchey, 2008; Stringer, 2014; Tomal, 2010); stakeholders' reluctance to interfere with other professional practices (Mills, 2011); resistance to change, fear of the unknown, and threats to security on the part of stakeholders (Mills, 2011; Tomal, 2010); and potential loss of power within an organization (Coghlan & Brannick, 2010; Hacker, 2013; Tomal, 2010). Many action research authors agree that understanding the change process is essential when undertaking action research because action research aims at solving problems and always implies change (Tomal, 2010). Finding appropriate solutions to be able to overcome these challenges is important. Often success of an implemented action/intervention depends on how stakeholders will accept and support the proposed action and get engaged with the change process.

Additional complexity of implementing action/intervention in an MMAR study may relate to the need for more expertise, time, and resources to collect and analyze both types of data for action/intervention planning, implementation, and evaluation. The quality of the initial assessment of the problem, using mixed methods during the reconnaissance phase, may influence the choice of an action/intervention focus, target participant groups, and selected activities and strategies. Failure to capture all stakeholders' perspectives or their incorrect interpretations may result in a weak intervention design and underrepresentation of the needs of those who need the action change most. Engaging community members

> Refer to the Further Readings at the end of this chapter for detailed information about potential challenges and possible solutions related to implementing action in action research.

and other stakeholders with the study may be more challenging due to a certain complexity of an MMAR study design, methodological procedures related to collection, analysis and integration of quantitative and qualitative data, and the intricacy of interpreting meta-inferences from the integrated results.

The challenges related to different aspects of designing and conducting an MMAR study and possible ways of addressing those aspects were discussed in related chapters throughout this book. Additionally, it is useful to consider the factors that accounted for successful interventions in the reviewed published MMAR studies. The successful outcomes of these interventions were assessed using rigorous quantitative and qualitative methods during the evaluation phases of these studies. These factors reflect the democratic nature of the intervention implementation, application of mixed methods in the action research process, an informed choice of targeted population and intervention strategies, empowerment of the study participants, support of the community, and feasibility of the intervention process.

 Revisit the discussions about the procedural pros and cons of MMAR designs in Chapter 5, the challenges of quantitative and qualitative methods' integration in Chapter 6, the issues related to data collection, analysis, and quality assessment in an MMAR study in Chapters 7 and 8.

For example, in Aubel and colleagues' (2004) MMAR study, discussed earlier, of a country-wide initiative in Senegal to promote improved maternal and child nutrition practices among grandmothers, the researchers provided an explanation of the factors that, in their opinion, accounted for the success of the implemented intervention. The realization of the critical importance of these factors emerged from a rigorous evaluation of the intervention outcomes using multiple quantitative and qualitative methods. Overall, the communities were highly receptive to the intervention; grandmothers felt honored by the respect and attention given to them and were inspired to participate and share their personal stories. In addition, the intervention united the grandmothers and helped strengthen the networking relationships among them. The choice of grandmothers as the focus for the intervention was based on the research findings that supported grandmothers' critical role in their households and their ability to influence the attitudes and practices of other household members with regard to health and nutrition of women and children. Furthermore, the grandmothers in the study conveyed a belief of empowerment and had an improved sense of self-esteem due to their increased knowledge and the ability to share this acquired knowledge. The intervention strategy was also appropriate for this population because it was theory-based and grounded in a transcultural and syncretistic approach to health education that acknowledges traditional values and practices in communities' popular health cultures, but challenges any integration of new knowledge and practices. The intervention employed a problem-posing educational methodology that empowered grandmothers to think of their own solutions to the posed scenarios. Finally, the success of the project was secured by employing committed and skillful community facilitators who were trained in the study protocols and helped develop trusting ongoing relationships with participating grandmothers.

Likewise, in their MMAR study, Kavanagh and colleagues (2010) indicated the following factors that accounted for the successful implementation of an appreciative inquiry approach to implementing pain management evidence in pediatric nursing practice in a Canadian hospital: acceptance by all study participants, feasibility in implementation, building on existing strengths, resources and practices in the organization, and a positive and democratic nature of the suggested change. Gosin, Dustman, Drapeau, and Harthun (2003) discussed another set of factors that were critical to the successful development and implementation of the drug prevention education program for youths in the southwestern United States: "(1) create a strong program combining the knowledge of researchers and the expertise of community to increase the relevancy of the program to local youth, (2) increase the effectiveness of the program by fostering ownership by teachers and students, (3) allow participants to serve as experts regarding the culture of their communities, and (4) promote a more rigorous evaluation of the intervention" (p. 376). Importantly, the authors mentioned a critical role that evaluation played in helping estimate the outcomes of the implemented action/intervention.

So, what role does evaluation and monitoring of the action/intervention play in an MMAR study? How can practitioner-researchers use this information to promote sustainability of the change effort?

EVALUATING AND MONITORING ACTION/INTERVENTION IN AN MMAR STUDY

Once the action/intervention is implemented, it should be evaluated to learn if the procedures that were informed by the initial assessment of the problem/issue in the reconnaissance phase led to the desired outcomes, and whether any revisions to the initial action plan are necessary. Tomal (2010) argued that without evaluation a practitioner-researcher "never knows if the results of the action were successful or if the problem has been resolved" (p. 135). Evaluation in action research can target a range of desired outcomes, such as knowledge acquisition, individuals' performance and behavior, organizational climate, cost-benefit, feasibility and utility of the action, as well as an overall effectiveness of the intervention. According to Stringer (2014), evaluation is also necessary when there is a need to submit a progress report to the sponsoring agency, professional group, or community stakeholders. Additionally, evaluation acts as a tool for empowerment because it enables practitioner-researchers to reflect on the direction of the action/intervention and assess the efficacy of the employed procedures to achieve the desired outcomes. It also gives another chance to actively engage stakeholders into the action evaluation process to ensure that their claims, concerns, and problems have been addressed. In general, evaluation helps inform further monitoring of the action/intervention and promotes sustainability of the change effort. For example, in their MMAR study, Hussaini and colleagues (2013) discussed how mixed methods evaluation used within the community-based participatory action research approach facilitated their understanding of the efficacy of "the first time motherhood" educational campaign aimed at revealing African American men and women's attitudes to preconception health in Arizona (p. 1863).

Revisit Figure 4.1 and the discussion in Chapter 4 about an MMAR Study Process Model.

Evaluation and monitoring of the intervention are the next steps in an MMAR Study Process Model. Stringer (2014) suggested that evaluation should be ongoing because it helps monitor the action/intervention and its progress. This process is reflected in Figure 4.1 by two reverse solid and dashed arrows, leading from the evaluating action phase (Phase V) to monitoring and revising action phase (Phase VI) and back. Consistent evaluation informs the subsequent revisions, implementation, and further testing of the action/intervention. It also helps promote the action/intervention sustainability efforts and integration of best practices into other existing programs (Evashwick & Ory, 2003).

As shown earlier in Figure 4.1, when the action/intervention is successful, Phases V and VI can be repeated iteratively to support the intervention further monitoring and promoting its sustainability and transferability to other contexts and community settings. For example, in Aubel and colleagues (2004) MMAR study, referred to earlier in this chapter, the researchers discussed how, based on the positive evaluation outcomes of the educational nutrition intervention in Senegal, they recommended that similar community health and nutrition interventions should be designed and tested in other cultural contexts. Consistent with the reported intervention, the recommended interventions should also include grandmothers in a leading role, but should employ research designs that are more rigorous in order "to either confirm or refute these findings regarding grandmothers' capacity to learn, to modify their advice and to influence community health/nutrition practices" (p. 957).

If the action/intervention is not successful and does not lead to desired outcomes, its evaluation will help detect it and indicate the direction for further in-depth investigation of the problem at stake. Ultimately, it may require the development and subsequent testing of a new action/intervention plan. Such interactivity of the phases in an MMAR study process reflects the cyclical nature of action research making action evaluation and monitoring the critical components of the action research cycle. Craig (2009) referred to this process as continuous improvement because practitioner-researchers use evaluation results to address the next prioritized problem or revealed issue and the inquiry process continues. Consider Box 10.4 that contains an excerpt from Buck and Cordes's (2005) MMAR study. In this excerpt the authors discuss the rationale for further monitoring of the new program for elementary- and middle-level science teachers that was implemented and evaluated using mixed methods.

Refer to Box 10.3 for the discussion of Buck and Cordes's (2005) action plan.

Hinchey (2008) pointed out that monitoring in action research is also important for the project development because it helps reveal if any critical information was missing. For example, Endacott, Cooper, Sheaff, Padmore, and Blakely's (2011) MMAR study reported on the evaluation of the new "18-week journey" policy of

---

BOX 10.4

Example of Action/Intervention Monitoring in an MMAR Study

"Action research is a cyclical process. Our newly developed program is but the second action plan. This second plan will also be carefully monitored to further inform our efforts in reforming our teacher preparation programs to better prepare teachers to foster science literacy for all students. This process must continue to focus on uncovering whether the program leads to the desired outcomes; however, we believe our focus must expand beyond the experiences of the preservice teachers. If we are to understand whether we are truly preparing these preservice teachers to meet the needs of youth populations underserved in science education, we must turn our focus to these children. This means we must take a longitudinal approach and follow our preservice teachers through their initial experiences as classroom teachers. These future inquires must continue to inform our practice."

Reprinted from Buck & Cordes (2005, p. 62).

regulating admissions of patients to a hospital emergency department with the purpose of reducing stress for its staff (p. 203). Project monitoring data were reported to the project board at monthly meetings to inform the board members about the intervention progress. However, as the researchers pointed out, not all data were promptly provided by the hospital: "Many of these data were not available until the end of the project, preventing the action research from making use of them. Hence, some of the data trends highlighted below were evident as the project progressed, whereas others were not" (p. 206). Qualitative interviews with the emergency department staff members helped fill in the gaps in the missing information and revealed frustration with the new policy implemented in the hospital. The pressures on the staff resulting from this policy initiative increased and "were in direct conflict with the goal of improving patient flow through the ED" (p. 207). Based on the study conclusions, recommendations were made for changes in practices and staffing of the hospital emergency department.

In an MMAR study, monitoring of the action/intervention requires adherence to meta-inferences that were generated during the evaluation phase of the study. These inferences help practitioner-researchers make informed decisions about whether the revisions or further testing of the action/intervention plan are needed. The process of evaluation follows the methodological steps for conducting an MMAR study discussed in Chapters 4 through 9 and includes the following procedures:

- Developing the evaluation phase purpose statement and research questions
- Selecting an MMAR design
- Identifying the sample, quantitative, and qualitative data sources
- Collecting and analyzing quantitative and qualitative data
- Validating the findings and creating meta-inferences

Similar to the reconnaissance phase, stakeholders including study participants should be engaged in all aspects of the evaluation process from identifying evaluation objectives to the interpretation of meta-inferences from the evaluation phase. Stringer and Genat (2004) highlighted the importance of engaging stakeholders into a range of evaluation activities as an important component of the collaborative evaluation process. They indicated that it is particularly important to share the evaluation phase results with stakeholders "to get the word out about what has been discovered" (p. 151). This enables stakeholders to provide their input into the action/intervention monitoring and solicit their reaction to potential unintended outcomes. Altogether it helps promote sustainability of the implemented change and support the dissemination of the positive outcomes.

So, what are the venues for disseminating the information from an MMAR study? How do practitioner-researchers report the results of an MMAR study?

DISSEMINATING MMAR STUDY RESULTS

Sharing the study results is one of the key characteristics of the action research process (Creswell, 2012). A practical focus of action research calls for an immediate dissemination of research findings so that they can be implemented in practice. Koshy and colleagues (2011) advised that no matter what reporting format is selected for an action research study, the purpose of such report is to disseminate knowledge "to improve practice or to implement change as a result of research" (p. 146). Similarly, Mertler (2012) argued that sharing the findings of action research studies can help "bridge the divide" between theory and practice (p. 219).

Disseminating action research findings can also narrow the gap that exists between research and its uptake by professional communities. Reporting the outcomes and procedures of action research "jump-starts" the process of translation and adoption of the generated evidence into practice (Hacker, 2013, p. 103). Importantly, applying mixed methods in action research can facilitate this process and meet the demands of implementation science and translational research which focus on promoting the adoption of research findings into clinical, community, and policy routine settings. MMAR studies have the capacity for addressing this challenge due to their scientific rigor and practical focus, thus contributing to generating both "local and public knowledge" (Herr & Anderson, 2005, p. 111). This makes the research findings more translatable to practice while being applicable in larger scientific and professional community settings. Moreover, advancing utilization of MMAR studies in implementation science and patient-centered outcomes research can help facilitate the integration of evidence-based and patient-focused results in health care, making the research findings more actionable, reliable, and thus more readily acceptable by the intended users (Damschroder et al., 2009; Gabriel & Normand, 2012). Mixed methods research was reported as a valuable and advantageous approach to use in implementation research. Based on the analysis of published mixed methods research studies in mental health, Palinkas and colleagues (2011) concluded that some of the reasons for using mixed methods were to examine the context of the implementation of a specific intervention and to incorporate the perspectives of potential consumers of research (both practitioners and clients). Integration of qualitative methods within traditional quantitative designs allowed for giving voice to these important stakeholders and for promoting their engagement with the study outcomes.

Different formats and venues of communicating and reporting action research studies were extensively discussed in the action research literature. Action research authors described various types of reporting, such as formal reports focusing on larger audiences (e.g., publishing in academic and professional journals, developing reports to funding agencies, writing theses and dissertations, presenting at professional and research conferences) and informal reports focusing on an immediate community (e.g., reporting to peers, colleagues, community groups). They also provided useful writing tips and practical guidelines for reporting action research study results. Some of the other recommendations include connecting action research findings with personal experiences: "Action research is a personal business" (Mills, 2011, p. 145). Stringer (2014) also advised on "writing reports collaboratively" with stakeholders (p. 157) to prevent from losing their interpretive perspective on the research findings. Practical suggestions for how to engage stakeholders in the process of interpreting the MMAR study results and developing the conclusions that are meaningful for their users were discussed earlier in this chapter.

Refer to the Further Readings at the end of this chapter for a detailed discussion and examples of different ways of reporting action research studies in different disciplines.

When reporting an MMAR study, practitioner-researchers can follow the format or incorporate the components of a traditional action research report; however, they should also adhere to the guidelines suggested for reporting mixed methods research studies. For instance, O'Cathain, Murphy, and Nicholl (2008) developed the guidelines for Good Reporting of a Mixed Methods Study (GRAMMS) that are listed in Box 10.5. These guidelines focus on the methodological rigor of mixed methods procedures used in a study and underscore

> **BOX 10.5**
>
> ### Guidelines for Good Reporting of a Mixed Methods Study (GRAMMS)
>
> - Describe the justification for using a mixed methods approach to the research question.
> - Describe the design in terms of the purpose, priority, and sequence of methods.
> - Describe each method in terms of sampling, data collection, and analysis.
> - Describe where integration has occurred, how it has occurred, and who has participated in it.
> - Describe any limitation of one method associated with the presence of the other method.
> - Describe any insights gained from mixing or integrating methods.
>
> ---
>
> From O'Cathain et al. (2008) with permission of Sage Publications Ltd.

the value and quality of integrating quantitative and qualitative methods. Likewise, Creswell and Plano Clark (2011) recommended relating the structure of a mixed methods report to specific mixed methods designs—that is, presenting the description of the methods and findings following the sequence of the data collection and analysis in concurrent and sequential designs. Creswell and Tashakkori (2007a) advised that mixed methods reports should be "well-developed in both quantitative and qualitative components" (p. 108). They also promoted integrating the inferences from the study strands and reporting the overall conclusions that are well-developed outcomes of such integration: "The expectation is that by the end of the manuscript, conclusions gleaned from the two strands are integrated in order to provide a fuller understanding of the phenomenon under study" (p. 108). Greene (2007) also emphasized an integrative character of a mixed methods report. Approaching mixed methods from a social inquiry perspective, she viewed mixed methods writing as interplay of "different perspectives, voices, understandings, representational forms" (p. 188), which supports the collaborative and engaging nature of reporting an MMAR study.

When reporting the results of an MMAR study, practitioner-researchers should consider using practical advice and recommended guidelines available for reporting both action research and mixed methods studies. At the same time, practitioner-researchers should decide on the reporting format that is best suitable for the purposes of their report, the needs of their audience, and their own rhetorical preferences. Importantly, the degree of transparency in reporting an MMAR study may influence how the reported results are accepted and adopted by stakeholders and professional communities. The more detailed the information that is provided about how the study was conducted and how the results were generated, the more credible the reported information may be perceived by the accepting audience.

Consider how the researchers structured their reports for different MMAR design studies (Examples A–E) provided in the Appendix. Kostos and Shin (2010; Example A) and Glasson and colleagues (2006; Example B) who used a concurrent Quan + Qual MMAR study design followed a concurrent reporting structure. Since the purpose of this design is to produce validated meta-inferences from triangulating the inferences from the analysis of multiple data sources, in both studies the researchers explained the methods and presented the findings from the quantitative and qualitative study strands within the same sections in the article. Specifically, they first explained how the study participants were recruited and how the data were collected and analyzed in both study strands. While the authors reported the findings from the quantitative and qualitative study strands separately, they discussed the quantitative and qualitative results together, emphasizing how they jointly informed meta-inferences from the entire study.

Alternatively, Craig (2011; Example C), who utilized a Qual → Quan MMAR design, followed a sequential reporting structure. Because in sequential designs the inferences generated in the initial study strand inform the design of the next study strand, the researcher first presented the methods and results from the qualitative study strand and then discussed how the inferences from the interviews and focus group analysis informed the development of the quantitative survey instrument that was administered to a larger sample in the second, quantitative strand. Sampson (2010; Example D), who applied a multistrand MMAR study design, used a blend of the concurrent and sequential reporting structures.

DEVELOPING A PROPOSAL FOR AN MMAR STUDY

As discussed in the previous chapters, much of a research study's success depends on how carefully the study is conceptualized and designed during its planning stage. Planning an MMAR study is not void of these considerations. Developing a proposal for an MMAR study may be complex due to the need to balance practical simplicity of action research and methodological complexity of mixed methods. To address this complexity and assist practitioner-researchers in the research proposal writing process, some guidelines for developing a proposal for an MMAR study are provided. These guidelines are based on the methodological considerations for conceptualizing, designing, and conducting an MMAR study guided by an MMAR Study Process Model.

Box 10.6 contains a suggested structure of a proposal for an MMAR study arranged by major topics reflecting a traditional organization of a research proposal: introduction or statement of the problem, review of the related literature, and description of the study methods and procedures. Each topic contains suggested guidelines for the content components to be included in the proposal with the purpose of achieving the necessary level of transparency in explaining the planned study details. While following the basic principles of the suggested proposal structure is important, practitioner-researchers can adjust the content of these guidelines to the specific needs of their proposals, depending on the nature of a proposed study. For example, graduate students may consider closely following these guidelines while developing an MMAR study proposal for a master's thesis or a doctoral dissertation to persuade their committees of the need and the feasibility of the study. Similarly, providing all the suggested details about a proposed study may be important when submitting a grant proposal to a funding agency. Consider how methodologically elaborate is a research protocol for a sequential Quan → Qual MMAR study as proposed by Montgomery and colleagues (2008; Example E). Besides a necessary level of detail, this protocol includes the discussion of the study significance and expected outcomes. Alternatively, practitioner-researchers may decide to skip some methodological details when presenting a proposed study to professional organizations and community boards so as to avoid overwhelming them with technical information. At the same time, it is critical to communicate all necessary study details to ensure the community's realization of the issue and stakeholders' buy-in and support of the proposed study.

BOX 10.6

Suggested Structure of an MMAR Study Proposal

Problem Statement: The focus is to present the problem and to justify the need for a planned change or improvement.

- Introduce the practical problem or issue that requires solution while providing justification for the need for change.
- Discuss how this issue was addressed as identified through the literature review.
- Identify missing information/knowledge that you think might help solve the issue, and discuss how your study may contribute to solving this issue.
- Explain how solving the issue may help participants, practitioners, community members, and other stakeholders.
- Include the study purpose statement following the suggested MMAR study purpose statement scripts but phrased in the future tense. Specify if the proposed study will address the reconnaissance or evaluation phase, or both phases of an MMAR Study Process Model.
- List the study research questions, including the integrated MMAR question addressing an overall purpose of the study and the research questions for each quantitative and qualitative study strand.

Literature Review: The focus is to identify how the problem or issue of interest was explored in the literature and what solutions to the problem were reported by other practitioner-researchers and professional communities in order to justify the need for a planned change or improvement.

- Provide detailed information about the sources of evidence gathered about the problem/issue explored (research and professional literature) including the procedures for searching, summarizing, and synthesizing the literature.
- Outline the main ideas that exist on the topic based on the gathered information, capturing a spectrum of divergent views on the issue and reported "best practices" or solutions to the problem.
- Critically review, synthesize, and interpret the gathered information on the topic organized by main ideas (subtopics).

Methods and Procedures: The focus is to explain the study methodology and to provide evidence that the study is grounded in sound methods. This chapter should include the following sections in the following order:

- MMAR Approach
  - ○ Describe the mixed methods and action research approaches; explain their major characteristics and purposes and how the two approaches will be combined in your study; explain the rationale for conducting your study using an MMAR approach and how it is advantageous over other research approaches, including mono-method (quantitative and qualitative).

- Specify the stage(s) in an MMAR process (refer to an MMAR Study Process Model) where mixed methods will be used for data collection and analysis.
- Discuss the importance of collaboration and stakeholders' role in an MMAR study; explain how stakeholders will be selected and engaged in the study.

- MMAR Study Design

  - Describe the selected MMAR study design in detail: discuss the key characteristics of the chosen design, such as priority of quantitative and/or qualitative methods, sequence or timing of the quantitative and qualitative data collection and analysis, and integration/mixing (specify the stage/stages in the research process where integration of the quantitative and qualitative data/approaches/results will occur; relate the integration procedures to the chosen MMAR study design).
  - Explain why and how this particular design suits your proposed study purpose and research questions.
  - Develop the visual diagram of the procedures for your proposed MMAR study, using the appropriate notation system; specify all the procedures and expected outcomes for each study phase.

- Sampling

  - Discuss the sampling scheme for the chosen MMAR design: describe the criteria for selecting the site and the participants for each quantitative and qualitative strand; justify the choice of the site, the number of participants to be selected, and participant inclusion criteria.
  - Describe the recruitment procedures, access, and necessary permissions.
  - Describe stakeholders' role in sampling the study participants.

- Data Collection

  - Describe how the data will be collected within the chosen MMAR design, types of data to be collected for each quantitative and qualitative strand, and the rationale for choosing these specific data sources; address the data collection issues that you think should be considered in your proposed study.
  - Explain the timeframe for data collection, recording procedures, and organization and storing of the data.
  - Describe stakeholders' role in the data collection process.

- Data Analysis

  - Discuss how the data will be analyzed within the chosen MMAR design; describe initial preparation of the quantitative and qualitative data in each study strand, preliminary exploration of the data, and specific procedures for the quantitative and qualitative analysis to address the study purpose and research questions.

(Continued)

(Continued)

- o Discuss specific forms of integrative mixed methods data analysis that relate to the study design, forms of quantitative and qualitative data representation (tables, figures, drawings, conceptual models), and computer software to assist with quantitative and qualitative data analysis.
- o Describe stakeholders' roles in data analysis and interpretation.

- Quality Assurance

  - o Describe how you plan to assess the quality of your proposed MMAR study: Explain how you plan to evaluate the methodological rigor of each quantitative and qualitative study strand; address data quality and interpretation issues that may be related to an action research nature of the study; describe ways to secure quality of mixed methods meta-inferences generated from the quantitative and qualitative results to inform action/intervention.
  - o Connect these procedures to specific phases in an MMAR Study Process Model.
  - o Describe stakeholders' role in the process of quality assurance for the study.

- Ethical Considerations

  - o Address American Psychological Association ethical principles for conducting research and the need for obtaining the IRB's approval and informed consent letters; discuss preserving the anonymity of participants, voluntary participation, and data storage.
  - o Note that in sequential MMAR designs you should seek IRB's approval for the initial phase of the study and submit an amendment for the subsequent phase because the design of this phase is informed by the results from the initial phase.
  - o Discuss any specific ethical issues that might be related to the MMAR nature of the study.

- Feasibility and Advantages/Disadvantages

  - o Explain why you think the proposed study is feasible; specify advantages and limitations of the chosen approach; explain your knowledge of related research methods and your research skills; describe access to the site and study participants.
  - o Discuss potential benefits and challenges of collaborating with interested stakeholders during the study design and implementation.

SUMMARY

Consistent with an MMAR Study Process Model planning, implementing, and evaluating an action requires practitioner-researchers to accurately interpret meta-inferences from the reconnaissance and evaluation phases, share these results with stakeholders, and develop or revise an action/intervention plan based on the reconnaissance and evaluation meta-inferences and input from stakeholders. In an MMAR study, the process of interpreting meta-inferences involves determining how the results from the quantitative and qualitative study strands answer the research questions and how the generated meta-inferences address an overall intent of an MMAR study. The importance of using critical reflection and sharing the study results with stakeholders is addressed. Examples of the interpretation of meta-inferences in five illustrative MMAR studies, as well as useful tips for practitioner-researchers to consider when interpreting the meta-inferences are provided.

The chapter discusses the development and implementation of action/intervention in an MMAR study in the context of an MMAR Study Process Model, the components of an action plan, and levels of action planning (individual, group, organization, community/district, regional, and country). The discussion is illustrated with examples of MMAR studies in different disciplines. Potential challenges and possible solutions when implementing action/intervention and the role of evaluation and monitoring of action/intervention in an MMAR study are further discussed. Continuous evaluation and monitoring of the action/intervention progress can help promote its sustainability and transferability of the MMAR study results to other contexts or community settings. Applying mixed methods in action research can also meet the demands of implementation science, translational research and patient-centered outcomes research initiatives. In reporting the results of an MMAR study, practitioner-researchers should consider using practical advice and suggested guidelines available for reporting action research and mixed methods studies. Practitioner-researchers should also decide on the reporting format best suitable for the purposes of their report, the needs of their audience, and their own rhetorical preferences. The chapter concludes with some guidelines for developing a proposal for an MMAR study. These guidelines are based on the methodological considerations for conceptualizing, designing, and conducting an MMAR study discussed in this book.

REFLECTIVE QUESTIONS AND EXERCISES

1. Select a published MMAR study in your discipline or area of interest. Determine what phase or phases in an MMAR Study Process Model are reported in the article and identify an MMAR study design for each phase. Describe the purpose, the research questions (if posted), and the expected outcomes of this MMAR study. If the research questions are not provided, write a potential integrated MMAR question and research questions for each quantitative and qualitative study strand. Carefully consider how meta-inferences were generated and used to meet the study goals in each phase. Discuss how meta-inferences help answer the posed research questions.

2. Discuss the components that should be included in an action plan in an MMAR study. Select a published MMAR study in your discipline or area of interest that focused on the reconnaissance phase of an MMAR study. Discuss the plan for the action/intervention that the authors developed based on the results from the initial assessment of the problem. If the action plan was not reported in the article, create your own plan of the action/intervention using the generated meta-inferences from the reconnaissance study phase.

3. Explain the levels of action planning in an MMAR study. Identify what level of action planning was employed in the published MMAR study you selected to address Question 2. Using an example of a hypothetical MMAR study in your area of interest, describe how this problem may be approached with different levels of action planning.

4. Discuss potential challenges to implementing action/intervention in an MMAR study. Select a published MMAR study in your discipline or area of interest that reported on an implemented intervention. Describe what challenges the researchers had to overcome when implementing this intervention and what factors accounted for the intervention success. Pay particular attention to how the authors made conclusions about the intervention's success or failure.

5. Discuss the role that evaluation and monitoring play in an MMAR study process. Select a published MMAR study in your discipline or area of interest that reported evaluation and monitoring of an implemented intervention. Explain how the evaluation results were used to monitor the intervention, what changes were recommended to the action/intervention plan, and what meta-inferences guided the researchers' decisions. Discuss how the study stakeholders were involved or should have been involved in the process of evaluation and monitoring.

6. Locate two published MMAR studies in your discipline or area of interest that used concurrent Quan + Qual and sequential Qual → Quan or Qual → Quan designs. Compare the reporting formats of the two studies, paying attention to how the authors presented information about each quantitative and qualitative study strand, how they reported the integrated study results, and how they discussed stakeholders' engagement with the study process and the dissemination of the results. Reflect on the level of detail of the provided information and how persuasive were the authors' conclusions.

FURTHER READINGS

To learn more about engaging stakeholders in the process of interpreting results, examine the following sources:

Stringer, E. T. (2014). *Action research* (3rd ed.). Thousand Oaks, CA: Sage, Ch. 5, pp. 148–156.

To learn more about developing and implementing an action plan, examine the following sources:

Craig, D. V. (2009). *Action research essentials.* San-Francisco, CA: Jossey-Bass, Ch. 9, pp. 219–233.
Hinchey, P. H. (2008). *Action research: Primer.* New York: Peter Lang, Ch. 5, pp. 101–104.
Mills, G. E. (2011). *Action research: A guide for the teacher researcher* (4th ed.). Boston: Pearson Education, Ch. 7, pp. 152–169.
Stringer, E. T. (2014). *Action research* (4th ed.). Thousand Oaks, CA: Sage, Ch. 6, pp. 166–175.
Stringer, E., & Genat, W. J. (2004). *Action research in health.* Upper Saddle River, NJ: Pearson, Ch. 7, pp. 138–146.

To learn more about evaluating and monitoring an action plan, examine the following sources:

Stringer, E., & Genat, W. J. (2004). *Action research in health.* Upper Saddle River, NJ: Pearson, Ch. 7, pp. 146–154.
Tomal, D. R. (2010). *Action research for educators* (2nd ed.). Lanham, MD: Rowman & Littlefield Publishers, Ch. 6, pp. 135–142.

To learn more about the dissemination of action research studies' results, examine the following sources:

Craig, D. V. (2009). *Action research essentials.* San-Francisco, CA: Jossey-Bass, Ch. 8, pp. 201–218.

Hinchey, P. H. (2008). *Action research: Primer.* New York: Peter Lang, Ch. 5, pp. 104–120.

Koshy, E., Koshy, V., & Waterman, H. (2011). *Action research in healthcare.* Thousand Oaks, CA: Sage, Ch. 7, pp. 145–168.

Mertler, C. A. (2012). *Action research: Improving schools and empowering educators.* Thousand Oaks, CA: Sage, Chs. 8–9, pp, 217–278.

Stringer, E. T. (2014). *Action research* (4th ed.). Thousand Oaks, CA: Sage, Ch. 5, pp. 157–162.

Stringer, E., & Genat, W. J. (2004). *Action research in health.* Upper Saddle River, NJ: Pearson, Ch. 6, pp. 115–137.

To learn more about reporting mixed methods research studies, examine the following sources:

Creswell, J. W., & Plano Clark, V. L. (2011). *Designing and conducting mixed methods research* (2nd ed.). Thousand Oaks, CA: Sage, Ch. 8, pp. 251–266.

Greene, J. C. (2007). *Mixed methods in social inquiry.* San Francisco, CA: Jossey-Bass, Ch. 10, pp. 179–188.

O'Cathain, A., Murphy, E., & Nicholl, J. (2008). The quality of mixed methods studies in health services research. *Journal of Health Services Research Policy, 13*(2), 92–98.

Teddlie, C., & Tashakkori, A. (2009). *Foundations of mixed methods research: Integrating quantitative and qualitative approaches in the social and behavioral sciences.* Thousand Oaks, CA: Sage, Epilogue, pp. 318–323.

APPENDIX

Example A: MMAR Study in the Field of K–12 Education (Kostos & Shin, 2010)

Using Math Journals to Enhance Second Graders' Communication of Mathematical Thinking

Kathleen Kostos • Eui-kyung Shin

Abstract As an action research project, using mixed methodology, this study investigated how the use of math journals affected second grade students' communication of mathematical thinking. For this study, math journal instruction was provided. The data gathering included pre- and post- math assessment, students' math journals, interviews with the students, and teacher's reflective journal. Findings of the study indicated that the use of math journals positively influenced the students' communication of mathematical thinking and the use of math vocabulary. Additionally, math journals served as a communication tool between the students and teacher and an assessment tool for the teacher. The implications of this study regarding students' writing ability and time constraints issues were also discussed.

Keywords Mathematical communication • Mathematical thinking • Math journal

Published online: 20 April 2010
© Springer Science+Business Media, LLC 2010

K. Kostos
Fearn Elementary School, Aurora, IL, USA

E. Shin (✉)
Department of Teaching and Learning, Northern Illinois University,
Gabel Hall 162, DeKalb, IL 60115, USA
e-mail: ekshin@niu.edu

INTRODUCTION

"Cross out the 5, make it a 4 and put a 1 in front of the 3, then subtract." Over the past 10 years, this has been the response I frequently received from my students when I asked them to explain the concept of subtraction with regrouping. It is an explanation of a method of calculation but not an explanation of the concept of subtraction with regrouping. The students' response does not demonstrate the mathematical thinking process; rather it merely demonstrates the students' ability to memorize and recall a method of solving a problem to find a correct answer. Subtraction with regrouping is not the only concept my students have had difficulty when demonstrating their mathematical thinking. This is often the case with many mathematical concepts.

It is important for students to be able to demonstrate their mathematical thinking as well as their method of solving a problem. In mathematics tests that ask students to demonstrate their mathematical thinking, many students can provide a correct answer without understanding how they achieved it. A simple correct answer in most mathematics programs is a result of mastery rather than a result of their mathematical thinking. In developing students' mathematical thinking, mathematical communication can encourage students to explain how they obtained an answer by describing their thinking process (Burns and Silbey 1999; Fried and Amit 2003).

Mathematical thinking and mathematical communication go hand-in-hand. For example, the National Council of Teachers of Mathematics (NCTM) emphasizes the importance of mathematical thinking through mathematical communication. NCTM suggests in its *Principles and Standards for School Mathematics* (NCTM 2000) that math programs should allow students to (1) organize and consolidate their mathematical thinking through communication; (2) communicate their mathematical thinking coherently and clearly to peers, teachers and others; (3) analyze and evaluate the mathematical thinking and strategies of others; and (4) use the language of mathematics to express mathematical ideas precisely. Based on the NCTM's guidelines, teachers are encouraged to provide students with these opportunities.

Students' understanding of a mathematical concept can be communicated in many ways: in writing, orally, through pictorial representations, and with manipulatives. Regardless of how they communicate, students should be able to clearly explain their reasoning and show their mathematical thinking. Mathematical communication can also be promoted through teachers' questioning. Teachers can pose questions that require students to explain their thinking to solve a math problem. If students have difficulty explaining, teachers can use additional probing questions to encourage a student's thinking. In addition, math communication can encourage the correct use of math terminology, which helps students clearly communicate their understanding of mathematical concepts.

Math communication is receiving even greater attention in the field of mathematics education today. Students are now required to demonstrate their ability to communicate their mathematical thinking on high stakes testing. For example, students in Illinois are required to demonstrate their ability to communicate their mathematical thinking effectively on the Illinois Standards Assessment Test (ISAT) using illustrations and writing. For the last 10 years, I have spent many weeks teaching students extensively how to communicate their mathematical thinking in writing because it has not been taught as an ongoing process. Often the results were not satisfactory. They seemed to have a difficult time transforming their long possessed "getting the right answer" mindset to a newly introduced "focusing on the process" mindset.

I teach second graders and hope to lay the groundwork for their future in building their understanding of important mathematical concepts. I want to lay a foundation for my students to effectively communicate their mathematical thinking, so my students can explain how and why they use a mathematical concept to solve a problem. In order to achieve this, I need to find an innovative way to help my students communicate their mathematical thinking effectively. I believe allowing my students to demonstrate their mathematical thinking through writing and drawing in a math journal would be a comfortable, non-threatening, and effective way to express their mathematical thinking. Math journals would allow students to convey their knowledge about math concepts in their own words and/or illustrations. They would also give students opportunities to demonstrate their knowledge or ask questions without fear of embarrassment. Therefore, the research question that guided this study was how the use of math journals affected the second grade students' mathematical thinking through math communication.

THE IMPORTANCE OF MATH COMMUNICATION

To demonstrate a true understanding of mathematical thinking, students should be able to do more than just calculate a correct answer. For decades, the emphases on teaching mathematical concepts and students' ability to communicate their understanding of math concepts have been promoted by math educators. In 1989, the NCTM introduced the *Curriculum and Evaluation Standards for School Mathematics*. In this document, the importance of communication in math was emphasized, and the inclusion of these ideas was recommended as a standard for each grade level. Later in 1991, the NCTM published the *Professional Standards for Teaching Mathematics. This* document also addressed how teachers can promote communication while doing math. It suggested that teachers should pose questions and use tasks that challenge student thinking. Then teachers are to ask students to clarify and justify their ideas both orally and in writing. In 2000, the NCTM presented new standards in the *Principles and Standards for School Mathematics*. Again, the standards specifically stated that students should be able to communicate their math ideas orally and in writing. With this emphasis from the NCTM, it is apparent that mathematical literacy should be a focus of all mathematical programs.

WRITING AND JOURNALING TO COMMUNICATE MATHEMATICAL THINKING

There are many benefits of using writing in mathematics to enhance students' mathematical communication and comprehension skills. According to Burchfield et al. (1993),

> Writing is a natural process, a method of communication between people and a way to express the thoughts and feelings that occur within a person. Its use as a tool for the teaching and learning of mathematics is a recent development, springing in part from the NCTM Standards on Communication. No longer the exclusive province of the humanities, writing is now in use in mathematics classes at all levels, K-12. (p. 1)

Langer and Applebee (1987) also asserted that writing can help students (1) gain relevant knowledge and experience in preparing for new activities (2) review and consolidate what is known or has been learned and (3) reformulate and extend ideas and experiences.

Much research has been completed illustrating the benefits of writing in mathematics (Adams 1998; Baxter et al. 2005; Borasi and Rose 1989; Burns 1995; Clarke et al. 1993). Most of this research was completed in the 1990s following the release of the NCTM *Curriculum and Evaluations Standards* (Adams 1998; Borasi and Rose 1989; Burns 1995; Clarke et al. 1993). For example, math educator, Marilyn Burns wrote many articles and a book in support of math journals to explain how journal writing helps students reason and make sense of math (Burns 1995; Burns and Silbey 1999; Burns 2005). In addition, using journals for math instruction helps students make sense of problems that were frustrating or confusing (Burns and Silbey 1999; Fried and Amit 2003).

Writing can be used both as a way to communicate and to learn mathematics. Writing to learn can make a classroom more student-centered (Gammill 2006). Written communication helps the students become active learners and improve their academic achievement because students use language to facilitate their understanding and writing provides students with opportunities to communicate what they know and do not know. One format of writing that allows students to experience these benefits is journal writing.

A journal is an ongoing record that people use to record their thoughts, occurrences, experiences, and observations. The use of journals in math classes provides students a tool to record their personal learning. Many educational resources (e.g., Pearson Education, Inc., teachervision.com, etc.) that are frequently accessed by teachers encourage the use of math journals. In reviewing educational resources, journaling is often described as a practice of recording on paper and a collection of thoughts, understanding, and explanations about mathematical ideas or concepts in a bound notebook (Pearson Education, Inc. 2008).

The use of writing and correct vocabulary enhances a student's mathematical thinking. In a study conducted by Quinn and Wilson (1997), journals were used to promote a better understanding and retention of mathematical concepts. Their findings indicated that students are more likely to develop an understanding of a concept that leads to a correct answer when they are asked to write their explanation. Thus, journal writing encouraged the correct use of mathematical vocabulary (Tuttle 2005). In reverse, teachers can identify whether students understood the concepts by reviewing students' journals, since students would not be able to fully explain the process or concept if they did not understand it.

Additionally, previous studies reported that journaling helps students reflect on their learning (Adams 1998; McIntosh and Draper 2001). According to Kelly (2008), journals provide students the opportunity (1) to sort out experiences, solve problems, and consider varying perspectives (2) to examine relationships with others and the world (3) to reflect on personal values, goals, and ideals and (4) to summarize ideas, experiences, and opinions before and after instruction. Incorporating journal writing into mathematics instruction can develop students' abilities to think and communicate mathematically.

Furthermore, journals are also a good tool to assess students' communication skills (Adams 1998; McIntosh and Draper 2001). For teachers, math journals can serve as an assessment tool. Journals can help to drive instruction for one student or the entire class and identify students' strengths and/or weaknesses. After reading student journals, teachers can determine additional opportunities and resources to benefit the learners. Journals can also be used as a communication tool between the teacher and student (Burns 1995; Burns and Silbey 1999; Goldsby and Cozza 2002; McIntosh and Draper 2001; Williams and Wynne 2000).

Math journals can benefit learners with various ability levels. Baxter et al. (2005) illustrated the benefits of math journals, particularly for low achieving math students. In their study, they found that the students who rarely participated in math instruction were willing to share their ideas in their journals. These low achieving students showed affective responses, strategic competence, and reasoning through drawings, symbols, and words. The journal helped the students make sense of math and facilitated their communication of mathematical thinking.

However, as beneficial as math journals are in a classroom, there are some negative aspects as well. In previous research, a couple of concerns have been identified (Baxter et al. 2005; McIntosh and Draper 2001; Quinn and Wilson 1997). Most teachers felt that time constraints were an issue. Specifically the two aspects of time constraints addressed are time for recording in journals and time for evaluating journals. Teachers reported that they did not have enough class time to use journals on a consistent basis (McIntosh and Draper 2001; Quinn and Wilson 1997)or to review and evaluate journals (Baxter et al. 2005).

Despite the issue of time constraints, the research on the use of math journals in the classroom showed many benefits. In the study by Goldsby and Cozza (2002), they concluded that

> these writings can be a window into the mind of the student who is engaged in mathematical activities, providing the opportunity to "see" the why, not just the how, of the student's thinking and enabling the student to clarify and extend that thinking. (p. 520)

Their assertion summarizes the purpose of math journals and the benefits to both the students and teacher. This research was to examine how using a math journal affected in building a necessary foundation for second grade students to communicate mathematical thinking.

METHODOLOGY

This research focused on how the use of math journals affected second grade students' communication of their mathematical thinking. This inquiry was an action research project in which the teacher participated as the researcher. According to Mills (2003), action research is "any systematic inquiry conducted by teacher researchers... to gather information about... how they teach and how well their students learn" (p. 5). The information gathered helps teachers gain insights, develop their reflective practice and improve student outcomes, in this case to improve the math practice in a second grade classroom. Since the researcher was the teacher of the classroom, the researcher was able to utilize the insights that can only be obtained as an insider to the setting. This insider insight helped the researcher capture the students' thinking process more closely and gather and analyze the data more in-depth.

This study used a mixed methodology with qualitative and quantitative approaches. Creswell (1994) explains that mixed methodology uses both quantitative and qualitative approaches in a single study. The benefit of using a mixed methodology is triangulation of the findings and adding scope and breadth to a study. This study utilized both quantitative and qualitative data gathering methods to triangulate findings and to provide a more in-depth look at how the students communicated their mathematical thinking when using math journals.

Participants and Setting

The setting for this research was a second grade mixed-ability classroom in a large suburb of Chicago. In the school, there were 640 students in the Kindergarten through fifth grade. There were twenty students in the targeted classroom. However, data from only sixteen students were collected because one student did not return the permission slip, two students were not in the classroom during journal writing due to special services, and one student withdrew from school two and half weeks into the research. The participants were composed of two Asian, one African-American, two Hispanic, and eleven Caucasian students. Eight girls and eight boys participated. All the students' names used to report findings are pseudonyms to maintain confidentiality.

The researcher is the teacher of this classroom. The teacher-researcher has taught for 12 years, 2 years non-consecutively in a second grade classroom. The teacher-researcher has also served as the district's elementary mathematics curriculum chairperson for 5 years.

Math Journaling Instruction

The instruction, which was developed by the teacher-researcher, was completed over a 5-week period. During the instructional period, the students wrote in their math journals on average three times a week, using sixteen different prompts. The prompts dealt with mathematical concepts previously taught as well as basic mathematical concepts, such as grouping, two digit by two digit addition and multi-digit subtraction. The first three prompts were modeled by the researcher during whole class instruction over a week. Modeling showed students the use of various math strategies to solve math problems, which included using manipulative, drawing pictures, making charts or tables, and writing number sentences. Instruction also included providing directions and examples of writing how to solve a math problem. The students were asked to write a step-by-step explanation of what they did to solve the math problem.

Throughout the remainder of the course of study, 13 additional math journal prompts were completed by the students over 4 weeks. During that period, three mini lessons were taught by the teacher-researcher. The first mini lesson instructed students on strategies to incorporate math vocabulary from the question and prompt into the explanation. The second mini lesson was taught to help students identify clues in the questions to help them better understand the math problem. Students were instructed to act like a detective and look for clues such as numbers, key terms and unrelated information. They were then instructed to use that information to explain their answers. The last mini lesson focused on explaining step-by-step how the problem was solved and why. Individual instruction and interventions were provided as necessary throughout the study.

Data Gathering

In this study, data gathering methods included (1) pre- and post- math assessments (2) students' math journals, (3) interviews with students and (4) the teacher-researcher's reflective journal.

First, an identical math assessment was administered at the beginning and end of the study. The math assessment was obtained from Illinois State Board of Education, Illinois Learning Standards Stage

A Mathematics Assessment 8C.A, *Going to School* (ISBE 1997). The assessment focused on a mathematical problem using patterns. In detail, students were asked to determine the extension of patterns using manipulatives or drawings to represent patterns systematically and predict the pattern and to explain what was done and why it was done. The math assessments were used to compare the differences in the student's mathematical communication between pre- and post-instruction.

Second, the students' math journals were collected to examine the students' progress in developing mathematical communication skills and their mathematical thinking. The journals were completed by the students to record their thoughts and explanation of math concepts. Writing prompts for the math journals were obtained from *Saxon Math Two* (Larson 2008). The teacher also created some of the prompts. Sample prompts included "Write your age. Is it even or odd? How do you know?" and "Bob wanted to give his five friends some stickers. If he gives each friend three stickers, how many stickers will he need? Explain how you got your answer." Students wrote in their journals on average three times a week throughout the study.

Third, eight students out of sixteen were chosen at random to participate in an interview at the end of the study. Interview questions included (1) Do you like writing in math journals? Why or why not? (2) Does writing in your math journal help you understand a problem better? Why or why not? (3) Does writing in a math journal help you to use more math words? Why or why not? and (4) What was your favorite part about writing in the math journal? Why? The interviews were used to examine the students' perceptions of the use of math journals. While conducting interviews, the researcher recorded students' responses, and they were later used for analysis.

Lastly, the teacher recorded a reflective journal on days that mini lessons were taught or students wrote in their math journals. The teacher's reflective journal was to record conversations, ideas, general observations, and problems encountered by the students and/or the teacher. Areas for further explanation or re-teaching were also recorded. The teacher's reflective journal was also used for analysis.

Data Analysis

First, the pre- and post- instructional math assessments were scored using the Illinois State Board of Education, *Mathematics Scoring Rubric: A Guide to Scoring Extended-Response Items* (ISBE 2005). The scoring rubric (scale 0–4, 4 being the most competence in each category) was categorized according to mathematical knowledge, strategic knowledge, and explanation. The scores were analyzed in two ways: (1) overall total score and (2) the category of explanation specifically. The area of explanation was chosen because it reflects the students' reasoning and communication of their mathematical thinking. Pre- and post-assessment scores were compared using a *t*-test and descriptive statistics. In addition, the score in the explanation category was analyzed separately using descriptive statistics.

Second, the students' math journals were evaluated with the *Saxon Math Teacher Rubric for Scoring Performance Tasks* (Larson 2008). The criteria used in the rubric included (1) process and strategies, (2) knowledge and skills understanding, and (3) communication and representation. Similar to the math assessment, the students' math journals scores were analyzed in two ways: (1) the overall total score including all three categories and (2) the communication and representation category separately, which requires an explanation of how the problem or task was solved. Each category was assigned a number from zero to two, two being the most competent. Each individual student's daily scores were recorded on a running record to monitor progress. The overall score for each journal entry as well as the communication categories from students' journals were analyzed using descriptive statistics to note changes.

Additionally, the students' math journal entries were grouped according to common themes by mathematical concepts to monitor the growth or consistency of competence in each theme. The themes included sums entries and equal groups entries. The entries were compared chronologically. Qualitatively, the math journal was analyzed using coding and categorizing to examine similarities and differences between responses and common occurrences such as increased math vocabulary use.

Third, the interviews with eight randomly selected students were analyzed by coding and memoing (Dana and Yendol-Silva 2003). The students' answers to the interview questions were read several times. The emerging themes focusing on consistencies and changes in the students' responses as well as relationships and connections between the responses were recorded and then placed in categories. These categories were reviewed carefully to establish patterns.

Lastly, the teacher's reflective journal was also analyzed qualitatively using coding and memoing techniques. The teacher's reflective journal entries were read and re-read several times to look for emerging themes and patterns that informed how the use of math journals affected the second grade students' communication of mathematical thinking.

FINDINGS

The three findings from this research regarding the use of math journals to enhance second grade students' mathematical thinking through math communication are presented.

Improvement on Students' Mathematical Thinking through Math Communication

On the pre- and post-assessment, students were asked to complete a pattern problem and write an explanation about their work. In reviewing students' overall total scores, the pre- and post-assessment scores showed a statistically significant difference ($t = -4.46599$, $p < .05$). The mean score on the pre-assessment was 7.25 (out of 12), and 10.0 on the post-assessment. Specifically, of the sixteen students, thirteen increased their overall score from the pre- to the post-assessment, two remained the same and one decreased.

Separately, the pre- and post-assessment scores for the explanation category were reviewed and analyzed using descriptive statistics. The mean score increased from 1.13 on the pre-assessment to 2.56 on the post-assessment. On the pre-assessment, eleven students scored below two (out of four), while on the post-assessment no students scored below two.

The students' journal entries were grouped by similar topics to make a more meaningful comparison of the scores. These topics were sums and equal groups. The scores in the area of communication and representation were compared using descriptive statistics. Regarding the topic of sums, two students scored zero and fourteen students scored one (out of two points) on their first entry. On their second entry, when they were asked to complete the similar task, two students scored zero, nine scored one, and five scored two. The mean score increased from 0.88 to 1.19 (see Table 1).

The scores on the topic of equal groups also showed an overall increase in the mean score from 1.00 to 1.33. On the first entry, five students scored zero, six students scored a one, and four students scored two out of two points. On the second entry completed, ten students scored one, and five students scored two and no student scored zero.

TABLE 1   **Changes of the individual students' score in their math journals**

Students' names	Sums		Equal groups	
	First entry	*Second entry*	*First entry*	*Second entry*
Joan	1	1	**0**	**2**
Ally	**1**	**2**		
Jessica	1	1	2	2
Sean	**0**	**1**	**0**	**2**
Megan	**1**	**2**	1	1
Nicole	1	1	**0**	**1**
Kate	**1**	**2**	2	2
Cory	1	1	1	1
Sue	1	1	**0**	**1**
John	**0**	**1**	**0**	**1**
Andy	1	1	1	1
Joe	*1*	*0*	1	1
Mark	1	1	2	2
Mary	**1**	**2**	2	*1*
Ned	**1**	**2**	1	1
Kristina	*1*	*0*	1	1
Mean	.88	1.19	1.00	1.33

Bold values indicate the increase of the score. Italic values indicate the decrease of the score. Roman values indicate no changes of the score

In addition, during the instruction, the researcher observed changes in the content of the students' explanations. The teacher's reflective journal noted that "the students are becoming more adept at writing, need less assistance." The students rarely used the word *pattern* on the first entry. However, on the second entry, the word *pattern* as well as an explanation of the word (e.g., *repeating, over and over, same,* etc.) was used frequently. During the fourth week of the study, the researcher noted that "detailed explanations are much better; step-by-step explanations include drawings; explanations of what they did to answer the problem." These observational notes indicated the improvement of students' communication of mathematical thinking.

Increased Use of Mathematics Vocabulary

Previous research (Tuttle 2005) found that journal writing encouraged the correct use of mathematical vocabulary, and this research confirms that. During the journal writing, the students increased the use of math vocabulary in their mathematical explanations. The students' math journals, student interviews, and the teacher's reflective journal provided documentation of student use of math vocabulary.

Students used math vocabulary, such as *sum, patterns, equal groups, some, some more problem, tally marks, least,* and *greatest* in many entries throughout their math journaling. For example, Megan wrote on a pattern problem in the first week that "the seventeenth house was red because the pattern was red yellow yellow red blue yellow yellow." On a later pattern problem, Megan, the same student, wrote, "the reason, I know it [is] because the patern [pattern] was ▲ ▲• ▲ ▲• and it keeps on going." Megan was able to use the correct vocabulary word, which was *pattern,* and to explain what the word meant, something that keeps repeating itself.

On the subtraction problem, Ned wrote that "first I minstste [minused] in the tens colme [column] and that would leave me with 27." He used place value vocabulary when distinguishing between the tens and ones place referring to the digits. He also used the word "minused" indicating the operation of subtraction. On an addition problem, Joan wrote that "I got the sum 46 and then added 8 more and it gave me the sum 53." She correctly identified the answer to an addition problem as a sum rather than just an answer. Another example is Sue's explanation using math terminology to prove why a number is even. She wrote that "18 is even because if you split it into two eacle gropes [equal groups] and have no leftovers then it's even."

Throughout the instructional period, instances of increased use of vocabulary were recorded in the teacher's reflective journal. A later entry noted students' use of math vocabularies throughout their journal entries like *counted,* and *groups,* and students used math vocabularies more readily, giving more explanation. For example, the students used math related words to explain the process they used to get their answers. They specifically stated how they solved basic operation problems by using appropriate math vocabulary, such as counted objects in addition problems or grouped the objects together in multiplication problems. A conversation with Ally about her reasoning for solving a problem led to her using the correct vocabulary in her journal entry.

Ally: I added the right side, then added the left side

Teacher: What do you mean?

Ally: I added 2 ? 2, then 8 ? 6 to get 5

Ally added the digits in the tens column then the digits in the ones column. She realized that the sum of 8 ? 6 gave her another ten so she added it to the other digits in the tens column. Originally, she was unable to explain this. With further questioning, she used the correct terminology for place value in her written explanation. In her journal, she wrote that "kounted [counted] the 6 and the 8 and it ='s 14 and then I put the tens together and then it was 54!"

In student interviews, all eight randomly selected students (out of sixteen) indicated that writing in a math journal helped them to use more math words. Kate said, "cause when I use them I underline them, and I think about using them more." John responded, "I understand them more because I use them more."

Math Journals as an Assessment Tool

The students' math journals provided insights into the students' thought process and understanding of mathematical concepts, rather than simply checking the right answers. A review of students' journals provided information about concepts that needed to be re-taught to individual students, groups of students or the whole class. The students' journal scores were recorded on a running record, and the running record allowed for a quick review of all students' scores. For example, students' math journal entry number nine showed that thirteen of the 16 students lacked full understanding of even and odd numbers. This information indicated a need for whole group instruction on even and odd numbers.

Another entry requiring students to add 26 ? 28, and the quick review of the running record helped the teacher identify some students who had difficulty adding large numbers. It allowed an opportunity to question the identified students individually regarding adding large numbers. This allowed the students the opportunity to explain their thinking in order to guide them through the problem.

Again, an entry in the teacher's reflective journal described the benefit of monitoring students' mathematical thinking demonstrated in their math journals. The teacher's reflective journal noted an analysis of Joe's math journal. He was asked to find the sum of 26 ? 28, and he chose to use tally marks to add the numbers together. Upon further review, the teacher was able to determine the errors in his work. His answer was 53, which was incorrect. He had used a valid process to solve the problem but was unable to obtain a correct answer. The following was recorded in the teacher's reflective journal.

Even though students are missing problems, I am able to use their answers and work to locate their errors and analyze their thinking. What is 26 ? 28? Joe drew 54 tally marks but didn't count one of them (skipped was mark 26, also noticed that he drew 2 groups of 6 not 5, but counted as 5's. (would need review of tally marks).

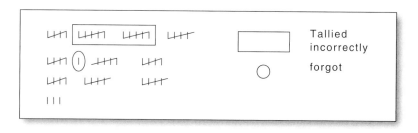

Joe forgot to count a single tally mark and therefore answered 53 instead of 54. The teacher was also able to determine that the student tallied incorrectly twice. Without the drawing, it would be difficult to determine the cause of the student's errors.

On another occasion, three students demonstrated confusion when the students were asked to determine how many cookies Bob and Joe had altogether if Bob had 50 and Joe had 30. Kristina wrote, "80 because an odd number ? odd number and 5 ? 2 = 7 sp [so] I add ne [one] more to 7 and I got 8." Cory wrote, "80 because it is an odd number. 50 ? 50 is 100 and you subtraked [subtracted] 20 cookies thany [then you] have 80 cookies." Both of these students recorded the correct answer to the problem, but neither demonstrated an understanding of the problem. A third student wrote, "first I dres [drew] my answer next I writ my sentine [wrote my sentence]." He had no work or answer. By reviewing these explanations, the teacher could see that these three students did not have full understanding of addition. Therefore, further instruction was provided for the students. The communication of students' mathematical thinking in their math journals allowed the teacher to determine the students' understanding of the math concepts.

IMPLICATIONS AND DISCUSSION

The research findings indicate that the use of math journals helped the students communicate their mathematical thinking and use math vocabulary more frequently. In addition, the teacher was able to use the math journals to assess students' mathematical thinking.

During the study, I learned that math journals can be a beneficial tool for my students and myself as a teacher. The math journals allowed the students opportunities to express their mathematical thinking through pictures and written explanations. They also allowed me to carefully observe how my students used problem-solving strategies and how they understood math concepts. Reviewing students' math journals allowed me to immediately assess a student's mathematical thinking process and adjust my teaching for individual and whole class instruction.

From this study, I believe that journal writing would benefit students' mathematical learning because it helps teachers to see the "how and why" of a student's mathematical thinking. It also allows students to write about their mathematical thinking on a continuous basis instead of just in preparation for high stakes testing, which is often the case. It also helps teachers assess their students' understanding of math concepts on an on-going basis.

While math traditionalists are correct that it is beneficial to memorize formulas, facts, and algorithms, the math reformists emphasize the need for students to have avenues such as journals, portfolios, or projects to demonstrate their understanding, which is also an important part of a math program. This study provided students with the opportunity to use math journals to demonstrate their mathematical thinking. The use of journal writing can be an important tool to learn about students' use of facts, algorithms, formulas and understanding of math concepts.

The importance of students being able to communicate their mathematical thinking has also been emphasized in previous studies, and scholars believe that using math journals can help students develop those communication skills. As stated by Schoen et al. (1999), "reports from business, industry and government suggest that, along with mathematical understanding and skills, students need to have well-developed abilities to analyze problem situations and to communicate ideas for solving those problems" (p. 445). Allowing students the opportunity to illustrate and write about their mathematical thinking in a math journal can benefit them in lifelong problem solving situations.

There were two aspects of the journal that I was concerned about before implementation. The first was the students' writing ability. I wondered whether second graders would have sufficient writing ability to demonstrate their mathematical thinking. However, it turned out that even though some students had difficulty writing, they were able to explain their steps in solving the problem through writing and illustrations. Students used multiple representations such as tally marks, individual pictures of each item, or tables to explain their answers. Some students explained their answers using a combination of pictures and written words such as showing tally marks to represent numbers and explaining in words what they drew and why.

If second graders with minimal writing skills could represent their thinking through pictorial representation, even younger students could begin to illustrate their thinking and understanding of numbers also. I have worked with numerous students who have had difficulty explaining the mathematical process they used to solve a math problem on high stakes testing. If students continuously write and talk about the mathematical processes they use, it may become a natural part of their process of problem solving in math.

Time constraints were also a concern, both the class time to write and the time to grade (Baxter et al. 2005; McIntosh and Draper 2001; Quinn and Wilson 1997). To address the classroom time element, the prompt was written on the board when students entered the classroom in the morning. It was the first assignment they did each day. Grading did take time. However, the benefits of being able to assess the students' understanding outweighed the time spent grading the task. In addition, by using a rubric, the time issue could be minimized.

The *Principles and Standards for School Mathematics* (NCTM 2000) encourages that math programs allow students the opportunities to communicate their mathematical thinking and ideas. As this study reports, the use of math journals can provide this opportunity for students. The use of math journals has become an important part of my classroom. My students look forward to writing in their journals, so we have begun to use them in our daily math lesson. If students are struggling with a math concept, they use their math journals to illustrate and think through the mathematical process.

In conclusion, when students write in mathematics, they are able to use multiple forms of representation to demonstrate their mathematical thinking. The use of math journals allows them to demonstrate a deeper understanding of a mathematical concept, since our understanding of any concept evolves and grows with continuous practice. The more students communicate their mathematical thinking process, the greater their understanding of math will become.

REFERENCES

Adams, T. L. (1998). Alternative assessment in elementary school mathematics. *Childhood Education,* 74(4), 220–224.

Baxter, J. A., Woodward, J., & Olson, D. (2005). Writing in mathematics: Communication for academically low-achieving students. *Learning Disabilities Research & Practice,* 20(2), 119–135.

Borasi, R., & Rose, B. (1989). Journal writing and mathematics instruction. *Educational Studies in Mathematics,* 20(4), 347.

Burchfield, P. C, Jorgenson, P. R., McDowell, K. G., & Rahn, J. (1993). *Writing in the mathematics curriculum.* Retrieved July 18, 2008 from http://www.woodrow.org/teachers/mi/1993/ 37burc.html.

Burns, M. (1995). *Writing in math class.* Sausalito, CA: Math Solutions Publications.

Burns, M. (2005). Looking at how students reason. *Educational Leadership, 63*(3), 27–31.

Burns, M., & Silbey, R. (1999). Math journals boost real learning. *Instructor,* 110(7), 18–20.

Clarke, D. J., Waywood, A., & Stephens, M. (1993). Probing the structure of mathematical writing. *Educational Studies in Mathematics, 25*(3), 235–250.

Creswell, J. W. (1994). *Research design: Qualitative & quantitative approaches.* Thousand Oaks, CA: Sage Publications.

Dana, N. F., & Yendol-Silva, D. (2003). *The reflective educator's guide to classroom research.* Thousand Oaks, CA: Corwin.

Fried, M. N., & Amit, M. (2003). Some reflections on mathematics classroom notebooks and their relationship to the public and private nature of student practices. *Educational Studies in Mathematics, 53,* 91–112.

Gammill, D. M. (2006). Learning the write way. *The Reading Teacher, 59*(8), 754–762.

Goldsby, D. S., & Cozza, B. (2002). Writing samples to understand mathematical thinking. *Mathematics Teaching in the Middle School, 7*(9), 517–520.

Illinois State Board of Education. (1997). *Going to school.* Retrieved July 25, 2008, from http://www.isbe.state.il.us/ils/math/stage_ A/8CA.pdf.

Illinois State Board of Education. (2005) *Mathematics scoring rubric: A guide to scoring Extended-response items.* Retrieved July 25, 2008, from http://www.isbe.state.il.us/assessment/math.htm.

Kelly, M. (2008). *Writing across the curriculum: The importance of integrating writing in all subjects.* Retrieved July 18, 2008, from http://712educators.about.com/cs/writingresources/a/journals. htm.

Langer, J. A., & Applebee, A. N. (1987). *How writing shapes thinking: A study of teaching and learning.* NCTE Research Report No. 22. Urbana, IL: National Council of Teachers of English.

Larson, N. (2008). *Saxon math 2.* Orlando, FL: Harcourt Achieve, Inc.

McIntosh, M. E., & Draper, R. J. (2001). Using learning logs in mathematics: Writing to learn. *Mathematics Teacher, 94(7),* 554–557.

Mills, G. E. (2003). *Action research: A guide for the teacher researcher* (2nd ed.). Upper Saddle River, NJ: Merrill Prentice Hall.

National Council of Teachers of Mathematics. (1989). *Curriculum and evaluation standards for school mathematics.* Reston, VA: NCTM.

National Council of Teachers of Mathematics. (1991). *Professional standards for teaching mathematics.* Reston, VA: NCTM.

National Council of Teachers of Mathematics. (2000). *Principles and standards for school mathematics.* Reston, VA: NCTM.

Pearson Education, Inc. (2008). *Journaling.* Retrieved July 18, 2008 from http://www.teachervision.fen.com/writing/letters-and-jour nals/48533.html.

Quinn, R. J., & Wilson, M. M. (1997). Writing in the mathematics classroom: Teacher beliefs and practices. *The Clearing House,* 71, 14–20.

Schoen, H. L., Fey, J. T., Hirsch, C. R., & Cxford, A. F. (1999). Issues and options in the math wars. *Phi Delta Kappan,* 80(6), 444–453.

Tuttle, C. L. (2005). Writing in the mathematics classroom. In J. M. Kenney (Ed.), *Literacy strategies for improving mathematics instruction* (pp. 24–50). Alexandria, VA: Association for Supervision and Curriculum Development.

Williams, N. B., & Wynne, B. D. (2000). Journal writing in the mathematics classroom: A beginner's approach. *The Mathematics Teacher,* 93(2), 132–135.

Example B: MMAR Study in the Field of Nursing (Glasson et al., 2006)

OLDER PEOPLE

Evaluation of a model of nursing care for older patients using participatory action research in an acute medical ward

Janet Glasson RN, CM DipAppScNurs, BNurs
MHlthSc (Hons) Candidate, School of Nursing, Family and Community Health, University of Western Sydney, Richmond, NSW, Australia

Esther Chang PhD, MEdAdmin, RN
Professor, School of Nursing, Family and Community Health, University of Western Sydney, Parramatta, NSW, Australia

Lynn Chenoweth PhD, BA, MA (Hons) M Ad.Ed., RN
Professor, Aged and Extended Care Nursing, University of Technology, Sydney, and Director, Health and Ageing Research Unit, South Eastern Sydney Area Health Service, NSW, Australia

Karen Hancock PhD, BSc (Hons)
Research Associate, School of Nursing, Family and Community Health, University of Western Sydney, Parramatta, NSW, Australia

Tracy Hall RN
Blue Mountains District Anzac Memorial Hospital, Katoomba, NSW, Australia

Submitted for publication: 1 June 2005
Accepted for publication: 23 June 2005
Correspondence:
Janet Glasson
16 Bordeaux Place
ORCHARD HILLS NSW 2748 Australia
Telephone: +61 2 4736 7070
E-mail: jbglasson@hotmail.com

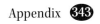

Frances Hill-Murray RN
*Blue Mountains District Anzac Memorial Hospital, Katoomba,
NSW, Australia*

Lesley Collier EN
*Blue Mountains District Anzac Memorial Hospital, Katoomba,
NSW, Australia*

GLASSON J, CHANG E, CHENOWETH L, HANCOCK K, HALL T,
HILL-MURRAY F & COLLIER L (2006) *Journal of Clinical Nursing* **15,** 588–598

Evaluation of a model of nursing care for older patients using participatory action research in an acute medical ward

Aims and objectives. The main aim of this study was to improve the quality of nursing care for older acutely ill hospitalized medical patients through developing, implementing and evaluating a new model of care using a participatory action research process.

Background. One of the challenges of nursing today is to meet the health-care needs of the growing older population. It is important to consider what quality of nursing care means to older patients if nurses are to address gaps between their own perceptions and those of older patients themselves and to consider conceptual models of care appropriate for older patients care in order to improve the quality of care provided.

Design. This study is a mixed method triangulated study, involving the use of both quantitative and qualitative methods through participatory action research methodology to establish an evidence-base for an evolving model of care.

Methods. The model was tested on 60 acutely ill patients aged at least 65 years. The medical ward nurses selected a key reference group including the researcher to facilitate the participatory action research process to develop, implement and evaluate a new model of care based on Orem's self-care model incorporating the Nurses Improving Care to Health System Elders Faculty (Am J Nurs 1994; 94:21) medication protocol to improve the nursing care provided for acutely ill older patients.

Results. The participatory action research process resulted in improved heath-care outcomes for the patients, such as significant improvements in activities of daily living capabilities between admission to discharge, significant improvements in knowledge levels regarding their medication regimes, as well as increased satisfaction with nursing care activities as perceived by older patients and nursing staff. The implementation of educational sessions during the model of care improved the older patient's functional activities and knowledge levels of their medication regime prior to discharge. In addition, by repeatedly explaining procedures, nurses became more involved with their individual patient's care, developing a patient-centred care relationship based on Orem's self-care model.

Conclusions. This study demonstrates the efficacy of a new model of nursing care in improving the quality of nursing care for older patients in the acute medical ward setting.

Relevance to clinical practice. This study is significant because of its evidence-base and demonstrates how the participatory action research process empowered nurses to make sustainable changes to their practice. The nurses in the study wanted to affect change. The planned change was not dictated by management, but was driven by the clinical nursing staff at the 'grass roots' level. Therefore, being involved in the decision-making process provided an incentive to actively implement change.

Key words: action research, activities of daily living, acute nursing care, efficacy of model of care, medication knowledge, older patients

INTRODUCTION

One of the challenges of nursing today is to meet the healthcare needs of the growing older population. Quality of nursing care is important for acutely ill older people who are the largest group of patients in terms of hospital admissions (Australian Institute of Health and Welfare 1999). Significant gaps have been found in nurses' knowledge and expertise in regards to older peoples' needs and the ageing process itself (Wilkes et *al.* 1998, Reed & Clarke 1999, Courtney et *al.* 2000). It is important to consider what quality of nursing care means to older patients if nurses are to address gaps between their own perceptions and those of older patients themselves and to consider conceptual models of care appropriate for older patients care in order to improve the quality of care provided.

Orem's self-care model (Orem 2001) advocates that a patient-centred approach to care is relevant to the care of older people in the hospital setting and has been widely applied in aged care nursing (Cavanagh 1991, Marriner Tomey & Alligood 2002). This model incorporates Orem's Self-care Deficit Theory, a theory composed of three related sub-theories consisting of the Self-care Theory, the Self-care Deficit Theory and the Theory of Nursing Systems (Orem 2001). When implementing Orem's model in practice (Cavanagh 1991), the nurses' role in caring for patients involves compensating for their self-care deficits (inabilities) and helping them to meet their universal self-care requisites (needs).

To facilitate the development and implementation of a model of care in the acute care setting, it is important to focus on the role of nursing staff and to introduce a variety of strategies to assist and support nurses to achieve their goal (Redman & Jones 1998). Clinical nurses require the support of nursing management and colleagues on the participating ward to introduce and sustain a patient-centred model of care in practice.

One way of evaluating a model of care is to use participatory action research (PAR; Hart & Bond 1995, Wadsworth 1997). It is an appropriate process for re-evaluating and changing nursing practice not only because of its reflecting process during the stages of planning, taking action in practice, observing, reflecting and replanning, but also for its similarity to the nursing process through the steps of assessment, planning, implementation, evaluation and replanning (Nolan & Hazelton 1996). PAR is also appropriate because it has been successfully employed to facilitate change and improve service provision in education and more recently in health care (Kemmis & McTaggart 1992, Greenwood 1994, Hart & Bond 1995, Binnie & Titchen 1999). The role of PAR is to empower nurses through the construction of their own knowledge, in a process of action and reflection (Reason & Bradbury 2001). That is, by nurses addressing clinical issues by reflecting on why certain procedures are performed: whether it is based on evidence or tradition, or whether the patients' best interests are being met by delivering care in a certain way. When nurses increase their knowledge through reflection, they can act on this through PAR. For example, they may participate in implementing a model of care in order to deliver more appropriate nursing care practices.

The main aim of this study was to improve the quality of nursing care for older acutely ill hospitalized medical patients through developing, implementing and evaluating a new model of care using a PAR process. This is the second phase of a study these previous phase of which identified important aspects of nursing care as perceived by nurses, older patients and their carers, and identified deficits in aspects of nursing care (Chang *et al.* 2003, Hancock *et al.* 2003; Table 1). This study sought to address older patients' specific issues in the acute medical ward setting. Issues related to encouraging self-care activities while in hospital and medication education.

Research questions:

1. Is the implementation of a model of care tailored to the nursing needs of older patients effective in enhancing outcomes such as functional activities of daily living and medication knowledge and management?

2. Were older patients who were admitted during model implementation more satisfied with the nursing care they received than premodel patients?

3. What are some of the key concepts relating to nursing care that emerged as a result of action research processes during implementation of a model of care for older patients?

METHOD

Design

A mixed method triangulation approach to data collection was used for this study, using both quantitative and qualitative methods. The advantages of using several methods to examine the same phenomenon are that it provides more in-depth information on the participants' experiences and feelings (Morse & Field 1996). Research instruments included: patient evaluation assessment instruments including a modified version of the Barthels ADL Index, Medication Regime Assessment and the satisfaction only component of the Caregiving Activities Scale (CAS) questionnaire developed by White (1972). Other sources of data collection included researcher field notes recorded continuously during the PAR process and minutes of meetings.

Stages of study

There were two stages to this study: the first stage identifies the aspects of nursing care that acutely ill older patients perceived as being important but were not satisfied with (occurring eight months before the second stage). The second stage (reported in this paper) is the development, implementation and evaluation of a model of nursing care designed to address two aspects of care that patients perceived as important but were not satisfied with. These were (i) increasing functional activities of daily living and (ii) increasing patient's knowledge of their medication regime both in hospital and at discharge.

TABLE 1	**Showing summary of the action research process for this study**

Action research step	Details
Reflecting	Findings from earlier stage presented to nurses and discussed Various models of care discussed
Planning	Key reference group formed to develop model Weekly inservice meetings with nurses and researcher Two issues to address in model: encouraging self care and increasing medication knowledge in patients Model of care chosen based on action research processes Evaluation tools chosen (Barthel's ADL's Index, Medication Regime
Implementing	Nurses use educative/supportive intervention with patients regarding ADLs and medication regime
Observing outcomes	Nurses encourage patients to attend to ADLs, measured patients' medication knowledge and administration
Feedback	Nurses reflect on observations during weekly meetings
Replanning	By key reference group to maintain or further develop model

Research setting and ethical clearance

The study setting was an acute medical ward located in a public hospital in Sydney, NSW. Nursing staff volunteered to participate in the PAR process to develop, implement and evaluate a model of care that would address older patients' issues that were identified in an earlier study. This study was approved by the relevant health services and university ethics committees.

Participants

Patients

There were two groups of patients:

Premodel group. Forty-one patients (mean age 78 years; 14 males, 27 females) were assessed on the acute medical ward in an earlier phase of the study prior to the model of care being implemented on this ward. This occurred approximately eight months prior to the model being implemented. Outcomes (discussed below) were compared with the model group. Four potential participants did not consent because they were undergoing procedures, were too ill or tired to participate. Six patients needed assistance in completing the questionnaire.

The patients were given a brief overview of the study. If interested in participating they were given a detailed information sheet and were asked to provide written, informed consent.

Model group. Sixty patients (mean age 76 years; 30 males, 30 females) who were hospitalized in the same medical ward as the earlier phase of the study were assessed while the model was being implemented on the ward. Twelve potential participants did not consent because they were undergoing procedures, were too ill or tired to participate. Four patients needed assistance in completing the questionnaire. The researcher consulted with nursing staff on the ward to identify patients who were eligible to participate in their study. The patients were also given an overview, a detailed information sheet and were asked to provide written, informed consent.

Criteria for selection for both groups included: aged 65 years or older; admitted for an acute illness; willing to participate in the study; hospitalized for at least two days; and meeting cognitive selection criteria of having no more than at the early stage of dementia, confusion/delirium or mental illness. Although it would be ideal only to assess patients who have no cognitive impairment, many older patients have dementia of some form (varying from slight to severe) and many develop confusion as a consequence of their hospital stay. Therefore, to exclude all patients with any form of dementia/cognitive impairment would limit the generalizability of the findings to older patients in acute care settings. All patients included in this study were assessed for cognitive status using the mini-mental state examination (MMSE) scale, a valid and widely used bedside instrument developed by Folstein *et al.* (1975). It was agreed by an expert panel and research team that any patients who scored less than 19 on the MMSE at the time of interview should be excluded from the study. If the patient had mild dementia, the family/carer consented for the patient to participate in the study.

The major diagnoses for both groups included chronic airways limitations or chronic obstructive airways disease, chest infection, pneumonia, congestive cardiac failure, chest pain for investigation, ischaemic heart disease and stabilization of diabetes.

Nurses

Premodel group. Fourteen nurses out of a possible 18 from the acute medical ward who met the following selection criteria registered permanent staff members of the medical ward (across the three shifts) and willing and able to give informed consent to participate in the study were assessed on satisfaction levels during the earlier phase of the study, approximately eight months prior to the model implementation.

Model group. All nurses working on the ward (n = 15) who met the selection criteria participated in the PAR process. However, 13 nurses volunteered to complete the survey during the implementation of the model.

Instruments

Barthel activity of daily living index modified

The Barthel activity of daily living (ADL) Index (Mahoney & Barthel 1965) was modified to incorporate Orem's self-care requisites (Orem 2001) during the model of care PAR process. The modified index was used to determine the patients' functional capacity pre-admission, on admission and prior to discharge in order to assess the older patients' self-care activities. The first 10 items on the index were similar to the 10 items on the Barthel ADL index applied during the earlier study. Only minor word changes were applied to incorporate Orem's requisites. Item 11 was added from Orem's self-care requisites, which states: 'balance solitude and social interaction', where a score of zero indicates 'not able to communicate concerns clearly', a score of one indicates 'willing to discuss concerns with nursing staff/family' and a score of two indicates 'independently seeks information and solitude'. An expert panel of nursing researchers, who was associated with the study, was consulted and agreed that the addition of the item was valid. Given that only one item was added and that the panel was consulted for validity, a reliability test was not performed.

Medication regime assessment

The medication regime assessment was designed to be employed by the ward clinical nurses to determine the patient's knowledge levels of their medications on admission and again prior to discharge from the selected medical ward during the model of care PAR process. This assessment instrument was based on the Nurses Improving Care to the Hospitalised Elderly (NICHE) Project Faculty (1994) medication protocol concepts and is therefore an evidence-based tool. It was used in conjunction with the administration of the pharmacy summary card (PSC). Nursing staff consulted with the hospital pharmacist to print Pharmacy Summary Cards (PSCs) for all older patients participating in the model of care study on admission, or the next day and prior to discharge. This was given to patients on the day of admission or the next day. The medication assessment tool consists of seven items for assessment of levels of knowledge on a four-point Likert scale in administration of medications by older patients.

Caregiving activities scale questionnaire

The satisfaction component only of the CAS questionnaire was administered to patients and nursing staff to determine their levels of satisfaction with nursing care. The CAS questionnaire was based on four dimensions of nursing care that includes items relating to: physical care, psychosocial care, implementation of doctor's orders and discharge planning. The questionnaire was comprised of 50 questions, in which patients were asked to rate their satisfaction with these nursing activities on a five-point Likert ordinal scale. Items that corresponded to the dimension were summated to provide a total score for that dimension. There was a prompt question following each item, which stated 'if not provided then why do you think this was the case?' Nursing staff were asked to rate the degree to which they had the opportunity to provide these aspects of nursing care. The scale has been used successfully and found to be valid and reliable by other researchers (Johnson 1987, Hudson & Sexton 1996).

Field notes

The researcher documented field notes during the PAR process. These notes documented observations of staff discussing why the model of care was needed, how the model of care was developed, what concerns were to be addressed, where the model of care would take place, and over what period of time and how these issues would be addressed and evaluated during the model of care process.

Procedure

Wadsworth's participatory action research process

Wadsworth's (1997) action evaluation research process was chosen by the KRG as an application of PAR, as it states the process clearly for nurses to follow. Wadsworth (1997) identifies the six steps in the PAR cycle in the following way: *reflecting* on the findings, *planning* (design) the actions, implementing these *actions* in practice (fieldwork), *observing* the outcomes of these actions (analysis and conclusions), *reflecting* on these outcomes (feedback) and *replanning* to maintain or further develop the model of care in a continuous cycle of improvement. Table 1 summarises the PAR procedure followed for this study.

Aspects of care to be addressed during the implementation of the PAR process were based on the empirical data gathered in an earlier phase of the study (see Table 2 showing patients' ratings of individual aspects of nursing care that were important items, but were rated low in satisfaction). These individual items included activities across the categories of physical and psychosocial care and discharge planning on the CAS questionnaire. There were two aspects of nursing that the nurses decided to address in this model of care. The first issue was the patients' request to 'teach me about the medications that I will be taking at home'. Nursing staff also decided to include medications taken in the hospital setting to increase the older patients' knowledge levels during hospitalization. The second issue addressed was the patients' request to 'encourage me to take more responsibility for my own care while in hospital'.

The third step in the action research cycle involved implementing these plans in action, with the fieldwork on the ward being facilitated by the KRG in collaboration with all ward nursing staff and recruitment of patients. The researcher facilitated the KRG nurses actions by encouraging them to identify older

TABLE 2	**Means scores for individual items on the CAS questionnaire for areas of importance for patients that they were not satisfied with, stage 1 (patient importance versus patient satisfaction)***

Item no.†	Question	Mean score
17	Help me maintain or restore normal elimination	3.97
22	Encourage me to take more responsibility for my own care while in hospital	3.96
11	Help me to assume a comfortable or appropriate position	3.93
39	Take time to talk with my family and answer their questions	3.65
24	Teach me about the medications that I will be taking at home	3.64

*Calculated by comparing patient importance scores above a mean of four to satisfaction scores below a mean score of four.

†Items noted to be important but were not satisfied with.

patients' issues through questioning, discussing and exploring the meaning of the feedback from the findings from the earlier study where the patients identified their issues. During this step in the cycle further nursing staff in-service ward meetings were conducted over a three-week period to present several models of care appropriate for the care of older patients for the nurses' consideration. These included the ACE Model developed by the NICHE project faculty (1994), a patient-centred care philosophy implemented by Binnie and Titchen (1999) and patient-centred care models – Neuman's system model, 1972 (Chinn & Kramer 1991) and Orem's self-care model, 1971 (Orem 2001). At these in-service meetings nurses were encouraged to act and identify for themselves a model that addressed the issues of older patients and was compatible with their clinical environment. The researcher then presented in-service meetings on how to apply this model of care in practice. To guide nursing care practice, the model selected was a patient-centred care philosophy based on Orem's self-care model and included the NICHE (1994)) faculty project medication protocol concepts.

Data collection procedure for patients

The patients' functional activities were assessed on admission to discuss their pre-admission activities, on admission activities and reassessed prior to discharge with the modified version of the ADL Index. The patients' knowledge levels of administration of medications were also assessed on admission, during their hospital stay and again prior to discharge from the selected medical ward with the MRA. This instrument included a section at the base of the form to indicate that the pharmacist was informed of the patients need for a pharmacy summary card (PSC). The PSC was given to all patients participating in the model of care study. This card assisted with the educational sessions by nurses when administering medications. These educational sessions were documented on the MRA. Red dots were placed on patients' charts and a red sheet placed on the front of the chart to alert staff members that the patient was participating in the model of care study.

Prior to discharge from the selected ward the patient was then asked to complete the satisfaction CAS questionnaire to determine whether the implementation of the model of care that was considered to address older patients' identified nursing care issues had resulted in increased patient satisfaction and improved patient care, such as improved satisfaction with the quality of nursing care received. Assistance, if required, was given to the patient to complete the questionnaire, although only a few patients required assistance in this medical ward. Questionnaires were filed according to the patient code number allocated.

Data collection procedure for nurses

During the last two weeks of the model of care implementation process, the nurses on the medical ward who had volunteered to participate in the model of care study were asked by the KRG members to give informed written consent and to complete the satisfaction CAS questionnaire in their own time. This time frame was chosen so that nurses' ratings reflected a uniform period of time. When completed nurses returned the questionnaire to one of the KRG members in a supplied sealed envelope. All questionnaires were place in a folder in the in-service room on the ward and filed according to their nurse code number.

Data analysis

Quantitative analysis

Outcomes of research instruments were analysed as follows:

1. Comparison of satisfaction scores premodel patient group outcomes with model group patients: A factorial between groups ANOVA (two categorical factors) was performed comparing satisfaction scores on each subcategory (the items within each of the four categories of the CAS were summed to provide a mean score for each of the four categories) for the premodel patient group and the model patient group. To avoid committing a type-1 error, a Bonferroni correction was applied of $P = 0.01$ to follow-up F-tests (0.05 divided by the number of dependent variables).

2. Comparison of premodel nurses group with model nurses: Data were compared descriptively only because of the low sample size.

3. Comparison of Barthel ADL scores premodel to model patient groups from admission to discharge: A repeated measures ANOVA was performed on premodel and model groups to determine whether implementation of the model resulted in improvements in Barthel ADL index scores on admission to discharge.

4. Medication assessment knowledge levels for model group: An ANOVA-test was also performed to determine whether implementation of the model resulted in improved medication assessment knowledge levels.

Qualitative analysis

After transcription, qualitative data were analysed using content analysis. Words and phrases were analysed and coded such that several concepts were abstracted. The research team collaborated to elicit consistent patterns of meaning of the text. The key concepts were presented within Wadsworth's (1997) six steps in the action research cycle.

RESULTS

Quantitative evidence of model efficacy

Caregiving activity scale questionnaire

The findings indicated significant differences between the premodel and the model groups in patient satisfaction with physical care [$F(1,100) = 174.4, P < 0.001$] and discharge planning [$F(1,100) = 89.79, P < 0.001$], with the model group more satisfied than the premodel group (see Tables 3 and 4).

| TABLE 3 | **Means, range and standard deviations for the four categories of satisfaction for the two premodel groups** | | | |

Variable	Mean	Min	Max	SD
Physical care				
Patient (n = 41)	3.35	2.00	5.00	0.71
Nurse (n = 14)	4.07	3.00	5.00	0.60
Psychosocial care				
Patient (n = 41)	3.87	3.00	5.00	0.71
Nurse (n = 14)	3.82	2.00	5.00	0.67
Doctors' orders				
Patient (n = 41)	4.79	4.00	5.00	0.37
Nurse (n = 14)	4.14	3.00	5.00	0.59
Discharge planning				
Patient (n = 41)	2.80	0.00	5.00	1.55
Nurse (n = 14)	3.86	2.00	5.00	0.77

Barthel activity of daily living index

Activity of daily living scores of patients in the earlier study were compared with the model of care group. There were overall significant differences between the two groups on scores, with only the model of care group showing significant improvements in ADLs between admission to discharge $[F(1,980) = 100.8, P < 0.001]$.

Medication regime assessment

Significant improvements in knowledge about medication regimes occurred during the period of hospitalization $(t = -18.78, d.f. = 59, P < 0 001)$, providing support for the use of the model of care education regime to improve patients' satisfaction by increasing their knowledge levels of medication regimes during an acute hospital stay.

Qualitative results

The evaluation of the model of care in this study during the PAR process yielded qualitative data from which several 'key concepts' emerged. The key concepts were as follows: barriers to change, enthusiasm to change, collaboration in planning, empowerment in planning, expanding knowledge and empowerment to change practice.

TABLE 4	Means, range and standard deviations for the four categories of satisfaction for the two model groups

Variable	Mean	Min	Max	SD
Physical care				
Patient (n = 60)	4.70	4.00	5.00	0.30
Nurse (n = 13)	4.03	3.00	5.00	0.58
Psychosocial care				
Patient (n = 60)	4.46	3.00	5.00	0.45
Nurse (n = 13)	3.85	3.00	5.00	0.56
Doctors' orders				
Patient (n = 60)	4.76	4.00	5.00	0.34
Nurse (n = 13)	4.40	4.00	5.00	0.42
Discharge planning				
Patient (n = 60)	4.80	3.00	5.00	0.44
Nurse (n = 13)	3.77	3.00	5.00	0.81

Barriers to change

The key concept 'barriers to change' emerged with the nurses' perception of their current nursing practice environment with several members of the nursing staff stating their concerns. These nurses' comments covered issues concerning time constraints and nursing staff levels that reduced their ability to perform nursing care procedures. The data suggested that the nurses were not confident about their ability to change their nursing care practice.

Enthusiasm to change

Another key concept involved the nursing staff's 'enthusiasm to change' the nursing care provided for these older patients. This concept emerged during meetings when the nurses related their perceptions of how to control work time issues. For example, the nurses claimed, 'as a group we can focus on one or two issues to change our nursing care.'

Collaboration in planning

The key concept of 'collaboration in planning' was evident when three nurses agreed to participate in the key reference group (KRG) facilitated by the researcher to collaborate to change the way they practice to improve nursing care. The KRG members also collaborated to focus on how to evaluate the impact of their new model of care. As a group, they designed the evaluation instruments in consultation with other clinical nursing staff on the selected ward.

Empowerment in planning

A further key concept that emerged from the data during the *plan* step was 'empowerment in planning'. This was manifested when the researcher presented several validated models of care for the nurses to select a model to address their individual ward issues. Nurse were given the power to choose which model best suited their needs and the environment in which they were working.

Expanding knowledge

'Expanding knowledge' emerged as a frequently recurring concept. This was evident when the nurses were consistently sharing their knowledge with other nurses on their ward concerning the model of care implementation strategies. Nurses were also educating patients about self-care and increasing patients' knowledge of their medication regime.

Empowerment to change practice

The key concept 'empowerment to change practice' emerged from the data. The nurses demonstrated their willingness to change practice and to control work time issues by incorporating the educational sessions into the medication rounds and encouraging self-care physical activities during the activities of daily living sessions. It emerged from the data that by permitting the patient to take an active part in the plan of care, nurses were able to support the patient's role in their acute care recovery and allow the patient to feel that they were an integral part of the team involved in the care plan.

DISCUSSION

The main aim of this study was to evaluate the efficacy of a model of care in enhancing patient outcomes and increasing satisfaction with nursing care provided. While it would be ideal to address all the issues raised in the earlier phase of the study, the nurses identified two issues to be addressed in the model of care, stating that it would be impossible to address more than two issues in the current ward environment. Nelson *et al.* (1996) and Berwick *et al.* (1990) propose that clinical nurses can achieve rapid improvements in results by making a series of limited changes and by carefully selecting process and outcome measures that evaluate the impact of these changes. The evidence suggests that this strategy worked extremely effectively in this ward.

For instance, the data confirm Orem's belief that a supportive—educative nursing intervention can increase an individual's self-care ability (Orem 2001). The underlying strategy guiding the intervention was that nurses allowed each older patient the time to express their individual capabilities regarding functional activities of daily living and medication knowledge levels, as they attended the modified Barthel ADL Index and the medication regime assessment (MRA) evaluation instruments. This is consistent with previous findings that indicate the importance of adopting an educative focus when caring for older patients to increase their activities of daily living prior to discharge from hospital (Covinsky *et al.* 1998, Stevenson 1999).

The MRA outcome of increased knowledge is consistent with a previous study to assess individual patients' medication knowledge levels by Ryan and Chambers (2000) who reported participants scored higher on the medication test after an educational programme compared with the pretest results. It may help patients to feel they have more control over their health when they understand their medication regime.

The data suggest that the added focus on individual care promoted more positive feedback from older patients. The emerging data from the meeting minutes and recordings made by the researcher from the field notes relating to the development, implementation and evaluation of the model of care confirm that older patients and nursing staff were more satisfied with the care provided during the implementation of the new model of care study. The finding that the patient model group was more satisfied with physical care than the premodel group may partly be due to the attention nurses paid to encouraging self-care in patients. The nurses were very pleased with the findings of increased satisfaction in the areas of care they had addressed during model implementation, and indicated they would continue to adopt the changes they had made to address the issues.

The barriers to change concept that described time constraints to perform procedures have also been noted in other studies (Duffield & Lumby 1994, Williams 1998, Fagin 2001, Janiszewski Goodin 2003, Gerrish & Clayton 2004). Considering the high dependency of many older patients with their comorbidities and rapid patient turnover, as well as the current staff shortage (Janiszewski Goodin 2003), the situation is unlikely to change in the short-term. However, the empowerment to change practice concept emerged when the nurses demonstrated their willingness to change practice and to control work time issues. At first, the nurses listed several barriers to implementing the model. This may have been a reflection of these particular nurses' tendency to resist change. The nurses did not seem confident in their ability to implement the changes. However, the sense of resistance to change was soon replaced by an empowerment to change some of the current nursing practices.

A major challenge for this study was to develop various strategies whereby the nurses were supported to change their nursing care practice to improve the quality of care provided as part of their clinical ward practice. Gerrish and Clayton's (2004) findings indicated that nurses perceived their various colleagues not to be particularly supportive of changing practice, with managers being seen as the least supportive. For the current study, the KRG members leading the changes in the nursing care were not in a position of authority, but data suggested that through the PAR process they were able to influence change. The managers on the medical ward were very supportive and encouraged the clinical nurses to create changes in their practice. The nurses needed encouragement and support to be enthusiastic in order to change their nursing care practice. According to the data the nurses were also encouraged by the KRG members to reflect on the nursing care they were providing, to plan the issues to be addressed to improve nursing care provided and to take action to develop and implement this change in their nursing care practice. The group action involved during the PAR process appeared to assist the nurses in identifying their strengths and increase their self-confidence to overcome barriers to change their nursing care practice to improve the quality of nursing care provided for their older patients. The empowerment in planning concept emerged when the researcher presented several models of care for the nurses to choose from to address their individual ward issues. This was consistent with other research that recommends the presentation of multiple strategies for the nurses to consider to facilitate and promote changes to their practice (Berwick *et al.* 1990, Short *et al.* 1993, Gerrish & Clayton 2004). Thus, nurses were given a choice of models to change their practice rather than being dictated by management or a research team.

The enthusiasm to change nursing care provided concept that was identified and initiated when the nurses changed their practice through collaboration and reflection as a group. It is likely that the group ownership of the process enhanced the change process. Collaboration in planning was evident when the nurses volunteer to form a KRG to develop, implement and evaluate the new model of care empowered the nurses through reflection and collaboration to gain strength to focus on the issues identified in the earlier study.

The expanding knowledge concept was evident when the nurses were consistently sharing their knowledge concerning the model implementation strategies. In this way, the role of PAR was to empower nurses through the construction of their own knowledge (Reason & Bradbury 2001). The nurses were also consistently sharing their knowledge with their patients during the educational sessions. Orem s theory of nursing systems was consistent with this action where a supportive/educative system was developed. It emerged from the data that the patients required repeated education, encouragement, reassurance and reinforcement of their activities of daily living when appropriate to regain their self-care activities during their acute medical ward stay. The data from the meeting minutes and field notes indicate that all nurses became more focused on their patients throughout the model of care process and, subsequently, became more involved in their individual patient care needs, ultimately providing a patient-centre philosophy of care (Binnie & Titchen 1999) based on Orem's self-care model (Orem 2001). The implementation of educational sessions during the PAR process not only improved older patients' functional activities and knowledge levels of their medication regime prior to discharge, but by repeatedly explaining procedures, nurses became more involved with their individual patient's care, developing a patient-centred care relationship. The findings suggest that the relationships between nurses and older patients were generally very agreeable and the nurses spoke positively about the support they offered the patients in helping them to manage their activities of daily living and education regimes regarding the administration of medications.

The researcher encouraged the KRG members to continue their meetings to reflect on the previous steps and to plan the next step in their model of care PAR cycle. This concept of reflection was emphasized at every stage during the model of care PAR process. The cyclical effect of the PAR process lends support to this process as a way to improve and sustain change. The KRG members' decision was to continue to administer the Pharmacy Summary Card not only to older patients but also to all patients on the ward on the day of admission or the next day if the staff considered the patient eligible, and to continue the educative supportive sessions regarding self-care.

Methodological considerations
and suggestions for future research

The findings from this study do not apply to acutely ill older patients with confusion, mental illness or more than early stage of dementia, or to non-acute hospital settings. The findings are further limited by fact that the model of care was developed, implemented and evaluated in only one acute medical ward that volunteered to participate. It is recommended that the findings of this study be applied to develop guidelines for acutely hospitalized medical patients, particularly for issues relating to educational sessions to increase the patient's functional activities and knowledge levels of their medication regimes prior to discharge. Further, only two issues were addressed in this model. Future models may focus on broadening their focus to additional issues relevant to the needs of older patients. It is further recommended that future research should focus on issues of sustainability of models of nursing care for older patients. Finally, it is recommended that future models focus on a multidisciplinary approach, involving physicians and allied health-care staff rather than simply nursing staff. However, this study did involve the collaboration of nursing staff with pharmacists in the use of the PSC.

CONCLUSION

There were various factors the researchers believe contributed to the efficacy of this model. These include:

- The group of nurses in this study wanted to affect change. The planned change was not dictated by management, but was driven by the nursing staff at the 'grass roots' level. Therefore, being involved in the decision-making process provided an incentive to actively implement change.
- The KRG members initiated encouragement of other nurses on the ward to be involved in the model of care study. They provided the motivation and communicated clearly how, when and where the model of care would be applied to their clinical practice.
- Nurses took ownership of the model of care. The researcher facilitated their ability to find solutions to the issues they wished to address.
- The model of care was built on evidence-base data gathered in an earlier study.
- The ward nurses had an incentive to see the model of care study through to completion, as they were aware that the effectiveness of the model would be evaluated.
- Most nurses employed on this medical ward were consistently employed during the model of care study. It can be difficult to implement changes that are sustainable when staff changes are constantly occurring.

This study demonstrates the potential that a new model of care has to improve the quality of nursing care for older patients in the acute medical ward setting. The study's involvement of patients and nurses follows the new public health approach that consumers are more active participants in their health care, and that disadvantaged groups, like the older population need better representation within the health-care systems (Australian Institute of Health and Welfare 2002).

CONTRIBUTIONS

Study design: EC, LChen, KH, JG; data collection and analysis: JG, TH, FHM, LColl, KH; manuscript preparation: JG, KH, EC, TH, FHM, LColl, LChen.

REFERENCES

Australian Institute of Health and Welfare (1999) *Australian Hospital Statistics 1997–1998.* Australian Institute of Health and Welfare, Canberra.

Australian Institute of Health and Welfare (2002) *Australia's Health 2002: The Eighth Biennial Health Report of the Australian Institute of Health and Welfare.* Australian Institute of Health and Welfare, Canberra.

Berwick DM, Godfrey AB & Roessner J (1990) *Curing Health Care. New Strategies for Quality Improvement.* Jossey-Bass, Francisco, CA.

Binnie A & Titchen A (1999) *Freedom to Practise: The Development of Patient-centred Nursing.* Butterworth Heinemann, Oxford.

Cavanagh SJ (1991) *Orem's Model in Action.* The Macmillan Press Ltd., London.

Chang E, Hancock K, Chenoweth L, Jeon Y, Glasson J, Gradidge K & Graham E (2003) The influence of demographic variables and ward type on elderly patients' perceptions of needs and satisfaction during acute hospitalization. *International Journal of Nursing Practice* **9,** 191–201.

Chinn PL & Kramer MK (1991) *Theory and Nursing: A Systematic Approach,* 3rd edn. Mosby, St Louis.

Courtney M, Tong S & Walsh A (2000) Older patients in the acute care setting: rural and metropolitan nurses' knowledge, attitudes and practices. *Australian Journal of Rural Health* **8,** 94–102.

Covinsky K, Palmer R, Kresevic D, Kahana E, Counsell S, Fortinsky R & Landefeld C (1998) Improving functional outcomes in older patients: lessons from an acute care elders unit. *Journal on Quality Improvement* **24,** 63–76.

Duffield C & Lumby J (1994) Caring nurses: the dilemma of balancing costs and quality. *Australian Health Review* **17,** 72–83.

Fagin C (2001) *When Care Becomes a Burden. Diminishing Access to Adequate Nursing. Millbank Report.* Millbank Memorial Fund, New York.

Folstein MF, Folstein SE & McHugh PR (1975) Mini-mental state, a practical method for grading the cognitive state of patients for the clinician. *Journal of Psychiatric Research* **12,** 189–198.

Gerrish K & Clayton J (2004) Promoting evidence-based practice: an organizational approach. *Journal of Nursing Management* **12,** 114–123.

Greenwood J (1994) Action research: a few details, a caution and something new. *Journal of Advanced Nursing* **20,** 13–18.

Hancock K, Chang E & Chenoweth L (2003) Nursing needs of acutely ill older people. *Journal of Advanced Nursing* **44,** 507–516.

Hart E & Bond M (1995) *Action Research for Health and Social Care: A Guide to Practice.* Open University Press, Buckingham.

Hudson K & Sexton D (1996) Perceptions about nursing care: comparing elders'and nurses'priorities. *Journal of Gerontological Nursing* **22,** 41–46.

Janiszewski Goodin H (2003) The nursing shortage in the United States of America: an integrative review of the literature. *Journal ofAdvanced Nursing* **43,** 335–350.

Johnson J (1987) Selected nursing activities for hospitalised clients. *Journal of Gerontological Nursing* **13,** 29–33.

Kemmis S & McTaggart R (1992) *The Action Research Reader,*3rd edn. Deakin University Press, Victoria.

Mahoney FA & Barthel DW (1965) Functional evaluation: the Barthel Index. *Maryland State Medical Journal* **14,** 61–65.

Marriner Tomey A & Alligood MR (2002) *Nursing Theorists and Their Work,* 5th edn. Mosby, Inc., St Louis.

Morse JM & Field PA (1996) *Nursing Research: The Application of Qualitative Approaches,* 2nd edn. Chapman & Hall, London.

Nelson EC, Mohr JJ, Batalden PB & Plume SK (1996) Improving health care: part 1: the clinical value compass. *Joint Commission Journal on Quality Improvement* **22,** 243–258.

Nolan A & Hazelton L (1996) *The Practising Nurse.* W. B. Saunders Bailliere Tindall, Sydney.

Nurses Improving Care to the Hospitalised Elderly (NICHE) Project Faculty (1994) Geriatric models of care: which one's right for your institution? *American Journal of Nursing* **94,** 21–23.

Orem DE (2001) *Nursing: Concepts of Practice,* 6th edn. Mosby- Year Books, St. Louis.

Reason P & Bradbury H (2001) *Handbook of Action Research.* Sage Publications, London.

Redman R & Jones KR (1998) Effects of implementing patientcentred care models on nurse and non-nurse managers. *Journal of Nursing Administration* **28,** 46–53.

Reed J & Clarke C (1999) Nursing older people: constructing need and care. *Nursing Inquiry* **6,** 208–215.

Ryan A & Chambers M (2000) Medication management and older patients: an individualized and systematic approach. *Journal of Clinical Nursing* **9,** 732–741.

Short SD, Sharman E & Speedy S (1993) *Sociology for Nurses an Australian Introduction.* MacMillan Education Australia Pty Ltd, South Melbourne.

Stevenson J (1999) *Comprehensive Assessment of Older People.* King's Fund Rehabilitation Programme Developing Rehabilitation Opportunities for Older People. Briefing Paper 2, London, pp. 1–21.

Wadsworth Y (1997) *Everyday Evaluation on the Run,* 2nd edn. Allen & Unwin, Melbourne.

White M (1972) Important of selected nursing activities. *Nursing Research* **21,** 4–14.

Wilkes L, LeMiere J & Walker E (1998) Nurses in an acute care setting: attitudes to and knowledge of older people. *Geriaction* **16,** 9–16.

Williams AM (1998) The delivery of quality nursing care: a grounded theory study of the nurse's perspective. *Journal of Advanced Nursing* **27,** 808–816.

Example C: MMAR Study in the Field of Social Work (Craig, 2011)

Precarious Partnerships: Designing a Community Needs Assessment to Develop a System of Care for Gay, Lesbian, Bisexual, Transgender and Questioning (GLBTQ) Youths

SHELLEY L. CRAIG

Factor-Inwentash Faculty of Social Work, University of Toronto, Toronto, Ontario, Canada

This article describes the planning and implementation of a mixed-method community needs assessment with the intent of creating a system of care for gay, lesbian, bisexual, transgender, and questioning (GLBTQ) youths in an urban area. Flowing from qualitative to quantitative research strategies, this needs assessment utilized key informant interviews, focus groups, and survey research in a countywide initiative. Rather than outline each set of findings, this article provides a brief description of the four phases of research activities and the action steps that were completed during each phase. Community context for the needs assessment is described in detail and a final system of care is proposed. Notable barriers and challenges associated with the community needs assessment are also articulated.

KEYWORDS community-based participatory research, sexual minority youth, lesbian, gay, bisexual, transgender, community needs assessment

BACKGROUND

Gay, lesbian, bisexual, transgender, and questioning (GLBTQ) youths are considered a population at risk. They are at increased peril for psychiatric disorders, substance abuse, and suicide (Bontempo & D'Augelli, 2002; Faulkner & Cranston, 1998; Gilman et al., 2001; Herrell et al., 1999; Meyer, 2003); discrimination and harassment from peers

This study was supported by a Service Partnership grant from The Children's Trust of Miami Dade County. We thank the members of The Alliance for GLBTQ Youth Service Partnership, particularly chairperson Michael Dentato, Key Informants, The Thurston Group and the Gay Advisory Board for their support and guidance. Above all, we are grateful for the adolescent participants who unabashedly shared their wisdom and experiences.

Address correspondence to Shelley L. Craig, Factor-Inwentash Faculty of Social Work, University of Toronto, 246 Bloor Street West, Toronto, Ontario, Canada M5V 1V4. E-mail: shelley.craig@utoronto.ca

Reprinted by permission of the publisher (Taylor & Francis Ltd, http://www.tandf.co.uk/journals). *Journal of Community Practice 19*, 2011, 274–291. Precarious partnerships: Designing a community needs assessment to develop a system of care for gay, lesbian, bisexual, transgender and questioning (GLBTQ) youths. Craig, S. L.

(D'Augelli & Grossman, 2001); and rejection from family (D'Augelli, Grossman, & Starks, 2008; National Youth Advocacy Coalition, 2004). Despite these challenges, few programs that target the specific needs of GLBTQ youths exist and little is known about such initiatives. Most research efforts have focused on youth risk factors, yet there is a critical need for inquiry into the ways in which service delivery systems could address these issues, particularly for minority GLBTQ populations. This article examines the stages in the implementation of a community needs assessment (CNA) developed in collaboration with local agencies. The challenges in balancing the perspectives of providers with multiple roles and agendas within this service partnership will be highlighted.

Community Needs Assessment

A CNA is used to identify the needs of a target population within a specific historical and geographical context (Berberet, 2006). Among other factors, it should involve the evaluation of existing health and mental health service delivery systems and their impact on the target population. Additionally, needs must be clearly defined and understood for truly effective programs and services to be created, implemented, and evaluated (Corona, Gonzalez, Cohen, Edwards, & Edmonds, 2009). Such an undertaking, particularly when it arouses deeply held community norms and values, is a complex and exhaustive task (Slaght & Schopler, 1994). Successful initiatives require research and collaboration between stakeholders (Siegel, Attkisson, & Carson, 1995). GLBTQ communities have not always undertaken CNAs due, in part, to resource scarcity that perpetually plagues organizations that serve marginalized populations. Furthermore, the competition between research and practice dollars is usually trumped by the high levels of community need for direct services. Miami Dade County (MDC) is no exception. MDC has a population of nearly 2.5 million (US Census Bureau, 2009) that is spread over 2,000 square miles and is serviced by a severely inadequate public transportation system. In 2007, MDC consisted of a majority of persons of Latino/Hispanic origin (62%) with significantly lower percentages of Blacks (20%), or non-Hispanic White (NHW) persons (18%). The service delivery system for this complex population is a very diverse mix of organizations, ranging from multimillion dollar institutions to community-based agencies run by volunteers. The GLBTQ population has been estimated at 123,000 (Olorunnipa, 2009) in MDC alone, and there are approximately 359,000 children and youths between the ages of 5 and 18 residing in the county (U.S. Census Bureau, 2009). MDC also has the fourth largest school district in the United States (Miami-Dade County Public Schools, 2009). This indicates that a great many youths and families that may be affected by GLBTQ-related issues. Although there are over 14 organizations that claim to serve GLBTQ youths in some capacity in MDC, most have budgets of less than $250,000 and nearly 60% have less than five staff members (Craig & Attonito, 2008). Thus, challenges such as a diverse and sprawling population and limited agency capacity were encountered when conceptualizing and implementing a comprehensive needs assessment.

Service Partnerships

Service partnerships (SP) are working groups that use techniques of community development and research to create systems of care. Such community-based interventions deliver coordinated and individualized services to address needs while highlighting family and child strengths (National Center for Youth Law, 2003). Frequently comprised of a loosely organized group of community and agency representatives from public and private sectors, SP coalesce around a shared belief that a collaborative approach could have greater impact on a perceived need. Eliminating an identified community health concern such as decreasing substance use in youth (Lubman, Hides, & Elkins, 2008), coordinating services for low income residents in neighborhood-based partnerships (Ahsan, 2008), and less frequently, developing services for a particularly vulnerable population (e.g., Latino youth; Corona et al., 2009) have culminated in SPs. Although GLBTQ community representatives are found within these existing SP, no examples were found of SP that specifically targeted this population. This article outlines the development of a CNA for GLBTQ youth and the concurrent expansion of a SP for this emerging vulnerable population in Miami-Dade County, Florida.

The first murmur of a SP began to circulate when a local funding agency released a request for proposals (RFP) for community planning grants. Six agencies then joined forces to advocate for inclusion of the GLBTQ youth population in the RFP process and to support an initial proposal (Dentato, Craig, & Smith, 2010). These agencies were a mixture of gay service organizations and larger mainstream organizations that had programs specific to GLBTQ youth. To increase the complexity of the process, the participating organizations had a multiplicity of mission-driven mandates such as education, public policy advocacy, mental health, resource and referral, and GLBTQ youth recreational services. As discussed in an earlier publication describing the initial formation of the SP, these issues represented ongoing challenges in establishing cohesion (Dentato, Craig, & Smith, 2010). Achieving and integrating support from all of these different stakeholders became of utmost importance as the SP progressed through the phases of the needs assessment.

Funding was initially granted to the SP for 1 year to support a combination of research and services. Of the approximately $210,000 in funding, the primary expenses included the salary of a full-time researcher (23%); research-related costs such as a laptop computer and travel for data collection, as well as gift cards and snacks for participants (7%); indirect costs paid to the fiscal agent (10%); and the delivery of existing services to GLBTQ youths (60%) through the six agencies involved in the SP. Once funded, the SP hired a researcher from a local public university to conduct a CNA from which to develop a system of care for GLBTQ youth. This particular principal investigator (PI) was selected because of her expertise in GLBTQ youth services, which represented an emic (insider) perspective but also had limited knowledge of the history of the local providers, which provided her a simultaneous etic (outsider) perspective (Creswell, 1998). The initial research scan found a profound need for the CNA due to a lack of any available data about GLBTQ youths in general, or service delivery systems particular to their needs. No substantive local data on sexual orientation, gender identity, or even same gender attraction existed. The questions simply were never asked. There were, however, plenty of anecdotes from service providers, a few stories from youth, and a great deal of energy and passion from the community to fuel the research process.

METHODS

Research Design

The CNA was based on a community-based participatory research (CBPR) design. CBPR has become increasingly utilized within North America as a result of its effectiveness and innovative approach to investigating the challenges of vulnerable populations (Tandon et al., 2007; Trinh-Shevrin et al., 2007). CBPR has been described as:

> a collaborative approach to research that equitably involves, for example, community members, organizational representatives, and researchers in all aspects of the research process. The partners contribute unique strengths and shared responsibilities to enhance understanding of a given phenomenon and the social and cultural dynamics of the community, and integrate the knowledge gained with action to improve the health and well-being of community members. (Israel, Schulz, Parker, & Becker, 1998, p. 3)

The CNA consisted of four primary phases which were relatively sequential and are visually depicted in Figure 1. The entire research process was designed to elicit rich qualitative data to contextualize and develop a comprehensive quantitative survey tool (Creswell, 2009; Denzin & Lincoln, 2008) from which to design an evidence-informed system of care. Such heterogeneous sources and approaches to data collection ensure trustworthiness (Clark, Creswell, Green, & Shope, 2008). Phase one included an environmental scan and key informant interviews (KII), and phase two consisted of focus groups comprised of GLBTQ youths from the community under study. With the information gleaned from the first two stages, phase three involved the development, implementation, and analysis of a survey of the target population called Youth Speak Out. Phase four consisted of solicited community feedback about the results of the CNA. To make this plan actionable, a series of steps (Table 1) were conceived and implemented in coordination with the SP. The entire process took approximately 13 months. Most of the qualitative and quantitative research was facilitated by the PI with the help of a research assistant.

Phase One: Environmental Scan and Key Informant Interviews

The first phase of the project included an environmental scan of national and local GLBTQ programs (this included eligibility criteria, utilization data, and types and locations of programs). Data about programs was gleaned following e-mails and phone calls to a variety of sources, including national GLBTQ organizations, members of the SP, the MDC Gay and Lesbian Chamber of Commerce, and an online social service resource database. Several local, national, and international organizations that did exceptional work with GLBTQ youth were identified through this research and visited to allow for a broad perspective on the creation of a system of care. Such destinations included Toronto, ON; San Francisco, CA; New York, NY; Boston, MA; Los Angeles, CA, Minneapolis, MN, Atlanta, GA and Washington, DC. The environmental scan served as the foundation for the initial list of potential interviewees.

During the next step, the KII were planned and initiated. Such qualitative methods are often utilized in prevention research (Patton, 1987, 2002) and are consistent with types of recommended evaluation research into programs that serve GLBT individuals (Kelly et al., 1991). The qualitative nature of KII is ideal for exploratory studies designed to better understand culturally-based beliefs and generate hypotheses for future research (Denzin & Lincoln, 2008). The criteria for participation in KII included: (a) knowledge of GLBTQ youth, preferably in Miami-Dade County; (b) potential access to the population or services; and (c) influence to advance the initiative (Berberet, 2006). Forty-five KII (n = 45) were conducted with local service providers, community leaders, and other stakeholders. Sites included mental health agencies, school counseling sites, after-school programs, homeless shelters, and delinquency and substance abuse facilities. The purpose of

| FIGURE 1 | Community assessment phases |

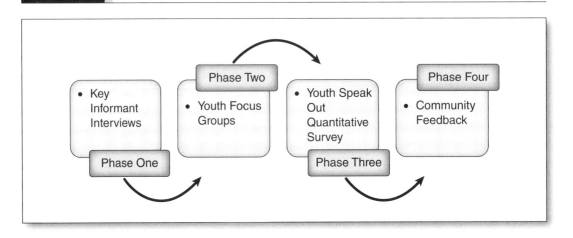

these KII were to: (a) assess the providers perception of youth needs and service availability, (b) build relationships with gatekeepers who could provide access to the population and programmatic support if needed, and (c) begin to develop the collaborative structure necessary for the development of a system of care (Berberet, 2006). Building these collaborative relationships is critical to the success of a CNA, as these key individuals are often in positions to either advance or impede the project and can also grant access to the target population. A series of open-ended guiding questions were asked in a semistructured format to enable key informants to share their ideas and experiences. Probes were used to encourage additional dialogue and clarification. Each KII lasted from 45 min to an hour-and-a-half. At the end of each KII, participants were asked for suggestions for other potential interviewees. It is notable that 100% of those contacted for KII agreed to participate in an interview. Each KII was transcribed and analyzed for themes using Atlas-Ti software. Findings indicated a need for safe homeless shelter services, education for adults within the youth system, family support, a public education campaign, mental health counseling, transportation, and health care.

Phase Two: Focus Groups With GLBTQ Youth

In the second phase of the research, focus groups were conducted to deepen relationships with the population of interest and to provide a richer understanding of the true needs of the population by building upon the perspective of the providers. Utilizing the new relationships with KII, the PI identified four sites (one in each region of the expansive county) and conducted focus groups. Youths were primarily recruited through existing gay—straight alliances in the schools or community youth groups. Upon completion of the original groups, both unanswered questions and a demand by the youths at various sites to be included in this project necessitated adding six more groups for a total of 10 focus groups with nearly 200 youth participants ($n = 180$). Results were transcribed, collated, and content analyzed for themes using Atlas-Ti qualitative software. The specific procedures and findings of these focus groups are reported in a different publication by this author.

TABLE 1 Research Activities: Community Needs Assessment (CNA)

Research phase	Research activity	Description	Plan	Outcome
Phase one	Local key informant interviews	Key informant interviews with community leaders and agency personnel to discuss providers perspective of GLBTQ needs, service gaps, community assets, and their opportunities for engagement Gather future and current partnership members	Initial goal of 10-20 key informant interviews using standardized protocol	45 key informant interviews completed and analyzed
	National key informant interviews	Identification of communities that are taking steps to create a system of care Assess national trends and build effective intrastate collaborations Identify practice models	Site visits planned: Toronto; Chicago; New York City; Boston; Los Angeles; San Francisco; Washington, DC; Minneapolis; and Atlanta	Site visits completed: Toronto; Chicago; New York City; Boston; Los Angeles; San Francisco; Washington, DC; Minneapolis; and Atlanta
Phase two	Focus groups	Focus groups are a good strategy to gather important context and history for prevention interventions in marginalized communities	4–6 focus groups planned with youth Transcribe, collate, and assess results	10 focus groups completed with youth ($n = 180$) Generate qualitative report

(Continued)

TABLE 1 (Continued)

Research phase	Research activity	Description	Plan	Outcome
Phase three	Literature review	Comprehensive literature reviews of risks and needs relative to the target population and tied to the domains addressed in both the needs assessment and focus groups	Literature review via PsychInfo, WebSPIRS, and PubMed databases	
	GAB (Gay Advisory Board)	Creation of a Youth Advisory Board (now named GAB) to engage consumers in the design and implementation of services	Monthly meetings with 10 core GLBTQ youth leaders from MDC initiated January, 2007	10 monthly meetings convened before CNA was completed and leaders graduated
		Such collaboration and oversight is critical to culturally competent practice	This community board reviews all issues related to the design and implementation of the CNA	
		Provides a great opportunity to empower young community leaders	Survey of needs and protective factors	Data collected and analyzed (N = 273)

Research phase	Research activity	Description	Plan	Outcome
	Youth Speak Out Survey	Creation of a full quantitative needs assessment for GLBTQ youth in MDC, including the following basic domains: Demographics School support Family support Health and mental health Social support Discrimination Service needs	Although online, primarily collected paper surveys Sample of 200 GLBTQ youth targeted Completion time: Approx 30 min	
Phase Four	Local Service Network Meetings	Identifying opportunities for community-resource sharing through the convening of all interested service partnerships and resource networks	Building of a service partnership consortium Monthly meetings	
	Community Stakeholder Feedback Loops	The final draft of the CNA was presented to a full convening of stakeholders and their feedback was integrated into the final plan.	Full meeting of service partnership research participants and interested community members	Full meeting convened

Note. GLBTQ = Gay, lesbian, bisexual, transgender, and questioning. MCD = Miami-Dade County

Phase Three: Youth Speak Out Survey

The third phase was the development of a quantitative survey instrument for youth. Based on the domains articulated by the qualitative research, the PI identified the relevant measures from the existing literature. A draft of the survey was constructed for review by the members of the SP. The design of the quantitative instrument was determined during three open meetings with staff from interested social service agencies. With an average number of 15 participants in attendance and 26 different people attending at least one of the meetings, these brainstorming sessions were infused with enthusiasm.

Several meetings were spent adding topics or questions that members wanted to include in the research. At the first meeting, more than 50 additional questions were suggested to the 200 already in the draft presented by the PI. Some agency representatives even requested individual meetings to discuss their specific research concerns. Many of the SP members wanted questions specific to their agency mission included (e.g., the school based programs wanted to ask about bullying). Such involvement led to opportunities to discuss the delicate balance between agency requests, youth needs, and overall feasibility. During the final full group meeting more questions were added and deleted and final consensus was reached on the survey contents.

Throughout this process, each version of the draft survey went to the newly created Youth Advisory Board (later renamed the Gay Advisory Board, by the youth participants). The Gay Advisory Board (GAB) consisted of 10 youths that had applied and been selected by the PI and the SP to oversee the CNA process. The PI felt that the GAB's insider knowledge and expertise as members of the target population was critical to both instrument validity and eventual program adoption. The youth members would review each draft of the survey and provide feedback to the SP. They met for one-and-a-half hours each month and were given gift cards to a local store as a reward for their participation. It should be mentioned that this unusual approach to construct validation caused some tension within the adult SP. As one participant stated, "I have worked with this population for 20 years—I probably know better than a group of 16-year-olds what they need." It is recognized that this process of adults' efforts being evaluated by adolescents should be carefully managed to preserve the relationships within the partnership. Such concerns were addressed through a training from a national expert in youth adult partnerships, but certainly represented a critical challenge to the construction of the final draft of the survey. Once finalized, the Youth Speak Out survey was implemented. A nonrandom sample of 273 GLBTQ youths from around MDC was collected using venue-based sampling. Building on the relationships established during the first two phases of the research, many of the KII organizations and focus group sites were willing venues for the quantitative survey. As data is understood and triangulated for accuracy, checks on the fidelity of the data are critical, especially from the perspective of the target population (Denzin & Lincoln, 2008).

Phase Four: Community Feedback

A key component of CPBR is the solicitation of community feedback on the findings of the CNA, as well as the identification of particular services for implementation. Participants were given opportunities to preview and give feedback through meetings with the SP and GAB, and presented to additional community members during a community wide meeting. Table 1 outlines a description of the plan for each of the specific research activities and related outcomes that were undertaken during the CNA to fulfill the expectations of each phase outlined in Figure 1.

SERVICE DOMAIN SELECTION

Conducting a needs assessment is an effective method of community empowerment and decision-making in the development of a plan for a system of care (Corona et al., 2009; Warheit, Bell, & Schwab, 1977). For the community members, the process of researching, selecting, and crafting a service system can be an engaging and inspirational process. These experiences are relatively uncommon for GLBTQ youths or youth providers who are often outside the margins of decision-making. The CNA supported the community-building intent of the planning process and ensured greater accuracy of the findings through the identification of youth needs. During all three phases, the data findings were taken back to the GAB and SP for confirmation of accuracy, which facilitated a continuous discussion of potential service domains; such as the need for housing, case management, mental health, medical services, and prevention services for GLBTQ youth. Once the primary service domains were envisioned, confirmed through data collection, and chosen by the planning committee, the selection of specific services was initiated. Even the Youth Speak Out survey was created in a way that allowed youths to prioritize services from a list generated from their qualitative responses (Berberet, 2006). The stakeholders recognized that inclusion of services would be contingent upon priorities, congruency with service domains, economic realities, and overall vision. During a half-day retreat that represented a community feedback loop, many were present to share their insights into services identified for inclusion in the system of care. At the end of this meeting, a decision was made to proceed with the following system of care.

A SYSTEM OF CARE: THE ALLIANCE FOR GLBTQ YOUTH

The following programs were identified through the CNA as the critical components of a system of care for GLBTQ Youth. This service continuum included several integrated programs for prevention and early intervention at the individual, family, and community level. Prevention Education workshops were designed to increase the awareness of GLBTQ youth issues and delivered in a variety of community environments. The flexible curriculum included an overview of GLBTQ youth development, direct strategies for program enhancement, and frank discussion of participant concerns. Workshops were tailored to both setting and audience. Youth Speaker Training consisted of public-speaking preparation to empower GLBTQ youth to share their stories. Trained youths then presented as part of the Prevention Education workshops. Youth Enrichment Events were safe socialization and skills-building programs that encouraged youth leadership development and self-expression. Activities such as dances, artistic workshops, and educational sessions were delivered through provider agencies. Care Coordination consisted of individualized guidance, support, and critical linkage to services in the community. Highly trained Care Coordinators helped GLBTQ youths navigate a range of challenges on the path to healthy adulthood. The care coordination philosophy was founded on a strengths-based model. One Care Coordinator was specifically trained to work with families in a Family Specialist role that provided services to the entire county. Community-Based Group Counseling consisted of six to eight sessions of prevention focused discussion. These groups were usually offered weekly in various locations throughout the county. Group counseling has been recognized as an effective means of developing resiliency among vulnerable youths (Thompson, 2005). In a group counseling session, adolescents discussed their experiences, feelings, and ideas facilitated by a mental health professional. Topics such as healthy relationships, substance abuse prevention, healthy decision making, and coping skills were discussed in these confidential group settings. Individual Counseling with a mental health professional was offered for youths at provider agencies throughout the county. Counseling was individualized to address the needs determined during an initial psychosocial assessment. Housing or Reunification Services consisted of safe and supportive short-term shelter services for homeless GLBTQ youths in a unique collaboration between a youth homeless shelter and the Alliance Care Coordinators. This system of care was initially planned for 5 years; however if the initial evaluation determined that services were necessary for a longer duration because of youth utilization and community feedback, other funding would be sought.

DISCUSSION

Designing and implementing a CNA that incorporates the perspectives of various stakeholders represents both a daunting task and an incredible opportunity. The ultimate outcome of this CNA was to suggest a model for a service system that was truly rooted in the needs of the GLBTQ youth community. Future articles will evaluate the stages of implementation and the specific programmatic outcomes. However, a brief discussion of some of the challenges in conducting the needs assessment may be useful for other communities undertaking such processes.

Identifying the Target Population

Although our quest was to learn about the issues impacting GLBTQ youths for the purpose of developing a service system, limiting our research to that population was impossible. This was due to the hidden nature of the population, the developmental identity stages that GLBTQ youths navigate in idiosyncratic ways, and the dependency that youths have on adults within the service delivery system. Even determining sexual minority status became a challenge. All participants in the focus groups, including those identifying as straight allies, were able to provide insight on the needs of GLBTQ youth. In many cases, straight-identified participants provided important evidence based on the experiences of their close friends and family members. As the value of this information was clearly recognized, the researcher decided to include this information. Although the data cannot be considered fully representative of the general population of GLBTQ youths, every effort was made to identify hard to reach subpopulations. Identifying the population was made easier because the funder restricted the scope of the CNA to GLBTQ youths in MDC.

Identifying Needs

Initially determining what *needs* meant was also a challenge. Needs may vary based on many factors: including age, sexual orientation status, region, culture, and gender identity. Furthermore, there were substantive differences between youth and adult perceptions of need. Many key informants openly stated that they did not understand the current needs of GLBTQ youths, however, also felt that adult-driven services, such as counseling, would fully address any possible youth concerns. Although there was a wide range of articulated issues, youths in focus groups identified their greatest need as a place for safe socialization. The proposed system of care incorporated both perspectives by suggesting point of entry socialization activities (Youth Enrichment Events) that could meet youth needs but also facilitate access to more intense services, such as counseling, when necessary.

Moreover, there seemed to be an element of projective identification that emerged for some adults that was of interest. Often these adults seemed to believe strongly that they knew exactly what the youths needed. It was helpful to compare these perceptions with the youth data collected during the community engagement process. On some issues, the adult providers were completely accurate about youth needs, at other times their perspectives may have been true of an earlier generation, and occasionally these perceptions seemed to be a projection of their own fears and concerns. For example, some providers spoke about how the youths should always remain closeted in high school for fear that they could jeopardize their future careers. Parental acceptance was also one need that all interviewed adults stressed as a critical focus for program development in the form of parent and family counseling; yet only about half of the youths even mentioned parental acceptance as a potential area of intervention. Many youths stated that "my parents will never accept me;" "it's a waste of time." Such contradictory beliefs could constitute a barrier to service delivery for GLBTQ youths, because adults have the power to design and implement programs for youths, and such initiatives may not fully comprehend youths' true needs, and thus be less successful in addressing them. A system of care that is not solidly based on the true needs of the population could face substantive implementation issues. Adults and youths also differed in their beliefs of the approach to service delivery. Youths strongly articulated that programs should delivered in field-based locations that they could easily access, which was in contrast to adult service providers who felt that agency-based counseling was the best type of delivery structure.

However, there were issues on which youths and adults concurred. Youths that lived outside the downtown core also articulated a lack of GLBTQ-friendly youth services in their neighborhoods, which were often in higher crime areas. Adults agreed that inadequate public transportation was a challenge for youths trying to obtain services. Both adults and youths also agreed that confidentiality concerns with parents and families can be barriers to service acquisition for youths. As such, strategies to minimize these potential barriers were incorporated into the design of the service continuum in the form of the provision of field-based services and public transportation cards for youths enrolled in the program, as well as training for staff about how to reinforce the confidential nature of services with youths.

Competing Agendas: Mavericks

There is limited literature on the population of activists that generate and sustain community-based organizations and programs for marginalized populations (Donaldson, 2007; Epstein, 1981). These passionate activists have often had to overcome significant resistance to their efforts to advance social change (Mizrahi & Rosenthal, 1998), a situation that often solidifies their identities as advocates. This approach may be particularly important for populations with limited representation, such as GLBTQ youth, that struggle with high levels of community-based stigma (Epstein, 1999). The advocates involved in the SP often had strong personalities articulating competing agendas, as well conflicting perceptions of needs. Such mavericks often had less experience working on community collaborations because such opportunities were less available to them. In many cases, these individuals had no experience working collaboratively on projects in which they were both part of the leadership and a component of the service delivery system. Although these maverick characteristics represent important and valuable catalysts to community development (Rubin & Rubin, 2008), there are times when competing agendas and personalities create challenges in developing community cohesion (Zald, 1969). To strengthen the SP, it became important to reiterate their individual efforts while stressing the overall research and program vision.

During many stages of research and program planning, the members of the community, many of whom represented particular organizations, would advocate for their agency's preferred approach to service delivery (e.g., the counseling agencies felt that the majority of the needs identified would be rectified through counseling). During these times, a significant amount of skilled facilitation was required. For example, during a SP forum convened to discuss the proposed service delivery plan, a traditional mental health agency brought three representatives, two with limited history of the community process. During the meeting, one of these individuals was incredibly disruptive and disrespectful because of her dissatisfaction with the amount of allocated services that were both adult-directed and mental health focused. This situation required strong limit setting on behalf of the facilitator and the opportunity for feedback from all of the invested parties, which meant that the meeting went over schedule until consensus was achieved. Because the objective was to design a service system for GLBTQ youths that was intended to have multiple levels of service across an expansive county, thus requiring significant interagency participation, extreme care was taken to ensure consensus among those involved. For example, two of the participating agencies had a long history of providing programs for adults to sensitize them about the needs of GLBTQ youth, and both wanted to be the sole agency providing those services for the SP. To address this conflict, several one-on-one meetings were facilitated where clearly defined service boundaries were articulated so that one agency provided sensitivity training within the school system and the other provided similar training in community-based agencies that were not schools. Such choreographed activities that incorporate the history and agendas of individual agencies while maintaining a vision of the collective potential are important to the slow and shaky development of a SP.

CONCLUSION

Developing service consortiums and programs designed to provide essential services for vulnerable and stigmatized populations with limited data is a challenge. It is essential to plan a system of care, yet strategies for community engagement in a community planning process need further development. Needs assessments can assist dramatically in the growth of community cohesion and the development and implementation of a system of care based on CBPR. Widespread CNAs for GLBTQ youths have been limited partially due to challenges in obtaining concurrent funding for both research and program development. This graduated CNA utilized both qualitative and quantitative approaches to elicit a significant amount of data about GLBTQ youth needs and available resources. Further, this CNA strove to fully engage both members of the target population and service providers as decision makers in the research to develop an applicable system of care for GLBTQ youth.

Such partnerships were often tenuous and possessed significant challenges in both implementing the needs assessment and uncovering the needs of the youth. In many cases, these efforts determined that needs were not being met by existing programs and that many of the needed programs simply did not exist. The CNA did not uncover services that existed yet were not needed, but this could be attributed to the general consensus that there was an overall lack of specific services for this population. Thus, as evidenced in the proposed service delivery model, new programs had to be created to meet the needs. The process of conducting a comprehensive and collaborative CNA is challenging, yet the process is critical to creating systems of care that are relevant for, and sensitive to, marginalized populations.

REFERENCES

Ahsan, N. (2008). *Sustaining neighborhood change*. Retrieved from http://www. aecf.org/~/media/PublicationFiles/ Authentic_guide_r14.pdf.

Berberet, H. M. (2006). Putting the pieces together for queer youth: A model of integrated assessment of need and program planning. *Child Welfare Journal.Special Issue: LGBTQ Youth in Child Welfare, 85*, 361–384.

Bontempo, D. E., & D'Augelli, A. R. (2002). Effects of at-school victimization and sexual orientation on lesbian, gay, or bisexual youths' health risk behavior. *Journal of Adolescent Health, 30*, 364–374.

Clark, V. L. P., Creswell, J. W., Green, D. O., & Shope, R. J. (Eds.). (2008). *Mixing quantitative and qualitative approaches: An introduction to emergent mixed methods research*. New York, NY: Guilford.

Corona, R., Gonzalez, T., Cohen, R., Edwards, C., & Edmonds, T. (2009). Richmond Latino needs assessment: A community-university partnership to identify health concerns and service needs for Latino youth. *Journal of Community Health, 34,*195–201.

Craig, S. L., & Attonito, J. (2008). *Community assessment report: Gay, lesbian, bisexual and transgender organizations in Miami-Dade County*. Unpublished manuscript.

Creswell, J. W. (1998). *Qualitative inquiry and research design: Choosing among five traditions*. Thousand Oaks, CA: Sage.

Creswell, J. W. (2009). *Research design: Qualitative, quantitative, and mixed methods approaches* (3rd ed.). Thousand Oaks, CA: Sage.

D'Augelli, A. R., & Grossman, A. (2001). Disclosure of sexual orientation, victimization, and mental health among lesbian, gay, and bisexual older adults. *Journal of Interpersonal Violence, 16*, 1008–1027.

D'Augelli, A. R., Grossman, A. H., & Starks, M. T. (2008). Families of gay, lesbian, and bisexual youth: What do parents and siblings know and how do they react? *Journal of GLBT Family Studies, 4*(1), 95–115.

Dentato, M., Craig, S. L., & Smith, M. (2010). The vital role of social workers in community partnerships: The Alliance for Gay, Lesbian, Bisexual, Transgender and Questioning Youth. *Child & Adolescent Social Work Journal, 27*, 323–324.

Denzin, N., & Lincoln, Y. (2008). *Strategies of qualitative inquiry* (3rd ed.). Thousand Oaks, CA: Sage.

Donaldson, L. P. (2007). Advocacy by nonprofit human services: Organizational factors as correlates to advocacy behavior. *Journal of Community Practice, 15,*139–158.

Epstein, I. (1981). Advocates on advocacy: An exploratory study. *Social Work Research and Abstracts, 17,* 5–12.

Epstein, S. (1999). Gay and lesbian movements in the United States: Dilemmas of identity, diversity, and political strategy. In B. Adam, J. J. Duyvendak, & A. Krouwel (Eds.), *The global emergence of gay and lesbian politics* (pp. 30–90). Philadelphia, PA: Temple University Press.

Faulkner, A. H., & Cranston, K. (1998). Correlates of same-sex sexual behavior in a random sample of Massachusetts high school students. *American Journal of Public Health, 88,* 262–266.

Gilman, S. E., Cochran, S. D., Mays, V. M., Hughes, M., Ostrow, D., & Kessler, R. C. (2001). Risk of psychiatric disorders among individuals reporting same-sex sexual partners in the National Comorbidity Survey. *American Journal of Public Health, 91*, 933–939.

Herrell, R., Goldberg, J., True, W. R., Ramakrishnan, V., Lyons, M., Eisen, S., & Tsuang, M. (1999). Sexual orientation and suicidality co-twin control study in adult men. *Archives of General Psychiatry, 56*, 867–877.

Israel, B. A., Schulz, A., Parker, E., & Becker, A. B. (1998). Review of community-based research: assessing partnership approaches to improve public health. *Annual Review Public Health,* 19,a173–202.

Kelly, T. A., St. Lawrence, J. S., Diaz, Y. E., Stevenson, L. Y., Hauth, A. C., Brasfield, T. L., et al. (1991). HIV risk behavior reduction following intervention with keya opiniona leaders of population: an experimental analysis. *American Journal of Public Health,* 81, 168–171.

Lubman, D. I., Hides, L., & Elkins, K. (2008). Developing integrated models of care within the youth alcohol and other drug sectors. Australasian *Psychiatry: Publication of The Royal Australian and New Zealand College of Psychiatrists, 16* , 363–366.

Miami-Dade County Public Schools. (2009). Miami *Dade County Public Schools:Profile of student enrollment.* Retrieved from http://www.dadeschools.net/StudentEnroll/Calendars/enroll_stats_aor.asp.

Meyer, I. H. (2003). Prejudice, social stress, and mental health in lesbian, gay, and bisexual populations: Conceptual issues and research evidence. *PsychologicalBulletin,* 129, 674–697. doi: 10.1037/0033–2909.129.5.674

Mizrahi, T., & Rosenthal, B. (1998). A whole lot of organizing going on: The status and needs of organizers in community-ty-based organizations. *Journal of Community Practice, 5*, 1–24.

National Center for Youthlaw. (2003). Katie A.v.Bonta: An overview—Components of wraparound services (Appendix A). Retrieved from http://www.youthlaw. org/fileadmin/ncyl/youthlaw/litigation/Katie_A.2/Katie_A_-_Appendix_A. pdf. National Youth Advocacy Coalition. (2004).

National *health survey of lesbian, gay.bisexual, transgender, and questioning* youth. Retrieved from www.nyac.org/ docs/ LGBTQ_whitepaper.pdf

Olorunnipa, T. (2009, October 4). South Florida gays more confident consumers. *Miami Herald.* Retrieved from http:// miamiherald.typepad.com/gaysouthflorida/2009/10/south-florida-gays-more-confident-consumers.html

Patton, M. Q. (1987). *How to use qualitative methods in evaluation.* Newbury Park, CA: Sage.

Patton, M. Q. (2002).Qualitative *research & evaluation methods* (3rd ed.). Thousand Oaks, CA.: Sage.

Rubin, H. J., & Rubin, I. (2008). Community *organizing and development* (4th ed.). Boston, MA: Pearson/Allyn & Bacon.

Siegel, L. M., Attkisson, C. C., & Carson, L. G. (1995). Need identification and program planning in the community context. In J. E. Tropman, J. L. Erlich & J. Rothman (Eds.), *Tactics and techniques of community intervention* (3rd ed., pp. 10–34). Itasca, IL: F. E. Peacock.

Slaght, E., & Schopler, J. H. (1994). Are quick and dirty community needs assessments better than no needs assessments? In M. Austin & J. I. Lowea(Eds.), *Controversial issues in communities and organizations* (pp. 142–157). Boston, MA: Allyn & Bacon.

Tandon, S. D., Phillips, K., Bordeaux, B., Bone, L., Bohrer, P., Cagney, K., et al. (2007). A vision for progress in community health partnerships. *Progress in Community Health Partnerships: Research, Education, and Action,* 11,a11–30.

Thompson,3R.%2005).Nurturing future generations: promoting resilience in children and adolescents through social, emotional, and cognitive skills (2nd ed.). New York, NY: Routledge.

Trinh-Shevrin, C., lslam, N., Tandon, S. D., Abesamis, N., Hoe-Asjoe, H., & Rey, M. (2007). Using communit-based participatory research as a guiding framework for health disparities research centers. Prog *Community Health Partnership,* 1, 195-205.

U.S. Census Bureau. *(2009).MapStats: Miami-Dade County* Flonda. Retxieved from http://www.fedstats.gov/qf/ states/12/12086.html

Warheit, G. J., Bell, R. A., & Schwab, J. J. (1977). *Needs assessment approaches:Concepts and methods.* Washington, DC: US Department of Health Education and Welfare.

Zald, M. (1969). Organizations as polities: An analysis of community organization agencies. In R. Kramer & Specht *(Eds.), Readings in community organization practice* (pp. 335–354). Englewood Cliffs, NJ: Prentice Hall.

Example D: MMAR Study in the Field of Higher Education (Sampson, 2010)

Student-negotiated Lesson Style

Richard J. Sampson
Gunma National College of Technology, Japan

Abstract

This paper presents an overview of action research conducted in an EFL university context, in which data was collected about students' past English learning experiences and hopes for college speaking classes. This data was then used to guide the lesson style for the semester. The study used three cycles of action research over one IS-week university semester, utilizing mixed-methods data collection and analysis. The results saw these groups of learners showing a strong preference for a communicative lesson style. Furthermore, the students' perception of their own speaking and communication ability showed a marked positive increase as a result of the change-actions involving student-centered experiential learning and goal-setting that evolved throughout the study.

Keywords

Action research, lesson style, motivation, negotiation, task-based learning

INTRODUCTION

Much has been written about the dearth of opportunity for students in Japanese secondary education to practically use English, as they need to commit six years studying English towards examination for university entrance (Aspinall, 2000; Clark, 2009; Fujimoto, 1999). Through this process, English is reduced in many cases to merely an artifact, much like data inputted into a mathematical formula (Ryan, 2009). The outcome is that many young adults, far from developing practical English communicative ability, instead develop a negative perception of their ability to use what they have spent so long memorizing. As Lightbown and Spada (1999) note, 'If the speaker's only reason for learning the second language is external pressure, internal motivation may be minimal and general attitudes towards learning may be negative' (56).

Corresponding author:

Richard J. Sampson, Gunma National College of Technology, 580 Toriba, Maebashi, Gunma, Japan 371–8530 [email: sampson@gen.gunma-ct.ac.jp]

Reprinted with permission from Sage Publications, Inc. Sampson, R. J. (2010). Student-negotiated lesson style. *RELC Journal*, 41(3), 283–299.

One challenge for teachers of university level English classes is to try to encourage students' self reflection of their abilities, to motivate students to use English language for free expression. This article will detail action research conducted between the author and a group of university students to this end – that is, identifying the problems and needs felt by the learners after previous learning experiences, exploring a change-action in methodology from the start of classes and follow-up change-actions throughout the semester, to try to address these recognized problems as a group.

LESSON STYLE

Literature detailing Asian learners' preferred approaches to learning falls into two broad camps – those arguing that set learning styles of Asian students disincline them towards communicative approaches (Kolarik, 2004; Park, 2002; Zhenhui, 2001), and those who assert that, when given the option, Asian students in fact prefer communicative approaches (Cheng, 2000; Falout, Murphey *et al:* 2008; Kikuchi, 2005; Littlewood, 2001).

In the first group, Kolarik (2004) contends that 'for Asian learners to adopt the communicative approach, they would have to make radical changes to some of their basic beliefs, values and consequent behaviour' (2). Furthermore, a review of literature detailing these Asian learning behaviours suggests that Asian students are subservient and passive, unwilling to volunteer opinions, do not participate fully in activities, and are less autonomous (Burrows, 2008; Xiao, 2006; Zhenhui, 2001). Indeed, Burrows (2008) argues that Japanese students will, 'if given the freedom to choose a preferred learning style...do so based on their own experience, thereby negating the purpose of being afforded the choice' (16). He continues that 'because of the strength of the cognitive and socio-cultural factors, they cannot be overcome regardless of the teaching methodology' (19).

In order for teachers to optimize lessons for Asian students, Zhenhui (2001) proposes that 'teachers may use assessment instruments such as the Myers-Briggs Type Indications Survey...the Keirsey Temperament Sorter...and the Classroom Work Style Survey, and then adapt their teaching style to match the results of such a student learning-style analysis (para. 15). However, in contrast to this, Clenton (1998) notes disparity between research that supports matching learning styles to teaching styles, and other research that suggests greater degrees of learning take place when there is a dissonance between learning style and teaching style.

Learners making up the learning group have a crucial impact on any learning experience. As Nunan (1989) states, 'the effectiveness of a language program will be dictated as much by the attitudes and expectations of the learners as by the specifications of the official curriculum' (176). Richards (2001), asserts the need to investigate learner factors as part of situation analysis, including such elements as:

- Learners' past language learning experiences.
- Learner expectations for the programme.
- Learners' views on language teaching.
- Learners' favoured learning approach (e.g., teacher-led, student-focused, group work).
- Learner expectations for roles of teachers, learners, and instructional materials.

(Adapted from Richards, 2001: 101–102).

Furthermore, Dornyei (2001a) discusses studies into learner demotivation (Chambers, 1993; Dornyei, 1998; Oxford, 1998; Ushioda, 1998) in which students noted teaching style and activities employed in lessons as the primary demotivating elements. This prompted Oxford to state, 'We must listen to our students. We must directly address the important teacher- and course-specific aspects mentioned by students if we want students to be motivated to learn' (1998, cited in Dornyei, 2001a: 150). Direct consultation with the learners might better inform the teacher of learners' expectations and preferences, as well as factors they might find motivating or demotivating, and allow the teacher to create a learning environment in which students feel more motivated to learn.

The preference to actually consult learners is apparent within literature which notes Asian students as supporting communicative methodology. Littlewood (2001) conducted research suggesting that, when asked, students from Asian cultures have positive attitudes towards more active, student-centered approaches to learning, and doubt traditional teacher-centered approaches. Kikuchi (2005) investigated, amongst other things, the preferred English lesson styles of Japanese university students and their expectations of teachers. The results indicated that these learners prefer 'to learn under so-called "communicative" conditions, with an emphasis on pair/group work, fun learning, individual help from teachers, with a positive classroom atmosphere' (11), and had a strong dislike of teacher-centered lessons. Falout, Murphey *et al.* (2008) asked Japanese university students to write 'advice letters' to their secondary-school English teachers. The results showed the majority 'expressed a desire for more chances and time to practice oral communication skills and less time on grammar...and less teacher-centered classrooms' (18). Cheng (2000) also questions assumptions about set learning-styles or behaviors of Asian students, and argues that, rather than being culturally-defined, learner behavior is more influenced by situation-specific elements. Such results tend to support the necessity of consulting directly with learners to construct the learning environment and lesson style.

ACTION RESEARCH

Classroom action research (AR) commences with the recognition of some problem or issue, development of a change process (the action) towards altering this reality, followed by reflection upon outcomes of this action. It may be cyclical, with reflection upon the change-action being used to instigate further change in a following cycle. As AR involves a specific problem in a specific context, results are not intended to be generaliz-able (Wallace, 1998); rather, it is more a process of group development and change, with the purpose of producing some benefit to the group.

The research described in this paper applied a number of different data-collection instruments to identify elements for change and assess effects of change-actions. Burns (2008, adapted from Altrichter, Posch & Somekh, 1993) asserts validity in AR as strengthened by triangulation, testing through practical action, research and educational aim compatibility, and ensuring fit between research design, data collection, and teaching (26). In particular, this final point led to selection of predominantly introspective methods in this research. Lack of an objective method for determining the extent information collected truly reflects processes conducted, thoughts, or perceptions of learners has seen validity of introspective methods questioned

(for discussion, see Nunan, 1992; Dornyei, 2007). However, as the project was largely participatory AR, that is to say, 'research which involves all relevant parties in actively examining together current action (which they experience as problematic) in order to change and improve it' (Wadsworth, 1998, para. 53), the subjective views of learners are of most importance in enacting change. Nunan (1992) states that diaries and journals as data collection tools 'provide insights into processes of learning which would be difficult, if not impossible, to obtain in any other way' (123). In order to collect views in a manner dovetailing teaching, learners were asked to complete a language learning autobiography to better inform design of the semester's classes, and the learning journal was suggested as a method for learners to reflect on their learning actions during classes, to think more deeply about their conduct in the learning process. In this way, it was hoped that the major data collection methods not only fit in with teaching, but attempted to enhance the learning process for students.

Burns (2008) argues that as AR focuses on a particular social situation, and does not try to produce results which may be generalized, statistical analyses are not used (11–12). As data collection is used to inform a change-action for a particular social group, detailed inferential statistics are somewhat beside the point. From a practical perspective, quantitative data elicitation methods were employed to provide triangulation, but kept relatively simple so as to most effectively inform the change-action without interfering with student learning.

During the course of the study, the following research questions evolved throughout three cycles (see further discussion below):

1. In what ways will information about students' past English learning experiences and hopes for college English lesson style guide design of motivating lessons? (CYCLE 1).

2. What elements of Task-based (TBL) lessons might students perceive as motivating? (CYCLE 2,3).

3. In what ways will students' perception of speaking ability be affected through introduction of TBL lessons? (CYCLE 2, 3).

4. In what ways will students' awareness of goal-motivated behavior be affected through introduction to a goal-setting framework? (CYCLE 3).

METHOD

Context and Participants

This research was conducted at a women's university in Japan through Interpersonal Communication classes, using the topically-organized Touchstone 4 textbook (McCarthy, McCarten and Sandiford, 2006). The medium of instruction was English. The first year students (average age 19) came from the Faculty of International Communication, and were in the researcher's classes. There were 24 students in 2 different classes, of which 22 agreed to take part in the research. The students' TOEIC scores ranged from 240 to 500 (TOEIC is a test of English language skills for business, administered by Educational Testing Service).

Sources of Data

In the course of this study, AR is used by the learning group to denote a problem with regards to learning in a classroom EFL setting. As a result of this, a total of three cycles of AR were conducted involving a number of data-collection instruments to provide triangulation, with each cycle building upon data from the previous cycle to implement some change action.

CYCLE I

In the initial class of the semester, students were asked to complete the Lesson Style Questionnaire, rating their preferences for lesson and teaching style on a semantic differential scale survey (see Appendix 1). Concurrently, students were asked to complete the Language Learning Autobiography, a free-writing exercise (see Appendix 2). A totaling of scores of the Lesson Style Questionnaire was conducted. The Language Learning Autobiography underwent qualitative content analysis – that is, the teacher-researcher read over the written texts a number of times, highlighting different phrases across the texts that reflected categories of interest to the change-action. These were allocated codes, and further refined into groupings to represent the main themes emergent from the texts. This data informed a change-action for the second cycle – used to discern the type of lesson style that students wanted to participate in.

CYCLE 2

Based on the data from Cycle 1, task-based lessons built around Nunan's (2004) and Willis and Willis' (2007) TBL conceptions were introduced. As such, lessons had students using language in context to complete a variety of tasks, individually or in small groups. Students were asked to complete an entry in the Learning Journal immediately after each lesson, with reflection upon the activities and learning during the class (see Appendix 3). These entries were collected after four weeks, exposed to qualitative content analysis, and used to determine change-action for Cycle 3.

CYCLE 3

As a result of data analysis from Cycle 2, students were asked to complete the Goal Setting outline by the following class and implement action to achieve their goals over the next 3 classes. Concurrently, students also continued to write in the Learning Journal. Again, after four classes, these two instruments were collected and underwent qualitative content analysis. The themes emergent from the Learning Journal were used to create a Learning Experience Questionnaire in an attempt at triangulating results. Due to restraints imposed by the assessment period for students, no new change-action was introduced after this. However, students continued to use the Learning Journal for remaining sessions. Finally, Learning Journals were collected, the Learning Experience Questionnaire was completed by students, and the data sources underwent qualitative content analysis and a totaling of scores.

RESULTS AND DISCUSSION

Research Question 1: *In what ways will information about students' past English learning experiences and hopes for college English lesson style guide design of motivating lessons? (CYCLE 1)*

Students' writing about past English learning experiences and hopes for college English lesson style allowed the teacher to more accurately match learner expectations. Firstly, the Language Learning Autobiography (LLA) provided a great deal of information about motivating and demotivating factors from students' previous experiences of English classrooms.

Noted demotivating elements included lack of student speaking during English classes, teacher-centered classes, and class-style being tailored towards preparation for university entrance exams. For example, one student noted the frustration of having no speaking activities in classes:

I studied English by mainly reading textbooks and writing some sentences by myself. I like writing very much. However, when speaking English, I am confused and can't speak well. Language is a communication tool, so it's useless if I can't make myself understood.

With regards to classes being teacher-centered, students noted bluntly that 'the teacher was speaking [for] one hour. We felt very very sleepy.' One student painted a clear picture:

Only the teacher talked in front of everyone during classes. It seemed a one-sided class for me. Some students listened very hard, but not all the students. Some students were studying another subject, sleeping, or even using their cellular phones.

Overall, students showed a strong aversion to the teacher-centered approach of secondary classes. Students perceived English studied at high school as being merely for exams, rather than practical English, and they were clear as to the effects:

I have learned English for entrance exams, so I studied only writing (including reading, grammar, words, etc...). Because of this, I can't speak English. I have no confidence in my speaking.

The main themes emerging that related to positive motivation towards English lessons involved (rare) occasions of student speaking and, interestingly, the generally negative nature of students' secondary English learning experience itself. With regards to speaking, one student noted:

I and my classmates did discussion in English. We exchanged our thinking about international relation. I always tried to speak English with native speaker. These experiences [gave] me a lot of knowledge.

Intriguingly, the lack of practical communication during secondary English classes led to many students commenting about conversely being motivated to learn in university speaking classes:

I didn't learn much [in high school], so I'm going to study speaking hard at university!

| FIGURE 1 | **Graphical Representation of Lesson Style Questionnaire Results** |

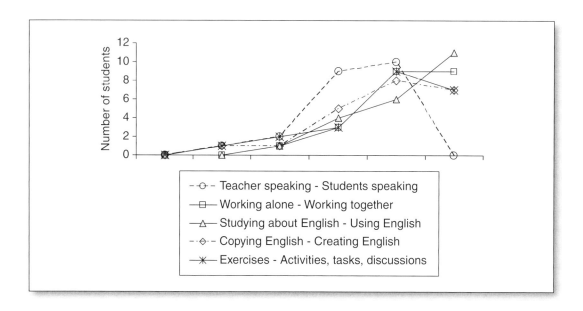

One student, after writing about the lack of speaking at high school, even remarked upon motivation towards career choice:

Thanks to boring English classes at high school, I became to want to become an English teacher who can teach English to students more interestingly. I think more and more students hate English classes if the boring classes continue.

The general theme apparent from the LLA was that students were dissatisfied with teacher-centered, non-communicative lessons, which led to almost every student writing negative perceptions of their speaking ability, such as:

I want to communicate in English, but I don't have that power.

I CAN'T speak English! I [have] no confidence in my speaking.

The Lesson Style Questionnaire (LSQ), inquiring about student hopes for college lesson style, produced results that seemed to confirm data from the LLA. As can be seen from Figure 1 above, students marked between two extremes on average closer to phrases reflecting a more student-centered, communicative lesson style.

This data collection guided the teacher-researcher in determining that, first, despite (or perhaps due to) years of teacher-centered English lessons with little communicative language usage, students wanted

| **FIGURE 2** | **Student Perception of Motivating Qualities of Tasks (LEQ)** |

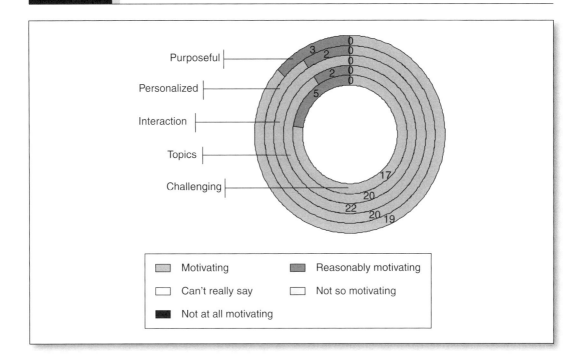

more student-centered, communicative lessons. Second, the qualitative data of the LLA allowed the teacher-researcher to glimpse the very apparent negative perception students held of their English speaking ability. Resultantly, the teacher-researcher was guided by information collected from students towards a lesson style providing students with more opportunity for student-centered, meaningful, communicative language use: that of TBL. It was hoped that the successful application of language that students experienced in this environment might lead to an alteration in perception of their own English communicative ability. As Dornyei (2001b: 57) states, 'we do things best if we believe we can succeed', and, in turn, 'the simplest way to ensure that students expect success is to make sure that they achieve it consistently' (Brophy, 1998: 60).

Research Question 2: *What elements of TBL lessons might students perceive as motivating? (CYCLE 2, 3).*

Through the Learning Journal (L J), there were a number of themes apparent regarding elements of TBL lesson style that students perceived as motivating. In order to confirm these themes at the end of the final cycle, a section of the Learning Experience Questionnaire (LEQ) was devoted to surveying these perceptions (see Figure 2 above), along with an open-ended section. As a result, three main themes emerged as significant from the data: that of personalization, topic-matching, and purposeful language use through interaction. Each of these will be discussed in turn below.

PERSONALIZATION

Students made frequent mention in the LJ of the enjoyment of using English to discover about classmates and the teacher through a range of activities that were personalized. Reasons were threefold: First, students felt more capable of interacting in English, as topics were directly related to themselves. As one student asserts: 'It was fun to talk about own experiences with each other. I felt free in the class, so I wasn't nervous.' Second, students focused not on language, but on the use of language to convey personalized meaning: 'Today's class was very fun because we were talking about other people. [Student 1] and I were talking about the present for [Student 2]. We thought the present to give her because we want her to be pleased. To think was very interesting!!!' Lastly, personalized language use gave rise to student realization about fundamental elements of communication, which in turn seemed to increase their motivation to talk with others: 'Today I was able to find a lot of common points with [Student]. I realized that it was important that I find out a common point to enliven conversation. So, I want to talk with more classmates and know their common points.'

TOPIC-MATCHING

There were some topics in the textbook mentioned by students as particularly interesting and motivating — one topic dealing with fashion, and two topics dealing with foreign cultures, the latter of which would be expected to a certain degree in an EFL setting. These topics provided motivation for students to further develop their English ability so that they might be able to go abroad and interact with speakers from other cultures. As one student remarked with reference to a section on different cultures:

Recently, we do some activities about a lot of foreign countries. So, I usually want to go there! Therefore, I must study and improve my ability of English. I feel I could use more English in today's class than ever before!

Another student mentions actually visualizing herself in a foreign country whilst studying these topics:

It was really interesting that there are a lot of different manners in the world. I didn't know people in Australia sometimes walk in bare feet. I would like to go to Australia, and be walking in a town in bare feet. I'll have great fun!

These topics seemed to awaken in students the realization that English might be a tool for communicating with people all around the world, and motivated them by giving a small glimpse of what lays beyond their own culture.

PURPOSEFUL LANGUAGE USE THROUGH INTERACTION

Purposeful language use through interaction became apparent as a motivational factor in three areas: First, through focusing upon a task or discussion rather than particular language forms, students used language purposefully and communicatively. This led to increased intrinsic motivation to complete the task, with students at times 'forgetting themselves' by getting so wrapped up in the task at hand:

> We tried to guess the secret information of other students. It was difficult, but it was so exciting!

> Today we thought about a party. Other groups' ideas were very funny, so I laughed a lot. For example, we have to wear three leaves at the party! However, if the party is held, I definitely wouldn't go there. This activity was so interesting, so I enjoyed learning!

Second, in many tasks students discussed some topic authentic for them, and had to make decisions together actually affecting something in the class or the university. This authentic, purposeful interaction was motivating for students:

> We discussed a topic in a group of four. Our topic was "this class." We discussed about "students use too much Japanese in class." We exchanged each opinion. Finally we came to the conclusion that we need to change our mind and take part in class more active. We presented to the class, and we want to translate ideas into action!

These kinds of real communication were motivating for students as they felt a strong attachment to topics affecting them everyday as students.

Last, although woven through the areas above, students found interaction itself stimulating. Through cooperation with classmates, students were able to encounter new ideas, thoughts, knowledge and ways of approaching tasks, providing motivation to further interact. As students commented:

> I learned various expressions from my partner. I found it is good activities to exchange my idea with my friends, so I want to express my idea more to classmates.

> I like group activities because it gives me new ideas. I'm always looking forward to the next activity.

The predominance of student-centered interaction in classes also led to students spending more time focused on learning, as, in the words of one student, they were spending no time 'staring into space,' as was noted in the LLA as common during teacher-centered learning at high school.

In general, students found the communicative, student-centered lesson style of TBL to be very appealing. There was a consensus which may be summarized best by the comment of one student:

> At last I know the fun of English. It was the class I looked forward to every week always. I usually didn't know what topic or activity we would do next week, but I knew I'd have a chance to be me in English. And I knew I could know about classmates.

This is mindful of Ushioda (2009), who discusses 'pedagogical practices which encourage students to develop and express their own identities through the language they are learning – that is, to be and become themselves' as being one aspect of autonomous learning (Ushioda, 2009: 223) – a factor that Dornyei (2001b) describes as promoting motivation.

The overwhelming response by students from the first cycle of action research was that they wanted a more student-centered, purposeful approach to English lessons. The positive feedback and noting of motivational elements of the introduced TBL lesson style discussed in this section provides at least some evidence that learners' instruction style preference which develops through socialization in learning institutes can be remolded. This would seem to refute, at least in part, generalized claims that particular teaching methods are not appropriate in certain contexts due to learners' instruction style preference (see, for e.g., Burrows, 2008). Students in this study seemed to want to adapt and become re-socialized into the new instructional style – they chose it from the start of the course, and consistently made positive comments about it throughout the course. As might be summarized by Brophy (1998):

> Each person has a unique motivational system, developed in response to experiences and to socialization from significant others [such as]...teachers. Therefore, rather than just accommodate classroom practices to students' existing motivational patterns, teachers can *shape* these patterns through socialization designed to develop students' motivation to learn (Brophy, 1998: 168 — italics in original).

Research Question 3: *In what ways will students' perception of speaking ability be affected through introduction of TBL lessons? (CYCLE 2, 3).*

| FIGURE 3 | **Student Speaking Perception at the End of Cycle 3 (LEQ)** |

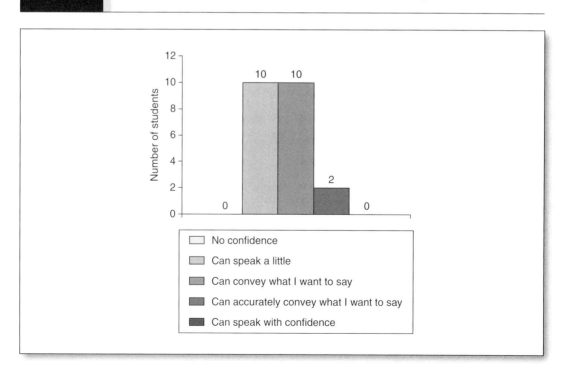

Words and phrases such as 'can't', 'not possible', and 'no confidence' were the mainstays of initial student attestations of speaking ability mentioned in reference to research question one. As a result, through change-actions introducing a lesson style with more opportunity for practical use of English, it was hoped by the teacher-researcher that a positive change in student perceptions of speaking ability might occur.

However, LJ entries from the initial weeks of the course saw students still reflecting negatively:

I couldn't understand when I heard [another student's] question.

I couldn't express myself in English, [even though] I tried hard.

You [the teacher] speak so fast, I don't know what to do.

As the weeks passed, and as students got used to the teacher and lesson style, comments changed:

Recently I can understand what you [the teacher] say!

I could talk with a lot of English compared to last week. I want to do my best with this condition!

I became to like speaking in English.

By the end of the course it could be seen that all students had a much more positive perception of their speaking ability, as partly evident in results from the corresponding section of the LEQ.

Entries from the open-ended section of the LEQ and final weeks of the LJ also confirmed a change in attitude towards spoken communication. Students noted 'my feeling of discomfort towards speaking has disappeared', and this was due to a new perception of using English for communication:

Before, I thought "They won't understand [what I want to say] anyway" so I hesitated to speak, but now, even if my grammar has lots of mistakes, I've become to just try to convey what I want to say somehow.

I don't really think my actual English knowledge has changed that much, but my motivation towards communicating in any way what I want to say has a lot!

The apparent degree to which students altered their perception, and indeed placed a new emphasis on trying to communicate over literal English speaking ability was a very positive outcome of the implemented change-action. Lack of any quantitative measure of student perception of speaking ability before the change actions commenced limits ability to compare degree of change through the corresponding LEQ section. However, it seems from qualitative data collected over the semester that students gained confidence in their ability to communicate by actually communicating. The importance of perceived ability has been noted in a study with Japanese students by Hashimoto (2002). Hashimoto concluded that 'the largest single effect was obtained from perceived competence to motivation' which suggested that 'increased perceived competence will lead to increased motivation which in turn affects frequency of L2 use in the classroom' (2002: 57). As such, it is hoped that students in this AR have made very positive progress through an upward-spiraling cycle that will see motivation, second-language use, and perceived ability all increasing concomitantly.

Research Question 4: *If students are introduced to a specific goal-setting framework, in what ways will students' awareness of goal-motivated behaviour be affected? (CYCLE 3).*

At the end of Cycle 2 it became apparent that many students were using the LJ to reflect upon what they did in lessons, and then setting goals for the following lesson(s) based on these reflections. Whilst this was a positive step in self-motivation, the goal-setting was predominantly rather vague:

I should speak more English.

I'm not good at listening. I'd like to improve it in this class, so I'll listen hard.

As a result, students were introduced to an outline sheet based on the goal-setting ideas of Alderman (1999, adapted in Dornyei, 2001b). This included sections for selection of a specific goal, intended action, goal accomplishment recognition, predicted challenges, and reflection on goal-attainment attempts. Initially, students struggled to set goals. As the teacher-researcher noted in his research journal:

Here was I, thinking that students might be motivated by goal-setting! About half of them hadn't even completed the sheet before class.

However, after further clarification of the process, students did manage to set goals for themselves. In a later entry:

Coming from a system where knowledge is just "poured in" from the outside, and then expecting students to make clear goals for themselves...was perhaps a bit too much. This said, it seemed like for all students, at least they could recognize something they wanted to work on, and tried to...make some effort towards this goal.

Evidence from students' LJ, LEQ, and Goal Setting outlines was altogether positive. All students marked that the goal-setting exercise had been useful on the LEQ. One student, who (amongst others) created a large sign for herself stating 'No Japanese – Only English!' as part of her goal-setting remarked:

Today I tried to speak only English!! It is my goal, but my friends worked together. Thanks to them, I was able to use English better. Speaking only English was really difficult, but English skill is not improved without it. At next class, I want to use English more and more!

Another student with a similar goal stated:

As might be expected, when we are in Japan, we feel hesitation or embarrassment to use English, but once [we'd] decided "No Japanese!" in goal-setting, it became easier to feel like speaking English.

Consequently, there was a noticeable change in attitude – it provided motivation to make positive changes to behaviour to try to meet the goal. Through goal-setting, students became more focused on the small steps they could take towards their overall goal of English development.

There was also a noticeable theme attesting to the motivational power students felt from goal-setting. One student notes that, even though the goal-setting exercise was intended for only three class periods,

It became my goal for every class. Compared with when I was just taking classes [with no goal], when I made a specific goal for myself, I tackled lessons more enthusiastically.

Another student relates that:

In order to move closer to my goal, I did things like looking up words or phrases I wanted to use, and then I'd make opportunities to talk [using them] in classes.

It appears that, after students' many years of externally-regulated learning, the goal-setting provided a useful first step on the road to realization that they themselves have control over their own learning.

Through the goal-setting exercise, students were able to realize their own locus of learning. This would seem to link to motivational concepts of self-determination, in which learners must feel autonomy and competence to be intrinsically motivated. Niemiec and Ryan (2009) assert autonomy as referring to 'the experience of behavior as volitional and reflectively self-endorsed,' and competence as 'the experience of behavior as effectively enacted' (2009: 135). This internal locus of causality, where people believe that they are the instigators of their learning behaviour, is asserted to promote intrinsic motivation (Stipek, 2002). The goal-setting exercise, in encouraging students to enact some action towards the achievement of their own goal, may well have drawn students' attention to *their* central place in the learning environment. As Dickinson (1995, cited in Dornyei, 1998: 124) argues, 'enhanced motivation is conditional on learners taking responsibility for their own learning...and perceiving that their learning successes and failures are to be attributed to their own efforts and strategies rather than to factors outside their control'. The goal-setting exercise may have given the students in these classes some insight into this concept.

CONCLUSION

This research grew out of an idea that consulting with students as to their past language learning experiences might better inform matching student hopes to lesson style. The first cycle of AR revealed a strong preference on the part of students for a student-centered, interactive and communicative lesson style, and an overall negative perception of English speaking ability, both of which were a reaction to previous language learning experiences. Based on these data, the second action cycle saw a communicative task-based lesson style initiated, with a subsequent cycle introducing a framework for students to produce and enact specific goal-setting. Over a total of three cycles, the study confirmed through initial consultation with learners that they showed a preference for communicative lesson style, resulting in change-actions that saw a great increase in the positive perception of learner speaking ability and assisted students in realizing the personal locus of control over learning through a goal-setting exercise. A number of elements that students related as motivating from the communicative lesson style implemented also became apparent.

It must be noted that the students in this study, being all Japanese females who had elected to study English at the university level, are not representative of the majority of university EFL situations. Furthermore, limitations due to the individual personality differences of students, teacher characteristics and their influence on the motivation of students, and the narrow purpose of the study might be admitted. However, as an AR framework was applied, the results of the study are not intended to be generalizable, applying specifically to the particular groups detailed. It is hoped, though, that the study might encourage other teachers to involve learners more fully in the process of course development. After all, it is the learners who should be central to learning.

REFERENCES

Aspinall R (2000) Policies for 'internationalization' in the contemporary Japanese education system. *Studies in Language and Culture* 21(2): 3–21.

Brophy J (1998) *Motivating Students to Learn.* Boston, MA: McGraw-Hill.

Burns A (2008) *Exploring teaching through action research.* Paper presented at Thailand TESOL 2008. Retrieved 6 January 2009 from: http://www.professoranneburns.com/downloads/thaitesol 2008.pdf

Burrows C (2008) Socio-cultural barriers facing TBL in Japan. *The Language Teacher* 32(8): 15–19. Cheng XT (2000) Asian students' reticence revisited. *System* 28: 435–46.

Clark G (2009) What's wrong with the way English is taught in Japan? *The Japan Times Online,* 5 February. Retrieved 7 February 2009 from: http://search.japantimes.co.jp/cgi-bin/ eo20090205gc.html

Clenton J (1998) *Learning styles and the Japanese.* Masters dissertation, University of Sussex, Sussex. Retrieved from http://www.sussex.ac.uk/languages/documents/learningstylesjapanese.pdf

Dornyei Z (1998) Motivation in second and foreign language learning. *Language Teaching* 31: 117–35.

Dornyei Z (2001a) *Teaching and Researching Motivation.* Essex: Pearson Education Limited.

Dornyei Z (2001b) *Motivational Strategies in the Language Classroom.* Cambridge: Cambridge University Press.

Dornyei Z (2007) *Research Methods in Applied Linguistics.* Oxford: Oxford University Press.

Falout J, Murphey T, Elwood J, and Hood M (2008) Learner voices: reflections on secondary education. *The Language Teacher* 32(10): 18–19.

Fujimoto H (1999) *The examination backwash effect on English language education in Japan.* Retrieved 16 February 2009 from: http://www.brookes.ac.uk/schools/education/eal/jl-archive/ jl-bestof/13.pdf

Hashimoto Y (2002) Motivation and willingness to communicate as predictors of reported L2 use: the Japanese ESL context. *Second Language Studies* 20(2): 29–70.

Kikuchi K (2005) Student and teacher perceptions of learning needs: a cross analysis. *Shiken:JALT Testing & Evaluation SIG Newsletter* 9(2): 8–20.

Kolarik K (2004) *Loosening the grip on the communicative ideal – a cultural perspective.* Paper presented at the 17th English Australia Educational Conference, Adelaide. Retrieved 13 May 2009 from: http://www.englishaustralia.com.au/ ea_conference04/proceedings/pdf/Kolarik.pdf

Lightbown PM, Spada N (1999) *How Languages are Learned.* Oxford: Oxford University Press, rev. ed.

Littlewood W (2001) Students' attitudes to classroom English learning: a cross-cultural study. *Language Teaching Research* 5(1): 3–28.

McCarthy M, McCarten J, and Sandiford H (2006) *Touchstone 4.* Cambridge: Cambridge University Press.

Niemiec CP, Ryan RM (2009) Autonomy, competence, and relatedness in the classroom: applying self-determination theory to educational practice. *Theory and Research in Education* 7(2): 133–44.

Nunan D (1989) Hidden agendas: the role of the learner in programme implementation. In: Johnson RK (ed.) *The Second Language Curriculum.* New York: Cambridge University Press: 176–87.

Nunan D (1992) *Research methods in language learning.* Cambridge: Cambridge University Press.

Nunan D (2004) *Task-based language teaching.* Cambridge: Cambridge University Press.

Park C (2002) Crosscultural differences in learning styles of secondary English learners. *Bilingual Research Journal 26(2):* 213–29.

Richards J (2001) *Curriculum development in language teaching.* Cambridge: Cambridge University Press.

Ryan S (2009) Self and identity in L2 motivation in Japan: the ideal L2 self and Japanese learners of English. In: Dornyei Z, Ushioda E (eds) *Motivation, Language Identity and the L2 Self.* Bristol: Multilingual Matters 120–43.

Stipek D (2002) *Motivation to Learn: Integrating Theory and Practice.* Boston, MA: Allyn & Bacon, Fourth ed.

Ushioda E (2009) A person-in-context relational view of emergent motivation, self and identity. In: Dornyei Z, Ushioda E (eds) *Motivation, Language Identity and the L2 Self.* Bristol: Multilingual Matters, 215–28.

Wadsworth Y (1998) What is participatory action research? *Action Research International, Paper 2.* Retrieved 3 January 2009 from: http://www.scu.edu.au/schools/gcm/ar/ari/p-ywadsworth98. html

Wallace MJ (1998) *Action Research for Language Teachers.* Cambridge: Cambridge University Press.

Willis D, Willis J (2007) *Doing Task-based Teaching.* Oxford: Oxford University Press.

Xiao L (2006) Bridging the gap between teaching styles and learning styles: a cross-cultural perspective. *TESL-EJ* 10(3): 1–15.

Zhenhui R (2001) Matching teaching styles with learning styles in East Asian contexts. *The Internet TESL Journal* 7(7). Retrieved 21 June 2009 from: http://iteslj.org/Techniques/ Zhenhui-TeachingStyles.html

APPENDIX I: LESSON STYLE QUESTIONNAIRE

Please read each pair of ideas, and check (☑) a box for what kind of lessons you want. Would you prefer:

1. Teacher speaking	Students speaking together
2. Students working together	Students working alone
3. <u>Using</u> English	Studying <u>about</u> English
4. Copying English	Creating <u>your own</u> English
5. Activities, tasks, discussions	English exercises

APPENDIX 2: LANGUAGE LEARNING AUTOBIOGRAPHY (INTRODUCTION)

What was your experience of secondary-school English classes? Please write any ideas about your experience, for example:

What happened in an average class?

What did the teacher(s) do?

What did the students do?

What was something positive about classes for you? Why?

What was something negative about classes for you? Why?

APPENDIX 3: LEARNING JOURNAL (INTRODUCTION)

In Interpersonal Communication 1 you will be asked to keep a learning journal – a kind of diary about your classes.

I'd like you to reflect about what we did in class – think back, and write about (for example):

something you learned

something you enjoyed

something that was motivating

something that was challenging

something you want to try next lesson...

Please write an entry the same day as your class, and bring the journal to next week's class.

Example E: MMAR Study in the Field of Health Care (Montgomery et al., 2008)

BMC Health Services Research

Technical advance

Supported housing programs for persons with serious mental illness in rural northern communities: A mixed method evaluation

Phyllis Montgomery*[†1], Cheryl Forchuk[†2], Craig Duncan[†1], Don Rose[†3], Patricia H Bailey[†1] and Ramamohan Veluri[†4]

Address: [1]School of Nursing, Laurentian University, Ramsey Lake Road, Sudbury, Ontario, P3E 2C6, Canada, [2]Faculty of Health Sciences, Lawson Health Research Institute, University of Western Ontario, 1151 Richmond Street, Suite 2, Health Sciences Addition, H38 London, Ontario, N6A5C1, Canada , [3]Daphne Cockwell School of Nursing, Ryerson University, 350 Victoria Street, Toronto, Ontario, M5B 2K3, Canada and [4]Department of Psychiatry, University of Western Ontario and Northern Ontario School of Medicine 680 Kirkwood Drive, Sudbury, Ontario, P3E 1X3, Canada

Email: Phyllis Montgomery* – pmontgomery@laurentian.ca; Cheryl Forchuk – cforchuk@uwo.ca; Craig Duncan – cduncan@laurentian.ca; Don Rose – donrose@ryerson.ca; Patricia H Bailey – pbailey@laurentian.ca; Ramamohan Veluri – rveluri@normed.ca * Corresponding author "Equal contributors

Published: 24 July 2008

Received: 30 June 2008

Accepted 24 July 2008

BMC Health Services Research 2008, 8:156 doi:10.1186/1472–6963–8–156

Accepted: 24 July 2008

This article is available from: http://www.biomedcentral.eom/l472–6963/8/l56

Reprinted from Montgomery, P., Forchuk, C., Duncan, C., Rose, D., Bailey, P., & Veluri, R. (2008). Supported housing programs for persons with serious mental illness in rural northern communities: A mixed method evaluation. *BMC Health Services Research, 8*(156). doi: 10.1186/1472-6963-8-156.

Abstract

Background: During the past two decades, consumers, providers and policy makers have recognized the role of supported housing intervention for persons diagnosed with serious mental illness (SMI) to be able to live independently in the community. Much of supported housing research to date, however, has been conducted in large urban centers rather than northern and rural communities. Northern conditional and contextual issues such as rural poverty, lack of accessible mental health services, small or non-existing housing markets, lack of a continuum of support or housing services, and in some communities, a poor quality of housing challenge the viability of effective supported housing services. The current research proposal aims to describe and evaluate the processes and outcomes of supported housing programs for persons living with SMI in northern and rural communities from the perspective of clients, their families, and community providers.

Methods: This research will use a mixed method design guided by participatory action research. The study will be conducted over two years, in four stages. Stage I will involve setting up the research in each of the four northern sites. In Stage II a descriptive cross-sectional survey will be used to obtain information about the three client outcomes: housing history, quality of life and housing preference. In Stage III two participatory action strategies, focus groups and photo-voice, will be used to explore perceptions of supported housing services. In the last stage findings from the study will be re-presented to the participants, as well as other key community individuals in order to translate them into policy.

Conclusion: Supported housing intervention is a core feature of mental health care, and it requires evaluation. The lack of research in northern and rural SMI populations heightens the relevance of research findings for health service planning. The inclusion of multiple stakeholder groups, using a variety of data collection approaches, contributes to a comprehensive, systems-level examination of supported housing in smaller communities. It is anticipated that the study's findings will not only have utility across Ontario, but also Canada.

BACKGROUND

Homelessness is a major health-related problem in Canada [1,2]. The number of homeless individuals reported ranges from 14,000 [3], "tens of thousands" [4]. Research also shows homelessness is more prevalent amongst persons living with severe mental illness (SMI) than in the Canadian population at large [1,4–6]. Kirby and Keon [7] suggest that approximately 30% to 40% of homeless people have mental health problems. Of those, as many as 25% also have an addiction problem. Such statistics, however, cannot begin to speak to the stigma and discrimination that persons with SMI encounter while trying to secure safe and adequate housing.

An intervention to prevent homelessness for people living with SMI is the supported housing approach [8]. This approach values the interplay of client choice, community integration, and flexible support with regard to housing. Emphasis on normal housing, work and social networks requires the implementation of individualized and flexible care processes delineated by the clients' goals and preferences [1,9,10]. Consumers, providers and policy makers recognize the effectiveness of supported housing for realizing positive health outcomes. According to Forchuk, Ward-Griffin, Csiernik and Turner [11], supported housing for homeless persons with mental illness allows for connections with significant others in addition to providing a sense of safety and purposefulness. Yet little is known about what supported housing elements, individually or in combination, are most significant for patient success [12,13].

To date, supported housing research has been conducted primarily in urban settings, focusing on indicators such as service utilization, housing stability, and other financial measures [1,12]. Until the late 1990s much of the supported housing research being conducted was descriptive and focused on consumer characteristics and outcomes [14–16]. Rog [17] reviewed the research evidence regarding the effects of supported housing on patient outcomes. He found that existing research, divergent as it is, strongly suggests that persons with SMI can live successfully in a range of housing types. Supporting this view are other Canadian researchers [11,18–20]. What remains unknown is the effect of supported housing intervention on outcomes for rural clients [21].

Researchers have also examined mitigating variables such as consumers' preferences for housing and support [22–25]. A shared finding is that consumers preferred to live in their own place, either alone or with a significant other rather than with other mental health consumers. Goldman et al. [22], however, suggests a cautious interpretation of such a finding since prior studies used professional- rather than client-designed measures of consumer preference.

Although limited, available evidence suggests housing with supports has positive effects on the clients' quality of life. Matching consumers' needs to specific services is the most cost-effective approach [26,27]. Housing combined with appropriate supports stabilizes the lives of persons characterized as chronically homeless. For example, a one-year study by Clark and Rich [28]examined the impact of supported housing and case management on measures of housing status, mental health symptoms, substance use, physical health and quality of life. The researchers found that persons with high psychiatric symptom severity achieved a higher quality of life with the supported housing program than with case management alone. As well, they reported that persons with low and medium levels of psychiatric symptoms did just as well as those with case management alone. These findings reinforce the importance of matching service type to clients' needs rather than delivering a prescriptive program; an emphasis challenged by northern and rural communities' lack of appropriate, accessible supportive services.

The success of the supported housing intervention is influenced by the characteristics, circumstances and resources of each community. As Lamb and Bachrach [29]state, "there is no single kind of housing that can effectively meet the needs of all long-term mental health patients" (p. 1043). Persons with SMI require a range of housing and support options. Salient policy documents such as *Respecting Housing and Support* [30] and *Out of the Shadows at Last* [7], assert that enabling people with mental illness to live safely in the community requires three interconnected elements. These include more housing units, more assistance so that people can afford existing units, and more supportive services. The interplay among these three factors is by no means prescriptive, thereby reinforcing the "non-cookie cutter" feature of implementing supported housing with a person coping with SMI.

Implementation of housing with supports in northern and rural communities is further confronted by factors such as small or non-existent housing markets, "aging" demographic trends, rural poverty, quality of housing, lack of mental health care services, lack of a continuum of housing services and economic and labor force changes [31,32]. Smaller communities have housing issues that often receive little attention in regards to policy [33]. As well, geography, population density, and the availability of mental health services offer unique challenges to evaluation research in northern and rural communities. Nevertheless, literature examining the methodological issues associated with assessing community mental health programs suggests a new role for evaluation in community mental health [8,34,35].

Objective and aims

The authors of this study contend that evaluation research fosters insight not only on how inquiry constructs knowledge but on how we create "formative narratives" for change. Despite the available evidence about the effects of supported housing, it is still unclear what elements within a particular supported housing approach and environmental context (rural setting) facilitate effective service provision for persons with SMI. Researchers [21,32,33] recommend further study on the processes of supported housing programs to identify the key elements of effective rural housing programs and their relationship to outcomes such as mental status, social functioning and quality of life. In addition, more research exploring the significance of these elements from the perspectives of consumers, families and service providers is needed [12,14,17].

The overall objective of this research is to describe and evaluate the processes and outcomes of supported housing programs for persons living with a serious mental illness (SMI) in northeastern Ontario from the perspective of clients, their families and community workers. The research questions guiding this inquiry are as follows:

1. What are clients' quality of life, housing stability, and housing preferences?

2. For clients residing in four Northeastern communities, what differences occur in their quality of life, housing stability, and housing preference?

3. What are the differences between Northeastern clients' quality of life, housing stability, and housing preferences and a Southwestern comparison group drawn from a Community University Research Alliance (CURA) sample from London, Ontario?

4. What are clients'/families'/providers' perceptions of the elements of effective supported housing programs?

5. What supported housing services need to be changed in order to make the most difference in the day-to-day lives of clients?

This study will also generate hypotheses for future research.

Theoretical Framework

This research will be guided by Forchuk, Ward-Griffin and Turner [11]conceptualization of *Getting, Losing and Keeping Housing* (Figure 1), originating from the housing experiences of 90 psychiatric consumers living in urban and rural areas in southwest Ontario. Their housing experiences involved three phases: losing ground related to limited control over their basic human rights and inappropriate housing conditions; struggling to survive with the support of various community services; and gaining stability as a result of securing personal space and rebuiding relationships. The model illustrates overlapping boundaries between processes and outcomes associated with housing. For example, achievement of housing stability requires accessing and receiving support services. To further understand the processes of securing housing and its outcomes such as quality of

| FIGURE 1 | The overlapping phases within the "tornado" of mental illness (Forchuk et al, 2006). |

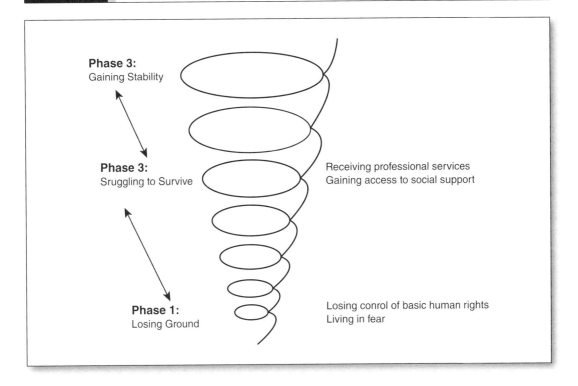

Phase 3:
Gaining Stability

Phase 3:
Sruggling to Survive

Receiving professional services
Gaining access to social support

Phase 1:
Losing Ground

Losing conrol of basic human rights
Living in fear

life, housing stability and housing preference, this conceptualization emphasizes listening to multiple perspectives (clients, families, and providers).

METHODS

Design

The study will use a mixed-methods design involving quantitative and qualitative methods that will be informed by participatory action research (PAR) (Figure 2). The combination of quantitative and qualitative methods will allow a more robust analysis [36] and provide multidimensional answers of maximum relevance to the research questions [37–39]. Quantitative data will provide baseline data related to sample characteristics, quality of life, housing stability and housing preference. The qualitative data will assist the researchers in further exploring the quantitative findings in relation to complex outcome variables such as quality of life [40]. Blending these approaches will allow for the findings to be considered within the context of perspectives of clients' and supported housing service providers. The study will be completed over a two-year period and will involve an iterative process

FIGURE 2	Sequential design procedure.

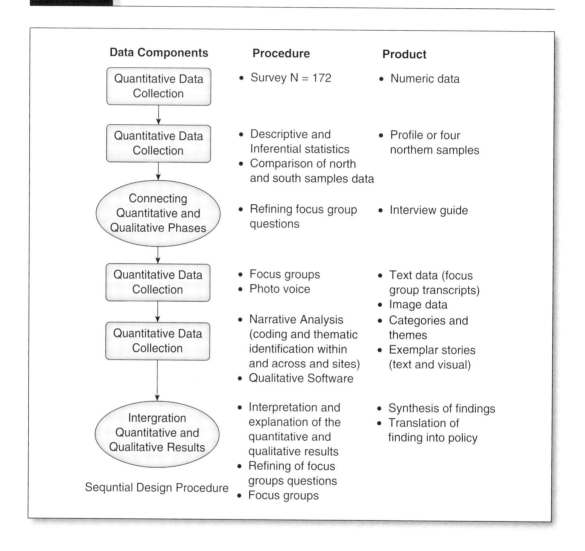

Sequntial Design Procedure

in four sequential stages: planning, two stages of data gathering, and knowledge synthesis and translation. Figure 3 illustrates more specifically how the project will be conducted in each phase. All phases will be conducted in consultation with an existing advisory committee, the Northern Homelessness Initiatives Network (NHIN): a committee established in 2000 for the purpose of creating, supporting, and sharing knowledge among housing services for persons with SMI. Their mandate is to build positive, professional relationships among supported housing agencies for people diagnosed with SMI who are living in northern Ontario. In preparation for this study, the network supported the pilot testing of photo-voice (a method detailed in Stage III below) in three housing programs.

Setting

The setting for this research is northeastern Ontario, a geographical area covering over 276,000 square kilometers. In each of the four districts, there is a variety of non-profit service or sets of services offering supported housing. Housing, scattered though each of the four communities, is not dependent on accepting support services, and the range of housing types varies across the four communities. Variation in supported housing implementation across the four communities is attributed to funding, availability and qualifications of service providers; knowledge uptake barriers; culture; and geography. Combined, over 500 persons with SMI are either receiving housing with supports or waiting to access such services. A shared program goal of all services is to assist persons with a SMI to integrate into the community by maintaining or improving a person's psychiatric functioning, independent living skills, and housing stability. This goal is consistent with both the elements and notions of preventing the "tornado" of mental illness [11]. Another shared feature is that the supported housing programs either operate under the mandate of the Canadian Mental Health Association, or the CMHA is at least involved with these programs and the agencies that administer them. Furthermore, each CMHA has an Executive Director who is a member of the NHIN, and all of these agencies will participate in the study.

Procedure

Stage I

This stage is particularly crucial as formal research has not been conducted in two of the four sites. Members of the research team, in consultation with the Executive Director and an identified research partner at each site, will collaborate concerning strategies to introduce the research to the supported housing service(s). Other activities include hiring a project coordinator and site data collectors; training research staff for data collection, data entry into software programs (SPSS and NVivo); meeting with NHIN; and securing ethical approval at each site (Figure 3).

Stage II

Stage II will address the first three research questions related to clients' quality of life, housing stability, and housing preference. A descriptive cross-sectional survey design and quota sampling will be used. To be eligible for inclusion in this study, participants must using or waiting for supported housing services, understand English, and be willing to provide informed consent. To be eligible for CMHA housing services, a client must have a SMI as defined by diagnosis, duration and disability [41]. A minimum sample size is 43 persons per site using the standard deviations and mean scores from the CURA data related to the Lehman Quality of Life scale with a power of .80 and an alpha of .05.

Data will be collected using four self-report survey tools: Demographic Profile; Lehman's Quality of Life Interview-Brief Version (LQOLI-BV) [42], Housing History Survey [43], and Consumer Housing Preference Survey Short Version (CHPSSV) [44]. The Demographic Profile consists of 10 items. The LQOLI measures clients'

FIGURE 3   **Project time-line.**

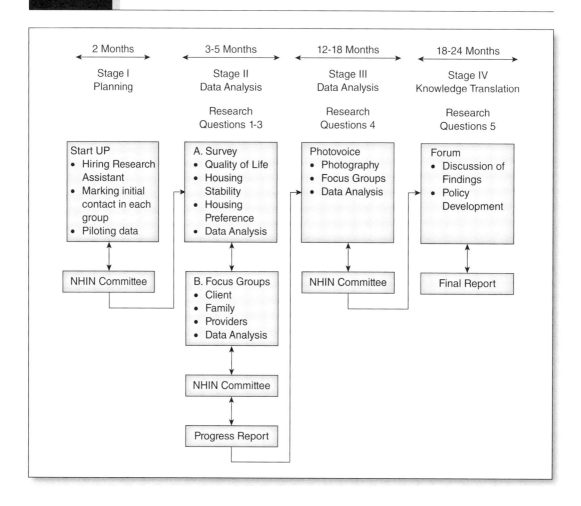

objective quality of life experiences and subjective feelings about these experiences in eight domains: residency, daily functioning, family relations, social relations, leisure activities, finances, safety and legal problems, work and school, and health. It is a structured self-report interview and takes approximately 30–45 minutes to complete. The brief version of the LQOLI to be used is reportedly easier to administer since clients are often more receptive to answering fewer questions. When used for individuals with chronic mental illnesses, the reported internal consistency of the LQOLI's various subscales, range from .86 to .90. The Housing History Survey was developed through a CURA on mental health and housing [43]. The form asks participants to list all their places of residency in the last two years, their duration at each residence, and whether the move was desirable. As well, they are asked to rate the housing on a 7-point satisfaction scale, 1 (delighted) to 7 (terrible). The fourth measure, the CHPSSV, was developed at the Centre for Community Change through Housing and Support (now known as the Centre for Community Change International). This is the same institute that pioneered Carling's notion supported housing [44]. The CHPSSV contains 22 questions about demographic information, current housing, preferred housing, preferred living companions and supports needed. All instruments will be administered by a trained researcher member in each site.

The study will be introduced to prospective client participants by familiar community mental health workers. Interested participants will be approached by a trained research member situated in each of the four sites. Informed consent will be obtained from all participants. During the consent process, participants will be informed that they may be contacted by the site's research member about participating in Stage III of the research study. Signed consent forms will be returned to the study's Project Coordinator for storage in a locked cabinet. Incentives for clients to participate will include strategies such as: transportation, forwarding of reminder letters for those with shared phone lines or no phones, and offering a $20.00 (Canadian) reimbursement.

Descriptive statistics will be used to describe the sample's characteristics and their quality of life, housing stability and housing preference. Results of the analysis will serve as the basis for discussion in the project's subsequent stages. A correlation matrix will examine the relationship between all major variables and selected demographic characteristics. Inferential statistics will be used to examine the differences and association among the four northern sites. The northern data will be matched to a comparison group drawn from a Community University Research Alliance (CURA) sample from London, Ontario. *T*-tests will be used to examine outcome differences between these groups.

Stage III

A participatory action method will explore research question four concerning clients', families', and providers' perceptions of supported housing in each community. Data will be collected through photo-voice and focus groups.

Photo-voice, a visual method, involves the use of cameras by participants. According to [45], the three goals of this strategy are: to enable individuals to record and reflect upon their everyday experiences; to promote discussion about their visual representations; and to heighten insight of the wider community including policy makers. This method has been shown to be effective for engaging vulnerable populations in research [46,47]. Quota sampling will be used to ensure that the resident sample is representative of the survey variables measured in Stage II. Eight clients from each site will be invited to participate in this stage of the study. Participants will be asked to take a minimum of 10 images addressing the following questions: Can you tell me a story about receiving housing services? What are the most important aspects of housing services for your housing stability? What are your concerns about the supported housing service? How might the supported housing services that you receive be improved? A focus group will be conducted at each site to allow participants to share and explain their photographs. The photographs will act as a visual cue for discussion about their supported housing experiences. It is anticipated that the focus group will run for less than two hours. Each focus group will be audiotaped and the stories relating the pictures to supported housing will be transcribed into text for the purpose of analysis.

Data will be entered into a software program. A narrative/ story analysis process will be used to analyze the partici- pants' interviews [48,49]. The underlying premise utilizing this analysis strategy is the recognition that individuals most effectively make sense of their everyday circumstances by telling stories [50]. This systematic story analysis process will help the researchers identify the processes of the supported housing programs that relate to quality of life, housing stability and housing preference within and across sites.

Focus groups [51] will be used to collect data from the perspectives of clients, their families and community mental health workers about their local supported housing program. Purposive sampling will be used to identify clients who are 18 years of age or older, family members and community mental health workers for separate focus groups. Focus group members will be recruited through announcements about the study posted in key locations such as libraries, survivor programs, housing services and psychiatric outpatient services. All potential participants who self-identify and meet the above-stated inclusion criteria will be contacted by the site research member, provided with more information about the study, and invited to participate. Incentives for participation will be included. The following questions for the focus groups will be discussed: What is the perception of receiving housing services? What are the aspects of the housing service that are most important and useful for housing stability? What are problems with the current approach? How can it be improved?

The size of each of the three focus groups will be eight to 10 participants. Each focus group will meet face-to-face once and the session will be facilitated by an experienced member of the research team. Another research member will take detailed notes and manage the process' mechanics, such as audio taping the session. It is anticipated that the focus group will run for approximately 1 1/2 to 2 hours. Food will be served at the focus group. Each focus group will be audio taped and transcribed into text for analysis purposes. The method of focus group data analysis will be the same process as used in photo-voice, narrative/story analysis.

Stage IV

Stage IV will address the remaining research question: What supported housing services need to be changed in order to make the most difference in the day-to-day lives of clients? In a one day forum involving clients, families, community workers, community mental health groups, mental health decision makers and politicians, focus group methodology will be used to translate the findings into meaningful policy. In preparation for the forum, the researchers, using a sequential explanatory strategy created by [52] (Figure 3) will synthesize the findings from stages II and III. A mixed group of participants will be asked to review current policies related to the study's findings and then they will be asked to discuss the perspectives to the following questions: What current policies are associated with the key findings? What policies are successful in preventing housing "tornados"? What changes are feasible? What new policies need to be developed and implemented? What support is needed for new policies to be effective? As above, each focus group will be audiotaped and transcribed into text for the purpose of analysis. Data analysis will be the narrative/story approach.

DISCUSSION

This project is relevant at a local and provincial level. There has been no evaluation of the supported housing programs for persons with SMI in the four Northeast Ontario communities participating in this project. At a provincial level, the lack of similar studies in rural SMI populations speaks to its originality. Involving the NHIN committee from the inception of this initiative resulted in a systems-level evaluation and an inclusion of a variety of data collection strategies. The project is also novel in that it will address a significant knowledge gap in the delivery of supported housing services in non-urban settings. It focus on the long-term needs of persons with SMI will contribute to understanding effective strategies within the boarder supported housing intervention.

COMPETING INTERESTS

The authors declare that they have no competing interests.

AUTHORS' CONTRIBUTIONS

All authors were involved in the writing and approving of the final manuscript.

ACKNOWLEDGEMENTS

This work is supported by the Ontario Mental Health Foundation. The authors acknowledge the ongoing support of NHIN and the community mental health clinical agencies involved in this project.

REFERENCES

1. Canadian Institute for Health Information: **Improving the Health of Canadians: Mental Health and Homelessness.** 2007 [http:// secure.cihi.ca/cihiweb/products/ mental_health_report_aug22_2007_e.pdf].
2. Vancouver Coastal Health: **A Mental Health & Addictions Supported Housing Framework.** 2006 [http://www. city.vancou ver.bc.ca/commsvcs/housing/supportivehousingstrategy/pdf/VCH-SuppHouFramework.pdf].
3. Statistics Canada: **Census Analysis Series, Collective Dwellings.** 2001 [http://www12.statcan.ca/english/census01 /Products/Analytic/ companion/coll/contents.cfm].
4. Hwang SW: **Homelessness and health.** *Canadian Medical Association Journal* 2001, **164(2)**:229–233.
5. Frankish CJ, Hwang SW, Quantz D: **Homelessness and health in Canada: Research lessons and priorities.** *Can J Public Health* 2005, **96(Suppl 2)**:S23-S29.
6. Public Health Agency of Canada: **The human face of mental health and mental illness in Canada.** 2006 [http:// www.phac-aspc.gc.ca/publicat/human-humain06/index-eng.php].
7. Kirby MJ, Keon WJ: **Out of the shadows at last: Transforming mental health, mental illness and addiction services in Canada.** 2006 [http://www.parl.gc.ca/39/1/parlbus/commbus/senate/com-e/soci-e/rep-e/rep-02may06-e.htm].
8. Perkins DV, Born DL, Raines JA, Galka SW: **Program evaluation from an ecological perspective: Supported employment services for persons with serious psychiatric disabilities.** *Psychiatric Rehabilitation Journal* 2005, **28(3)**:217–224.
9. National Association of State Mental Health Program Directors: **Mental health and recovery: What helps and what hinders: A national research project for the development of recovery facilitating system**

performance indicators. 2002 [http:// www.nasmhpd.org/nasmhpd_collections/collection5/publications/ntac_pubs/reports/MHSIPReport.pdf].

10. Nelson G, Hall BW, Walsh-Bowers T: **The relationship between housing characteristics, emotional well-being and the personal empowerment of psychiatric consumers/survivors.** *Community Mental Health Journal* 1998, **34(1)**:57–69.

11. Forchuk C, Ward-Griffin C, Csiernik R, Turner K: **Surviving the tornado of mental illness: Psychiatric survivors' experiences of getting, losing, and keeping housing.** *Psychiatric Services* 2006, **57(4)**:558–562.

12. Culhane DP, Metraux S, Hadley T: **Public service reductions associated with placement of homeless persons with severe mental illness in supportive housing.** *Housing Policy Debate* 2002, **13(1**107–163 [http://repository.upenn.edu/cgi/viewcontent.cgi?arti cle=I067&context=spp_papers].

13. Rog DJ, Randolph FL: **A multisite evaluation of supported housing: Lessons learned from cross-site collaboration.** *New Directives for Evaluation* 2002, **94**:61 –72.

14. Chilvers R, MacDonald GM, Hayes AA: **Supported housing for people with severe mental disorders.** *Cochrane Database Syst Rev* 2006:CD000453.

15. Fakhoury WKH, Murray A, Shepherd G, Priebe S: **Research in supported housing.** *Social Psychiatry and Psychiatric Epidemiology* 2002, **37**:301–315.

16. Fakhoury WKH, Priebe S, Quraishi M: **Goals of new long-stay patients in supported housing: A UK study.** *International Journal of Social Psychiatry* 2005, **51(1)**:45–54.

17. Rog DJ: **The evidence on supported housing.** *Psychiatric Rehabilitation Journal* 2004, **27(4)**:334–344.

18. Parkinson S, Nelson G, Horgan S: **From housing to homes: A review of the literature on housing approaches for psychiatric consumers/survivors.** *Canadian Journal of Community Mental Health* 1999, **18**:145–164.

19. Clarke J, Febbrara A, Hatzipantelis M, Nelson G: **Poetry and prose: Telling stories of formerly homeless mentally ill people.** *Qualitative Inquiry* 2005, **11(6)**:913–932.

20. Nelson G, Clarke J, Febbraro A, Hazipantelis M: **A narrative approach to the evaluation of supportive housing: Stories of homeless people who have experienced serious mental illness.** *Psychiatric Rehabilitation Journal* 2005, **29(2)**:98–104.

21. Forchuk C, Jensen E, Berman H, Csiernik R, Gorlick C, Ward-Griffin C, Montgomery P: **Rural issues and homelessness.** 2007.

22. Goldman HH, Rachuba L, VanTosh L: **Methods of assessing mental health consumer's preferences for housing and support service.** *Psychiatric Services* 1995, **46:**169–172.

23. Nelson G, Hall B, Forchuk C: **Current and preferred housing of psychiatric consumer/survivors.** *Canadian Journal of Community Mental Health* 1993, **22(1)**:5-I9.

24. Schutt RK, Goldfinger SM, Penk WE: **Satisfaction with residence and with life: When homeless mentally ill persons are housed.** *Evaluation and Program Planning* 1997, **20(2):** 185–194.

25. Tanzman B: **An overview of surveys of mental health consumers' preferences for housing and support services.** *Hosp Community Psychiatry* 1993, **44(5)**:450–455.

26. Goering P, Boydell K, Butterill D, Cochrane J, Durbin J, Rogers J, Trainor J, Wasylenki D: **Review of best practices in mental health reform.** 1997.

27. Goering P, Sylph J, Boyles S, Babiak T: **Supported housing: A consumer evaluation study.** *International Journal of Social Psychiatry* 1992, **38(2)**:107-119.

28. Clarke C, Rich AR: **Outcomes of homeless adults with mental illness in a housing program and in case management only.** *Psychiatric Services* 2003, **54(1)**:78–83.

29. Lamb HR, Bachrach LL: **Some perspectives on deinstitutionalization.** *Psychiatric Services* 200I, **52(8):** I039–1045.

30. Housing Task Force on the Policy Advisory Committee: **Policy document: Respecting housing and support.** 1995.

31. Bruce D: **Housing needs of low-income people living in rural areas.** 2003:1–6 [https://www03.cmhc-schl.gc.ca/b2c/b2c/init.do?lan guage=en&z_category=0/0000000012/0000000030/0000000032].

32. Canadian Mortgage and Housing Corporation: **Research highlights: Housing needs of low-income people living in rural areas: Literature review.** 2003:03–023 [http://www.cmhc-schl.gc.ca/publications/en/rh-pr/socio/socio03–012-e.pdf].

33. Seychuk C: **The invisibility, visible homelessness in a rural BC community.** 2004 [http://www.bcifv.org/resources/newsletter/ 2004/fall/invisible.shtml].

34. Hutchinson DS, Razzano L: **Multifaced perspectives on program evaluation for psychiatric rehabilitation services.** *Psychiatric Rehabilitation Journal* 2005, **28(3)**:207–208.

35. Kirsh B, Krupa T, Horgan S, Kelly D, Carr S: **Making it better: Building evaluation capacity in community mental health.** *Psychiatric Rehabilitation Journal* 2005, **28(3)**:234–241.

36. Burke Johnson R, Onwuegbuzie AJ, Turner LA: **Toward a definition of mixed methods research.** *journal of Mixed Methods Research* 2007, **1(2):**112–133.

37. Flemming K: **The knowledge base for evidence-based nursing: A role for mixed methods research?** *Advances in Nursing Science* 2007, **30(1)**:41–51.

38. Cloke P, Milbourne P: **Homelessness and rurality: 'Out-of-place' in purified space?** *Environment and Planning D: Society and Space* 2000, **18**:715–735.

39. Cloke P, Widdowfield RC, Milbourne P: **The hidden and emerging spaces of rural homelessness.** *Environment and Planning* 2000, **32**:77–90.

40. Creswell JW, Fetters MD, Ivankova NV: **Designing a mixed methods study in primary care.** *Ann Fam Med* 1999, **2(1**):7–12.

41. Ontario Ministry of Health and Long-Term Care: **Making it happen: Operational framework for the delivery of mental health services and supports.** 1999 [http://www.health.gov.on.ca/english/ public/program/mental health/mental reform/ makingithappen_mn.html].

42. Lehman AF: **Quality of life interview for the chronically mentally ill.** *Evaluation and Program Planning* 1988, **11(1**):51 –62.

43. Forchuk C, Turner K, Hall B, Wiktorowicz M, Hoch JS, Schofield R, Nelson G, Evoy L, Levitan E, Ward-Griffin C, Perry S, Csiernik R, Speechley M: **Partnerships in capacity building: Housing, community economic development, and psychiatric survivors.** 2001.

44. Carling P: *Return to community: Building support systems for people with psychiatric disabilities* New York, New York: Guilford Press; 1995.

45. Wang CC, Cash JL, Powers LS: **Who knows the streets as well as the homeless? Promoting personal and community action through photovoice.** *Health Promotion Practice* 2000, **1**:81–89.

46. Wang CC, Burris MA: **Photovoice: Concept, methodology, and use for participatory needs assessment.** *Health Education & Behavior* 1997, **24(3)**:369–387.

47. Deacon SA: **Creativity with quality research on families: New ideas for old method.** 2000, **4(3/4):** [http://http//www.nova.edu/ ssss/QR/QR4–3/deacon.html].

48. Bailey PH: **Death stories: Acute exacerbations of COPD.** *Qualitative Health Research* 2001, **11(3)**:322–338.

49. Bailey PH, Tilley S: **Storytelling and the interpretation of meaning in qualitative research.** *journal of Advanced Nursing* 2002, **38(6)**:574–583.

50. Bruner J: **The narrative construction of reality.** *Critical Inquiry* 1991, **18**:1–21.

51. Morgan D, Kreuger R: *The focus group kit: Thousand Oaks* California: Sage; 1997.

52. Ivankova NV, Creswell JW, Stick SL: **Using mixed methods: Sequential explanatory design: From theory to practice.** *Field Methods* 2006, **18(1)**:3–20.

PRE-PUBLICATION HISTORY

The pre-publication history for this paper can be accessed here: http://www.biomedcentral.com/1472-6963/8/156/pre pub

Publish with **BioMed Central** and every scientist can read your work free of charge

"BioMed Central will be the most significant development for disseminating the results of biomedical research in our lifetime."

Sir Paul Nurse, Cancer Research UK

Your research papers will be:

- available free of charge to the entire biomedical community
- peer reviewed and published immediately upon acceptance
- cited in PubMed and archived on PubMed Central
- yours — you keep the copyright

Submit your manuscript here: **BioMed**central
http://www.biomedcentral.com/info/publishing_adv.asp

GLOSSARY

Acting phase is a phase in the mixed methods methodological framework for action research during which an action/intervention plan that was informed by mixed methods inferences from the reconnaissance phase is implemented.

Action plan is "a framework or blueprint that is implemented to improve practice, conditions, or the environment in general" (Craig, 2009, p. 237).

Action research "is a participatory process concerned with developing practical knowing in the pursuit of worthwhile human purposes. It seeks to bring together action and reflection, theory and practice, in participation with others, in the pursuit of practical solutions to issues of pressing concern to people, and more generally, the flourishing of individual persons and their communities" (Reason & Bradbury, 2008, p. 4).

Advocacy lens is synonymous with **transformative-emancipatory framework.**

Between-strategies mixed methods data collection involves collecting quantitative and qualitative data using different methods (Teddlie & Tashakkori, 2009).

Capacity building in action research involves training of community members about the study goals and research methods to be employed in the study.

Change theory was presented by Kurt Lewin through a three-step model to a planned change: (1) "unfreezing" the existing situation to create conditions for the new behavior/change adoption, (2) "moving" to a planned action using an action research approach, and (3) "refreezing" or stabilizing the community to ensure sustainability of the taken action and new behavior/change (Burnes, 2004).

Codebook is a list of codes and their groupings into emergent categories and themes (Guest et al., 2012).

Coding is "identifying a meaningful segment of text [that] calls for some minimal representation of that meaning" in qualitative data analysis (Guest et al., 2012, p. 52).

Combined mixed methods data analysis is implemented to assess whether the results from the quantitative and qualitative study strands converge or diverge in addressing the posed research questions, and if any further analysis should be conducted to decrease the discrepancies in the joint data interpretation (Creswell & Plano Clark, 2011).

Community is defined broadly as inclusive of all types of communities from educational to professional to public. Community in this context includes any professional (e.g., an educational institution, a business firm, a hospital), charitable (e.g., a shelter for homeless people), or religious (e.g., a church) organization; neighborhoods made up of area residents (e.g., city, region, street, subdivision); or groups of people who share cultural, political, social, economic, and other interests (e.g., skinheads, gays, and lesbians).

Community-based action research "builds on the tradition of action research by embedding change oriented projects within a larger community of practitioners, consultants, and researchers" (Senge & Scharmer, 2001, p. 238).

Confirmability refers to the extent to which the study findings are shaped by participants' views and not by a researcher's bias (Lincoln & Guba, 1985).

Connected mixed methods data analysis is implemented by sequentially connecting or interlinking the results from the two chronological study strands with the purpose of explaining the joint results and creating a more in-depth understanding of the studied issue (Creswell & Plano Clark, 2011).

Constant comparative method involves comparing the data from all data sources in a given study segment by segment during the coding process in qualitative research (Strauss & Corbin, 1998).

Constructivist refers to "a perspective that defines knowledge as dependent upon human perception, and thus as never free from such influences as culture, history, and belief" (Hinchey, 2008, p. 20).

Credibility refers to the extent to which the study findings are believable and promote confidence in their "truth" (Lincoln & Guba, 1985).

Dependability refers to the extent to which the study findings are consistent and could be repeated (Lincoln & Guba, 1985).

Descriptive statistics focuses on describing and summarizing quantitative data with the purpose of identifying trends and patterns in the data and uncovering potential relationships among the variables.

Diagnosing phase is a phase in the mixed methods methodological framework for action research during which practitioner-researchers conceptualize the problem that requires solution in the workplace or other community setting and identify the rationale for investigating it by using both quantitative and qualitative methods.

Dialectic stance refers to a philosophical position that allows for the juxtaposition of different perspectives from multiple paradigms (Greene, 2009).

Epistemological refers to ways for knowing how the world/scientific investigation should work.

Evaluation phase is a phase in the mixed methods methodological framework for action research during which an action/intervention is evaluated using mixed methods to learn whether it produces the desired outcomes.

Fundamental principle of mixed methods research implies that "methods should be mixed in a way that has complementary strengths and nonoverlapping weaknesses" (Johnson & Turner, 2003, p. 299).

In vivo coding refers to using participants' actual words for code labels in qualitative data analysis.

Incompatibility thesis refers to the view that it is inappropriate to integrate quantitative and qualitative methods due to fundamental differences in the philosophical paradigms underlying those methods (Teddlie & Tashakkori, 2009).

Inductive data analysis in qualitative research aims at reducing the volume of information by systematically organizing the data into categories and themes from specific to general (Creswell, 2014; Mertler, 2012).

Inference quality refers to "standards for evaluating the quality of conclusions that are made on the basis of research findings" in a mixed methods study (Teddlie & Tashakkori, 2003, p. 287).

Inferential statistics focuses on making predictions or drawing conclusions about a larger population based on the data collected from a sample of this population (Vogt, 2005).

Integrated mixed methods action research (MMAR) question addresses an overall practical intent of an MMAR study, and foreshadows an integrated or a mixed methods approach to exploring the issue. It is answered by developing meta-inferences based on the collection and analysis of multiple forms of quantitative and qualitative data in the process of the whole MMAR study.

Integration refers to an explicit interrelating of the quantitative and qualitative methods in a study (Creswell & Plano Clark, 2011; Teddlie & Tashakkori, 2009).

Inter-coder agreement refers to the process when several researchers independently code select pieces of text data, and then compare the codes and emergent themes to resolve discrepancies.

Intermethod mixing refers to concurrent or sequential use of two or more methods, such as using questionnaires and observations in the same study (Johnson & Turner, 2003).

Interpretive consistency in Teddlie and Tashakkori's (2009) integrative framework for inference quality indicates the extent to which each conclusion follows the results obtained from the quantitative and qualitative study strands.

Intramethod mixing refers to "the concurrent or sequential use of a *single* method that includes both qualitative and quantitative components," such as using a questionnaire consisting of both open- and closed-ended items (Johnson & Turner, 2003, p. 298; emphasis in original).

Literature review map is "a visual picture (or figure) of the research literature on a topic that illustrates how a particular study contributes to the literature" (Creswell, 2014, p. 244).

Mental model is "the set of assumptions, understandings, predispositions, and values and beliefs with which a social inquirer approaches his or her work" (Greene, 2009, p. 53).

Merged mixed methods data analysis through data transformation implies transforming one type of data into another type for further analysis (Creswell & Plano Clark, 2011; Teddlie & Tashakkori, 2009).

Meta-inferences refer to study conclusions grounded in the integrated quantitative and qualitative results from the entire study (Teddlie & Tashakkori, 2009).

Mixed methods action research (MMAR) refers to action research studies that employ both quantitative and qualitative research methods within a mixed methods approach.

Mixed methods data analysis refers to methodological procedures related to integrating quantitative and qualitative analytical strategies in a mixed methods study (Creswell & Plano Clark, 2011; Greene, 2007; Teddlie & Tashakkori, 2009).

Mixed methods research is "research in which the investigator collects and analyzes data, integrates the findings, and draws inferences using both qualitative and quantitative approaches or methods in a single study or program of inquiry" (Tashakkori & Creswell, 2007, p. 4).

Mixed methods research question is an overarching integrated question that addresses an overall intent of a mixed methods study (Creswell & Plano Clark, 2011; Teddlie & Tashakkori, 2009).

Monitoring phase is a phase in the mixed methods methodological framework for action research during which practitioner-researchers make decisions about whether the revisions or further testing of an action/ intervention plan is needed based on mixed methods inferences from the evaluation phase.

Mono-method approaches refer to research approaches that employ either quantitative or qualitative methods.

Nonprobability sample refers to selecting large numbers of individuals in a nonrandom manner from those who are easily accessible; the focus is on potential study participants' accessibility and availability, although they may not be well representative of the studied population (Babbie, 2005; Creswell, 2012).

Philosophical assumptions are basic set of beliefs or assumptions that guide individuals' actions and research.

Planning phase is a phase in the mixed methods methodological framework for action research during which an action/intervention plan is developed based on mixed methods inferences from the reconnaissance phase.

Point of interface describes "the position in which the two methods join" in the process of the mixed methods study implementation (Morse & Niehaus, 2009, p. 25).

Pragmatism is a philosophical position that underscores the idea that what has practical and functional value is ultimately important and valid (Johnson & Onwuegbuzie, 2004; Maxcy, 2003).

Priority or weighting is the relative importance or weighting of quantitative and qualitative methods for answering the study's questions (Creswell & Plano Clark, 2011; Teddlie & Tashakkori, 2009).

Probability sample refers to selecting a large number of individuals from the population in a manner that provides equal opportunity for each individual to be chosen; the focus is on selecting study participants who are representative of the studied population (Babbie, 2005; Creswell, 2012).

Purpose statement is a succinct statement that conveys the overall intent of the study and advances its overall direction (Creswell, 2014; Johnson & Christensen, 2012).

Purposeful sample refers to intentionally selecting a small number of "information-rich" participants from those who have knowledge of or experience with the studied phenomenon; the focus is on generating in-depth information and understanding of individual experiences (Creswell, 2012; Patton, 2002).

Qualitative methods refer to the methods that collect and analyze narrative or text data expressed in words and images.

Qualitizing refers to the process when quantitative data are first analyzed using statistical methods to identify trends and relationships, then narrative categories are identified within each variable based on the distribution of scores (Creswell & Plano Clark, 2011; Teddlie & Tashakkori, 2009).

Quantitative methods refer to the methods that collect and analyze numeric data expressed in numbers or scores.

Quantitizing refers to the process when qualitative data are first analyzed inductively for codes, categories, and themes; then, depending on the level of data transformation, codes, categories, and/or themes are assigned numeric values, or frequency counts and are merged with the original quantitative data set for joint analysis (Creswell & Plano Clark, 2011; Teddlie & Tashakkori, 2009).

Quasi-mixed designs are designs "in which two types of data are collected (QUAL, QUAL), with little or no integration of the two types of findings or inferences from the study" (Teddlie & Tashakkori, 2009, p. 142).

Reconnaissance refers to the process of identifying a general idea and then examining "the idea carefully in the light of the means available" (Lewin, 1948b, p. 205).

Reconnaissance (fact-finding) phase is a phase in the mixed methods methodological framework for action research during which a preliminary assessment of the identified problem or issue is conducted using mixed methods in order to develop a plan of action/intervention.

Reliability is referred to as "the degree to which a test consistently measures whatever it is measuring" (Gay et al., 2006, p. 139).

Research ethics is a set of moral principles that are aimed at assisting researchers in conducting research ethically, particularly research involving human beings (Mertler, 2012).

Research hypotheses are statements that contain predictions about the outcomes of a relationship among variables and are used in a quantitative research approach (Creswell, 2012; Plano Clark & Badiee, 2010).

Research objectives are statements of intent that identify the goals researchers plan to achieve by undertaking the study (Creswell, 2012).

Research problem is a problem or issue that leads to a research study (Creswell, 2012; Johnson & Christensen, 2012).

Research questions stated in the question format narrow the study purpose to specific questions that researchers seek to answer in the research project (Creswell, 2012).

Sampling is the process of selecting units (e.g., events, people, groups, settings, artifacts) "in a manner that maximizes the researcher's ability to answer research questions that are set forth in a study" (Tashakkori & Teddlie, 2003, p. 715).

Saturation refers to the point in data collection and analysis when additional individuals or cases do not provide new information (Guest et al., 2006).

Stakeholders are those who have a stake in the issue engaged in the process of investigation to find effective solutions to resolve the problem (Stringer, 2014).

Statistics is "a set of procedures for describing, synthesizing, analyzing, and interpreting quantitative data" (Gay et al., 2006, p. 301).

Strand is component of a mixed methods study that encompasses the basic process of conducting quantitative or qualitative research: posing a question, collecting and analyzing data, and interpreting results (Creswell & Plano Clark, 2011; Teddlie & Tashakkori, 2009).

Sustainability in action research refers to reaching some level of human, social, economic, ecological stability through the development of competencies out of the action and the creation of new knowledge from the study (Coghlan & Brannick, 2010).

Timing is temporal relationship between the quantitative and qualitative strands within a study (Creswell & Plano Clark, 2011; Teddlie & Tashakkori, 2009).

Transferability refers to the extent to which the study findings are applicable to other contexts (Lincoln & Guba, 1985).

Transformative-emancipatory framework refers to a perspective that defines knowledge as influenced by "historical and contextual factors, with special emphasis on issues of power that can influence the achievement of social justice and avoidance of oppression" (Mertens, 2003, p. 120).

Triangulation is the process of finding corroborating evidence across multiple forms of data, study participants, researchers' views, and interpretations (Creswell, 2012; Denzin, 1978; Teddlie & Tashakkori, 2009).

True mixed methods designs are mixed methods designs in which there is an integration of quantitative and qualitative approaches at different stages in the study process (Teddlie & Tashakkori, 2009, p. 142).

Trustworthiness refers to accuracy or validity of the findings in a qualitative study instead of conventional validity and reliability used in quantitative research (Lincoln & Guba, 1985).

Validation refers to the process of assessing the rigor of the methodological procedures used in the study.

Validity is "the degree to which a test measures what it is supposed to measure, and, consequently, permits appropriate interpretation of the scores" (Gay et al., 2006, p. 134).

Variable is a characteristic or attribute that can be measured and that can change or vary (Creswell, 2012; Vogt, 2005).

Within-strategy mixed methods data collection refers to collecting both quantitative and qualitative data employing one strategy, such as using a survey instrument that includes close- and open-ended questions (Teddlie & Tashakkori, 2009).

Worldview is a basic set of beliefs or assumptions that guide the research process (Lincoln & Guba, 1985).

REFERENCES

Adelman, C. (1993). Kurt Lewin and the origins of action research. *Educational Action Research, 1*(1), 7–25.

Akintobi, T. H., Yancey, E. M., Daniels, P., Mayberry, R. M., Jacobs, D., & Berry, J. (2012). Using evaluability assessment and evaluation capacity-building to strengthen community-based preventive initiatives. *Journal of Health Care for the Poor and Underserved, 23,* 33–48.

Aldridge, J. M., Fraser, B. J., Bell, L., & Dorman, J. (2012). Using a New Learning Environment Questionnaire for reflection in teacher action research. *Journal of Science Teacher Education, 23,* 259–290.

Alise, M., & Teddlie, C. (2010). A continuation of the paradigm wars? Prevalence rates of methodological approaches across the social/behavioral sciences. *Journal of Mixed Methods Research, 4*(2), 103–126.

Anderson, G. L., & Herr, K. (1999). The new paradigm wars: Is there room for rigorous practitioner knowledge in schools and universities? *Educational Researcher, 28*(5), 12–21.

Arcidiacono, C., Velleman, R., & Procentese, F. (2010). A synergy between action-research and a mixed methods design for improving services and treatment for family members of heavy alcohol and drug users. *Journal of Community & Applied Social Psychology, 20,* 95–109.

Armstrong, D., Gosling, A., Weinman, J., & Marteau, T. (1997). The place of inter-rater reliability in qualitative research: An empirical study. *Sociology, 31* (3), 597–606.

Arnold, R., Maticka-Tyndale, E., Tenkorang, E., Holland, D., Gaspard, A., & Luginaah, I. (2012). Evaluation of school- and community-based HIV prevention interventions with junior secondary school students in Edo State, Nigeria. *African Journal of Reproductive Health, 16*(2), 103–125.

Aubel, J., Toure, I., & Diagne, M. (2004). Senegalese grandmothers promote improved maternal and child nutrition practices: The guardians of tradition are not averse to change. *Social Science and Medicine, 59,* 945–959.

Aylward, P., Murphy, P., Colmer, K., & O'Neill, M. (2010). Findings from an evaluation of an intervention targeting Australian parents of young children with attachment issues: The "Through the Looking Glass" (TtLG) project. *Australian Journal of Early Childhood, 35*(3), 13–23.

Babbie, E. R. (2005). *The basics of social research* (3rd ed.). Belmont, CA: Wadsworth.

Baker, D. L., Melnikow, J., Ly, M. Y., Shoultz, J., Niederhauser, V., & Diaz-Escamilla, R. (2010). Translation of health surveys using mixed methods. *Journal of Nursing Scholarship, 42*(4), 430–438.

Berg, B. L. (2004). *Qualitative research methods for the social sciences* (5th ed.). Boston: Pearson Education.

Blackford, J., & Street, A. (2012). Is an advanced care planning model feasible in community palliative care? A multi-site action research approach. *Journal of Advanced Nursing, 68*(9), 2021–2033.

Blackstone, D. (2011). *An evaluation of community college transfer student support services at a four-year institution: A multistrand mixed methods action research study.* Unpublished research proposal, University of Alabama at Birmingham.

Blanco, M., Pino, M., & Rodriguez, B. (2010). Implementing a strategy awareness raising programme: Strategy changes and feedback. *Language Learning Journal, 38*(1), 51–65.

Boeije, H. R. (2009). *Analysis in qualitative research.* Thousand Oaks, CA: Sage.

Bond, C., Cole, M., Fletcher, J., Noble, J., & O'Connell, M. (2011). Developing and sustaining provision for children with motor skills difficulties in schools: The role of educational psychologists. *Educational Psychology in Practice, 27*(4), 337–351.

Bradley, H. A., & Puoane, T. (2007). Prevention of hypertension and diabetes in an urban setting in South Africa: Participatory action research with community health workers. *Ethnicity & Disease, 17,* 49–54.

Brewer, J., & Hunter, A. (1989). *Multimethod research: A synthesis of styles.* Newbury Park, CA: Sage.

Brown, L. D., & Tandon, R. (1983). Ideology and political inquiry: Action research and participatory research. *Journal of Applied Behavioral Science, 19*(3), 277–294.

Bryman, A. (1988). *Quantity and quality in social research.* London: Routledge.

Bryman, A. (2006). Integrating quantitative and qualitative research: How is it done? *Qualitative Research, 6,* 97–113.

Bryman, A., Becker, S., & Semptik, J. (2008). Quality criteria for quantitative, qualitative and mixed methods research: A view from social policy. *International Journal of Social Research Methodology, 11*(4), 261–276.

Buck, G. A., & Cordes, J. G. (2005). An action research project on preparing teachers to meet the needs of underserved student population. *Journal of Science Teacher Education, 16,* 43–64.

Burnes, B. (2004). Kurt Lewin and the planned approach to change: A re-appraisal. *Journal of Management Studies, 41*(6), 977–1002.

Campbell, D., & Fiske, D. W. (1959). Convergent and discriminant validation by the multitrait-multimethod matrix. *Psychological Bulletin, 54,* 297–312.

Caracelli, V, J., & Greene, J. C. (1993). Data analysis strategies for mixed methods evaluation designs. *Educational Evaluation and Policy Analysis, 15*(2), 195–207.

Carboni, L. W., Wynn, S. R., & McGuire, C. M. (2007). Action research with undergraduate preservice teachers: Emerging/merging voices. *Action in Teacher Education, 29*(3), 50–59.

Carr, W., & Kemmis, S. (1986). *Becoming critical: Education, knowledge and action research.* Philadelphia: Falmer.

Christ, T. W. (2009). Designing, teaching, and evaluating two complementary mixed methods research courses. *Journal of Mixed Methods Research, 3*(4), 292–325.

Christ, T. W. (2010). Teaching mixed methods and action research: Pedagogical, practical, and evaluative considerations. In A. Tashakkori & C. Teddlie (Eds.), *SAGE handbook of mixed methods in social & behavioral research* (2nd ed.) (pp. 643–676). Thousand Oaks, CA: Sage.

Clark, M. A., Lee, S. M., Goodman, W., & Yacco, S. (2008). Examining male underachievement in public education: Action research at a district level. *NASSP Bulletin, 92*(2), 111–132.

Cochran-Smith, M., & Lytle, S. L. (1993). *Inside/outside: Teacher research and knowledge.* New York: Teachers College Press.

Coghlan, D., & Brannick, T. (2010). *Doing action research in your own organization* (3rd ed.). Thousand Oaks, CA: Sage.

Collins, K. (2010). Advanced sampling designs in mixed research: Current practices and emerging trends in the social and behavioral sciences. In A. Tashakkori & C. Teddlie (Eds.), *SAGE handbook of mixed methods in social & behavioral research* (2nd ed.) (pp. 353–377). Thousand Oaks, CA: Sage.

Collins, K., Onwuegbuzie, A., & Jiao, Q. (2007). A mixed methods investigation of mixed methods sampling designs in social and health science research. *Journal of Mixed Methods Research, 1*(3), 267–294.

Craig, D. V. (2009). *Action research essentials.* San Francisco: Jossey-Bass.

Craig, S. L. (2011). Precarious partnerships: Designing a community needs assessment to develop a system of care for gay, lesbian, bisexual, transgender and questioning (GLBTQ) youths. *Journal of Community Practice, 19,* 274–291.

Creswell, J. W. (1994). *Research design: Qualitative and quantitative approaches.* Thousand Oaks, CA: Sage.

Creswell, J. W. (2003). *Research design: Qualitative, quantitative, and mixed methods approaches* (2nd ed.). Thousand Oaks, CA: Sage.

Creswell, J. W. (2009). *Research design: Qualitative, quantitative, and mixed methods approaches* (3rd ed.). Thousand Oaks, CA: Sage.

Creswell, J. W. (2010). Mapping the developing landscape of mixed methods research. In A. Tashakkori & C. Teddlie (Eds.), *SAGE handbook of mixed methods in social & behavioral research* (2nd ed., pp. 45–68). Thousand Oaks, CA: Sage.

Creswell, J. W. (2012). *Educational research: Planning, conducting, and evaluating quantitative and qualitative research* (4th ed.). Upper Saddle River, NJ: Merrill Prentice Hall.

Creswell, J. W. (2013). *Qualitative inquiry and research design: Choosing among five approaches* (3rd ed.). Thousand Oaks, CA: Sage.

Creswell, J. W. (2014). *Research design: Qualitative, quantitative, and mixed methods approaches* (4th ed.). Thousand Oaks, CA: Sage.

Creswell, J., Fetters, M., & Ivankova, N. (2004). Designing a mixed methods study in primary care. *Annals of Family Medicine, 2*(1), 1–6. PMID: 15053277

Creswell, J. W., Klassen, A. C., Plano Clark, V. L., & Clegg Smith, K. (2011). *Best practices for mixed methods research in the health sciences*. Bethesda, MD: National Institutes of Health.

Creswell, J. W., & Miller, D. L. (2000). Determining validity in qualitative inquiry. *Theory Into Practice, 39*(2), 124–130.

Creswell, J. W., & Plano Clark, V. L. (2007). *Designing and conducting mixed methods research.* Thousand Oaks, CA: Sage.

Creswell, J. W., & Plano Clark, V. L. (2011). *Designing and conducting mixed methods research* (2nd ed.). Thousand Oaks, CA: Sage.

Creswell, J. W., Plano Clark, V. L., Gutmann, M., & Hanson, W. (2003). Advanced mixed methods research designs. In A. Tashakkori & C. Teddlie (Eds.), *Handbook of mixed methods in social & behavioral research* (pp. 209–240). Thousand Oaks, CA: Sage.

Creswell, J. W., & Tashakkori, A. (2007a). Developing publishable mixed methods manuscripts. *Journal of Mixed Methods Research, 1*(2), 107–111.

Creswell, J. W., & Tashakkori, A. (2007b). Differing perspectives on mixed methods research. *Journal of Mixed Methods Research, 1*(4), 303–308.

Crilly, T., & Plant, M. (2007). Reforming emergency care: Primary Care Trust power in action research. *Health Services Management Research, 20,* 37–47.

Cunningham, J. L. (2011). *A sequential explanatory mixed methods action research design to examine factors related to intent for HPV vaccination among collegiate males in Alabama.* Unpublished research proposal, University of Alabama at Birmingham.

Currall, S. C., & Towler, A. J. (2003). Research methods in management and organizational research: Toward integration of qualitative and quantitative techniques. In A. Tashakkori & C. Teddlie (Eds.), *Handbook of mixed methods in social & behavioral research* (pp. 513–526). Thousand Oaks, CA: Sage.

Curry, L. A., O'Cathain, A., Plano Clark, V. L., Aroni, R., Fetters, M., & Berg, D. (2012). The role of group dynamics in mixed methods health sciences research teams. *Journal of Mixed Methods Research, 6*(1) 5–20.

Damschroder, L. J., Aron, D. C., Keith, R. E., Kirsh, S. R., Alexander, J. A., & Lowery, J. (2009). Fostering implementation of health services research findings into practice: A consolidated framework for advancing implementation science. *Implementation Science, 4*(50), 1–15. doi:10.1186/1748–5908–4–50

Datta, L. (1994). Paradigm wars: A basis for peaceful coexistence and beyond. In C. S. Reichardt & S. F. Rallis (Eds.), *The qualitative-quantitative debate: New perspectives* (pp. 53–70). San Francisco: Jossey-Bass.

Davidson, P., Digiacomo, M., Zecchin, R., Clarke, M., Paul, G., Lamb, K., . . . Daly, J. (2008). A cardiac rehabilitation program to improve psychosocial outcomes of women with heart disease. *Journal of Women's Health, 17*(1), 123–134.

Davies, J. (2010). Preparation and process of qualitative interviews and focus groups. In L. Dahlberg & C. McCaig (Eds.), *Practical research and evaluation: A start-to-finish guide for practitioners* (pp. 126–144). Thousand Oaks, CA: Sage.

Davis, W. (2011). *Parent involvement technology use program: A concurrent mixed methods action research study.* Unpublished research proposal, University of Alabama at Birmingham.

Dellinger, A. B., & Leech, N. L. (2007). Toward a unified validation framework in mixed methods research. *Journal of Mixed Methods Research, 1*(4), 309–332.

Denzin, N. K. (1978). *The research act: A theoretical introduction to sociological methods.* New York: McGraw-Hill.

Denzin, N. K., & Lincoln, Y. S. (2011). Introduction: The discipline and practice of qualitative research. In N. Denzin & Y. Lincoln (Eds.), *The SAGE handbook of qualitative research* (4th ed., pp. 1–19). Thousand Oaks, CA: Sage.

DeVellis, R. F. (2011). Scale development: Theory and applications. *Applied social research methods series, 26* (3rd ed.). Thousand Oaks, CA: Sage.

Dillman, D. A., Smyth, J. D., & Christian, L. M. (2009). *Internet, mail, and mixed-mode surveys: The tailored design method* (3rd ed.). New York: Wiley & Sons.

Downs, T. J., Ross, L., Patton, S., Rulnick, S., Sinha, D., Mucciarone, D., . . . Goble, R. (2009). Complexities of holistic community-based participatory research for a low income, multi-ethnic population exposed to multiple built-environment stressors in Worcester, Massachussetts. *Environmental Research, 109,* 1028–1040.

Edmonds, W. A., & Kennedy, T. D. (2013). *An applied reference guide to research designs: Quantitative, qualitative, and mixed methods.* Thousand Oaks, CA: Sage.

Eisinger, A., & Senturia, K. (2001). Doing community-driven research: A description of Seattle Partners for Healthy Communities. *Journal of Urban Health, 78,* 519–534.

Elliott, J. (1991). *Action research for educational change.* Buckingham, UK: Open University Press.

Endacott, R., Cooper, S., Sheaff, R., Padmore, J., & Blakely, G. (2011). Improving emergency care pathways: An action research approach. *Emergency Medicine Journal, 28,* 203–207.

Evashwick, C., & Ory, M. (2003). Organizational characteristics of successful innovative health care programs sustained over time. *Family & Community Health, 26,* 177–193.

Fink, A. (2005). *Conducting research literature reviews: From the Internet to paper.* London: Sage.

Fleiss, J. (1981). *Statistical methods for rates and proportions.* New York: Wiley.

Forchuk, C., Ward-Griffin, C., Csiernik, R., & Turner, K. (2006). Surviving the tornado of mental illness: Psychiatric survivors' experiences of getting, losing, and keeping housing. *Psychiatric Services* 2006, *57*(4): 558–562. Quoted in Montgomery, P., Forchuk, C., Duncan, C., Rose, D., Bailey, P., & Veluri, R. (2008). Supported housing programs for persons with serious mental illness in rural northern communities: A mixed method evaluation. *BMC* [BioMed Central] *Health Services Research, 8*(156), 1 -8. doi:10.1186/1472 -6963 -8 -156.

Fowler, F. (2009). Survey research methods (4th ed.). *Applied Social Research Methods* series, 1. Thousand Oaks, CA: Sage.

Fueyo, V., & Koorland, M. A. (1997). Teacher as researcher: A synonym for professionalism. *Journal of Teacher Education, 48*(5), 336–344.

Gabriel, S. E., & Normand, S.T. (2012). Getting the methods right—the foundation of patient-centered outcomes research. *The New England Journal of Medicine, 367*(9), 787–790.

Galini, R., & Efthymia, P. (2010). A collaborative action research project in the kindergarten: Perspectives and challenges for teacher development through internal evaluation process. *New Horizons in Education, 58*(2), 18–33.

Gay, L. R., Mills, G. E., & Airasian, P. (2006). *Educational research: Competencies for analysis and applications* (8th ed.). Upper Saddle River, NJ: Merrill Prentice Hall.

Giachello, A., Arrom, J., Davis, M., Sayad, J., Ramirez, D., Nandi, C., & Ramos, C. (2003). Reducing diabetes health disparities through community-based participatory action research: The Chicago Southeast Diabetes Community Action Coalition. *Public Health Reports, 118,* 309–323.

Glasson, J., Chang, E., Chenoweth, L., Hancock, K., Hall, T., Hill-Murray, F., & Collier, L. (2006). Evaluation of a model of nursing care for older patients using participatory action research in an acute medical ward. *Journal of Clinical Nursing, 15,* 588–598.

Gosin, M. N., Dustman, P. A., Drapeau, A. E., & Harthun, M. L. (2003). Participatory action research: Creating an effective prevention curriculum for adolescents in the Southwestern U.S. *Health Education Research, 18*(3), 363–379.

Grant, J., Nelson, G., & Mitchell, T. (2008). Negotiating the challenges of participatory action research: Relationships, power, participation, change and credibility. In P. Reason & H. Bradbury (Eds.), *The SAGE handbook of action research: Participative inquiry and practice* (2nd ed., pp. 589–601). Thousand Oaks, CA: Sage.

Greene, J. C. (2007). *Mixed methods in social inquiry.* San Francisco: Jossey-Bass.

Greene, J. C. (2008). Is mixed methods social inquiry a distinct methodology? *Journal of Mixed Methods Research, 2*(1), 7–22.

Greene, J. C., & Caracelli, V. J. (1997). Defining and describing the paradigm issue in mixed-method evaluation. In J. C. Greene & V. J. Caracelli (Eds.), *Advances in mixed-method evaluation: The challenges and benefits of integrating diverse programs.* New Directions for Evaluation 74, pp. 5–17. San Francisco: Jossey-Bass.

Greene, J. C., Caracelli, V. J., & Graham, W. F. (1989). Toward a conceptual framework for mixed-method evaluation designs. *Educational Evaluation and Policy Analysis, 11*(3), 255–274.

Greenwood, D., & Levin, M. (2007). *Introduction to action research: Social research for social change* (2nd ed.). Thousand Oaks, CA: Sage.

Greysen,S. R., Allen, R., Lucas, G. I., Wang, E. A., & Rosenthal, M. S. (2012). Understanding transitions in care from hospital to homeless shelter: A mixed-methods, community-based participatory approach. *Journal of General Internal Medicine, 27*(11), 1484–1491. doi:10.1007/s11606–012–2117–2

Guest, G. (2013). Describing mixed methods research: An alternative to typologies. *Journal of Mixed Methods Research 7*(2), 141–151.

Guest, G., Bunce, A., & Johnson, L. (2006). How many interviews are enough? An experiment with data saturation and variability. *Field Methods, 18*(1), 59–82.

Guest, G., MacQueen, K. M., & Namey, E. E. (2012). *Applied thematic analysis.* Thousand Oaks, CA: Sage.

Hacker, K. (2013). *Community-based participatory research.* Thousand Oaks, CA: Sage.

Hales, B. (2011). *A mixed methods action research study of a Tier 3 reading intervention program with a quantitative focus.* Unpublished research proposal, University of Alabama at Birmingham.

Hemmings, A., Beckett, G., Kennerly, S., & Yap, T. (2013). Building a community of research practice: Intragroup team social dynamics in interdisciplinary mixed methods. *Journal of Mixed Methods Research, 7*(3), 261–273.

Herbert, A., Stephen, K., Robin, M., & Ortrun, Z.-S. (2002). The concept of action research. *The Learning Organization, 9*(3/4), 125–132.

Herr, K., & Anderson, G. L. (2005). *The action research dissertation: A guide for students and faculty.* Thousand Oaks, CA: Sage.

Hesse-Biber, S. N., & Leavy, P. (2011). *The practice of qualitative research* (2nd ed.). Thousand Oaks, CA: Sage.

Hesselink, A. E., Verhoeff, A. P., & Stronks, K. (2009). Ethnic health care advisors: A good strategy to improve the access to health care and social welfare services for ethnic minorities? *Journal of Community Health, 34,* 419–429.

Hicks, S., Duran, B., Wallerstein, N., Avila, M., Beloni, L., Lucero, J., . . . White Hat, E. (2012). Evaluating community-based participatory research to improve community-partnered science and community health. *Progress in Community Health Partnerships: Research, Education, and Action, 6*(3), 289–299.

Hinchcliff, R., Greenfield, D., Moldovan, M., Pawsey, M., Mumford, V., Westbrook, J. I., & Braithwaite, J. (2012). Evaluation of current Australian health services accreditation processes (ACCREDIT-CAP): Protocol for a mixed-methods research project. *BMJ Open.* doi:10.1136/bmjopen-2012–001726

Hinchey, P. H. (2008). *Action research: Primer.* New York: Peter Lang.

Howe, K. R. (1988). Against the quantitative-qualitative incompatibility thesis or dogmas die hard. *Educational Researcher, 17,* 10–16.

Hussaini, K. S., Hamm, E., & Means, T. (2013). Using community-based participatory mixed methods research to understand preconception health in African American communities of Arizona. *Maternal and Child Health Journal, 17*(10), 1862–1871.

Israel, B. A., Schulz, A. J., Parker, E. A., & Becker, A. B. (2001). Community-based participatory research: Policy recommendations for promoting a partnership approach in health research. *Education for Health: Change in Learning & Practice, 14*(2), 182–197.

Ivankova, N. (2014). Implementing quality criteria in designing and conducting a sequential QUAN→QUAL mixed methods study of student engagement with learning applied research methods online. *Journal of Mixed Methods Research, 8*(1), 25–51. First published on May 20, 2013. doi:10.1177/1558689813487945

Ivankova, N. V., Creswell, J. W., & Stick, S. (2006). Using mixed methods sequential explanatory design: From theory to practice. *Field Methods, 18*(1), 3–20.

Ivankova, N., & Kawamura, Y. (2010). Emerging trends in the utilization of integrated designs in social, behavioral, and health sciences. In A. Tashakkori & C. Teddlie (Eds.), *SAGE handbook of mixed methods in social & behavioral research* (2nd ed., pp. 581–611). Thousand Oaks, CA: Sage.

Ivankova, N., & Stick, S. (2007). Students' persistence in a Distributed Doctoral Program in Educational Leadership in Higher Education: A mixed methods study. *Research in Higher Education, 48*(1), 93–135. doi:10.1007/s11162–006–9025–4

Jacobson, W. (1998). Defining the quality of practitioner research. *Adult Education Quarterly, 48*(3), 125–139.

James, E. A., Milenkiewicz, M. T., & Bucknam, A. (2008). *Participatory action research for educational leadership: Using data-driven decision making to improve schools.* Thousand Oaks, CA: Sage.

Jick, T. D. (1979). Mixing qualitative and quantitative methods: Triangulation in action. *Administrative Science Quarterly, 24,* 602–611.

Johnson, B., & Christensen, L. (2012). *Educational research: Quantitative, qualitative, and mixed approaches* (4th ed.). Thousand Oaks, CA: Sage.

Johnson, B., & Gray, R. (2010). A history of philosophical and theoretical issues for mixed methods research. In A. Tashakkori & C. Teddlie (Eds.), *SAGE handbook of mixed methods in social & behavioral research* (2nd ed., pp. 69–94). Thousand Oaks, CA: Sage.

Johnson, B., & Onwuegbuzie, A. (2004). Mixed methods research: A research paradigm whose time has come. *Educational Researcher, 33*(7), 14–26.

Johnson, B., Onwuegbuzie, A., & Turner, L. A. (2007). Toward a definition of mixed methods research. *Journal of Mixed Methods Research, 1*(2), 112–133.

Johnson, B., & Turner, L. (2003). Data collection strategies in mixed methods research. In A. Tashakkori & C. Teddlie (Eds.), *Handbook of mixed methods in social & behavioral research* (pp. 297–320). Thousand Oaks, CA: Sage.

Johnson, C. V., Bartgis, J., Worley, J. A., Hellman, C. M., & Burkhart, R. (2010). Urban Indian voices: A community-based participatory research health and needs assessment. *Journal of the National Center, 17*(1), 49–70.

Johnson, J. C., & Weller, S. C. (2001). Elicitation techniques for interviewing. In J. F. Gubrium & J. A. Holstein (Ed.), *Handbook of interview research: Context & method* (pp. 491–514). Thousand Oaks, CA: Sage.

Kavanagh, T., Stevens, B., Seers, K., Sidani, S., & Watt-Watson, J. (2010). Process evaluation of appreciative inquiry to translate pain management evidence into pediatric nursing practice. *Implementation Science, 5*(90). doi:10.1186/1748–5908–5–90

Kemmis, S. (Ed.). (1982). *The action research reader.* Geelong, Australia: Deakin University Press.

Kemmis, S., & McTaggart, R. (2007). Participatory action research: Communicative action and the public sphere. In N. Denzin & Y. Lincoln (Eds.), *Strategies of Qualitative Inquiry* (3rd ed., pp. 271–330). Thousand Oaks, CA: Sage.

Kilbride, C., Meyer, J., Flatley, M, & Perry, L. (2005). Stroke units: The implementation of a complex intervention. *Educational Action Research, 13*(4), 479–504.

Kilbride, C., Perry, L., Flatley, M., Turner, E., & Meyer, J. (2011). Developing theory and practice: Creation of a community of practice through action research produced excellence in stroke care. *Journal of Interprofessional Care, 25,* 91–97.

King, K. P. (2010). Advancing educational podcasting and faculty inquiry with a grounded research model: Building on current mixed-methods research across contexts. *Journal of Continuing Higher Education, 58,* 143–155.

Koshy, E., Koshy, V., & Waterman, H. (2011). *Action research in healthcare.* Thousand Oaks, CA: Sage.

Kostos, K., & Shin, E. (2010). Using math journals to enhance second graders' communication of mathematical thinking. *Early Childhood Education Journal, 38,* 223–231.

Kreuger, R., & Casey, M. (2008). *Focus groups: A practical guide for applied research* (4th ed.). Thousand Oaks, CA: Sage.

Krieger, J., Rabkin, J., Sharify, D., & Song, L. (2009). High Point Walking for Health: Creating built and social environments that support walking in a public housing community. *American Journal of Public Health, 99*(S3), Suppl. 3, S593–S599.

Krueger, P. (2010). It's not just a method! The epistemic and political work of young people's lifeworlds at the school-prison nexus. *Race, Ethnicity and Education, 13*(3), 383–408.

Leman, J. (2010). Different kinds of quantitative data collection methods. In L. Dahlberg & C. McCaig (Eds.), *Practical research and evaluation: A start-to-finish guide for practitioners* (pp. 159–171). Thousand Oaks, CA: Sage.

Lewin, G. (1948a). Action research and minority problems. In G. Lewin (Ed.), *Resolving social conflicts: Selected papers on group dynamics by Kurt Lewin* (pp. 201–216). New York: Harper & Brothers Publishers.

Lewin, G. (1948b). (Ed.). *Resolving social conflicts: Selected papers on group dynamics by Kurt Lewin.* New York: Harper & Brothers Publishers.

Lewin, K. (1951). *Field theory in social science: Selected theoretical papers.* D. Cartwright (Ed.). New York: Harper & Row.

Lincoln, Y. S., & Guba, E. G. (1985). *Naturalistic inquiry.* Beverly Hills, CA: Sage.

Lingard, L., Albert, M., & Levinson, W. (2008). Grounded theory, mixed methods, and action research. *British Medical Journal, 337,* 459–461.

Lustick, D. (2009). The failure of inquiry: Preparing science teachers with an authentic investigation. *Journal of Science Teacher Education, 20,* pp. 583–604.

Lyons, A., & DeFranco, J. (2010). A mixed-methods model for educational evaluation. *The humanistic psychologist, 38,* 146–158.

Macaulay, A. C., Commanda, L. E., Freeman, W. L., Gibson, N., McCabe, M. L., Robbins, C. M., & Twohig, P. L. (1999). Participatory research maximizes community and lay involvement. *British Medical Journal, 319*(7212), 774–778.

Maritz, R., Pretorius, M., & Plant, K. (2011). Exploring the interface between strategy-making and responsible leadership. *Journal of Business Ethics, 98,* 101–113.

Mason, J. (2006). Mixing methods in a qualitatively driven way. *Qualitative Research, 6*(1), 9–25.

Maxcy, S. J. (2003). Pragmatic threads in mixed methods research in the social sciences: The search for multiple modes of inquiry and the end of the philosophy of formalism. In A. Tashakkori & C. Teddlie (Eds.), *Handbook of mixed methods in social & behavioral research* (pp. 51–89). Thousand Oaks, CA: Sage.

Maxwell, J., & Loomis, D. (2003). Mixed methods design: An alternative approach. In A. Tashakkori & C. Teddlie (Eds.), *Handbook of mixed methods in social & behavioral research* (pp. 241–272). Thousand Oaks, CA: Sage.

Maxwell, J., & Mittapalli, K. (2010). Realism as a stance for mixed methods research. In A. Tashakkori & C. Teddlie (Eds.), *SAGE handbook of mixed methods in social & behavioral research* (2nd ed.; pp. 145–167). Thousand Oaks, CA: Sage.

McKellar, L., Pincombe, J., & Henderson, A. (2009). Encountering the culture of midwifery practice on the postnatal ward during action research: An impediment to change. *Women and Birth, 22,* 112–118.

McKernan, J. (1988). The countenance of curriculum action research: Traditional, collaborative, and emancipatory-critical conceptions. *Journal of Curriculum and Supervision, 3*(3), 173–200.

McNiff, J., & Whitehead, J. (2011). *All you need to know about action research* (2nd ed.). London: Sage.

Medves, J., Paterson, M., Chapman, C. Y., Young, J. H., Tata, E., Bowes, D., . . . O'Riordan, A. (2008). A new inter-professional course preparing learners for life in rural communities. *Rural and Remote Health, 8* (1), 1–8.

Merriam, S. B. (1998). *Qualitative research and case study applications in education.* San Francisco: Jossey-Bass.

Mertens, D. M. (2003). Mixed methods and the politics of human research: The transformative-emancipatory perspective. In A. Tashakkori & C. Teddlie (Eds.), *Handbook of mixed methods in social & behavioral research* (pp. 135–164). Thousand Oaks, CA: Sage.

Mertens, D. M. (2005). *Research and evaluation in education and psychology: Integrating diversity with quantitative, qualitative, and mixed methods* (2nd ed.). Thousand Oaks, CA: Sage.

Mertens, D. M., Bledsoe, K. L., Sullivan, M., & Wilson, A. (2010). Utilization of mixed methods for transformative purposes. In A. Tashakkori & C. Teddlie (Eds.), *SAGE handbook of mixed methods in social & behavioral research* (2nd ed., pp. 193–214). Thousand Oaks, CA: Sage.

Mertler, C. A. (2012). *Action research: Improving schools and empowering educators.* Thousand Oaks, CA: Sage.

Miles, M., & Huberman, M. (1994). *Qualitative data analysis: An expanded sourcebook* (2nd ed.) Thousand Oaks, CA: Sage.

Mills, G. E. (2011). *Action research: A guide for the teacher researcher* (4th cd.). Boston: Pearson Education.

Mirza, M., Anandan, N., Madnick, F., & Hammel, J. (2006). A participatory program evaluation of a systems change program to improve access to information technology by people with disabilities. *Disability and Rehabilitation, 28*(19), 1185–1199.

Montgomery, P., Forchuk, C., Duncan, C., Rose, D., Bailey, P., & Veluri, R. (2008). Supported housing programs for persons with serious mental illness in rural northern communities: A mixed method evaluation. *BMC* [BioMed Central] *Health Services Research, 8*(156), 1–8. doi:10.1186/1472–6963–8–156.

Morgan, D. L. (1998). Practical strategies for combining qualitative and quantitative methods: Applications to health research. *Qualitative Health Research, 3,* 362–376.

Morse, J. M. (1991). Approaches to qualitative-quantitative methodological triangulation. *Nursing Research, 40*(1), 120–123.

Morse, J. M., & Niehaus, L. (2009). *Mixed method design: Principles and procedures.* Walnut Creek, CA: Left Coast.

Morton-Cooper, A. (2000). *Action research in health care.* London, UK: Blackwell Science.

Nastasi, B. K., Hitchcock, J. H., Brown, L. M. (2010). An inclusive framework for conceptualizing mixed methods design typologies: Moving toward fully integrated synergistic research models. In A. Tashakkori & C. Teddlie (Eds.), *SAGE handbook of mixed methods in social & behavioral research* (2nd ed., pp. 305–338). Thousand Oaks, CA: Sage.

National Cancer Institute. (2005). *Theory: A guide for health promotion practice* (2nd ed.). Washington, DC: U.S. Department of Health and Human Services, National Institutes of Health.

National Institutes of Health. (1999). *Qualitative methods in health research: Opportunities and considerations in application and review.* Retrieved from http://obssr.od.nih.gov/pdf/Qualitative.pdf

National Institutes of Health. (2009). *Code of federal regulation: Protection of human subjects.* Retrieved from http://www.hhs.gov/ohrp/humansubjects/guidance/45cfr46.html

Newman, I., Ridenour, C. S., Newman, C., & DeMarco, G. M. P. Jr. (2003). A typology of research purposes and its relationship to mixed methods. In A. Tashakkori & C. Teddlie (Eds.), *Handbook of mixed methods in social & behavioral research* (pp. 167–188). Thousand Oaks, CA: Sage.

Newman, S. D., Andrews, J. O., Magwood, G. S., Jenkins, C., Cox, M. J., & Williamson, D. C. (2011). Community advisory boards in community-based participatory research: A synthesis of best processes. *Preventing Chronic Disease, 8*(3), A70.

Nolen, A. L., & Vander Putten, J. (2007). Action research in education: Addressing gaps in ethical principles and practices. *Educational Researcher, 36*(7), 401–407.

O'Cathain, A. (2010). Assessing the quality of mixed methods research: Toward a comprehensive framework. In A. Tashakkori & C. Teddlie (Eds.), *SAGE handbook of mixed methods in social & behavioral research* (2nd ed., pp. 531–555). Thousand Oaks, CA: Sage.

O'Cathain, A., Murphy, E., & Nicholl, J. (2008). The quality of mixed methods studies in health services research. *Journal of Health Services Research Policy, 13*(2), 92–98.

O'Leary, Z. (2004). *The essential guide to doing research.* London: Sage.

Onwuegbuzie, A. J., & Combs, J. (2010). Emergent data analysis techniques in mixed methods research: A synthesis. In A. Tashakkori & C. Teddlie (Eds.), *SAGE handbook of mixed methods in social & behavioral research* (2nd ed., pp. 397–430). Thousand Oaks, CA: Sage.

Onwuegbuzie, A. J., & Johnson, R. B. (2006). The validity issue in mixed research. *Research in the Schools, 13*(1), 48–63.

Onwuegbuzie, A. J., & Leech, N. L. (2006). Linking research questions to mixed methods data analysis procedures. *The Qualitative Report, 11*(3), 474–498.

Onwuegbuzie, A. J., & Leech, N. L. (2007). A call for qualitative power analyses: Considerations in qualitative research. *Quality & Quantity: International Journal of Methodology, 41*(1), 105–121.

Oxford Dictionaries (n.d.). Oxford University Press. Retrieved from http://www.oxforddictionaries.com/us/

Padgett, D. (2009). Qualitative and mixed methods in social work knowledge development. *Social Work, 54*(2), 101–105.

Padgett, D. (2012). *Qualitative and mixed methods in public health.* Thousand Oaks, CA: Sage.

Palcanis, K. G., Geiger, B. F., O'Neal, M. R., Ivankova, N. V., Evans, R. R., Kennedy, L. B., & Carera, K. A. (2012). Preparing students to practice evidence-based dentistry: A mixed methods conceptual framework for curriculum enhancement. *Journal of Dental Education, 76*(12), 1600–1614.

Palinkas, L. A., Aarons, G. A., Horwitz, S., Chamberlain, P., Hurlburt, M., & Landsverk, J. (2011). Mixed method designs in implementation research. *Administration and Policy in Mental Health, 38*(1), 44–53.

Patton, M. Q. (1980). *Qualitative evaluation and research methods.* Newbury Park, CA: Sage.

Patton, M. Q. (2002). *Qualitative research and evaluation methods* (3rd ed.). Thousand Oaks, CA: Sage.

Payne, Y. A. (2008). "Street life" as a site for resiliency: How street life-oriented black men frame opportunity in the United States. *Journal of Black Psychology, 34*(1), 3–31.

Perry, J. (2009). A combined social action, mixed methods approach to vocational guidance efficacy research. *International Journal of Educational Vocational Guidance, 9,* 111–123.

Pettit, J. (2010). Learning to do action research for social change. *International Journal of Communication, 4,* 820–827.

Phillips, J., & Davidson, P. M. (2009). Action research as a mixed methods design: A palliative approach in residential aged care. In S. Andrew & E. J. Halcomb (Eds.), *Mixed methods research for nursing and the health sciences* (pp. 195–216). Hoboken, NJ: Wiley-Blackwell.

Pickard, J. (2006). Staff and student attitudes to plagiarism at University College Northampton. *Assessment & Evaluation in Higher Education, 31*(2), 215–232.

Plano Clark, V. L. (2010). The adoption and practice of mixed methods: U.S. trends in federally funded health-related research. *Qualitative Inquiry, 16*(6), 428–440.

Plano Clark, V., & Badiee, M. (2010). Research questions in mixed methods research. In A. Tashakkori & C. Teddlie (Eds.), *SAGE handbook of mixed methods in social & behavioral research* (2nd ed., pp. 275–304). Thousand Oaks, CA: Sage.

Punch, K. F. (1998). *Introduction to social research: Quantitative and qualitative approaches.* London: Sage.

Ragin, C. C., Nagel, J., & White, P. (2004). *Workshop on scientific foundations of qualitative research.* Washington, DC: National Science Foundation. Retrieved from http://www.nsf.gov/pubs/2004/nsf04219/nsf04219.pdf

Reason, P., & Bradbury, H. (2008). Introduction. In P. Reason & H. Bradbury (Eds.), *The SAGE handbook of action research: Participative inquiry and practice* (2nd ed., pp. 1–10). Thousand Oaks, CA: Sage.

Reese, D. J., Ahern, R. E., Nair, S., O'Faire, J. D., & Warren, C. (1999). Hospice access and use by African Americans: Addressing cultural and institutional barriers through participatory action research. *Social Work, 44*(6), 549–559.

Reichardt, C. S., & Rallis, S. F. (1994). Qualitative and quantitative inquiries are not incompatible: A call for a new partnership. In C. S. Reichardt & S. F. Rallis (Eds.), *The qualitative-quantitative debate: New perspectives* (pp. 85–92). San Francisco: Jossey-Bass.

Reutzel, D. R., Fawson, P. C., & Smith, J. A. (2006). Words to go!: Evaluating a first-grade parent involvement program for "making" words at home. *Reading Research and Instruction, 45*(2), 119–159.

Richardson, L., & Reid, C. (2006). "I've lost my husband, my house and I need a new knee . . . why should I smile?": Action research evaluation of a group cognitive behavioral therapy program for older adults with depression. *Clinical Psychologist, 10*(2), 60–66.

Robertson, J. (2000). The three Rs of action research methodology: Reciprocity, reflexivity, and reflection-on-reality. *Educational Action Research, 8*(2), 307–326.

Rossman, G. B., & Wilson, B. L. (1985). Numbers and words: Combining quantitative and qualitative methods in a single large-scale evaluation study. *Evaluation Review, 9*(5), 627–643.

Royal Society of Canada. (1995). *Guidelines and categories for classifying participatory research projects in health.* Retrieved from http://lgreen.net/guidelines.html

Sagor, R. (2005). *The action research guidebook: A four-step process for educators and school teams.* Thousand Oaks, CA: Corwin.

Sampson, R. J. (2010). Student-negotiated lesson style. *RELC Journal, 41*(3), 283–299.

Schulz, A. J., Israel, B. A., Selig, S. M., Bayer, I. S. & Griffin, C. B. (1998). Development and implementation of principles for community-based research in public health. In R. H. MacNair (Ed.), *Research strategies for community practice* (pp. 83–110). New York: Haworth.

Schwandt, T. A. (2001). *Dictionary of qualitative inquiry* (2nd ed.). Thousand Oaks, CA: Sage.

Senge, P., & Scharmer, O. (2001). Community action research: Learning as a community of practitioners, consultants and researchers. In P. Reason & H. Bradbury (Eds.), *Handbook of action research: Participative inquiry and practice* (pp. 238–249). Thousand Oaks, CA: Sage.

Seymour, J. E., Almack, K., Kennedy, S., & Froggatt, K. (2011). Peer education for advance care planning: Volunteers' perspectives on training and community engagement activities. *Health Expectations.* doi:10.1111/j.1369–7625.2011.00688.x

Shattuck, J., Dubins, B., & Zilberman, D. (2011). MarylandOnline's inter-institutional project to train higher education adjunct faculty to teach online. *International Review of Research in Open and Distance Learning, 12*(2), 41–61.

Shavelson, R. J., & Towne, L. (Eds.). (2002). *Scientific research in education.* Committee on Scientific Principles for Education Research. Washington, D.C.: National Research Council.

Shenton A. K. (2004). Strategies for ensuring trustworthiness in qualitative research projects. *Education for Information 22,* 63–75.

Shortt, K. (2002). The benefits of negotiating student versus staff control over learning. *Psychology Teaching Review, 10*(1), 61–67.

Shulha, L. M., & Wilson, R. J. (2003). Collaborative mixed methods research. In A. Tashakkori & C. Teddlie (Eds.), *Handbook of mixed methods in social & behavioral research* (pp. 639–669). Thousand Oaks, CA: Sage.

Sieber, S. D. (1973). The integration of fieldwork and survey methods. *American Journal of Sociology, 78,* 1335–1359.

Smith, J. K. (1983). Quantitative versus qualitative research: An attempt to clarify the issue. *Educational Researcher, 12*(3), 6–13.

Stake, R. (1986). An evolutionary view of educational improvement. In E. R. House (Ed.), *New directions in educational evaluation* (pp. 89–102). London: Falmer.

Strand, K., Marullo, S., Cutforth, N., Stoecker, R., & Donohue, P. (2003). *Community-based research and higher education: Principles and practices.* San Francisco: Jossey-Bass.

Strang, K. D. (2011). Radioactive manufacturing projects and politics: Scientist and politician normalized risk decision process. *International Journal of Management and Decision Making, 11*(3/4), 231–248.

Strauss, A., & Corbin, J. (1998). *Basics of qualitative research: Techniques and procedures for developing grounded theory* (2nd ed.). Thousand Oaks, CA: Sage.

Stringer, E. T. (2014). *Action research* (4th ed.). Thousand Oaks, CA: Sage.

Stringer, E., & Genat, W. J. (2004). *Action research in health.* Upper Saddle River, NJ: Pearson Education.

Stripling, J. D. (2011). *Parental involvement in secondary schools: It's effect on student discipline and academic achievement.* Unpublished research proposal, University of Alabama at Birmingham.

Tanke, E. D., & Tanke, T. J. (1982). Regulation and education: The role of the institutional review board in social sciences research. In J. E. Sieber (Ed.), *The ethics of social research: Fieldwork, regulation, and publication* (pp. 131–149). New York: Springer-Verlag.

Tashakkori, A., & Creswell, J. (2007). The new era of mixed methods. *Journal of Mixed Methods Research, 1*(1), 3–8.

Tashakkori, A., & Creswell, J. (2008). Mixed methodology across disciplines. *Journal of Mixed Methods Research, 2*(1), 3–6.

Tashakkori, A., & Teddlie, C. (1998). *Mixed methodology: Combining qualitative and quantitative approaches.* (Applied Social Research Methods Series, 46). Thousand Oaks, CA: Sage.

Tashakkori, A., & Teddlie, C. (Eds.). (2003). *Handbook of mixed methods in social & behavioral research.* Thousand Oaks, CA: Sage.

Tashakkori, A., & Teddlie, C. (Eds.). (2010). *SAGE handbook of mixed methods in social & behavioral research* (2nd Ed.). Thousand Oaks, CA: Sage.

Taut, S. (2007). Studying self-evaluation capacity building in a large international development organization. *American Journal of Evaluation, 28*(1), 45–59.

Teddlie, C., & Tashakkori, A. (2003). Major issues and controversies in the use of mixed methods in the social and behavioral sciences. In A. Tashakkori & C. Teddlie (Eds.), *Handbook of mixed methods in social & behavioral research* (pp. 3–50). Thousand Oaks, CA: Sage.

Teddlie, C., & Tashakkori, A. (2009). *Foundations of mixed methods research: Integrating quantitative and qualitative approaches in the social and behavioral sciences.* Thousand Oaks, CA: Sage.

Teddlie, C., & Tashakkori, A. (2010). Overview of contemporary issues in mixed methods research. In A. Tashakkori & C. Teddlie (Eds.), Sage *handbook of mixed methods in social & behavioral research* (2nd ed., pp. 1–41). Thousand Oaks, CA: Sage.

Teddlie, C., &Yu, F. (2007). Mixed methods sampling: A typology with examples. *Journal of Mixed Methods Research, 1*(1), 77–100.

Teram, E., Schachter, C., & Stalker, C. (2005). The case for integrating grounded theory and participatory action research: Empowering clients to inform professional practice. *Qualitative Health Research, 15,* 1129–1140.

Tesch, R. (1990). *Qualitative research: Analysis types and software tools.* Bristol, PA: Falmer.

Thomas-MacLean, R., Hamoline, R., Quinlan, E., Ramsden, V., & Kuzmicz, J. (2010). Discussing mentorship: An ongoing study for the development of a mentorship program in Saskatchewan. *Canadian Family Physician, 56,* e263–e272.

Thorndike, R. M. (1997). *Measurement and evaluation in psychology and education* (6th ed.). Upper Saddle River, NJ: Prentice-Hall.

Thorndike, R. M., & Thorndike-Christ, T. M. (2011). *Measurement and evaluation in psychology and education* (8th ed.). Upper Saddle River, NJ: Pearson Education.

Thornewill, J., Dowling, A. F., Cox, B. A., & Esterhay, R. J. (2011). Information infrastructure for consumer health: A health information exchange stakeholder study. *American Journal of Preventive Medicine, 40*(5S2), S123–S133.

Tomal, D. R. (2010). *Action research for educators* (2nd ed.). Lanham, MD: Rowman & Littlefield Publishers, Inc.

Torre, M. E., & Fine, M. (2005). Bar none: Extending affirmative action to higher education in prison. *Journal of Social Issues, 61*(3), 569–594.

Tritter, J. (2007). Mixed methods and multidisciplinary research in health care. In M. Saks & J. Allsop (Eds.), *Researching health: Qualitative, quantitative and mixed methods* (pp. 301–318). Thousand Oaks, CA: Sage.

VanDevanter, N., Kwon, S., Sim, S-C., Chun, K., & Trinh-Shevrin, C. (2011). Evaluation of community–academic partnership functioning: Center for the Elimination of Hepatitis B Health Disparities. *Progress in Community Health Partnerships, 5*(3), 223–233.

Vecchiarelli, S., Prelip, M., Slusser, W., Weightman, H., & Neumann, C. (2005). Using participatory action research to develop a school-based environmental intervention to support healthy eating and physical activity. *American Journal of Health Education, 36*(1), 35–42.

Vogt, P. W. (2005). *Dictionary of statistics and methodology: A nontechnical guide for the social sciences.* Thousand Oaks, CA: Sage.

Wang, C. (1997). Photovoice: Concept, methodology, and use for participatory needs assessment. *Health Education and Behavior, 24*(3), 369–387.

Warren, S. R., Noftle, J. T., Ganley, D. D., & Quintanar, A. P. (2011). Preparing urban teachers to partner with families and communities. *School Community Journal, 21*(1), 95–112.

Westhues, A., Ochocka, J., Jacobson, N., Simich, L., Maiter, S., Janzen, R., & Fleras, A. (2008). Developing theory from complexity: Reflections on a collaborative mixed method participatory action research study. *Qualitative Health Research, 18*(5), 701–717.

White, R., & Wafra, N. (2011). Building schools of character: A case-study investigation of character education's impact on school climate, pupil behavior, and curriculum delivery. *Journal of Applied Social Psychology, 41*(1), 45–60.

Williamson, G. R., Webb, C., & Abelson-Mitchell, N. (2004). Developing lecturer practitioner roles using action research. *Journal of Advanced Nursing, 47*(2), 153–164.

Willis, G. (2005). *Cognitive interviewing: A tool for improving questionnaire design.* Thousand Oaks, CA: Sage.

Winter, R. (1987) *Action research and the nature of social inquiry.* Aldershot, UK: Gower.

Wisniewska, D. (2011). Mixed methods and action research: Similar or different? *Glottodidactica, 37,* 59–72.

Wolcott, H. F. (1989). *Kwakiutl village and school.* Prospect Heights, IL: Waveland.

Wright, D. B., & London, K. (2009). *First (and second) steps in statistics* (2nd ed.). London: Sage.

Yin, R. K. (2006). Mixed methods research: Are the methods genuinely integrated or merely parallel? *Research in the Schools, 13*(1), 41–47.

Young, L., & Higgins, J. W. (2010). Using participatory research to challenge the status quo for women's cardiovascular health. *Nursing Inquiry, 17*(4), 346–358.

Zoellner, J., Zanko, A., Price, B., Bonner, J., & Hill, J. L. (2012). Exploring community gardens in a health disparate population: Findings from a mixed methods pilot study. *Progress in Community Health Partnerships: Research, Education, and Action, 6*(2), 153–165.

AUTHOR INDEX

Aarons, G. A., 319

Abelson-Mitchell, N., 66, 83, 224

Abesamis, N., 363

Adams, T. L., 331

Adelman, C., 29, 49, 307

Ahern, R. E., 142, 143, 160, 195, 231

Ahsan, N., 362

Airasian, P., 219, 223, 229, 230, 231, 256, 260, 261, 292

Akintobi, T. H., 66, 147, 161, 195, 222

Albert, M., 27

Aldridge, J. M., 193, 207

Alexander, J. A., 319

Alise, M., 14, 58

Allen, R., 66, 142, 236t, 238, 240, 241, 242, 251, 267, 304

Alligood, M. R., 344

Almack, K., 66, 137, 213

Amit, M., 331

Anandan, N., 69t, 83

Anderson, G. L., 27, 28, 29, 32, 33, 34, 35, 37, 45, 47, 53, 55, 56, 57, 58, 59, 96, 101, 102, 116, 196, 233, 259, 260, 265, 268, 270, 271, 272, 273, 274, 291, 292, 304, 305, 314, 319

Andrews, J. O., 267

Applebee, A. N., 331

Armstrong, D., 242

Arnold, R., 66, 225, 246

Aron, D. C., 319

Aroni, R., 55

Arrom, J., 35, 36, 37, 44, 45, 46, 47, 103, 105, 186t, 189, 198, 209, 309, 313

Aspinall, R., 376

Attkisson, C. C., 361

Attonito, J., 361

Aubel, J., 203, 313, 315, 317

Avila, M., 251

Aylward, P., 69t, 83

Babbie, E. R., 63, 183, 184, 185

Babiak, T., 395

Bachrach, L. L., 395

Badiee, M., 21, 107, 108, 116, 164, 180

Bailey, P., 70, 77–80, 91, 97, 137, 173, 175f, 186t, 193, 213, 224, 228, 249, 307, 313, 321, 393–406

Baker, D. L., 97, 260

Bartgis, J., 190, 210, 211, 222, 230

Barthel, D. W., 347

Batalden, P. B., 354

Baxter, J. A., 331, 332, 340

Bayer, I. S., 31, 32, 36, 49, 58, 104

Bazeley, P., 256

Becker, A. B., 363

Becker, S., 30, 259

Beckett, G., 55

Bell, L., 193, 207

Bell, R. A., 369

Beloni, L., 251

Berberet, H. M., 361, 363, 364, 369

Berg, B. L., 205

Berg, D., 55

Berman, H., 395, 396

Berry, J., 66, 147, 161, 195, 222

Berwick, D. M., 354, 356

Binnie, A., 344, 350, 356

Blackford, J., 187t, 202, 205, 238t, 240

Blackstone, D., 169, 170, 252

Blakely, G., 317

Blanco, M., 67t, 82, 158, 192, 204, 247

Bledsoe, K. I., 55, 82

Boeije, H. R., 233

Bohrer, P., 363

Bond, C., 187t, 188

Bond, M., 344

Bone, L., 363

Bonner, J., 66, 187t, 231, 234t

Bontempo, D. E., 360

Borasi, R., 331

Bordeaux, B., 363

Born, D. L., 394, 395

Bowes, D., 67*t*

Boydell, K., 395

Boyles, S., 395

Bradbury, H., 28, 344, 356

Bradley, H. A., 199, 206

Braithwaite, J., 188, 314

Brannagan, K. B., 293

Brannick, T., 314

Brasfield, T. L., 363

Brewer, J., 14

Brophy, J., 383, 386

Brown, L. D., 27

Brown, L. M., 57, 82, 209

Bruce, D., 395

Bruner, J., 401

Bryman, A., 13, 56, 259

Buck, G. A., 66, 83, 186, 189, 309, 310, 311, 317

Bucknam, A., 46, 49, 51, 56, 58, 102, 189, 199, 207, 225, 274

Bunce, A., 183

Burchfield, P. C., 330

Burke Johnson, R., 397

Burkhart, R., 190, 210, 212, 222, 230

Burnes, B., 28

Burns, A., 378, 379

Burns, M., 329, 331

Burris, M. A., 401

Burrows, C., 377, 386

Butterill, D., 395

Cagney, K., 363

Campbell, D., 13

Caracelli, V. J., 10, 11*t*, 13, 14, 21, 24, 59, 124, 135, 152, 208

Carboni, L. W., 27

Carera, K. A., 140, 251

Carling, P., 399, 401

Carr, S., 395

Carr, W., 29, 95

Carson, L. G., 361

Casey, M., 202

Cash, J. L., 401

Cavanagh, S. J., 344

Chamberlain, P., 319

Chambers, M., 355

Chang, E., 66, 70, 71–73, 74*f*, 91, 92, 93, 95, 131, 157, 188, 189, 204, 212, 223, 230, 234, 305, 312, 320, 342–359

Chapman, C. Y., 67*t*

Chenoweth, L., 66, 70, 71–73, 74*f*, 91, 92, 93, 95, 131, 157, 188, 189, 204, 212, 223, 230, 234, 305, 312, 320, 342–359

Chilvers, R., 395, 396

Chinn, P. L., 350

Christ, T. W., 51, 54

Christensen, L., 16, 99, 104, 230

Christian, L. M., 197, 264

Chun, K., 238*t*, 242

Clark, G., 376

Clark, M. A., 67*t*, 267

Clark, V. I. P., 363

Clarke, C., 344, 395

Clarke, D. J., 331

Clarke, J., 395

Clarke, M., 66, 68*t*, 83, 223, 246

Clayton, J., 355, 356

Clegg Smith, K., 6, 7, 15, 57

Clenton, J., 377

Cloke, P., 397

Cochran, S. D., 360

Cochrane, J., 395

Cochran-Smith, M., 27

Coghlan, D., 314

Cohen, R., 361, 362, 369

Cole, M., 187*t*, 188

Collier, L., 66, 70, 71–73, 74*f*, 91, 92, 93, 95, 131, 157, 188, 189, 204, 212, 223, 230, 234, 305, 312, 320, 342–359

Collins, K., 191, 216

Colmer, K., 69*t*, 83

Combs, J., 245

Commanda, L. E., 209

Cooper, S., 317

Corbin, J., 239, 241

Cordes, J. G., 66, 83, 186, 189, 309, 310, 311, 317

Corona, R., 361, 362, 369

Counsell, S., 355

Courtney, M., 344

Covinsky, K., 355

Cox, B. A., 66, 188, 192, 207, 268

Cox, M. J., 267

Cozza, B., 331, 332

Craig, D. V., 239, 245, 302, 303, 306, 307, 308, 312, 317, 321, 326

Craig, S. L., 66, 70, 73–75, 76*f*, 91, 92, 95, 96, 141, 154, 174, 176*f*, 188, 194, 203, 204, 208, 214, 360–375

Cranston, K., 360

Creswell, J. W., 4, 5, 6, 7, 9, 10, 11*t*, 13, 14, 15, 18, 19, 20, 21, 22, 24, 34, 44, 46, 51, 55, 56, 57, 58, 63, 75, 96, 97, 98, 99, 100*f*, 102, 104, 105, 106, 107, 108, 113, 116, 118, 119, 120*t*, 124, 125, 129, 131, 132, 133, 135, 136, 137, 138, 140, 141, 143, 150, 152, 155, 159, 171, 172, 180, 182, 183, 184, 191, 193, 194, 197, 198, 200, 201, 202, 203, 204, 205, 208, 211, 216, 217, 219, 221, 222, 223, 232, 233, 235, 239, 240*f*, 245, 246, 247, 249, 250, 256, 257, 259, 264, 268, 269, 270, 275, 276, 279, 284, 289, 292, 293, 299, 320, 327, 332, 362, 363, 397, 402

Crilly, T., 312

Csiernik, R., 97, 394, 395, 396, 397*f*, 399, 400

Culhane, D. P., 395, 396

Cunningham, J. L., 127, 167, 261, 264, 269, 270, 276, 278

Currall, S. C., 58

Curry, L. A., 55

Cutforth, N., 189

Cxford, A. F., 339

Daly, J., 66, 68*t*, 83, 223, 246

Damschroder, L. J., 319

Dana, N. F., 335

Daniels, P., 66, 147, 161, 195, 222

Datta, L., 16

D'Augelli, A. R., 360

Davidson, P., 66, 68*t*, 83, 223, 246

Davidson, P. M., 59, 60, 200, 232, 304

Davies, J., 184, 216

Davis, M., 35, 36, 37, 44, 45, 46, 47, 103, 105, 186*t*, 189, 198, 209, 309, 313

Davis, W., 125, 126, 286, 289

Deacon, S. A., 401

DeFranco, J., 58, 83

Dellinger, A. B., 259, 278, 282*t*, 293

DeMarco, G. M. P., Jr., 162

Dentato, M., 362

Denzin, N. K., 13, 69*t*, 75, 232, 299, 363, 368

DeVellis, R. F., 143

Diagne, M., 203, 313, 315, 317

Diaz, Y. E., 363

Diaz-Escamilla, R., 97, 260

Digiacomo, M., 66, 68*t*, 83, 223, 246

Dillman, D. A., 197, 264

Donaldson, L. P., 371

Donohue, P., 189

Dorman, J., 193, 207

Dornyei, Z., 378, 379, 383, 385, 388

Dowling, A. F., 66, 188, 192, 207, 268

Downs, T. J., 83, 196, 305

Drapeau, A. E., 315

Draper, R. J., 331, 332, 340

Dubins, B., 66

Duffield, C., 355

Duncan, C., 70, 77–80, 91, 97, 137, 173, 175*f*, 186*t*, 193, 213, 224, 228, 249, 307, 313, 321, 393–406

Duran, B., 251

Durbin, J., 395

Dustman, P. A., 315

Edmonds, T., 361, 362, 369

Edmonds, W. A., 88

Edwards, C., 361, 362, 369

Efthymia, P., 67*t*, 200, 209, 225, 312

Eisen, S., 360

Eisinger, A., 31

Elkins, K., 362

Elliott, J., 39, 41*f*, 99

Elwood, J., 377, 378

Endacott, R., 317

Epstein, I., 371

Epstein, S., 371

Esterhay, R. I., 66, 188, 192, 207, 268

Evans, R. R., 140, 251

Evashwick C., 316

Evoy, L., 399, 400

Fagin, C., 355

Fakhoury, W. K. H., 395

Falout, J., 377, 378

Faulkner, A. H., 360

Fawson, P. C., 66, 225, 232, 249, 260

Febbrara, A., 395

Fetters, M., 55, 140, 397

Fey, J. T., 339

Field, P. A., 345

Fine, M., 188, 208, 211, 212

Fink, A., 96, 97, 116

Fiske, D. W., 13

Flatley, M., 68*t*, 83, 208, 209, 212, 237*t*, 238

Fleiss, J., 242

Flemming, K., 397

Fleras, A., 68*t*, 304

Fletcher, J., 187*t*, 188

Folstein, M. F., 347

Folstein, S. E., 347
Forchuk, C., 70, 77–80, 91, 97, 137, 173,
        175f, 186t, 193, 213, 224, 228, 249, 307,
        313, 321, 393–406
Fortinsky, R., 355
Frankish, C. J., 394
Fraser, B. J., 193, 207
Freeman, W. L., 209
Fried, M. N., 331
Froggatt, K., 66, 137, 213
Fueyo, V., 34
Fujimoto, H., 376

Gabriel, S. E., 319
Galini, R., 67t, 200, 209, 225, 312
Galka, S. W., 394, 395
Gammill, D. M., 331
Ganley, D. D., 268
Gaspard, A., 66, 225, 246
Gay, L. R., 219, 223, 229, 230, 231, 256,
        260, 261, 292
Geiger, B. F., 140, 251
Genat, W. J., 183, 189, 204, 205, 221, 224, 260, 272, 318, 326
Gerrish, K., 355, 356
Giachello, A., 35, 36, 37, 44, 45, 46, 47, 103, 105, 186t, 189,
        198, 209, 309, 313
Gibson, N., 209
Gilman, S. E., 360
Glasson, J., 66, 70, 71–73, 74f, 91, 92, 93, 95,
        131, 157, 188, 189, 204, 212, 223, 230,
        234, 305, 312, 320, 342–359
Goble, R., 83, 196, 305
Godfrey, A. B., 354, 356
Goering, P., 395
Goldberg, J., 360
Goldfinger, S. M., 395
Goldman, H. H., 395
Goldsby, D. S., 331, 332
Gonzalez, T., 361, 362, 369
Goodman, W., 67t, 267
Gorlick, C., 395, 396
Gosin, M. N., 315
Gosling, A., 242
Gradidge, K., 345
Graham, E., 345
Graham, W. F., 10, 11t, 13, 14, 21, 24,
        124, 152, 208
Grant, J., 103

Gray, R., 9, 16, 17, 25
Green, D. O., 363
Greene, J. C., 5, 9, 10, 11t, 13, 14, 21, 24, 54, 55, 59, 119, 122t,
        124, 129, 135, 140, 144, 150, 152, 161, 208, 245, 257,
        259, 299, 320, 327
Greenfield, D., 188, 237t, 238, 241, 242, 314
Greenwood, D., 26, 34, 37, 49, 54, 56, 82
Greenwood, J., 344
Greysen, S. R., 66, 142, 236t, 238, 240, 241, 242, 251, 267, 304
Griffin, C. B., 31, 32, 36, 49, 58, 104
Grossman, A. H., 360
Guba, E. G., 208, 265, 267, 269, 273, 274
Guest, G., 119, 183, 239, 240, 241, 256
Gutmann, M., 171

Hacker, K., 207, 209, 221, 241, 314, 319
Hadley, T., 395, 396
Hales, B., 164, 165
Hall, B., 395, 399, 400
Hall, B. W., 394
Hall, T., 66, 70, 71–73, 74f, 91, 92, 93, 95, 131, 157, 188, 189,
        204, 212, 223, 230, 234, 305, 312, 320, 342–359
Hamm, E., 190, 316
Hammel, J., 69t, 83
Hamoline, R., 186t, 233, 236t, 238, 241, 242
Hancock, K., 66, 70, 71–73, 74f, 91, 92, 93, 95, 131, 157, 188,
        189, 204, 212, 223, 230, 234, 305, 312, 320, 342–359
Hanson, W., 171
Hart, E., 344
Harthun, M. L., 315
Hashimoto, Y., 387
Hauth, A. C., 363
Hayes, A. A., 395, 396
Hazelton, L., 344
Hazipantelis, M., 395
Hellman, C. M., 190, 210, 212, 222, 230
Hemmings, A., 55
Henderson, A., 66
Herbert, A., 27
Herr, K., 27, 28, 29, 32, 33, 34, 35, 37, 45, 47, 53, 55, 56, 57, 58,
        59, 96, 101, 102, 116, 196, 233, 259, 260, 265, 268, 270,
        271, 272, 273, 274, 291, 292, 304, 305, 314, 319
Herrell, R., 360
Hesse-Biber, S. N., 110
Hesselink, A. E., 304
Hicks, S., 251
Hides, L., 362
Higgins, J. W., 59, 69t, 250

Hill, J. L., 66, 187*t*, 231, 234*t*

Hill-Murray, F., 66, 70, 71–73, 74*f*, 91, 92, 93, 95, 131, 157, 188, 189, 204, 212, 223, 230, 234, 305, 312, 320, 342–359

Hinchcliff, R., 188, 237*t*, 238, 241, 242, 314

Hinchey, P. H., 26, 29, 33, 44, 45, 46, 47, 49, 56, 96, 101, 102, 197, 208, 219, 233, 267, 268, 274, 304, 308, 314, 317, 327

Hirsch, C. R., 339

Hitchcock, J. H., 57, 82, 209

Hoch, J. S., 399, 400

Hoe-Asjoe, H., 363

Holland, D., 66, 225, 246

Hood, M., 377, 378

Horgan, S., 395

Horwitz, S., 319

Howe, K. R., 14, 16

Huberman, M., 232, 233, 241, 242

Hudson, K., 348

Hughes, M., 360

Hunter, A., 14

Hurlburt, M., 319

Hussaini, K. S., 190, 316

Hutchinson, D. S., 395

Hwang, S. W., 394

Islam, N., 363

Israel, B. A., 30, 31, 32, 36, 49, 58, 104, 363

Ivankova, N., 3, 6, 7, 8, 9, 10, 12, 14, 15, 18, 20, 21, 22, 25, 58, 63, 66, 135, 136, 137, 140, 147, 159, 171, 172, 180, 193, 249, 251, 259, 275, 397, 402

Jacobs, D., 66, 147, 161, 195, 222

Jacobson, N., 68*t*, 304

Jacobson, W., 259

James, E. A., 46, 49, 51, 56, 58, 102, 189, 199, 207, 225, 274

Janiszewski Goodin, H., 355

Janzen, R., 68*t*, 304

Jenkins, C., 267

Jensen, E., 395, 396

Jeon, Y., 345

Jiao, Q., 191

Jick, T. D., 13

Johnson, B., 4, 9, 12, 13, 16, 17, 24, 25, 53, 54, 55, 58, 59, 60, 99, 104, 153, 212, 217, 230, 279

Johnson, C. V., 190, 210, 212, 222, 230

Johnson, J., 348

Johnson, J. C., 201

Johnson, L., 183

Johnson, R. B., 259, 270, 275, 276, 277, 278, 281*t*, 289, 293

Jones, K. R., 344

Jorgenson, P. R., 330

Kahana, E., 355

Kavanagh, T., 236*t*, 238, 241, 242, 315

Kawamura, Y., 3, 14, 15, 25, 58, 63, 275

Keith, R. E., 319

Kelly, D., 395

Kelly, M., 331

Kelly, T. A., 363

Kemmis, S., 27, 29, 32, 33, 34, 37, 38, 40*f*, 49, 57, 95, 344

Kemp, L., 256

Kennedy, L. B., 140, 251

Kennedy, S., 66, 137, 213

Kennedy, T. D., 88

Kennerly, S., 55

Keon, W. J., 394, 395

Kessler, R. C., 360

Kikuchi, K., 377, 378

Kilbride, C., 68*t*, 83, 208, 209, 212, 237*t*, 238

King, K. P., 68*t*, 269

Kirby, M. J., 394, 395

Kirsh, B., 395

Kirsh, S. R., 319

Klassen, A. C., 6, 7, 15, 57

Kolarik, K., 377

Koorland, M. A., 34

Koshy, E., 27, 33, 49, 51, 56, 66, 95, 96, 97, 98, 101, 102, 103, 104, 112, 116, 197, 199, 200, 201, 202, 203, 204, 205, 206, 208, 216, 221, 225, 232, 233, 235, 239, 256, 259, 260, 273, 292, 303, 318, 327

Koshy, V., 27, 33, 49, 51, 56, 66, 95, 96, 97, 98, 101, 102, 103, 104, 112, 116, 197, 199, 200, 201, 202, 203, 204, 205, 206, 208, 216, 221, 225, 232, 233, 235, 239, 256, 259, 260, 273, 292, 303, 318, 327

Kostos, K., 66, 70, 71, 72*f*, 93, 94, 99, 100, 101, 132, 154, 173, 174*f*, 188, 189, 192, 199, 207, 211, 228, 237*t*, 238, 305, 312, 320, 328–341

Kramer, M. K., 350

Kresevic, D., 355

Kreuger, R., 202, 402

Krieger, J., 205, 207, 209

Krueger, P., 66, 83, 313
Krupa, T., 395
Kuzmicz, J., 186*t*, 233, 236*t*, 238, 241, 242
Kwon, S., 238*t*, 242

Lamb, H. R., 395
Lamb, K., 66, 68*t*, 83, 223, 246
Landefeld, C., 355
Landsverk, J., 319
Langer, J. A., 331
Larson, N., 334
Lawrence, J. S., 363
Leavy, P., 110
Lee, S. M., 67*t*, 267
Leech, N. L., 107, 164, 191, 259, 278, 282*t*, 293
Lehman, A. F., 399
Leman, J., 184, 216
LeMiere, J., 344
Levin, M., 34, 37, 54, 56, 82
Levinson, W., 27
Levitan, E., 399, 400
Lewin, G., 28, 38, 39*f*, 53, 55, 61, 88, 92, 93, 298, 307
Lewin, K., 30
Lightbown, P. M., 376
Lincoln, Y. S., 75, 208, 232, 265, 267, 269, 273, 274, 363, 368
Lingard, L., 27
Littlewood, W., 377, 378
London, K., 189
Loomis, D., 53, 119
Lowery, J., 319
Lubman, D. I., 362
Lucas, G. I., 66, 142, 236*t*, 238, 240, 241, 242, 251, 267, 304
Lucero, J., 251
Luginaah, I., 66, 225, 246
Lumby, J., 355
Lustick, D., 207
Ly, M. Y., 97, 260
Lyons, A., 58, 83
Lyons, M., 360
Lytle, S. L., 27

Macauley, A. C., 209
MacDonald, G. M., 395, 396
MacQueen, K. M., 239, 240, 241, 256
Madnick, F., 69*t*, 83
Magwood, G. S., 267
Mahoney, F. A., 347
Maiter, S., 68*t*, 304

Maritz, R., 66, 132, 247, 260, 261
Marriner Tomey, A., 344
Marteau, T., 242
Marullo, S., 189
Mason, J., 59
Maticka-Tyndale, E., 66, 225, 246
Maxcy, S. J., 16, 25, 54
Maxwell, J., 16, 53, 119, 275
Mayberry, R. M., 66, 147, 161, 195, 222
Mays, V. M., 360
McCabe, M. L., 209
McCarten, J., 379
McCarthy, M., 379
McDowell, K. G., 330
McGuire, C. M., 27
McHugh, P. R., 347
McIntosh, M. E., 331, 332, 340
McKellar, L., 66
McKernan, J., 29, 49, 53
McNiff, J., 44, 51, 56, 57, 58, 96, 101, 200, 259, 273, 292
McTaggart, R., 27, 32, 33, 34, 37, 38, 40*f*, 49, 57, 344
Means, T., 190, 316
Medves, J., 67*t*
Melnikow, J., 97, 260
Merriam, S. B., 265, 269
Mertens, D. M., 55, 60, 82, 183
Mertler, C. A., 101, 108, 110, 116, 210, 222, 223, 225, 228, 229, 231, 233, 256, 261, 270, 308, 319, 327
Metraux, S., 395, 396
Meyer, I. H., 360
Meyer, J., 68*t*, 83, 208, 209, 212, 237*t*, 238
Milbourne, P., 397
Milenkiewicz, M. T., 46, 49, 51, 56, 58, 102, 189, 199, 207, 225, 274
Miles, M., 232, 233, 241, 242
Miller, D. L., 270
Mills, G. E., 30, 33, 34, 42, 43*f*, 46, 49, 51, 55, 56, 66, 95, 96, 97, 101, 102, 104, 106, 108, 116, 197, 198, 216, 219, 221, 223, 228, 229, 230, 231, 233, 245, 249, 251, 256, 260, 261, 265, 268, 269, 273, 292, 293, 302, 308, 309, 314, 319, 326, 332
Mirza, M., 69*t*, 83
Mitchell, T., 103
Mittapalli, K., 16, 275
Mizrahi, T., 371
Mohr, J. J., 354
Moldovan, M., 188, 237*t*, 238, 241, 242, 314

Montgomery, P., 70, 77–80, 91, 97, 137, 173, 175*f*, 186*t*, 193, 213, 224, 228, 249, 307, 313, 321, 393–406
Morgan, D., 402
Morgan, D. L., 14, 135, 138, 140
Morse, J. M., 10, 11*t*, 12, 13, 14, 20, 21, 68*t*, 119, 121*t*, 124, 129, 132, 135, 136, 137, 138, 140, 141, 143, 150, 152, 153, 155, 171, 180, 193, 216, 345
Morton-Cooper, A., 272
Mucciarone, D., 83, 196, 305
Mumford, V., 188, 237*t*, 238, 241, 242, 314
Murphey, T., 377, 378
Murphy, P., 69*t*, 83
Murray, A., 395

Nagel, J., 15
Nair, S., 142, 143, 160, 195, 231
Namey, E. E., 239, 240, 241, 256
Nandi, C., 35, 36, 37, 44, 45, 46, 47, 103, 105, 186*t*, 189, 198, 209, 309, 313
Nastasi, B. K., 57, 82, 209
Nelson, E. C., 354
Nelson, G., 103, 394, 395, 399, 400
Neumann, C., 66, 146, 195, 252, 303
Newman, C., 162
Newman, I., 162
Newman, S. D., 267
Niederhauser, V., 97, 260
Niehaus, L., 10, 11*t*, 12, 21, 119, 121*t*, 124, 129, 132, 135, 136, 137, 138, 140, 141, 143, 150, 152, 153, 155, 171, 180, 193, 216
Niemiee, C. P., 389
Noble, J., 187*t*, 188
Noftle, J. T., 268
Nolan, A., 344
Nolen, A. L., 112
Normand, S. T., 319
Nunan, D., 377, 379, 380

O'Cathain, A., 55, 275, 279, 282*t*, 293, 319, 320, 327
Ochocka, J., 68*t*, 304
O'Connell, M., 187*t*, 188
O'Faire, J. D., 142, 143, 160, 195, 231
O'Leary, Z., 44, 45, 46, 57
Olorunnipa, T., 361
Olson, D., 331, 332, 340
O'Neal, M. R., 140, 251
O'Neill, M., 69*t*, 83

Onwuegbuzie, A., 4, 16, 24, 53, 54, 55, 58, 60, 107, 164, 191, 245, 259, 270, 275, 276, 277, 278, 281*t*, 289, 293, 397
Orem, D. E., 344, 347, 350, 354, 356
O'Riordan, A., 67*t*
Ortrun, Z. S., 27
Ory, M., 316
Ostrow, D., 360

Padgett, D., 4, 57
Padmore, J., 317
Palcanis, K. G., 140, 251
Palinkas, L. A., 319
Palmer, R., 355
Park, C., 377
Parker, E., 363
Parker, E. A., 30
Parkinson, S., 395
Paterson, M., 67*t*
Patton, M. Q., 12, 13, 16, 184, 363
Patton, S., 83, 196, 305
Paul, G., 66, 68*t*, 83, 223, 246
Pawsey, M., 188, 237*t*, 238, 241, 242, 314
Payne, Y. A., 242
Penk, W. E., 395
Perkins, D. V., 394, 395
Perry, J., 59
Perry, L., 68*t*, 83, 208, 209, 212, 237*t*, 238
Perry, S., 399, 400
Pettit, J., 56
Phillips, J., 59, 60, 200, 232, 304
Phillips, K., 363
Pickard, J., 66, 136, 159, 312
Pincombe, J., 66
Pino, M., 67*t*, 82, 158, 192, 204, 247
Plano Clark, V. L., 4, 5, 6, 7, 9, 10, 11*t*, 13, 14, 15, 18, 19, 20, 21, 24, 55, 56, 57, 102, 104, 107, 108, 113, 116, 118, 119, 120*t*, 124, 125, 129, 131, 132, 133, 135, 137, 138, 140, 141, 143, 150, 152, 155, 164, 171, 180, 191, 193, 194, 211, 217, 245, 246, 247, 250, 257, 259, 276, 279, 284, 289, 293, 299, 320, 327
Plant, K., 66, 132, 247, 260, 261
Plant, M., 312
Plume, S. K., 354
Powers, L. S., 401
Prelip, M., 66, 146, 195, 252, 303
Pretorius, M., 66, 132, 247, 260, 261

Price, B., 66, 187*t*, 231, 234*t*
Priebe, S., 395
Punch, K. F., 247
Puoane, T., 199, 206

Quantz, D., 394
Quaraishi, M., 395
Quinlan, E., 186*t*, 233, 236*t*, 238, 241, 242
Quinn, R. J., 331, 332, 340
Quintanar, A. P., 268

Rabkin, J., 205, 207, 209
Rachuba, I., 395
Ragin, C. C., 15
Rahn, J., 330
Raines, J. A., 394, 395
Rallis, S. F., 14, 16
Ramakrishnan, V., 360
Ramirez, D., 35, 36, 37, 44, 45, 46, 47, 103, 105, 186*t*, 189, 198, 209, 309, 313
Ramos, C., 35, 36, 37, 44, 45, 46, 47, 103, 105, 186*t*, 189, 198, 209, 309, 313
Ramsden, V., 186*t*, 233, 236*t*, 238, 241, 242
Randolph, F. L., 395
Razzano, L., 395
Reason, P., 28, 344, 356
Redman, R., 344
Reed, J., 344
Reese, D. J., 142, 143, 160, 195, 231
Reichardt, C. S., 14, 16
Reid, C., 51, 188
Reutzel, D. R., 66, 225, 232, 249, 260
Rey, M., 363
Rich, A. R., 395
Richards, J., 377
Richardson, L., 51, 188
Ridenour, C. S., 162
Robbins, C. M., 209
Robertson, J., 209
Robin, M., 27
Rodriguez, B., 67*t*, 82, 158, 192, 204, 247
Roessner, J., 354, 356
Rog, D. J., 395, 396
Rogers, J., 395
Rose, B., 331
Rose, D., 70, 77–80, 91, 97, 137, 173, 175*f*, 186*t*, 193, 213, 224, 228, 249, 307, 313, 321, 393–406
Rosenthal, B., 371

Rosenthal, M. S., 66, 142, 236*t*, 238, 240, 241, 242, 251, 267, 304
Ross, L., 83, 196, 304
Rossman, G. B., 14, 16
Rubin, H. J., 372
Rubin, I., 372
Rulnick, S., 83, 196, 305
Ryan, A., 355
Ryan, R. M., 389
Ryan, S., 376

Sagor, R., 46
Sampson, R. J., 66, 70, 75–77, 78*f*, 89, 91, 92, 95, 144, 177*f*, 178, 198, 214, 236*t*, 238, 253, 306, 312, 321, 376–392
Sandiford, H., 379
Sayad, J., 35, 36, 37, 44, 45, 46, 47, 103, 105, 186*t*, 189, 198, 209, 309, 313
Schachter, C., 32
Scharmer, O., 30, 49
Schoen, H. L., 339
Schofield, R., 399, 400
Schopler, J. H., 361
Schulz, A., 363
Schulz, A. J., 30, 31, 32, 36, 49, 58, 104
Schutt, R. K., 395
Schwab, J. J., 369
Schwandt, T. A., 241
Seers, K., 236*t*, 238, 241, 242, 315
Selig, S. M., 31, 32, 36, 49, 58, 104
Semptik, J., 259
Senge, P., 30, 49
Senturia, K., 31
Sexton, D., 348
Seychuk, C., 395, 396
Seymour, J. E., 66, 137, 213
Sharify, D., 205, 207, 209
Sharman, E., 356
Shattuck, J., 66
Shavelson, R. J., 15
Sheaff, R., 371
Shenton, A. K., 265, 268
Shepherd, G., 395
Shin, E., 66, 70–71, 72*f*, 93, 94, 99, 100, 101, 132, 154, 173, 174*f*, 188, 189, 192, 199, 207, 211, 228, 237*t*, 238, 305, 312, 320, 328–341
Short, S. D., 356
Shortt, K., 302

Shoultz, J., 97, 260

Shulha, L. M., 57, 82

Sidani, S., 236*t*, 238, 241, 242, 315

Sieber, S. D., 13

Siegel, L. M., 361

Silbey, R., 329, 331

Sim, S. C., 238*t*, 242

Simich, L., 68*t*, 304

Sinha, D., 83, 196, 305

Slaght, E., 361

Slusser, W., 66, 146, 195, 252, 303

Smith, J. A., 66, 225, 232, 249, 260

Smith, J. K., 14

Smith, M., 362

Smyth, J. D., 197, 264

Song, L., 205, 207, 209

Spada, N., 376

Speechley, M., 399, 400

Speedy, S., 356

Stake, R., 274

Stalker, C., 32

Starks, M. T., 360

Stephen, K., 27

Stephens, M., 331

Stevens, B., 236*t*, 238, 241, 242, 315

Stevenson, J., 355

Stevenson, L. Y., 363

Stick, S., 6, 7, 8, 9, 10, 12, 18, 20, 21, 22,
    66, 135, 136, 137, 159, 171, 172, 180,
    193, 249, 402

Stipek, D., 389

Stoecker, R., 189

Strand, K., 189

Strang, K. D., 66, 83

Strauss, A., 68*t*, 239, 241

Street, A., 187*t*, 202, 205, 238*t*, 240

Stringer, E. T., 27, 30, 40, 42*f*, 44, 47, 49, 53, 54, 55, 66, 101,
    103, 111, 182, 183, 185, 187, 189, 200, 202, 203, 204,
    205, 206, 208, 209, 210, 216, 221, 224, 239, 260, 265,
    272, 274, 292, 308, 309, 314, 316, 318, 319, 326

Stripling, J. D., 167, 168

Stronks, K., 304

Sullivan, M., 55, 82

Sylph, J., 395

Tanaka, H., 293

Tandon, R., 27

Tandon, S. D., 363

Tanke, E. D., 112

Tanke, T. J., 112

Tanzman, B., 395

Tashakkori, A., 4, 5, 7, 9, 10, 11*t*, 13, 14, 16, 17, 18, 19, 21, 24,
    51, 54, 56, 63, 68*t*, 69*t*, 107, 112, 119, 120*t*, 124, 125,
    128, 129, 133, 135, 136, 137, 138, 140, 141, 143, 144,
    150, 152, 153, 154, 171, 180, 182, 184, 191, 197, 198,
    199, 201, 202, 211, 216, 259, 261, 275, 276, 280*t*, 289,
    293, 298, 299, 320, 327

Tata, E., 67*t*

Taut, S., 66, 83

Teddlie, C., 4, 9, 10, 11*t*, 13, 14, 16, 17, 18, 19, 21, 24, 54, 56,
    58, 68*t*, 69*t*, 107, 112, 119, 120*t*, 124, 125, 128, 129, 133,
    135, 136, 137, 138, 140, 141, 143, 144, 150, 152, 153,
    154, 171, 180, 182, 184, 191, 197, 198, 199, 201, 202,
    211, 216, 223, 245, 246, 247, 248, 250, 251, 252, 257,
    259, 261, 275, 276, 289, 289*t*, 293, 298, 299, 327

Tenkorang, E., 66, 225, 246

Teram, E., 32

Tesch, R., 232

Thomas-MacLean, R., 186*t*, 233, 236*t*, 238, 241, 242

Thorndike, R. M., 260, 263, 264, 292

Thorndike-Christ, T. M., 260, 292

Thornewill, J., 66, 188, 192, 207, 268

Tilley, S., 401

Titchen, A., 344, 350, 356

Tomal, D. R., 38, 56, 196, 197, 198, 199, 220, 221, 222, 228,
    229, 256, 260, 298, 314, 316, 326

Tong, S., 344

Torre, M. E., 188, 208, 211, 212

Toure, L., 203, 313, 315, 317

Towler, A. J., 58

Towne, L., 15

Trainor, J., 395

Trinh-Shevrin, C., 238*t*, 242, 363

Tritter, J., 57

True, W. R., 360

Tsuang, M., 360

Turner, E., 237*t*, 238

Turner, K., 97, 394, 395, 396, 397*f*, 399, 400

Turner, L. A., 4, 12, 13, 53, 54, 55, 59, 153,
    212, 217, 279, 397

Tuttle, C. L., 331, 337

Twohig, P. L., 209

Ushioda, E., 378, 385

Vander Putten, J., 112

VanDevanter, N., 238*t*, 242

VanTosh, L., 395

Vecchiarelli, S., 66, 146, 195, 252, 303
Veluri, R., 70, 77–80, 91, 97, 137, 173, 175*f*, 186*t*, 193, 213, 224, 228, 249, 307, 313, 321, 393–406
Verhoeff, A. P., 304
Vogt, P. W., 220, 221, 222, 223, 228, 229, 230, 231

Wadsworth, Y., 344, 349, 379
Wafra, N., 66, 69*t*
Walker, E., 344
Wallace, M. I., 378
Wallerstein, N., 251
Walsh, A., 344
Walsh-Bowers, T., 394
Wang, C., 205, 216
Wang, C. C., 401
Wang, E. A., 66, 142, 236*t*, 238, 240, 241, 242, 251, 267, 304
Ward-Griffin, C., 97, 394, 395, 396, 397*f*, 399, 400
Warheit, G. J., 369
Warren, C., 142, 143, 160, 195, 231
Warren, S. R., 268
Wasylenki, D., 395
Waterman, H., 27, 33, 49, 51, 56, 66, 95, 96, 97, 98, 101, 102, 103, 104, 112, 116, 197, 199, 200, 201, 202, 203, 204, 205, 206, 208, 216, 221, 225, 232, 233, 235, 239, 256, 303, 318, 327
Watt-Watson, J., 236*t*, 238, 241, 242, 315
Waywood, A., 331
Webb, C., 66, 83, 224
Weightman, H., 66, 146, 195, 252, 303
Weinman, J., 242
Weller, S. C., 201
Westbrook, J. I., 188, 237*t*, 238, 241, 242, 314
Westhues, A., 68*t*, 304
White, M., 345
White, P., 15
White, R., 66, 69*t*
White Hat, E., 251
Whitehead, J., 44, 51, 56, 57, 58, 96, 101, 200, 259, 273, 292

Widdowfield, R. C., 397
Wiktorowicz, M., 399, 400
Wilkes, L., 344
Williams, A. M., 355
Williams, N. B., 331
Williamson, D. C., 267
Williamson, G. R., 66, 83, 224
Willis, D., 380
Willis, J., 380
Wilson, A., 55, 82
Wilson, B. L., 14, 16
Wilson, M. M., 331, 332, 340
Wilson, R. J., 57, 82
Winter, R., 54
Wisniewska, D., 51, 82
Wolcott, H. F., 42
Woodward, J., 331, 332, 340
Worley, J. A., 190, 210, 212, 222, 230
Wright, D. B., 189
Wynn, S. R., 27
Wynne, B. D., 331

Xiao, L., 377

Yacco, S., 67*t*, 267
Yancey, E. M., 66, 147, 161, 195, 222
Yap, T., 55
Yendol-Silva, D., 335
Yin, R. K., 21, 53, 107, 153, 154, 180, 212
Young, J. H., 67*t*
Young, L., 59, 69*t*, 250
Yu, F., 191

Zald, M., 372
Zanko, A., 66, 187*t*, 231, 234*t*
Zecchin, R., 66, 68*t*, 83, 223, 246
Zhenhui, R., 377
Zilberman, D., 66
Zoellner, J., 66, 187*t*, 231, 234*t*

SUBJECT INDEX

Acting phase:
    action research, 42–43, 45*f*
    mixed methods in action research, 61*f*, 62, 72*f*, 74*f*, 76*f*, 78*f*, 80*f*
    MMAR Study Process Model, 90*f*, 92
    validation process, 287*t*
Action plan, 47, 308–314
Action research:
    action plan for, 47
    action research model, 39, 41*f*
    change theory, 28–29
    collaboration, 33
    community-based action research, 27, 30
    community-based participatory research, 27, 30–32
    community of interest, 30
    community orientation, 29–32
    conceptual models, 37–43
    cyclical nature, 44–46
    defining characteristics, 27–29
    dialectic spiral model, 42, 43*f*
    emancipatory framework, 34
    empowerment of, 34–35
    ethics, 111–112, 114 (box)
    features of, 29–35
    flexible nature, 46
    four-stage model, 38
    interacting spiral model, 40–41, 42*f*
    methodological characteristics, 44–47
    methodological steps model, 38, 39*f*
    multiple data sources for, 46–47
    participation, 33
    practical focus of, 32–33
    reconnaissance, 38, 39*f*
    reflective practice, 33–34
    research approaches, 27, 30–32
    research process steps, 42–43, 45*f*
    research study example, 35–37
    spiral model, 38–39, 40*f*

    stakeholders, 30
    sustainability, 31
    systematic inquiry, 44
    triangulation, 46–47
    worldview, 27
    See also Mixed methods in action research; Mixed methods action research (MMAR)
    See also Introduction, 26–27; Reading resources, 49; Reflective questions, 48–49; Summary, 47–48
Action research assessment:
    catalytic validity, 271 (box)
    characteristics of, 270, 272
    democratic validity, 271 (box)
    dialogic validity, 272 (box)
    generalizability, 274–275
    insider-outside perspectives, 272–273
    objectivity, 273–274
    outcome validity, 271 (box)
    process validity, 271 (box)
    subjectivity, 273–274
    transferability, 274–275
    validity criteria, 271–272 (box)
    See also Qualitative data assessment; Quantitative data assessment; Validation process
    See also Reading resources, 292–293; Reflective questions, 291–292; Summary, 290–291
Action research model, 39, 41*f*
Action research process model. *See* MMAR Study Process Model
Agency for Healthcare Research Quality, 15
American Educational Research Association, 15
American Evaluation Association, 15
Analysis of covariance (ANCOVA), 227*t*
Analysis of variance (ANOVA), 226*t*, 229–230 (box)
Assessment quality of research. *See* Validation process
ATLAS.ti software, 243*t*
Audiovisual material, 205–206 (box)
Australia, 15

Barthel Activity of Daily Living (ADL) index, 72, 73, 345, 347–348, 350, 352

Best Practices for Mixed Methods Research in the Health Sciences, 5–6, 7 (box), 15

Between-strategy mixed methods data collection, 211–214

Bias, 268–269

BioMed Central, 406

Bottom-up approach, 51

Bracketing technique, 268–269

British Journal of Health Psychology, 15

Canada, 15

Capacity building, 103, 209

Caregiving Activities Scale (CAS), 72–73, 345, 348, 349*t*, 350, 351

Catalytic validity, 271 (box)

Change theory, 28–29

Chicago Southeast Diabetes Community Action Coalition, 35–36 (box), 209, 313

Chi-square test, 227*t*, 231–232 (box)

Cluster sampling, 184 (box)

Codebook, 240–241

Coding, 239–244

Coefficient alpha, 263

Coefficient of equivalence, 263

Coefficient of stability, 263

Collaboration, 33, 57

Combined methods:
  integrating quantitative and qualitative methods, 19 (box), 21–22, 156–157, 159, 160, 161
  mixed methods data analysis, 246–247

Community action/intervention:
  action plan, 47
  action plan development, 308–309, 310–311 (box)
  action planning levels, 309, 312–314
  evaluation process, 316–318
  Good Reporting of a Mixed Methods Study (GRAMMS), 319, –320
  implementation challenges, 314–316
  implementation process, 307–316
  interpretive consistency process, 299
  meta-inferences, 298–307
  reflection process, 302–303
  research dissemination, 318–321
  research interpretation process, 299–305
  research outcomes, 300–302
  research proposal, 321–324
  research purpose, 300–302
  research questions, 300–302
  research study examples, 305–307
  stakeholder involvement, 303–305
  See also Introduction, 298; Reading resources, 326–327; Reflective questions, 325–326; Summary, 324–325

Community-based action research, 27, 30, 31–32 (box)

Community-based participatory research, 27, 30–32, 362–363

Community of interest, 30

Community orientation, 29–32

Comprehensive research, 53

Concurrent Quan + Qual study design:
  advantages/disadvantages, 132–133
  applications, 131–132
  conceptual model, 130f
  data collection, 198 (box), 199 (box), 200 (box), 202 (box), 203 (box), 204 (box), 205–206 (box), 209, 213t
  decision flowchart, 134f
  evaluation phase example, 165 (box)
  integration points, 156–158
  integration strategies, 156–158
  methodological characteristics, 128–131
  mixed methods data analysis, 246–247, 248f, 253 (box)
  quantitative data analysis, 222 (box), 223 (box), 224 (box), 228 (box), 230 (box), 231 (box), 232 (box)
  research purpose, 129 (box)
  sampling, 191–192
  validation process, 289 (box)
  visual diagram, 173, 174f

Concurrent timing, 19 (box), 20

Confirmability, 265, 266 (box)

Connected methods:
  mixed methods data analysis, 247–249, 250f, 253–254 (box)

Constant comparative method, 241

Constructivist worldview, 54

Construct validity, 260, 262 (box)

Consumer Housing Preference Survey Short Version, 399, 400–401

Content validity, 260, 262 (box)

Convenience sampling, 184 (box), 186*t*

Correlation coefficient, 223 (box)

Credibility, 265, 266 (box)

Criterion validity, 260, 262 (box)

Cronbach's alpha, 263

Curriculum and Evaluation Standards for School Mathematics (NCTM), 330, 331
Cyclical nature:
 action research, 44–46
 mixed methods in action research, 56–57

Data analysis. *See* Mixed methods data analysis; Qualitative data analysis; Quantitative data analysis
Data collection:
 assessment process, 198–199 (box)
 audiovisual material, 205–206 (box)
 between-strategy mixed methods data collection, 211–214
 capacity building, 209
 concurrent Quan + Qual study design, 198 (box), 199 (box), 200 (box), 202 (box), 203 (box), 204 (box), 205–206 (box), 209, 213*t*
 considerations, 206–211
 data quality, 210
 documents, 204–205 (box)
 focus group interview, 202–203 (box)
 intermethod mixing, 212–214
 interviews, 201–203 (box)
 intramethod mixing, 212–214
 key informant interview, 201 (box)
 multistrand study design, 198 (box), 200 (box), 213t
 observation, 203–204 (box)
 observation checklist, 199–200 (box)
 photo-voice, 205–206 (box)
 prioritizing data sources, 206–208
 qualitative data sources, 200–206
 quantitative data sources, 196–200
 sequential Qual-Quan study design, 203 (box), 204-205 (box), 213*t*
 sequential Quan-Qual study design, 202 (box), 204 (box), 213t
 surveys, 197–198 (box)
 triangulation, 208
 within-strategy mixed methods data collection, 211–214
 See also Introduction, 182; Reading resources, 216–217; Reflective questions, 215–216; Summary, 214–215
Democratic validity, 271 (box)
Demographic Profile, 399–400
Dependability, 265, 266 (box)
Descriptive statistics, 220–224
Diagnosing phase:
 action research, 42–43, 45*f*

mixed methods in action research, 61, 72*f*, 74*f*, 76*f*, 78*f*, 80*f*
 MMAR Study Process Model, 89, 90*f*, 91
 validation process, 286*t*
Dialectic action research spiral model, 42, 43*f*
Dialectic stance, 54–55
Dialogic validity, 272 (box)
Discriminant function analysis, 227*t*
Discriminant validity, 262 (box)
Documents, 204–205 (box)
Dynamic Indicators of Basic Early Literacy Skills (DIBELS), 105, 106 (box), 108–110, 163 (box), 301

Early Interventions in Reading (EIR) Tier 3 program, 164, 165 (box), 166
Educational Leadership in Higher Education (ELHE-DE), 8–9 (box), 12
Elder nursing care study (example B):
 acting phase, 92
 Barthel Activity of Daily Living (ADL) index, 72, 73, 345, 347–348, 350, 352
 Caregiving Activities Scale (CAS), 72–73, 345, 348, 349*t*, 350, 351
 community action/intervention, 305–306, 312, 320–321
 conclusions, 357
 concurrent Quan + Qual study design, 131–132, 157
 data analysis, 351
 data collection, 212, 350
 diagnosing phase, 91
 evaluation phase, 93
 field notes, 348
 full text, 342–359
 introduction, 344–345
 Medication Regime Assessment, 345, 348, 352
 mini-mental state examination (MMSE) scale, 347
 mixed methods approach, 345–351
 mixed methods in action research, 71–73, 74*f*
 monitoring phase, 93
 overview, 343–344
 participants, 346–347
 participatory action research (PAR), 344–345, 346*t*, 349–350
 Pharmacy Summary Card (PSC), 348
 planning phase, 92
 qualitative data analysis, 234–235, 351
 qualitative results, 352–354
 quantitative data analysis, 223 (box), 230 (box), 351
 quantitative results, 351–352, 353*t*

recommendations, 356–357
research design, 345
research implications, 354–357
research instruments, 345, 347–348
research problem identification, 95
research questions, 345
results, 351–354
sampling, 188, 189
Self-care Deficit Theory, 344
Self-care Theory, 344
setting, 346
Theory of Nursing Systems, 344
Emancipatory framework:
action research, 34
mixed methods in action research, 55–56
Emic data, 58
Empowerment, 34–35
English as a Foreign Language (EFL) study (example D):
abstract, 376
acting phase, 92
action research, 378–379
community action/intervention, 306–307, 312, 313, 321
conclusions, 389–390
data collection, 214, 380
diagnosing phase, 89
full text, 376–392
introduction, 376–377
Language Learning Autobiography, 144, 146, 380, 391–392
Learning Experience Questionnaire (LEQ), 77, 146, 380, 383f, 386f
lesson style, 377–378
Lesson Style Questionnaire, 144, 146, 380, 382f, 391
methodology, 379–380
mixed methods in action research, 75–77, 78f
multistrand study design, 144, 146, 177f, 178
participants, 379
planning phase, 92
qualitative data analysis, 236t, 253
reconnaissance phase, 91–92
research cycles, 379, 380
research problem identification, 95–96
research questions, 381, 383, 386, 388
research results, 381–389
setting, 379
Epistemological similarities, 51–52
Equal priority, 19 (box), 20–21
Equivalent forms reliability, 260, 263

Ethics:
action research ethics, 111–112, 114 (box)
general research ethics, 110–111, 113 (box)
mixed methods action research (MMAR), 110–114
mixed methods research, 112–113, 114 (box)
Etic data, 57–58
Evaluation phase:
action research, 42–43, 45f
mixed methods in action research, 61f, 62, 72f, 74f, 76f, 78f, 80f
MMAR Study Process Model, 90f, 92–93
validation process, 288t
Expected outcomes, 104–105
Extreme case sampling, 184–185 (box)

Feasibility, 103–104
Flexible nature, 46
Focus group interview, 202–203 (box)
Four-stage action research model, 38
Fundamental principle of mixed methods research, 12
Funding organizations, 15

Gay, Lesbian, Bisexual, Transgender and Questioning (GLBTQ) Youth study (example C):
acting phase, 92
community action/intervention, 306, 312–313, 321
community assessment phases, 363–364, 365–367t, 368
community-based participatory research, 362–363
community feedback, 367t, 368
community needs assessment (CNA), 361, 365–367t
conclusions, 372–373
data collection, 203 (box), 204–205 (box), 208, 214
environmental program scan, 363
focus groups, 364, 365t
full text, 360–375
Gay Advisory Board (GAB), 366t, 368
key informant interviews, 363–364, 365t
literature review, 97, 366t, 368
methodology, 362–368
mixed methods in action research, 73–75, 76f
planning phase, 92
reconnaissance phase, 91
research background, 360–362
research design, 362–363
research implications, 370–372
research problem identification, 95
sampling, 188, 194–195

sequential Qual-Quan study design, 141–142, 154–155, 174, 176*f*, 178

service domain selection, 369

service partnerships (SP), 361–362

service system programs, 369–370

Youth Speak Out survey, 367t, 368

Generalizability, 274–275

General research plan, 101–104

Good Reporting of a Mixed Methods Study (GRAMMS), 319, –320

Handbook of Mixed Methods in Social & Behavioral Research (Tashakkori & Teddlie), 4–5, 14, 16, 182–183

Health Services Research, 15

Homogeneous case sampling, 185 (box), 187*t*

Housing History Survey, 399, 400

Housing intervention study (example E):

abstract, 394

community action/intervention, 307, 321

Consumer Housing Preference Survey Short Version, 399, 400–401

data collection, 213, 399–400

Demographic Profile, 399–400

diagnosing phase, 91

full text, 393–406

Housing History Survey, 399, 400

Lehman's Quality of Life Interview-Brief Version, 399–400

literature review, 97

methodology, 397–402

mixed methods data analysis, 249

mixed methods in action research, 77–80

participatory action research (PAR), 397, 398*f*

project time-line, 400*f*

quantitative data analysis, 224 (box), 228 (box)

research background, 394–397

research design, 397–398

research implications, 402–403

research objectives, 396

research stages, 399–402

sampling, 186*t*, 193

sequential design procedure, 398*f*

sequential Quan-Qual study design, 137, 173, 175*f*

setting, 399

theoretical framework, 396–397

HPV vaccination study (Alabama), 127 (box), 166–167 (box), 263–264 (box), 269–270 (box), 277–278 (box)

HyperRESEARCH software, 243*t*

Illinois Standards Assessment Test (ISAT), 100, 329

Illinois State Board of Education, 333–334, 334

Incompatibility thesis, 14

Independent-measures *t*-test, 226*t*, 228 (box)

Inductive approach, 233

Inference quality, 275

Inferential statistics, 221, 224–225, 228–232 (box)

Insider-outside perspectives, 57–58, 272–273

Integrated mixed methods action research (MMAR) question, 108

Integrative Framework for Inference Quality, 276, 280*t*

combined methods, 19 (box), 21–22, 156–157, 159, 160, 161

concurrent Quan + Qual study design, 154, 156–158, 173, 174*f*

connected methods, 19 (box), 21–22, 158–160, 161

data collection, 211–214

defining characteristics, 152–153

evaluation phase, 154–155, 161–171

illustrated diagram, 22*f*

integration points, 153, 155–161

integration strategies, 19 (box), 21–22, 155–161

merged methods, 19 (box), 21–22, 156*t*, 157–158, 161

meta-inferences, 154–155

mixed methods in action research, 56

mixed methods research, 19 (box), 21–22

multistrand study design, 160–161, 177*f*, 178

point of interface, 153

purpose statement, 161–171

purpose statement script, 163 (box)

quasi-mixed design, 153

reconnaissance phase, 154–155, 161–171

research questions, 161–171

research study examples, 154–155, 164–171, 173–178

sequential Qual-Quan study design, 154–155, 159–160, 174, 176*f*, 178

sequential Quan-Qual study design, 158–159, 173, 175*f*

true mixed methods design, 153

visual diagram notations, 171, 172 (box)

visual diagram rules, 172 (box)

visual diagrams, 173–178

See also Introduction, 152; Reading resources, 180; Reflective questions, 179; Summary, 178–179

Interacting action research spiral model, 40–41, 42*f*

Inter-coder agreement, 241–242

Intermethod mixing, 212–214

Internal consistency reliability, 260, 263 (box)

International Journal of Multiple Research Approaches,
    14–15
Internet resources:
    BioMed Central, 406
    international organizations, 15
    mixed methods research, 15
    research funding, 15
    software programs, 220, 243t
Interpretive consistency process, 299
Interviews, 201–203 (box)
Intramethod mixing, 212–214
In vivo coding, 239

JMP software, 220
Journal of Mixed Methods Research, 4, 5, 14–15, 51

Key informant interview, 201 (box)
Kruskall-Wallis test, 227t
Kuder-Richardson 20 (KR-20), 263

Language Learning Autobiography, 144, 146, 380, 391–392
Learning Experience Questionnaire (LEQ), 77, 146, 380, 383f, 386f
Legitimation Model, 276, 277–278 (box), 281–282t
Lehman's Quality of Life Interview-Brief Version, 399–400
Lesson Style Questionnaire, 144, 146, 380, 382f, 391
Literature review, 96–98
Literature review map, 98
Logistic regression, 227t

Mann-Whitney U test, 227t
Math education study (example A):
    abstract, 328
    communication skills, 330
    community action/intervention, 305, 312, 320
    concurrent Quan + Qual study design, 132, 154, 173, 174f
    data analysis, 334–335
    data collection, 199 (box), 207, 211, 333–334
    evaluation phase, 93
    full text, 328–341
    introduction, 329–330
    journaling, 331–332
    journaling assessment, 338–339
    journaling instruction, 333
    mathematics vocabulary, 337–338
    mixed methods approach, 332–335
    mixed methods in action research, 70–71, 72f

monitoring phase, 93, 94
    participants, 333
    qualitative data analysis, 237t
    quantitative data analysis, 228 (box)
    research implications, 339–340
    research problem statement, 99–101
    results, 335–339
    sampling, 188, 189, 192
    setting, 333
    student improvement, 335–337
    writing skills, 330–332
Mathematics Scoring Rubric (ISBE), 334
Maximal variation sampling, 184 (box), 187t
MAXQDA software, 243t
Mean, 221 (box)
Measures of association, 223–224 (box)
Measures of central tendency, 221–222 (box)
Measures of variability, 222–223 (box)
Median, 221 (box)
Medication Regime Assessment, 345, 348, 352
Member checking, 267–268
Mental models, 54
Merged methods:
    mixed methods data analysis, 246, 247
Meta-inferences:
    community action/intervention, 298–307
Methodological steps action research model, 38, 39f
Mixed methods action research (MMAR):
    capacity building, 103
    conceptualization of, 94–114
    defined, 63
    ethics, 110–114
    expected outcomes, 104–105
    feasibility of, 103–104
    general research plan, 101–104
    integrated mixed methods action research (MMAR) question, 108
    literature review, 96–98
    literature review map, 98
    mixed methods research question, 107
    MMAR Study Process Model, 88–94
    problem identification, 95–96
    purpose statement, 104–105, 106 (box)
    researcher skills, 102
    research hypotheses, 108
    research objectives, 105–106
    research problem statement, 99–101
    research questions, 106–110

research study example, 105, 106 (box), 108–110
resource availability, 102–103
results dissemination, 104
software programs, 103
stakeholders, 103
timeline, 102
See also Introduction, 87–88; Reading resources,
116; Reflective questions, 115;
Summary, 114–115
Mixed methods data analysis:
combined mixed methods data analysis, 246–247
concurrent Quan + Qual study design,
246–247, 248f, 253 (box)
connected mixed methods data analysis,
247–249, 250f, 253–254 (box)
defined, 245–246
merged mixed methods data analysis, 246, 247
multistrand study design, 252–253, 254 (box)
qualitizing quantitative data, 247
quantitizing qualitative data, 247
sequential Qual-Quan study design, 250–251, 252*f*,
254 (box)
sequential Quan-Qual study design, 247–249, 250*f*,
253–254 (box)
triangulation matrix, 245
See also Introduction, 218–219; Reading resources,
256–257; Reflective questions, 255–256; Summary,
254–255
See also Qualitative data analysis; Quantitative data
analysis
Mixed methods in action research:
advantages of, 58–59, 60 (box), 65, 67–69*t*
advocacy lens, 55–56
application of, 59–80
bottom-up approach, 51
collaboration, 57
comprehensive research, 53
constructivist worldview, 54
cyclical nature, 56–57
dialectic stance, 54–55
emic data, 58
epistemological similarities, 51–52
etic data, 57–58
insider-outside perspectives, 57–58
integrative features, 52–58
mental models, 54
MMAR Study Process Model, 59, 61–62, 72*f*,
74*f*, 76*f*, 78*f*, 80f

participatory action research, 51
pragmatism, 53–54
reflective practice, 55
research study examples, 62–80
systematic inquiry, 53
transformative-emancipatory framework, 55–56
triangulation, 51
See also Introduction, 50–52; Reading resources, 82–83;
Reflective questions, 81–82*;* Summary, 80–81
Mixed Methods International Research Association, 15
Mixed methods methodological framework. *See* MMAR
Study Process Model
Mixed methods research:
advantages of, 10–12
best practices approach, 5–6, 7 (box), 15
conceptual model, 7f
current status, 14–16
defining characteristics, 4–6, 7 (box)
fundamental principle of mixed methods research, 12
funding organizations, 15
historical development, 13–14
incompatibility thesis, 14
international recognition, 14–15
Internet resources, 15
methodological characteristics, 18–22
mono-method approach, 5
multimethod approach, 13–14
paradigm debate, 14
philosophical assumptions, 16, 17 (box)
pragmatism, 16, 17 (box)
priority, 19 (box), 20–21
professional journals, 14–15
qualitative methods, 3–4
quantitative methods, 3–4
research study example, 6–10, 12
strands, 18, 19 (box), 20
third methodological movement, 4
timing, 19 (box), 20
weighting, 19 (box), 20–21
See also Introduction, 3–4; Reading resources, 24–25;
Reflective questions, 23–24; Summary, 23
Mixed methods research question, 107
MMAR Study Process Model:
acting phase, 42–43, 45*f*, 61*f*, 62, 90*f*, 92
action research, 42–43, 45*f*
diagnosing phase, 42–43, 45*f*, 61, 89, 90*f*, 91
evaluation phase, 42–43, 45*f*, 61*f*, 62, 90*f*, 92–93
mixed methods action research (MMAR), 88–94

mixed methods in action research, 59, 61–62, 72*f*, 74*f*, 76*f*, 78*f*, 80*f*
model illustration, 45*f*, 61*f*, 90*f*
monitoring phase, 42–43, 45*f*, 61*f*, 62, 90*f*, 93–94
planning phase, 42–43, 45*f*, 61*f*, 62, 90*f*, 92
reconnaissance phase, 38, 39*f*, 42–43, 45*f*, 61–62, 90*f*, 91–92
research study examples, 70–80
validation process, 284–288
Mode, 221 (box)
Monitoring phase:
action research, 42–43, 45*f*
mixed methods in action research, 61*f*, 62, 72*f*, 74*f*, 76*f*, 78*f*, 80*f*
MMAR Study Process Model, 90*f*, 93–94
validation process, 288*t*
Mono-method approach, 5
Multimethod approach, 13–14
Multiple analysis of variance (MANOVA), 227*t*
Multiple regression, 227*t*, 230 (box)
Multistrand combination, 19 (box), 20
Multistrand study design:
advantages/disadvantages, 147
applications, 144, 146–147
conceptual model, 146*f*
data collection, 198 (box), 200 (box), 213*t*
evaluation phase example, 169–170 (box)
integration points, 160–161
integration strategies, 160–161
methodological characteristics, 143–144
mixed methods data analysis, 252–253, 254 (box)
research purpose, 129 (box)
sampling, 195–196
visual diagram, 177*f*, 178

National Council of Teachers of Mathematics (NCTM):
Curriculum and Evaluation Standards for School Mathematics, 330, 331
Principles and Standards for School Mathematics, 329, 330, 340
Professional Standards for Teaching Mathematics, 330
Standards on Communication, 330
National Institutes of Health (NIH), 5–6, 7 (box), 15
National Research Council, 15
Non-parametric methods, 225
Nonprobability samples, 183, 184 (box), 186*t*, 189, 191–196

Nurses Improving Care to the Hospitalized Elderly (NICHE) Project Faculty, 348, 350
NVivo software, 243*t*

Objectivity, 273–274
Observation, 203–204 (box)
Observation checklist, 199–200 (box)
One-way analysis of variance (ANOVA), 226*t*, 229 (box)
Outcome validity, 271 (box)
Out of the Shadows at Last (Kirby & Keon), 395

Paired *t*-test, 226*t*, 228 (box)
Paradigm debate, 14
Parametric methods, 225
Participation, 33
Participatory action research (PAR):
defined, 51
elder nursing care study (example B), 344–345, 346t, 349–350
housing intervention study (example E), 397, 398f
Patient-Centered Outcome Research Institute, 15
Pearson correlation, 223 (box), 226*t*
Pfizer Foundation Southern HIV/AIDS Prevention Initiative, 147
Philosophical assumptions, 16, 17 (box)
Photo-voice, 205–206 (box)
Planning phase:
action research, 42–43, 45f
mixed methods in action research, 61*f*, 62, 72*f*, 74*f*, 76*f*, 78*f*, 80*f*
MMAR Study Process Model, 90*f*, 92
validation process, 287*t*
Point of interface, 153
Pragmatism:
mixed methods in action research, 53–54
mixed methods research, 16, 17 (box)
Principles and Standards for School Mathematics (NCTM), 329, 330, 340
Priority:
equal priority, 19 (box), 20–21
mixed methods research, 19 (box), 20–21
qualitative priority, 19 (box), 20–21
quantitative priority, 19 (box), 20–21
Probability samples, 183, 184 (box), 186*t*, 189, 191–196
Problem identification, 95–96
Professional journals, 14–15
Professional Standards for Teaching Mathematics (NCTM), 330

Purposeful samples, 183, 184–185 (box), 186–187*t*, 191–194, 195–196

Purpose statement:
mixed methods action research (MMAR), 104–105, 106 (box)

QDA software, 243*t*

Qualitative data analysis:
analytic process, 233–235, 239, 240f
approaches to, 232–233
codebook, 240–241
coding, 239–244
constant comparative method, 241
inductive approach, 233
inter-coder agreement, 241–242
in vivo coding, 239
research considerations, 244 (box)
research study examples, 236–238*t*
software programs, 242, 243 (box)
theme development, 234*t*, 239–244
See also Mixed methods data analysis; Quantitative data analysis
See also Introduction, 218–219; Reading resources, 256–257; Reflective questions, 255–256; Summary, 254–255

Qualitative data assessment:
assessment strategies, 267–270
bias, 268–269
bracketing technique, 268–269
confirmability, 265, 266 (box)
credibility, 265, 266 (box)
dependability, 265, 266 (box)
member checking, 267–268
sequential Quan-Qual study design, 269–270 (box)
transferability, 265, 266 (box)
triangulation, 268
trustworthiness, 265, 266 (box), 267–270
validation process, 261, 264
See also Action research assessment; Quantitative data assessment; Validation process
See also Reading resources, 292–293; Reflective questions, 291–292; Summary, 290–291

Qualitative Inquiry, 15

Qualitative methods, 3–4

Qualitative priority, 19 (box), 20–21

Qualitative Research in Accounting & Management, 15

Qualitizing quantitative data, 247

Quality Framework for Mixed Methods Research, 279

Quantitative data analysis:
concurrent Quan + Qual study design, 222 (box), 223 (box), 224 (box), 228 (box), 230 (box), 231 (box), 232 (box)
correlation coefficient, 223 (box)
descriptive statistics, 220–224
inferential statistics, 221, 224–225, 228–232 (box)
mean, 221 (box)
measures of association, 223–224 (box)
measures of central tendency, 221–222 (box)
measures of variability, 222–223 (box)
median, 221 (box)
mode, 221 (box)
non-parametric methods, 225
parametric methods, 225
Pearson correlation, 223 (box), 226*t*
procedures, 219–220
research considerations, 244 (box)
research study examples, 222 (box), 223 (box), 224 (box), 228 (box), 230 (box), 231 (box)
sequential Qual-Quan study design, 222 (box), 230 (box), 231 (box)
sequential Quan-Qual study design, 224 (box), 228 (box), 232 (box)
Spearman correlation, 223 (box), 226*t*
standard deviation, 222 (box)
statistical tests, 226–227*t*
statistics, 219, 220–232
variables, 220
variance range, 222 (box)
See also Mixed methods data analysis; Qualitative data analysis
See also Introduction, 218–219; Reading resources, 256–257; Reflective questions, 255–256; Summary, 254–255

Quantitative data assessment:
coefficient alpha, 263
coefficient of equivalence, 263
coefficient of stability, 263
construct validity, 260, 262 (box)
content validity, 260, 262 (box)
criterion validity, 260, 262 (box)
Cronbach's alpha, 263
discriminant validity, 262 (box)
equivalent forms reliability, 260, 263
internal consistency reliability, 260, 263 (box)
introduction, 259–260
Kuder-Richardson 20, 263

reliability, 260–261, 262–264 (box)

sequential Quan-Qual study design, 263–264 (box)

test-retest reliability, 260, 263

validity, 260–261, 262 (box), 264 (box)

See also Action research assessment; Qualitative data assessment; Validation process

See also Reading resources, 292–293; Reflective questions, 291–292; Summary, 290–291

Quantitative methods, 3–4

Quantitative priority, 19 (box), 20–21

Quantitizing qualitative data, 247

Quasi-mixed design, 153

Quota sampling, 184 (box), 186t

Racial and Ethnic Approaches to Community Health (REACH) 2010 Initiative, 35–36 (box)

Reconnaissance phase:

action research, 38, 39f, 42–43, 45f

mixed methods in action research, 61–62, 72f, 74f, 76f, 78f, 80f

MMAR Study Process Model, 90f, 91–92

validation process, 287t

Reflective practice, 33–34, 55

Regression analysis, 227t, 230–231 (box)

Reliability, 260–261, 262–264 (box)

Repeated-measures ANOVA, 226t, 229 (box)

Research design:

basic study designs, 128–147

concurrent Quan + Qual study design, 128–133, 134f

features of, 148 (box)

methodological dimensions, 125–128

MMAR study designs, 124–147

multistrand study design, 129 (box), 143–144, 146–147

recent mixed methods designs, 118–124

research study designs, 124–128

research study examples, 126 (box), 127 (box)

sequential Qual-Quan study design, 129 (box), 138, 140–143, 145f

sequential Quan-Qual study design, 129 (box), 133, 135–138, 139f

See also Introduction, 117–118; Reading resources, 150; Reflective questions, 149; Summary, 148–149

Researcher skills, 102

Research hypotheses, 108

Research in the Schools, 15

Research objectives, 105–106

Research problem statement, 99–101

Research questions:

community action/intervention, 300–302

mixed methods action research (MMAR), 106–110

Residential-Palliative Approach Competency (R-PAC) project, 59, 60 (box), 304

Resource availability, 102–103

Respecting Housing and Support (1995), 395

Robert Wood Johnson Foundation, 15

Rorty, Richard, 16

SAGE Handbook of Action Research (Reason & Bradbury), 28, 275

Sampling procedures:

concurrent Quan + Qual study design, 191–192

considerations, 185, 187–190

mixed methods approach, 191

multistrand study design, 195–196

nonprobability samples, 183, 184 (box), 186t, 189, 191–196

overview, 184–185 (box)

probability samples, 183, 184 (box), 186t, 189, 191–196

purposeful samples, 183, 184–185 (box), 186–187t, 191–194, 195–196

recruitment considerations, 189–190

research study designs, 191–196

research study examples, 186–187t, 188, 189, 191–196

sample size, 188

saturation point, 183

sequential Qual-Quan study design, 194–195

sequential Quan-Qual study design, 193–194

stakeholder representation, 185, 187–188

strategies, 182–185, 186–187 (box)

typology, 182–185, 189

See also Introduction, 182; Reading resources, 216–217; Reflective questions, 215–216; Summary, 214–215

Saturation point, 183

Saxon Math Teacher Rubric for Scoring Performance Tasks (Larson), 334

Saxon Math Two (Larson), 334

Self-care Deficit Theory, 344

Self-care Theory, 344

Sequential Qual-Quan study design:

advantages/disadvantages, 142–143

applications, 141–142

conceptual model, 140f

data collection, 203 (box), 204–205 (box), 213t

decision flowchart, 145f

integration points, 159–160

integration strategies, 159–160

methodological characteristics, 138, 140–141

mixed methods data analysis, 250–251, 252f, 254 (box)

quantitative data analysis, 222 (box), 230 (box), 231 (box)

reconnaissance phase example, 168 (box)

research purpose, 129 (box)

sampling, 194–195

visual diagram, 174, 176f, 178

Sequential Quan-Qual study design:

advantages/disadvantages, 137–138

applications, 136–137

conceptual model, 135f

data collection, 202 (box), 204 (box), 213t

decision flowchart, 139f

integration points, 158–159

integration strategies, 158–159

methodological characteristics, 133, 135–136

mixed methods data analysis, 247–249, 250f, 253–254 (box)

qualitative data assessment, 269–270 (box)

quantitative data analysis, 224 (box), 228 (box), 232 (box)

quantitative data assessment, 263–264 (box)

reconnaissance phase example, 166–167 (box)

research purpose, 129 (box)

sampling, 193–194

validation process, 277–278 (box)

visual diagram, 173, 175f

Sequential timing, 19 (box), 20

Simple random sampling, 184 (box), 186t

Simple regression, 227t, 230 (box)

Simple t-test, 226t, 228 (box)

Snowball sampling, 185 (box), 187t

Software programs, 103, 220, 242, 243 (box)

Spearman correlation, 223 (box), 226t

Spiral action research model, 38–39, 40f

SPSS, 220

Stakeholders:

action research, 30

community action/intervention, 303–305

mixed methods action research (MMAR), 103

sampling, 185, 187–188

Standard deviation, 222 (box)

Standards on Communication (NCTM), 330

Statistical tests, 226–227t

Statistics, 219, 220–232

Strands, 18, 19 (box), 20

Stratified sampling, 184 (box)

Subjectivity, 273–274

Surveys, 197–198 (box)

Surviving the Tornado of Mental Illness (Forchuk, Ward-Griffin, Csiernik, Turner), 396–397

Sustainability, 31

Systematic inquiry, 44, 53

Systematic sampling, 184 (box)

Technique of Social Investigation, The (Fry), 13

Test-retest reliability, 260, 263

Theoretical sampling, 185 (box)

Theory of Nursing Systems, 344

Third methodological movement, 4

Timeline, 102

Timing:

concurrent timing, 19 (box), 20

mixed methods research, 19 (box), 20

multistrand combination, 19 (box), 20

sequential timing, 19 (box), 20

Transferability:

action research assessment, 274–275

qualitative data assessment, 265, 266 (box)

Transformative-emancipatory framework, 55–56

Triangulation:

action research, 46–47

data collection, 208

mixed methods data analysis, 245

mixed methods in action research, 51

qualitative data assessment, 268

Triangulation matrix, 245

True mixed methods design, 153

Trustworthiness, 265, 266 (box), 267–270

*T-test, 226t, 228 (box)

Two-way ANOVA, 226t, 229 (box)

Typical case sampling, 184 (box)

United Kingdom, 15

University of Alabama, Birmingham, 15–16

University of Nebraska, Lincoln, 8–9 (box), 15–16

U.S. National Academy of Sciences, 15

U.S. National Science Foundation, 15

Validation Framework, 278–279, 282–283t

Validation process:

acting phase, 287t

approaches to, 276–284

assessment frameworks, 276–279, 280–283t

assessment process, 284–290

concurrent Quan + Qual study design, 289 (box)
defined, 258–259
diagnosing phase, 286*t*
evaluation phase, 288*t*
guidelines for, 290 (box)
inference quality, 275
Integrative Framework for Inference Quality, 276, 280*t*
Legitimation Model, 276, 277–278 (box), 281–282*t*
MMAR Study Process Model, 284–288
monitoring phase, 288*t*
planning phase, 287*t*
quality considerations, 275–276
Quality Framework for Mixed Methods Research, 279
reconnaissance phase, 287*t*
sequential Quan-Qual study design, 277–278 (box)
Validation Framework, 278–279, 282–283*t*

validity threats, 279, 284
See also Action research assessment; Qualitative data assessment; Quantitative data assessment
Validity:
action research assessment, 271–272 (box)
quantitative data assessment, 260–261, 262 (box), 264 (box)
Variables, 220
Variance range, 222 (box)

Weighting, 19 (box), 20–21
William T. Grant Foundation, 15
Within-strategy mixed methods data collection, 211–214
Worldview, 27, 54

Youth Speak Out survey, 367*t*, 368

⊛SAGE research**methods**

The essential online tool for researchers from the world's leading methods publisher

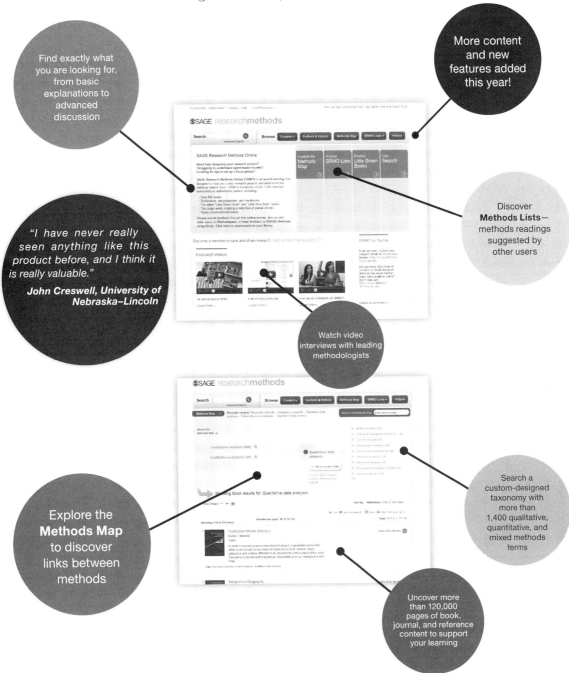

Find exactly what you are looking for, from basic explanations to advanced discussion

More content and new features added this year!

"I have never really seen anything like this product before, and I think it is really valuable."

John Creswell, University of Nebraska–Lincoln

Discover **Methods Lists**— methods readings suggested by other users

Watch video interviews with leading methodologists

Explore the **Methods Map** to discover links between methods

Search a custom-designed taxonomy with more than 1,400 qualitative, quantitative, and mixed methods terms

Uncover more than 120,000 pages of book, journal, and reference content to support your learning

Find out more at
www.sageresearchmethods.com